HebrewS

VERSE - BY - VERSE

A Classic Evangelical Commentary

To Andy and Cindy
My Love in Christ Jesus
Resting in Him

Marie K.

5/9/00

Col 1:9.

Heb 3:4-16

Books by William R. Newell
Romans: Verse-by-Verse
Hebrews: Verse-by-Verse
Revelation: Chapter-by-Chapter

HEBREWS

VERSE - BY - VERSE

A Classic Evangelical Commentary

WILLIAM R. NEWELL

kregel
CLASSICS

Grand Rapids, MI 49501

Hebrews: Verse-by-Verse by William R. Newell.

Published in 1995 by Kregel Classics, an imprint of Kregel Publications, P.O. Box 2607, Grand Rapids, MI 49501. Kregel Classics provides trusted, time-proven publications for Christian life and ministry. Your comments and suggestions are valued.

Cover Design: Alan G. Hartman

Library of Congress Cataloging-in-Publication Data
Newell, William R. 1865–1956.
   Hebrews verse-by-verse: a classic evangelical commentary / William R. Newell.
      p.   cm.
   Originally published: Chicago: Moody Press, c1947.
   1. Bible N.T. Hebrews—Commentaries. I. Title. II. Title: Hebrews.
BS2775.3.N48   1995   227'.087077—dc20   94-37701
                                                 CIP

ISBN 0-8254-3327-4 (paperback)

2 3 4 5 Printing / Year 99 98

Printed in the United States of America

CONTENTS

FOREWORD

The object of HEBREWS is to set forth CHRIST, above angels —their Creator, indeed; above Moses—as Son, not servant; above Abraham—who paid tithes to Melchizedek; Christ, not connected with Aaron; of wholly different order, for earthly tabernacle, priest-hood, sacrifices are **done away** in HEBREWS; not priest on earth, but Christ our Great Priest at God's right hand in Heaven itself— **who ever liveth to make intercession for us.**

All earthly "religion," therefore is superseded—even Levitical, though given by God Himself!

Since the Holy Spirit came at Pentecost, we "worship by the Spirit of God" (Phil. 3.3); glorying "in Christ Jesus", through Whom we **offer up a sacrifice of praise to God continually** (Heb. 13.15).

Believers, therefore, are directed to constant access to God's throne by Christ's blood and **through the veil . . . His flesh;** partaking, as they do, of **a heavenly calling:** belonging to and in Heaven, though at present engaged in pilgrimage through this world.

If Hebrew believers have **not here an abiding city** now, surely Gentiles have none. All believers (along with Abraham), **look for the city which hath the foundations—the city of the Living God.**

The *great object* of HEBREWS, then, is to set before these be-lievers' eyes, CHRIST, the Son of God; the Son of Man; the Great High Priest in Heaven; and to cause them constantly to occupy their thought and worship with God, into Whose presence Christ by His blood has brought them:

Without the camp: WITHIN THE VEIL!

CHAPTER ONE

1 In many parts, and in many manners of old, God, having
2 spoken to the fathers in the prophets, at the end of these
   [Old Testament] days did speak to us in [the person of
   His] Son, Whom He appointed Heir of all things,
   through Whom also He made the ages; Who, being the
3 effulgence of His glory, and the exact expression of His
   substance, and upholding all things by the word of His
   power, when He had made purification of sins, sat down
   on the right hand of the Majesty on high;

WE BEG THE READER'S permission thus to begin the opening words of this great epistle with a literal arrangement of the
order of the Greek words, which may at first appear strange; but
which will profit us as we remember that God *thus spake.*

God did not, as does our English version, place His Name as the
very opening word of the epistle. But He sets forth His many Old
Testament *words,* and His divers *manners* of speaking in that time
past to the fathers by the prophets— as *contrasted* with His speaking to us at the end of these [Old Testament] days . . . in a Son!

Now this is a strange manner of speech; to speak in a Son! But
thus, in a word, is set before us the great message of Hebrews.

God hath spoken to us! How? Not after the former messages
in the Old Testament prophets; but in a *Person,* a *Son*—Who is
now declared to be God, Creator, Upholder, Lord, Heir of all
things!

In the "Four Gospels," as four "books of the Bible," Christ is
set forth; for in these records God speaks to us *in His Son!* In
Matthew He walks before us as the King of Israel; in Mark as the
Servant of Jehovah; in Luke as the Son of Man; and in John as the
Eternal Word, "the Only Begotten Son," Creator-God! So it is not
in the New Testament as in the former Old Testament **portions**

or **manners.** In the Old Testament God spake by **prophets. Now God hath spoken unto us in** [the Person of] **His Son.** "God was manifest in the flesh."

And here at the beginning let us bow our whole being at this word, **God.** God has spoken! An old Puritan preacher used to say there were just two things he desired to know: "First, Does God speak (concerning any matter)? Second, What does God say?" Atheists—fools, deny God's being. Deists deny that He has revealed Himself—that He has spoken. The great multitude of humanity ignore Him, living their little selfish earth-lives, to hear at last the fearful words, "Depart from Me." "Hear, and your soul shall live" is the constant message of Scripture. Nor is God named in **Hebrews 1.1** as "The God and Father of our Lord Jesus Christ," as in Paul's epistles to the Church as such. For the subject immediately taken up in **Hebrews 1** is not our salvation or blessing, but *the Person and place of God's Son!*

First, the whole Old Testament revelation is compassed in simple words: **Having of old time spoken unto the fathers* in the prophets by divers portions and in divers manners** (literally, multi-partedly and multi-manneredly). This of course refers to God's revelation of Himself in the Old Testament, especially the period following Abraham and Genesis 12 through Malachi—before the Son was sent. We remember that in these thirty-nine books of the Old Testament there are various **parts** or "books": history, biography, genealogy, legislation, religious ordinances, spiritual experiences, prophecy. And God spoke in various **manners:** sometimes by the Spirit directly upon His servants; sometimes through angels, or even in theophanies (appearances of

---

*In reading **Hebrews,** Gentile believers naturally and correctly, though unconsciously, assume that "the fathers" belong to them. For a Gentile believer is told that "Abraham is the father of us all," that is, of all true believers: "If ye are Christ's then are ye Abraham's seed, heirs according to promise." (Rom. 4.16, Gal. 3.29).

It will not do at all to view the writer of **Hebrews** as building up that which God has destroyed, as regards the present standing of national Israel in His sight. We repeat over and over that today Israel is Lo-ammi—"not God's people" (Hos. 1.9); that the Kingdom of God has been "taken away" from that nation (Matt. 21.43); that nation having crucified their Messiah, their Messianic promises and hopes were deferred to a remnant at the Lord's return. Meanwhile, God had raised up Christ His Son, and set Him at His own right hand, in a priesthood compared to which Moses and Levi and Aaron were but "shadows." National Israel was left behind at the Cross—as were indeed all men! The Cross was the end of man; God was manifest in the flesh, and they spat in His face and crucified Him.

God Himself as the Angel of Jehovah, as to Abraham in Genesis 18); sometimes by conferred Divine wisdom, as Proverbs and Ecclesiastes; sometimes through putting His words in the mouth of His prophets; and sometimes through prophetic visions or dreams of the night.

Verse 2: At the end of these days God did speak unto us in [the person of His] Son, Whom He appointed Heir of all things, through Whom also He made the ages—Astonishing it was, indeed, even in that "old time," that the infinite, eternal, glorious God should speak unto dust and ashes such as man is! But this wondrous fact of God's having spoken in past days is to prepare us (vs. 2) for a more stupendous statement: [God] did at the end of these days speak unto us in [the person of His] Son!*

It should be noted that the words, did speak unto us in Son, (which great fact carries throughout the epistle) refer to the Son at His incarnation and onward. John, indeed, defends His absolute, eternal Sonship in his opening verse: "In the beginning was the Word, and the Word was with God, and the Word was God . . . All things were made through Him; and without Him was not anything made that hath been made." God spoke indeed *through* the Old Testament writers. But this was before God spake unto us IN [His] Son.

It is, in these first two verses of Hebrews, not the fact that God hath "spoken": but that, having spoken to the fathers by divers portions and in divers manners, He has gone beyond these former "portions" and "manners" of speaking and did speak in [the person of His] SON!

Nor is it to have this Son Himself here speak to us. God speaks: and lo, the Son is there! "This is My Beloved Son!" Nay, infinitely beyond this: for God does not in Hebrews say, "Hear Him." Nay: the Son does not speak to us in Hebrews. But God speaks *concerning* Him. And it is after the Cross, after the resurrection, after the post-resurrection salutation to Christ: "Thou art a Priest forever after the order of Melchizedek."

---

*"In Son": there is no article, there is no possessive pronoun, in the Greek. Again we feel the poverty of English idiom, and must translate, "His Son," or "a Son". But if we say over and over to ourselves the very words, God did speak unto us in Son, our hearts will feel the meaning, though our words cannot translate it.

It is in view of the Divine glory of the Person of Christ, the
SON, Heir of all things, addressed as *God, Lord, Creator* and
Upholder of all things; also, indeed, as *Son of Man*—for as man
He is to be set over all things! And we even now behold Him,
"because of the suffering of death crowned with glory and
honor." Thus is He, the Son, set before us at the very first in
Hebrews!

How utterly different is this from Old Testament "words" and
"portions." Truly this is another "manner of speaking" than those
messages of old time unto the fathers in the prophets. Here is
the only begotten Son Who declares the Father! (Jno. 1.18).
I repeat, Christ does not speak in the book of **Hebrews.**
He, Himself, is God's message to us here!

And now we behold the snare into which so many have been
drawn. They go back to Matthew, Mark, Luke, and John and
study "the teachings of Jesus," as they call them. They dream to
honor Him in terming Him "the Great Teacher."

But the fundamental truth set forth in **Hebrews** is that Christ
Himself, the Son of God, *is* God's message, His voice to us.
Herein the message of **Hebrews** resembles John 3.16, "God so
loved the world that He gave His only begotten Son"; and again,
"He that *hath* the Son *hath* the life; he that hath not the Son of
God *hath not the life*" (I Jno. 5.12).

There comes for everyone who has *believed* on the Lord Jesus
Christ a moment when he HEARS—when God the Father speaks
by the blessed Spirit to his heart. Christ, therefore, is no mere
Teacher, but the personal Voice and eternal Gift of God to him!
Such an one knows what the words before us mean, **God hath
spoken to us in** [the person of His] **Son.**

The presence of the Son comes steadily before us in the Bible.
First the prophecy of "the Seed of the woman" (Gen. 3.15);
then, "Behold, a virgin shall conceive, and bear a Son, and shall
call His name *Immanuel*" (God with us)—Isaiah 7.14; next, the
manner of fulfillment: Gabriel announces to Mary: "The Holy
Spirit shall come upon thee, and the power of the Most High
shall overshadow thee: wherefore also the holy thing which is
begotten shall be called the Son of God" (Lk. 1.35). Then, the

angelic rapture, and the song the shepherds heard: "Glory to God
in the highest!" The star, and company of worshiping wise men
from the East; the voice from Heaven, "This is My beloved Son,
in Whom I am well pleased; hear ye Him"; the years of
His ministry of mercy; Gethsemane—and the accepting of *the
cup* from the Father's hand; the laying down of His life at
Calvary; the final word, "Father, into Thy hands I commend My
spirit"; the resurrection, and the message to Mary Magdalene,
"Go unto My brethren, and say to them, I ascend unto My Father
and your Father, and My God and your God" (John 20.17).

Now all these things are familiar to us; but look again at the
language: **God hath spoken unto us in Son.** We naturally expect
to hear that Son speaking to us in this book of **Hebrews.** From
the beginning to the end He is before us, there at God's right
hand. The Holy Ghost inspires the writer of **Hebrews** to portray
His eternal deity and glory; His real humanity; and His session at
the right hand of the Majesty on high, where He "ever liveth to
make intercession." Over the house of God as Son, not servant;
greater infinitely than the host of angels, or the servants of God
on earth; appearing "before the face of God for us," a *seated*
Priest!—His one offering for redemption forever over! And, in
the infinite power and worth of that sacrifice as known by God
alone, a *"Great High Priest"*: One able to be "touched with the
feeling of our infirmities," having been "in all points tempted
like as we are—sin apart."

Thus **God hath spoken to us in Son.** In the silent depths of our
hearts we either hearken to God speaking in this Son, and
respond to God's invitation to enter in boldly, by the blood of
Jesus, to the throne of grace, in a life of faith and praise and
worship; or, we "neglect", "drift away", and finally "refuse"—
what? The voice of God Himself, speaking to us in His Son!

So, it is not the "voice of words," as at Sinai, that comes to
us. God speaks to us **in a Person,** His dear, only-begotten One:
Jesus Christ, "the same yesterday, and today, and unto the ages."

Now let us consider the seven marvelous utterances (vss. 2-3)
concerning this Son in Whom **God hath spoken unto us.**

1. **Whom He appointed Heir of all things.**
2. **Through Whom also He made the ages [*aiōnas*].**

3. **Being the effulgence of** [God's] **glory.**
4. [Being] **the exact-expression of His substance.**
5. **Upholding all things by the word of His power.**
6. **He . . . made purification of sins.**
7. **He sat down on the right hand of the Majesty on high.**

First, Whom He appointed Heir of all things—This great
revelation naturally evokes a threefold inquiry: First, as to the
place of God in appointing Christ Heir. Second, Why Heir, and
appointed when? Third, What do **"all things"** embrace?

The Son shared the Divine glory before the world was. He
"emptied Himself"* when He came into the world. Throughout
Hebrews (and the whole Word of God, indeed!) we find God
the Father and God the Son equal in fact of Deity, yet the Son
constantly doing willingly, yea, gladly, the will of the Father;
and the Father, just as gladly, constantly exalting the Son.

Now heirship follows sonship: among men, naturally; between
God the Son and God the Father, eternally. It is therefore as
Son—He having come into the world at the end of the Old
Testament revelations; and God "having spoken" to us in that Son
—that His appointment as **Heir of all things** is announced. Indeed,
He thus regarded Himself: Mark 12.1-12: They said, "This is
the Heir."

Now that "all things" are spoken of, let us reflect that "all
things have been created through Him and unto Him." (Col. 1.16,
Heb. 1.2; cf. Prov. 8, Jno. 1). We find God's plan for the future
also in Ephesians 1.9, 10: "According to His good pleasure which He
purposed in Him [Christ]" looking forward "unto a dispensation of
the *fullness* of the times, to sum up *all* things in Christ, the things in
the heavens, and the things upon the earth" (not the things of the
world below, the lost, though they will bow the knee to Him as
Lord—Philippians 2.10).

---

*Philippians 2.7, Revised Version. That is, He laid aside His glory, His power, and His
wisdom, leaving them with the Father, and taking the "form of a servant" down here. He
spoke of the glory He had with the Father before the world was. He said, "The Son
can do nothing of Himself, but what He seeth the Father doing"; and "I by the Spirit
of God cast out demons." This Self-Emptying as to the fact of it, affords no difficulty
to simple faith; although the process of it is Divinely inscrutable. Christ when on earth
continued just as certainly Deity as from all eternity: "Before Abraham was born, I AM."
This voluntarily self-emptied state continued. He said to Peter in Gethsemane, "Thinkest
thou that I cannot beseech My Father, and He shall even now send Me more than twelve
legions of angels?" He did not make the request. And at another time, He saw a fig tree
afar off, and came "if haply" He might find fruit thereon, refraining from using His power.

Christ—**Heir of all things,** through Whom God created the ages; "all things were made through Him;" "all things were created through Him and unto Him . . . and in Him all things hold together"! (Col. 1.16, 17). We opened our eyes from sleep— and lo, the created light! But it was Christ's voice that spoke, "Let there be light," when darkness had thralled a ruined world. We arose to dress, and lo, for all our clothing He had prepared the materials. We sat down to eat, and lo, all our food had been made by Him. We passed through the garden, and lo! every plant beautiful to the eye or good for food, Christ had created for us. We saw afar the mountains, and lo, it was His strength that had set them fast! We looked beyond the mountains, and the sea was there; but again, "The sea is His and He made it." We looked above the mountains and the sea, and there was the sky, blue and wonderful; but lo! His voice had spoken: "Let there be a firmament!" And as for the clouds, they are "His chariot," and "Behold, He cometh with the clouds," just as a cloud received Him out of the sight of the gazing apostles on Olivet. And He has ascended "far above all the heavens"! He has "passed through the heavens," as the appointed **Heir of all things.** For as the Son, He inherits all things, which as we have seen, He made, created— and also the very ages *(aiônas),* each with its order of things and its Divine purpose.

But someone is weary of all this recital. Someone objects, "I believe *man* has *his* place, and *his* powers, and *his* planning and thinking." Well, O puppet, what hast thou created? Ye "brought nothing into the world; and can carry nothing out." O dust, living a little while, to dust returning: can you get on without breathing, a day, an hour? Nay, you must depend for every breath, nay every heart beat, on the God "in Whose hand thy breath is"; and He has spoken in His Son—even Christ!

Let us meditate deeply and frequently upon this stupendous statement: *God's Heir is Christ!*

a. This is for eternity: there will be no change in God's mind and the blessed Spirit's delight in this matter.

b. Men agree that the surest title known on earth is that by inheritance. By the Divine pleasure and decree, the Son of God comes into possession, forever and ever, of all things. They are His. He is *Heir!*

c. Note the peculiar fitness and safety of Christ's being **Heir of all things.** With men, inheriting a fortune is the occasion, often, of the development of inherent selfishness. But Christ, while possessing (even in Gethsemane) the power of self-deliverance, absolutely rejected, even unto death, the path of selfishness. Language utterly fails us to express the boundless, unselfish devotion which said to the very end, "The cup which the Father hath given Me, shall I not drink it?" The Son of God proved what He claimed: "I am come down from Heaven, not to do Mine own will, but the will of Him that sent Me." Mark the sweat falling down as blood in Gethsemane where the Father gave Him to *taste* the cup of wrath for our sins, ere sin was laid upon Him! And even when forsaken of God, He held fast His claim, "My God!" Oh, for language here, but we have none for the unselfishness and devotion! For all eternity, His death, toward which He "steadfastly set His face to go to Jerusalem," has proven Him the fit and safe **Heir of all things!**

d. He shares with those He calls "His brethren" with the same infinite readiness, (as we shall find in Ch. 2), so that we read, "joint-heirs with Christ" (Rom. 8.17). It is as Man that all things will be subjected to Him. And we find (Heb. 2.13-14) that in order for this, God is manifest in the flesh—Christ steps in among men, His creatures, in a body "prepared" by God (Ch. 10.5).

Yes, the Son of God has fellow-heirs! And God speaks to us redeemed sinners, delivered from "the hole of the pit," thus: "The Spirit Himself beareth witness with our spirit, that we are children of God: and if children, then heirs; heirs of God, and joint-heirs with Christ; if so be that we suffer with Him, that we may be also glorified with Him" (Rom. 8.16-17). And again, "Thou art no longer a bondservant, but a son (adult son—*huios*); and if a son, then an heir through God" (Gal. 4.7).

Alas, this poor, poor world! In the words, "We brought nothing into the world . . . neither can we carry anything out," Paul wrote the biography of every man! Men have struck gold, heaped it up, and left it—to be paupers eternally! Men have labored, and with genius, to "accumulate," as they say, and have left it forever—paupers. Xerxes of Persia had no limit to his earthly possessions, but dying without Christ, to what was he heir? An eternity with nothing! For *Christ* has been appointed **Heir of all things!** The proud millionaire, yea, they say the billionaire, is with us today. For a few years he is rich and then leaves it all and is poor forever! While some humble servant of his, who had Christ, dying, steps out into an unspeakably glorious eternity, rich beyond all imagination. Why? He is an "heir of God, and joint-heir with Christ," who was **appointed Heir of all things.** Yea, indeed, let us meditate much on these words. I am writing these words in sight of the most elegant private mansion in all of the United States; but was the builder, who is gone from it now, an heir with Christ? There is no other eternal good!

2. **Through Whom also He made the ages**—We have this action illustrated in the opening verse of the Bible: "In the beginning God created the heavens and earth." Then after the judgment period of verse 2, we have, "And God said, Let there be light: and there was light." Here spoke the eternal Word Who gives creative utterance to the counsels of the Deity: "For all things were made through Him" (Jno. 1.3).

Made the ages *(aiôns)*—An *aiôn,* (English *aeon*) as we know, is a space of time during which God is developing some special phase of His purpose.

For example, in Genesis 1 there is brought before our eyes an earth surrounded by the "deep," with "darkness" upon its face. That this was not the original condition of the world when created is shown in Isaiah 45.18:—"For thus saith Jehovah that created the heavens, the God that formed the earth and made it, that established it and created it *not* a waste, (Heb. *tohu*) that formed it to be inhabited" (or, *habitable*). That the "darkness" and "deep" were a judgment upon a former condition is also brought out in the words of Genesis 1.2: "And the earth was (Heb., *"became")* *tohu and bohu*—waste and empty," whereas God says He created it not *tohu,* a waste, but *habitable,* as we just saw.

Note also, when man is created, he is told to replenish the earth, just as Noah was commanded at the end of the Flood:

Genesis 9.1: "And God blessed Noah and his sons, and said unto them, Be fruitful and multiply, and replenish the earth"—which had been emptied of population.

Therefore, the words of Hebrews 1.2, **He made the** *aiôns,* refer to those processes in each age by which God is bringing to pass His great purpose. It is a solemn word indeed, that "now once at the end (literally, consummation) of the ages *(aiôns)* hath He been manifested to put away sin by the sacrifice of Himself" (9.26). The "evil age" that crucified Him is still on, to be ended by His return to earth when the *aiôn* to come, the Millennium, will begin. How unutterably wonderful are the words of Revelation 22.4, 5, concerning the saints: "They shall see His face; and His name shall be on their foreheads. And there shall be night no more; and they need no light of lamp, neither light of sun; for the Lord God shall give them light: and they shall reign *unto the ages of the ages.*"

Be it noted now that while in Hebrews 1.2 we are told that the "ages" were "made" *(poieô)* through Christ, when we come to the original of calling creation into being, a different Greek word is used—*ktidzô,* create: but the same Person, Son of God, is declared to have "created all things." Indeed, it is further asserted that: "In Him were all things created, in the heavens and upon the earth, things visible and things invisible, whether thrones or dominions or principalities or powers; all things have been created . . . in Him . . . through Him, and unto Him." (Let all note these three words, in the Greek, *en, dia, eis,* of Colossians 1.16. They mean, in view of Him, through His direct action, with respect to His honor and glory!)*

Verse 3: Who, being the effulgence of His glory, and the very image of His substance, and upholding all things by the word of His power, when He had made purification of sins, sat down on the right hand of the Majesty on high—
3. **Being the effulgence of His glory**—We are reminded at once of, "No man hath seen God at any time; the only begotten Son, Who is in the bosom of the Father, He hath declared Him"

**Will,* we may say, lies with God; *creative command,* with Christ, the Word; and the *execution of the command,* with the Spirit: "Thou sendest forth *Thy Spirit,* they are created" (Ps. 104.30). We see the Spirit present in Gen. 1.2, also.

(Jno. 1.18). In John 1, He is therefore the Word by Whom God is declared unto us. The term "effulgence," used in verse 3, pre-sents the Son as the Person of the Deity in and by Whom the glory of that Deity is manifested. And the glory *(doxa)* "is the expression of the Divine attributes collectively."

"All that God is—not merely in His ways, but in His being—is expressed absolutely by the Son . . . No one has grasped what the Son of God is until he has prostrated his soul before Him 'God over all, blessed forever'! (Rom. 9.5). I would that I could put it so strongly that every soul would bow to the truth of it, the absolutely essential, perfect divinity of the Son of God, our Lord Jesus Christ. We admit not one iota of a question, not one shadow of a doubt, not one bit of tarnish upon that glory which God has spread before us on this page."—Ridout, **Lectures on Hebrews.**

4. **And the exact-expression* of His substance**—From our Lord's words, "God is a Spirit," many unconsciously conceive spirit, and, consequently, God, as not having "substance." But we must not confuse "substance" here with matter as we know it. In Deuteronomy 4.15, 16, Jehovah indeed protested to Israel, "Ye saw *no manner of form* on the day that Jehovah spake unto you in Horeb out of the midst of the fire; lest ye corrupt yourselves, and make you a graven image in the form of any figure." But this was a protection against idolatry, as see the verses which follow, especially verse 25. But in Exodus 24, in connection with the rati-fication of the first covenant, we read:

"Then went up Moses, and Aaron, Nadab, and Abihu, and seventy of the elders of Israel: and they saw the God of Israel; and there was under His feet as it were a paved work of sap-phire stone, as it were the very heaven for clearness. And upon the nobles of the children of Israel He laid not His hand: and *they beheld God,* and did eat and drink" (vss. 9-11).

This in no wise contradicts God's word to Moses in Exodus 33.

---

*The very image of His [God's] substance: Two words in this phrase instantly awaken intense interest. In their order they are, (a) "image", or better, **impress:** the Greek word is *charaktēr.* Primarily this word denotes the instrument used in engraving or carv-ing, and from this, the impression made by the die or engraver: "The exact expression (the image) of any person or thing"; in our verse, literally, **the exact-expression of sub-stance of Him** (of God); (b) "substance"; see comment on #4, text.

Moses had said, "Show me, I pray Thee, Thy glory." God in answer promised to "make all His goodness" pass before him, saying:

"Thou canst not see My face; for man shall not see Me and live. And Jehovah said, Behold there is a place by Me, and thou shalt stand upon the rock: and it shall come to pass, while My glory passeth by, that I will put thee in a cleft of the rock, and will cover thee with My hand until I have passed by: and I will take away My hand, and thou shalt see My back; but My face shall not be seen" (vss. 20-23). See also Exodus 34.5 ff. This agrees also with the visions of Ezekiel, Chapters 1.26-28, 3.12-14, 8.2, 9.3; 10; 11.22. These Scriptures reveal the Triune God, enthroned upon the cherubim. We see in Revelation 5.6 our Lord's essential place there, "In the midst of the throne and of the four living creatures, and of the elders." Although being also the Son of Man, He is a Lamb (lit., "a little lamb") "as though it had been slain"—about to take the kingdom on earth (but His place is in the glory that He had with the Father before the world was).

This word "substance" in Hebrews 1.3 relates to Deity itself—the "exact expression" of which, the Man Christ Jesus is!

5. **Maintaining* all things by the word of His power—** John Owen said, "Our Lord Jesus Christ, as the Son of God, hath the weight of the whole creation upon His hand."

Men talk of "the *laws* of nature"; of the "*laws* of being." In the absolute there are no such things! In the light of this all-embracing, overwhelming word, **maintaining all things,** and the method and means by which Christ does it **by the word of His power,** to talk of the "laws" resident in things is simply infidelity, or sublime ignorance.

Certainly there were creative *commands* in Genesis: "Let the earth put forth grass . . . Let there be light . . . Let the waters swarm with swarms of living creatures, and let birds fly above the earth . . . Be fruitful, and multiply, and fill the waters in the seas, and let birds multiply on the earth . . . Let the earth bring forth living creatures after their kind." Again, after making man

---

*See Vincent, who says, "It implies sustaining, but also movement." It deals, as Weiss puts it, "with the all, in all its changes and transformations throughout the aeons."

in His own image, after His likeness, God said "*Be* fruitful, and multiply, and replenish the earth, and subdue it."

Nevertheless, man *is* utterly dependent! As God said to Belshazzar, "The God in Whose hand thy breath is, and Whose are all thy ways"; or Paul to the Athenians, "In Him we live, and move, and have our being"; and, "He Himself giveth to all life, and breath, and all things"; or as Job utters it: "In Whose hand is the soul of every living thing, and the breath [spirit] of all mankind" (Job 12.10); so it is, not only with man, but with every living creature and with the plants of the field, which if God command, shall come up "in a night" (Jonah 4.10)—*every living thing is sustained in being* by the Lord Jesus Christ, the eternal Son. Humbling, but true, O proud man! Yea, blessedly true! say God's saints.

When the Son of God acted in creation by His Word, did He resort to the "laws" of non-existent things? You say, Impossible. "By faith we understand that the worlds have been framed by the word of God, so that [as a result of which] what is seen [the visible universe] hath not been made out of things which appear." People of simple faith accept it: and there is no other sort of faith: for, "Except ye turn and become as little children . . ."!

So the same Person Whose word created still upholds (maintains). Mighty wonder! You object, "Christ Himself said, 'Not a sparrow falleth without My Father' "—making the first Person of the Deity exercise what we call "providence." Alas, how quickly, unless deeply and constantly taught of God, does the human mind become unitarian, rejecting Christ's Deity!*

The Greek word translated "upholding" *(pherô)* is found, for instance, in Mark 2.3, 4 when they came *bringing* the paralyzed man. Again, our Lord said in Mark 12.15, 16: "*Bring* Me a denarius . . . And they *brought* it" *(pherô* twice). It is used seven times in one chapter, John 15, concerning bearing fruit, the

---

*The Jews knew better, who heard His words, "I and the Father are one." (Jno. 10.30). They took up stones to cast at our Lord when He asserted His eternity of being, in Jno. 8.58-59; and again, when He stated His Divine unity with the Father, John 10.30, 31. Our Lord's saying that He had come from Heaven, from the Father, divided the multitude, as we see in Jno. 7.25-44, and 8.23; as His frequent claim that the Father that sent Him was with Him, aroused their blind enmity (Jno. 8.16, 20-27).

emphasis being upon the branch's bearing fruit, and not the fruit,
the branch. This is the word used in Hebrews 1.3 of our Lord's
upholding the universe in every, even the minutest, particular! He
maintaineth all things.

Confess that He is God the Son, and as being so He would
have all power as part of His eternal glory. Then **the word of
His power** becomes an overmastering thought, beyond the conception of mind, but the delight of faith, like that of a babe
trusting its mother. We are not permitted here, as it seems to me,
to let a created universe "run along," after giving it certain
trends. But **the word of His power** ("The creating, omnipresent
Word"—Ohlshausen) is certainly as much His word as that with
which He created all things in the beginning.

The word of His power was constantly spoken of by our blessed
Lord in His ministry among men; and He is the same, "yesterday,
and today, yea, and forever." He "cast out the spirits with *a word*"!
"I will, be thou made clean," He said to the leper. "Young man, I
say unto thee, arise," He said to the widow of Nain's son.
"Lazarus, come forth!" He cried at Bethany, "and he that was dead
came forth." The centurion of Matthew 8.8-13 entered into *faith*
in the word of His power: "Only say the word, and my servant
shall be healed!"

Certainly it is true that our Lord could command an order of
things, as we read in Psalm 119.90-91:

"Thou hast established the earth, and it abideth,
They abide this day according to Thine ordinances;
For all things are Thy servants."

But do not dream that there are any "ordinances" which leave out
the direct and constantly exercised power of the Lord Jesus Christ.
"In Him (Christ) all things *consist*," or "hold together"* (Col.
1.17).

To conceive that the Son of God can **maintain all things by
the word of His power,** and at the same time or for an instant,

---

*Bishop Lightfoot says concerning this word: "Hold together, *cohere:* He is the principle
of cohesion in the universe. To take one instance, the action of gravitation, which keeps
in their places things fixed, and regulates the motions of things moving, is an expression
of His mind. Similarly, in Heb. 1.3, Christ the *Logos* is described as *sustaining* the
universe."

be absent from His creation (in the sense in which evolutionists'
claim) is hideous infidelity which would banish God from His
own creation if it could! An example dear to us is our Lord Jesus'
constant care for all His saints. Thousands upon thousands are
asking Him daily for this and that: and He is able to speak the
word of power to all and to each. How? He is God! There is no
limit to His power.

> "All, all that buds, and blossoms, and rejoices,
>   hath My Beloved made;
>   His wisdom and His tenderness and gladness
>   told forth in leaf and blade.
>   All, all that buds, and blossoms, and rejoices,
>   hath My Beloved made;
>   All moves unto the music of His power
>   that fills the woodland glade."
>
>   Gerhardt Ter Steegen

Such a song is that of the Christian: not of the pantheist or
the atheist, neither of whom want God. Ghastly wonder of all
the ages: man, a creature, whose very name is need, need, need;
who must be "kept" from outside himself, like a newborn babe
supplied with breath, with food, with air; kept in balance by a
power wholly without himself; who must be warmed by a created
sun; the temperature of his body kept by a marvelous adjustment;
his blood kept circulating; his heart kept beating—yet the constant effort of human "science" and "philosophy" is to get as far
away as possible from the consciousness of this creating, pro-
viding, maintaining Lord God!

6. **When He had made purification of sins**—This is the most
brief and comprehensive statement in all Scripture of our Lord's
work at His first coming. "Purification" here is to be conceived
of in the largest sense as including not only believers' sins
expiated on the Cross, where propitiation and remission were
secured; but also the whole task of Christ as to the removal of
sins from God's sight*—described in one word! Looking at the
work done Godward, it is "the Lamb of God taking away the sin
of the world." Note that it is **purification of** sins, not, from

---

*"In the thought of making *purification of sins* is already foreshadowed the work of Christ
as High Priest, which plays so prominent a part in the epistle."—Vincent.

sin: it is the great work of the Cross, effective everywhere and forever, whereby God pardons and remits the sins of individual believers, and brings in a new creation where righteousness is "at home." But, here used, it is a great word preparing the way, laying the foundation, for the priestly work of Christ revealed in this epistle.

7. Sat down on the right hand of the Majesty on high—These words present the last of the seven revelations concerning the Person of that Son in Whom God has "spoken unto us." Lack of much reverent consideration of these wondrous words of God concerning the Son accounts for the shallow, doubting "Christianity" everywhere. My first visit to London came just at the season when favored persons were being "received" by royalty (Edward VII). I marked the conduct of those Americans who were preparing to be "received at court," their assiduous daily study of the proper attire, address, and every detail they thought would be important. My heart sank at the contrasting heedlessness of these same human creatures towards their *God*, and towards *that Son* in Whom He has now "spoken."

Ah, the supernal dignity of these words, sat down . . . Majesty . . . on High!* It is indeed a seated Priest, after an accomplished work, Whom we are to find in Hebrews! But now the infinite greatness of His Person and position is before us. Indeed the word "Majesty" is simply the Greek word "great" formed into a capital noun, used in Scripture only of the majesty,

---

*Four times in Hebrews is Christ seen as having sat down on the right hand of God:
   1. In Ch. 1.3, as Son, Heir, Effulgence, Upholder—after "purification of sins," He sat down on the right hand of the Majesty on High. This is in view of His Person.
   2. In Ch. 8.1, 2 we have the High Priest's ministry described: "Who sat down on the right hand of the throne of the Majesty in the heavens, a minister of the sanctuary, and of the true tabernacle, which the Lord pitched, not man."
   3. In Ch. 10. 12, contrasted with earthly priests, that keep standing "day by day ministering . . . He . . . sat down on the right hand of God." Here, His sitting down is in view of His one sacrifice. The sacrifice is never to be repeated, therefore the Priest is seated.
   4. In Ch. 12.2 He is seen as the Leader *(Archegos)* of the "great cloud of witnesses" who lived, walked and conquered by faith (Ch. 11): "Jesus, the Leader and Perfecter of the faith, Who for the joy that was set before Him endured the Cross, despising shame, and hath sat down at the right hand of the throne of God." Here neither His Person, His ministry, nor His finished work is before us, but His *inner motives* in view of the "joy set before Him"; and His consequent "race"—enduring the Cross, despising the shame."
   Reflection upon these four wondrous views of Christ's session at God's right hand will greatly edify the believer.

the greatness, of God (Heb. 1.3, 8.1; Jude 25. Compare II Sam. 7.22, Ps. 145, 3, 6; I Chron. 29.11). THERE IS NO OTHER GREATNESS! May we be brought into this consciousness!

Verse 4: Having become by so much better than the angels, as He hath inherited a more excellent name than they: "Better" (the Greek word *kreitton*) is used thirteen times in this book of **Hebrews,** out of nineteen times in the whole New Testament. Beginning here in Chapter 1.4 with Christ Himself **better than the angels*** we have "better things" (6.9); "better person" (than Abraham (7.7); "better hope" (7.19); "better covenant" (7.22); "better covenant . . . better promises" (8.6); "better sacrifices" (9.23); "better possession" (10.34); "better country" (11.16); "better resurrection" (11.35); "better things" (11.40 and 12.24). No wonder Paul uses the same word "better" in Philippians: "To depart and be with Christ . . . is very far better"! (1.23).

This blessed Son having in His humanity the "body" which, He said, His Father prepared for Him (10.5), was "made for a little while lower than the angels" (2.9). Astonishing fact! (—which, by the way, eternally protects the elect angels from the pride by which the others were lost, following the dragon in his pride—Rev. 12.4, 8, 9). Now this Son is said to have **become so much better than the angels, as He hath inherited a more excellent name than they.†** Of course no moral or spiritual excellence is

---

*Jewish minds thought much of angelic glory. They had received the Law as ordained by ministry of angels (Acts 7.53). They were wont, therefore, to regard with awe and wonder those obedient messengers of God's power. There can be no stronger proof of this than John's temptation to worship one (Rev. 19.10, 22.8-9). Hence the weight of the further testimony here to Christ's glory, He having become by so much better than the angels, as He hath inherited a more excellent name than they.

†And this was as MAN, remember! For He is here set before us as the Son in Whom God—at the end of the Old Testament days—had spoken! So He is "the Word made flesh" and having as such, "tabernacled among us" (Jno. 1.14), of whom God is here speaking! Read Chapter 1 over and over!

Now, how much better than the angels had He, though Man, "become"?

1. He is the Son of God; they are "servants" (1.5, 7).
2. He is to be worshiped by the angels! (1.6).
3. He is addressed as *"God"* by God the Father! (1.8).
4. He is addressed as "King"—Whose "sceptre" is that of uprightness" (1.8).
5. For His love of righteousness, and hatred of iniquity, His God had "anointed Him with the oil of gladness above His fellows"—whoever they be! (1.9).
6. He is addressed as "Lord," Who "in the beginning did lay the foundations of the earth," and the works of Whose hands the very Heavens are! (1.10).
7. He shall *continue*, though these Heavens shall pass away: "They shall perish, but Thou continuest . . . Thou art the same; Thy years shall not fail" (1.11, 12).

indicated here, for He was ever perfect. But He was, we read, "perfected through sufferings" (2.10, 5.9, 7.28). He went on from trial to trial, from testing to testing, to perfect obedience to God's will—which involved His death, and that as a Sin-offering. But thence God raised Him, and thus He must be held in our minds—from the words of Chapter 1.3, "When He had made purification of sins," as a Risen One, seated on the right hand of God! He has taken that place above the angels which belonged to Him eternally as Son and Heir of all things, and now belongs to Him as the "one Mediator between God and men, the MAN Christ Jesus" (I Tim. 2.5). Few believe in their very hearts that there is a MAN in the glory!—and that Paul wrote of "Christ concerning *the flesh*," the words, "Who is over all, God blessed forever"!

Note especially that word "become." As God the Son, He could not *"become."* He could say, "Before Abraham was born, I AM!" But, as having emptied Himself, having taken the form of man, and humbled Himself, even to "obedience unto death, yea, the death of the Cross"—it is thus He is seen in the words before us. His "becoming" took Him for a little while "lower than the angels." Now, raised from the dead through the glory of the Father, and being by the right hand of God exalted, He has taken His seat as Man (none the less God, but as Man) **on the right hand of the Majesty on High.** And this phrase, **become by so much,** measures the distance—infinite and incomprehensible to us—between the Risen Christ and the angelic host. How much better? **As He hath inherited a more excellent name than they.** This "Name" is never for a moment to be thought of as in com-petition with the angels or other beings. Competition with their Creator? Subjection is their delight! "Glory to God in the highest," they sang when He was born in Bethlehem—to be for "a little while *lower* than the angels"! How happy is their sweet ministry, "sent forth to do service for the sake of them that shall inherit salvation," which service they delight to do. But, brother, it

---

8. "Of which of the angels hath He said at any time, Sit Thou at My right hand, till I make Thine enemies the footstool of Thy feet?" (1.13).

9. "Are they not all ministering spirits, sent forth to do service for the sake of them that shall inherit salvation?" (1.14).

10. "Not unto angels did He [God] subject the world to come" (whereof in Hebrews we speak, and to which we look forward) (2.5).

is not the vote of the heavenly beings that makes the Son of God
become by so much better than the angels. It is the facts in the
case. He is *God.* They are *creatures.* The cleavage is infinite, between Him and all creatures and between His work and that of any
creature, forever—much as God loves His faithful servants.

Note that it is **by so much*** and not merely so much better.
That is, it is a measure of place, or degree; not of quality of
being. The great mystery we must never forget is even that
when He became "for a little while lower than the angels," He
was still the same in Deity as when He created all things. We must
make careful distinction here between "having become" and
"having inherited a name." This "inheriting" compels us to
regard Him as Man, as the Word made flesh, as the Son, perfected forevermore, and ascended to Heaven. Indeed, the language of the whole verse sets this forth. He "sat down," the
previous verse tells us; and now, "having become," and having
"obtained by inheritance," are spoken of Him.

After these seven utterances concerning our Lord's Person
(vss. 2, 3), God cites *seven Old Testament Scriptures,* elucidating
and proving verse 4. Let us examine these seven quotations made,
as usual in Hebrews, from the Septuagint.†

**Verse 5: For unto which of the angels said He at any time,
Thou art My Son, This day have I begotten Thee?** (Ps. 2.7).
That Christ's Deity is here before us leaps into utterance in this
verse. These angels are creatures, with the same creature-responsi-
bility possessed by all creatures, a fact which is readily seen
in God's pronouncement of future judgment upon the fallen

---

*This comparative phrase, in its four occurrences in Hebrews, really sets forth infinity.
The measure in each case is beyond measure! Ch. 3.3, 5 says Moses was faithful in all
God's house but Jesus was "counted worthy of more glory than Moses by so much
as He that built the house hath more honor than the house." Ch. 7.22: "Inasmuch as
it is not without the taking of an oath . . . by so much also hath Jesus become the
Surety of a better covenant." (Not until Ch. 13.20 will the great announcement of
that "eternal covenant" between God and Christ, by which He was "brought again
from the dead," be definitely set forth; but it is doctrinally involved throughout the
book from Ch. 1.3-4, on.) And Ch. 8.6 "He hath obtained a ministry the more
excellent, by so much as He is also the Mediator of a better covenant."

†"The Septuagint was a translation of the O. T. from the Hebrew into the Greek
language, made about 270 to 285 B.C.; so-called because of the 70 translators said to
have been engaged in making it. It is the most ancient of all versions of the Hebrew
O. T."—Angus, *Cyclopedic Handbook to the Bible.*

angels in Psalm 82.6-7 (see Jno. 10.34-36). Though called "sons" as created beings—as, indeed, Adam is called, being Divinely created (Lk. 3.38), yet no angel is ever addressed as is Christ.* Here (Ps. 2.7) Christ is addressed in an entirely different man-ner. *First* of all, He is the eternal Son. The relationship of Father, Son, and Spirit always existed in the Deity. *Second,* when He was born in Bethlehem, that is, in the incarnation, He is also called "Son of the Most High" and "Son of God" (Lk. 1.32, 35; see also Isa. 9.6, "Unto us a Child is born, unto us a *Son* is given"). *Third,* when He was raised from the dead He was so saluted, as we read in Acts 13.33: "The promise made unto the fathers . . . God hath fulfilled . . . unto our children, in that He raised up Jesus."

To what occasion, then, of our Lord's life, do the words in Hebrews 1.5 refer? To His eternal Sonship? To His incarnation? Or to His resurrection-ascension, and session at God's right hand? Evidently to the last named. Paul said plainly to the Jews in Pisidia:

"In that He raised up Jesus; as also it is written in the second psalm, 'Thou art My Son, this day I have begotten Thee.' And as concerning that He raised Him up from the dead, now no more to return to corruption, He hath spoken on this wise, 'I will give you the holy and sure blessings of David.' (Isa. 55.3). Because He saith also in another psalm (16.10), 'Thou wilt not give Thy Holy One to see corruption.' "

Here Paul clearly connects the words of the Second Psalm, "This day have I begotten Thee," with our Lord's resurrection and His salutation by the Father as risen.

In the address, **Thou art My Son, This day have I begotten Thee,** are these two distinct elements: first, the fact that He *is* the Son eternally; and second, His public recognition as such afterwards, and most especially at His resurrection, when He was "declared to be the Son of God with power"—as is so emphasized in Romans 1.4.

But in Hebrews 1.5 the question is not when He was called

---

*"In O. T., 'sons' is applied to angels collectively but never individually. See Ps. 29.1, 89.6. Similarly, 'son' is applied to the chosen nation: Ex. 4.22, Hos. 11.1; but to no individual nation."—Vincent.

Son, but the fact that He was so called, as over against the fact
that no angel was ever thus addressed! We find God speaking to
David in the great royal covenant (I Chron. 17.13; II Sam. 7.14)
whereby He promised him a Son, the throne of Whose kingdom
He would establish forever, of that One of David's house Who
should inherit his throne forever:

> I will be to Him a Father,
> And He shall be to Me a Son.

How wonderfully the Spirit of God brings out the thought of
God, where our poor minds could not have followed! The words,
He shall be to me a Son, are of course spoken of Christ as a Son
of David—as Man. As God He was eternally in the relationship
of Son. Again we would warn against seeking to probe into this
mystery, which faith and faith alone can receive.* When our
Lord was born, He was *Emmanuel,* God with us (Isa. 7.14); and
He was Man, yea, a babe, Who by the spirit of prophecy said,
"Thou didst make me trust when I was upon My mother's breasts"
(Ps. 22.9).

There are in Matthew 11.27 three great facts shown unto us by
our Lord: first: "All things have been delivered unto Me of My
Father" (of this we do not now speak). Second, "No one knoweth
the Son, save the Father." Of this we must speak with profoundest
emphasis: for this "knowing" is that of which only God, and no
creature, is capable. Third, "Neither doth any know the Father,
save the Son, and He to whomsoever the Son willeth to reveal
Him." This He has willed for us who, begotten of God, born of His
Spirit, are of God's family (I Jno. 2.13). But it is upon the
Father's knowledge of the Son that we must ponder especially in
Hebrews 1.

To sum up, Christ being the Son of God, greeted thus before
incarnation and constantly afterwards, is "declared to be the Son

---

*A godly and deeply instructed brother has written: "We cannot fathom what He was.
Our hearts should not go and scrutinize the Person of Christ as though we could know
it all. No human being can understand the union of God and man in His Person:
'No one knoweth the Son, save the Father' . . . All that is revealed, you may know;
we may learn a great deal about Him . . . but when I attempt to fathom the union of
God and man . . . no man can."

of God with power . . . by the resurrection from the dead"
(Rom. 1.4), and thus preached.*

Verse 6: And when He again bringeth in THE FIRSTBORN
into the world, He saith, And let all the angels of God worship
Him: In this, the third of these great Old Testament words
concerning Christ, the Spirit goes back to Psalm 97.7: "Worship
Him, all ye gods." (Perhaps also there is a reference to Deut.
32.43, Sept.) The 97th is one of the psalms of the second coming
and millennial reign of Christ. Note first the beautiful name of
Christ here (Heb. 1.6): THE FIRSTBORN. It is in itself an
absolute *title*, a name. He is The Firstborn—the immediate
expression of the rights and the glory of God. He has universal
pre-eminence. Instead of looking at this wonderful Name† from
the creature's viewpoint, as do the Unitarians, modernists, and all
infidels, let us view this Name from its only proper viewpoint,
that of God Himself. Then indeed does it begin to teach us
marvelous things of blessing!

You remember that in our Lord's prayer in the 17th of John,
He asks that the Father will glorify Him "with the glory which I

---

*" 'Thou art my Son, this day have I begotten Thee,' is His relationship in time with
God. It depends, I doubt not, on His glorious nature; but this position for man was
acquired by the miraculous birth of Jesus here below, and demonstrated as true and
determined in its true import by His resurrection."—J. N. Darby.

†When we quote Col. 1.15, "Who is the image of the invisible God, The Firstborn
of all creation," Unitarian hosts rush to cry, "Yes, the Firstborn, the highest—but a
creature, evidently." But let them read the next verse, "For in Him were all things
created in the heavens and upon the earth." We press upon the reader that there is no
faintest hint of Christ's being a creature, but the exact opposite: *"God* was manifest
in the flesh." The movement is from God toward us, in infinite condescension. The
Creator is coming among His creatures. The Second Person of the Deity has stepped
into the creature place: not at all *becoming* a creature, for He Himself created all things!
But the Father prepared Him a body (Heb. 10.5) and from the womb of the virgin,
according to the word of prophecy, it could now be said, "Unto us a Child is born,
unto us a Son is given . . . and His name shall be called Wonderful, Counsellor, Mighty
God, Father of eternity, Prince of peace." O sinner! O saint! Read this and adore.
In proceeding out into His creation should He not have the title, "The Firstborn"?
He is not of creation in His origin, but He is one with us in grace.

This name, Firstborn *(Prototokos)* is applied seven times to our Lord (although in
Matt. 1.25 and Lk. 2.7 it concerns His birth: "She brought forth her firstborn son").
In Rom. 8.29, "The Firstborn among many brethren"; Col. 1.15, "The Firstborn of all
creation," because "by Him were all things created"; Col. 1.18, "The Firstborn from
among the dead" (in resurrection, of course); Heb. 1.6, *When He again bringeth in The
Firstborn into the World;* Rev. 1.5, "The Firstborn of the dead" (for Christ
did not go back, as did Lazarus, into the life of earth, but was raised in "newness
of life": Rom. 6.4).

It is, we repeat, a title—not the eldest son of a family. See Ps. 89.27, where God,
in speaking of David's *tenth* son (I Chron. 3.1-5) Solomon, declares, "I will make
[or, appoint] him *firstborn* the highest of the kings of the earth" (II Chron. 9.22-24).

had with Thee," He said, "before the world was." He was there in all eternity past, one Person in the ineffable Trinity, Father, Son, and Holy Spirit. To that eternal past the title, The First-born, cannot belong. Where, then, do we begin to find it? In God's motion toward creatures—even ourselves—not angels but men! Why this coming forth into creation and toward creatures? Was not the triune God sufficient in Himself? Were not His attributes all glorious? Was not the fellowship of Father, Son and Spirit enough—infinitely enough?

Nay. God is *Love!* And He would bestow that love upon crea-tures, who, by that bestowal, would be forever blessed. And He would reveal the absoluteness of that love in sending the Son of His love to redeem those who were otherwise guilty, lost, and forever undone. So God "brought in" His Son "into the world" first at Bethlehem. Again and again our Lord testified that He had not come of Himself, but that the Father had *sent Him:* "I came forth and am come from God; for neither have I come of Myself, but He *sent* Me" (Jno. 7.28, 29; 8.42; 10.36). Now this was His first coming. And, according to hundreds of passages in the New Testament, as well as those in the old prophets, He is to be sent again into this world. God will **again bring in THE FIRSTBORN into the habitable world,** where He was once rejected: mark that! God will bring Him back to earth again,* and in revealed glory. Paul says in I Thessalonians 4.14, "If we believe that Jesus died and rose again, even so them also that are fallen asleep in (Gr., *through*) Jesus will God *bring with* Him." Not only will God bring Christ back but the Saints with Him! See I Thessalonians 3.13: "The coming of our Lord Jesus *with all His Saints"!*

Second, "the angels" are to be taken into a higher place than they have ever had, even that of worshipers, a new and under-standing place, where they will know God's love, and His electing Grace, seen in the redeemed, the members of Christ's Body! The words, **Let all the angels of God worship Him,** we find mar-

---

*Of the adverb translated "again" *(palin),* Thayer says, "Joined to verbs of all sorts, it denotes renewal or repetition of the action . . . In Heb. 1.6, *palin* is tacitly opposed to the time when God *first* brought His Son into the world." And Alford: "In this epistle, when *palin* is joined to a verb, it always has the sense of "a second time." The A. V. reading, "And again, when He bringeth in," makes "again" a simple particle, not an adverb, and so obscures this reference to *Christ's second coming.*

velously carried out in Revelation 5.7-12. There is deep
instruction for us in this passage. After the Lamb has taken the
governmental seven-sealed book, the four Living Ones and the
twenty-four Elders fall down before Him, having each one a
harp, for it is the day of Heaven's joy, celebrating His death and
His purchasing [men] unto God with His blood out of "every
tribe, and tongue, and people, and nation," to "reign upon the
earth." Then come the angels. Their time of serving the saints
is over, and their time of worship of the Lamb continues. "And
I saw, and I heard a voice of many angels round about the
throne," John tells us, "and the number of them was ten
thousand times ten thousand, and thousands of thousands; saying with a great voice, Worthy is the Lamb that hath been slain"
(Rev. 5.11, 12).

Someone may ask, Have not the angelic beings always worshiped Christ the Son, through Whose word they were created?
Doubtless they have always worshiped the Triune God. But
when in the eternity past did God reveal Himself as at the incarnation when the only begotten Son, Who was in the bosom of the
Father, "declared Him"? (Jno. 1.18). It was not that God dwelt
in Heaven in thick darkness as He appeared on Sinai. On the
contrary, it is written of Him, "Who only hath immortality,
dwelling in light unapproachable" (I Tim. 6.16). Read again
the footnote regarding "again" on Hebrews 1.6.

In the various "theophanies" of the Old Testament, the Son
was the Speaker—as He was the Speaker of the creative word
of Genesis 1.3. And we know Isaiah saw Christ's glory, as God
(Isa. 6; Jno. 12.41). Yet not to the Old Testament fathers did
God speak "in a Son," as now. Nor do we read in Scripture of
any other being than man created in God's image and likeness.
For God's counsels were connected with Christ *as man.**

---

*God will "sum up all things in Christ, the things in the heavens, and the things upon
the earth"—which is the "secret of His will" made known in Eph. 1.9, 10. Vss. 11-14
and following show our direct connection with Christ as God's "inheritance" (vs. 18);
while Eph. 3.10, 11 tells us that it was God's intent that now "unto the principalities
and powers in the heavenlies might be made known through the Church [the Assembly,
the Bride of Christ,] the manifold wisdom of God, according to the purpose of the ages
[margin] which He purposed in Christ Jesus our Lord."

These "ages" run back to the beginning of God's creation, including, we believe,
all things God has created. So this "purpose of the ages"—God's great ultimate object
in them all, was to *reveal Christ,* in Whom dwelleth all the fullness of the Godhead, and
the Assembly, as Christ's fullness (Eph. 1.22, 23).

Just how much the angels knew of our Lord as the Eternal
Word, we may not know. What a celebration there was on the
night He was born in Bethlehem as God manifest in the flesh!
But here in Hebrews 1.6 the angels will be called, we believe, into a
ministry of intelligent worship such as they never knew before.
Read carefully here I Peter 1.11-12: "Which things angels desire
to look into"! What things? Those things concerning "the sufferings
of [appointed unto] Christ, and the glories that should follow
them." Those matters which concern God's redemptive plan reveal
His nature as *Love:* which things are shown directly to the objects
of redemption, lost men; but which must be learned by observation by sinless heavenly beings. Christ "took hold of" (or "gave
help to") the seed of Abraham, "not of angels" (Heb. 2.16). So
that the pardoned sinner knows the heart of God as no angel,
cherub or seraph can!

Having, therefore, beheld God's love in sending His dear Son
to the Cross, the angels enter with delight unimaginable upon
the worship of that Son, when He takes over the kingdom things,
as we said above.

Verse 7: In the fourth Old Testament citation concerning the
Son's place above the angels, we see their former ministry described thus:

> And of the angels He saith,
>   Who maketh His angels winds,
>   And His ministers a flame of fire:

This is quoted from Psalm 104.4, the word "maketh" indicating, according to a revered expositor, "He created them so."
"The thought expressed here is that God employs His angels in
the physical operation of the universe"—Conybeare. Here the
angels are servants,* whereas in the following verse, the Son is

---

*"It will be well to trace through the Revelation the very remarkable, often wholly
unexpected, and hitherto unrevealed angelic activity.

"We have already noticed . . . the constant and prominent part angels have in the
ministration of affairs in Heaven: Rev. 5.2-11, 8.3-5; then (8.6-11) the seven angels
with the trumpets, sending terrible direct judgment from Heaven. How God places in
angels, 'mighty in strength,' the execution of His plans, is concretely suggested in Rev.
10.7. In Rev. 14.18 we find the angel 'that hath power over fire'. In Rev. 16.5, 'the
angel of the waters'; in 16.8, an angel the agent that gives power to the sun to 'scorch
men with fire; and in 19.17, an angel standing in the sun, speaking His message.
These are instances of the remarkable powers and offices possessed through Divine gift
by these beings called angels. God continually and personally ministers the affairs of this

addressed as God. For it is a state of being, not a ministry, that is in view in all this passage. It is the Son of God above the angels, although God created them able "to fly swiftly" (Dan. 9.21) and to be His ministers Whose throne is "fiery flames." See again in Daniel 7.9, 10, and Revelation 8.2 God surrounded by these ministers, as Gabriel said (Lk. 1.19), "I am Gabriel, that stand in the presence of God."

In the fifth and sixth citations of Scripture here in Hebrews 1, we have several marvelous features. In the first place, both these quotations, (first, vss. 8-9, from Ps. 45; second, vss. 10-12, from Ps. 102) are assertions of our Lord's Deity: the first, with respect to His Person; the second, with respect to His creatorship. In the second place, these quotations are taken out of their Old Testament context by the Holy Spirit, and applied to Christ in a manner that is startling. Finally, like all the seven citations of Scripture we are considering, they are utterances of God the Father, concerning, or directly unto, God the Son.

8 But of the Son He saith,
    Thy throne, O God, is forever and ever;
    And the sceptre of uprightness is the sceptre of Thy kingdom.
9 Thou hast loved righteousness, and hated iniquity;
    Therefore God, Thy God, hath anointed Thee
    With the oil of gladness above Thy fellows.*

This, as we have said, is from the beautiful 45th Psalm (which read), a rapturous welcome of the Lord at His second coming in glory, by the saved remnant of Israel: as the first verse says,

"I speak the things which I have made touching the King."

Notice the enraptured words addressed to Christ:

"Thou art fairer than the children of men;
Grace is poured into Thy lips:
Therefore God hath blessed Thee forever."

Here Christ is plainly addressed as Man—as note "Thy fellows," in the preceding verse.

---

earth; and we learn from such verses as Rev. 7.1, that He does it through angelic ministers. He loves to delegate His power to His faithful servants."—The author's book, **The Revelation,** pp. 109-110.

*Here, as Deity, He is addressed as God by God the Father, and, as also Man, by the words, "Thy God." For as Man, He "emptied Himself"—of His glory, power and wisdom (Phil. 2.6-8).

But we come to the sixth verse in this 45th Psalm, and He is addressed as *God!* The Spirit of God quotes this verse in Hebrews 1.8, and addresses it to Christ: **Thy throne, O God, is for ever and ever.*** No Unitarian evasion can escape it. Here God goes away back before the incarnation. Vain and dangerous indeed it is for the human mind to speculate on the union of Deity and humanity. Christ is both. Faith receives it!

Now we proceed, in Psalm 45.6, 7, quoted in Hebrews 1.8, 9:

And the sceptre of uprightness is the sceptre of Thy kingdom: Both in the psalm and here, we may see the righteousness of Christ's millennial reign.

Thou hast loved righteousness and hated iniquity;
Therefore God, Thy God, hath anointed Thee
With the oil of gladness above Thy fellows.

We shall note what this word "fellows" *(metochoi)* means. It occurs five times in **Hebrews.**

We must remember that the 45th Psalm, which is here before our eyes, is "a goodly matter touching the king"—that is, con-cerning Christ at His coming to reign. Verses 3-5 of this psalm see Him with His sword upon His thigh, riding on prosperously, His "arrows sharp," the "peoples falling under Him," "the King's enemies." This corresponds with our Lord's coming as "KING

---

*Here are three things: First, the Son addressed as God by the Father. Our Lord's walk, words, and works were in full consciousness of this: "Therefore the Jews sought the more to kill Him, because He not only brake the sabbath, but also called God His own Father, making Himself equal with God" (Jno. 5.18). There are no degrees in Deity!

Second, the Son as the Lamb shares the throne of Deity. Nor does this conflict with I Cor. 15.28: "When all things have been subjected unto Him [Christ], then shall the Son also Himself be subjected to Him that did subject all things unto Him, that God may be all in all." "For He must reign till He hath put all His enemies under His feet" (vs. 25). It is an administrative throne (rather than "mediatorial," as it has been sometimes called) on which He "must reign till"—. It is not the throne of Heb. 1.8. Therefore when that work of administering judgment to the enemies is completed, Christ voluntarily "shall deliver up the kingdom of God, even the Father." The fact, however, that He has (a) become man, and (b) had all things delivered unto Him of the Father for the task of putting down foes, does not detract from His own essential, eternal Deity. Even in the final revelation to us, the throne of God (Rev. 22.1, 3) is "The throne of God and of the Lamb"—a precious word! For the words "The Lamb" show Him *Man*, as we know Him to be God!

Third, the Lamb, seen in the midst of the throne in Rev. 5.6, does not retire into that throne of the triune God again, but is "the Lamp" of the glory of God in the new Jerusalem forever (Rev. 21.23). He is Man forever, being God from eternity to eternity. He sits "forever" upon the throne with God: "equal with God." Yet His eternal delight, as when upon earth, is to do the will of the Father; and the Father's eternal delight is to glorify the Son!

OF KINGS AND LORD OF LORDS" (Rev. 19.11-16). There, "the armies which are in Heaven followed Him." They are seen as companions, "fellows." But the words: **God, thy God, hath anointed Thee with the oil of gladness,** gives us a blessed view of that day of delight when our blessed Lord comes upon that glorious hour appointed by the Father (Acts 1.6, 7) when He enters upon His kingdom. He will indeed say on that day to His faithful servants, "Enter thou into *the joy* of thy Lord" (Matt. 25.21, 23).

But His joy will abound "above" theirs, in these respects:

(a) He is God the Son; they are creatures.

(b) He has therefore infinitely **loved righteousness and hated iniquity.**

(c) He has been looking forward to that day (the millennial coming) which Psalm 45 depicts, from ages past.

(d) As Psalm 2 and Hebrews 10.13 and many Scriptures show, the holy purpose of God involves the overthrow in wrath of all His final enemies. And when the day comes, it will be measureless joy to the Son to clear the unrighteous away—just as it was a delight to do the Father's will in bearing the sin of the world.

In the Millennium, our Lord will "rule *in the midst* of His enemies," for although all obey, it is written that they "yield *feigned* obedience" (Ps. 18.44, 81.15, 66.3), and rush to Satan's banner when he is loosed (Rev. 20.7-9).

We must receive into our thinking the fact that His infinite joy includes the removal of final foes.

Note further the holy love and holy hate which marked Christ's course on earth, resulting in that **anointing with the oil of gladness** to which our Lord refers in the words, "Enter thou into the joy of thy Lord" or in Hebrews 12.2, "Who, for the *joy* that was set before Him." The eternal, immeasurable gladness of Christ as having *done to the utmost* the Father's will, and having been *anointed of Him*—ponder upon it—His "fellows" share it in due measure.

Come now to the sixth of these great Old Testament citations, from Psalm 102.25-27:

10 And, Thou, Lord, in the beginning didst lay the foundation of the earth,

And the heavens are the works of Thy hands:
11   They shall perish; but Thou continuest:
    And they all shall wax old as doth a garment;
12   And as a mantle shalt Thou roll them up,
    As a garment, and they shall be exchanged:
      But Thou art the same,
      And Thy years shall not fail.
13   But of which of the angels hath He said at any time,
    Sit Thou on My right hand,
    Till I make Thine enemies the footstool of Thy feet?
14   Are they not all ministering spirits, sent forth to do
    service for the sake of them that shall inherit salvation?

**Verse 10: Thou, Lord, in the beginning didst lay the founda-
tion of the earth,**

And the heavens are the works of Thy hands:

The circumstances of this passage are profoundly moving to
a spiritual heart. For in Psalm 102.23, 24, our Lord Jesus in
speaking thus to the Father:
"He weakened My strength in the way;
He shortened my days.
I said, O My God, take Me not away in the midst of My days:
Thy years are throughout all generations."

How blessedly human are such words! At thirty-three a man
has just found his vigor, and the things of earthly life have their
greatest interest and power. This beautiful, touching appeal is
made by the Man Christ Jesus to God as *His God*, when it is revealed to Him that His days are to be shortened, that His strength
is to be weakened—for, "He was crucified through weakness"
(II Cor. 13.4). "Take me not away in the midst of My days,"
pleaded the Man Christ Jesus. And then the argument with His
God: "*Thy* years are throughout all generations." How this must
have touched the very heart of God His Father! And what answer
does He make to His Son? Now, have simple faith and be prepared
for what the Spirit of God does at this place. For, though Christ
is speaking in Psalm 102.23, 24, God answers Him in verses 25-27!
We should look upon the earth and the heavens as becoming
"old" (Heb. 1.11). Thus shall we become occupied with Him to
Whom God says, **But Thou art the same, and Thy years shall
not fail.**

Again we remark that these mighty words of comfort are ad-dressed by God the Father to His dear Son then in humiliation, in answer to His cry, "Take Me not away in the midst of My days." The Father declares to His Son, pointing to the eternity past, that He, the Son, Whom He addressed as Lord (Heb. 1.10), made the earth and the heavens! Then, pointing to the eternity coming, He assures Him, **But Thou art the same, and Thy years shall not fail.** It is God the Father's answer to His Son's cry—and what an answer!

And what a testimony by the Father to the Son's Creatorship is this verse of Hebrews 1!* The Father willed creation, the Son spake it, the Spirit executed it! (Ps. 104.30).

Verse 11: They shall perish; but Thou continuest;
And they all shall wax old, as doth a garment.

Here self-existent Deity is ascribed to Christ. Then as to what He has made, the earth, the heavens: **They shall perish,** as con-trasted with Christ's continued existence. Our Lord Himself said, "Heaven and earth shall pass away." It is not in God's mind to preserve forever this present creation. Its end is revealed in **they shall perish . . . wax old . . . be rolled up . . . exchanged!** How brief is the existence of present created things! Poor man, in all his thinking and living, treats the present earth and heavens as abiding. The mockers of the last days make what they regard as the fixed permanence of the universe the basis of their scoffing at Christ's coming, with the stupendous changes it involves, say-ing, "Where is the promise of His coming? for, from the day that the fathers fell asleep, all things *continue as they were* from the beginning of the creation" (II Pet. 3.4). Every believer should read often the two closing chapters of the Revelation, and remember that the present creation is to be *exchanged*, as our next verse in **Hebrews** tells us. Before the face of the Sitter upon the Great White Throne of final judgment, "The earth and the heaven fled away; and there was found no place for them . . . He that sitteth on the throne said, Behold, I am making all things new."

---

*Fosdick, the infidel who has publicly, in print and by voice, denied all the fundamentals of the faith of the gospel, has a sermon on "The Danger of Worshipping Jesus of Nazareth." What will God say to the Fosdick atom in that day—in view of this verse, where God addresses Jesus as, "Thou, *Lord,*" and makes Him the *Creator?*

Verse 12: And as a mantle shalt Thou roll them up,
As a garment, and they shall be exchanged:
What an expression and prophecy! Christ will be the One
before Whose face earth and Heaven flee away. Note the word
exchanged, rather than *changed*,* for there shall be a new Heaven
and a new earth, in place of the old, which shall utterly pass away.†

But Thou art the same, and Thy years shall not fail. Here we
see Christ's uncaused continuance of being. Every creature
changes, every creature's years fail, for creatures are dependent.
God the Father, God the Son, and God the Holy Spirit, three in
One, are not dependent, but are seen to all eternity—past, and to
come!

Verse 13: But of which of the angels hath He said at any time,
Sit Thou on My right hand, Till I make Thine enemies the
footstool of Thy feet?
This is the seventh of these wonderful citations concerning the
Son of God's position above all angelic creation. Angels and saints
are much in the mouths of Romanists, as with the early Gnostics,
who built up a series of higher and higher powers they called
"demiurges"—finally to reach God! How we praise God for the
simplicity of His Word! Christ, and Christ alone, God's dear Son,
is the Word of God! As to God's purposes for the future,
Christ's enemies shall be by God placed beneath His feet. For
this we see our Lord waiting, in Chapter 10.13. Note this word

---

*"To cause one thing to cease, and another to take its place."—Thayer.

†As Stuart well remarks, "The heavens are often represented as an expanse, and to roll
them up, is of course to remove them. The language, however, in the case before us,
is borrowed from the custom of folding up, laying aside, garments that have become
unfit for use."

Govett says of the new heavens and the new earth: "Both heavens and earth are
'new.' They are of new materials: not merely a purifying of the old. They are not new
because they are a fresh modification of the old materials! This verse teaches us that the
heavens and earth are new in their materials, as well as in their form. 'The earth is new,
for the old earth passed away.' If I say 'A new man-of-war graced the port of Plymouth,
for the old Victory foundered in the Atlantic'—none would suspect me of asserting
that the old vessel was fished up, and that its timbers, rearranged, constituted the new
vessel. 'The former earth and heaven passed away.' The former chapter exhibited the
destruction of the old creation; it had no longer any locality. Now we are presented with
the final state which succeeds."

We hear also Isa. 51.6: "Lift up your eyes to the heavens, and look upon the earth
beneath; for the heavens shall vanish away like smoke, and the earth shall wax old
like a garment."

"The course of thought is easily traced: as the garment which has grown old is
rolled up and changed, so the former heavens and earth shall give place to the new
heavens and the new earth."—Moulton.

"enemies." We have it here in Chapter 1.13, from Psalm 2; and in Chapter 10.13: "Henceforth expecting till His *enemies* be made the footstool of His feet"; and again, Chapter 10.27, "A fierceness of fire which shall devour the *adversaries.*" We shall not pause here to describe these "adversaries," except to say that they are those who "will not that *this* Man reign over them" (Lk. 19.14, 27).

Perhaps no utterance of Scripture is more misunderstood than this 13th verse, yet see how plain it is:

1. The Son of God is asked to sit at the Father's right hand.

2. It is promised, as to His enemies, not that they shall be converted, but that they shall be **made the footstool of His feet.**

3. The Father is seen bringing back His Son to this earth, for it is *on earth* that both human enemies and Satan himself are, at Christ's coming, put beneath His feet. See Revelation 19.11-21. Compare I Corinthians 15.25, which we have noted above; and see that Psalm 110.1 is quoted by our Lord in Matthew (22.44), Mark (12.36), and Luke (20.42); and by Peter at Pentecost (Acts 2.34, 35)—besides here in Hebrews 1.13.

4. At the time when God the Father will bring back His Son into this world, men are seen arrayed against Him: His "enemies." Only the willfully blind can possibly deny this. This absolutely contradicts the mouthings of "Modernists" that this world is going to be won by "moral suasion," and what they call "the kingdom," by human effort: "movements," "uplifts," man's appeals to "what is best in humanity." No less does this Scripture give the lie utterly to "Postmillennialism," together with the horrid bastard, "A-millennialism."

"Enemies"! Yes, this world has not changed, except every day for the worse, since "both Herod and Pontius Pilate, with the Gentiles and the peoples of Israel, were gathered together, against the Lord, and against His Anointed" (Acts 4.26). "The mind of the flesh is enmity against God." We have not words, nor this book pages, to paint the picture! The Son believes exactly what the Father tells Him of His future "enemies," and that they shall be **made the footstool of His feet,** and therefore is "expecting" this event. This 13th verse of Hebrews looks forward to the stupendous scene of Revelation 19.5 ff., when, against the glorious Lord Who comes riding with the armies of Heaven to tread "the winepress of the fierceness of the wrath of God, the Almighty," we find the kings of the earth lined up, under God's great enemy, the Beast, the Antichrist (Rev. 19.19).

But "Modernism," along with the wretched sect-slaves whose "standards" declare that *man* will make a "better world," that "the kingdom is already here," and that this world shall be prepared for Christ by being better instructed, better exampled and led, until it is so turned to God that Christ will be welcomed here!—all this, the first chapter of **Hebrews** proclaims to be *a lie!* That any so-called "great denominations" and their Bible-ignorant "standards" hold it, only proves it is false. "Great"? In whose eyes, pray you? In His Who forbade sects? Great in numbers, property, worldly religious influence, yes. But all that is *Laodicea!* Christ will *spue it out.*

Verse 14: Are they not all ministering spirits, sent forth to do service for the sake of them that shall inherit salvation? What a ministry for the "angels of His power," the "mighty in strength"! To them, service is a delight. The thought of a seat above others —to "be as the Most High" indeed entered the heart of the "anointed cherub" (who is now Satan), the Adversary. But it is farthest from the imagination of "the elect angels." Even to little children these love to belong, as "their angels," always "beholding the face of the Father," in their interest. They fulfill God's word, hearkening unto the voice of His word (Ps. 103.20), and His word at present is that they shall *serve* creatures *beneath* them, **them that shall inherit salvation,***— with a humble fulfillment of this ministry that we should meditate upon. *God will duly reward it.*

---

*Ministration—Salvation: In these two words appears the measureless difference between angels and the redeemed. Michael, the archangel, is seen in Dan. 10 and 12 sent to instruct that prophet. Gabriel, who "stands before God," was sent to Zacharias to announce the birth of John the Baptist, and to the virgin Mary, foretelling Christ's birth. All angels are seen in such "service."

But as for **them that shall inherit salvation,** these (although in themselves sinners, such as the angels were preserved from being) are made objects of value, worth and dignity, only to be measured by the infinite price paid in their redemption, and by the place God assigns them—to be directly connected with His own person and glory in Christ, forever!

So the first chapter of *Hebrews* sets forth the Son, "having made propitiation of sins," and having "sat down on the right hand of the Majesty on High," as "having become by so much better than the angels as He hath inherited a more excellent name than they," as we have seen. But **they that shall inherit salvation**—those sons He brings to glory—are so absolutely connected with Him that it is written, "He that sanctifieth and they that are sanctified are **all of one.**"

You may say the question in verse 13 was, What angel did God ever command to sit at His right hand till He made his enemies his footstool? True, there was no such angel, as we know. But we desire to emphasize, at the close of this first chapter: First, that believers are *inheritors* of salvation—what a heritage! And second, that such "heirs of God" are constantly being served by heaven-sent angels! But remember always the great word of this first chapter— that God's Son is Heir of all things—God, Lord, Creator and Upholder of all things!

CHAPTER TWO

1   Therefore we ought to give the more earnest heed to the
2   things that were heard, lest haply we drift away from
     them. For if the word spoken through angels proved
     steadfast, and every transgression and disobedience re-
3   ceived a just recompense of reward; how shall we escape,
     if we neglect so great a salvation? which having at the first
     been spoken through the Lord, was confirmed unto us
4   by them that heard; God also bearing witness with them,
     both by signs and wonders, and by manifold powers,
     and by gifts of the Holy Spirit, according to His own will.

**Verse 1: Therefore we ought to give the more earnest heed
to the things that were heard**—This word "therefore" means,
because of all that has been spoken in Chapter 1 of the glorious
person of the Son of God; and His infinite height above His
creation; especially, as the argument proceeds to declare, that to
us God hath spoken **through the Lord.** This refers evidently to
the Four Gospels, and to the Acts; as we saw in Chapter One.

More earnest heed.—If the Old Testament prophets should
be heard, how much more the Lord of glory Himself! He having
come to earth, become Man, and speaking to men! **To the things
that were heard**—These Hebrew believers had *read* the Old
Testament, and *heard* the gospel. Many were like Apollos, who
had been "taught by word of mouth" (Acts 18.25, R. V. margin).
Compare also Theophilus (Lk. 1.4, R. V. marg.).

We are in a different position, in that we have the complete,
living, written *record* of our Lord's earthly ministry, the apostles'
witness in the book of Acts, and also the *epistles.* That these Hebrew
believers, however, had been accurately and thoroughly instructed,
even if "by word of mouth," is taken for granted by the apostle.

Lest haply we drift away [from them]. It was not the gospel
that might "slip away" but the people who heard it might by inattention drift away from *it!* The world is ever tugging at the
believer, and that so often unconsciously to him, to go along with

its false hopes. Satan likes nothing better than a *neglecting* Christian! We all know, too, that the tendency of our natures is to drift along with earthly things away from the gospel. The Hebrew believers to whom the great exhortation of this book is directed, had *heard*. They were familiar, first of all, with what we call the Old Testament Scriptures, and with their own history as a nation. They were also familiar with the coming and death of Jesus, their Messiah, together with His glorious resurrection and ascension. Possibly some were not ignorant of His *priestly* work. For at that time the preaching of Christ did not omit, as largely today, the mention of His present priestly ministry and their dependence thereupon for their walk. But that the Levitical economy was *entirely ended;* and that the Son of God was Priest after *another order* than Aaron, and that *forever*—even "the order of *Melchizedek*," this epistle is designed to teach them!

Howbeit, the desperate danger was that they should "drift away."*

Alas, how many thousands have heard the word of the gospel— only to drift away from their moorings forever,—through sluggishness and neglect! *Drifting* is the quietest, easiest, most delightful way of dying!

Let us remember all through this book of Hebrews that it is not called an *epistle,* but a "word of *exhortation*" (Heb. 13.22). In fact, this verse contains the word "exhort" twice: "I beseech [Gr., *exhort*] you, brethren, bear with the word of *exhortation*." In Romans 12.7, 8 we find exhorting distinct from teaching: "He that teacheth *(let him give himself)* to his teaching; *or* he that exhorteth,

---

*In driving from Buffalo to Toronto, one passes very close to the great falls of Niagara. I stopped there one day several years ago and asked a guard concerning a beautiful large yacht which had lodged upon the brink of the great falls.

"How came that yacht there?" I asked.

The guard said, "The owner of that vessel was a patriotic millionnaire who lent it to the government for use in World War I. It was turned back to him after the war. He and a company of his friends were sailing down the Niagara below Buffalo, and the party, and all the crew, had gone ashore for refreshments. What was their astonishment and dismay, when they came back, to find their vessel gone! The employee responsible admitted he had tied it up hastily and insecurely—not reckoning the force of the current! And their vessel was gone!"

I asked the guard whether it could not be recovered.

"No machinery known to man could rescue that vessel," he replied.

Had the party been aboard it, and had fallen into slumber, not one could have been rescued!

to his exhorting." Barnabas, you remember, whose first name was Joseph (Acts 4.36), was "by the apostles surnamed Barnabas (which is, being interpreted, Son of exhortation)."

Now an exhorter's gift is to persuade those who have heard into *obedience to what they have heard.* Such, therefore, is **Hebrews.** And so at the very beginning (Ch. 2.1) we find, **We ought to give the more earnest heed to the things that were heard, lest haply we drift away.** But to "bear with" a word of exhortation, that may *shout its warnings* into our heavy ears, is not easy. Many will *not bear* with such a word!

Verse 2: For if the word spoken through angels—That is, the Law, whether or not we fully understand yet Galatians 3.19, "The Law . . . was ordained through angels by the hand of a mediator"; or, "This is he [Moses] that was in the assembly in the wilderness with the angel* that spake to him in the Mount Sinai" (Acts 7.38). We may have overlooked this truth, as it is not brought out till after Jehovah had pronounced the commandments (the "ten words") with a great voice from the top of Sinai. God's word to man, also was frequently delivered by angels, as to Lot (Gen. 19.1-22), or Daniel (Dan. 9.21; 10.4-14). God does not tell us in what manner **the word was spoken through angels;** but it **proved steadfast.** The argument of the verse is: If the Law ordained through angels, who were *creatures,* brought **just recompense,** how much rather when the Lord Himself comes and speaks, and men reject or neglect *His* word!

We know from the terrible experience of Israel in the wilderness something of what it is to **receive a just recompense** of reward for every transgression and disobedience. "Transgression" (Gr. *parabasis*) here means willful overstepping of a commandment; "disobedience" *(parakoē),* failing to hear through "neglect." But note the emphasis is upon "angels." Angels have just been seen to be creatures, servants; yet God backed up His word He had spoken through them!

Now we come to the first of the long series of great warnings in **Hebrews.** It is in the form of a question:

---

*"Behold, I send an angel before thee, to keep thee by the way, and to bring thee into the place which I have prepared. Take ye heed before him, and hearken unto his voice; provoke him not; for he will not pardon your transgression: for My name is in him." (Ex. 23, 20, 21). See also Ex. 32.34, and Acts 7.53: "Ye who received the Law as it was ordained by angels, and kept it not."

Verse 3: How shall we escape, if we neglect* so great a salvation which having at the first been spoken through the Lord, was confirmed unto us by them that heard;—

How shall we escape? (2.3). "They escaped not"! "Much more shall not we† escape"! (See Ch. 12.25.)

In these three searching sentences in **Hebrews** we are face to face with man's responsibility, the coming unavoidable issue. God delights in the death of no man! This must be believed. He would rather they turned from their way and lived. But God is "the Judge of all' (12.23). Although He *has* judged human sin once upon a Substitute, Christ, God will not "save every one," as the Universalists claim. For human choice is not invaded: "I would," said Christ, "but ye would not." Neglecting, despising, turning away, most men do despite God's goodness.

The word "escape" emphasizes that great crisis to which morally responsible human beings are travelling on. If *true believers*, they have already escaped! Our Lord said, "Verily, verily, I say unto

---

*See an extreme translation of the same Greek word in Matt. 22.5; "They made light of it."

†How shall we regard this epistle to the Hebrews in view, for example, of the "we" four times, and the "us" of the first three verses? There are those that say that the writer speaks "only as a Hebrew to Hebrews," and that as we are not Hebrews, most of us, it was not spoken to us! How fallacious and dangerous is such talk! *"Whatsoever* things were written aforetime were written for our learning." And again, the "holy brethren" to whom this epistle was directed were, as we shall often repeat, not at all the Israelitish nation as such, but those believing Hebrews who were "partakers of a heavenly calling" (3.1).

Gentile believers, therefore, should "give the more earnest heed" to the things of the Epistle to the Hebrews. For God had not of old sent His word to Gentiles! (Ps. 147.19-20). Therefore the nations (for Heb. *goyim* and Gr. *ethnē* always mean *nations* as over against Israel, God's elect nation), were wholly ignorant of the "shadows" and "types" of God's great salvation set forth in the O. T. Instead of superciliously handing over the Hebrews epistle "to the Jews," they should read it with profound reverence and humility. For by Israel's disobedience "salvation is come unto the Gentiles, to provoke them [Israel] to jealousy." We "now have obtained mercy by their [Israel's] disobedience . . . that by [the example of] the mercy shown to you [Gentiles] they also may now obtain mercy" (Rom. 11.11, 30, 31).

Gentiles, who now have the O. T. (a part of the grace and mercy God is now showing to us!) are tempted two ways: First, under burden of conscience to go back for relief to the *Law* which God gave *Israel*; second, to "hand over" to unbelieving Israel the O. T. as belonging only to them, and speaking about them; and not to Gentiles.

Mark carefully then: God spake in the Old Testament to Israel. Gentile believers of the New Testament gospel, hearing the same God whom they have believed explaining the Old Tesament to Hebrew believers are at once *edified*,—as is anyone who hears God speak; *instructed,* both by the types of the Old Testament and their contrast with the heavenly realities into which both Hebrew and Gentile believers have now entered; and *warned* by God's dealing with the disobedient of those past days!

you, he that heareth My word, and believeth Him that sent Me, *hath* eternal life, and *cometh not into judgment.*" That is, God's judgment against him has been already executed upon a Substitute, the news of which great event i̇ called The Gospel, or "good tidings": "He that believeth on Him is not judged" (Jno. 3.18). The "second death," which is the "lake of fire," hath no power (Rev. 20.6: Gr. *exousia*,—authority: R. V. marg.) upon him who is thus pronounced "blessed and holy . . . those who have part in the first resurrection"!

But *if they are neglecters and despisers,* there is terrible warning for them in this searching word, **HOW SHALL WE ESCAPE?** God's dealing with triflers—with those who **neglect so great a salvation,** will not be merely judicial, but *personal!* Those who "lay up wrath against the day of wrath" will discover, when the moment comes for the revelation of the righteous judgment of God, that they have fallen "into the hands of the Living God"—which is what we are told in Hebrews 10.31 is "a *fearful* thing"! He says, "I will recompense." In Malachi 1.4 we read of those against whom "Jehovah hath indignation *forever.*"

Our Lord uses the same Greek word for "escape" in Luke 21.36: "Watch ye at every season, making supplication, that ye may prevail to ESCAPE all these things." Paul uses it in that searching question of Romans 2.3: "Reckonest thou this, O man . . . who judgest them that practice such [evil] things, and doest the same, that thou shalt ESCAPE the judgment of God?" And again, in I Thessalonians 5.3, concerning the great and terrible Day of the Lord that is coming: "When they are saying, Peace and safety, then sudden destruction cometh upon them, as travail upon a woman with child; and they shall in no wise ESCAPE."

The prospect is appalling! We are looking today upon a time like that which preceded the Flood, as our Lord said: "As it came to pass in the days of Noah, even so shall it be also in the days of the Son of Man [at His second coming to earth]. They ate, they drank, they married, they were given in marriage, until the day that Noah entered into the ark, and the Flood came and destroyed them all." Again, He likens it to the days of Lot: eating, drinking, buying, selling, planting, building; "but in the day that Lot went out from Sodom it rained fire and brimstone from Heaven,

and destroyed them all: after the same manner shall it be in the day
that the Son of Man is revealed" (Lk. 17.26-30).* Unjudged
lust and violence we see to be filling the earth. A properly
separated Christian, one filled with the Spirit, fears the boasted
"progress" of this age, abhors the bolder and bolder flaunting of
naked abominations before the eyes, and knows from Scripture that
all the nations of the earth (and America especially) are "polluted"
by unjudged murder (Num. 35.33), by unnumbered adulteries,
and by despising of the *marriage vow* (Jer. 3.1), that "putting
away" which God *hates*. (See also Mal. 2.16; Matt. 19.3-9.)

God over and over declares that He will visit this earth for its
iniquity with terrible judgments. Read Isaiah 24, and remember
that the seals, trumpets, and bowls of wrath of Revelation 6 to 16
all *precede* the coming of the Great Day of Wrath of Revelation 19,
when our Lord returns as King of kings to tread the winepress
of the fierceness of the wrath of God, the Almighty.

But let us mark that the flaming question in Hebrews 2.3 is *not*
how shall they, the nations, escape, but how shall WE escape?
Hebrews, like the rest of the epistles, is spoken not to the world,
but to those who have professed faith in the Lord Jesus!

How shall we escape if we neglect so great a salvation?—
Since **Hebrews,** we repeat, is addressed to professing Christian
believers, "neglect," among many phases, would include:

1. Ceasing to give the attention and earnestness to the things
of God and of salvation that once we gave; a growing distaste for
Bible reading; willingness to be absent from the assemblies of
the saints of God (Heb. 10.25).

2. Absorption in earthly, selfish interests.

3. Increasing deadness of heart toward Christ, His sacrifice, and
to the love of God, Who gave Him.

4. Occupation with the affairs and news of this world, rather
than of the world to come, and our coming Lord.

5. Loss of God-consciousness.

6. Putting away of the thought of a "judgment to come."

7. Finally, living like the "beasts that perish," so far as
eternity is concerned.

---

*Of course the warning of Lk. 17.31 does not refer directly to the Church, which will
be raptured away before "the end," the "Tribulation," in a moment, "in the twinkling
of an eye" (I Thess. 4.16-18; Rev. 3.10).

All these are phases of **neglecting so great a salvation.***

Which having at the first been spoken through the Lord— That is, this "salvation" is regarded as having been spoken by the Lord Himself in the Four Gospels. His own words were, "The Son of Man came to seek and *to save* that which was lost"; "The Son of Man came to give His life a ransom for many."

Was confirmed unto us by them that heard [HIM]—That is, by the twelve apostles, and by all who knew and believed the Lord Jesus.

Verse 4: God also bearing witness with them, both by signs and wonders, and by manifold powers—So we have (1) the Lord Himself, (2) those that heard from His lips, (3) the direct "confirming" witness from God, from Pentecost on (Mk. 16.20): the "greater" works which Jesus said His disciples would do after He should go to the Father (Jno. 14.12); the "many signs and wonders wrought among the people" by Stephen; the "signs which Philip did"; the catching away of Philip by "the Spirit of the Lord"; Peter's healing of Aeneas and raising Dorcas from the dead; the deliverance of Peter from prison; the healing of the cripple at Lystra by Paul; the "special miracles" at Ephesus; and the "signs and wonders"† God wrought everywhere among both Gentiles and Jews where the gospel came!

---

*Among *causes* of spiritual negligence, or neglect, we note:

1. A shallow work at the beginning—conscience not awakened to the lost, guilty state; but only "feelings" stirred. Such persons are those "sown upon the rock"—no depth of soil. They hear with immediate joy: but in a true work of the Spirit, conviction of *sin* comes first—and "godly sorrow" (II Cor. 7.10).

2. Lack of chastening—of which all God's real children are made "partakers" (Heb. 12.8; Ps. 94.12-13).

3. Prosperity in this world: Ps. 73.3-9. "The prosperity [*careless ease*, R. V.] of fools shall destroy them" (Prov. 1.32).

4. Inattention to Divine warnings: (Prov. 29.1; I Ki. 13.20-24). God says, "In the day of prosperity, be joyful: and in the day of adversity, *consider*" (Eccles. 7.14).

5. Blindness to relative values and actual spiritual states, like Laodicea, in Rev. 3; following postponement of remembering whence we have fallen, and so of repentance (Rev. 2.5).

6. Conformity to surrounding indifference—which is to "follow a multitude to do evil"—forbidden of God (Ex. 23.2). The world "lieth in the evil one" (like a babe in its mother's arms!) indifferent to coming judgment (Gen. 19.14).

7. Keeping hold of some darling sin.

†**Signs** (Gr., *sēmeion*): "Miracles and wonders by which God authenticated the men sent by Him, or by which men prove that the cause they are pleading is God's" (Thayer). Thus our Lord had the Divine seal placed upon His works: "This beginning of His signs did Jesus in Cana of Galilee, and manifested His glory; and His disciples believed on Him" (Jno. 2.11). Again, "This is again the second sign that Jesus did,

And by gifts [lit., "distributions"] of the Holy Spirit, according to His own will: This takes us to I Corinthians 12, where the "gifts" of the Spirit are set forth fully: "All these worketh the one and the same Spirit, dividing to each one severally, even as He will" (vs. 11). Here we have the same two thoughts together, the Spirit "dividing" various gifts to individual believers, and doing this according to His will—the will of God. See also here verses 4,7. It will not do to confine this statement to the apostolic days; nor, for that matter, can any part of verse 4 be restricted to that period. For when there has been faith, throughout the Christian centuries, God has wrought signs and wonders and powers, the records of which, alas, are withheld if discovered, by a "respectable" Christianity!*

Returning now to the contrast of Christ with the angels (which Heb. 2.1-4, the *first* of the *seven great warnings of* Hebrews, interrupted), we read:

Verse 5: For not unto angels did He subject the world to come, whereof we speak: From the subject of the measureless height

---

having come out of Judea into Galilee" (Jno. 4.54). And, "Many other signs therefore did Jesus in the presence of the disciples, which are not written in this book: but these are written, that ye may believe that Jesus is the Christ, the Son of God; and that believing ye may have life in His name" (Jno. 20.30, 31).

Wonders (Gr.: *terasin*), is found only in the plural and joined with signs. "A miracle regarded as a portent or prodigy awakening amazement" (Vincent).

Powers (Gr. *dunamesin*), the third word, means energy, or work of power. These three are seen together sometimes, as here in Heb. 2.4, in Acts 2.22, and in II Cor. 12.12. Speaking generally, signs indicate miraculous deeds authenticating the doer; wonders, such evident operations as indubitably indicate God's presence and working (see Acts 2.19); powers, the energy which is put forth in such deeds. Note that the Antichrist is said to use "all power and signs and lying wonders" (lit., "wonders of falsehood"—II Thess. 2.9). Therefore two things should be considered: (1) whether signs, or wonders, or powers, they are beyond human power to exercise or to understand; (2) their character, whether of God or of Satan, must be determined by their correspondence to God's holy Word, and by their results.

*Read the account, in The Scots' Worthies, a book that no one of Christian judgment thinks of contravening, of how John Welch, son-in-law of John Knox, of Scotland, raised a young man from the dead in France; or again, in that remarkable series of books, now out of print, The Annals of the American Pulpit the account of William Tennant, raised from the dead; or the testimony of Dr. John L. Nevius, a godly Presbyterian missionary in China for over forty years, in his book Demon Possession and Allied Themes, of the Chinese casting out demons in wonderful simplicity of faith, never dreaming that there had been any cessation of this authority given by our Lord (Mark 16.17). See also the remarkable testimony of beloved Dr. A. J. Gordon, pastor of Clarendon Street Baptist Church, Boston, in The Ministry of Healing, concerning such nam~ rs Pastor Blumhardt, Dorothea Trudell, and others.

above angels occupied by our Lord, we pass here to God's plans concerning the millennial age that will follow this present age, wherein the Son of God will come forth to exercise on earth His Melchizedek priesthood. **Not unto angels**—First, let us consider that angelic control by which God orders matters behind the scenes in this present dispensation, as in the Old Testament. Angels are "mighty in strength, fulfilling His word, hearkening unto the voice of His word" (Ps. 103.20). Angels ministered unto Christ in His earthly life; at the tomb an angel descended from heaven, rolled away the stone;* and angels sat "one at the head, and one at the feet, where the body of Jesus had lain." The "two men" spoken of in Acts 1.10, 11, were perhaps angelic. An angel of the Lord opened prison doors for "the apostles" (Acts 5), for Paul (Acts 16), and for Peter (Acts 12, in which chapter two angels smite—one in mercy, and one in judgment). Although Satan is the prince of this world and god of this age, he can do nothing without Divine permission. God interferes in answer to the prayers of His saints by means of the angels; and thus is the present world subject to them. But it will not be so in **the world to come,** the millennial age.

The thought of **the world to come** pervades the book of **Hebrews,** and cannot here refer to present things! See Chapter 6.5, "the powers of the age (aiôn) to come"; also Chapter 10.1, "the Law, having a shadow of the coming good things." Thayer defines **the world to come:** "That consummate state of all things which will exist after Christ's return from Heaven." Andrew Murray's definition is: "That world to which the psalm (Ps. 8) looks forward, the Kingdom of the Messiah, the Kingdom of Heaven upon earth." Conybeare's comment is interesting: "The 'world to come' here corresponds with 'the city to come' of Chapter 13.14. The subjection of this to the Messiah (though not yet accomplished, see vs. 9) was another proof of His superiority to the angels."

---

*This remarkable passage (Matt. 28.2-5) reads.

"And behold, there was a great earthquake; for an angel of the Lord descended from heaven, and came and rolled away the stone, and sat upon it. His appearance was as lightning and his raiment white as snow: and for fear of him the watchers did quake, and became as dead men. And the angel answered and said unto the women, Fear not ye; for I know that ye seek Jesus, Who hath been crucified."

The apostle here in verse 5 is speaking, as he insists, (*laloumen, we are speaking*) of the world (the "inhabited earth," see Chapter 1.6) when He, the Son Who created all things, shall return to this world with His enemies "the footstool of His feet." So the argument goes right on from Chapter 1.14 to Chapter 2.5 (as you see, vs. 5 begins with "For," connecting it with Ch. 1.14), having in view the subjecting of the habitable earth to the Son of man, and proceeding immediately to quote in proof of this, the wonderful Eighth Psalm. We shall, therefore, repeating verse 5, quote on through verse 8, b; (but not the last sentence of verse 8, **But now we see not yet**—which refers to the state of things at present, contrasted with those when all things shall actually be subjected under the feet of the Son of Man, at His coming).

5   **For not unto angels did He subject the world to come,**
6   **whereof we speak. But one hath somewhere testified, saying,**
     What is man, that Thou art mindful of him?
     Or the Son of man, that Thou visitest him?
7   **Thou madest Him for a little while lower than the angels;**
     Thou crownedst Him with glory and honor,
     And didst set Him over the works of Thy hands:
8   **Thou didst put all things in subjection under His feet.**
     For in that He subjected all things unto Him, He left nothing that is not subject to Him.

Verse 6: What is man, that Thou art mindful of him? Or the son of man, that Thou visitest him? Here the Spirit takes the Eighth Psalm, quoted also in Ephesians 1.22 and I Corinthians 15.27, and applies it to Christ. This Eighth Psalm is one of the great Messianic psalms. At the first reading we can see David at night, gazing at the heavens, and saying (Ps. 8.3, 4):

"When I consider Thy heavens, the work of Thy fingers,
The moon and the stars, which Thou hast ordained,
What is man, that Thou art mindful of him?
And the son of man, that Thou visitest him?"

David seems to be thinking of Adam the first, to whom indeed God gave dominion. But, "The first man is of the earth, earthy: the Second Man is of Heaven," as Paul tells us (I Cor. 15.47). Adam being a type of Him Who was to come, as we read David's words in New Testament light, the first Adam disappears upon his failure; and the Second Man, the last Adam, is before our eyes.

Verse 7: Thou madest Him for a little while lower than the angels.*

The angels referred to in verses 7 and 9 are of course "the holy angels," "the elect angels," whose ministry to human "heirs of salvation" is seen in Chapter 1.14. Now in what respects was our Lord **made for a little while lower than the angels?**

First, in becoming man, the Son of God entered fully into man's limitations. Jesus, "being wearied with His journey," sat by Jacob's well, in John 4. "He Himself was in the stern, asleep on the cushion—" after a long day's preaching (Mk. 4.38, R.V.). He ate and drank to replenish strength, just as any man would do. Angels are not thus dependent. When man attains to that (coming) age, and the resurrection from among the dead," he will be "equal unto the angels" (Lk. 20.35, 36) in manner of being.

Our Lord's undergoing the **suffering of death, and tasting death for every one,** (vs. 9) is the *second* great element in His becoming **for a little while lower than the angels.** They are not subject to death. He, by the Father's will, and His own ready willingness, became so.

In the *third* place, perhaps we ought to mention our Lord's subjection to temptation, which is so emphasized in **Hebrews.** After His temptation, for example, as narrated in Matthew 4, we read, "Then the devil leaveth Him; and behold, angels came and ministered unto Him." "The elect angels" were not only preserved from the original apostasy with Lucifer, but evidently from temptation, in the sense that evil did not become attractive, in the least,† unto them!

7   Thou crownedst Him with glory and honor,
    And didst set Him over the works of Thy hands:
8   Thou didst put all things in subjection under His feet.
    For in that He subjected all things unto Him, He left
    nothing that is not subject to Him. But now we see not
9   yet all things subjected to Him. But we behold Him Who
    hath been made a little lower than the angels, even Jesus,

---

*But at His birth as such, the heavenly host filled the air not with shouts that He had been made lower than they, but with shouts of "Glory to God *in the highest.*"

†The fact that Michael contended with the devil, as seen in Jude, does not imply that he was "tempted." There was no personal tempting approach to the archangel in any sense; but on his part, firm resistence and rejection of Satan's claim concerning the body of Moses.

**because of the suffering of death crowned with glory
and honor, that by the grace of God He should taste of
death for every man.**

Verses 7, 8: Here God's purpose becomes manifest concerning
our Lord's millennial position, the time unto which the Lord Himself looks—"expecting" (Ch. 10.13). Man is to be placed over
everything. All things are to be put in subjection under the feet of
Christ as *Man*. Of course we at once understand from the following
verses that it is to Jesus—"very God and very Man," that all things
are to be subject. But we are to find that others, whom He calls His
"brethren," are to be associated with Him.

Mark again the purposes of God. His eternal counsels were not
connected with the first man, but were announced after that man's
failure—in the words to the serpent, "He [the Seed of the
woman] shall bruise thy head." The Seed, Christ, the Second
Man, was to be connected with us, not by generation of man, but
by Divine action in what we call the incarnation.* It is the same
person Who in Hebrews 1 was seen as Son of God and Heir of
all things, Who is seen in this second chapter as *Man*—just as truly
Man now, as from all eternity He was God!

Having in mind, then, that future subjection of all things to the
Second Man, we see already the *present* state of things, in the
words, **But now we see not yet all things subjected to Him**
(vs. 8.c). They will be subject, but are **not yet.** The Millennium's
opening scene is future: see Revelation 20.1-3. Satan is today
"the prince of this world"—still unbound. "The whole world
lieth in the evil one" is yet true (I Jno. 5.19).

Verse 9: But praise God for these great words in Hebrews 2.9:
**But we see Jesus, the One Who for a little lower than the angels
was made, for the suffering of death, with glory and honor
crowned: to the end that by the Grace† of God He might taste
of death for every one.** The eyes of believers immediately go to
Him upon Whom they have believed; and lo, **we behold Him . . .
crowned with glory and honor,** at God's right hand!

---

*Words about the incarnation are always addressed to faith. Gabriel said to Mary, "The
Holy Spirit shall come upon thee, and the power of the Most High shall overshadow thee;
Wherefore also the holy thing which is begotten shall be called the Son of God" (Lk. 1.35).

†By the Grace of God taste of death for everyone. It cannot be rendered *"everything"*—
as this word *grace* would have no meaning thus! "Grace" is not for "things," but for
people, for unworthy *sinners!*

Now it will be supremely necessary for us to remember, as the following verses open to us, that *we* are *one with Him*. It is not possible unto reason, but only unto faith, to conceive that such unworthy ones, such weak ones as we, should be elevated above the mighty, holy angels!* We are ready to consent that our blessed Lord, sinless in life and victorious over death, should take His place "far above all rule, and authority, and power, and dominion, and every name that is named, not only in this age, but also in that which is to come." It is a constant and subtle temptation to allow freely that the Lord Himself has passed "far above all the heavens," but with false humility to say: "That is not for *me*. Angels are glorious heavenly beings, and I am a poor, earthly sinner." For in the very passage just quoted (Eph. 1.21-23) we read that God gave Christ "to be Head over all things to the Church, *which is His Body*, the fullness of Him that filleth all in all," that is, the filling up of Christ Himself! As we read in I Corinthians 12.12: "For as the body is one, and hath many members, and all the members of the body, being many, are one body; *so also is Christ*." To reject this is not humility, but unbelief, or unwillingness to let go earthly things and admit our position by God's sovereign grace, as *one with Christ*, seated in the heavenlies with Him. We are about to read in Hebrews 2.11 that Christ and those in Him are "all of one." Blessed indeed is the man who has seen an end of his old place in Adam, at Calvary, where "our old man was crucified with Him," Christ having been "made to be sin on our behalf; that we might become the righteousness of God *in Him*" (II Cor. 5.21)! Christ on the Cross died unto sin, thus breaking the relationship between Himself and sin, forever. For we read, "The life that He liveth, He liveth *unto God*." And we are likewise to reckon ourselves dead, being in Christ as the last Adam, and His death to sin becoming thus federally ours. (We must revert often to these preceding revelations, for the fact of them is *taken for granted* in the book of **Hebrews.)**

---

*It is well to remember here, (and it will help to humble us) that the Greek word *aggeloi*, translated "angels," literally means *messengers*. Rotherham's translation effectively renders it "messengers" constantly. We have the verb *aggelo*, meaning to announce; and from this comes *aggilos*, a messenger, plural *aggeloi*, translated, or transliterated, "angels," occurring some 75 times in the N. T. Once there is *aggelia* (1 Jno. 1.5) meaning "message."

So note that in Chapter 2.5-8 we have Christ as Man **set over the works of God's hands**—angels, principalities, powers, all things. We do not speak thus to create a false elation or sense of self-importance in any human breast. But, in this great book of **Hebrews** which reveals Christ as our Great High Priest on high, we have this destiny of Christ as Man placed over all things, at the very outset; and, second, our *oneness with this Man,* even Jesus! We are not yet glorified; Christ *is* glorified—**is crowned with glory and honor** (cf. Phil. 2.9-11). He Himself, therefore, is the object of our "beholding." But it is as *connected with Him,* that we see Him. All our interests have passed from earth. This is necessarily true, for we read that it is **because of the suffering of death**—that He **has tasted of death** for us, that the eyes of our hearts turn to Him, crowned in the Father's delight because **He** became obedient to death, yea, the death of the Cross.

That by the grace of God He should taste of death for every one: What words are these! What a compass in this verse! First, Jesus **made for a little while lower than the angels.** Then **the suffering of death;** then, because of that, at present **crowned with glory and honor** at God's right hand. Then the sweet word of explanation of His death: **that by the grace of God He should taste of death for every one.** "Grace," the source of all blessing, but how feebly grasped by us! Let faith lay fast hold here! Just as on a passenger train there are steps and handles to enter into the cars, so do there come along such verses as these, for faith to step upon and hold fast to, and climb up on the train for glory! Make verses like this, O believer, personal possessions! If Christ did **taste of death for every one,*** if God's grace extended to that, it means you, and it means me. *Only believe!*

---

*The genitive of *pas (pantos),* "every," is here used. But the world may be either masculine or neuter. Some insist that the expression "every one" should be every **thing;** but we object that the translation "every thing" looks toward Universalism. Furthermore, the following vs. (2.10) explains the expression as referring to Christ's **bringing many sons** to glory, and His being **made perfect through sufferings as the Captain of their salvation.** Nor does Col. 1.20—"reconcile all things," a passage sufficient in itself, change the translation of Heb. 2.9 *(pantos):* "every one."

So that we have in vs. 9, **for every one;** vs. 10, **many sons;** vs. 11, **they that are sanctified** called "brethren"; vs. 12, both "brethren" and **congregation (or Assembly);** vs. 13, **I and the children God hath given me;** vs. 14, **the children sharers in blood and flesh** and Himself in like manner partaking of the same; vs. 15, **all them who through fear of death were subject to bondage,** delivered; vs. 16, **the seed of Abraham** (see Gal. 3.29); vs. 17, again "**His brethren**"; and then, "**a merciful and faithful High Priest . . . to make propitiation for the sins of the people.**"

10 For it became Him for Whom are all things, and through
   Whom are all things, in bringing many sons unto glory,
   to make the Author of their salvation perfect through
11 sufferings. For both He that sanctifieth and they that
   are sanctified are all of one: for which cause He is not
   ashamed to call them brethren, saying,

12   I will declare Thy name unto My brethren,

      In the midst of the congregation will I sing Thy praise.
13 And again, I will put My trust in Him. And again, Behold, I and the children whom God hath given Me.

Verse 10: For it became Him for Whom all things, and through
Whom are all things, in bringing many sons unto glory, to make
the Captain of their salvation perfect through sufferings. For
both He that sanctifieth [Christ] and they that are sanctified
[the saints] are all of one: This verse tells both how God's grace
has extended to us; and what it became this God to do, in bringing many sons unto glory, into His very presence Who dwelleth
in *light unapproachable!** Here we go back to what we might call

---

*He was to bring them to glory. Therefore, He must go where they were, and (a)
become one with them as to their guilt, which He must bear; and (b) become sin on
their behalf. So bringing many sons unto glory would involve sufferings—the most terrible of all, to be forsaken of God,— made a curse for us! Nothing else could "become"
God as regarded our sin and our sinful state.
    1. It became His *being*, as God. It was into God's presence we were to be brought.
    2. It became His *Holiness*: with an infinite abhorrence He hated sin.
    3. It became His *righteousness*: He must deal righteously in bringing sons to glory.
    4. It became the God Whose name is LOVE to do this amazing thing—bring to
glory many sons. Only a God of Love would want us there.
    5. It became His *Wisdom*, "of Whom are all things and for Whom are all things."
He sees the eternities and has planned for them as it "became" Him.
    6. It became His *Lordship* over all things. Knowing all things about all creatures,
He could place them all where He would. And He chose to place *first* those redeemed
by Christ!
    7. It became Him because Christ's obedience unto death *revealed God* for all ages.
He is worthy to be obeyed, said His Son, even unto forsaking, anguish, and death!
    Finally, God infinitely loved His Son, the "Captain" of these "sons." And thus it
"became" Him to plan for that Son a path of *sufferings* untold and unutterable, in
walking in which day by day that Son's fidelity to God His Father became manifest
to all eternity. The wounds that now are in Jesus' hands and feet and side will declare
to the ages of the ages that it is good to obey God, at all cost. And God will forever
remember the Son's sufferings, as if they were of yesterday.
    Thus, it became God to make the Leader of our salvation perfect through sufferings.
And remember, if we suffer with Him, it is because we are redeemed by His sufferings
and sacrifice. Satan hates redeemed ones, those trusting Christ's one offering. So he makes
them suffer, whether by temptation to doubt Christ's sacrifice; or by calling attention to
their weak faith, or inconsistent experience. But Christ's accepted work (accepted of God!)
and not our grasp of it, is the question! We know that God has accepted Christ's sacrifice,
because He raised Him from the dead!

the first causes: what *became* the counsels of God, both in sending
Christ, and in His dealings with Christ upon earth. What it was
"becoming," fitting, for the infinitely holy God to do—ah, what a
subject for our poor human grasp! It is *God* Who is before us, for
Whom all things exist. Whatever the works or the words of our
Lord Jesus Christ, we must refer their *cause* to that which was
"becoming to God." It is not the arbitrary *will* of God that is here
in view, but that which was "becoming" to God Himself—to His
being.

Would it have *become* God, the holy One, even to admit to His
presence sinners of the human race who had been merely "in-
fluenced" (as some would teach) by the "perfect example" of the
"beautiful life" of Jesus?

Would it have been becoming to the *government* of God to admit
to His presence enemies who had infracted all the righteous edicts
of His throne, and with no penalty imposed for that disobedience?

Would it have been becoming to the throne of infinite Majesty
and glory to have about that throne—all unatoned for—those who
had been in closest sympathy with God's arch-enemy, Satan?

This important tenth verse in Chapter 2 is the second great
general word concerning God in **Hebrews.** The first is, "God has
spoken to us in [the Person of His] Son" (1.2). And this second
word is that the Son, having partaken of blood and flesh, become
man, yea God's Lamb, **it became God . . . to make Him perfect
through sufferings.** "It *behooved* Christ to suffer, and to rise again
from the dead" (Acts 17.1-3). We insist that the very foundation
of the Gospel appears in this word, **it became God!** It became
Him to judge sin; it *became* Him to give His own Son to *bear* sin;
it *became* Him to lay before that Son a path of obedience involving
suffering—even unto death.

Oh, how different is what "became" God here from what becomes us! It becomes us
to protect our sons. It "became" God to hand over His only, well-beloved Son to sufferings; to be "driven by the Spirit into the wilderness to be tempted," until Satan had
"completed every temptation"; to have not "where to lay His head"; to choose disciples
who would all forsake Him; betray Him; one deny knowing Him! To be forsaken by the
untold thousands He had blessed and healed; yea, to be forsaken of *God!*

When at last He said, "It is finished," and, "Father, into Thy hands I commend My
spirit," it was over! He had been "perfected through suffering." He had "learned
obedience through the things that He suffered" (Heb. 5.8-9); and having been made
perfect, He became unto all them that obey Him the *cause* of eternal Salvation—named of
God a High Priest after the order of Melchizedek."

While we now "behold . . . Jesus . . . crowned with glory and honor," let us not only see His present place as God's reward to Him for His path of obedience; but also regard His path of sufferings thereto, as the only path which could *become* a holy God!

The Captain of their Salvation—This "Captain" (Gr.: *Archêgos;** cf. Ch. 12.2 and comment there) is Christ. Thus the first view we have here of Christ, connected with these "sons being brought to glory," is as the File-Leader of the company. It is as if God were saying, "Hebrew believers, do not stumble, as most of your nation are doing, at a suffering Messiah.† Your lot is now far above that of mere Hebrews. *You* partake of a *heavenly* calling! You are journeying to Heaven, home to God, Who is bringing you as sons unto glory. Do you not see from all Scripture that the Blessed One Who should become the Captain of sons going forth from earth to Heaven, must have suffered, yea, have been made perfect through sufferings? It *becomes* Me that the Captain of their salvation has so yielded to all My will as to have suffered all things."

They were to be "sons," and were to be brought "unto glory." Who was to bring them, and how? One must go where they were, have their guilt charged to Him, bear the wrath due to them. Our Lord's course from Bethlehem to Calvary is looked

---

**Archêgos:* "(1) Chief, Leader, Prince: of Christ (Acts 5.31); (2) One that takes the lead in anything, and thus affords an example: of Christ, Heb. 2.10, 12.2."—Thayer. "A word difficult, not to understand, but to render in English. It is a leader, but it is more, It is used for one who begins, and sets a matter on: originator."—Darby.

Archêgos is a combination of two Greek words meaning *to begin* and *to lead.* It occurs four times in the N. T.: Acts 3.15, 5.31; and twice in *Hebrews:* Chs. 2.10 and 12.2. As used here in Ch. 2.10, it does not refer to our Lord as a Sin-Offering, but as the Captain or *File-Leader* of those that are to be saved, whom He calls His "brethren" (2.11, 12), and "the children [of God] whom God hath given" Him (vs. 13); and as the Deliverer through death of those children, having brought to nought at the Cross the devil, who had the power of death, setting free from fear-of-death-bondage, all those over whom the devil tyrannized, Christ as the *Archêgos,* therefore, is the Leader, the Deliverer, among His brethren, becoming Himself "perfected through sufferings." Bloomfield interprets *Archêgos* by *aitios* in Heb. 5.9: "the *Cause* of eternal salvation." There is reason for this as the word "Prince" (Acts 3.15 5.31) would indicate place, position, rather than source, supply.

†Alford calls attention to Bleek's excellent remarks "on the lingering of the offense of the cross among these Jewish Christians, who, although their ideas of the glory and kingly triumph of the Messiah had been in a measure satisfied by the resurrection and exaltation of Christ, and their hopes awakened by the promise of future glory at His second coming, —yet, in the procrastination of this great event, felt their souls languishing, and the old stumbling-block of Christ's sufferings recurring to their minds. To set forth then the way of suffering and the cross as one worthy of God's high purpose, would be a natural course for the argument of the writer to take."

at in the words: **made perfect through sufferings.** Yes, such a journey from the glory that He had with the Father, down to earth and back to that glory, would involve on the part of that great Captain of their salvation "emptying Himself," taking the "form of a servant," becoming in the "likeness of men," humbling Himself "unto death, yea, the death of the Cross"!

But think Who He was! "Is not this the carpenter?" the people of Nazareth asked. Yes, but He was the Creator also. And He was in a path that would shortly make Him "an alien to His mother's children," "despised and rejected of men, a Man of sorrows, and acquainted with grief," in all these sufferings, *learning** obedience (5.8).

Verse 11: For both He that sanctifieth and they that are sanctified are all of one:—† Look at once at the words "sanctifieth" and "sanctified." **He that sanctifieth** evidently is Christ; **they that are sanctified** are the **sons** (of God) being "brought unto glory." This is a use of the word "sanctify" common in the book of **Hebrews.** And this passage, it seems to me, allies itself most intimately with the great high-priestly prayer of John 17, where our Lord prayed: "Sanctify them in the truth: Thy word is truth . . . And for their sakes I *sanctify Myself,* that they themselves also may be *sanctified in truth.*" This verse removes at once all thoughts of sanctification in the sense of removal of defilement, for Christ had none. Yet He says, "I sanctify Myself, that they themselves also may be sanctified in truth."

---

*Note this word *learn.* Being God, He had not to *obey,* but participated in the counsels of the Trinity from all eternity. Even when He came to earth, *"He* emptied Himself"— it was not compulsion. But. He having become man, the Father was now His *God:* and He "learned obedience." Our Lord was morally and spiritually perfect at all times and in all ways; He was *God!* But through sufferings he *"learned* obedience." And, since the sufferings were infinite, the perfection is glorious and eternal! (We shall see more of this in Chs. 5-7-9; 7.28. Compare also Lk. 13.32.)

†Note that the word "For" introducing vs. 11 argues from vs. 10 the **reason why the** Captain of the "many sons being brought to glory" was made **perfect through sufferings.** We find that Christ that **sanctifieth and they that are sanctified are** ALL OF ONE. Now as we have indicated, the oneness, the unity of Christ and believers, is well known from other passages. But the form of the expression here "all of one" is unique. It speaks of *kind or quality* of being, rather than mere unity.

But our blessed Lord's becoming "all of one" in quality of being with those whom the Father had given Him, did not at all mean that He shared Adam's nature, or became united with the sinful human race. He did not become a son of Adam. But the Holy Spirit, as we have seen, "came upon" His virgin mother, and the power of the Most High kept "over-shadowing" her. Christ, therefore, took part in "blood and flesh" life *directly from God,*—all *sinless,* entirely *separate* from the Adamic race.

In this very prayer our Lord is devoting Himself to that *identification with His own,* which would be consummated the next day on the Cross! He set Himself apart unto that death, in order that His disciples might share His risen life. For He testified, "Except a grain of wheat fall into the earth and die, it abideth by itself alone." The oneness of believers with Christ described here is not that of being members of the Body of Christ, but it is a deeper truth still, or rather, preliminary to the forming of the Body of Christ, implying union with Himself. In John 17.16, again, He said, "They are not of the world, *even as I* am not of the world"—and verse 21, "that they may all be *one, even Thou, Father, art in Me, and I in Thee,* that they also may be *in Us.*"

So in Hebrews 2.11 the great announcement is made that Christ and they that are sanctified **are all of one!** They *share His life* Who died and rose! **For which cause He is not ashamed to call them brethren.*** Its being connected with His sufferings makes this verse one of the most wonderful of many Scriptures concerning the identification of believers with their Lord. They are so much of one with Him that He is not ashamed to call them brethren. Amazing, overwhelming fact! Let faith lay hold of Him and rejoice in Him.

Verse 12: saying,
I will declare Thy name unto My brethren,
In the midst of the congregation [lit., "assembly"; Gr.: *ecclêsia*] will I sing Thy praise!

To all who know the 22nd Psalm, from which this passage is

---

*There is what we can but feel to be a carnal, presumptuous name given to the Son of God in the mouths of some: "Our Elder Brother." We have never heard one speak thus who understood our identification with Him in death and resurrection, as taught in Rom. 6, 7; Col. 3, and elsewhere. To call Christ your "Elder Brother" is to reduce Him to your human, Adamic standing, rather than seeing yourself condemned in Adam, and Christ dying for your guilt, and you, as connected with Adam, *identified with that death.* If you object that Christ called us "brethren"; why may we not call Him "Brother"? I answer, Find a hint that any of the holy apostles addressed Him thus. If He calls us brethren, it is because He became identified with us poor, wretched, lost creatures by infinite Divine grace; and, now He leads the worship of His saints as "The Firstborn of many brethren," indeed: but in heavenly worship. You may say, "Lord Jesus," but no believer finds himself saying, "Brother Jesus." Yet when we turn to God and Heaven, and join the praise and worship (which we should be doing—Heb. 13.13), we know it is true that He calls *us* "brethren." Let Him speak thus in limitless *grace:* for God has made us all of one with Him! But we will call Him Lord, for (a) He is eternally God the Son; (b) He is the "Second Man"—the "Last Adam" (I Cor. 15.47, 45); (c) but He is called "the Man from Heaven," and those in Him are eternally heavenly!

brought to us by the Spirit, these words are captivating to the heart.
For the 22nd Psalm has two parts: verses 1-21, and verses 22-31.
The quotation here begins with the *second* part, at verse 22; but the
psalm begins:

"My God, My God, why hast Thou forsaken Me?

Why art Thou so far from helping Me, and from the words
of My groaning?

. . . I cry in the daytime [the first three hours of the crucifixion day (Mark 15.25): 9 to 12 o'clock] but Thou
answerest not:

And in the night season [the second three hours, when
the absolute darkness of Divine forsaking fell upon Him
(Mark 15.33)] and am not silent.

But Thou art holy.

. . . Thou hast brought Me into the dust of death . . .

A company of evil-doers have enclosed Me;

They pierced My hands and My feet . . .

They part My garments among them,

And upon My vesture do they cast lots . . .

Save Me from the lion's mouth!

"Yea, from the horns of the wild-oxen *Thou hast answered Me!*"

Thus was He cut off, suffering from the hand of God the judgment of our sin; but delivered "from the lion's mouth." Our Lord
as He died committed His spirit to the Father (Lk. 23.46), Who
received it to the disappointed hate of Satan and the hosts of hell,
"the wild-oxen."

Thus ends the first half of this blessed psalm. The second half,
immediately following, is our *Risen* Lord in resurrection-life,
speaking:

I will declare Thy name unto My brethren:

In the midst of the Assembly will I praise Thee.

Now we know, from John 20, the message the risen Lord sent
by Mary Magdalene to the disciples: "But go unto My brethren,
and say to them, I ascend unto My Father and your Father, and
My God and your God." Astonishing words, "Brethren"! "My
Father and your Father"! "My God and your God"!

Note then the two parts of this great verse, Hebrews 2.12:
first, He will **declare God's Name unto His brethren**: then, second, **In the midst of the Assembly will He praise God!** We con-

stantly find our Lord among His disciples speaking of His Father, even saying to them, "When ye pray, say, *Our* Father." We find them at the last supper asking, "Show us the Father, and it sufficeth us." But when the Holy Ghost came, *they knew!*

Now the last part of verse 12: **In the midst of the Assembly will I praise Thee!** This brings us to the revelation of our Lord's *ETERNAL* PRIESTLY WORK! The first priestly work is *prayer for us* (Lk. 22.32; Jno. 17); the *second* is, that He bore our sins on the Cross; the third is, that He will *get us home* through this God-hating world, making "intercession for us," "compassed about" as we are with "infirmity"—He will get us home *where He is!* Upon this element of His priesthood most of our thoughts, naturally, indeed, are centered. Sad to say, we fall even below this! In our failure or sin we think of our Lord only as our *Advocate*— which is indeed connected with priesthood, thank God! But as to thinking of Him as Priest in the fourth phase, as eternally revealing God's name to us as His "brethren"; and as Himself singing eternally the praises of God *among the saints,* "in the midst of the Assembly"—many Christians have not even considered it!

Yet He says, **In the midst of the congregation** (of all His redeemed ones) **will I sing Thy praise:** Let us meditate upon this word. The question instantly comes, When and for how long will this praising be? Some have thought it will cease when all the redeemed are brought to glory. With this we cannot for an instant agree. Will Christ ever cease to lead the praise of His blood-bought saints? Will He ever cease to be the Lamb "that hath been slain"? It is the *glorified* saints whom Christ is leading in praise, and will lead forever! In our poor weak assembling here below, we thrill and rejoice at any consciousness of His presence, and of access to God through Him. Is His priesthood only to last until He gets us all to Heaven? Nay, it will be fully active then! Remember, God is infinite, infinite, infinite! (How lame is language!) Shall we ever come to know Him so fully that there will be no further need of our Great High Priest's "declaring God's Name" more deeply and fully unto us? Is not the *Lamp* of that city to which we are going the Lamb Himself? "In the ages to come" God will indeed "show the exceeding riches of His grace in kindness toward us," but it will still be *"in Christ Jesus"!* (Eph. 2.7).

This glorious phase of Christ's priesthood, His leading the ever-lasting singing, has only begun. Thank God, it will never cease!

"O Home of God My Father's joy and gladness,
        O riven Veil whereby I enter in!
There can my soul forget the grave, the weeping,
        The weariness and sin.
O chamber, all thine agate windows open
        To face the radiant east—
O holy temple, where the saints are singing,
        Where Jesus is the Priest—
Illumined with the everlasting glory,
        Still with the peace of God's eternal now,
Thou, God, my Rest, my Refuge, and my Tower—
        My home art Thou."
                (T. S. M., in Ter Steegen).

No, to affirm that the priesthood of Christ as leading His re-deemed in their worship and praises will have an end when the saints see God's face, is to forget the Lamb Who is eternally there, as "The Lamb that hath been slain," leading those He has bought, in worship!

"And I saw no temple therein: for the Lord God the Almighty, and the Lamb, are the temple thereof. And the city hath no need of the sun, neither of the moon, to shine upon it: for the glory of God did lighten it, and the lamp thereof is the Lamb" (Rev. 21. 22, 23).

It is the conciousness that will prevade the New Jerusalem for-ever: God so loved us that He gave His Son! Christ so loved us that He bought us with His own blood! We are here in this place of ineffable bliss, enjoying forever the unhindered outflow of the infinite love of God, because the Son of God loved us and gave Himself for us! We are forever here *in Him!* Our God, Who is *love*, has fully and eternally expressed that love in the infinite sacrifice of His Son, in Whom we are. And Christ leads our praises forever!

Now comes a further citation from Scripture:

Verse 13: And again, I will put My trust in Him:—These words occur in the remarkable passage in Isaiah (8.16-17) where, after the nation has stumbled (vs. 15), the testimony, the teach-ing, is "bound up, sealed," among Christ's disciples. The word is: "Bind thou up the testimony, seal the Law among My disciples [which God had done when He took it from the Jewish nation as a whole and committed to our Lord's "disciples." See the four Gospels.]. And I will wait for Jehovah, that hideth His face from the house of Jacob, and I will *look for Him*" (put My trust in Him, Septuagint translation). This is the whole spirit of our Lord in the prophetic word. It is His spirit especially in the Psalms and most especially in Psalm 16, when, in dying, Christ says,

"Thou wilt not leave My soul to Sheol;
Neither wilt Thou suffer Thy holy One to see corruption:
Thou wilt show Me the path of life."

The very words I will put My trust in Him, His enemies taunted Him with, on the Cross: "He trusted on God."

I will put My trust in Him—What a word, for One Who is Himself *God*, to say! It reminds us of II Corinthians 13.4: "He was crucified through weakness, yet He liveth through the power of God." For the Son, as Man, walked in the path of *faith*, looking, in weakness, wholly to *Another* for all things—just as "His brethren," the saints, now do, or should do, toward *Him* (Gal. 2.20). I will put My trust in Him was His blessed attitude. Let it be ours!

And then a citation from the next verse of Isaiah 8:

And again, Behold, I and the children whom Jehovah hath given Me: Primarily these "children" were Isaiah's two sons which were to be "for signs and for wonders": Shear-jashub and Maher-shalal-hash-baz.* But God uses them here to represent those "brethren," those "sons of God being brought to glory," of whom the preceding verses in Hebrews 2 speak.

14 Since then the children are sharers in blood and flesh, He also Himself in like manner partook of the same; that
15 through death He might bring to nought him that had the power of death, that is, the devil; and might deliver all them who through fear of death were all their life-
16 time subject to bondage. For verily not to angels doth He give help, but He giveth help to the seed of Abra-

---

*Their names, given by God (Isa. 7.3; 8.1) sum up Isaiah's prophecy concerning Israel: Shear-jashub, "A remnant shall return"; Maher-shalal-hash-baz, "The spoil speedeth, the prey hasteth"—the judgment that was coming on the nation prior to the final restoration of the Remnant. So these children were "for signs and for wonders"—if Israel could perceive them!

**17 ham.   Wherefore it behooved Him in all things to be
made like unto His brethren, that He might become a
merciful and faithful High Priest, in things pertaining to
18 God, to make propitation for the sins of the people. For in
that He Himself hath suffered being tempted, He is able
to succor them that are tempted.**

This first mention in **Hebrews** of Christ's death looking toward
His priesthood, shows it as compassing two great things: (a) the
complete overthrow of the one having **the power of death, that
is, the devil:** the "prince of this world" and "god of this age";
(b) Christ's taking hold, according to Divine purpose and promise,
not of angels, but **of the seed of Abraham,** who is named of God
"the father of all them that believe."*

**Verse 14: Since then† the children are sharers in blood and
flesh.**

The "children" here are the children of God, given to Christ
(vs. 10; see Jno. 17.9, 10). But we must examine closely what is
said. There is no loose statement in Scripture. Therefore **sharers
in blood and flesh** (the Greek order) should be translated exactly
that way. For God said, "As to the life of all flesh, the blood
thereof is all one with the life thereof" (Lev. 17.14). Marvel of

---

*Thus Christ is Priest—not of the human race, but of "them that are of **faith"** (Gal..
3.7; Rom. 4.11).

†The words "since then," which begin vs. 14, open out to us one side of the meaning of
the words, "all of one." For we read: **Since then the children** [the "sons He is bringing
unto glory"] **are sharers in blood and flesh, He also Himself in like manner partook of
the same.** The nature He takes is *absolutely human,* though unconnected with Adam the
First. For, as we have noted, He was the "Seed of the woman," and that by God's direct
power! Let this *humanity* of our blessed Lord captivate us wholly. We can enter no
possible human condition or circumstance with which He is not immediately and perfectly familiar!

Then, second, our *resurrection-oneness* with Christ, the teaching of which permeates
Paul's epistles, is included in these words "all-of-one"! "If then ye were raised together
with Christ, seek the things that are above, where Christ is, seated on the right hand of
God . . . For ye died, and your life is hid with Christ in God" (Col. 3.1, 3). This marvelous *oneness* is asserted over and over, though never *explained:* for how can such a
marvel be addressed to anything but to simple faith?

So then both in the fact that *He is a man* "partaker of blood and flesh in like manner" with us; and also that He died, and *we died with Him;* He was raised, and *we were
raised with Him,* the great words, "ALL OF ONE" are ours.

Out of the two facts comes the revelation of the mystery of the Body of Christ: first,
our Lord's actual *humanity;* and second, our sharing *His Risen life.*

His **taking part in blood and flesh** and that **in like manner with us,** did not enable
Him to greet us as "brethren"; but when He was raised from the dead, "The last Adam
became a life-giving spirit"! (I Cor. 15.45). Then He could and did, greet them as
"brethren" (but not before resurrection). Believers have "died with Christ," and are
no longer **in** that first Adam in which they were born. What a salvation!

marvels, of both Divine mercy and Divine wisdom! Our Lord was
to be the "Seed of the woman" that should "bruise the serpent's
head." The Seed of the *woman*, whom Satan first deceived and who
led her husband into sin!—ah, how God's *grace* triumphs! *Christ*
was given as "her Seed"—to bruise Satan's head! Here the preparation for that "bruising" (by means of death upon the Cross) is
shown us. The first step of infinite condescension *is*, **He took
part in blood and flesh.** God did not give our Lord, as He did
Adam, a body complete, full-grown. In the miracle of His infinite
mercy, the Holy Ghost came upon Mary and Christ's word was
fulfilled (Ps. 40.6; Heb. 10.5), "A body Thou hast *prepared* for
Me." This was uttered through David over a thousand years before
Christ's day by the Spirit of God: "For the testimony *of Jesus* is
the spirit of prophecy" (Rev. 19.10). God willed to "prepare a
body" for His Son after the same manner as that in which our
bodies are prepared, except that God by the Holy Spirit, and not
a human father, communicated the life to the ovum in the womb
of the virgin. Thus our Lord **partook of blood and flesh . . . in
like manner** as we:* how marvelous!

**Verses 14, 15: . . . that through death He might bring to
nought (Gr.: *katargeo*) him that had the power of death,† that**

---

*This first step of infinite condescension, He took part in blood and flesh, mystifies those
who do not know their lost state, their guilt, their helplessness. The second step of
equally gracious condescension is, He laid down this blood-and-flesh life: "He bare our
sins in His own body on the tree." For, "without shedding of blood there is no remission." In dying, He poured out His blood, and *left behind* the blood-and-flesh sphere!
But, "God raised Him up"—yet not back into "blood and flesh" existence. He had
"flesh and bones," indeed, (Lk. 24.39). But He was raised to "newness of life" "by the
glory of the Father." Only living faith follows Him there!—faith given by God, and by
the Holy Spirit.

†Two words must be looked at here: *kratos*—which means *might;* and *exousia,* which
includes the right to use might or power.
  Darkness is essentially the result of sin—connected therewith constantly by God (Gen.
1.2; I Sam. 2.9; Prov. 4.19; 20.20; Jer. 13.16; Matt. 8.12; II Peter 2.4, 17—contrast
here I Peter 2.9). Darkness has a *right (exousia),* therefore, over sinners: so that in
Col. 1.12, 13, the saints are seen to be by the Father "made meet to be partakers of the
inheritance of the Saints in *light,* having been delivered out of the power *(exousia, right)*
of *darkness,* and translated into the Kingdom of the Son of His love."
  Now Satan had no *right* but he did seize the power *(kratos)* of death—a third of the
heavenly beings—"stars of Heaven" the dragon is seen to drag down with him (Rev.
12.3, 4). And after Adam sinned Satan seized the might *(kratos)* of death, and he
became the acknowledged *prince*—yea and the *god* of those sinners over whom *darkness*
now had the right *(exousia).*
  The fact that Satan is to be bound in Hades the thousand years of the Millennium
shows that he had no *right (exousia)* over the human race. For though the race is *not*

is, the devil; and might deliver all them who through fear of death were all their lifetime subject to bondage.

Several questions confront us here. *First,* How, or on what ground, did the devil have **the power of death?** *and what means this expression? *Second,* How did our Lord through His death nullify, remove, put-out-of-business, bring to nought the devil? (These are some of the meanings of the word *katargeo*.) *Third,* What is the "bondage" to which the **fear of death** subjects people, and how does Christ deliver them?

Questions I and III: First, it is to be remembered that the devil was not an angel, but the "anointed cherub that covered" (God's throne, evidently), of the highest order of beings in Heaven. He "walked up and down in the midst of the stones of fire" (Ezek. 28.14). He was regarded by Michael, the archangel as a "dignity" compared to himself! (Jude 8, 9). Upon his sin (as revealed to us in Ezek. 28 under the type of the king of Tyre), he was ejected from Heaven: "I have cast thee as profane out of the mountain of God" (Ezek. 28.16). Our Lord described this ejecting of Satan in the words: "I beheld Satan fallen as lightning from Heaven" (Lk. 10.18). He became the deceiver who would displace God, and, inasmuch as the first Adam was to be tested, was permitted to visit the earthly Eden.* His chief role, so far as the saints of God

converted during the Millennium but rushes back to Satan's banner the moment he is "released for a little season," at the end of the thousand years (Rev. 20.7-10), it is evident that *living* in sin, *darkness* having the *right* over them, they are helpless and willing slaves of Satan, the arch-leader of sin's hosts—as in Heaven, so on earth!

Now Satan having seized **might** *(kratos)* over the human race concerning whom darkness has *right*—it is most fitting indeed that in **Hebrews** the very first recorded result of our blessed Lord's death is, that that death brought to nought him that was exercising on earth the might *(kratos)* of death!

For in **Hebrews** believers are constantly exhorted to hold fast their "**confidence,**" their "**boldness,**" toward God. Yea, to "draw near, by the blood of Jesus," to come, (by the Spirit, certainly) where their Great Priest, their "Forerunner" has gone—through the veil, a new and living way which He dedicated for us (Heb. 10.19, ff). Believers are to became *worshipers,* in **Hebrews,** and to press on to full growth.

So Satan's utter overthrow is the first result of Christ's death shown in **Hebrews!** For the saints are to do business in Heaven—not here where Satan reigns!

*Might of death: Gr., *Kratos,* "might"; consistently translated thus of God's might: Eph. 1.19, Col. 1.11; and of Christ's might in Eph. 6.10. Note the same word in the doxologies of I Tim. 6.16, I Pet. 4.11, 5.11; Jude 25; Rev. 1.6, 5.13.

*Being himself a creature, Satan had no right over other creatures, our first parents, or the race. We see that in Rev. 12.9b, when he is finally ejected from Heaven and is cast down to earth, one third of the angels fall with him. It is instructive to mark his two names and the three great characters in which he is shown, in Rev. 12.9: As the "great dragon,"

are concerned, is that of the *accuser* of the saints before God. If the angels, who are below the cherubim, are called "mighty," how much greater was the "might" of this anointed one of the cherubim when, his heart "lifted up in pride," and having sinned, he turned against God in that terrible *endless* pride which his fall brought in! That "might," all of it, he now turns against God and His creatures; and God permits him to use this fearful might against those who have chosen sin and darkness.

He did not have a right (Gr. *exousia,* authority), we repeat, over *unfallen* Adam. He secured that right *(exousia)* over *fallen* man, who had now turned against God. And he uses *might (kratos)* after man's fall. This "might" or "power" of death, then, of the devil, is a Divinely permitted exercise of power.* A slave of sin himself, like Spartacus, the Roman slave, he became the *leader* of slaves, which now included the human race. For of sin, our Lord Jesus said, "Every one that committeth sin is the bondservant (Gr., *doulos*) of sin"; as again Paul, "Know ye not, that to whom ye present yourselves as servants unto obedience, his bondservants ye are whom ye obey; whether of sin unto death, or of obedience unto righteousness?" (Rom. 6.16).

Therefore Satan's hold upon man, however unjust, could be broken only by removing that sin which held man as a slave in *"bondage."* Let us give all our soul's attention then, to *the judgment on the Cross.*

With the righteous judgment of sin, and the bearing of it, at the Cross, Satan had *nothing to do.* The transaction was altogether between God as the Judge, and Christ, the Lamb of God, (1) bearing our sins, which were transferred to Him; and (2) made to be sin on our behalf, "that we might become the righteousness of God in Him" (II Cor. 5.21).

he is contrasted with his former estate: when God said to him, "Thou sealest up the sum, 'ull of wisdom, and perfect in beauty" (Ezek. 28.12). As "the old serpent" he is seen using his marvelous wisdom to destroy. As "the devil" (*diabolos,* lit., the underflinger, slanderer), he is the *accuser.* As Satan, he is the direct enemy or *adversary* of God and His people. (See I Chron. 21.1; Job 1 and 2.) And lastly, he is the *deceiver* of the whole habitable earth: he deceives as to man's conceits of his own righteousness; of his creature ability (for man has none); as to all dreams of human greatness and progress without God; and especially in his "blinding the minds of the unbelieving" as to their doom (II Cor. 4.4).

*No creature has *independent* power—even to obey God! God's holy angels, indeed, are called "the *elect* angels"—God having in inscrutable sovereignty protected their state of obedience.

As regards Satan, our blessed Lord said, "Now is the *judgment of* this world ["judgment" referring to His own death]: now shall the *prince of this world be* cast out. And I, if I be lifted up from the earth [at Calvary] will draw all men unto Myself" [the future kingdom triumph]. There is coming a judgment day at the Great White Throne of Revelation 20.11-15. The preceding verse (20.10) sees the devil cast into the lake of fire and brimstone. He has *no part* in this Great White Throne judgment.

Nor has he any part in the judgment day of Calvary! There God, the first Person of the Trinity, laid on Christ, Whom He names as Son, God, Lord, in Hebrews 1, our actual sins, as it is written: "Jehovah hath *made to light* [Heb., R.V. margin] on Him the iniquity of us all" (Isa. 53.6); and, "Who His own self bare our sins in His body upon the tree" (I Pet. 2.24).

But sins, having been transferred to Him, must be judged according to the holy being of God, as really as the sins of the wicked will be judged at the last judgment day of Revelation 20. Therefore Christ on the Cross was *forsaken* of God. Oh, behold this! Thank God, He, as innocent, still had His faith, for He cried, "*My God!*" But the *forsaking* was real and absolute, for there was no relieving answer to His cry: "Jesus therefore . . . said, It is finished: and He bowed His head, and gave up His spirit" (Jno. 19.30). He bore our sins in His *body,* not His spirit, and His spirit was free—innocent!

This yielding up His spirit was evidently after or upon His death in the flesh, as a comparison of the four Gospels will reveal: for note: (a) "the ninth hour" had come; (b) "the veil of the temple was *rent* in the midst," signifying that the article of death was past for Christ. Those words, "Father, into Thy hands I commend My spirit," are not said while He is under the curse for sin. For John 19.30 reads, "When Jesus therefore had received the vinegar, He said, *It is finished:* and He bowed His head and gave up His spirit," while Luke adds, "Jesus, crying with a loud voice, said, Father, into Thy hands I commend My spirit: and having said this, He gave up the ghost." The spirit of the Lord Jesus was of course infinitely innocent, for He was the Son of God, though He had just borne our fearful judgment!

The judgment, then, of sins on Calvary was as absolute as the judgment of the Great White Throne will be; because it is God Who laid our sins upon Christ. It is God Who forsook Him, our Substitute, instead of us. It is God Who declares, "Our old man was crucified with Him"—that He was, we repeat, "made to be sin on our behalf; that we might become the righteousness of God in Him." Marvelous—but written! The result of this judg- ment was, of course, overwhelming disaster for Satan and his hosts, as announced in Hebrews 2.14: **He also Himself in like manner partook of blood and flesh, that through death He might bring to nought him that had the power of death, that is, the devil.**

Question II: By what means and manner did Christ **bring to nought** . . . the devil, who, wrongly indeed, but actually, was exercising **the might of death**, and making all **subject to bondage through fear of death?**

Let us first notice several things by which our Lord Jesus Christ did *not* bring Satan to nought and deliver men. It was *not* by the spiritual beauty and moral excellence, infinite as that was, of our Lord's life on earth, that He brought Satan to nought. Mod- ernist preachers, befooled by the very devil whose existence they deny or ignore, would preach the "beautiful life of Jesus," to be "imitated": would preach the "standards, the ethics of Jesus," even the "unselfishness of Jesus," saying that these are all men need! If men will consider the question, "What would Jesus do?" and do it, *they say*, "everything will be all right." Poor dupes, poor slaves, yea, beguiled slaves beguiling other slaves to their doom!

Our Lord did *not* annul or bring to nought the devil, in the wilderness, by refusing to yield to his temptations. Certainly our Lord by His wilderness victory "bound the strong man," and then went about "spoiling his house," "casting out demons," "healing all that were oppressed of the devil" (Acts 10.38). But after the wild- erness temptation we read: "When the devil had completed every temptation, he departed from Him *until* a season" (Lk. 4.13)— literally, "until a fitting opportunity." Satan, far from being "brought to nought" then, even wrought through the Lord's own, as in Peter, when the Lord rebuked him (in Matt. 16.23) with "Get thee behind Me, Satan!" and on *until,* as we have noted,

Jesus came forth from the Garden and said to the priests and soldiers led by Judas, "This is your hour, and the power [authority, *exousia*] of darkness."

No, *not* by His life, *not* by His example, *not* by His teachings, *not* by His miracles, did Christ bring the devil *to nought*. But, as the Word says, **He partook . . . of blood and flesh, that THROUGH DEATH He might bring to nought him that had the might* of death, that is, the devil.** This glorious truth, that **through death** Christ brought to nought the devil, is emphasized throughout Paul's epistles. In Romans we see Christ having become a propitiation "through faith in His *blood*" (3.25), bearing our sin, putting its guilt away; and we read, "We *died* to sin" (6.2); "Our old man *was crucified* with Him, that the body of sin might be done away, that so we should no longer be *in bondage* to sin" (6.6); "For he that *hath died* is righteously-released from sin" (6.7); "We *died* with Christ" (6.8); "Even so reckon ye also yourselves to be *dead* unto sin, but alive unto God in Christ Jesus" (6.11); "Ye also were *made dead* to the Law through the body of Christ" (7.4); "We have been *discharged* from the Law" (annulled—*katargeo*: 7.6).

If this great word *katargeo*, "brought to nought," is to be used concerning the bondage in which Satan held us, it must include both the removing of sin with its guilt and power, and the taking us out of that Adam in whom was involved our responsibility.

"We must look intently upon this Christ on the Cross," as Luther used to say, "made to be sin on our behalf." During our Lord's earthly life He was "tempted in all points like as we are, sin apart." But at Calvary, by God's act, He was made *to become sin, the thing itself,* for us! Satan was deluded at that hour into jubilance! Christ's lips had testified that God had forsaken Him. He had lifted not a hand to defend Himself. He had committed Him-

---

*An example of Satan's having **the might of death,** and *not* the right or authority, is seen in the case of Job. Only when God permitted was Satan able to work: "And Jehovah said unto Satan, Behold he *is* in thy hand; only spare his life." (Compare II Sam. 24.1, and I Chron. 21.1. Here we see God's *permissive* use of Satan, as in Job's case—Job 1 and 2.) Again, "Your adversary, the devil, as a roaring lion, walketh about, seeking whom he may devour" (I Pet. 5.8). He has the devouring might, but only when *permitted*—thank God! The tense of the verb in Heb. 2.14 is in the past: **"had the might of death."** Believers are **not under this might or power!** But as to those out of Christ, "The whole world lieth *in* the evil one."

self to "Him Who judgeth righteously." At last He said, "It is finished!" and "He bowed His head and gave up His spirit." Thus He "suffered for sins once . . . being put to death in the flesh, but made alive in the spirit."

What now could Satan do? Of those he *had* held in bondage, the *sin,* the guilt, that liability to death under judgment which made the "bondage" possible, had all been *borne by a Substitute;* and He of God's appointing! Those who believed on Christ were *free*— as free as their Substitute! And Him God raised up from the dead, and received at His right hand—"crowned with glory and honor!" What *right* then had Satan over believing ones? *None whatever!* Let them be "subject to God," and *believe,* thus *resisting* the devil, and he will flee from them. Astounding witness to Satan's defeated condition!* (Note *exact* words of Jas. 4.7.)

When our Lord rose from the dead, and was received up into glory, He went up as the Victor Who had **brought the devil to nought!** Nothing now but unbelief or disobedience, or ignorance of their liberty, can hold men in bondage to Satan. All his basis of accusation before God, all his power to terrorize believers on earth is nullified, for the judgment for believers was over at the Cross. Do you see that, O believer? Satan has no power, no rights over you. None! He may hinder you; he may oppose you—he did and does oppose all testimony in Christ's Name. But God has reckoned to you the full value of Christ's whole work; and neither *guilt,* nor *bondage,* nor *fear* belongs to you at all! You are *in Christ,* and are *as Christ* in God's reckoning! "The sting of death is sin," but Christ bore the sin, and put it away. "The power of sin is the law," but those in Christ died unto law that they might live unto God (Gal. 2.19). And you are *in a Risen Christ,* Who is all in all to you: "righteousness, sanctification, and redemption"! If, therefore, you are not as free from the devil's bondage of fear as Christ is, it is either from ignorance of Christ's work, or lack of reliance thereon!

---

*The Holy Spirit, our Lord told us, would convict the world of three things: sin, righteousness, and judgment (Jno. 16.8): Men know, as to the first, that *it is a sin* not to believe on Christ; second that Christ is *righteous,* because He has left the world and gone to the Father; third, that the prince of this world, Satan, has been *judged.* When men realize this, it is like the cry going over a battlefield, "Our commanding general has been killed!" This world is an armed camp against God. A Holy Ghost revival shatters the world's sense of security, takes away all their confidence. Their hearts are like water. God grant such revivals!

All their lifetime subject to bondage, is a summary of the history of most people you know. "It is appointed unto men once to die, and after this cometh judgment" (Heb. 9.27). That double engagement lies ever before men out of Christ! Drown their convictions in pleasure, debauchery, infidelity, as they may, there is ever bondage to fear of death! Peculiarly is this bondage felt by those whose consciences have been awakened to the fearful character and consequences of human guilt, and to their own inability to change their moral state. By these we mean true souls, who may not yet have learned the full truth of the deliverance Christ accomplished at the Cross in their behalf.*

Verse 16: For verily not of angels doth He take hold but He **taketh hold of the seed of Abraham:** The angels, whatever their past has been, were created with moral responsibility. At least one-third of them revolted with Satan in Heaven (Rev. 12.4), yet the rest, named "the holy angels," were preserved—not by creature power, but by Divine sovereign will. These are called the "elect angels" (I Tim. 5.21). The point here is that, of these beings called *angels,* Christ did not "take hold." While there are profound mysteries in this subject, yet perhaps we may say this much:

First, God's purposes were always connected with *man,* because

---

*Through fear of death were all their lifetime subject to bondage. From the time you were born your mother was afraid you would *die;* the household kept in touch with doctors—"through fear of death;" funerals passed your house, often carrying loved ones, over whom you wept; the reports that came of whole communities smitten with disease filled with *dread;* the cemeteries you passed cried out, "You will soon be here!" The philosophers and the poets you read made your life "a brief passing moment,"—and then death.

The human race is today SUBJECT TO BONDAGE. They may talk peace—but yonder comes the *undertaker!*

Now—to hear the astounding NEWS that death and judgment for the believer on Christ are PAST THINGS! that they have been borne by *Another,* for us; and that the believer is not coming into judgment but has passed out of death into life! also that God has raised His dear Son from the dead; and that He has passed as our Great High Priest through the heavens and is now seated at the right hand of God! and that our standing is perfect and glorious in Christ! that even if a believer should sin, he has "an Advocate—Jesus Christ the righteous"—I say, that the contemplation in faith of these glorious truths sets the heart singing in joy! And that "bondage" which arose "through fear of death" is gone forever! For the believer has died with Christ, and is raised with Him; and Christ has entered God's presence as the Forerunner of believers: where God's saints are, in their *standing,* and shall be shortly in *personal presence forever!*

So He **delivered all those who through fear of death were all their life subject to bondage!**

the eternal Son was to *become man,* in the eternal Divine plan! And the first man was made "in the image" of God (Gen. 1.22).

Second, "My delight was with the *sons of men,*" God said. As the angels themselves sang:

"Glory to God in the highest,

And on earth peace among *men in whom His delight is*" (Lk. 2.14).

Third, "God *so loved* the world that He gave His only begotten Son." We quote over and over words that, freely *believed,* would cast us on our faces weeping for joy and wonder! It was not pity, it was not self-interest—not merely to redeem back to Himself creatures who should become His servants, that God gave His Son. Nor is this wonderful verse pronounced concerning God's elect. But that "God so loved *the world*" is our Lord's explanation of His presence here!

Fourth, God had a sovereign right to pass by those fallen angels that had been in His presence, and to come to take hold of man, a creature far below the mighty angels!

Fifth, the GRACE of God is revealed as nowhere else in all eternity in His coming down to the lowest of His morally conscious beings—*sinners* and *lost,* as they were—and not only pardoning, but raising up those believers to sit in the heavenlies in Christ, members of Christ Himself!

Verse 17: Wherefore it behooved Him in all things to be made like unto His brethren, that He might become a merciful and faithful High Priest in things pertaining to God, to make propitiation for the sins of the people:

Here we find that in order to become "a merciful and faithful High Priest," **it behooved Him in all things to be made like unto His brethren.** This involved (1) Partaking of the "blood and flesh" life that they had; (2) Being thus made "a little lower than the angels" (though their Creator); (3) Being "perfected through sufferings"—even suffering death under Divine forsaking! He **made propitiation for the sins of the people,** being a **merciful and faithful High Priest in things pertaining to God.**

Our hearts grieve over those (and there are many) who deny that Christ's priestly work began until He was saluted by God after resurrection, "Thou art a Priest forever." But He laid down

His life in *priestly* manner! (Note Jno. 10.) We are amazed that
some have said that His high priesthood did not begin until He
presented His blood in Heaven. Some have even pointed to our
Lord's words to Mary Magdalene, "Touch Me not; for I am not
yet ascended unto the Father": declaring that He was on His way
on that day of resurrection, to fulfill the type of the high priest in
placing His blood before God, as the Levitical high priest sprinkled
the blood in the Holy of Holies on the Day of Atonement, quoting:
"There shall be no man in the tent of meeting when he goeth in
to make atonement" (Lev. 16.14-17).* I would ask, What then
mean our Lord's words on the Cross, "It is finished"? If the
sprinkling of His blood before God in Heaven was necessary to
complete the work of atonement, what mean the words, "It is
finished"? What was finished? Atonement! The putting away of
sin (before God) by the sacrifice of Himself!

Over 700 years before Christ came, the Spirit spoke by Isaiah
of what His priestly work would involve, and "He was not re-
bellious." We quote the wondrous words of preparation, that
"morning by morning" the Father "opened His ear to hear" words
of His coming priestly sacrifice. He was born King of the Jews;
and He was the great Prophet Whom Moses foretold; but He
was no less Priest—yea, High Priest, on His way to the Great Day
of Atonement at Calvary! Hear our blessed Lord speaking:

"The Lord Jehovah hath opened Mine ear, and *I was not re-
bellious, neither turned away backward. I gave My back to the
smiters, and My cheeks to them that plucked off the hair; I hid not
my face from shame and spitting"* (Is. 50.5, 6).

Of course priesthood is based upon *sacrifice,* upon *poured out*
blood. But as our Lord said in John 17, "Now I come to Thee, and
these things I am speaking *in the world,* that they may have My
joy made full in themselves." He desired them to hear His priestly
words, to recognize His priestly relationship to them! If Isaiah
could say over seven hundred years before the event, as if the event
were past, "He *was* despised and rejected," surely our blessed Lord

---

*Note: *it was the High Priest,* and none other, who, alone in the tabernacle on the
Day of Atonement, killed the bullock and the goat. So our Lord *laid down His own life*
—no one "taking it from Him." He "laid it down" as our High Priest, and we must so
regard Him!

might speak within a few hours of His offering Himself on the Cross as if the event had already taken place, as in this same John 17.4, "I glorified Thee on the earth, having accomplished the work which Thou hast given me to do."*

Before we close our study of this wonderful 17th verse, we must meditate in detail upon two phrases, **Wherefore it behooved Him,** and, **in things pertaining to God.**

The word "behooved" in the first of these phrases, does not involve, as among men, the idea of duty or obligation, but that of a necessary condition to achieve a result. His being **made like unto His brethren,** "sons whom God was bringing unto glory," was necessary in His undertaking priesthood for them. Now in what particulars did His being **made like unto His brethren** consist? In His partaking of blood and flesh; in His being subject at Nazareth to "His parents"; in His "increasing in wisdom and stature"; engaging in carpentry work with Joseph; in His being "made for a little while lower than the angels," and traveling the troubled pathway of humility here below—"in all points tempted like as we are, sin apart," in His traversing the path the Father gave Him, "a Man of sorrows and acquainted with *sickness*" (Hebrew); daily, hourly, applied to by human need and suffering, and bringing His matters before God in daily prayer. (See Mk. 1.35; Lk. 3.21, 4.42, 6.12, 9.28, 29.)

Here were men, utterly unable to deal with God, Whom they infinitely, hourly, needed. And here was Christ, "laying His hand upon us both" (Job 9.33). These things **it behooved Him** to do and to be, until, "through the eternal Spirit," He should have offered Himself without blemish unto God, to shed His blood at the Cross. A Priest at Calvary, He *"offered up Himself."* It matters not who slew Him: "No man took His life from Him" (Jno. 10.17, 18) : He laid it down *of Himself,* by command of His Father. No one else offered Him up: He offered up *himself,* a *priestly* act! Then after He rose, He "passed through the heavens,"

---

*Mr. Darby well says "As having once for all completed His work for the putting away of sin, our Priest offered His sacrifice once for all when He offered up Himself." (synopsis, in loc.) As also F. W. Grant: "It is certain that Christ was a merciful and faithful High Priest to make propitiation; and therefore He was High Priest *before* propitiation was, or could be, made . . . Propitiation is by blood, and that was shed *on earth!*"

being *then, a Great High* Priest *before* He "passed through the heavens" (Heb. 4.14). Note, it was a High Priest who *passed* through. **It behooved Him in all things to be made like unto His brethren:**

1. In "emptying Himself," as Deity, of glory, power, wisdom (Phil. 2.5-8).

2. In incarnation—"sharing in blood and flesh" (Heb. 2.14).

3. In *individual sympathy* with each of His own.

4. In sharing, in His ministry, the circumstances of His disciples.

5. In being "perfected through sufferings" (vs. 10).

Thus **He became a merciful and faithful High Priest in things pertaining to God.**

Things pertaining to God *(ta pros ton Theon)* is used by Paul in Romans 15.17, and in Hebrews 2.17 and 5.1, these places only in the New Testament. This phrase is a characteristic one, both as to its form and its content. It is remarkable that Paul in Romans 15.17 should connect it with that priestly "offering up of the Gentiles" in which he "ministered in sacrifice" the gospel of God, "in the power of signs and wonders, in the power of the Holy Spirit: . . . glorying in Christ Jesus in *things pertaining to God.*"

Things pertaining to God: What were these things in Hebrews 2.17?

1. Things which were necessary for Christ to do (that is to die) for us *as sinners.*

2. His presenting Himself Risen before the face of God for us, giving us thus a place in Him in Heaven, and rights and priviliges of worship in God's immediate presence—at the "throne of Grace."

3. His Divine intelligence, and priestly sympathy *unlimited,* concerning our needs, temptations and trials; and constant unwearied attendance thereunto, obtaining help for us from God; for, although all blessing is *through* Christ, "all things are *of* God (Rom. 11.36).

4. Finally, that adoration of God in which Christ the Son Himself delights, and in which He will eternally lead His redeemed "brethren," "the congregation" of redeemed ones. All this, at

least, is included in this word, **things pertaining to God.*** "In the midst of the congregation will I sing Thy praise!"

Concerning this eternal worship, we repeat over and over that it will be the supreme delight of the redeemed. For they will be brought to apprehend more and more, forever, of the "kindness of God," Whose Name is Love, and Who is in every attribute infinite in perfection! In His presence there is fullness of joy; in His right hand there are pleasures for evermore. Sin and self left behind, with our former limited apprehension while on earth, we shall throughout the endless ages of eternity find ever new delight in Him Who through and in His blessed Son is "our Portion forever."

And even today, we *draw near* in our Lord Jesus Christ, our

---

*Distinguish carefully between the *result* of accepted propitiation and the thing itself. Note that **things pertaining to God** just precedes **to make propitiation for the sins of the people**. We must learn and believe in our very hearts that this task of making **propitiation for the sins of the people** was a transaction between Christ, as Sin-offering, and God, as God.

Comparing the frequency of use in Scripture of a word, fact, or doctrine is often the best means of arriving at the truth set forth. Let us note in **Hebrews**, twenty or more statements referring to our Lord's propitiatory death: (We quote the most telling words only, to conserve space; hunt them out in Chs. 1, 2, 5, 7, 9, 12, 13.

When He had made purification of sins (1.3).

Because of the suffering of **death** crowned . . . that He should taste of **death** for every man (2.9).

Made perfect through sufferings (2.10).

Through death He might bring to nought him that had the power of death (2.14).

To make propitiation (2.17).

Every high priest . . . is appointed . . . that he may offer . . . sacrifices for sins (5.1).

Prayers and supplications unto Him that was able to save Him out of **death** (5.7).

He (offered up sacrifices) once for all, when He offered up Himself (7.27).

Christ . . . **through His own blood,** entered . . . into the holy place, having obtained eternal redemption (9.12).

The blood of Christ, Who through the Eternal Spirit **offered Himself** unto God (9.14).

He is the **Mediator** of a New Covenant, a **death** having taken place for the redemption of the transgressions that were under the first covenant. (9.15).

Once at the end of the ages hath He been manifested **to put away sin by the sacrifice of Himself** (9.26).

Christ . . . **once offered** to bear the sins of many (9.28).

By one offering He hath perfected forever them that are sanctified (10.14).

He . . . offered one sacrifice for sins forever (10.12).

Enter into the holy place **by the blood of Jesus** . . . through the veil, that is to say, His flesh (10.19, 20).

Jesus **endured the Cross,** despising shame (12.2).

Jesus, that He might sanctify the people also **through His own blood, suffered** without the gate (13.12).

The God of peace . . . brought again from **the dead** the Great Shepherd of the sheep **in the blood** of a covenant eternal (13.20).

Read and re-read these wondrous passages concerning the death of Christ. They draw out our hearts.

Great High Priest, and come by the power of the blessed Spirit to "the Throne of Grace," and enter upon that blessed and glorious worship which will have its consummation in eternity. *This worship is set before us in* **Hebrews!**

Verse 18: For in that He Himself hath suffered being tempted, He is able to succor them that are tempted: What a marvel is here! Isaiah calls Him "Immanuel, God with us;" and "Wonderful, Counsellor, Mighty God, Father of Eternity"! But when He was on earth, He was *tempted:* **He suffered, being tempted.** As the Holy One, He loved righteousness and hated iniquity, so that even the presence of evil caused Him suffering. Having then been, through the appointed sufferings, perfected, He becomes a High Priest Who **is able to succor them that are tempted.**

Dear friend, you and I might be in the presence of someone who is suffering peculiar and agonizing temptation. But, poor things that we are, we would not know it; and did we know it, who has the power to deliver another soul? *Christ,* having Himself suffered being tempted, is able to succor them that are tempted.

Rely on this *Great High Priest* of Whom we are reading in this book of **Hebrews.** Thank God, He is "a Priest forever," as we shall see! There is one God, one Mediator between God and men, the Man Christ Jesus! Rely upon His past work and His present priestly work in your behalf, and *go directly by Him to God;* knowing first, that "God is *for* us" (Rom. 8.31); and that Christ Jesus "is at the right hand of God—Who also maketh intercession for us" (Rom. 8.34); and that our Great High Priest is **merciful and faithful . . . for in that He Himself hath suffered, being tempted, He is able to** succor them that are tempted. Thank God!

We shall learn much more in **Hebrews** of this Great High Priest!

CHAPTER THREE

1   WHEREFORE, holy brethren, partakers of a heavenly calling, consider the Apostle and High Priest of our
2   confession, Jesus; Who was faithful to Him that appointed Him, as also was Moses in all His [God's] house.
3   For He hath been counted worthy of more glory than
Moses, by so much as He that built the house hath more
4   honor than the house. For every house is builded by
5   some one; but He that built all things is God. And Moses
indeed was faithful in all His [God's] house as a ministering servant for a testimony of those things which
6   were afterward to be spoken; but Christ as a Son, over
His [God's] house; Whose house are we, if we hold fast
our boldness and the glorying of our hope firm unto the
end.

Verse 1: WHEREFORE—GOD'S WORD is INSPIRED! So
we do well to weigh every term He uses. This "wherefore" is
like, for example, the "therefore" of Romans 5.12. It means that
what has already been written in **Hebrews** calls us to consider
Christ as God (Ch. 1); and as Man (Ch. 2); especially in His
willingness "to be made in all things like unto His brethren"
(2.17).

Holy brethren—The apostles addressed the Jews generally as
"brethren" (Acts 2.29; 13.38); as indeed, Paul and Barnabas
were addressed by the Jews (before they understood the message of grace: Acts 13.15). But this address, **holy brethren**, in
this verse, is not a reference to brethren by race, but to those
believing on Christ—which is very far different! They are
"brethren" in the sense of Hebrews 2.11, 17; and they are "*holy*
brethren" not because of their holy walk (though they may have
had a good walk), but because they were in Christ—"sanctified
in Christ Jesus."

Partakers of a heavenly calling—Here are indeed great words!
words which connect this epistle with the prayer our Lord made

in John 17 (vss. 14, 16, 21-24), and with His coming for His heavenly saints as He promised in John 14.2, 3; and shown by Paul in I Corinthians 15.50-57; Ephesians 1.3; 2.5, 6; 5.30, 32; I Thessalonians 4.16, 17. "Calling" here, as always in the epistles, has reference not to an invitation to go to Heaven, but to a *present* heavenly state, and manner of being. For Christians, according to Colossians 1.12, have already by Christ's work, *been* made "meet to be partakers of the inheritance of the saints in light," and their *citizenship* is in Heaven (Philippians 3.20). The Hebrews naturally had an earthly calling.* To them was given an earthly land,

---

*The fearful plight of "Israel after the flesh" is brought to mind by the fact that saved Hebrews no longer partake even of the earthly calling of Israel! Language almost fails us here! It is deeply impressive that this epistle is addressed not to "Jews" or "Israel," but to Hebrews.

In unfathomable grace, God presented His Son as "born King of the Jews," partaking of "blood and flesh." National Israel, led on by blind priests and Pharisees, despised and rejected their only true Messiah. They poured out His life-blood, and thus "Israel *after the flesh*" forever lost their Messiah. For God had said "the life of the flesh was all one with the blood thereof." Christ poured out His *soul* (Lev. 17.11) unto death, laying down His life. He was not coming back into the blood-and-flesh life. When He was raised from the dead, it was in "newness of life"; life out of death; resurrection life; of which "Israel after the flesh" knew nothing.

Therefore, at that time, Israel was lost; and as it was then, when they said, "Crucify Him!"—so it is today.

When a Hebrew is "enlightened" and saved now, it is as a common sinner. God has declared "There is no distinction between Jew and Greek"; for all sinned. There are no "Hebrew-Christians"; they are just *pardoned sinners.*

For the fact that God has today an elect "Remnant" of Israel whom He will by and by save by *Sovereign mercy* and grace, just as He does Gentiles now, brings no hope to the present national "Israel after the flesh." Today they build their synagogues and have their "religious" teachings. Tomorrow, after the Church is raptured, they will have their temple in Jerusalem, and there again begin their sacrifices—though in utter unbelief! Concerning that temple God has said:

"What manner of house will ye build unto Me? . . . He that killeth an ox is as he that slayeth a man; he that sacrificeth a lamb, as he that breaketh a dog's neck; he that offereth an oblation as he that offereth swine's blood: he that burneth frankincense, as he that blesseth an idol" (Isa. 66.1-3).

It will be in this temple, soon to be built by the Jews, that Paul writes, "The man of sin, the son of perdition . . . *sitteth in the temple of God,* setting himself forth as God" (II Thess. 2.3, 4). This is the Antichrist, the "abomination of desolation" referred to by our Lord (Matt. 24.15; Jno. 5.43).

The Jews today are carrying on their synagogue ceremonies in darkness, having slain their Messiah, Who has been raised from the dead and is seated at the right hand of the Majesty on high; and is over the true "house of God," which does not at all contain the "fleshly" nation of the Jews!

Of *mercy,* this Jewish *nation knows nothing yet, nationally.* And when the fearful "Tribulation" arises to its height and they are about to be "cut off from being a nation" (Ps. 83.4) at Armageddon, and there is poured upon the Remnant the "spirit of grace and supplication" and they look, by Divine illumination, *"unto Him Whom they have pierced"* (Zech. 12.10), there will be "a very great *mourning!*" That Remnant will see what they have done and what God has done in opening a door of faith to the Gentiles. They will see, by the "mercy" shown toward us, Gentiles, that they must be cast upon the same *sovereign mercy* (Rom. 11.30-32). "For God hath shut up all

with earthly blessings wonderful indeed, with Jehovah's dwelling in their midst, in His temple in Jerusalem! But their sin drove Jehovah from that temple. It was destroyed, the city taken, the people placed under Gentile rule. And, though they rebuilt their temple, and, at the time of this epistle worshiped there, they were *under the Romans,* so that, although never to be nationally *forsaken* of God, they were not yet nationally *forgiven!* But these individual *believing* Hebrews, addressed in Hebrews 3.1, had been *transferred from an earthly to a heavenly calling and destiny,* an entirely different "calling," ending their fleshly hopes; called to a rejected Saviour—and lo! a priesthood announced *on high,* at God's *right hand:* for those *who believed and left all earthly hopes*—who were willing to be "without the camp" (of earthly religious things) and to be the earth-rejected but Heaven-received worshipers "within the veil" above! On earth they would be persecuted, despised. In Heaven they were received, welcomed, invited to "the throne of Grace," of which, alas, the Jewish *nation* knew nothing!

Remove from your mind the idea of any difference before God between these Hebrews and anyone else who comes to God by Jesus Christ. For (we say it over and over), although God had given these Hebrews a "religion," the book of **Hebrews** sees God *taking it all away!* The Hebrews were indeed to learn lessons from their former history, and God will exercise great gentleness and grace now toward them. But Aaron *disappears;* yea, Moses *disappears;* yea, the Law is *"disannulled—the priesthood being changed";* the scene is changed *from earth to Heaven!* And these Hebrew believers are saluted as "partakers of a *heavenly* calling." In this "calling" there are no Hebrew or Jewish things, which distinctions belong *wholly to earth!* (Col. 2.16, 17; Heb. 8.5).

It will be found difficult to view a Hebrew believer as "having nothing"; and most difficult to the Hebrew believer himself!* Union

---

unto disobedience, that He might have *mercy* upon all!" Let both Jew and Gentile ponder that!

*Let us Gentiles reflect that *with God* there are no "Episcopalians," "Presbyterians," "Methodists," "Baptists." It was the writer's great privilege in the Moody Church in Chicago to teach a Bible class in which one night at my request they all wrote down the "churches" they came from, and the "denominations" or "sects" they represented. There proved to be over two hundred churches, or assemblies; for Chicago is a large city. But they called themselves by forty-one different denominational names! Yet with God they were simply *believers.* We are *not* "fighting denominations, having the gospel to preach! We

with Christ, resurrection, heavenly position, this was the "heavenly calling." They are no longer Hebrews, no longer Gentiles, for they are "new creatures in Christ." New creatures are no more Hebrews than new Englishmen or new Chinese. Creation is *creation*, not *change!* (I Cor. 7.19; Gal. 6.15).

There is but one heavenly calling revealed.* Those to whom Ch. 3.1 was addressed were "partakers" of it. They were in a Risen, heavenly Christ. It matters not whether or not they fully realized these glorious facts, or whether or not they enjoyed them. The writer of **Hebrews,** indeed, here *defines* their heavenly calling, (as is done in Ephesians). But he does assert that they, being partakers of a heavenly calling, are through with earthly things, not having here on earth even an abiding city! They are to be approached as those who once had such a city, and temple, and sacri-

---

allude to those things only to illustrate how difficult it is to *hold only heavenly things, as partakers of a heavenly calling.* It is so easy to say, "*I* am of Paul; and *I* of Apollos!"

*The word *kaleo*, "*I call*," and its noun, *klesis*, calling, are used in the N. T. over 50 times, as, Rom. 1.1-7; 8.28, 30; I Cor. 1.2, 9, 24; Jude 1; Rev. 17.14.

The "calling" of God is a sovereign act, which determined the position and privileges of these believers:

1. It is the description both of the order of life and being into which God has created a creature, and also of that order of life befitting such creation. Angels, for example, were created into the angelic state and mode of being. Certain of them "kept not their first principality but left their proper habitation" (Jude 6).

2. Of them who are "saints" by calling, Rom. 8.30 says that they were foreordained before this calling.

3. Scripture also asserts that these were "called with a holy calling, not according to our works, but according to His own purpose and grace, which was given us in Christ Jesus before times of ages" (II Tim. 1.9, literally).

4. It is written of the Corinthians, who at that time were "babes in Christ," that they were "sanctified in Christ Jesus, called saints"; and that God, "Who is faithful," would also "confirm them unto the end," that they might be "unreprovable in the day of our Lord Jesus Christ" (I Cor. 1.2, 8).

5. While the saints are exhorted to "walk worthily of the calling wherewith they were called" (Eph. 4.1; II Thess. 1, 11, 12) yet note, they did not obtain the "calling" by excellent behavior, nor lose it by failure, but enjoyed it in a faithful walk. Note also the same in II Peter 1.5-11: the great exhortation to diligence on our part, by such diligence making "our calling and election sure" (which is the great exhortation in **Hebrews,** is it not?), God guarding us against stumbling, and guaranteeing assurance of an "entrance richly supplied . . . into the eternal kingdom of our Lord and Savior Jesus Christ."

6. See also II Pet. 3.17, 18: It was not the intention of God, in revealing to us a marvellous "calling" into which He had foreordained us, to have us become negligent. Peter exhorts us to "grow in the grace and knowledge of our Lord and Savior Jesus Christ" (not grow "in grace," as often wrongly quoted, but grow in *the* grace and experimental favor and acquaintanceship of our Lord Jesus Christ Himself).

7. Finally, those believers who have been most quietly certain of their own heavenly calling have most constantly given God praise for their own *election!* For they know Whom they have trusted! In view of the unutterable *Grace* that had formed such purposes toward their unworthy selves they are filled with rapturous thanksgiving!

fices, but are now without them, without any earthly religion whatever. And they are called to come boldly to the throne of of grace *in Heaven*, by the blood of Jesus; having Him as Great High Priest! In short, the object of **Hebrews** is to call to a heavenly worship, people who now have **a heavenly calling!**

Of course to think that the apostle in thus lovingly exhorting the Hebrew believers, is admitting any "special character" of theirs, would be to deny other Scriptures. Unless we keep in mind the great facts revealed in Paul's epistles, we shall not, in our study of **Hebrews,** be ready at its great exhortation in Chapter 13, to go forth to our rejected Lord "without the camp" (which is not only Judaism,* but all human "religion" as such), "bearing His reproach." We all know, if we are honest with ourselves, that to glory in a despised, rejected, crucified Christ is not the message Christendom† honors or will bear with. "Without the camp" below; "within the veil" above: what does the world know of *that?*

No, there was no "other gospel" for Hebrews. The Lord told Ananias that Saul was to bear His name "before the Gentiles, and kings, *and the children of Israel.*" (Acts 9.15). Peter says Paul wrote "Scriptures" unto the Jews who were of the *Diaspora*, the "Dispersion" (I Pet. 1.1). See also II Peter 3.1, 15-16: "Our beloved brother Paul . . . wrote unto you; as also in all his epistles, speaking in them of those things; wherein are some things hard to be understood, which the ignorant and unsteadfast wrest, as they do also the other *Scriptures,* unto their own destruction."

---

*The Hebrews had had a Divinely given religion, *Judiasmos*, which we translate "Judaism" (Gal. 1.13, 14); which Paul, as a Jew, also calls "our religion" (threskeia, Acts 26.5). †The very name "Christians"—whence came it? From the *world*, not from God! It was a taunt. In Antioch of Syria, a city with a reputation for cynicism and human "smartness," the disciples "were called *Christians* first" (Acts 11.26). "Christian"—a remarkable word! A *Hebrew* idea (Messiah-Anointed), expressed in Greek *(Christos)* with a Latin ending anos: thus worldwide! See also I Pet. 4.16: "If any man suffer *as a Christian*, let him not be ashamed; but let him glorify God *in this name."* We might translate "Christians," "Christ-ones"; compare "Jesus-men," as true believers were mockingly called by unbelieving Chinese. It is the world's name, not God's. God's name for His saints with respect to His truth, is *"believers."* "Believers were the more added to the Lord, multitudes both of men and women" (Acts 5.14). The characteristic of believers is bowing to God's Word, believing it just as it stands.

How many of God's saints do you know who habitually think of themselves as simply *believers?* There has been a mighty work at Calvary; they have a Risen Lord and a heavenly calling which they, as believers, entered. The world, in its Satan-ruled ignorance, calls them "Christians," Christ-ones, as over against the Jews. The "Christian *religion"* has supplanted, in what they call "Christendom," the Jews' religion! But saints are simply *"believers."*

Doubtless, having had a Divinely given religion, they were, as are all having a "religion," slow to apprehend the break, the end of all "religion" at the Cross, with the end of all Levitical things, of all earthly things; and their place "without the camp," and the present worship "within the veil" in Heaven. Furthermore, Paul is not "the apostle to the circumcision" (Gal. 2.8, 9). Even James, writing to "The Twelve Tribes which were of the Dispersion," describes "pure *religion* and undefiled before our God and Father" to be visiting the fatherless and widows in their affliction, and keeping oneself unspotted from the world (Jas. 1.27). How about this, Jew? Romanist? Denominationalist? Reformed theologian? Any place left for the Mosaic economy? Furthermore, religionist: have *you* been visiting the fatherless and widows? Are you "un-spotted from the world"?

Consider the Apostle and High Priest of our confession, Jesus —While the word "our" here is directed to Hebrew believers, it includes *all* believers, all partakers of a "heavenly calling."

Each of the four Gospels ends the account of the despising and rejection and crucifixion by national Israel of that Messiah Whom God had sent to them—for it is evident that He was first sent, not to the Gentiles, but to the Jews. He said, (Matt. 15.24): "I was not sent but unto the lost sheep of the house of Israel." In the sending forth of the twelve, He charged them, "Go not into any way of the Gentiles, and enter not into any city of the Samaritans: but go rather to the lost sheep of the house of Israel" (Matt. 10.5). In the words of John, "They that were *His own* received Him not" (1.11).

Remember Matthew 21.43: "The kingdom of God shall be taken away from you, and shall be given to a *nation* bringing forth the fruits thereof." This coming "nation" is not the Church, nor Gen-tiles, but that nation described in Isaiah 66.7-9, to be "brought forth at once": that is, the national Israel, which, though "a very small Remnant" (Isa. 1.9; 10.20-22; 11.11, 16; 37.31, 32; 46.3 marg.; Dan. 12.1), "shall look unto Him Whom they have pierced."

That day has not yet come, and although God does, in this epistle, explain to these Hebrews their past history, we find Christ as set forth here, *not* belonging to the Hebrews as such, but on the contrary, to Heaven itself! with a heavenly life, and carrying on a worship altogether heavenly!

Therefore when we read, **Consider the Apostle and High Priest of our confession**—we must not think in Jewish terms. **And High Priest**—For fifteen centuries, from Moses to Christ, God taught the Hebrew nation to depend on their high priest, upon his work, and upon his year by year acceptability to God. This was especially true on the Great Day of Atonement, once a year, when, in the wilderness, the nation would gather round the tabernacle, waiting, while the high priest went in with the blood of the slain goat, to see him reappear. Their hopes (before their idolatry and apostasy) were based on this: that the high priest would come out from the Holy of Holies, place his hands upon the head of the live goat, and confess over its head all the iniquities and sins of the nation, and send it away into an uninhabited land, never to be found. (For the slain goat, and that "sent away," *together* are the type of shed blood bringing man into God's presence, and also dismissing forever their sins.) Read Leviticus 16 again—unless you remember well all facts of the Great Day of Atonement.

Of course, most of my readers will be Gentiles, and concerning the priestly work of Christ there has been a lamentable lack of teaching. Would that all of us, Hebrew or Gentile believers, were alike fully instructed in the Old Testament setting forth of the office and ministry of the high priest. For these men, types as they were, become in their ministry a wonderful help to appreciate this book of **Hebrews,*** which deals with that Great High Priest, "Who ever liveth to make intercession for us."

---

*It was Divinely intended that the *result* of the reading of the book of Hebrews would be that these Hebrews should (a) abandon all reliance on the old Covenant, or Levitical things; and (b) know that the New Covenant with the house of Judah and Israel lies in the future—is not yet made—so that they shall not attach their hopes to it.

(c) That they should know that Christ was *"another* Priest . . . not after the order of Aaron"—but of an order Israel had never known, even that of Melchizedek, who preceded Abraham, the patriarch, therefore indescribably greater than Abraham; and that Christ was after Melchizedek's order of *never-ending* priesthood, established by Divine oath.

(d) And know that the only worship God is now accepting is heavenly and unseen, not connected at all with earthly things, whether buildings, forms, or ordinances.

(e) And that inasmuch as Christ, rejected by the world and particularly by human "religion," suffered "without the gate," fulfilling the type of the *body* of the sin-offering; we whose hopes are *in Heaven*, should "go forth unto Him without the camp" of human religion "bearing His reproach."

(f) That such believers should know their sins forgiven *forever!*

Of our confession—The word "confession," (Gr. *homologia*) is used six times in the New Testament, three of which are in Hebrews. It is unfortunately, in this text, in the King James Version, rendered "profession." (Its use in I Timothy 6.12, 13, shows how inadequate this translation is.) Christ before Pilate did not make a "profession," but *confessed:* "Pilate said unto Him, 'Art Thou a king, then?' Jesus answered, 'Thou sayest that I am—a *king!*" See John 18.37. Our Lord's "Thou sayest" was the most emphatic "YES!" The Apostle and High Priest of our confession, then, is One Whom you have *confessed,* One with Whom your relationship is personal, as connected with His Lordship: as Paul says: "If thou shalt *confess* with thy mouth *Jesus as Lord.*" See verbal form in Matthew 10.32; Luke 12.8, etc.

"Consider the Apostle and High Priest of our confession, Jesus." In this verse every word needs comment! "Consider the Apostle." When we note Whom we are to "consider," and what He is here, we are convicted of neglect at once! The word "consider" means to fix the mind with all attention. Here, as we see, it is upon the person of our Lord. We are asked to fix our attention on Jesus in the double character of Apostle and High Priest. We may say that perhaps Christians have "considered" these two characters of our Lord less than any others!

Now an "apostle" was *one sent.* Here our Lord is called "the Apostle of our confession." Who sent Him forth? *The Father,* certainly!— as He so constantly told the Jews, *to whom* He was sent first (Matt. 15.24); and then to *all* (I John 4.10, 14). Were there other "apostles?" Certainly—but *Christ* sent *them* forth. And people who heard them were to believe on *Christ,* and confess—not any earthly apostle, but Christ Himself—"the Saviour of the world." In our confession, we are constantly to remember that He is the Apostle sent forth to us from the Father, and that He is to be confessed by us constantly before the world. What could be meant by the words "our confession?" First, it acknowledges Jesus as Son of God, Creator, Upholder; second, the reality of His humanity; third, the infinite efficacy of His atoning work; fourth, the marvelous union which enables Him to call believers "brethren"; fifth, the new and eternal priestly "order" of Melchizedek—as we shall see in Hebrews Seven.

In short, the book of **Hebrews** is *given* to "our confession" of Him, "Who was faithful to Him that appointed Him."

Jesus—How wonderful that God had known Him in His conception by this precious, personal name, Jesus! (Matt. 1.21; Lk. 1.31). Therefore let us not fear, but have this name, "Jesus," ever in our hearts, as we go through **Hebrews**. We saw Him in Chapter 1 as Son, Heir, Creator, high above even heavenly creatures; and then in Chapter 2 we saw Him just as truly *Man!* He is not ashamed to call us brethren"! So let us hold fast that tender name, *Jesus!* We shall find Him in Chapter 6 called *Christ.* Let us remember what is written in Chapter 13: "Jesus Christ, the same yesterday, and today, and unto the ages" (13.8).

Verse 2: Who was faithful to Him that appointed Him, as also was Moses in all His [God's] house: This faithfulness to the God Who appointed Him "the Apostle and High Priest of our confession," should be the subject of our most attentive consideration. While not developed fully here as later in the book, God's appointing Jesus our High Priest in Heaven must claim our first attention. You may have noticed that the Gospel of John, taking for granted our Lord's rejection by Israel (Jno. 1.11 previously quoted), proceeds to develop His Deity, and the fact that anyone believing may have life in His Name; and gives again and again our Lord's word as to whence He came: "Him Whom the Father sanctified and *sent* into the world"; "He that honoreth not the Son, honoreth not the Father that *sent* Him;" "I seek not Mine own will, but the will of Him that *sent* Me"; Whom He *sent,* Him ye believe not"; "My teaching is not mine but His that *sent* Me"; "I am not come of Myself, but He that *sent* Me is true"; and many other like statements. (It will profit you greatly to mark throughout John this appointment by God of Jesus to be "The Saviour of the world.")

This earnest word, "Consider *Him,*" must apply, first, to His appointment by God; and second, to His faithfulness to Him that appointed Him. Even in Gethsemane His prayer was, "My Father, if this [cup] cannot pass away, except I drink it, Thy will be done" (Matt. 26.42). Faithful unto death was He!

Verse 3: For He hath been counted worthy of more glory than Moses, by so much as he that built the house hath more honor

than the house: Jehovah testified to Miriam and Aaron, who claimed revelations from God equally with Moses, "My servant Moses is faithful in all My house: with him will I speak" (Num. 12.7, 8). When we consider the "ten thousand things of God's Law" with which Moses had to deal, we see a little of the vast administration of what God calls His "house." Even the little household affairs of bits of dust like us need faithful servants. Such a servant in God's house was Moses! And he indeed was honored of God, and had glory, and shall have it. He and Elijah appeared "in glory" on the Mount of Transfiguration. Yet Moses was not, and no creature could be, the *builder* of God's house. His offices, and the glory due him, even to his being "king in Jeshurun," were all from God.

Westcott well says, "The point of comparison lies in the fact that Moses and Christ were both engaged, not, as other Divine messengers, with a part, but with the *whole* of the Divine economy. The prophets dealt severally with this or that aspect of truth; the kings with another region of life; the priests with another. But Moses and Christ dealt with the *whole house of God.*"

Verse 4: For every house is builded by some one; but He that built all things is God: We have seen that God has a "house" in human affairs, with which "house" all that faithfully confess Christ's name are connected. This is to be borne in mind by every Christian. The *Builder* of the house, therefore, is God. As Paul says of the present saints, "Ye are God's *building*" (I Cor. 3.9). And Peter: "Ye also, as living stones, are built up a *spiritual house,* to be a holy priesthood, to offer up spiritual sacrifices, acceptable to God through Jesus Christ" (I Pet. 2.5). And Paul directs Timothy: "That thou mayest know how men ought to behave themselves in *the house of God,* which is the Church of the living God, the pillar and ground of the truth" (I Tim. 3.15).

Verse 5: And Moses indeed was faithful in all His house as a ministering-servant—What a great testimony, this! God loves to record the devotion to His will exhibited by His servant* Moses, as

---

*The following note on Greek terms for various orders of *servants,* from Vine's Expository Dictionary of New Testament Words is excellent:

"*Diakonos* views a servant in relation to his work; *doulos,* a bondservant, slave, views him in relationship to his master.

"As to synonymous terms, *leitourgos* denotes one who performs public duties:

we have seen. But notice that concerning Moses, the preposition is "in"; not "over"—as we read concerning Christ. Moreover, Moses was in God's house as a *ministering-servant,* not as a son.†

We must pause and trace more fully the subject of "God's house" in Scripture. What this expression means will be perhaps best seen in God's command to Moses in the wilderness: "Speak unto the children of Israel . . . and let them make Me a sanctuary, that I may dwell among them." Never had God *dwelt* among men before. He had visited, even walked with and talked with such men as Enoch, Noah, and Abraham; but there had been never a hint of God's coming to *live* among them! We become familiar with marvelous heavenly truth, yet many never really consider deeply the meaning thereof. Did not God have Heaven and the Heaven of heavens? Did He not say through Isaiah, "I dwell in the high and holy place"? That God should desire to dwell with men, we do not fully consider, perhaps do not really believe.

God dwelt *first* in the midst of Israel in the wilderness, in the tabernacle; *second,* afterwards, in the temple of Solomon, until the idolatry and sin of that nation drove Him away (Ezek. 8-24). *Third,* after the seventy years captivity, the glory having departed, and the ark having been lost at the burning of the temple by Nebuchadnezzar, He dwelt in the similar, restored temple, where, although the glory did not return, and there was no ark, yet God said, "Build the house; and I will take pleasure in it, and I will be glorified . . . For I am with you, saith Jehovah of hosts" (Hag. 1.8; 2.4. See also Mal. 3.10.) *Fourth,* however obscure God's manifestation there, yet the temple in the days of the Maccabees (second century before Christ) is called "the sanctuary" (Dan. 11.31). *Fifth,* after many years again of man's unfaithfulness, even

---

misthios and *misthotos,* a hired servant; *oiketes,* a household *servant; huperetes,* a subordinate official waiting on his superior . . . *therapon,* one whose service is that of freedom and dignity."

It is this last word, *therapon,* that God uses to describe Moses in Ch. 3.5: his service was "that of freedom and dignity."

We have rendered *therapon* "ministering-servant."⁵ (See Num. 12.7, 8.)

†You cannot perhaps better see the spirit in which Moses wrought than in the last chapter of Exodus. He had built the tabernacle, according to the pattern shown him in the mount. And then follow the words, "Thou *shalt,*" twenty times in the first fifteen verses, and then: "Thus did Moses: according to all that Jehovah commanded him, so did he" (Ex. 40.16). "As Jehovah commanded Moses" is written eight times in this chapter; 22 times in the account of the work, Chapters 35-40 of Exodus!

to their allowing Herod the Edomite to enlarge the temple, so that the carnal Jews boasted, "Forty and six years was this temple in building," Christ came to it, and in astonishing grace, still called it, "My Father's house"! This at the beginning of His ministry! While at the end of His ministry, at the second cleansing of the temple, again driving out the profiteers, He still said, "Is it not written, My house shall be called a house of prayer for all nations?"

The week of His crucifixion, He announced to the apostate nation, "Behold, your house is left unto you desolate"! (Matt. 23.38). And Matthew 24 begins, "And Jesus went out from the temple." All this was two days before the Passover.

Thus ended for the time the dwelling of God with national Israel.

Sixth, the real "temple" where God dwelt when Christ was here, was the temple of Christ's body—His own Person (Jno. 2.21). "He spake of the temple of His body." And John 14.10: "The Father abiding in Me doeth His works." The deluded, priest-ridden nation crucified Him, and lo, on the day of Pentecost, came the Holy Ghost to the upper room, to dwell within the believers in that distinct-from-Israel form of the "House of God," the Assembly of the Living God—the Church! Note that our Lord had looked forward to this in Matthew 16.18, prophesying that He would build it. And He had prophesied that the Comforter would "come unto you . . . abide with you . . . shall be in you." In the book of Acts from Pentecost on, and in the epistles, this blessed abiding Presence is before us. And today as then, the Assembly of God, administered by the double-indwelling of the Holy Ghost in the individual believer and in the Assembly, is "the house of God."*

For a testimony of those things which were afterward to be spoken. What "things" are these? We know that Moses was himself a type of Christ (Deut. 18.15, 18). We also know that the

---

*Again, at the prophetic end of the Church's history in Laodicea, our Lord, on the outside, says "Behold, I stand at the door and knock; if any man hear My voice and open the door, I will come in to him, and will sup with him, and he with Me." Then comes the judgment of the Apocalypse, (the Church having been raptured at end of Revelation 3). And finally comes the Last Judgment, and the New Creation—with what announcement?

"Behold, the tabernacle of God is with men, and He shall dwell with them, and they shall be His people [note plural, R. V.] and God Himself shall be with them, and be their God" (Rev. 21.3).

There is no accounting for God's desiring to dwell with men, except His love!

things that happened to Israel "happened unto them by way of example; and were written for our admonition" (I Cor. 10.11)! But we must see that the "things spoken" which the Mosaic economy witnessed to in its offerings, feasts, and prophetic fea' tures, looked forward not only to the time of Christ, but further on, to the time of Christ's second coming, Israel's redemption, "the good things to come."

Verse 6: But Christ as a son, over His house; Whose house are we, if we hold fast our boldness and the glorying of our hope firm unto the end. This "house," as we have seen, is constantly called in Scripture "the house of God," but over this house of God is Christ, viewed not only as the Head of the Body, the Church, but also as Himself actively *building.*

If we hold fast—The aversion which many have to **Hebrews** arises from the "ifs"—that is, from the *warnings.* And many say, "These warnings are not for *us,* because this epistle was written to the Hebrews, not to us Gentiles; they were 'under Law'; we are not."

But Chapters 3 and 4 do not touch the question of being under the Law, but the question of personal attitude toward God and His Word! (The word "law" does not occur in Chapters 3 and 4: but the words "His Voice," [3.15]; "a promise," (4.1); "the word of God," (4.12); "the Holy Spirit saith," [3.7]; are found.)

Our boldness* and the glorying of our hope—That hope which belongs to our salvation in Christ was to be held fast . . . firm unto the end, by these Hebrew believers. The danger was that of turning back to that Judaism, that *religion,* which their friends, relatives, and prominent Hebrew ecclesiastics held, and which, originally given of God, was now superseded by the Son of God—a Priest not even of Aaron's *"order,"* and not *of,* or *on* earth! If Hebrew be'

---

*"Boldness" (lit., *all-spokenness*—a spirit of utter, confident openness), is taken from two Greek words *pan,* meaning all; and *brema,* meaning speech. We have a similar meaning in our term, "speak out." The Apostle John uses it over and over: "If our heart condemn us not, we have **boldness** (same Gr. word) toward God." Herein is love made perfect, that we may have **boldness** in the day of judgment; because as He is, so are we in this world." "This is the **boldness** which we have toward Him, that, if we ask anything according to His will, He heareth us." "Abide in Him, that, if He shall be *manifested,* we may have **boldness** and not be ashamed before Him at his coming" (I Jno. 2.28; 3.21; 4.17; 5.14). The verb is also illustrated in Eph. 6.20; I Thess. 2.2; Acts 13.46; 14.3; 18.26 and other places. It means to speak out all the heart, without fear or reserve.

lievers, who had had a God-given religion, were not to glory, except in a *heavenly hope,* and "go forth unto Jesus without the camp" (of human religion), how much more Gentiles, to whom God had never given either the ten commandments or any "religion" whatever!*

Alas, how few Gentile "professing Christians" do we know who really constitute God's *House,* glorying only in Christ, worshiping only by the Spirit!—the true "circumcision," whose citizenship is in Heaven; whence also they wait† for a Saviour, the

---

*The exact truth of such a passage as Psalm 147.19-20 must be received and borne in mind. Let us read it:
"He showeth His word unto Jacob,
His statutes and His ordinances unto Israel.
He hath not dealt so with any nation;
And as for His ordinances, they have not known them.
Praise ye Jehovah."
Not to the Egyptians, the mightiest nation of that day, did God reveal Himself. He testified, by Moses; and upon Egypt's proud rebellion He sent plagues and brought His people out.
Not to Babylon, the great royal empire: He testified to Nebuchadnezzar and to Belshazzar, but did not reveal *Himself* nor His *ordinances.*
Not to Persia, which replaced Babylon: Cyrus and Darius acknowledged Jehovah's direction, but they did not have the ordinances.
Not to Greece, brilliant-minded, courageous: God did not make known Himself or His ordinances to Greece.
Nor to all-conquering Rome: they were as ignorant of God as the others. Pilate crucified Christ, and Nero martyred Paul and Peter:—which was but the beginning, as read church history.
Psalm 147 also reads in verses 12 and 13:
"Praise Jehovah, O Jerusalem;
Praise thy God, O Zion.
For He hath strengthened the bars of thy gates;
He hath blessed thy children within thee."³
Then note again the verses with which we begin. Paul indeed writes concerning Israel in Romans 9.4, 5:
"Whose is the adoption, and the glory, and the covenants, and the giving of the Law and the religious-service of God, and the promises; whose are the fathers, and of whom is Christ as concerning the flesh, Who is over all, God blessed forever. Amen."
It is good that the apostle immediately explained, "They are not all Israel, that are of Israel: . . . That is, it is not the children of the flesh that are children of God; but the children of the promise are reckoned for a seed" (Vss. 6, 8).
And why? We know why. Not only did this nation Israel rebel against Jehovah's Law and ordinances but they rejected and horribly slew their Messiah; and their house is left to them "desolate."
Nevertheless, here is this great epistle, directed—to whom? To *Hebrews.* No, not to Judah nor Israel, nor to the nation as such. But the title is, to *Hebrews;* and in Chapter 3.1 we see *what Hebrews:* those who in Divine sovereignty had been enlightened as to Christ, and had confessed His name in salvation.

†Remember that in the last chapter of The Revelation, our Lord three times repeated, "Behold I come quickly!" Meanwhile, Paul says, "Set your mind on the things that are above, not on the things that are upon the earth. For ye died and your life is hid with Christ in God. When Christ, [Who is] our life, shall be manifested, then shall ye also be

Lord Jesus Christ": who "have no confidence in the flesh" (Phil. 3.3, 20), or in earthly things, whether creeds, "standards," denominational "programs," "church work," or great buildings! These things become a deadly snare, so that many no longer hold fast their "boldness" toward God, or the "glorying of their hope" in a *heavenly Christ*—and especially in His *speedy coming!* (See I Thess. 4.13-18.)

There are those who have true faith, represented by the good ground in the parable of the Sower: "These are such as in an honest and good heart, having heard the Word, *hold it fast,* and bring forth *fruit* with *patience."* But our Lord in the same parable said concerning the rocky ground hearers, "These have no root, who *for awhile believe,* and in time of temptation *fall away."* These warnings of Hebrews are not given to create uncertainty, but to avoid presumption and carelessness. At the Last Supper, when He had announced that one of *them* would betray Him, each of the true disciples said, *"Is it I, Lord?"* Note that it was our *Lord Himself* Who had caused this question. *So here in* Hebrews.

Notice that the Israelites had not what is here called "boldness toward God." This was the very opposite of that which they knew under Law, with the veil unrent. Only the priests of the tribe of Levi were permitted to come even past the first veil; and the high priest alone, once a year only, came past the second, into God's immediate presence. *Behaving* was the consciousness toward God under Law; *believing*—freedom, unreserve, "boldness," came only through *Christ's* work. Now the believer comes into the presence of God, gladly resting in Christ's blood, with which (blood) Christ "entered into the holy place—*into Heaven itself,* now to appear before the face of God for us." There was nothing for sinners to hide but sin; and sin had been put away by the blood of Christ; which was now *trusted in!* Satan's continual effort is to obscure the work of Christ, and bring sins to remembrance; and thus "put (us) in fear by . . . terror," as Peter says (I Pet. 3.6).

Under the Old Covenant no one had nor could have, the consciousness that his sin was forever and entirely put away. But God has provided *us* a *"better* hope, through which we *draw nigh unto*

---

manifested with Him in glory" (Col. 3.2, 3). How closely these Scriptures connect themselves with the exhortations in Hebrews!

God"! Indeed, the exhortation to "hold fast our boldness and the
glorying in our "hope," of Chapter 3.6, runs right through the
book of Hebrews: "Having then a Great High Priest, who hath
passed through the heavens, Jesus the Son of God, let us *hold fast
our confession*" (4.14). "Be not sluggish, but imitators of them
who through faith and patience inherit the promises" (6.12).
"Having therefore, brethren, boldness to enter into the holy place
by the blood of Jesus" (10.19), and then the great exhortation
(vs. 23) : "Let us *hold fast the confession of our hope* that it waver
not; for He is faithful that promised."

In Chapter 3.6 (and also vs. 14), we find expressed by God a
definite condition of blessing—nay, of salvation itself: which we
must study with great care.*

  7 **Wherefore, even as the Holy Spirit saith,**
      Today if ye shall hear His voice,
  8 **Harden not your hearts, as in the provocation,**
      Like as in the day of the trial in the wilderness,
  9 **Where your fathers tried Me by proving Me,**
      And saw My works forty years.
 10 **Wherefore I was displeased with this generation,**
      And said, they do always err in their heart:
      But they did not know my ways;
 11 **As I sware in My wrath,**
      They shall not enter into My rest.

Verse 7: Even as the Holy Spirit saith, Today if ye shall hear
His voice, harden not your hearts—TODAY! Mark its repetition
five times over: verses 7, 13, 15; and twice in Chapter 4.7. Speak
it over, and then write it: Today! Today! Today! Today! Today!
and let the conscience and heart feel its full effect. How infinitely
solemn it is! As Paul says to the Corinthians: "We entreat also
that ye receive not the grace of God in vain (for He saith,

    At an *acceptable time* I hearkened unto thee,
    And in a day of salvation did I succor thee:

---

*It will not do to wave away, with the ultra-Calvinist, honest considerations of these "if"s
conditions upon the ground that they are inconsistent with God's sovereign election. Reader,
God is not here speaking of His sovereign election. And it *is* sheer evasion not to receive
the truth as here spoken because "God has His elect to whom conditions do not apply."
That is God's business, and He will speak of it when He pleases. He does not please to
speak of election in the verses we are considering.

    Nor will it do, with the Arminians, to base God's operations upon the actions and
choices of the human will—and to ignore His Sovereignty.

    It is our duty to find, if we are able, what God says here, and the exact meaning thereof.

Behold, *now* is the acceptable time; behold, *now* is the day of Salvation)" (II Cor. 6.1, 2).

It is the Holy Spirit that saith "Today." Our Lord wept over Jerusalem, saying, "O that thou hadst known *in this day,* even thou, the things which belong unto peace! but *now* are they hid from thine eyes . . . because thou knewest not the time of thy visitation!" (Lk. 19.42, 44). Note that present tense, "Saith." These third and fourth chapters of **Hebrews** are no mere historical narration, but an exhortation to those who in Chapter 3.1 are said to be "partakers of a heavenly calling"—partakers of the *presence* of and *speaking* by the Holy Spirit in the Word!* Now, as we have said, these Hebrews had had a past history with God. Therefore both they and we must learn, as God applies the lesson of that history, what the Holy Spirit is *now* saying.

Verse 8: The words the Holy Spirit here quotes, **Today if ye shall hear His voice, harden not your hearts, as in the provocation**—were spoken nearly a thousand years before **Hebrews** was written, to David (Ps. 95.7, ff). But God makes them live, not in Hebrew believers' ears only, but in our hearts, your heart and mine, if we are true believers, and wise. Does anyone deny the possibility of a Gentile's hardening his heart† and closing his

---

*We may note seven mentions of the Holy Spirit in **Hebrews:** (1) "Gifts (distributions) of the Holy Spirit" (2.4); (2) "As the Holy Spirit saith" (3.7); (3) "Made partakers of the Holy Spirit" (6.4); (4) "The Holy Spirit this signifying" (9.8); (5) "Through the eternal Spirit offered Himself" (9.14); (6) "The Holy Spirit also beareth witness" (10.15); (7) "Done despite unto the Spirit of grace" (10.29). The careful believer will notice that those operations of the Holy Spirit which are involved in our conviction of sin, new birth, sealing and witness to sonship, His guidance; and "the sanctification of the Spirit" (II Thess. 2.13) and "renewing" (Tit. 3.5) *are not once referred to in the seven passages quoted above!* Speaking with the utmost reverence, we must say, "God . . . hath spoken to us **in a Son**," in **Hebrews.** There are in the New Testament accurate and intimate accounts of the Spirit's coming and operations, as Rom. 8, Gal. 4.4-6, I Cor. 12-14, Jno. 14-16; but not so in **Hebrews**, though He is present, jealously present, for it is His unwearied desire to "take the things of Christ and show them unto us."

But even sanctification, in **Hebrews**, is not seen as the work of the Spirit, but as that separation unto God effected by the death of Christ. (For example, 10.10; 10.14; 13.12.) Ch. 12.14 is seen not to be an exception—in view of Ch. 10.29, where sanctification to God, though "tasted," entered upon, was finally refused rather than "followed after."

†"This word 'Today' is the expression of the patient activity of God's grace toward Israel even unto the end. The people were unbelieving; they have hardened their hearts; they have done so, and will, alas! do so to the end, until judgment come in the Person of the Messiah-Jehovah, Whom they have despised. But until then God loves to reiterate. 'Today if ye will hear My voice.' It may be that only a few will hearken; it may be that the nation is judicially hardened, in order to admit the Gentiles; but the word 'Today' still resounds for every one among them who had ears to hear, until the Lord shall appear

ears? Then, let every one pay attention to what the Holy Spirit here SAITH, **Today if ye shall hear His voice, harden not your hearts.** Daily, hourly, to all His saints God speaks, by His Spirit.

Verse 9: Where your fathers tried Me by proving Me—At Massah and Meribah, "The people murmured against Moses, and said, Wherefore hast Thou brought us up out of Egypt, to kill us and our children and our cattle with thirst? . . . And he called the name of the place Massah [margin, that is, Tempting, or Proving], and Meribah [that is, Chiding, or Strife], because of the striving of the children of Israel, and because they tempted Jehovah, saying, Is Jehovah among us, or not?" (Ex. 17.3, 7). Yet God had brought them out from Pharaoh's bondage, through the Red Sea, and was giving them manna from Heaven daily for their needs! To "try" God by "proving" Him is to say, deep in the heart, "I am going to do such and such things, which He has forbidden and threatened against, and see whether anything will overtake me!" Thus a lad might say, "Father has forbidden the very thing I want to do, and says he will whip me if I disobey. But I do not believe he will punish me: I'll do what he forbade, and see if he will." So he disobeys, and such disobedience is "trying by proving."

And saw My works forty years: In Moses's great discourse in Deuteronomy, we read, "It is *eleven days' journey* from Horeb by the way of Mount Seir unto Kadesh-Barnea." But we read "And it came to pass *in the fortieth year,* in the eleventh month, on the first day of the month, that Moses spake unto the children of Israel, according unto all that Jehovah had given him in commandment unto them." *Forty years to make an eleven days' journey! Why?* The awful, presumptuous wickedness is described in our verse in Hebrews 3: **Your fathers tried Me by proving Me.** God had commanded Israel to go into the land of Canaan. Forgetting all His goodness and the displays of the resistless might of His power, they listened at Kadesh-Barnea to the cowardly report of the un-

---

in judgment . . . For the Remnant who had believed, it was an especial warning not to walk in the ways of the hardened people who had refused to hearken—not to turn back to them, as Israel did in the wilderness.

"As long as the 'Today' of the call of grace should continue, they were to exhort one another, lest unbelief should glide into their hearts through the sublety of sin."—J. N. Darby, *Synopsis,* pp. 261-2.

faithful spies, with the marvelous fruit of Canaan before their eyes at the time.* Read Numbers 13 and 14—astonishing!

Paul, Peter, and Jude all warn us against the sin of testing God's judgments: (I Cor. 10.5, 10; II Pet. 2.4, 7; Jude 5, 7). Hear Jude's solemn words: "Now I desire to put you in remembrance, though ye know all things once for all, that the Lord, having saved a people out of the land of Egypt, afterward destroyed them that believed not." Our Lord said, "Remember Lot's wife." Meditate on some of the terrible words used in the texts above, of God's judgments on the Israelites who believed not: "over-thrown," "destroyed," "bodies (Gr., *limbs*) strewn down along [Vincent's translation] in the wilderness."

This generation does not believe in a God of judgment! And the lack of assurance of eternal salvation in Christendom today springs naturally from lack of preaching the truth about Divine judgment at the Cross! But we beg of you to remember that it is written of God that He *"spared* not *His own Son,* but delivered *Him* up for us all." Behold Christ, the sinless One—forsaken, *spared not,* when our iniquities were laid on Him! There we see what sin deserves and must surely have, at the hands of a holy God!

Verses 10, 11:
Wherefore I was displeased with this generation,
And said, they do always err in their heart:
But they did not know My ways;
So I sware in My wrath,
They shall not enter into My rest.

Verses 8, 9, 10, and 11 speak directly to these Hebrew believers —it is the story of the *trial of God* by their fathers, and their displeasing Him and erring **in their heart,** ignorant of His *ways:* with the result that He sware they should not enter into His rest. What that means, we shall consider. But remember here the rea-

---

*Note in vss. 8-12 (1) The state of *heart* Israel was in. (2) God's gracious voice, which if heard, would bring blessing. (3) Their attitude: hardening their hearts, by "proving" God wilfully, and thus "trying" Him. (The word "try" or "tempt," of their presump-tion toward God, is the same word used concerning Satan's tempting man to do evil). (4) The arousing of God's settled *wrath,* causing His oath to exclude them from that "rest" into which He would have led them. (5) The possibility of a like "evil heart of unbelief" today. (6) The sign of it, falling away from a Living God, whether to a life of sin, or to a life of "religion" which walks in forms, merely, shutting out God's fellowship.

sons God gives. People, alas, accustomed from old days to hand
over searching passages "to the Jews," say, "That does not apply to
us." Dear friend, "As face answers to face in water, so the heart
of man to man." *Profit* by God's loving warning to these Hebrew
believers! Ah, the possibilities of sin and rebellion in *any* human
heart! Men say, "I have my *personal* opinion." "He that trusteth
in his own heart is a fool," *God says*.

God pays no attention to what you have in your *head* of so '
called "education." His eyes are upon the *heart*. Our Lord removed
its cover: and lo, we read: "From *within*, out of the *heart* of men,
evil thoughts proceed, fornications, thefts, murders, adulteries,
covetings, wickedness, deceit, lasciviousness, an evil eye, railing,
pride, foolishness: all these evil things proceed from within, and
defile the man" (Mk. 7.21-23).

And the Holy Spirit said through the prophet of old, "The
heart is deceitful above all things, and it is exceedingly corrupt:
who can know it? I, Jehovah, search the mind, I try the heart"
(Jer. 17.9, 10). Note that God speaks here of *all* human hearts—
not those of Jews only. Remember I Corinthians 10.5, 6, 12,
written to *Gentile* believers: "With most of them [Israel in the
wilderness, as here in **Hebrews**] God was not well pleased: for
they were overthrown in the wilderness. Now in these things they
became figures [or *types*, R.V., margin], of *us* to the intent *we*
should not lust after evil things, as *they* . . . Wherefore let him
that thinketh he standeth, take heed lest he fall."

All this said to Gentile believers!—I *Corinthians* 10.6.

To return to verses 10-11, God said of the Israelites, **They do
always err in their heart: But they did not know My ways; As I
sware in My wrath, they shall not enter into My rest.** They
erred in their hearts, not their heads. You remember Psalm 103:
"He made known His *ways* unto Moses, His *doings* unto the
children of Israel." Why did He make known His ways to Moses?
Hearken to Moses' prayer (Ex. 33.13), pleading alone with God
at Sinai after the calf-worship: "Now therefore, I pray Thee, if I
have found favor in Thy sight, show me *Thy ways*, that I may
know Thee"! (See also Ps. 25.4; 86.11; and Hos. 14.9.) Consequently, God made known His *ways* unto Moses. But unto the

children of Israel* He made known only "His *doings*." Now it is of our personal friends that we say, "I know his or her *ways*." A person's "ways" arise from and express his personality. It is one's delight to be acquainted with the "ways" of our friends, of those we love; to understand their feelings toward us, and to be able in general to predict what their opinions, actions, or reactions, will be. But how many among Israel cried to God when Moses did, to *know* HIS "ways"—to be acquainted with HIM?

Jehovah had come on Sinai and delivered to Israel a religious system; and after they had completed the tabernacle He asked them to make, He Himself abode in the Holy of Holies—screened, indeed, from their curious sight by the veil. His presence, nevertheless, was there. The vast multitude of Israelites were content to have the Levitical *system:* but did they ever inquire concerning the *Person* Who dwelt among them? They became accustomed to calling themselves (as they do today), "The Chosen People." But become personally an hungred for His *fellowship*—they did not.

Most professing Christians today are quite content to belong to some association of Christians, and be known by its name, and to hold a credal form which relates the *doings* of God and Christ. But do they *know* His *ways*? Do they desire a personal relationship and walk with their God? Are they eager to know the ways of the blessed Spirit Whom God has sent to take charge of things till our Lord's return? Judge if a godly preacher, filled with the Spirit and urging to a life of devotion to God, comes among you: how large a hearing will *he* have? Judge honestly, and do not forget! Let none of Baal's lying prophets tell you that "things are

---

*Israel had been in the midst of Egypt—a most idolatrous people. And they had never given up the idols of Mesopotamia. Remember Stephen's terrible charge:
    "But God turned and gave them up to serve the host of heaven; as it is written in the book of the prophets,
    Did ye offer unto Me slain beasts and sacrifices
    Forty years in the wilderness, O house of Israel?
    And ye took up the tabernacle of Moloch,
    And the star of the god Rephan
    The figures which ye made to worship them:
    And I will carry you away beyond Babylon" (Acts 7.42, 43).
    In view of the fearful idolatry of both Israel and Judah in the past (II Chron. 33, II Ki. 17.9-18), we tremble to read (Matt. 12.43-45) that seven demons of idolatry worse than the former will come into them when they (except the Remnant) shall worship the Antichrist, knowing and triumphing in the fact that he is from a lost world (Isa. 28.14, 15). "And the . . . prince that shall come [the Antichrist] . . . shall make a firm covenant with the many for one week" (*heptad*, seven, i. e., 7 years—Dan. 9.26, 27).

going well," when, God having revealed Himself as *Love* and in the sacrifice of His dear Son, professing Christians are content to remain ignorant of *His ways!*

You ask, "What do you mean by knowing God's ways?" Well, listen to His friend Abraham, pleading for Lot in Sodom: "That be far from Thee, to do after *this manner,* to slay the righteous with the wicked, that so the righteous should be as the wicked."

Or Moses, on Sinai, when God said, "Let Me alone . . . that I may consume them: and I will make of thee a great nation." And Moses' answer: "Wherefore should the Egyptians speak, saying, For evil did He bring them forth?" And at Paran: Jehovah said unto Moses, "I will smite them with the pestilence, and disinherit them, and will make of thee a nation greater and mightier than they. And Moses said unto Jehovah, Then the Egyptians will hear it . . . and they will tell it to the inhabitants of this land . . . The nations which have heard the fame of Thee will speak, saying . . . Jehovah was not *able* to bring this people into the land which He sware unto them." How often was it recorded of God, "I have pardoned according to thy word"—*Moses'* word! Elijah and Elisha also walked in such fellowship with God that they would *say,* and expect God to do! So was Joseph in Egypt, Joshua at Gibeon, Samuel the prophet—indeed all the prophets—and David.

Jonah desired Nineveh, Israel's rising enemy, to be destroyed. You know his story. When God repented of the judgment of that city and did it not, Jonah cried, "I pray Thee, O Jehovah, was not this my saying, when I was yet in my country? Therefore I hasted to flee unto Tarshish; for I knew that Thou art a gracious God, and merciful, slow to anger, and abundant in loving kindness, and repentest Thee of the evil." Jonah knew God's *ways* so well that he feared to preach in Nineveh lest it repent: for Israel feared Assyria, and its capital, Nineveh.

The wicked say to God, "We desire not the knowledge of Thy ways" (Job 21.14). The angel said to Daniel, "The people that *know their* God shall be strong, and do exploits." Since not knowing God's ways is shown as the vital lack in Israel of old, and assured their failing to enter God's rest, let us ask, How shall *we* know the ways of God? Mark it well: do as Moses did. Ask, and seek to have His *ways* shown to you. Or, with David, plead Psalm

27.11, and the like. We *must* know our God and His ways. Otherwise, we shall be mere "professing" Christians.

> 12 Take heed, brethren, lest haply there shall be in any
>   one of you an evil heart of unbelief, in falling away from
> 13 the Living God: but exhort one another day by
>   day, so long as it is called Today; lest any one of you be
> 14 hardened by the deceitfulness of sin: for we are become
>   partakers of Christ, if we hold fast the beginning of our
> 15 confidence firm unto the end: while it is said, Today if ye
>   shall hear His voice, harden not your hearts, as in the
>   provocation.

**Verse 12: Take heed, brethren, lest haply there shall be in any
one of you an evil heart of unbelief, in falling away from the
living God:**

It is "*the Living* God" by whom these Hebrew believers were
warned that "falling away" from Him was a danger. This must be
noted and remembered.

1. It was the *Living* God, the Father, who gave His Son. It
was the *Living* God, the Son, who bore our sins, and returned to
the Father's right hand. It was the *Living* God, the Holy Spirit,
who came at Pentecost and *is here now,* to indwell every believer,
to be the conscious Leader and Power in every spiritual activity!
"It seemed good to the Holy Ghost and to us" (Acts 15.28) were
the words of the apostles in those days when they were dealing
with God, conscious of His presence and power!

2. Note, these Hebrews were not warned of any danger of
falling away from "religion." Just so, today, people are "Methodists," "Baptists," "Presbyterians," and so regard themselves.
They never think of "falling away" from a *religious profession*—
any more than the Roman Catholics. But as to the *Living God*—
having to do with *Him* daily, hourly, yea, moment by moment—
they may have never *thought of that,* either!

3. Now think of a God who knows our every thought, and
who has loved us all along the way—who gave His Son in His
love for us, Who finds those who professed His name and confessed His Son, so indifferent to His constant overtures of love,
as to fall away from the Living God! Note this does not say, or
mean, fall into *sin,* merely: but to fall away from *a Person,* "the
Living God!" Have you ever had any one whom you valued and

loved fall into utter neglect of you? Nothing wounds so deeply.

4.   Note that it is **an EVIL heart of unbelief,** that falls **away from the Living God.** As we have noted in Mark 9.24, the man desiring the Lord's blessing cried, "I believe; help Thou mine unbelief!" We may have much consciousness of, and struggle with, unbelief, but could our hearts be described as evil hearts of un- belief—that is, hearts willfully inclined to a state of unbelief and rejection of the fellowship of the "Living God"?

5.   Now this awful state was national Israel's. They heard God's voice, but they hardened their heart against hearing, know- ing, and obeying, this "living" and loving God!

6.   For this reason, we believe God does not set forth in the book of **Hebrews,** the *doctrines* of Christianity (for this had al- ready been done by Paul and the other apostles, both by preaching and epistles), but it is God's *person* and *His Way* that are in question here. People are afraid of the *ifs* of **Hebrews**—foolishly thinking that it is the *conduct* of professing Christians that en- dangers them. No! It is their attitude toward "The Living God"!

7.   Over against that "hardening through deceitfulness of sin" of Chapter 3.13 is set forth in **Hebrews,** the blessed person of a Great High Priest, in Heaven, perfected down here through suf- ferings, filled with every knowledge of our need of unmeasured sympathy and eternal constancy; infinitely ready to see us through all difficulties, trials and temptations. Ah, if we could all learn to *keep considering Him!* God wants us in Heaven. He is not willing that any should perish. Thus viewed as the great and constant picture of God's tender love, Christ in His high-priestly ministry in Heaven, based on His all-atoning work on Calvary, draws the heart toward God and away from the hardness that a "religion," a sense of "duty," may beget.

8.   For it must be constantly remembered that the Hebrews had a God-given *religion,* that they had a religious *history* of which they were proud, and in which they were confident. Now to bring "the Living God" into an already "religious" though ceremonial scene—how shall we describe it? Ah, we do not need to describe it! For the history of this exact thing is written in the four Gospels. "The Father, abiding in Me is doing His works." "I and the Father are one." "He that hath seen Me hath seen the Father." "The

Word was God." And what did *man's "religion"* do? Behold the marks in Christ's hands and feet and side!

Therefore, hardening, in the sense the book of **Hebrews** uses it, is against God, "The Living God"—His presence, His holiness, His control of sinful man's *will*.

The *hardening* was against a *person*—even "The Living God." No one is a *compelled* victim to such hardening!

This is no earnest heart-struggle with unbelief, such as the father of the demoniac boy had (Mk. 9.24): "Straightway the father of the child cried out, and said, "I believe; help Thou mine unbelief!" He bowed to the Lord's word, and put as it were his believing foot forward, though tremblingly! His was *not* **an evil heart of unbelief.** That spoken of in Hebrews 3.12 is a heart that abides in unbelief because it desires to retain its evil! "And this is the judgment, that the light is come into the world, and men loved the darkness rather than the light; for their works were evil" (Jno. 3.19).

And what is the result? **Falling away from the Living God.** Little by little, day by day, from *God,* Whose presence and power had been known, they "fall away." Satan once "walked up and down in the midst of the stones of fire" of God's presence (Ezek. 28.14), but chose sin, and fell "as lightning from Heaven" (Lk. 10.18). Slowly, but not less surely, do these fall! Our Lord describes them in Luke 8.13: "Those on the rock are they who, when they have heard, receive the word with joy; and these have no root, who *for awhile believe,* and in time of temptation fall away." How awful!

That generation of Israelites spoken of in Hebrews 3.12 "tried God by proving him," and their carcasses fell in the wilderness "forty years." They did not desire to deal with the LIVING GOD. Forms and ceremonies they might endure, though never enjoy. The gods (demons) they had served in Egypt were represented by inanimate idols: "Neither is there any breath in their mouths."* All through Scripture, from Deuteronomy to The Revelation (28 times, seven, multiplied by the earth number, four),

---

*Probably it is given, that is, allowed of God, to the terrible trinity of evil at the close of this age (Satan, Antichrist, and his false prophet) to give *breath* to the image of Rev. 13.15, as a final, inescapable, "strong delusion" (II Thess. 2.11), that the unbelieving world in that day may believe the devil's lie (Jno. 5.43).

is found this blessed but awful name THE LIVING GOD. Perhaps the thing above all others that makes the book of **Hebrews**
so solemn is that in it we are dealing with a *Living* God. It is no
matter here of "creed" or "church connection," but of *reality*.
Four times in this great epistle these words, the Living God, are
used concerning Him: twice in connection with those finally lost
(3.12; 10.31), twice in connection with the saints (9.14; 12.22),
as we shall see.

The fearful thing is that, with a soul **falling away from the
living God,** there is the certainty of a future meeting with a disobeyed—yea, despised God, "the Judge of all"! A human bit of
dust with no help, with no Intercessor, and a nature eternally
alienated from all that God is! If you say that you believe in
"eternal security," thank God if you have it! But you have solemn
need of all the warnings God is giving in **Hebrews.** Remember the
words, "Elect . . . according to the foreknowledge of God the
Father, in sanctification of the Spirit, *unto obedience* and sprinkling
of the blood of Jesus Christ: Grace to you and peace be multiplied" (I Pet. 1.1, 2).

**Verse 13: But exhort one another day by day, so long as it is
called Today; lest anyone of you be hardened by the deceitfulness
of sin:** Here is set before us a Christian service quite uncommon
—unless in times of real revival.* The duty of exhorting one
another is, alas, neglected by most of us. We judge, and criticize
others, but do not faithfully exhort and rebuke. Some professing
Christians never mention to others the things of the Lord, though
eternity lies right ahead! Instead, we should have our fellow
Christians upon our hearts constantly, in solicitous love, so that
we would have tender boldness to "exhort" them if we saw them
going astray or tempted to turn aside. Instead of criticizing one
another, we should care for one another: "Brethren, even if a man

---

*Jonathan Edwards described the great revival at Northampton as follows: "There were
remarkable tokens of God's presence in almost every house . . . Our public assemblies
were then beautiful. The congregation was alive in God's service—every one earnestly
intent upon the public worship; every hearer eager to drink in the words of the minister
as they came from his mouth . . . The assembly in general were from time to time in
tears, while the Word was preached; some weeping in sorrow and distress, others with joy
and love, others with pity and concern for neighbors . . . We have kept from year to
year days of public confessing and prayer to God, to acknowledge our backsliding and
humble ourselves for our sins, and to seek of God forgiveness and reformation."

be overtaken in any trespass, ye who are *spiritual*, restore such a one in a spirit of gentleness; looking to thyself, lest thou also be tempted" (Gal. 6.1). Read also Leviticus 19.17 in the Revised Version "Thou shalt *surely rebuke* thy neighbor, and not bear sin because of him." This shows that failure directly to exhort a brother is a guilt-bringing neglect on our part.

We know from Chapter 13.22 that **Hebrews** is an epistle, and the whole epistle is an "exhortation." But the writer could not himself be present day by day with each of them, so that this most solemn duty of *caring for one another* is laid upon each and every one of them. Believers are of course supposed to be *assembling as believers:* Chapter 10.25: "Not forsaking our own assembling together." But in both that verse and the one preceding, there is the exhortation to "consider one another," and "keep exhorting one another." Assemblies of believers find their patterns, for example, in the assemblies at Jerusalem (Acts 2.42, 46, 47), and at Troas (Acts 20.7), and at Ephesus (Acts 20.17-25). Gatherings indeed of joy they were—but of holy fear, for God the Holy Spirit was there, and Christ Himself was constantly recognized—the Center of all. Therefore this solemn, blessed duty and privilege of exhorting one another was laid upon them all. They were to care for each other, as the members of one body—as, for example, one hand cares for the other (I Cor. 12.12, 13, 27).

Alas, it is often the consciousness of our own weakness and failures that makes us fail to exhort others. We say, Did not Jesus warn us against casting out motes from others' eyes while having a beam in our own? Certainly. But He went further: He said, "*Cast out first* the beam out of thine own eye; and then shalt thou see clearly to *cast out the mote* out of thy brother's eye" (Matt. 7.5). The duty toward the brother remains!

Lest any one of you be hardened by the deceitfulness of sin— Three great questions are before us here: (1) What is sin?* (2)

---

*Concerning sin, note these things: Sin brings *guilt*, sin *defiles*, sin *enslaves*.

Sin's *guilt:* God created us and sustains our being. He is the absolute sovereign of this creation. Independency is not only the act of a traitor, but God being a holy God, it is the *choice* of evil—a choice of all that God's holiness infinitely abhors, and His government forbids. Therefore the least sin brings *guilt* on the sinner, on account which God must settle according to Himself and the infinite demands of His own throne. Even conceive the act or thought of lawlessness to be a single act, and not to become a habit (which is impossible)—the guilt, the liability to Divine punishment, would be the same:

How does sin deceive? (3) How does the deceitfulness of sin harden?

1.   What is sin? (a) "Sin is lawlessness" *(anomia)*. This is a state of refusal to be controlled by God. The Authorized Version here (I Jno. 3.4), "Sin is transgression of the Law," is inadequate and misleading. The Greek word *anomia* means *lawlessness*. Transgression of the Law would be *parabasis nomou,* an *action,* but *anomia,* lawlessness, is a *state.* Again, the translation is misleading, because it puts all the race under the Ten Commandments,* which were given to Israel only (Ps. 147.19, 20; Mal. 4.4; Rom. 9.4): and for life on *earth.* "Do not commit adultery, steal, kill . . . covet" do not pertain to !ife in *heaven!* The translation is inadequate—utterly so! For when God said, "Sin is *anomia*—lawlessness," He spake of the creature's inner refusal to Divine *control.* Sin is that departure from the Creator which follows *a will of its own.* So it was with Satan (Ezek. 28). The end of such a course is seen in Isaiah 14.12 ff., in the Antichrist's (figured by the king of Babylon) saying, "*I will* be like the Most High" (Isa. 14.14).

---

just as one proven treachery to his country in time of war by a traitor, condemns him to judgment.

Sin *defiles.* While guilt is the result of lawlessness toward God's throne, and courts judgment, *defilement* is that state abhorrent to God's holy *nature,* into which sin brings the creature: "Thou art of purer eyes than to *behold* evil" (Hab. 1.13). To one first studying carefully God's use in His Word of the terms "clean" and "unclean," and the teachings on impurity, defilement, and the necessity for cleansing, there comes astonishment! Leprosy was Jehovah's type of sin's defilement. Lepers had to be *cleansed,* not cured. This offended men (II Ki. 5.11) who dreamed of "recovering" the leper instead of cleansing. But cleansing from sin's defilement is just as impossible to the sinner as pardoning his own sin's guilt!

Sin *enslaves,* as we have said before. Man dreams of delivering himself from sin's slavery by an act of his will. But Jesus said, "If the *Son* shall make you free, ye shall be free indeed" (Jno. 8.36). Reflect, then, reader, on the three-fold fact that man can neither pardon, cleanse, nor deliver himself. For you are surrounded by a world deceived by Satan, its prince, into believing man can do all three—by good works! Damning delusion!

---

*The Ten Commandments, "holy, just and good," were fitted to the life of an earthly nation. Paul could get on with them till he came to the tenth—"Thou shalt not covet" (lit., *desire*). This slew him; or rather, indwelling sin, obtaining this means, "beguiled" him. "Through the commandment," as he says, "sin became exceedingly sinful." This was God's object: "The Law was given that the trespass might abound." Mr. Darby well says:

"Sin is equivalent to the spirit of self-will and unrestrainedness, whether man's will or not. When there was Law, its acts were actual transgressions; but without this, sin was there, though there were no such actual transgressions till Law entered . . . There can be no transgressions when there is no law. What is there to transgress? But self-will and lust, lawlessness, there may be. It is the state of fallen man: only the Law made it 'exceedingly sinful.' "

When Adam *willed* to eat the fruit, he departed from God into what is called *sin*.

Scripture says:

(b) "Whatsoever is *not of faith* is sin."

(c) "The thought of *foolishness* is sin."

(d) "*All unrighteousness* is sin."

Sin is an entity, a power! It is a *thing*, having *energy!*

2. How does sin "deceive"? Sin deceives in many ways. It has every advantage. (a) It has "pleasures." It invites with charms, false glamor. (b) Sin is a great promiser—of all earthly successes. It blinds the eyes, stifles the conscience, hardens the heart, and says all shall be well. Its prophets keep promising sinners liberty— "promising them liberty, while they themselves are bondservants of corruption" (II Peter 2.19—a solemn chapter, which please read). Most of the people you meet are hardened and blinded by some form of sin—terrible thought! (c) The creature is most forgetful of unpleasant warnings. (d) The creature has self-confidence —unlimited! "I can quit" (some habit) is in his heart, and how often in his mouth! But our Lord warned, "Everyone that committeth sin is the *bondservant* of sin" (Jno. 8.34).

3. How does **the deceitfulness of sin** *harden?* (a) Because of delayed judgment. "Because sentence against an evil work is not executed speedily, therefore the heart of the sons of men is fully set in them to do evil" (Eccl. 8.11). God's long suffering is therefore despised. Thousands around about the sinner keep sinning and are not immediately stricken: thus comes false peace! (b) Sin deceives by appearing harmless, promising good or enjoyment; by the fact that its victims think, "Others are doing it"; by taking advantage of ignorance of the Word of God: so that the victim listens to the voice of false teachers, who say, "You are all right if you are sincere!" Millions are thus being *sincerely* lost, like those who sailed *sincerely* on the Lusitania, and sailed to their death. Sin looks so fair—before it is committed! And after one has committed it, it so deceives and hardens that at the worst, like Adam and Eve, we try to shield ourselves from the consequences of our nakedness till GOD comes upon the scene. (c) Conscience unheeded is slowly stupefied—finally "seared as with a hot iron." Unless God sends immediate poignant conviction, it is more easy

to sin the second time than the first. At last comes the fearful state described to Moses by Jehovah:

"Lest there should be among you man, or woman, or family, or tribe, whose heart turneth away this day from Jehovah our God, to go to serve the gods of those nations; lest there should be among you a root that beareth gall and wormwood; and it come to pass, when he heareth the words of this curse, that he **bless himself in his heart,** saying, I shall have peace, though I walk in the stubbornness of my heart, to destroy the moist with the dry" (Deut. 29.18, 19).

No wonder we read after this last state, "Then the anger of Jehovah and His jealousy will smoke against that man, and all the curse that is written in this book shall lie upon him"! (vs. 20).

Verse 14: For we are become partakers of Christ, if we hold fast the beginning of our confidence firm unto the end: For these Hebrew believers, what was the "beginning of their confidence"? Without doubt, their first faith in Christ, accompanied by the "confidence" that faith begot. This word "confidence" (Gr., *hupostasis*) is used five times, always by Paul. In its use in II Corinthians 11.17, it is accompanied by boasting: "confidence of boasting." That is, Paul, hearing the good report of the Corinthian believers, was filled with *confidence* in his boasting of their faith. The Hebrew believers could not have been believers unless there had been such a revelation of Christ and His work to their hearts that a state of joyful *confidence* had been entered into! This *"confidence"* was to be held *fast.* That argued satanic, worldly, and "religious" opposition, certainly. But the redeeming Saviour was not to be abandoned, but "confidence" in Him held firm to the end. The "end" was when they should enter upon their life above. Meanwhile, "faith" would be a confidence" (Ch. 11.1, this same word *hupostasis*) of the "things hoped for."

Thus they would become **partakers of Christ.** The translation of this word "partakers" *(metochoi)* must be governed by its use. In Luke 5.7 it is merely "partners." In Hebrews 3.1, *"partakers* of a heavenly calling," it indicates the "calling" of all true believers in this dispensation; and again in Chapter 12.8, "chastening, whereof all [sons] have been made *partakers."* But on the other hand, in Chapter 6.4, certain were made "partakers *(metochoi)* of the Holy Spirit,' who afterwards fell away and were lost.

There was, as we shall find, a presence and an operation of the Holy Spirit short of final sealing and salvation. Certainly Hebrews 1.9 finds our blessed Lord at His glorious second coming accom- panied by *"partakers" (metochoi),* or "fellows." But the path to that day is no careless one, as Chapter 3.14, and, indeed, most of both Chapters 3 and 4 solemnly warn.*

15 While it is said,
    Today, if ye shall hear His voice,
    Harden not your hearts, as in the provocation.
16 For who, when they heard, did provoke? nay, did not all
17 they that came out of Egypt by Moses? And with whom was He displeased forty years? was it not with them that
18 sinned, whose bodies fell in the wilderness? And to whom sware He that they should not enter into His rest, but
19 to them that were disobedient? And we see that they were not able to enter in because of unbelief.

Chapter 4.1: LET US FEAR, THEREFORE, lest haply, a promise being left of entering into His rest, any one of
2 you should seem to have come short of it. For indeed we have had good tidings preached unto us, even as also they: but the word of hearing did not profit them, be- cause it was not united by faith with them that heard.
3 For we who have believed do enter into that rest; even as He hath said,
    As I sware in My wrath,
    They shall not enter into My rest:
although the works were finished from the foundation of the world.
4 For He hath said somewhere of the seventh day on this wise, And God rested on the seventh day from all His
5 works; and in this place again,
    They shall not enter into My rest.
6 Seeing therefore that it remaineth that some should enter thereinto, and they to whom the good tidings were be- fore preached failed to enter in because of disobedience,

---

*"I suppose it has been true of us all that there was a time when we shrank from all Scriptures that spoke of *conditions.* Well can many of us remember when we looked with fear and trembling upon this chapter, or at the sixth chapter, or the closing portion of the tenth chapter."—Ridout, **Lectures on The Hebrews,** p. 61 (an excellent book" Loizeaux, N. Y.

7 He again defineth a certain day, TODAY, saying in
   David so long a time afterward (even as hath been said
   before),
       TODAY if ye shall hear His voice,
       Harden not your hearts.
8 For if Joshua had given them rest, He would not have
9 spoken afterward of another day. There remaineth there-
10 fore a sabbath rest for the people of God. For he that
   is entered into His rest hath himself also rested from his
11 works, as God did from His. Let us therefore give diligence to enter into that rest, that no man fall after the
12 same example of disobedience. For the word of God is
   living, and active, and sharper than any two-edged
   sword, and piercing even to the dividing of soul and
   spirit, of both joints and marrow, and quick to discern
13 the thoughts and intents of the heart. And there is no
   creature that is not manifest in His sight: but all things
   are naked and laid open before the eyes of Him with
   Whom we have to do.

We have printed the Scripture above, making no division between the close of Chapter 3 and the beginning of Chapter 4, so
that there may be no interruption of our study of the great subject
of the "rest" of God. Going back, now, to Chapter 3.15, let us
note in the following verses, that the opposite of holding fast the
"beginning of their confidence" (Ch. 3.6, 14) was "hardening their
hearts" (Ch. 3.8, 15), "provoking" God (Ch. 3.8, 15, 16), and
"displeasing" Him (Ch. 3.10, 17); thus coming short of entering
His rest (Ch. 3.11, 18; 4.1). The solemn fact is that in this book
of **Hebrews** *eternal salvation* is constantly contrasted with "*neglect*," "*sluggishness*," "*falling short*" of a promise; mere "*tasting*"
of the heavenly gift" (eternal life), sinning "willfully after that
we have received the knowledge of the truth," and afterward
"falling away," "*treading under foot* the Son of God . . . counting
the blood of the covenant a *common thing*"! It could not be otherwise, for God in **Hebrews** is speaking unto us *in His Son!* (Heb.
1.2).

What God in *sovereign grace* may do (as in the case of the man
in I Cor. 5.1-5, and in I Cor. 11.29-33), is God's affair. But the
book of **Hebrews** is not the place in which He sets it forth.
Hebrews, unlike Romans, does not proclaim the way of Salva-

tion; but places before us the *Person* of Christ, Son of God, Son of Man; His oneness with His saints, His victory over Satan; His one offering for sin; His blessed heavenly priesthood; His headship as Son over the house of God: and God sets before us all these in view of *the holy walk on earth they involve* in true saints!

Verses 7 and 15 of Chapter 3 say: TODAY if ye shall hear His voice!—Three times are these words quoted in Chapters 3 and 4; and of course they are always connected with the very voice of God: **the Holy Spirit saith, (3.7); while it is said, (3.15); as hath been said before, (4.7).**

Furthermore, in Chapter 4.7 occur the words, **He again defineth a certain day, TODAY, saying in David so long a time afterward**—We learn then immediately, that the sovereign God speaks in special ways and at times chosen by Him. Five times in Chapters 3 and 4, the Hebrew believers to whom Paul wrote are addressed with the solemn word "TODAY." Blessing is conditioned in Chapter 3.6 on "their holding fast their boldness and the glorying of their hope firm unto the end"; and in verse 14, on "holding fast the beginning of their confidence firm unto the end." That the present dispensation is indicated, is plain from verse 13: "Exhort one another day by day, so long as it is called TODAY." There is present, then, the danger of "falling away from the Living God," and of being "hardened by the deceitfulness of sin" (Ch. 3.12, 13).

To individuals, therefore, "Today" would cover all that time in which "a promise is left" of entering into "His rest" (4.1)—that is, all the season of the Spirit's gracious wooing. Some would indeed become "hardened by the deceitfulness of sin," and "fall away." If that were not a possibility, these Scriptures would be causeless. God does not speak in vain! This whole dispensation, ending with the rapture of the church, is called "TODAY."* Sinners are being welcomed; Grace is reigning. The word is, "He that will, let him take the water of life freely."

16 **For who, when they heard, did provoke? nay, did not**

---

*" 'Today' is whilst the Spirit invites, and continues to this present time. It is always 'today' until we enter the bright 'tomorrow' that is before us; and 'while it is called Today' we are to exhort one another lest any of us should be 'hardened through the deceitfulness of sin.' "—Ridout.

17 all they that came out of Egypt by Moses? And with
   whom was He displeased forty years? was it not with
   them that sinned, whose bodies fell in the wilderness?
18 And to whom sware He that they should not enter into
19 His rest, but to them that were disobedient? And we
   see that they were not able to enter in because of
   unbelief.

**Verse 16: For who, when they heard, did provoke? nay, did
not all they that came out of Egypt by Moses?** As to *Israel*, "Even
so then at this present time also there is a remnant according to
the election of grace" (Rom. 11.5). But they are received by *grace*
alone, as sinners only! As to this word, "TODAY," let Israel be
our warning! Israel came to Kadesh-Barnea, and being *permitted*
(let Deuteronomy 1.22 interpret Numbers 13.1) to send spies into
the good land God's word had vouchsafed them, they hearkened to
the evil report of the ten unbelieving spies: "It is a good land . . .
but the giants are there, and cities walled up to heaven." No attention was given to the testimony of Joshua and Caleb: "The land
is an exceeding good land . . . Rebel not against Jehovah, neither
fear ye the people of the land . . . Jehovah is with us: fear them
not." Nay! "All the congregation bade stone them with stones"!
" 'Let us make us a captain,' said they, 'and let us return into
Egypt!" (Num. 14.4-10). This was "the provocation" of our text.
Then the glory of Jehovah appeared; and but for the intercession
of Moses they would have been smitten with pestilence and disin-
herited, and Moses alone would have taken their place. (Read
again, we beg you, Num. 13 and 14, and Deut. 1.)

**Verse 17: And with whom was He displeased forty years?
was it not with them that sinned, whose bodies fell in the wilderness?**—The question arises concerning the "forty years" in the
wilderness, in this verse in Hebrews 3, and I Corinthians 10.1-5:
Were all these with whom He was displeased eternally lost?
Were any of the Israelites whose carcasses fell in the wilderness
saved? The same question arises concerning professing believers
today. Are those like the Corinthians (I Cor. 11.30-32) who fail
to judge their own lives, to be accounted rejected by God? In
this latter case, No! For God here says, "When we are judged
[by sickness or death], we are chastened of the Lord, that we
may *not* be condemned with the world." (*Note* verse 32.) God's

grace prevailed even in the case in Corinth of the man who had his own father's wife (I Cor. 5, II Cor. 2.5-11). Salvation is by God's *grace* always!

These Hebrews, as we have said, belonged to a nation concerning which God says,

"He showeth His word unto Jacob,
His statutes and His ordinances unto Israel.
He hath not dealt so with any nation;
And as for His ordinances, they have not known them"
(Ps. 147.19-20).

They were *"near* unto Him" (Ps. 148.14; Deut. 4.7), as compared with the Gentiles, who were "far off" (Eph. 2.12, 13, 17). But— who shall say how many of that nation had or had not *personal faith* in the God Who had given His statutes and ordinances unto Israel? We may speak of three points here:

First, in reading Scripture, we must constantly use spiritual discernment. Our verse speaks of **them that sinned.** Paul says, *"All* sinned"; but there (Rom. 3.23), he is opening up to sinners the glorious news of justification through Christ's blood. But "sinned" in Hebrews 3.17 has no reference to man's general state; but to conscious, willful rebellion, persisted in.

Second, the Israelites were perpetually conscious of what their leader, Moses, expresses in the great 90th Psalm entitled: "A Prayer of Moses the man of God": "Thou hast set our iniquities before Thee, our secret sins in the light of Thy countenance." Being *under the Law,* the more sincere they were, the greater their consciousness of failure. See Paul's own experience under the Law even after his salvation, Romans 7.7-24.*

Third, the word **"sinned"** of Hebrews 3.17 has a peculiar and

---

*Anyone desirous of finding God's way of grace can see what *the Law* will do, the ministration of *death* and *condemnation* (II Cor. 3.7, 9). Study the 90th psalm further: Moses' prayer: "Return, O Jehovah, how long? and let it repent Thee concerning Thy servants." And His words, "Make us glad according to the days wherein Thou hast afflicted us, And the years wherein we have seen evil" (vss. 13, 15).

Moses had been constituted "mediator" for Israel (Gal. 3.19), and had been identified with them by God. They were all sharing the afflictions and the wilderness wanderings, and seeing the "evil." He says further, "For we are consumed in Thine anger, and in Thy wrath are we troubled . . . All our days are passed away in Thy wrath: We bring our years to an end as a sigh" (vss. 7.9).

We learn, therefore, if we are willing to learn, that not under an admixture of Law and Grace can there be real Divine *perfecting.* (For Moses' *heart* was right with God; but Christ had not yet died, putting sin out of God's sight!)

terrible meaning. There are acts of willfullness and rebellion, the effects of which will go on forever. Sweet is the message, "If we confess our sins, He is faithful and righteous to forgive us our sins, and to cleanse us from all unrighteousness" (I Jno. 1.9). But John in the same epistle declares, "There is a sin *unto death: not concerning this do I say that he should make request" (I Jno. 5.16).

Moses and Aaron at Kadesh (Num. 20.9, 11, 12, 24) acted in such unbelief (Moses using his own rod instead of Aaron's) that both he and Aaron were shut out of the land, despite Moses' pleadings. Thus also David, concerning the child of his sin, was forgiven, as he celebrates in Psalm 32; but the *governmental* judgment remained, and the child died (II Sam. 12).*

Read Moses' supplication for these wilderness rebels, and God's immeasurably gracious answer: "Pardon, I pray Thee, the iniquity of this people according unto the greatness of Thy loving kindness, and according as Thou hast forgiven this people, from Egypt even until now." "And Jehovah said, I have pardoned, according to thy word" (Num. 14.19, 20).†

Here we see the Divine purpose of eternal mercy towards anyone that should desire it of Him; the while His governmental glory demanded that they should not reach God's *"rest"*—which to *them* was the promised *Canaan* (Deut. 12.9; 25.19). For whatever we

---

*Owen, the great Puritan commentator, well says: "There is a repentance and humiliation that may free the soul from eternal ruin, and yet not remove a temporal judgment threatened against it. Such was the repentance of David upon his adultery. The Lord put away the guilt of his sin, and told him that he should not die penally, but would not be entreated to spare the life of the child, nor David in those other sore afflictions which afterward befell him on the same account. And thus it might be with some, yea, with many of those Israelites. God might give them repentance to make way for the pardon and forgiveness of their persons; nevertheless, He would so far take vengeance on their inventions as to cause their carcasses to fall in the wilderness.

"But yet this must be acknowledged, that their punishment was a great *representation* of the future judgment, wherein ungodly believers shall be cast off forever, for, as they fell visibly under the wrath and displeasure of God, and their carcasses were cast out in the wilderness as a loathsome abomination, so their judgment overtook them under this formal consideration, that they were excluded out of the rest of God. And these things together gave an excellent *resemblance* of the judgment to come, when sinners shall perish eternally under the wrath of God and be forever excluded out of His rest."—Com. on Hebrews.

†"So in Exodus: when God threatened to destroy all the people, He recalled His threat when Moses pleaded His promises, and sent His angel to guide them, but declared, Nevertheless in the day when I visit I will visit their sin upon them. And Jehovah plagued the people, because they made the calf, which Aaron made. (Ex. 32.34, 35). But their falling in the wilderness had nothing to do with the saving of their souls: Moses and Aaron died in the wilderness too, and we know they were saints of Jehovah."— J. N. Darby.

find revealed further upon God's "rest" in **Hebrews**, it is evident that, first of all, for *Israel*, it was their *getting into the land* that Jehovah had promised to their fathers. This "rest" must not be confused with their eternal salvation. Moses, indeed, yes, and Miriam and Aaron, as we have said, all failed to enter the promised "rest." Yet Moses was with the Lord on the Mount of transfiguration! We dare not say, therefore, that Caleb and Joshua were the *only* ones in whom saving faith dwelt! They were the only ones that entered the land and attained unto the "rest" (so far as it was then attained).

Jude indeed says, "The Lord, having saved a people out of the land of Egypt, afterward destroyed them that *believed* not." And he associates them with the fallen angels that "kept not their own principality" (Gen. 6), and are "kept in everlasting bonds under darkness unto the judgment of the great day"; and with Sodom and Gomorrah, which are "set forth as an example, suffering the punishment of eternal fire" (Jude 5-7). But who would dare to assert of believers *today* that only those Christians who were fully surrendered to the Lord and were filled with the Holy Spirit, were to be saved? There are in **Hebrews** a number of profoundly difficult questions—this one as to the destiny of those who **fell in the wilderness,** being one of the most serious of them!

God hates the self-imagined "charity" which refuses to believe His words concerning His wrath, yea, His eternal wrath, upon the finally impenitent; and it is frightful how ready people are to follow this deathful teaching! To believe the letter of all of God's words concerning "the eternal fire prepared for the devil and His angels," of which our Lord spoke (Matt. 25.41); into which the wicked will be sent forever; and yet, on the other hand, to follow with equal fidelity His revelations of sovereign grace toward those whom we would naturally deem should be condemned, is a work of faith which only those can do who in their measure can say with Paul, We have "obtained mercy of the Lord to be faithful."

The great lesson for us today—what is it? Compare our state with that of the believers of the early church. It is true that many Christians are *wilderness Christians* and will be so to the end— as to this experience of *the rest of faith?* This is a most solemn question!

Victory in the Risen Christ, the infilling of the Spirit, power for service, unselfish love toward everybody, especially toward all Christians—if this is your yearning desire, if you thirst after these things, thank God!

Verse 18: And to whom sware He that they should not enter into His rest but to them that were disobedient? The question at once arises, How could God expect man to rest in a creation which had already been judged on account of man's sin, a creation in which God no longer rested? The answer is, as it seems to me, simple. It was none of man's business, none of Israel's business in the wilderness, to inquire about the permanence or otherwise of the first creation. Their business was to exercise faith in and obedience to the merciful Jehovah-God who had not only brought them out of Egypt's bondage by blood redemption, and brought them through the Red Sea, swallowing up their enemies, but had sustained them right up to the border of Canaan, defending them, despite their murmurings, from Amalek and from all their enemies.

Their business, I repeat, was to go forward gladly in faith. Caleb and Joshua did this, and entered Canaan. Others entered not into God's rest. They were disobedient (vs. 19): **They were not able to enter in because of unbelief.** "TODAY" for them, is over. The ten evil spies, leaders in unbelief and rebellion, died of the plague, and the people were told they must go back into the wilderness, where their dead bodies should fall. *Presumption,* the next day, was not *faith.* **They were not able to enter in.** To multitudes of those whose bodies fell in the wilderness, the solemn words of A. B. Simpson apply:

> "They came to the gates of Canaan,
>   But they never entered in.
> They came to the land of promise,
>   But they perished in their sin.
> And so we are ever coming
>   To the place where two ways part:
> One leads to the land of promise,
>   And one to a hardened heart".

"Unbelief" is an attitude of the heart, not of the mind. So we read an "evil heart of unbelief" (3.12). And in **Chapter 3.19,** "**unbelief**" lies at the root—is the cause of that "**disobedience**" which brings on Divine judgment. Unbelief is not inability to understand, but *unwillingness* to *trust*, for *trusting* God puts the creature into *God's* hands. It is the will, not the intelligence, that is involved. The unbeliever *chooses* to remain in his *own* hands. Also, the unsurrendered unspiritual believer will suffer great loss —though he may be *saved*. He would like eternal bliss, of course. But God hath made Jesus both *Lord* and Christ—whereas the unbeliever chooses to remain lord of his own life.

It is not for lack of evidence that unbelief exists. Every heart beat, every breath, tells man he is nothing but a creature—utterly insufficient in himself for a moment's existence. And his conscience says there is a God; and the creation under his feet and above him witness it. But "an *evil* heart of unbelief" says, I want to live *for myself*, which is the essence of evil, of sin.

There is a character of "unbelief," an essential character, not always emphasized: that is, the attitude of neglect or forgetfulness of God, a treating of the ever-present gracious One as if He did not exist; a forgetfulness of past blessing that is inexplicably fathomless. The attitude of the disciples in Mark 8.1-4 will illustrate. Some little time before (Mk. 6), Christ had fed the five thousand with five loaves and two fishes, and they had been rewarded with a basketful of fragments apiece. But when a great multitude came together again, and had nothing to eat, and the Lord said, "I have compassion on the multitude, because they . . . have nothing to eat," His disciples answered Him, "Whence shall one be able to fill these men with bread here in a desert place?" (Mk. 8.4).

Exactly the same circumstances; precisely the same need; and the Lord of glory taking them into partnership with His infinite power: For "He asked them, How many loaves have ye? And they said, Seven." But utter blindness on their part.

"He took the seven loaves, and having given thanks, He brake . . . and they set them before the multitude. And they had a few small fishes: and having blessed them, He commanded to set these also before them." And four thousand men were filled, and seven baskets of fragments taken up. No wonder our Lord "sighed deeply in His spirit," and asked the searching questions, "Have ye [the disciples] *your heart* hardened? Having eyes see ye *not*? and having ears, hear *ye not?* and do *ye* not remember?"—"Do *ye* not yet understand?"

God is present *now* with *you*, believer, wherever and whoever you are. Are you able, are you willing, to reckon on His presence and His help? This is *faith*. Unbelief sees nothing, learns nothing, gets nothing, is **not able to enter in.**

CHAPTER FOUR

1   LET US FEAR therefore, lest haply, a promise being
left of entering into His rest, any one of you should seem
2   to have come short of it. For indeed we have had good
tidings preached unto us, even as also they: but the
word of hearing did not profit them, because it was
3   not united by faith with them that heard. For we who
have believed do enter into that rest; even as He hath said,

As I sware in My wrath,

They shall not enter into My rest:
although the works were finished from the foundation
4   of the world. For He hath said somewhere of the seventh
day on this wise, And God rested on the seventh day
5   from all His works; and in this place again,

They shall not enter into My rest.

THOUSANDS UPON THOUSANDS of earnest souls have
misread **Hebrews**, and have fallen into doubt, darkness, and even
despair. The reason was, their failure to read aright these great
warnings which **Hebrews** holds.

There are indeed in **Hebrews** constant and solemn warnings
against inattention towards God's message; "neglect" of God's
Son and His "so great salvation"; spiritual sluggishness and
sloth. These states of soul, all, are shown to tend to final
apostasy and eternal woe. Neglecters easily become rejecters;
unbelief hardens; and shallow dealing with Divine things becomes despairing of Divine things.

But on the other hand—according to God's Word, "Ye have
grieved the heart of the righteous, whom I have not made sad"
(Ezek. 13.22). There are honest hearts of the family of "Littlefaith" who have applied to themselves, with terrible self-ac-
cusation, words intended for others than themselves. Satan delights to roar continuously in the ears of a trembling soul: "You
have trampled under foot the Son of God, you have 'done despite

to the Spirit of grace'! You have been 'hardened by the deceitfulness of sin.' It is 'impossible to renew you to repentance!' "

Let such timid souls remember and reflect upon God's past
ways with them, His graciousness, His long-suffering, His
goodness. And even in their state of trembling let them read
such a verse as **Chapter 4.1; Let us fear, therefore, lest haply, a
promise being left of entering into His rest.** Let them dwell
upon these latter words, **a promise being left.** Let them cast
themselves upon the mercy of God, and look, even in their
fearfulness, for this promise that is *"left"!* For this verse does
indeed apply, first of all, to those who may have sorely neglected
God's promises and providences. Yet even for such, the words
are: **a promise being left.** Let them take up Bunyan's *Pilgrim's
Progress* (which God has so blessed to souls), and in the second
part become acquainted with "Mr. Ready-to-halt," "Mr. Fearing,"
yea, with "Mercy," and, as we have said, with all whose name
may be called "Littlefaith." One has well said, "Little faith brings
the soul to Heaven, while great faith brings Heaven into the
soul!"

In all their soul-exercising also, let them remember that "Mr.
Legality" is their great enemy! It was from "dead works" that the
consciences of these Hebrew saints were delivered by the blood
of Christ to serve the Living God. Let them stay within sight
of Calvary, and not be driven by the enemy to undertake to get
deliverance through "serving" God.

Yes, God, being infinitely loving and long-suffering, constantly
"leaves" for the believer some promise which he may lay hold of by
faith, if he will. The warning here, however, is that such a
gracious promise may be neglected, overlooked, **come short of.**

Now you may have failed to lay hold of one promise after
another; and your life may have become more and more perplexed. But do not despair! For it is God's habit to "leave" a
promise! There is such a one for you! Search for it prayerfully,
carefully, humbly. And when you find your heart drawn out to
any Scripture, thank God for that, praying that there may be
in your heart a "mixture of faith," graciously given by Him.

**For we see verse 2: For indeed we have had good tidings
preached unto us, even as also they** [Israel of old]: **but the word**

of hearing did not profit them, because it was not united by faith ["mixed with faith", A.V.] with them that heard.

Faith, reading a promise, says, "This means *me!*"

I remember a meeting many years ago, where presents were being given out to poor children. From a great heap of presents on the table, the leader would read out names of those who were to receive gifts, and such ones were expected to come forward and receive them thankfully. There came the reading of the name of a certain boy, and no one came forward. Someone sitting beside me said, "There's that boy, over there by the aisle."

I watched him. His name was repeated several times. At first he looked forward at the announcer; then, as his name was re-peated, he looked to the right and to the left; and then stood half up and looked all around over the back part of the building, ex-pecting to see the favored one. But someone near him called out, "He means *you, Jimmy!*"

Jimmy kept his seat, clutching the chair in front of him. He was not used to receiving presents! Not until the speaker looked right at him, reading his name, and asked, "Is that your name?" did he tremblingly get up and go forward and accept his present!

Thus we act toward God. We quote promises—never really *claiming* them. Do not forget that the last word in Chapter 3 is "unbelief." We have seen that Israel lost their promised land (Num. 14) through simply not believing! Just as they fell short of Canaan, so many professing Christians today, though a promise is left them of entering into His rest, fail of it:—of that spirit-ual "rest" which belongs to all who hear and believe that Christ has borne their sin; that He made peace by the blood of His Cross.*

Verse 3: But God says, We who have believed do enter into that rest. Dear brother, it is of infinite importance to you and to me just to BELIEVE!—to believe God's "promises" that are

---

*The most of the nation of Israel in the future will not "profit" by the voice of the two witnesses of Revelation 11.3-12, warning them of the fearful results of worshiping the Antichrist and his image. Most of them will not attend to the voices of the three angels who warn in Revelation 14.6, 8, 9. A "Remnant" shall indeed "return to the mighty God," but it will be a "very small Remnant" that shall be saved (Isa. 1.9; 7.3; Rom. 9.27, 28). It will (Isa. 66.8) be with this Remnant, called "a nation brought forth *at once,*" that God will make His future covenant "with the House of Israel and with the House of Judah," as we shall find in Heb. 8, He will do.

"left" us! The work was finished on the Cross, and our Lord is
in the glory on the ground of that perfect work for sinners. Do
not try to become worthy by any works, or change of your "character," but just *believe*. And do not rest upon any "church" forms or
ceremonies: for God does not rest there, but *in Christ alone!*

Verse 3 (contd.):

> Even as He hath said,
> As I sware in My wrath,
>   They shall not enter into My rest:

although the works were finished from the foundation of the
world.

As we continue to take up the great subject of what God calls
"My rest" (brought before us by the Spirit from Chapter 3.11
to 4.11), let us consider what this "rest" of God is, and what it
is not.

God Himself entered upon rest after the seven days of
creation:

"For in six days Jehovah made Heaven and earth, and on the
seventh day He rested, and was refreshed" (Ex. 31.17).

Let these words mean precisely what they say: Jehovah rested.
Jehovah was *refreshed*. Let none dare to object that God, being
infinite and almighty, could not be "refreshed." God's word is, that
He *was!*

"And God saw everything that He had made, and behold, it
was very good . . . And on the seventh day God finished His work
which He had made. And He rested on the seventh day from all
His work which He had made." Note, *"He rested* on the seventh
day." So also state the next verses in Hebrews 4:

> 4 For He hath said somewhere of the seventh day on this
>   wise, And God rested on the seventh day from all His
> 5 works; and in this place again,
>   They shall not enter into My rest.

See Genesis 1.31 to 2.3. Sin entered; God's rest was broken. All
creation was subjected to "vanity." God could not rest where sin
was. For it is well to reflect that there is in God, from all eternity
unto all eternity, the infinite complacency which belongs to the
Absolute Good.* Therefore there was creation, and, in order that

---

*All our human restlessness, our incapacity for rest, arises from sin: "The wicked are like
the troubled sea; for it cannot rest, and its waters cast up mire and dirt". (Isa. 57.20).

His creatures might know Him, to man was given free will. When sin entered God's creation (though not from Him Who "cannot be tempted with evil, and Himself tempteth no man"), there resulted a *necessity* and an *opportunity*. The *necessity* was *judgment*: God sparing not angels when they sinned! The *opportunity* was *love:* God so *loved* that He gave His Son. Consequently, there is the exhibition of the nature of God Himself: "Herein is love." (Not that when sin entered, God's purposes or counsels failed: for these were all connected with Christ, and His redemptive work to come.) Therefore He began *working* toward redemption. (This is what our Lord meant when He said: "My Father *worketh* even until now, and I *work*"—Jno. 5.17.)* Indeed, from the time that Adam sinned, God had prophesied (Gen. 3.15) a great struggle between the woman's Seed (Christ) and the seed of the serpent, in which the Seed of the woman (Christ) should "bruise the serpent's head": a struggle not over until Satan is cast into the lake of fire forever! (Rev. 20.10).

And so we come to the Cross. In Christ crucified we find God's holiness and righteousness that could not spare His well-beloved Son, sin being laid upon Him; and also that fathomless *love* that reached us in redeeming power. You and I may not yet have found full rest or constant rest in the work of the Cross. *God has!* May His grace enable us so to "rest" in what was done at the Cross and in resurrection, as to glorify God in finding *peace* (Col. 1.20).

Our blessed Lord on the Cross cried, "It is finished!" Sin had been laid upon Him; He had been forsaken, smitten by God's hand as a Substitute for our sin, the wages of which was death. His death met that penalty perfectly and forever! "Through His own blood" as our Great High Priest "He entered in once for all into the Holies [Heaven], having obtained eternal redemption" (Heb. 9.12). "He, when He had offered one sacrifice for sins forever, *sat down* on the right hand of God" (Ch. 10.12).

Now becomes possible the first phase of God's "rest" for the

"The sea is no more" in John's vision (Rev. 21.1), for the sea could not *rest!* All is REST in the New Creation; all is absent that suggests unrest.

*The Jews, like the present "Seventh Day Adventists," sticklers for the seventh day observance, said of Christ, "This man keepeth not the Sabbath." They, like the Adventists today, chose to remain under the Law that God says *condemns* them! (Gal. 3.10).

believer: we rest where God rests, in the shed blood of Christ! This spiritual rest arises from *accepting God's announcement* of Christ's finished work on our behalf. Hezekiah spake to his people when the Assyrians came against them:

"With him is an arm of flesh: but with us is Jehovah our God to help us, and to fight our battles. And the people *rested themselves upon the words* of Hezekiah king of Judah" (II Chron. 32.8).

Let Hezekiah's subjects be a lesson to us!

The tenth verse of Hebrews 4 also has a reference to this spiritual rest: **For he that is entered into His rest hath himself also rested from his works as God did from His.** (a) There is a time when spiritual anxiety ceases in view of the work of the Cross; (b) and also (generally some time later, when struggle to live a holy life *in one's own strength* ceases: and a "Thanks be to God, Who giveth us the victory through our Lord Jesus Christ!" rises from the heart), there is *ever-deepening* "rest," as His *yoke* is fully accepted by the believer: as the Lord Jesus said (Matt. 11.28, 29), "Take My yoke upon you, and learn of Me; for I am meek and lowly in heart: and ye shall find *rest* unto your souls"—rest from self, from anxiety, from depending on one's own planning. Sad to say (c) there are, as we shall see, many who do not go on with God, who remain "*babes.*" (See Heb. 5.12.)

This is the present rest of faith, the *found* rest of Matthew 11.29. This is a subjective state called "the peace *of* God" (Phil. 4.6, 7), the believer already, through faith in Christ's shed blood, having "peace *with* God" (Rom. 5.1; 8.1).

There is a *second* phase of rest, set forth by Paul in II Thessalonians 1.6-10. The Thessalonian Christians were being afflicted by persecution and every earthly wrong. They were still in the trials of this world, and the enemy was tempting and opposing them. So Paul writes that, consequent upon the second coming of Christ, "If so be that it be a righteous thing with God to recompense affliction to them that afflict you, and to you that are afflicted *rest with us,* at the revelation of the Lord Jesus from Heaven with the angels of His power in flaming fire."

Here will be a cessation of temptation, trial, and all infirmity. Satan having been cast down to earth, there will also be rest from conflict with him.

But we must note further here, for there are those who claim (most earnestly) that the rest into which believers enter is *only* the "rest of faith" in believing on Christ (Heb. 4.3), and so beholding His blood as to have the conscience "cleansed from dead works to serve the living God," thus having rested from their works as God did from His (Chs. 4.10; 9.14). To this I would say, while deeply appreciating the high and holy purpose, yea, and walk, of such dear saints, that our chapters state over and over (from 3.11 to 4.11) that it is *God's* rest into which believers are to enter. Now God does indeed rest, in a sense none of us fully appreciate, in the work of His beloved Son at Calvary. Yet, to carry out the figure of Hebrews 3 and 4 (which is Israel's entering Canaan): let us suppose we have come up out of the wilderness, and crossed over Jordan in the power of the death of Christ, as the ark brought Israel over (Josh. 3). What about the "Canaanites"? the "inhabitants of the land"? Israel's *"rest"* involved *the conquest of these possessing enemies!* But the book of Judges is the record of their *failure* through *unbelief, compromise,* and even, in the case of Dan, *rebellion and idolatry!* In Judges 2.20-23, we read that on account of this failure, this disobedience of unbelief: "Jehovah left those nations, without driving them out hastily; neither delivered He them into the hand of Joshua."

Indeed in Joshua's old age Jehovah said to him: "Thou art old and well stricken in years, and there remaineth yet very much land to be possessed" (Josh. 13.1).

And although later we read:

"So Jehovah gave unto Israel all the land which He sware unto their fathers; and they possessed it and dwelt therein. And Jehovah gave them rest round about, according to all that He sware unto their fathers: and there stood not a man of all their enemies before them; Jehovah delivered all their enemies into their hand. There failed not aught of any good thing which Jehovah had spoken unto the house of Israel; all came to pass" (Josh. 21.43-45), yet the emphasis here is upon *Jehovah's* faithfulness when Israel pressed on against their enemies. In the very last chapter of Joshua we find Joshua gathering all the tribes of Israel to Shechem, and solemnly enjoining "the elders . . . their heads . . . their judges . . . and their officers . . . *Put away the gods* which your fathers served beyond the River, and in Egypt; and serve ye Jehovah" (vs. 14).

But the declaration of the Spirit in Hebrews 4.6, 7, 8 is:

6 **Seeing therefore it remaineth that some should enter
thereinto, and they to whom the good tidings were before preached failed to enter in because of disobedience,**

7 **He again defineth a certain day, Today, saying in David
so long a time afterward [hundreds of years afterward]
(even as hath been said before),**
     Today if ye shall hear His voice,
     Harden not your hearts.

8 **For if Joshua had given them rest, He would not have
spoken afterward of another day—**
of the rest as still future.

So, still carrying out the figure of Chapters 3 and 4, our rest,
like that of Israel, involves the *conquest* of *enemies*. However deep
and abiding our rest in Christ's work on the Cross and His priesthood in Heaven, the conflict with the hosts of darkness is *still on,*
and *will* be on till Christ comes for us—for His Church! Even then,
though (as we have seen) those "afflicted" by the enemy will have
rest—the rest of the Millennial Kingdom*—*yet God's* final REST
awaits the *last overthrow of Satan,* who is to be released after the
1000 years and lead those who come to his banner from the four
corners of the earth, in the greatest rebellion earth has ever seen,

---

*The Millennium in a vast degree illustrates the rest of God's people, both of those of the
heavenly calling, and of redeemed national Israel. As we know, "They that are Christ's"
are taken up in the Church's Rapture, at the *first* phase of His coming. Then after the
Antichrist's covenant with Israel (Dan. 9.2) (Daniel's seventieth week of years), occurs
the revelation or manifestation to earth (Rotherham: "forthshining") of Christ's coming
—the *second* phase. The event makes possible rest, both for the spared remnant of
Israel and, of course, for the Church. All the enemies of God's saints must be dis-
posed of if those saints are to have rest! Satan is cast into the abyss in the center of the
earth, and it is sealed over him for one thousand years. Of Satan's host of angels
(evidently one-third of the angels of God), we read in Isaiah:

"And it shall come to pass in *that day,* that Jehovah will punish the host of the high
ones on high, and the kings of the earth upon the earth. And they shall be gathered
together as prisoners are gathered in the pit [margin, dungeon], and they [Satan's host] shall
be shut up in the prison; and after many days [that is, after the Millennium] shall they
be visited" (Isa. 24.21, 22).

"That day" is the day of Christ's coming in *wrath.* If anyone is ignorant of the time
that this will occur, let him read the next verse:

"Then the moon shall be confounded, and the sun ashamed; for Jehovah of hosts will
reign in mount Zion, and in Jerusalem; and before His elders shall be glory"—that is,
at the beginning of the Millennium.

Lastly, as to evil men: they will be dealt with by the Lord at that time, and during
the Millennium. Even one who slanders in secret will be "cut off" with "all the wicked
of the land . . . all the workers of iniquity" (Ps. 101.5, 8); for our Lord will rule with
a rod of iron, in the 1000 years!

at the close of the Millennium (Rev. 20.7-10). After that, he will be cast forever into the "lake of fire and brimstone," where the Antichrist and the false prophet shall have been during the Millennium; and the last judgment (that of the Great White Throne) and the final eternal separation of the wicked from among the righteous will take place.*

So the "rest of God" into which His saints shall *finally* enter, and unto which He directs them, is that state of things in which *God Himself* is at rest, and in which He takes delight! This can only be at the *New Creation*, as Peter says: "According to His promise, we look for new heavens and a new earth, wherein dwelleth† righteousness' (II Pet. 3.13).

(1) To rehearse then, what has been said: The believer should rest fully in Christ's work for him, with a conscience cleansed by Christ's blood from dead legal works, or from hoping anything from the flesh. He should come to say with Paul, "I know that in me, that is, in my flesh, dwelleth no good thing" (Rom. 7); and should see the deliverance, saying also with Paul, "I thank God through Jesus Christ my Lord!" and so recognizing the work of the Spirit as to say: "The law of the Spirit of life in Christ Jesus made me free from the law of sin and of death" (Rom. 8.2).

These present elements—rest from guilt in the blood of Christ, and deliverance from the power of sin and the Law through identification with Christ in His death and burial, should be shared by every believer. Thus only doth he press on to full growth.‡

---

*Revelation 21.3-4 will then describe one company:
"God Himself shall be with them, their God: and He shall wipe away every tear from their eyes; and death shall be no more; neither shall there be mourning, nor crying, nor pain, any more: the first things are passed away."
And Revelation 21.8 describes the other:
"But for the fearful, and unbelieving, and abominable, and murderers, and fornicators, and sorcerers, and idolaters, and all liars, their part shall be in the lake that burneth with fire and brimstone; which is the second death." For, concerning the New Jerusalem: "And there shall in no wise enter into it anything unclean, or he that maketh an abomination and a lie; but only they that are written in the Lamb's book of life" (Rev. 21.27).

†Or, we may paraphrase: "Wherein righteousness *is at home*." Thayer says, "In the Septuagint the rendering of the Greek word for dwelleth *(katoikeô)*, meaning to settle, to dwell, differs from *paroikeô*, meaning to sojourn, as the *permanent* differs from the *transitory.*"

‡There is also another phase not often thought of:
"Blessed are the dead who die in the Lord from henceforth: yea, saith the Spirit, that they may *rest* from their labours; for their works follow with them" (Rev. 14.13, see

(2) Believers should expect (and that at any moment, for there is no unfulfilled condition), being caught up to meet the Lord in the air, and transformed into His likeness, receiving our resurrection bodies. Thus the present conflict with the devil, the world, and the flesh, will be over forever.

But (3) we must also look forward, and that with a sure hope, away beyond the Millennium, to *the eternal state,* unto which we already belong ("If any man is in Christ, he is a new creation":) but for which an outward Heaven and earth remain *to be* created! How comfortable were God's closing words by His angel to Daniel: "But go thou thy way till the end be; for thou *shalt rest,* and shalt stand in thy lot, at the end of the days"! (Dan. 12.13). Whatever God does in the "ages to come," there will be no longer necessary any dispensational revealing of Himself, and unfolding to all holy creatures of His nature as *Love!* That was done once for all at the Cross, and is being continued now in Christ's tender sympathetic priesthood in Heaven. There will be no longer need for warning against enemies, eternal separation from them having then taken place. There will be no longer need of preaching or prophesying that the will of God is the creature's true bliss; the praises of those blessed holy ones who by Divine grace have chosen God's will, will be proof that the creature's only true happiness is to know and serve the God Whose name is Love. As for God, the following beautiful words from Zephaniah express His "rest" of the ages to come, do they not? "He will rejoice over thee with joy; He will *rest* in His love; He will joy over thee with singing" (Zeph. 3.17).

As long as there is a problem unsettled, a saint not yet glorified, transformed into Christ's image; as long as God's enemies are permitted to "destroy the earth," even to use His blessings of light, air, food, health—God's "rest" will not, cannot, be completed. Concerning the present earth, God says, "The heavens are the heavens of Jehovah; but the earth hath He given to the children of men" (Ps. 115.16). But the "New Creation," the "New Heavens and the

---

author's book The Revelation, p. 225).
   This is a vivid example of the ending of our work for God, called by Paul "accomplishing our course". Our Lord Jesus Himself said to the Father, "I glorified Thee on the earth, having *accomplished the work* which Thou hast given me to do." There comes time when earthly labor for God ends, and the heavenly state is begun.

New Earth," are absolutely *according to God*—not in any sense an "adjustment" of the old, but entirely *new,* with Sin, and Trial, *banished forever!*

God says: "Behold, I create new heavens and a new earth; and the former things shall *not be remembered, nor come into mind*" (Isa. 65.17).

"The first heaven and the first earth are *passed away,*" (Rev. 21.1): "every tear . . . death . . . mourning . . . crying . . . pain . . . passed away" (vs. 4).

"The new heavens and the new earth, which I will make, shall remain before Me" (Isa. 66.22).

What is wrapped up in the marvelous words, "He that sitteth on the throne saith, Behold I make *all things new*" (Rev. 21.5), we cannot even feebly *grasp:* any more than we can fully understand the new birth—so puzzling to Nicodemus, "the teacher of Israel." New creatures are those *in Christ.* But while we already belong to the New Creation, how little we know of it! "All things new": a new nature, a new kind of existence of what we call material things; new laws of being of which men know nothing. Did not our Risen Lord come and "stand in the midst," "when the doors were shut," and say, "Handle Me, and see; for a spirit hath not flesh and bones, as ye behold Me having"? The New Creation, though material and tangible as was our Lord's resurrection body, will evidently bear a relation to the old, as we read:

"The first man is of the earth, earthly; the second Man is of Heaven . . . If there is a natural body, there is also a spiritual body"* (I Cor. 15.47, 44).

This New Creation is founded upon the blood of the Cross, as we read in Colossians 1.20. In the New Jerusalem the Lamb is the light. They shall see God's face: (no temple-worship: no distance from God). "His name shall be in their foreheads," . . . and they shall reign forever and ever (Rev. 22.4-5). How wonderful! (There are two great amazements when we think of God: first, He is infinite; second, He loves US!)

From this study of God's "rest," let us return to take up more particularly

---

*A "natural" body: literally, a body adapted for the soul—*psychikos;* and also "a spiritual body,"—that is, a body adapted for the spirit—*pneumatikos.*

**Verse 6, ff: Seeing therefore it remaineth that some should
enter thereinto, and they to whom the good tidings were before
preached failed to enter in because of disobedience**—The Hebrew
Christians addressed in this epistle had been brought up to reverence their national election—just as "Presbyterians" and other
sects do their history and "standards." But such reverence blinds
men to the facts. The Israelites **failed to enter in** through unbelief
and hardness of heart. God's mercy had spared the nation; but
only Caleb and Joshua, as we have seen, entered Canaan! This
awful failure would be the very things never mentioned in the
talks of their rabbis!

But since these Hebrew Christians were now dealing directly,
by Christ, with God, their true history as a nation must be shown
to them. As a nation, they had **failed to enter in.** (Imagine any
synagogue today teaching this national failure: the rest of the
Jews would mob such a synagogue! Yet such teaching would be
the truth.) Israel has **failed to enter in,** and the kingdom of God
has been "taken away" from that nation, to be given to the
coming Remnant of it—to "a nation bringing forth the fruits"
of God's kingdom (Matt. 21.43)—a nation not yet born, but
which "shall be born in a day"! (Isa. 66.8; Zech. 12.10-13.6).

It is striking in **Hebrews,** and also characteristic of the book,
that the sin called to the attention of these believers is not that of
the rejection and crucifixion of their Messiah, but the national
attitude of unbelief shown by them at the first offer of "rest"
in the land Jehovah had promised them in their early national
history!

Christ was now in Heaven, over God's house as a Son—with
rights even the faithful servant Moses had never known. Thus
to take their minds back to that great outburst of unbelief against
God's servant Moses would indeed show up their own history to
their hearts! Would these Hebrew Christians hold fast their
"boldness," and the "glorying" of their hope in Christ—thus
obeying the voice of the blessed Spirit not to harden their hearts?
Or would they treat the Son as their fathers had treated the
servant Moses—and rebel?*

---

*Yet God had dealt with them in utter grace each time. He had brought them to Sinai, and
said to them, "If ye will . . . keep My covenant, then ye shall be mine own possession

It was not because they were under an imperfect covenant that Israel failed to enter in. It was because their hearts were bent to evil, and thus to unbelief. They did not desire the acquaintance of the God Who had opened the door to the promised land for them. "Let us make a captain, and let us return into Egypt," they said. So at Sinai, when Moses was upon the mountain they had said to Aaron:

"Up, make us gods, which shall go before us; for as for this Moses, the man that brought us up out of the land of Egypt, we know not what is become of him"! (Ex. 32.1).

It is this frightful readiness, yea, eagerness, to do without God —not, indeed, without "religion"—forms, ordinances, and the like; but without the Living God, that is the mark of the Laodicean stage of the Church's history, also—just as of that failing, unbelieving generation of Israel whose "limbs" were "strewn down along in the wilderness" (Heb. 3.17). If people, being what are called "church-members," find themselves able and quite willing to do without the fellowship of God and Jesus Christ His Son day by day; if people do not know what it is to be "led of the Spirit," it may be a dream that they are sons of God! Hell will be filled with false professors, those who deceived themselves.

I tell you, beloved, the story of "the day of the trial in the wilderness," "the provocation," needs to be laid to heart by you and me! Let no one dare to say that the great warnings of Hebrews 3 and 4 do not concern, and directly, every believer today! Shall these Hebrew believers be solemnly warned by recalling their own history of unbelief and failure to enter in, and Gentile believers have no such heart-dangers to be warned of? Where should God go for warnings for *all* believers, if not to the history of His dealings with *the children of men?*

You say, "Since Christ died and rose and is gone to Heaven, things are entirely different." We grant at once that sin has been put away, and Christ is indeed in Heaven. But Peter warned those

---

from among all peoples: for all the earth is Mine." And in supreme self-confidence they had promised, "All that Jehovah hath spoken, we will do." And so at Sinai they had signed, by note of hand as it were, *a covenant,* to which God will yet held them—when in the last days He brings them "into the bond of the covenant." (See Ezek. 20.33-38.) For the fulfillment of this prophecy lies in the immediate future, when the nations shall turn against Israel, and become toward them "the wilderness of the peoples." This is the universal anti-Semitism that is *already arising!*

to whom he wrote (the "elect . . . of the Dispersion," surely) to
make their "calling and election *sure*"—not to God, but to *them-*
selves! "*Watch* ye," also pleads Paul with the Ephesian elders
(Acts 20.31); and,

"I know that after my departing grievous wolves shall enter in
among you, *not sparing the flock;* and from among your own selves
shall men arise, speaking perverse things, *to draw away the dis-*
ciples after them" (vss. 29, 30).

"In the last days grievous times shall come. For men shall be
lovers of self, lovers of money, boastful, haughty . . . lovers of
pleasure rather than lovers of God; holding *a form of godliness,*
but having *denied the power thereof*" (II Tim. 3.1-5).

Again, "But shun profane babblings: for they will proceed further in ungodliness, and their word will eat as doth a gangrene:
of whom is Hymenaeus and Philetus; men who concerning the truth
have erred, saying that the resurrection is past already, and overthrow the faith of some" (II Tim. 2.16-18).

Paul also told Timothy, "The time will come when they *will not*
endure the sound doctrine." And (II Tim. 1.15) "This thou
knowest, that all that are in Asia [Ephesus being the center]
turned away from *me;* of whom are Phygelus and Hermogenes."*
These turned away, not necessarily from all Christian profession,
but at least from that heavenly doctrine, "the mystery," committed
to Paul, which is the only truth that establishes and protects saints.

So now there is set before our eyes, in this great book of **Hebrews,**
all the frightful scene of Divine judgments. For Israel (though
nationally pardoned in answer to Moses' prayers) turned back into the wilderness, knowing that they would never see the land of
milk and honey!

How solemn, then, the warnings of Hebrews 3 and 4! You who
say so glibly, "This story of failing to enter into Canaan belongs

---

*Notice how Paul *tells* out the *names* of false or dangerous teachers. No other practice is
safe in protecting the saints! The saints know the names of Jones or Smith, though they
may not yet have Scripturally discerned the evils that Smith or Jones may be teaching. It
is my business (and it is yours and Paul made it his), if we are teaching the saints, to
warn them of dangerous men. It is reported that someone asked John Darby what books
he had in his library. He replied, "I have the Bible, and bad books." I do not report
this story as a fact; but I can understand from his own writings Mr. Darby's concern
about all books that he read! I do not know anyone more zealous, or jealous, for truth,
Biblically set forth, since the days of Paul. You say, "It got Mr. Darby hated" Certainly!
What of that? So was *Paul!*

to the Jews, not to us"—wait! You and I were told, since the Spirit came at Pentecost, to be *filled with the Spirit* (Eph. 5.18). *Have we been?* Again,

"Now the God of hope *fill you* with all joy and peace in believing, that ye may abound in hope, in the power of the Holy Spirit" (Rom. 15.13). Are *you* filled with all joy and peace, abounding in hope, walking in the power of the Holy Spirit? If so, thank God! If not, be still and hearken to the Spirit's searching words concerning Israel's **failure to enter in**—and learn of what *your* heart, like theirs, is capable.

God has promised, when He saves national Israel, to "take away the stony heart out of their flesh, and give them a heart of flesh" (Ezek. 36.26). With us Christians, *Christ* is to be received into the heart, and dwell there by faith. Mark, *that only* is a normal Christian condition. Paul is praying for it for the Ephesians, even though they had been "sealed with the Holy Spirit of promise" (Eph. 1.13). Still "he bows his knees unto the Father . . . that He would grant them . . . that *Christ might dwell* in their hearts through faith"—a definite thing; only upon condition of which could they be "filled unto all the fullness of God" (Eph. 3.14-19).

Be reasonable! To whom could God speak with unavoidable plainness and warning except to the Hebrews? There is *one* Body: we know that. Before God since Calvary there is no difference between Jew and Greek; all are sinners. But God, Who has declared all human hearts alike, had already for over 1500 years had direct dealings with Hebrew hearts, even the hearts of those who had received promises, and had had many blessings and deliverances. And the record of it is already written in the Old Testament. It would be pride and self-importance, yea, presumption, for a Gentile professing Christian to say, "Inasmuch as this epistle is addressed to Hebrews, it is not addressed to me." But have you not seen from this very book of Hebrews that it lifts hearers completely away from earth into a heavenly calling? Just as you, Gentile believer, though a "sinner of the Gentiles," have by unexpected, limitless grace been sought, and brought into the same calling.

For you or me to pass this epistle over "to the Jews," is to blind ourselves to, and deny, its whole message. A Hebrew believer, reading it and from the heart believing it, would become as free as Paul, and could say, along with that great apostle (to the Gentile Galatian believers), "I beseech you, brethren, become as I am, for I also am become as ye are." He was wholly a heavenly man, and no racial or religious distinctions were left in his heart or life!

Frankly speaking, brother, if after reading **Hebrews** you say, "That epistle is written to the HEBREWS," and you keep Hebrew believers as a distinct class in your heart, it is you that have missed the great Divinely intended effect of **Hebrews**. *You* are the loser. You do not believe that all are one in Christ! Also, you have missed the joy of being enlightened by the blessed Holy Spirit concerning God's past ways on earth.

We now come again to one Scripture quoted and re-quoted three times in these chapters: Psalm 95.7:

Verse 7: Today if ye shall hear His voice, Harden not your hearts. The argument for the present, peculiar attention of the Hebrew believers is, that **Today if ye shall hear His voice, harden not your hearts,** was said **in David so long a time afterward:** that is, after the sad events of the wilderness forty years. So that, if the Spirit took the wilderness overthrow as a warning for those who should read David's writings hundreds of years later—with how much force should the warning come to believers today—a warning of the treachery of the human heart. We have been examining the "rest" of God, together with such facts as that Joshua* did not give them rest, or God (vs. 8) **would not have**

---

*As for Joshua himself, his words in Joshua 24.15, "As for me and my house we will serve Jehovah," summarize his wonderful life. But concerning Israel, read Joshua 23:1-4:

"And it came to pass after many days, when Jehovah had given rest unto Israel from all their enemies round about, and Joshua was old and well stricken in years, that Joshua called for all Israel, for their elders and for their heads, and for their judges and for their officers, and said unto them,

"I am old and well stricken in years: and ye have seen all that Jehovah your God hath done unto all these nations because of you; for Jehovah your God, He it is that hath fought for you. Behold, I have allotted unto you these nations that remain."

But alas, in the book of Judges, after Joshua's death, we read,

"Manasseh did not drive out the inhabitants of Beth-shean . . . Ephraim drove not out the Canaanites . . . Zebulun drove not out . . . Asher drove not out . . . Naphtali drove not out the inhabitants . . . but he dwelt among the Canaanites . . . The Amorites forced the children of Dan into the hill-country" (1.27-34), and the like.

Then comes the heart-breaking message from the angel of Jehovah: (2.1-23).

"Ye have not hearkened unto My voice: why have ye done this? . . .. I will not drive them out from before you; but they shall be as thorns in your sides, and their gods shall be a snare unto you."

And then:

"And also all that generation were gathered unto their fathers: and there arose another

spoken afterward of another day. Now let us take *moral* warning of this oft repeated word, TODAY. The writer himself testifies, as he has heard others testify, to the *losing of years* by the failure to hear some Spirit-spoken "TODAY" message, either from the Word directly, or from some faithful messenger, or from what we call "circumstances." May I speak humbly and reverently here? But is not God's long-suffering from the very manner of His dealing with Israel, even now saying again and again, "Today"? This is a word of patient, tender Divine *love*. Creatures of the dust that we are, we should *spring* to obey the voice of the heavenly glory! Some, indeed, have, like Israel, "fallen," "hardened by the deceitfulness of sin"—yea, by that self-deceiving which makes promises to self of a *future* hearkening or obedience, while living in *present* disobedience. I would to God that both you and I and all of us could read Hebrews 3 to 6 with that testimony in our own hearts that God gave to His servant Moses, "My servant Moses—is *faithful* in *all* My house"!

We are more and more impressed that the book of **Hebrews** stands between that salvation set forth in Romans, and the judgment depicted in the book of The Revelation. For the Judge in The Revelation is our blessed Lord Himself (Rev. 1). He stands as Priest-Judge among the seven assemblies called by His name on earth. Then, Chapter 5, He takes the seven-sealed book of universal judgment from God's hand in Heaven. And finally, He comes in Person in the Great Day of the wrath of God the Almighty (Rev. 19). God *does not want us* in the judgment, my friend. Judgment is His "*strange* work" (Isa. 28.21). And He says, "As I live . . . I have no pleasure in the death of him that dieth . . . Wherefore turn yourselves and live"! (Ezek. 33.11; 18.32).

---

generation after them, that knew not Jehovah, nor yet the work which He had wrought for Israel.

"And the children of Israel did . . . evil in the sight of Jehovah, and served the Baalim; and they forsook Jehovah . . . followed other gods . . . provoked Jehovah to anger . . . forsook Jehovah and served Baal and the Ashtaroth. And the anger of Jehovah was kindled against Israel, and He delivered them into the hands of spoilers . . . sold them into the hands of their enemies . . . The hand of Jehovah was against them for evil . . . they were sore distressed."

Graciously, "Jehovah raised up judges . . . Yet they hearkened not unto their judges . . . they turned back, and dealt more corruptly than their fathers . . . they ceased not from their doings, nor from their stubborn way" (2.16-19).

What a sad history!

Do you remember our Saviour's great words in John 5.24?

"Verily, verily, I say unto you, He that heareth My word, and believeth Him that sent Me, hath eternal life, and cometh not into judgment, but hath passed out of death into life."

And His great closing public message in John 12.47:

"If any man hear My sayings and keep them not, I judge him not: for I came *not to judge* the world, but to save the world."

(Christ will be Judge at last! But *now:* "The Father hath given Me a commandment what I should say . . . and His commandment is Life Eternal"!)

Therefore after those blessed epistles, that proclaim the way of Salvation, and before The Revelation, the book of judgment, comes this wonderful *exhortation-epistle* of **Hebrews.** In it God sets His Son and His priestly work before us, and the heavenly worship which alone is real, and in which God yearns that we should join. No wonder, therefore, if He warns us again and again of the treachery of the human heart. *"Let us take heed,"* as we are exhorted in **Hebrews**—for *eternity* is at stake!

9   **There remaineth therefore a sabbath rest for the people**
10   **of God. For he that is entered into his rest hath himself**
11   **also rested from his works, as God did from His. Let us**
     therefore give diligence to enter into that rest, that no
12   **man fall after the same example of disobedience. For the**
     Word of God is living, and active, and sharper than any
     two-edged sword, and piercing even to the dividing of
     soul and spirit, of both joints and marrow, and quick to
13   **discern the thoughts and intents of the heart. And there**
     is no creature that is not manifest in His sight: but all
     things are naked and laid open before the eyes of Him
     with Whom we have to do.

Verse 9: There remaineth therefore a sabbath rest [*sabbatismos*] **for the people of God:** Note (1) that this "rest" is for "the people of God"—here meaning especially the Christ-confessing Hebrews, in view of the past history of their nation. But of course including all "partakers of the heavenly calling." Note (2) this rest "remaineth": that is, it is *future*—not present rest in Christ's work, blessed as that is. For rest in Christ's atoning work for us is constantly attacked by Satan; and often also by reproofs and disturbing of conscience. There must also, as we have seen, be watchfulness against "an evil heart of unbelief." And real rest in Christ's atoning work is accompanied by a godly walk; where the enemy's "devices" must be watched against.

The "rest" itself is here called *sabbatismos,* a "state-of-rest" (cessation from labor or employment). Not in the sense of a weekly occurrence, but in the sense of that eternal state entered into by those who, already new creatures in Christ, enter that New Creation of Revelation 21-22; to which they already *belong,* where all things are *according to God,* where God Himself is at rest: For this is *what is meant by God's rest!**

Verse 10: See pages 119-123

Verse 11: Let us therefore give diligence to enter into that [His] rest—For to these Hebrew believers and to us, God has told how the nation which He brought out of Egypt fell short of even the rest of Canaan. "Diligence" is opposed to that lack of "earnest heed" with its consequent "neglect" (Ch. 2.1-3); and of course to the lack of use of the spiritual "senses" of Chapter 5. 14; and that state of dullness into which their negligence and spiritual sloth, that lack of energy in appropriating Divine grace, had brought them. See II Peter 1.5, 10; and II Corinthians 7.11, 12, where the same word is translated "earnest care." Here the Corinthians were aroused from a state of puffed-up self-satisfaction, to what God calls "godly sorrow," which wrought "earnest care" in them. Read this passage, and note the wonderful seven-fold change in them, which brought the apostle to say that he

---

*"The sabbath was made for man," that is, as a mercy to his *body*, which is part of the *old* creation.

"The Sabbath-rest *(Sabbatismos)* is the consummation of the New Creation in Christ, through whose priestly mediation reconciliation with God will come to pass—the rest of perfect adjustment of all things to God."—Vincent, p. 424.

"Into God's rest, Hebrews 4 teaches us, man in creation never entered. Such natural peacefulness without combat as he may have had then for a moment, cannot be on earth now . . . The rest of God, after the first creation, was short. The rest of men with God passed away like a morning dream.

"God's rest will have its sabbath in the Millennium . . . What is the rest of the New Creation, to which I belong as having died and risen, Christ being my life, the heavenly rest of the Lord's day is the intimation, the day of Christ's resurrection . . . The Lord's day is the happy witness, as far as a day can be, of a better and perfect rest."—J.N.D., Vol. X.

Excellent! But the "rest of God" is in the New Creation (Rev. 21-22), where all is of God, where all not of Him is banished forever, from this NEW CREATION in which those in Christ already are!

was "comforted and of good courage" toward them. This meaning must be brought into Hebrews 4.11, and 6.11.*

We shall find that this "universal earnestness" is a great secret of progress, and the great guardian against the sad condition of the Hebrew believers; who, we are to see in Chapter 5, became "needers of *milk*, and not of solid food . . . without experience of the word of righteousness," instead of teachers of others. Remember, believer, that this world is an "Enchanted Ground." Here again **Pilgrim's Progress,** which astonishes us by its pictures of spiritual *facts* and *folks,* illustrates the danger of lack of diligence in our Christian path. See note† below!

To enter into that rest—Here "that rest" is seen to be a spiritual thing, a Divine return for "diligence" toward the things of God. Then we have, **that no man fall**—Let me quote here Charles Hodge, the Calvinistic theologian: I copy from his **Commentary on Romans,** p. 422, published in Edinburgh, 1875—valued highly in Britain:

"Believers [the elect] are constantly spoken of [in Scripture] as in danger of perdition. They are saved only if they continue steadfast [in faith]. If they apostatize, they perish. If the Scriptures tell the people of God what is the tendency of their sins as to themselves, they may tell them what is the tendency of such sins as to others. Saints are preserved not in spite of apostasy, but from apostasy."

After the same example of disobedience: The last word in Chapter 3, "unbelief," or want of faith, described a condition of heart—not having God and His power and former blessing in view.

---

*"This word 'diligence' indicates universal earnestness in accomplishing, promoting, or striving after anything."—Thayer.

The translation in the old version, **Let us labor therefore to enter into that rest,** is not exact. The true meaning is, to be roused from sloth, and give *all attention.*

†"I saw then in my dream that they went till they came into a certain country, whose air naturally tended to make one drowsy, if one came a stranger into it. And here Hopeful began to be very dull and heavy of sleep. Wherefore he said unto Christian, 'I now begin to grow so drowsy that I can scarcely *hold up* mine eyes; let us lie down here and take one nap.'

" 'By no means,' said the other, 'lest sleeping, we never wake more.'

"*Hopeful.* 'Why, my brother? Sleep is sweet to the laboring man: we may be refreshed if we take a nap.'

"*Christian.* 'Do you not remember that one of the shepherds bid us beware of the Enchanted Ground? He meant by that, that we should beware of sleeping; 'Wherefore let us not sleep as do others, but let us watch and be sober' (I Thess. 5-6).

"*Hopeful.* 'I acknowledge myself in a fault; and, had I been here alone, I had by sleeping run the danger of death!' "

"Disobedience" is the action of the natural heart in this condition. Compare verse 6, in our present chapter. "Lord, increase our faith," was the apostles' prayer. Their Lord rebuked often their lack of faith: "Why are ye fearful, O ye of little faith?" And, "O foolish men, and slow of *heart* to *believe* in all that the prophets have spoken!" Nevertheless, none but Judas had an *"evil* heart of un' belief." Analyze this carefully. All unbelief is evil; but an *"evil heart of unbelief"* is that set over, in the parable of the sower, against the good-ground hearers: "These are such as in an honest and good heart, having heard the word, hold it fast and bring forth fruit." An *evil heart* of unbelief is one that holds fast to sin, and tries to believe at the same time! But this terrible state Paul shows up, in the words, "Holding faith and *a good conscience;* which some having thrust from them made shipwreck concerning the faith" (I Tim. 1.19).

You cannot ride two horses going in different directions; you must let one go. So "an *evil* heart of unbelief" has *chosen evil.* Let us remember that Paul says an apostate is not a backslider: an apostate is one who has, by his own will, turned his back on Christ and Christianity. Having "tasted" all things, he has "fallen away," as we show elsewhere (Ch. 6.4-8).

Whatever God's rest may be, and however we consider it, all who read Hebrews 3.17 to 4.13 honestly, will consent, as we have said, that the prevailing spirit of it is *warning:*

"*If* we hold fast our boldness . . . Harden not your hearts . . . Take heed . . . Not able to enter in because of disobedience . . . Let us fear . . . lest any one of you should seem to have come short of it" . . . **Let us give diligence to enter into that rest, that no man fall after the same example of disobedience.**

The very vision of Israel today, a people without a land, and a land without a people, should warn every believer. Let those who take trips to Palestine, go to the Jews' Wailing-Wall, and listen and take heed!

God is the same God in this day of grace that He was with them under the Law. Then He saved people in mercy: today He does likewise. Then he rejoiced in and blessed men of faith; to' day He does likewise. The Joshuas, Samuels, Davids, Hezekiahs, Jehoiadas and Josiahs; with the Sarahs, Rahabs, Ruths, Hannahs,

and Shunammite women—all who really loved Him and sought
His face, He brought into peculiar blessing: just as He does today.*

But take heed that your bones do not fall in the wilderness!
The early church, as pictured in the book of Acts—are you of it?

"Continuing steadfastly with one accord . . . breaking bread at
home, they took their food with gladness and singleness of heart,
praising God . . . And the Lord added to them day by day those
that were being saved . . . Believers were the more added to the
Lord, multitudes both of men and women" (2.46, 47; 5.14).

And remember our Lord's words, "They [His disciples] are
not of the world, even as I am not of the world." And Paul, to
the Colossians:

"If then ye were raised together with Christ, seek the things
that are above, where Christ is, seated on the right hand of God.
Set your mind on the things that are above, not on the things
that are upon the earth. For ye died, and your life is hid with
Christ in God" (3.1-3).†

Unless a man walks with a tender conscience, he does not want
to be warned or rebuked. To be told, "Give diligence," hints that
he is slothful; "Take heed," that he is thoughtless, if not reck-
less; "Let us fear," that he has false confidence; "Harden not your
heart," that he is capable of that. Most Christians are content

---

*You who have been troubled by your lack of inward rest; who are worried about your
failures and your sins, and are tempted to say, "This passage in Hebrews convicts me:
I am not one of those who shall 'enter into rest.' " Let me ask you: Who were those who
displeased God? Were they not saying, in rebellion, "Let us make a captain, and let us
return into Egypt"? Were they not refusing even to face the path of faith, God being their
mighty Leader, before Whom giants and walled cities are nothing? Did they not talk of
stoning Caleb and Joshua?

Now let us compare *your* condition. Are *you* saying, "The Christian path is too irksome
for me; the difficulties and trials are too great: I am going back into the world"?

You know you are not saying that! The thought fills you with horror. Satan is the prince
of this world—this world which crucified the Son of God!

Do not, therefore, I beg you, misuse this passage of Scripture, (confessedly difficult
though it be). You belong to *Christ*: Your very horror at the thought of relinquishing the
Christian path and returning to the world, proves that.

†A Chicago preacher, a godly man, told me an experience of his:

He said, "Brother Newell, last Sunday morning, I announced my text. 'If any man be
in Christ, he is a new creature: the old things are passed away; behold, they are become
new!' The church, holding about 1000, was full. I said, 'How many of you are Christians?
Please rise.' The audience rose, in the main floor and gallery. I said, 'Please be seated.'
Now I will read my text again: 'If any man be in Christ, he is a new creature.' Will all
the *new creatures* please rise? Here and there, some arose; a few, quite readily; more,
hesitantly; and most of the audience, not at all."

I have never forgotten that incident, the more so that I have seen it corroborated through
many years.

with "church membership," general approval of pastor and people, and such "church duties" as are requested of them.

But will you please tell me how, with only these things, they differ from the Jew, with his synagogue, rabbi, observances, and approvals?

You may answer, "I hold orthodox Christian teachings concerning the Scriptures and the Person and atoning work of Christ." But this, my friend, will not satisfy the book of **Hebrews**; and this, too, is the reason that very many Christians are not satisfied with the book of **Hebrews**—"Written to the Jews," they say!

One of the most solemn passages of the whole Bible follows:

Verse 12: For the word of God is living, and active—Remark that they of old, as well as we, have to do with His *Word*—that which God has magnified above all His Name (Ps. 138.2). For those having to do with God, have to do with that *Word!* All His being and attributes are behind it. It is of eternal consequence that we should have a right perception of the Word of God! It is not merely a book of 66 books, bound between two covers, which you may pick up and lay down as you might any writing of man. Our Lord Jesus said of His own words, "The words that I have spoken unto you *are spirit,* and *are life.*" It will be impossible in the compass of this comment to trace all that God says of the Scripture that "cannot be broken." Notice that the word "For" begins the verse, because verses 12 and 13 give the great reason why there must be earnest *diligence* in this matter of entering into the rest of faith, and going on with God. It might be supposed that the "diligence" in verse 11 concerns man's activity only—diligence in prayer, or any special activity. But this word, "For," brings in God. And how, God? you ask. The answer is astonishing: **For the word of God is living, and active.*** God deals with men not by mere "influences," nor through human "thinking," but through His word, whether written or preached. Compare verse 2.

First, it is "living." That is an amazing statement. It may be be-

---

*The A.V. rendering, "quick and powerful," is doubly unfortunate. First, "quick," as meaning living, is an old word not now commonly used or understood. Second, "powerful" is not a good translation of the Greek word, *energês.* Thayer renders it, "that which is *at work.*"

yond our grasp to know just in what manner the Word of God is "living," except to remind ourselves:

a. That it is the word of *God,* not of a creature. Therefore it can never pass away: "Forever, O Jehovah, Thy word is settled in Heaven" (Ps. 119.89).

b. That the Word of God, being the utterance of living Deity, and as we have seen, not passing away, must abide perpetually in the same vitality and energy as when first spoken, because the Spirit of God Who inspired the words, *does not leave them:* "The Word of God, which *liveth* and *abideth*" (I Pet. 1.23.) This is why believers grow: they feed upon the words that "are life"; and why unbelievers, modernists, who actively reject the Bible as "God spake all these words," find it "a savor of death unto death." For the Holy Spirit, Who alone can impart life, *lives in the words they reject!*

While the Word of God is for *life,* thousands are slain by it; while sadly few hearken and live. The same Word was preached in the parable of the Sower (Matt. 13) to the wayside hearer, the rocky ground hearer, and the thorny ground hearer—that was preached to the good ground hearer. But only the last, "in an honest and good heart," received it. It were better for the others had they never heard.

c. Being the Word of God, it is the utterance of infinite wisdom. Here is no chaff, no possible element of decay. It will be as fresh a billion ages from this moment as now. Spurgeon said, "If, when I go to Heaven, God should say, 'Spurgeon, I want you to preach for all eternity,' I would simply say, 'Give me a Bible, Lord; this is all I shall need.' " Let everyone who has a Bible in his house remember that he has a *living* book there! Being the *logos* (Word) of God, it becomes the *hrêma* (saying) of God,—by the quickening power of the Holy Spirit Who inspired it and indwells it.

Second, it is "active." There are things alive that are not active. I saw a large tortoise at a neighboring zoo the other day. It had life, but hardly activity. Near it was a cage of golden eagles, whose very existence was activity. But the Word of God is not only living, but active. This, people will not believe. But concerning this word, our Lord said, "Take heed how ye hear." That is, the Word of God is always *doing something* to those who hear or read it! When

Jonah cried out to that great city of Nineveh, "Yet forty days, and Nineveh shall be overthrown!" how active God's word through His prophet became!*

We emphasize this example of the activity of the Word of God. It is the **word of God** that has gone forth and searched them out, the activity of **the word of God** only.

And sharper than any two-edged sword—Paul must have been familiar with the sight of the bronze Roman sword of the first century: "Among early double-edged swords, the Roman pattern stands out as a workmanlike and formidable weapon for a close fight," the **Encyclopaedia Britannica** tells us. But how much sharper is the Word of God than any man-made weapon!

And piercing even to the dividing of soul and spirit—At a great camp-meeting I attended many years ago, there was a great deal of prayer. Some 1500 Christians had come together from all over the United States and Canada. I remember Fanny Crosby sitting in the second seat from the front, a dear saint, with Heaven upon her face. One day some one had preached the Word with power in the afternoon, and the people were dispersing. But a negro came running up to the altar, dropped on his knees, and began to cry mightily to God. I truly believe his voice could have been heard a mile. We gathered around him to comfort him, but it was as if we were not in existence. The Word of God had pierced even to the dividing of soul and spirit. Our singing, our talk, meant nothing to the man. He had been a backslidden church member, and as he afterwards told it, "*I saw myself before God's judgment bar! yea, slipping into hell, and the voices of earth meant nothing.*"

Alas, we forget that many come to meetings, enjoy the singing and the organ, yea, the eloquence of the preacher; but never experience **dividing of soul and spirit**. All is "soulical" to them. There is no direct dealing with God.

---

*"The people of Nineveh *believed God;* and they proclaimed a fast, and put on sackcloth, from the greatest of them even to the least of them. And the tidings reached the king of Nineveh, and he arose from his throne, and laid his robe from him, and covered him with sackcloth, and sat in ashes. And he made proclamation . . . Let neither man nor beast, herd nor flock . . . feed nor drink water; but let them be covered with sackcloth, both man and beast, and let them cry mightily unto God: yea, let them turn every one from his evil way, and from the violence that is in his hands . . . And God saw their works, that they turned from their evil way; and God repented of the evil . . . and He did it not" (Jonah 3.5-10).

Here is a church "service": in comes the "choir," who, with "most acceptable performance," and "skillful accompaniment," "render" a musical "number," which, using probably Bible words, brings the audience under a *religious spell*. But is it *spiritual*—of the Holy Spirit? Hear one of them earnestly describe it:

"Hearing God's message while the organ rolls

It's mighty message to *our very souls*."
Certainly, it is to their *souls*, not to their *spirits!*

Then (let us hope), comes a godly preacher, who uses "the sword of the Spirit, the Word of God." He calls sinners to "flee from the wrath to come," to the Cross, where judgment on sin has already fallen. Men, women and even children fall under the power of the Holy Spirit, so that God becomes a living Person with Whom they have to deal. Real conviction has seized them. They have no peace until they are led by the Spirit of God to rest in the blood of Jesus, shed for them. Those who believe God (and none others are ever saved), flock forward, entirely forgetting their "religious" condition of awhile ago, when "the organ rolled," and concerned only with their *spiritual* state before God. The **Word of God, living and active,** has pierced **to the dividing of soul and spirit.** Men deal with God, and God deals with men, not in "soulical" music and eloquence, but in SPIRIT. Those saved have dealt with God as spirits, and will worship Him in their spirits. "God is my witness," cries Paul, "Whom I serve *in my spirit* in the gospel of His Son!" "The Spirit of God" is said to "bear witness with our *spirits* that we are born-ones of God"—not with our soulical faculties, which may *hear the organ roll, feel religious,* and go to hell!*

---

*We repeat, **soul and spirit,** Heb. 4.12, is one of the Scripture proofs that soul and spirit are not one and the same. Another is I Thess. 5.23: "May your spirit and soul and body be preserved entire." Man is here seen as a tripartite being, not merely body and soul. (See author's book, **Romans Verse By Verse,** pp. 11, 211, 306-8.)

This comes out first in Eden: "Jehovah God formed man of the dust of the ground"— there is the body; "and breathed into his nostrils the breath (Heb., *ruach* spirit) of *lives;* and man became a living soul." There is the being, or mode of life, formed by the combination of spirit with body, and the spirit could now look forth upon the creation and take part in its activities. "Mind," as we call it, found its activity in the soul-life, as we read in Gen. 2.19, that "Jehovah God formed every beast . . . every bird . . . and brought them unto the man to see what he would call them." Man had a perception of the respective places in creation assigned to the creatures by their Creator, with Whom he was at that time in blessed relationship.

So in this **dividing of soul and spirit** by the living and active Word of God, people become, praise God, spiritual Christians! In I Corinthians 2.12 to 3.3, there are seen three classes: (1) *natural* men, not born of God; (2) babes in Christ, born of God, but still *carnal*, under prevailing *fleshly* impulses; and (3) *spiritual*, that is, those controlled in mind and life by the blessed Spirit of God, toward Whom, by us, account must be rendered. The Holy Spirit does not present the truth to the soul, to the sensibilities, or to the reason, but *directly* to the human *spirit*.

Of both joints and marrow—The opposite effect from dividing and judging is seen in Ephesians 4.16 and Colossians 2.19:

"From Whom all the Body fitly framed and knit together through that which every joint supplieth, according to the working in due measure of each several part, maketh the increase of the Body unto the building up of itself in love." "The Head, from Whom all the Body, being supplied and knit together through the joints and bands, increaseth with the increase of God."

Physicians have long known that the purpose of the marrow "appears to be to increase the red corpuscles." In the joints is no life: in the marrow, there is. But here in Hebrews 4.12, it is a work of searching out (even for judgment) and for ultimate salvation. It is no mere figure of speech, but just as **soul and spirit** of this verse denote different parts of man, so the body is, as it were, opened up, even in **both joints and marrow,** by the judging, living Word of God."*

And quick to discern the thoughts and intents of the heart:

The doctrine that man is only "body and soul" has enabled fallen man to exalt this "mentality" of his, and to dream that it is the spirit. So there are theological seminaries today that claim to "prepare men for the ministry" by a course of mental exercises in theological lessons in "church history," and other studies. But this leaves out the Holy Ghost Who came at Pentecost! It does not treat man as a *spirit*, which spirit alone has communion with God. A theological "training" that leaves out the Holy Ghost, is a daily insult to the God of Pentecost!

*Many years ago, I was called to the home of a beloved and very prominent Christian worker to talk to his daughter, it being hoped that I might lead her out of her attitude of despair of salvation. Both she and her father told me her story.

She had engaged in Christian service in another land along with her parents, and had become deeply infatuated with a Christian writer known the world over. When assurance of her own salvation began to fail her, she saw this man as *her idol*. As I quoted to her several Scriptures which spoke of God's sovereignty in grace, and His willingness to receive any, and reminded her that His Word is living, and active . . . piercing even to

We have known people suddenly arrested in their deepest being by reading a verse of Scripture. The thoughts, and necessarily, the intents of the heart, they found discerned, and themselves the object of an infinite Intelligence, but yet an Intelligence not like that at Siani, when the glory and power and majesty of God were openly displayed; but in the written Word of God, which, being "living and active," had pierced them. This piercing may have resulted in their conviction of sin, and accepting Christ and salvation; or it may have been resisted. Nevertheless, the power of the Word of God is here seen, and we greatly need to meditate upon it in these days.

Verse 13: The Word of God brings everything out into the light: **All things are naked and laid open before the eyes of Him with Whom we have to do.** As David said to Solomon, "Know thou the God of thy father, and serve Him with a perfect heart and with a willing mind; for Jehovah searcheth all hearts, and understandeth all the imaginations of the thoughts" (I Chron. 28.9). And Hannah, in her great prayer: "Jehovah is a God of knowledge, and by Him actions are weighed." And Solomon, in his prayer of dedication: "Render unto every man according to all his ways, whose heart Thou knowest (for Thou, even Thou only, knowest the hearts of all the children of men)."

14 **Having then a Great High Priest, Who hath passed through the heavens, Jesus the Son of God, let us hold**

15 **fast our confession. For we have not a high priest that cannot be touched with the feeling of our infirmities; but One that hath been in all points tempted like as**

16 **we are, sin apart. Let us therefore draw near with boldness unto the throne of grace, that we may receive mercy, and may find grace to help us in time of need.**

Verse 14:   These Hebrew believers are here exhorted to "hold fast" their confession. "Confession" of what? First, that Jesus is the Son of God; second, that as the Son of God He is our Great

---

the dividing of soul and spirit, of both joints and marrow; and said that we may throw ourselves completely upon His mercy, she suddenly screamed to her father:
    "Do you not see? I am *dying!*" She stretched forth her arms: "See! they are *dead!* My *bones* are drying up! God has forsaken me, and I know it!"
    No persuasion of either her father or myself availed in the least.
    "I am nothing but *soul*—I'm *all* soul! My *spirit is dead!*" she would scream.
    I kept in touch with her father. He wrote me that she died, despairing!

High Priest; and, third, that He has put away, at the Cross, all our sins forever; and fourth, that, raised from the dead, He **passed through the heavens.** The connection of this last clause with Chapter 7.26, "Such a High Priest became us, holy, guile-less, undefiled, separated from sinners, and made *higher than the heavens,*" is very manifest.

Now what does **passed through the heavens,** mean? It means that all earthly priesthood and ceremony and temple are abandoned by God during this dispensation, and that worship is carried on in Heaven alone! It was one thing for Jesus to be born King of the Jews and to go about "doing good, and healing all that were oppressed of the devil," God manifestly with Him, calling Israel to receive their Messiah: they refused—they crucified Him.

It is another thing that now He has been "declared to be the Son of God with power, according to the Spirit of holiness, by the resurrection from the dead." The "mystery of godliness" writ-ten by the Spirit through Paul in I Timothy 3.16 is "without con-troversy great." But its first term reads, "He Who was manifested in the flesh"; its fourth, "preached among the nations"; and its sixth, "received up in glory."

We repeat, worship is now carried on in Heaven alone, for since Christ's death, the worshiper is *nigh* to God. That is, he is to go into the holiest of all, "by the blood of Jesus, by the way . . . a new and living way, through the veil, that is to say, His flesh," as we shall see in Chapter 10.19 ff, the great exhortation passage of **Hebrews.** "We [believers]" says Paul, "are the [real] circumcision, [those identified in death with Christ, Who was cut off out of the land of the living] *who worship by the Spirit of God,* and glory in Christ Jesus, and have no confidence in the flesh" (Phil. 3.3).

We cannot therefore state too strongly that there is no earthly worship now; that true worship is in the Spirit, Who, blessed be God, is here with us, but is also in Heaven. He acts in, for, and through believers wholly and only on the ground of Christ's ac-complished work, and of His being received up in glory, and of His having **passed through the heavens.** The believer has the same blessed rights in the presence of the Father as belong to the Son in Whom he is, and Who "appears before the face of God" for him.

Certain further conclusions follow the fact that our **Great High Priest, Jesus the Son of God, hath passed through the Heavens:**

1. All worship or pretended connection with God by men calling themselves "priests" on earth, whether Romish priests or pagan priests, involves sin and rebellion far more blasphemous than that of Korah, Dathan, and Abiram, whom the earth, opening, swallowed up. For by this pretension the Son of God and His one sufficient sacrifice of Himself are despised; and the Most High God is openly insulted by profane wretches.

2. Such worship as is fully pleasing to God is patterned in the book of Acts where the constant presence, superintendence, and guidance of the Holy Spirit are openly confessed by all believers. In those days there were no great "cathedrals," no "ecclesiastical" edifices or titles or forms; but believers *went in to God*, glorying in Him through Christ their Great High Priest. Any variation from this, or from Paul's description in his epistles of the heavenly calling, character, and ministry of the Church of God, must be finally rejected of God, although in His long suffering and grace He may deign for awhile to allow earnest believers to make use of means and methods not set forth in His Word. The believer will be rewarded for all really done in the name of the Lord Jesus; yet all not set forth in the Scriptures must finally be rejected by a Holy God. Wise Christians will ever be most careful, therefore, to "prove all things; hold fast that which is good"—that is, according to the Scriptures.

3. Since the world has crucified the Son of God, **who hath passed through the heavens,** and is awaiting His own return in glory (Ch. 10.13), we well know that no kingdom, no state, will be "conquered by the gospel," but the very contrary! Believers are termed by our Lord in His absence a "little flock." Christendom and the world are fast preparing to bow to Satan's Christ: "All that dwell on the earth shall worship him" (Rev. 13.8). This is no "failure of the gospel," or of the Church, as some, arguing in the flesh, assume! But it is God's permitting man to show what he really is, and on whose side he is. "Popular" religious movements will be judged by the wise believer in the light of all Scripture. Let us take heed, brethren, lest in our heart of hearts we be found "building up a work," rather than waiting

for our Lord from Heaven. One of the articles in the ritual of the Moravians—godly and missionary saints—reads thus: "From the unhappy desire of becoming great, Gracious Lord, deliver us!"

We might illustrate the indifference of Christendom to our **Great High Priest Who hath passed through the heavens,** and to the worship now going on in Heaven, by an imagined visit to the camp of Israel of old.

Every Israelite knew that a morning and an evening lamb were offered daily as burnt offerings to Jehovah; and that four other great sacrifices (two of them having to do with the forgiveness of sin) had been provided, and minutely described by God to Moses and Aaron; in addition to the Great Day of Atonement once a year, the great yearly feasts, the weekly Sabbath, and other celebrations. They had been told to teach their children the meaning of these things, especially of the Passover, by which they had been delivered from Egypt by the shedding of the lamb's blood.

Let us in imagination step up to this man calling himself an Israelite, and hold converse with him.

"No," he says, "I don't give any thought to the daily offerings. The priest is supposed to attend to all that! I do not see anything in it anyhow but a form. And so with the Great Day of Atonement. As for the Passover feast, and the others, I meet my friends there. But as for remembering that the blood of the lamb down in Egypt long ago kept the destroyer from smiting the Israelites whose tents were marked with it—I rather regard that as a fable. The weekly Sabbath also, frankly, would get to be a burden to me were it not for the social feature—meeting friends and acquaintances."

"Yet you call yourself an Israelite?" we ask. "Oh, yes, certainly!" Here then is a man who does not *regard* the presence of the Creator God in yonder tabernacle, though he owes life, breath, and all things to Him. Furthermore, all the priestly functions going on there, meant to teach him deep truths, and draw him close to the God of Israel, mean nothing to him!

Alas, it is so in the professing church! There is a great priesthood being exercised in Heaven. Sacrifices are not now being offered up, because the Son of God and Son of Man offered Himself once for all, at infinite cost, to put away man's sin. But there is a worship going on in Heaven: the Holy Ghost has come. The saints delight to remember Him Who died for them—not only on the Lord's Day, at the Lord's table, in remembrance of Him, but every day! Christ is for them, as it were, the "morning and evening sacrifice." The value, power and infinite blessedness of this acceptance before God in their behalf is ever before them. These are *the saints of God.*

But, alas, there are those who "go to church," and "sit . . . as My people," as God said to Ezekiel; and sing the songs, hear the sermon, greet their friends, praise the preacher, then go home, to feast at dinner, and "enjoy themselves," as best they may.

But where is God, where is Christ, where is the Holy Spirit in all this? *The Living God, they know not.* The Great High Priest, and the worship belonging to the heavenly calling, they care not for. The Holy Ghost, they have not.

Ah, if it were only one here and there! But there are thousands upon thousands, to whom the sense of the fearful need of the shed blood of Christ on their behalf has never come; to whom the un-utterable rest of faith in that blood, and the ecstatic sweetness of a purged conscience have never come; to whom the "entering in by the new and living way," and the "drawing near to God" by the blood of Christ, with Him as a **Great High Priest Who hath passed through the heavens,** mean nothing; to whom the glad singing that has begun in Heaven to go on for all eternity, has never opened on their ears! "Church membership," the selection of a "denomination," the following of some petty "program," even jealousy for certain "standards,"—that is all there is to it.

Once in awhile, in marvellous mercy, God puts forth a hand in sovereign grace and rescues some soul from this unconscious death and damnation, and there is joy in Heaven!

In contrast to cold, indifferent, professing Christians, neglectful of the priesthood and worship in Heaven, there are earnest, gra-cious souls who find hindrances and difficulties in laying hold of Christ's benefit to us as *Priest.* For to those who have heard and believed the true gospel of Christ's having fully settled their ac-count, actually borne their judgment, and put away their sin by His blood at the Cross, unless the doctrine of Christ's priesthood

in Heaven has been thoroughly explained, there will arise per-
plexity and self-condemnation, when assaults and accusations of
Satan are made upon the soul, and experimental peace is destroyed.

For the question arises in such a heart: "Since Christ 'made peace
by the blood of His Cross,' why do I not experience peace?" And
further, when God's providence permits to arise circumstances
which, looked at in themselves, test the faith and seem to hide His
face; and most especially when upon searching their hearts they
can find no cause for such Divine withdrawal of comfort; and
even earnest supplication seems to avail nothing; I say, unless the
true doctrine of Christ's work as Priest on our behalf in Heaven
be diligently taught and received, there will be much spiritual
trouble.

For almost universally the human heart expects a priest to *do*
something God-ward. The thought that *all has been done,* that
Christ at God's right hand is NOT making propitiation for us,
but is acting upon the basis of propitiation *already made*—His
work God-ward having been finished; that He has entered in,
"having obtained eternal redemption"; that there is "no more
offering for sin"—this great fact tests the reality of our faith in
Christ's work to the very utmost.

I have met thousands upon thousands of Christians, but, as I
look back, I can remember few indeed whose presence gave one a
consciousness that they had untroubled *rest.* Many, of course, were
relying upon Christ and His work and had learned to view their
own righteousnesses as filthy rags. But among even the most earnest
and "consecrated" of these, the majority seemed yet to be engaged
in what one might call an inward struggle, or were at least longing
after a "higher state of grace" in themselves.

Yet there have been souls who have come into an unbroken
abiding in God according to I John 4.16: "He that abideth in love
abideth in God, and God abideth in him." I remember in particular
many years ago sitting on the bank of the Hudson, above New
York, having a long talk with a Christian gentleman from England.
In this man I found no vestige whatever of struggle or aspiration.
The very atmosphere of his presence was one of quietness, of satisfaction, of utter absence of all apprehension, or creature-fear. Rest,
depth, devotion—all these breathed forth from him, quite unknown
to himself.

For I found, as we talked and talked, that rest in Christ was perfected in him to a degree I had never thought possible! Faith with
him was no effort: was not Christ God the Son? Had not Christ
put away sin for ever on the Cross? Did Christ not live at God's
right hand, and live *for him* and *in* him *as* "the hope of glory?"
Whatever struggles over these matters he may have had, they were
all past. The verse that seemed to sum up his life was the third verse
of our present chapter in **Hebrews**: "We who have believed *do
enter into that rest.*" The influence of that conversation was to me
a revelation—became to me a voice.

You may say, Among all the twelve there was only one such
disciple. Yes, I know it. And the others recognized it (Jno. 13.23-
26). But did not John's attitude of simplicity of *faith* make true in
his experience, "We know and *have believed* the love *which God
hath in our case*"? And see Stephen in Acts 7.

It is hard indeed for our poor legal hearts to surrender to this
mighty fact: that *not* our devotion or consecration, or will to serve
or suffer, but our FAITH is addressed, when our Lord says, "All
things are possible to him that *believeth*" (Mk. 9.23); and, "As
therefore ye received Christ Jesus the Lord [by simple faith], so
keep walking in Him" (Col. 2.6).

And who, I pray you, has the right to believe? Well, Paul wrote,
in the Spirit, "sinners; of whom I am chief" (I Tim. 1.15); and,
"The life that I now live in the flesh I live by the faith of the Son
of God, Who loved me and gave Himself for me."

"Thou sayest, Fit me, fashion me for Thee.
    Stretch forth thine empty hands, and be thou still:
O restless soul, thou dost but hinder Me
    By valiant purpose and by steadfast will.
Behold the summer flowers beneath the sun,
    In stillness His great glory they behold;
And sweetly thus His mighty work is done,
    And resting in His gladness they unfold.
So are the sweetness and the joy Divine
    Thine, O beloved, and the *work is Mine.*"—Ter Steegen.

Now tell me why all the mighty priestly work of Christ in
Heaven should not be made good in your case. Do you plead you
are unworthy? That is a plea of one who does not yet know *grace*.

Grace is for the *unworthy*! As long as you and I are disappointed in ourselves, we show that we have been hoping in ourselves. When we have failed, it is our own strength we have, in our folly, leaned upon. If you are one of "them that are tempted" (2.18), one of the "ignorant and erring" (5.2), you are one of those to whom our Great High Priest freely affords His infinite blessing, as our next verse reads:

Verse 15: For we have not a High Priest that cannot be touched with the feeling of our infirmities; but One that hath been in all points tempted like as we are, without sin.*

This is what we longed for! You remember how old Eli, the high priest of Israel, misjudged Hannah, who was in deep affliction and earnest prayer. As she prayed, he "marked her mouth . . . and thought she had been drunken." Not so with our High Priest! He never misjudges, always understands. How tenderly He restored Peter after his denial. What a blessed comfort, in our weakness and infirmities, to know that we have a Great High Priest able to be touched with the feeling of our infirmity!" No matter how weak and failing we realize ourselves to be, our position in Him never changes. No matter what the darkness may be, our Great High Priest ever appears before the face of God for us; and He is the same yesterday and today and unto the ages, able as when on earth to be **touched with the feeling of our infirmities**—yea, all the infirmities of His own!†

---

*"May God in His mercy give us a true insight into the glory of what is offered us in these words—even this, that our High Priest, Whom we have in heaven, is One Who is able to sympathize with us, because He knows, from personal experience, exactly what we feel!

"For we have not a high priest who is not able to sympathize with our weaknesses. The writer uses the two negatives to indicate how common the thought is which he wishes to combat. A rich king, who lives every day in luxury,—can he, even though he hear of it,—*can* he fully realize what it means for the poor sick man, from year to year, never to know where his daily bread is to come from? Hardly! And God, the glorious and ever-blessed, can He truly feel what a poor sinner experiences in his daily struggle with the weakness and temptations of the flesh? God be praised! *Jesus* knows, and is able to sympathize. He is one who hath been in all things tempted like as we are, without sin." And He is *God the Son!*—Murray, *"The Holiest of All."* p. 168.

†I recently had a talk with a dear friend who has had much infirmity of body, but who was at this time deeply concerned with another phase of infirmity. "So often," he said, "for days at a time, I do not seem to be able to get hold of anything. Even my hold on God seems gone, and a sense of weakness which is indescribable overwhelms me. Whether it is nervous weakness, or mental collapse, or a direct attack of the enemy, I do not know. What shall I do?"

I read to this friend Paul's words in II Corinthians 12.9, 10, with the Lord's answer to

"Touched"—what a beautiful word! What a continual tenderness! And it is not the emotion of pity here, nor feeling *for* us, as of one far off from us, but of feeling *with* us— sympathy. For we read further, but **One that hath been in all points tempted like as we are.** Tempted directly by Satan, assailed by all the wiles of our great enemy, passing sinless and holy through all; tempted by circumstances so adverse as to seem as if God had forgotten Him: no place to lay His head. Tempted by the continual unbelief of the Jews, and of His mother's children; tempted and tried constantly by the little faith and slowness of heart of His own disciples, for whom He cared as the very children of the bridechamber. We praise God for this word, **in all points tempted like as we, sin apart.**

The word "yet" inserted in both the Authorized and the Revised versions here, "yet without sin," is an utter hindrance, instead of a true translation. The Greek reads, "tempted like as we, *without sin*," or, "*sin apart.*" The Greek word for without, *chōris*, signifies having no connection with, no relationship to. Temptation does not involve sin. Twice in this epistle, here and at Chapter 9.28, occurs this remarkable expression, *chōris hamartias*, apart from sin.

It may throw light on the first occurrence to look at the other, where we read that Christ, "having been once offered to bear the sins of many, shall appear a second time, apart from sin, to them that wait for Him, unto salvation" (Ch. 9.28). Every thoughtful reader will at once see the meaning of *chōris hamartias* here, for we know that our Great High Priest, Jesus the Son of God, hath been "manifested to put away sin by the sacrifice of Himself" (9.26), so that, having been thus "once offered to bear the sins of many," when He appears the second time, it will be **apart from sin.**

---

his three times beseeching that his "thorn in the flesh" might be removed—(a physical infirmity, but a "messenger of Satan" to keep "buffeting" him: that he "might not be exalted overmuch"): "He hath said unto me, My grace is sufficient for thee"; and Paul's wonderful response:

"Most gladly therefore will I rather glory in my weaknesses, that the power of Christ may rest upon me. Wherefore I take pleasure in weaknesses, in injuries, in necessities, in persecutions, in distress, for Christ's sake: for when I am weak, then am I strong."

I rejoice to say that my friend seemed comforted. He had never thought of glorying in weaknesses, taking pleasure in infirmities. It is for such cases as this that our Great High Priest, the Forerunner for us, has entered in, and supplies to us His strength—HIS—His OWN strength!

Clearly, whether we read here the expression *chôris hamartias,*
apart from sin, as referring to Christ Himself or to us, whose
sins He bore, the sin question will not come up for the saints at
His coming. Therefore the phrase, *choris hamartias,* denotes an
entire absence of sin, in Chapter 4.15, as in Chapter 9.28.

Our Lord was tempted by Satan to fall down and worship Him.
Does this mean that there was an inclination in Christ to do such
a thing? What folly to think of it! He was the "True Light"
which shone in the darkness, and the darkness "overcame it not."
This is the testimony of the Spirit in John 1.5, 9. There was nothing of the inward struggle that we know when tempted. It is a
Satanic delusion, and next door to blasphemy, to assert that in
order to be **in all points tempted like as we,** Christ must have had
an inward inclination to the evil! There are two great truths you
must hold fast; the truth about our Lord's *Person,* the truth about
His *Work.* In all His temptations—and He endured them all—He
was *God,* Who had spoken the word of creation of the worlds,
and upholds them "by the word of His power" (Heb. 1.2, 3).

Though our Great High Priest is man, it is blessed indeed to
have Him called in this great passage **Jesus the Son of God,** able
to be touched with the feeling of our infirmities, having passed
through the path of temptation—suffering therein because He
was the infinitely Holy One, loving righteousness and hating iniquity, and being of course **apart from, without, sin.** Even in our
little life on earth we know of temptations of virtuous, high-
minded persons who have been approached by those who would
ensnare them; and the very suggestion of the evil they abhorred
has made them suffer, for they hated the evil. Now One infinitely
above us, our blessed Lord, has this testimony borne to Him as
man: "Thou hast loved righteousness and *hated iniquity*" (Ch.
1.9).

The perpetual object of the devil is to malign Christ to every
believer, and to deny His work. But "Jesus Christ is the same yesterday and today, yea and forever"—the *Jehovah* character. Loving
righteousness and hating evil marked every moment of our Lord's
existence on earth, as well as before He came. Therefore leave out
the dishonoring "yet" of the translations of Chapter 4.15; and
behold your Lord, assaulted by every evil which Satan, or the world

of evil men, or poor faltering disciples could bring to bear upon Him, going steadily on, delighting to do the will of God. Such is the Captain of your salvation!

Verse 16: Let us therefore draw near with boldness unto the throne of grace—This is the throne of God in all His holiness, righteousness, and truth. It is to *Him* we come. The word "There' fore" refers us to verses 14 and 15, which we have just studied. Our Great High Priest is there, at God's right hand, and of course believers are in Him, as brethren. (See Ch. 2.11.) Thence our boldness. "He appears before the face of God for us," and "ever liveth to make intercession for us." Our Priest does not stand between us and God, as did Israel's; but He is Head over the house of God, of which we are a part; and in the midst of the saints He leads our worship and our praise.

But note that it is not to Him we are told to draw near, but **unto the throne,** unto *God:*

1. God must be on His throne.

2. God's name is not mentioned here, but the throne only. The whole passage (vss. 14-16) is filled with the presence of our Great High Priest, and it is His presence there that gives us boldness.

3. But it is **a throne of Grace.** Here is an amazing word, for Grace means favor, and **a throne of grace** is dispensing favor. It is in the value of the finished work of Christ on our own be' half that the believer is welcomed to the throne of Grace. It is the throne of the infinitely holy God, twice in this epistle called "the throne of the Majesty in the heavens," where is the blessed and only Potentate, the only God, called in Chapter 12 "the Judge of all," Who has judged our sin in His own Son and has chosen to place believers in Christ Risen, making them thus the righteousness of God Himself, in Christ. This is immeasurable, yea, unutterable grace. Grace is always sovereign. There are only two principles: grace and "merit," as it is called. But of merit we have none: "There is none righteous." We must not, cannot avoid this, that we, no matter what we have been or what we have done, are being received (by Divine sovereign grace) as Christ our Lord was received. There are *no degrees* of acceptability or acceptance before God. Every believer is received *according to the full, finished work of Christ!*

This is without doubt the hardest (though most simple and most insisted upon) truth for believers to grasp, in all the book of **Hebrews.**

But we must conceive of God's throne being now **a throne of grace**—yea, that Grace which gave His Son to bear sin, made to be sin in our behalf. For us to hang back is to doubt God's heart of mercy; to limit Christ's unspeakable sacrifice, and secretly to conceive that God must have something against us because of past sin or failure: and this is that unbelief which is the great secret foe of the God of truth and grace. Believer, exercise your heart over and over on this wonderful phrase, **the throne of grace.** To the most of even real Christians, it is a throne where possible judgment awaits them, or a throne which puts them "on probation," or (as the Reformed Theology will have it), a throne where, behind and beyond everything else, Law, and not Love, reigns and must reign.*

It is called a **throne of grace** in view of the *purposes* of God. In us is to be exhibited, for all eternity, age after age, and more and more in each age, the infinite kindness of God Whose name is Love (Eph. 2.7). It is a throne at which no charges against sinners are made. For we read, "God was in Christ [at the Cross] reconciling the world unto Himself, *not* reckoning unto them their trespasses" (II Cor. 5.19). That dispensation is on, in which our Lord Jesus Christ said,

"If any man hear My sayings, and keep them not, I judge him not . . . the word that I spake, the same shall judge him in the last day" (Jno. 12.47-8). But the "Last Day" is not yet; the day of *Grace* is here, and, praise God, has not yet closed, as it will close! In all the unspeakable blessedness of that friendship toward sinners which the Friend of sinners displayed when in this world, **the throne of grace** exists. Now if God chooses to sit in grace, not judgment, let poor sinners hasten! and let believers, no matter

---

*In the Church time of Rev. 2 and 3, indeed, our Lord Jesus says, "I also overcame, and sat down with My Father in His throne." But when the dispensation changes from grace to judgment at Rev. 4.1, there is the throne of the thrice holy One surrounded by the four-and-twenty thrones of the elders, and before Whom they and the four living ones fall, crying out, "Holy, holy, holy!" Again at the close of the Millennium, there is the Great White Throne, of the Last Judgment; and finally, the "throne of God and of the Lamb" of the eternal state (Rev. 21, 22).

how faint of heart or how failing in life, hasten into this throne room! There can be no mistake: God cannot lie.

Let us come boldly—As we have seen (cf. Ch. 3.6, and see comment there) the word "boldness" is literally, *all-spokenness* —meaning, "Unreservedness in speech; freedom, frankly, without concealment; fearless confidence: the diametric opposite of being covered with shame" (Thayer). So let us not be ashamed or fearful, but *have boldness* before such a throne.

To close, then, this wonderful verse, we have the object to be obtained in thus **coming boldly to a throne of grace**: first, **that we may receive mercy**—special favor, Divine blessing; second, that we **may find grace to help in time of need.** Let us analyze these briefly.

Paul speaks of himself as one who had "obtained mercy" at his salvation; and again, as one who had "obtained mercy" to be faithful—in his ministry. National Israel also in the future is to obtain what she has *never yet* obtained—mercy (Hos. 2.19). Now here in **Hebrews** the believer is exhorted, having this Great High Priest touched with the feeling of his infirmities, to come boldly **unto the throne of grace, to receive mercy.** This is not the mercy of salvation, for he has already received that.* Unsaved people are not told that they have a Great High Priest, for they have not, till they have believed the marvelous news of the gospel. But, you say, when is the believer then to come to **receive mercy?** Well, let him come according to the example given in Scripture. David said:

"Evening, and morning, and at noonday, will I complain, and moan;

And He will hear my voice" (Ps. 55.17);

and,

"At midnight I will rise to give thanks unto Thee
Because of Thy righteous ordinances" (Ps. 119.62).

The "mercy" referred to in Hebrews 4.16 is explained by what follows: Here is a faithful, praying believer, daily going to God, pouring out his soul—for he is always in a state of dependence, as we know. Then suddenly, unexpectedly, there comes a

---

*Mark that "mercy" here is a noun. The verb, which we know in Lk. 18.13, *"Be Thou merciful* [or propitiated] to me a sinner," sets forth initial salvation. See Rom. 9.15, 16, 18; I Tim. 1.13, 16. But it is special *mercy* to a saved person that Heb. 4.16 speaks of.

time of need, need of special grace for special testings or even chastenings (see Ch. 12). False friends betray, or weak Christians try his spirit. Testings of all kinds come. But peculiarly does the saint find **times of need** when the great enemy is permitted specially to attack him. But lo, such a one has already **obtained mercy** for just such a **time of need:** so that when they arrive, he **finds grace to help** him. Grace in this sense is the direct supplying by the almighty power of God, by the indwelling Spirit, of such Divine help as the believer needs at any time.

Alas, perhaps all of us will give ready testimony that we can trace our spiritual failures to a lack of prayer* beforehand—a lack of a **drawing near with boldness unto the throne of grace.** One who has "obtained mercy" is written down in God's book for help when "time of need" arises. This is most important. We ought not to postpone our appeals until the time of *need*. Then we may be distraught, we may be perplexed; then we may be bereaved, ill in body, or overwhelmed by some tremendous call or opportunity for service. But if we obey this great command of verse 16, and, outside the time of need, **draw near with boldness unto the throne of grace,** we shall find ourselves made inwardly conscious of a Divine "yes" which will give us wonderful confidence when the **time of need** comes and we need **grace.**†

---

*It is to be carefully noted that that operation of the Holy Spirit within us which enables us to pray is not here set before us, as elsewhere. Why? Because in Hebrews God is speaking to us *in a Son*. It is the Person and work of Christ that are in view. We should, however, remember such verses as Eph. 2.18: "Through Him [Christ] we both [Jew and Gentile believers] have our access in one Spirit unto the Father." Here the Trinity is before us: we come *through Christ, the Spirit* having the enabling power in prayer, unto *God as Father*. Neither of these relationships is set before us in Hebrews. But, as we said, the Person and work of Christ, by Whom and by which we have the right to, and do, draw near to God in Heaven, are set forth.

†Many years ago, in the Moody Institute, it fell to me to direct the afternoon and evening gathering of all the students. Together with my helpers, some eleven men, I made the celebration a missionary one. There was manifest blessing.

When all was over, at about ten at night, I said to the young men who had helped, "Let us go into my office and thank the Lord." We went in and knelt to pray. It was in none of our minds to remain long, but just to thank the Lord ere we retired.

But it pleased God to take the meeting in charge. His Spirit filled us. In a few minutes we were on our faces praising God and weeping with joy. How His love melted and overwhelmed us! All sense of distance from God, yea, all sense of self, was gone. Only measureless joy in God, as we knew ourselves the objects of His intimate kindness and love, remained.

There we were until half past three in the morning! And when we dispersed, we were more refreshed, in body and spirit, than at the beginning. After the brethren left, I marked stain after stain of tears upon the floor, where men had wept with joy. Four men,

Not only justification through the blood of Christ, not only our position *in* Christ, do we find in **Hebrews**, but spiritual activity on the part of those who have been "enlightened." There is an entering in, in **Hebrews:** not an entering in to mere doctrines, but into God's *presence.* There is a boldness enjoined throughout the book which is a boldness toward God, in view always of Christ's having put away our sin by His one sacrifice, and having Himself entered within the veil as our Forerunner, appearing before the face of God for us.

And in **Hebrews**, activity of believers culminates in *worship.* To be satisfied with "joining the church," holding "correct doctrine," or engaging in "church activities" or "programs" is far, far from **Hebrews** teaching. In **Hebrews** the believers are all to be *acquainted* with God, to be godly, to be worshipers,* to be pressing on to full growth, to be "imitators of those who through faith and patience inherit the promises."

It is sadly true that many Christians never on earth become such worshipers and praisers of God. Thus they doubly lose. For it is Christ's business in Heaven to see that our needs are supplied, and our trials and temptations met. But God's plan is that we should come *habitually* to the throne of grace. Thus all things are supplied, and we are delivered from this world, and our minds set on the things that are above, as we are enjoined in Colossians 3.1-3.

But the greatest result, infinitely the greatest, is the glory God

---

if not five, became missionaries as a result of that night's visitation.

God may not at all times overwhelm us, as on that occasion, with a sense of His blessedness and love. We walk by faith, not by sight (lit., appearance, vision, or experience). But at all times, under all circumstances, God is love, and believers are invited **to come boldly to a throne, a throne of GRACE!**

*We may note that:

1. *Salvation* brings joy and gratitude: delightful to God, yet not properly worship.
2. A sense of *sonship* brings filial affection, rather than worship.
3. *Union* with Christ (and God) brings a sense of liberty—and blessedness of life.
4. The relation of *Bride*, "espoused to one Husband," Christ, brings a sense of separation from the world to Him: the "first love" (Rev. 2.4).
5. Taking Christ as *Lord* brings a sense of being owned by Him, and delight in service. Christ died and rose again "that *He* might be *Lord*", "Whom I *serve* in my spirit in the gospel of His Son," as said Paul.
6. But *worship* belongs to God as God; and the redeemed will worship forever!

Even Christ said, "My Father" (as being one of the Godhead) but, "My *God*", as having become *man.* Indeed, though He was "equal with God," yet will Christ, Who has, as Man, entered into the holies above "through His own blood," as our Great High Priest, lead the praises and worship of "the great congregation" of His saints forever.

receives from a life filled with prayer and praise. A "heavenly minded" Christian is noted by the world and remembered by the saints. Oh, let us become occupied with this wondrous life of worship and praise!

It is related of the saintly Duncan Matheson in Edinburgh, by a friend who was walking with him one day, that Matheson turned gently to him, saying, "Gang alang, Jimmie, for the Lord ha' a word wi' me. Wait for me." So the friend walked on for several blocks, while Matheson was occupied in some business with God. Then he caught up with his friend.

The great barrier to the love of worship in most hearts is the thought of *distance*—of a gulf between us and our God. Judging in our hearts our nearness to God by our own inner sense of that nearness, we fail to look at Christ (in Whom we are) as having entered in through His own blood into the holies above. *He* is our nearness! We are created in Him, the Risen Christ, and made to "sit with Him in the heavenlies, in Christ Jesus."

How many Christians should daily be "drawing near" the **throne of Grace** in Heaven? Absolutely all! It will never do merely to say, "I am saved. I have believed Romans' truth—justification by faith. And I have believed Ephesians' truth, that I am raised up with Christ and made to sit with Him in the heavenlies." For **Hebrews** takes the heavenly calling for granted, and then says, **Draw near**. Do you yourself, do this? Are *you* offering up "a sacrifice of praise to God continually"? Are *you* a constant worshiper within the veil?

CHAPTER FIVE

1   For every high priest taken from amongst men is ap-
    pointed for men in things pertaining to God: that he
2   may offer both gifts and sacrifices for sins; who can bear
    gently with the ignorant and erring, for that he himself
3   also is compassed with infirmity; and by reason thereof
    is bound, as for the people, so also for himself, to offer
4   for sins. And no man taketh the honor unto himself,
5   but when he is called of God, even as was Aaron. Thus
    also the Christ glorified not Himself to be made a high
    priest, but He [did] that spake unto Him:
        Thou art My Son, This day have I begotten Thee!
6   As He saith also in another place, Thou art a priest
    forever after the order of Melchizedek.

7   Who in the days of His flesh, having offered up prayers
    and supplications with strong crying and tears unto Him
8   that was able to save Him out of death, and having been
9   heard for His godly fear, though He was a Son, yet
    learned obedience by the things which He suffered; and,
    having been made perfect, He became unto all them that
10 obey Him the Author [or Cause] of eternal salvation;
    named of God a High Priest after the order of Mel-
    chizedek.

THIS PASSAGE, THROUGH verse 10, grows out of Chapter
4.14-16. We see in it, first, that the high priests of Israel were
appointed for men in things pertaining to God, to offer both
gifts, and sacrifices for sins. So with us: it is all through Christ.
Second: An earthly high priest could bear gently, because of
being himself compassed with infirmity, and so bound . . . to offer
both for himself and his own sins. Here contrast him with Christ—
Whose sympathy arose not out of His infirmities—for He had none!
(as see Chapter 7.28 and comment there), nor sins (see Ch. 9.14).
Christ's sympathy grew out of His passing all along the path of
suffering to "perfecting": and so being able to be "touched with

the feeling of *our* infirmities"—though *He had no infirmity!* Read again and again Chapter 7.28: "The Law appointeth men high priests, having infirmity; but the word of the oath, which was *after the Law,* [appointeth] a Son, *perfected forevermore!"*

Verse 1: The argument is this: That the high priests of Israel were **taken from among men,** because they were appointed **for men in things pertaining to God.** The word "For," which opens the chapter, while it refers back to the priesthood of Christ (Ch. 4.14-16) both compares and contrasts Him with Aaronic high priests. There are, first in general, **things pertaining to God** which men must have attended to, but which men cannot them-selves attend to. They must have a *priest;* and for us Christ is that Priest,* because, although Son of God, He became man, and was **appointed for men in things pertaining to God.** (See this ex-pression, **in things pertaining to God,** in Rom. 15.17; and in Heb. 2.17, and comment there. Cf. I Chron. 26.32, II Chron. 19.11.)

Both gifts and sacrifices for sins: Note that "gifts" precedes "sacrifices," both here and in other places where this expression occurs (Chs. 8.3 and 9.9), because the chief and normal business of a priest was to receive the gifts and direct the worship of the people. Of course, we know that priesthood is based on sacrifice, and this will be emphasized: see Chapters 7.27; 10.11. But just as in **Hebrews** our Great High Priest leads the worship and songs of the saints, who have access by His blood, and through the veil, His flesh; and by His presence, unto God's very throne: so the high priest of Israel, in all except one day of the year, was "appointed for" Israel **in things pertaining to God:** "first-fruits," "thank-offerings," "gifts," and all manner of wor-ship. On the one day excepted, the Great Day of Atonement, all the sins and iniquities of Israel were confessed by him. All **sacri-fices for sins** throughout the year were under his direction.

It is blessed to reflect that Christ, having offered "one sacrifice for sins forever," is at God's right hand, ready to receive and welcome all gifts from the saints—of praises or of "doing good." See carefully Chapter 13.15, 16.

---

*Even William Kelly says concerning Ch. 5.1-5, "The description of priesthood is general, but with Aaron in view, in order to bring in the wondrous contrast of Christ." Yes, that contrast is brought out in **Hebrews,** but not, we feel, in this passage, for vss. 1-10 set forth the office, work, character, and attitude toward God of a priest, be it Aaron or Christ. It is a description, rather than a contrast, here.

To sum up and continue:

1. Priests are **taken from among men.**

2. Priests are **appointed for men.** A prophet comes forth from God representing God *to men.* A priest goes in on man's behalf *to God.*

3. The priest is occupied with **things pertaining to God.**

4. The priest offers **both gifts and sacrifices for sins.**

5. The priest must be one **who can bear gently with the ignorant and erring.** In the earthly priest's case, the reason is that he himself also is compassed with infirmity; and by reason thereof is bound, as for the people, so also for himself, to offer for sins (vss. 2, 3). In Christ's case (see vss. 7-10), being Himself sinless, He needed not to offer for Himself, **yet learned obedience by the things which He suffered;** thus having been made perfect, He became a High Priest that can be "*touched* with the feeling of *our* infirmities"; but having been "in all points tempted like as we are, sin apart," as we saw in Chapter 4.15. We repeat, He Himself had no infirmity!

6. (Vs. 4): The priest must be **called of God, even as was Aaron.** It is an honor that **no man taketh unto himself. Even Christ also, though He was a Son (vs. 8),** with blessed humility glorified not Himself to be made a high priest, but He [glorified Him] that spake unto Him—that is, the Father!

Thou art My Son,* this day have I begotten Thee:

Verse 6: as He saith also in another place, Thou art a priest forever after the order of Melchizedek. Thus the Father spoke to Christ, according to Psalm 2.7; saluting Him thus, according to Psalm 110.4.

Verse 7: Who in the days of His flesh—This refers, of course, to our Lord's life on earth, from the time He "in like manner partook of blood and flesh," till the time the Father raised Him from the dead. After the resurrection, His consciousness looked

---

*"The name here expresses the same relationship, but it is to the Messiah born on earth that this title is here applied. For Ps. 2, as establishing Him as King in Zion, announces the decree which proclaims His title: Thou art My Son; this day have I begotten Thee, is His relationship *in time,* with God. It depends, I doubt not, on His glorious nature; but this *position for man* was acquired by the miraculous birth of Jesus here below, and demonstrated as true and determined in its true import by His resurrection."—Darby's Synopsis.

back to these **days of His flesh,** as we remember His saying just
before His ascension, "These are My words which I spake unto
you, *while I was yet with you*" (Lk. 24.44). We know, of course,
even from this same chapter in Luke, vss. 39-43, that He had, *after*
His resurrection, flesh and bones—a real human body!

Having offered up prayers and supplications with strong cry-
ing and tears—Our Lord's life was one of prayer, as for example
in a single Gospel, Luke, see Chapters 3.21; 5.16; 6.12; 9.18, 28, 29;
11.1; 22.39-46. But the two Greek words for prayer used here in
Hebrews 5.7 are unusual: one, *deêsis,* meaning *supplication in great*
need; and the other, *hiketêrias,* used only here in Scripture, meaning, *entreating for aid.*

Unto Him that was able to save Him out of death—Here we
evidently have Gethsemane. And what was the conflict in Gethsemane? We have had to turn away from frightful misinterpreta-
tions of the scene there. Some have insisted that our blessed Lord
in Gethsemane was having a struggle with Satan; and some that He
prayed to be delivered from dying! Now I cannot see any persons
present in Gethsemane other than Scripture presents—that is, the
Son and the Father (and a helping angel, at the close: Lk. 22.43).

Nor did our Lord ask the Father to save Him *from (apo)* dying,
but out of [*ek***] death,** into which He was to come. We know
from Psalm 16.10 that He stepped off, at the Cross, into death,
with full faith!

"For Thou wilt not leave My soul to Sheol [Hades];
Neither wilt Thou suffer Thy Holy One to see corruption.
Thou wilt show Me the path of life."

Had He not prayed there on the Cross, "Let not the pit shut its
mouth upon Me"? (Ps. 69.15 is Messianic—see vss. 9 and 21.) It is
the Father (not Satan!) Who is presenting the "cup" to our Lord's
lips in Gethsemane—not to drink at that moment, but that He may
taste, in all the awfulness of it, what it will mean to drink it fully
on the Cross. For the "cup" is the cup of infinite holy wrath against
human sin, involving that *forsaking* concerning which our Lord
cried with such anguish, "My God, My God, why hast Thou forsaken Me?" For from all eternity, in love inconceivable, there had
been the fellowship of the Father and the Son upon the Father's
bosom!

In Gethsemane the Father would have Him *taste* that cup, and *choose* it, while still in fellowship with the Father. Consequently there are those agonizing cries, "My Father, if it be possible, let this cup pass away from Me: nevertheless, not as I will, but as Thou wilt." And as our Lord goes on (the sleeping disciples never helping His prayer), His sweat becomes as great drops of blood falling to the ground!

The Son of God, being Himself God, as the Creator and Upholder of all things, had never had to *obey!* But as we read in Chapter 2.10, "It became Him, for Whom are all things, and through Whom are all things, in bringing many sons unto glory, to make the Captain of their salvation perfect through sufferings." Therefore we read that His entreaties in Gethsemane were "in an *agony*" (Lk. 22.44). But He gets the victory! He consents to the Father—to being *forsaken* by Him. (See the comment on Heb. 13.20, 21.)

So He said, when they came to arrest Him, and Peter's sword was drawn, "Put up the sword into the sheath: the cup which the Father hath given Me, shall I not drink it?"

There is no mention of Satan in that holy struggle. His time was not come. Over those of Adam's race who were sinners, Satan "had the might of death," as we have seen in Chapter 2.14. But Christ had not sinned! Neither was our sin yet laid upon Him. And it is frightful slander to say that our Lord prayed to be saved from *dying!* He had steadily *chosen* the path to the Cross: He began "to show unto His disciples, that He must go unto Jerusalem . . . and be killed, and the third day be raised up" (Matt. 16.21). And read and re-read these verses:

"When the days were well-nigh come that He should be received up, He steadfastly set His face to go to Jerusalem" (Lk. 9.51). No! He expected to die, and He would not even pray for deliverance. In John 12.24ff He said, "Except a grain of wheat fall into the earth and die, it abideth by itself alone; but if it die, it beareth much fruit."

And in verse 27 He definitely states the question:

"Now is My soul troubled; and what shall I say? Father, save Me from this hour."

And His answer is, "But for this cause came I unto this hour Father, *glorify Thy name*."

Be ashamed, all who ever dreamed that our Lord was praying to be kept from dying, or of the fantastic thought that He was praying that Satan might not kill Him, so that He *might* die on the Cross! These things are far from this scene. Our Lord, Who had "emptied Himself," and had trodden the path of poverty, unselfishness, and nothingness in Himself, now was brought to death. He was tasting now in Gethsemane what it would mean on the Cross to be forsaken under wrath by God, with the awful load of our sin upon Him. And He would obtain from **Him that was able to save Him out of death,** the present assurance that He would do this. To what a degree of weakness, then, in His path of obedience in order to become our Saviour and Priest, was the Lord Jesus Christ reduced. As He says in Psalm 22.15, "Thou hast brought Me into the dust of death."

Never one of the human race that had stepped off *with sin upon him,* into physical death, heretofore, but had gone down to doom—no coming back! What our Lord prayed for was that upon His dying such Scriptures might be fulfilled as:

"Thou wilt not leave My soul to Sheol;

Neither wilt Thou suffer Thy Holy One to see corruption.

Thou wilt show Me the path of life:

In They presence is fullness of joy;

In Thy right hand there are pleasures forevermore" **(Ps.** 16.10, 11).

And having been heard for His godly fear—That is, He was not heard merely because He was the Son of God and spotless, but He was about to step into the place of guilty creaturehood: He was to be "crucified through weakness,"* and to live by "the power of God" **(II Cor. 13.4).** Therefore His attitude is, "Thy will be done": this absolutely, finally. His "fear," therefore, was not dread of God, but that reverence to the utmost which belonged to the place of obedience into which He had stepped when He said, "Lo, I am come to do Thy will, O God."

---

*"For Him, death was death. Man's utter weakness, and God's just vengeance [against sin], and alone, without one sympathy, forsaken of those whom He had cherished, Messiah delivered to Gentiles and cast down, the judge washing his hands of condemning innocence; the priests interceding against the guiltless instead of for the guilty,—all *dark,* without one ray of light even from God."—Darby's **Collected Writings.**

Verse 8: Though being a Son, He learned from the things He suffered, obedience. As the Eternal Son, the Second Person of the Deity, One in the counsels of creation itself, the Executor thereof, He needed not to learn anything! But He must "learn *obedience*," even though a Son!

Therefore we read,

"He counted not the being on an equality with God a thing to be grasped, but emptied Himself, taking the form of a servant, being made in the likeness of men; and being found in fashion as a man, He humbled Himself, becoming obedient unto death, yea, the death of the Cross!" (Phil. 2.6-8).

We dwell upon this, our Lord's preparation for Calvary; otherwise the believer, urged by a weak conscience, will be seeking to substitute his own obedience, not realizing that One has already obeyed, "even unto death," as the passage quoted above concludes, "yea, the death of the Cross." Meditate much here. **The Son learned obedience* by the things which He suffered.** Reflection upon the relations of Father, Son, and Holy Spirit, at Calvary, is an ever-flowing spring to the believer's heart: God the Father, holy and righteous, about to take the judgment-seat against human sin; Christ, the Son, Creator, Heir, about to become the Victim, the Bearer of the creature's sin, in, as it were, the creature's place (though ever God)! And all this "through the Eternal Spirit," through Whom all our Lord's ministry was carried out. (See Heb. 9.14.) One reflecting deeply upon this astonishing spectacle, is "lost in wonder, love, and praise"—and this is the Divine desire!

True obedience on our part is an outflow of love, as was Christ's. We also, in the things that we suffer, learn obedience—submission, patience, trust. Nevertheless our obedience, be it what it may, purchases nothing as to salvation—nothing whatever. In this path Christ is alone. We all know this, but it ever bears repeating! Let us remove at this point all thoughts of our obedience

---

*The "obedience" which our Lord learned by the things which He suffered was not legal obedience—that is, to the letter of the Law, which Israel had broken. Those who view Christ as having obeyed the Law, where man had failed and thus giving us His righteousness, miss the great motive of our Lord's obedience—to do the Father's will! And also that great, ever-present love, which chose to lay His life down for the sheep.

It is this constant choosing of the will of the Father that is called *learning obedience*.

to God, or consecration to Him, now or in the future, as "meritorious." It *is* Christ in this passage Who is about to become **the Cause of eternal salvation** (vs. 9)—*Christ*, I say—not Christ's obedience plus our surrender, or even our faith as purchasing aught!

Verse 9: Then we come to the marvelous ninth verse: **And having been made perfect**—Of course, this was not moral perfection, which was His always, eternally, in every moment, every circumstance. He was *perfect* as a babe and as a child; but He "grew, and waxed strong, filled with wisdom." He was *perfect* sitting among the doctors in the temple at twelve years of age.*

But it was most especially in the path of obedience, when He set His face to go to Jerusalem, that His "perfecting" came. As He sent word to Herod: "Go and say to that fox, Behold, I cast out demons and perform cures today and tomorrow, and the third day *I am perfected.*" Christ's moral and spiritual perfection only emphasizes this word concerning the end of the prescribed path of humiliation and suffering culminating at the Cross.† His quench-

---

*He did not assume at that time to teach, nor, indeed, until anointed with the Holy Spirit when He was thirty years of age. But when He was twelve, His simple but profound questions, and His understanding and answers to the questions of the doctors, amazed all that heard Him. And so does the verse following (Lk. 2.51) amaze us: "He went down with them, and came to Nazareth; and He *was subject unto them*" (His parents).

†On His drinking that cup, all consciousness of God as the Father was withdrawn. He was *forsaken!* What fearful three hours of darkness they were to Him—"from the sixth to the ninth hour," with the load of the world's sin, and the guilt thereof, transferred to His shoulders! Others had *committed* the sins. But when laid upon Him, the sins became His, with their guilt. While He cried on the Cross:

"They that hate Me without a cause are more than the hairs of My head" (conscious personal innocence), yet the next verse in that prophetic Psalm 69 reads:

"My sins are not hid from Thee."

He had accepted this fearful bestowment from God's hand—sins, ours, by commission; His now in atonement.

But faith remained: He cried, *"My* God, *My* God!" And hear Him say, as they were nailing Him on the cross, "Father, forgive them"; for He was not yet forsaken (as it seems to me) during the first three hours—the third to the sixth hours upon the Cross. He could still say "Father" to God.

Then came the darkness—corresponding to the outer darkness into which those go who die with sin upon them!

As an accursed thing, as One made sin, as One forsaken, drinking the cup of wrath, He could not speak the word, "Father," but only "My God." For Him to have the witness not only that He pleased the Father ("He that sent Me is with Me, for I do always the things pleasing unto Him"), but the very witness that God was Father; to be reduced to that human consciousness which could only say, "My God," and, "I am a worm, and no man" (Ps. 22.6); there must have been, just as His spirit was departing, a sweet whisper from God, unto which His instant response was, "Father, into Thy hands I commend My Spirit." His blood had been shed. The human spirit leaves the body as the *result* of death

less devotion to the Father's will and word reached its peak there. At the very end He remembered one more prophecy of Scripture, and cried, "I thirst!"

"After this Jesus, knowing that all things are now finished, that the Scripture might be accomplished, saith, I thirst. There was set there a vessel full of vinegar: so they put a sponge full of the vinegar upon hyssop, and brought it to His mouth. When Jesus therefore had received the vinegar, He said, It is finished: and He bowed His head, and gave up His spirit" (Jno. 19.28-30).

Had He not said in His great prayer, "I glorified Thee on the earth, having accomplished the work which Thou hast given Me to do"? (John 17.4).

Therefore we read, **having been made perfect:** tested in every path, tried by every circumstance, tempted with the offer of all earth's kingdoms; denied by one disciple, betrayed by another, forsaken of them all; what fault can we find? None! *God* found none! God raised Him up the third day—eternal testimony to the perfect obedience of His spotless Son!

Verse 9 (contd.): And now, what is the result? **Having been made perfect, He became unto all them that obey Him the Cause** [Gr., *aitios*] **of eternal salvation:** Here two results—both most precious—are announced, flowing from our Lord's **having been made perfect.** First, **He is the Cause of eternal salvation.** The word "Cause" was used to denote that which constitutes an occasion of action, whether favorable or otherwise; that in which the reason and procuring power of anything resides. Note the same word in Luke 23.4, 14, 22. To translate the word "Author" is to look at Christ as an originator, whereas the salvation is of and from *God*—Christ and His work being *the procuring cause* of it. Further, note that it is **to them that obey Him** that He Himself is this procuring Cause. He is the *Lord* Jesus Christ: *Jesus* is His personal name; *Christ* is His official title—God's *Anointed;* and He is *LORD of all!* Because of the suffering of

---

(Lk. 8.55).

He had "borne our sins in His body on the tree." He laid His life down, but He could not cease to be God the Son. Nevertheless, He passed, in bearing sin, in putting it away, into a place where God could not "look upon" Him as "made *sin,*" "become a *curse.*"

How we do thank God for that faith which, even in Divine forsaking, still said, "My God"! Our eternity depended wholly upon that sacrifice—wholly upon that!

death, "God highly exalted Him, and gave unto Him the name
which is above every name" (Phil. 2.9). How wonderful to have
a Cause of salvation, and that eternal, lying completely outside
ourselves in Another!

10 —named of God a High Priest after the order of Melchizedek.

11 Of whom we have many things to say, and hard of
interpretation, seeing ye are become dull of hearing.

12 For when by reason of the time ye ought to be teachers,
ye have need again that some one teach you the rudiments of the first principles of the oracles of God; and
are become such as have need of milk, and not of solid

13 food. For every one that partaketh of milk is without
experience of the word of righteousness; for he is a babe.

14 But solid food is for fullgrown men, even those who
by reason of use have their senses exercised to discern
good and evil.

Verse 10: See Chapter 6.20.

Verse 11: **hard of interpretation**—Difficulty of interpretation
may lie in one of three directions: (1) in the teacher, not fully
instructed, (2) in the subject, often in itself deep and difficult,
or (3), in the hearers who are **dull of hearing.** In this case number
1 was not true—Paul had **many things to say.** Number 2, many
will affirm, was a fact, because of the "difficult" statements concerning Melchizedek. But Paul asserts that neither of these two
was the trouble. It was the hearers, who **by reason of the time
ought to have been teachers,** who through spiritual sloth and neglect had **become dull of hearing.**

Of the subject of Melchizedek, of the "order" of our Lord's
priesthood (see Ch. 7 and comment there), Paul is full, and desirous to speak, but the **many things to say** were **hard of interpretation seeing they were become dull of hearing.** It is not said
that the matters concerning Melchizedek were in themselves
difficult to a spiritual, alert, Bible-absorbed Christian. But those to
whom Paul was writing were **become dull** (sluggish) **of hearing,**
not constitutionally, but dispositionally. Compare "By hearing
ye shall hear," and, "Their ears are dull of hearing," of Matthew
13.14, 15 (lit., "With their ears heavily they have heard"). We
must *apply* this: when God's Word is read or preached publicly,

how many people crowd to the front seats, or cup their ears with
their hands in eagerness? Or, how many hang back (if they come
at all), clinging to the back seats, amused possibly with the least
distraction?—a cat or dog getting into the building and walking
across the platform!

Verse 12: **For when by reason of the time ye ought to be
teachers**—The gospel had been first published to the Hebrews at
Jerusalem at Pentecost, and spread by those who heard it everywhere. We are familiar with the list of some fourteen places mentioned in Acts 2.9-11, of those who heard in their own tongues "the
mighty works of God." Over thirty years after Pentecost comes
the writing of the Epistle to the **Hebrews!** They **ought to be
teachers,** *indeed!* God counts the time since a man has heard the
truth and believed it. He rightly expects progress in Divine things.
Years, months, days, hours, yea, moments, are precious to professing Christians, since the Holy Ghost came down from Heaven
to "enlighten" us, to "lead us into all truth," to empower us in
things Divine, and to bring forth through us and in us that
precious "fruit" for which the Husbandman (the Father) looks
with yearning from those in Christ, the True Vine. Is there
anyone reading these lines who **ought to be a teacher*** who is
still, after a long time, needing re-teaching in the **rudiments of
the first principles of the oracles of God?**

**And are become such as have need of milk, and not of solid
food.** Here are two sad, most solemn, and in the light of what
comes in Chapter 6, terrible facts. First, these long-ago believers
were milk-users—**had need of milk, and not of solid food.** Second,
they had **become** such *again!* Reader, we are always *becoming!*
Not one of us is where he was yesterday. If an unbeliever, you
are further in unbelief today than yesterday. For:

"To sow an act is to reap a tendency,
    To sow a tendency is to reap a habit;
    To sow a habit is to reap a character,
    To sow a character is to reap a destiny."

---

*This of course does not mean that all the saints are to have that special *gift* of teaching
of Eph. 4.11. Yet it does set forth what God expects of those that hear the good news.
"They . . . that were scattered abroad" (and they were NOT the apostles) "went about
preaching the Word" (Acts 8.4). If you have believed and know "the truth of the
gospel," you ought to be a teacher, a witness. And some day the Lord will ask you about
this.

If a believer, you have either become "a bondservant of God," or, you may have **become such as have need of milk,** unable to bear, or undesirous of, the **"strong meat"** which belongs to the word of Christ Risen, and the saints risen with Him—and, to Christ leading the heavenly worship, and you one of the saints entering into that heavenly song, "giving thanks always for all things." Or, you have, as we shall see in Chapter 6.12, been "sluggish," not an imitator "of them who through faith and pa' tience inherit the promises." God, by His blessed Spirit, is ever exhorting us to "*follow on,*" to *grow* in the grace and acquaintance' ship of our Lord Jesus Christ; to "abound in every grace," to be "filled unto all the fullness of God."

It is tragic beyond utterance that this great epistle of **Hebrews** is addressed to Hebrew believers who had **become such as have need of milk**—tragic that Paul had to talk to "babes"! It was indeed difficult to interpret to them the mighty and glorious Melchizedek priesthood, of which the Levitical system could be only a "shadow." "Babes"? Users of milk? Turning back to earthly priests and forms? When only a few brief years had passed since the Son of God walked on earth, Who had put away sin forever at the Cross, and sat down on the right hand of the Majesty on high, a High Priest forever! *Babes?* in need of *milk?* when just now the holy apostles, who had *walked and talked* with this now Risen and Glorified Christ, had been *speaking* to them? *Men,* the apostles were, not babes! Filled with the energy of faith, not "sluggish," were *they! Strong men,* ready for *martyrdom,* "filled with all joy and peace in believing."

Brethren, I am filled with trouble at all this. Can it be possible that human hearts are capable of such shallowness, indifference, ingratitude, sluggishness, unbelief?

"Yes," they say, "Peter was here but now, full of eagerness, putting us in remembrance. But give us a little *milk, warm* milk, and let us sleep! Apollos we heard, mighty in the Scriptures! He stirred us at the moment, but give us just a little *milk* now, and we shall get to *sleep!* Paul we knew, whose presence made Christ real, whose eyes were always ready to weep. We often heard him, and now this letter comes from Italy, from him and those with him. Yes, we remember his holy influence, his deep, wonderful words.

But we have settled down. We no longer like arousing words. Once, perhaps, we did; but we have certain 'standards' that are good enough for us now. Our creed is all written out and settled; we have only to say 'Yes' to it. We find a need, true, in our souls; but it is for *milk*, for the simple *fundamentals* of the gospel. Others may like Peter's, Paul's and John's talk of suffering with Christ, of being filled with the Spirit, of being not under Law but Grace, and of waiting for our Lord's return.

"But we believe there's a middle path. We do not believe in excitement about religious matters. Too, we have relatives and close friends among the Jews, who do not believe as we do that Jesus was the Messiah. But they are good citizens, and we wish to live in peace with them, to be *tolerant!* So give us a little more *milk*, and do not ask us to be roused up!"

Verse 13: For every one that partaketh of milk is without experience of the word of righteousness: for he is a babe. Now what mean these words? It is a tragic thing if we do not know. **Without experience of the word of righteousness,** does not mean merely inexperience in the fact of righteousness by faith, justification. But, as the apostle goes on to show, it is an ignorance, an inexperience, that results from *the lack of use of the spiritual senses!* It refers more particularly to *walk*—that walk of holiness and uprightness belonging to the children of God, which is the true path of every eager, obedient believer!

For he is a babe: Let me seek in a brief footnote to give some of the characteristics of these babes.* There is, however, this vital

---

*Babes: that is, those who have *become* babes. Every one delights in a true babe in Christ, eager, hungry, trustful, discovering a fresh world! But these *became* milk-users, babes. Have they marks? Oh, yes. To name a few:

1. They are "tossed to and fro and carried about with every wind of doctrine" (Eph. 4.14 ff), as a babe is carried about and handed from one to another.

2. They "belong," as they say, to some particular denomination—which they call, like a baby his crib, "My church."

3. They glory in men: "Dr. So-and-so's preaching." They do not know what the Church of God is, the one Body of Christ, and that "membership" is only *in Christ*. Paul had to minister to the Corinthians as unto babes in Christ, feeding them on milk only, not because he had not told them deeper things, but because they had turned aside to be carnal, saying, *"I am of Paul," "I am of Apollos," "I of Cephas,"* and (condemned alike because they said "I," not "We") "I of *Christ*" (I Cor. 12.13). So today: "I am of Wesley," "I am of Calvin." "Are you," says Paul, "not *carnal*, and walk *as men?" Men* choose to say, "I am a conservative," or, "a liberal," "a Republican," "a Democrat."

Such things are all abhorrent to the one Spirit Who has baptized us into the one Body of Christ! Furthermore, we are *"members one of another,"* that is, of all saints, not of some little narrow denomination!

difference between natural life and spiritual life. In natural life, a babe needs to be carried about, needs to be fed with milk, and needs to be left often to sleep. Thus he will grow. Not so with spiritual life! The proper babe in Christ needs milk but for a little while, and needs to be told, and that soon, and fully, the stronger things: needs to be pointed to a glorified as well as a crucified Christ, the Great High Priest; and to Christ as coming again. He needs to be told that he cannot be *carried,* that he *must press on,* if he is to attain full growth. The regenerated *will* is involved in spiritual growth.

Verse 14: But solid food is for fullgrown men, even those who by reason of use have their senses exercised to discern good and evil: "Fullgrown men" here has no reference to six feet of height and two hundred pounds of weight. But, as Paul says, "In *malice*

---

4. Again, mark how much a babe must *sleep.* Do you realize the trouble of heart a preacher or teacher of the Word of God experiences when he stands up to declare the eternal truth which infinitely concerns his audience, and knows that they do not follow him? Babes must sleep a great deal; and so do these Christians!

Years and years ago I was preaching in a large church in the United States on the atonement. The subject was, "The Three Crosses," and God greatly enlarged and helped. Three rows from the front there sat a delightful gentleman for many years an elder in that church, very prominent in business, who had been vice-mayor of that large city. I noticed him in these meetings, settle himself to sleep every time! The moment the singing and announcements were over, to sleep he would go, with his knees braced against the seat ahead, and hunched down in his pew.

But one Lord's day morning, suddenly he opened his eyes, straightened in his seat, grasped the seat in front, and listened with great intentness, without moving. The minute the service was over he almost ran to the front, grasped my hand, and said,

"I never heard that before in all my life! I did not know that all my sins were laid on Christ and put away forever. This is most wonderful!"

"Yet," I said, "my dear Mr. H., it is the truth."

"He said, "I see it's the truth, and I have been asleep all these years!"

From that moment that man's life was transformed, as everybody testified. No more sleeping for him! I presented to him a special copy of the New Testament, which he treasured. Coming to that city several years afterwards, I heard, "Mr. H. is very ill." I hastened to see him.

His wife said, "Slip up quietly: I think he is asleep. But he has that Testament you gave him, and reads it day and night."

I stepped quietly to the bedroom door, and there he was, lying asleep, yet with the peace of Heaven on his face, and with the Testament I had given him open! No more *spiritual* sleep for him, I repeat. Shortly after, he went to glory!

5. Then there are spiritual babes who fuss over this and that, just as babies fuss. They are the quarrelers, the dividers, those who, like a petulant child, "want my own way."

6. Finally and alas, there are vast thousands who once were wakened, perhaps in revival times, who once were drawn to the Word of God, who once were stirred by earnest prayer and teaching, who once had family prayer and thanksgiving. Today they are "church members," respectable, unspiritual, unfruitful, dull, uninterested in the study of Scripture, unfavorable toward revival or "special measures" which might arouse them.

Draw out a lamentation for those who *become* "babes"!

be ye babes, but in mind be *men*" (Gr., *of full age*), those who, according to Hebrews 6.1, "press on unto perfection," or *full growth.* The whole thought here is of spiritual development. When you were born into your earthly family, your parents were eager to know whether all your senses were perfect—sight, hearing, smelling, feeling, taste. In the verse we have in hand, the spiritual senses are in view. **Men of full age are those who have their senses exercised,** and are able to take "solid food."

It is striking that all five bodily senses have their counterparts in the spiritual realm! (1) *Taste:* "If indeed ye have *tasted* that the Lord is gracious"; "O taste and see that the Lord is good." (2) *Hearing:* "*Hear* and your soul shall live"; "He that hath ears to hear, let him hear."* (3) *Sight:* "Open Thou mine *eyes,* that I may behold wondrous things out of Thy law." "Having the eyes of your heart enlightened." (4) *Smell:* the Holy Spirit said of Christ, "He shall be of *quick scent* in the fear of Jehovah" (Isa. 11.3, R.V., margin): and Paul wrote to the Philippians, "I am filled, having received . . . the things from you, an odor of a sweet smell,† a sacrifice acceptable, well-pleasing to God." There are also spiritual sins, which to the quickened spirit become foul and stenchful—

---

*Lack of use of senses from lack of interest is described by our Lord in Matt. 13.13-15:
"Therefore speak I to them in parables; because seeing they see not, and hearing they hear not, neither do they understand. And unto them is fulfilled the prophecy of Isaiah, which saith,
By hearing ye shall hear, and shall in no wise understand;
And seeing ye shall see, and in no wise perceive:
For this people's heart is waxed gross,
And their ears are dull of hearing,
And their eyes they have closed;
Lest haply they should perceive with their eyes,
And hear with their ears,
And understand with their heart,
And should turn again,
And I should heal them."

"Fatty degeneration of the heart," as the doctors call it, they have, due to too much fat in the whole body (from over indulgence in earth's foods and follies; and spiritual inactivity), and their ears are dull of hearing, and their eyes they have dozily closed! This lack of interest in Divine things which comes like a creeping paralysis upon those remaining inactive, when God is calling, is, in this passage, quoted by our Lord (Isa. 6.9-10) laid directly to the blame of the hearer.

†There is no sense so subtle and certain as that of scent. It is beautifully set forth as concerning God, in that Christ offered Himself up for a sweet smelling savor! His life, walk, and ministry were a constant fragrance of delight to the Father. Turning it about, Christ was and shall be, we repeat, "of quick scent in the fear of Jehovah," discerning the least inclination of His will.

unclean things of the world. (5) *Feeling:* Of King Josiah, God said
He sent the gracious message "because thy heart was *tender*."
Toward one another we are told to be "tender-hearted." Again,
we are cautioned against wounding the conscience which is weak
(I Cor. 8.12); while the awful word is spoken of some, that
"being past feeling," they "gave themselves up to lasciviousness,
to work all uncleanness with greediness" (Eph. 4.19). Like our
Lord, we should be "able to be *touched*."

To discern good and evil: To discern good and evil, to refuse
the evil and choose the good, describes a holy walk. Brother,
brother, have you not discovered that this world, as regards your
feet, is a labyrinth of snares? As regards your hearing, is full of
false voices? Its wisdom is foolishness—its promises are empty
and vain—its philosophy is a puffball. But the most of even professing Christians are steeped in the thought that this world
has something, educationally, socially, even religiously, to benefit them. Paul cried, "We are not ignorant of his [Satan's]
devices"! Over and over we are counseled, "Be not deceived."
A fullgrown man will **discern good and evil,** with **exercised senses.**
But alas, most professing Christians are described in the verses
we have been looking at. They cannot discern—they are **without
experience in the word of righteousness;** they are **become dull
of hearing**—they need to be taught—they can take only milk!

Ere we close the chapter, it is imperative that we here see,
acknowledge, and hold, the Bible doctrine of *Christian perfection.*

First, we remember that there was no such thing as being perfected under the Law (Heb. 7.19). David cried, "I have seen an
end of all perfection . . . Thy comandment is exceeding broad"!
(Ps. 119.96). The Law, being holy and just, as well as good, must
demand and keep demanding from the creature—not what the
creature in a fallen state may be able to supply, but what God, in
His infinite holiness and righteousness must require. Alas, if only
the legalists all might see this! Does not Moses cry,

"Thou hast set our iniquities before Thee,

Our secret sins in the light of Thy countenance"?
This was the very purpose of the Law. Sin was there all the time,
but the Law made it known to the sinner. "The Law was given
that the trespass [of it] might abound." And since, in man and in

the flesh, there is no moral ability, therefore, there is no attainment
of perfection, and those who in any sense whatever hold themselves under Law, remain infants, just where the Jews remain who
were placed under Law by God: "So we also [writes Paul as a
Jew], when we were *minors (nêpioi,)** were held in bondage under
the rudiments of the world" (Gal. 4.3).

Second, we read that for those in Christ, they being not under
Moses' Law, but *dead* to it and *discharged therefrom* (Rom. 6.14;
7.4, 6, R.V.); and being indwelt by the Holy Spirit, there is the
"law of the Spirit of life in Christ Jesus," which makes us "free
from the law of sin and of death." This "freedom" does not mean
that the flesh is changed (Rom. 8.2), for we are "waiting for . . . the
redemption of our body," groaning within ourselves until that
day (Rom. 8.23); but it does mean that we may "by the Spirit . . .
put to death the doings of the body," and live by and be led by the
Spirit of God (Rom. 8.13, 14). "But I say, Walk by the Spirit,
and *ye shall not* fulfill the lust of the flesh" (Gal. 5.16). Again,
"They that are of Christ Jesus have crucified the flesh with the
passions and the lusts thereof." These are such as are described also
in Galatians 5.25: "If we live by the Spirit, by the Spirit let us
also walk."

Paul was one of the **fullgrown (perfect) men** Hebrews 5.14
speaks of, and such was Stephen, and all the apostles! Such are
some saints today. For there is set before the believer constantly
the command to "grow in the grace and knowledge of our Lord
Jesus Christ." Nay more: there is commanded, as in Ephesians
4.13, 14; Colossians 3.14, a state of adulthood, arriving at a
"fullgrown" man, being "no longer children *(nêpioi),* tossed to
and fro and carried about with every wind of doctrine."

When in II Corinthians 13.11 Paul says, "Finally, brethren . . .
be *perfected,*" he uses the second word for perfecting, *katartidzō.*
It is illustrated beautifully in Matthew 21.16: "Out of the mouths
of babes and sucklings Thou hast *perfected* praise." These two
words, *katartidzō,* meaning fundamentally to render fit, or sound—
to put in order, make complete; and *teleios,* which has reference to
maturity, as a finished product—of full age, fullgrown, mature

---

*See the same word in I Cor. 3.1, babe; 13.11, child, five times; Eph. 4.14, children;
Heb. 5.13, babe.

(as in Eph. 4.13; Phil. 3.15), are set before the believer. To full growth, completeness, maturity, both the Word of God and the indwelling Spirit urge us. The believer should be no more content to remain a babe, than a lad have no urge to become a man! To press on to *full growth* is the Divine command; to fail therein through neglect, unbelief, or earthly "religious" influence, fear of men, or yielding to the world, invites spiritual decline, and is the path to apostasy!

Alas, "perfection" and "perfecting" are words many Christians shy from, because they connect them with "perfection in the flesh," which of course does not exist. When believers understand that the great desire of God is that "Christ may be formed in them" and that "perfecting" is the operation of *God:* and that they are simply to present their bodies a living sacrifice, acceptable to God, that they may be "transformed by the renewing" of their mind, that they may prove "what is the good and acceptable and perfect will of God," all is changed! The only question is, Are they *willing* for this transformation? For, as Paul puts it (II Cor. 3.18), "We all, with unveiled face, beholding as in a mirror the glory of the Lord, are transformed into the *same image* from glory to glory, even as from the Lord the Spirit."*

Let us close our study of Hebrews 5 by searching out other Scriptures on "perfecting," (1) as to *faith,* (2) as to *holiness,* (3) as to *love,* (4) as to *knowledge,* especially of God's will:

1. Paul writes, "Night and day praying exceedingly that we may see your face, and may *perfect* that which is lacking in your *faith*" (I Thess. 3. 10). And he says to the Corinthians, "This we also pray for, even your *perfecting.*" James also recognizes the perfecting of faith, saying, "Thou seest that faith wrought with his (Abraham's) works, and by works was faith made *perfect;*

---

*As the sainted Andrew Murray wrote: "It is only the full and perfect knowledge of what Christ is and does for us that can bring us to a full and perfect Christian life. The knowledge of Jesus Christ that we need for conversion does not suffice for growth, for progress, for sanctification, for maturity. Just as there are two dispensations, the Old Testament and the New, and the saints of the Old, with all their faith and fear of God, could not obtain the more perfect life of the New, so with the two stages in the Christian life of which the Epistle (Hebrews) speaks. Those who, through sloth, remain babes in Christ, and do not press on to maturity, are ever in danger of hardening their heart, of coming short and falling away. Only those who hold fast the beginning firm to the end, who give diligence to enter *the rest,* who press on unto *perfection,* do in very deed inherit and enjoy the wonderful New Covenant blessings secured to us in Christ."

and the Scripture was fulfilled which saith, And Abraham *believed*
God, and it was reckoned unto him for righteousness." How often
our Lord lamented the "weak" or "little faith" of those who
sought His help, even of the disciples! Do you and I expect to be
perfected in faith, as God desires?

2. Perfecting in holiness:

"Having therefore these promises, beloved, let us cleanse ourselves from all defilement of flesh and spirit, *perfecting holiness*
in the fear of God" (II Cor. 7.1).

The preceding verses (II Cor. 6.14-18) indicate separation
from "unequal yokes" with unbelievers, from all fellowship with
unrighteousness or darkness, having no concord (being in Christ)
with Belial; remembering that a believer has *no portion* with an
unbeliever, nor a temple of God (which every believer, being indwelt by the Spirit, *is*) with *idols:* remembering that *separation
unto Him* which God expects of His people, saying:

"Come ye out from among them, and *be ye separate, saith the
Lord,*

And touch no unclean thing; and I will receive you,

And will be to you a Father, and ye shall be to Me sons and
daughters, saith *the Lord Almighty*" (II Cor. 6.17-18).

"The Lord Almighty" corresponds to the name He revealed to
Abraham in Genesis 17.1: "I am *God Almighty;* walk before
Me, and be thou *perfect."* God *furnishes the power* for a separated
life! "This is the will *of God,* even your sanctification" (I Thess.
4.3).

3. Perfecting in *love:*

"*Perfect love* casteth out fear . . . he that feareth is not made
perfect in love" (I Jno. 4.18); "If we love one another, God
abideth in us, and His love is perfected in us" (I Jno. 4.12).
Here, on the negative side, is deliverance from the fear of judgment; and on the positive, a walk in love with one another. The
pathway to love is entered in I John 4.16 (R.V., margin):

"We know and have believed the love which God hath *in our
case."* Again, "Herein is love, *not that we loved God,* but that *He
loved us,* and sent His Son to be the propitiation for our sins"
(vs. 10); and, "We love, *because* He first loved us" (vs. 19);
"Above all these things put on love, which is *the bond of perfect-*

ness" (Col. 3.14); I Corinthians 13.1-13 and Chapter 14.1: "*Follow after* (pursue) *love;* yet desire earnestly spiritual gifts."

4. In *knowledge:*

"We . . . do not cease to pray and make request for you, that ye may be *filled* with the knowledge of His will in *all* spiritual wisdom and understanding" (Col. 1.9).

"Epaphras . . . saluteth you, always striving for you in his prayers, that ye may stand *perfect* and fully assured in *all* the will of God" (Col. 4.12).

The above are some of the passages of these blessed epistles which describe the heavenly calling and walk of the Church, the Assembly of God.

Let us "press on unto perfection," unto "full growth." "He Who began a good work in you *will perfect it* until the day of Jesus Christ" (Phil. 1.6). *Rely* on that! Let us beware that our Lord does not say of us as of Sardis, "I have found no works of thine *perfected* before My God" (Rev. 3.2). Let our ambition daily be that we, "*dealing truly* in love, may *grow up* in all things into Him, Who is the Head, even Christ"! (Eph. 4.15, R.V., margin.)

CHAPTER SIX

1   On this account, leaving the word of the beginning of
     Christ, unto full growth let us be pressing on! not lay-
     ing again a foundation of repentance from dead works,
2   and of faith toward God, of the teaching of baptisms,
     of laying on of hands, of resurrection of the dead, and of
3   judgment eternal. And this will we do—if God permit.

YOU MAY WELL ASK concerning these six things how they
constituted the word of the beginning of Christ. First of all, we
must remember that the epistle is addressed to Hebrews. Second,
that these Hebrews addressed had, as indicated here, received the
word of the beginning of Christ (as set forth in the Gospels),
that is, what to them were fundamentals concerning Christ. Third,
leaving these things which are enumerated, they were to press
on unto full growth, out of their state of babehood.*

As we inquire then concerning this word of the beginning of
Christ, which these Hebrew believers had embraced, we must
put ourselves into their position, tracing truth as they would hear
and embrace it; and not from the Gentile believers' experience or
point of view.

For we remember that our Lord Jesus gave to Peter "the keys
of the kingdom of the heavens." This must have a certain meaning. We open ourselves unto the snare of Romanism if we deny
or neglect the fact! These "keys" were not keys to salvation
(which is of course based wholly on the shed blood of Christ), but

---

*We are astonished to find some authors whom we love asserting that the word of the
beginning of Christ was Judaism. But Paul tells us in Gal. 1.13, using the very word Judaism
(Joudaismos), that so far from Judaism's being the word of the beginning of Christ, it was
the religion of Christ's chief hater and persecutor of the saints! "Ye have heard of my
manner of life in time past in the Jews' religion (Joudaismos), how that beyond measure I
persecuted the Church of God, and made havoc of it; and I advanced in the Jews' religion
[same word] beyond many of mine own age among my countrymen, being more exceedingly zealous for the traditions of my fathers. But when it was the good pleasure of God,
Who separated me, even from my mother's womb, and called me through His grace, to
reveal His Son in me, that I might preach Him among the Gentiles; straightway I conferred not with flesh and blood," etc.

the office of announcing those *conditions* under which Jews first (Acts 2.37-38), and afterwards Gentiles (Acts 10.43, 44), should receive the benefits of Christ's redemption—and thus enter the Kingdom.*

Moral delinquency is not charged against these Hebrew believers, but what is infinitely more serious, spiritual rebellion. For they were not at all in the same category with their fathers, to whom the Law had been spoken and the Levitical shadow system had been *prescribed*—for now the Son of God had come. (There should be constant reference by each of us who reads Hebrews to the glory of the Son, in Whom God had now spoken: the Heir of all things: Creator, Upholder, the Effulgence of the Divine glory: God, Lord!)

Nor was it merely that He had come and walked as the Son, as related in the Gospels; but that, according to prophecy, He had died, as David wrote of Him in Psalm 22: "They pierced My hands and My feet." He had died, forsaken of God! Divine wrath against human sin had been fully expiated. Then "He hath been raised"—"raised from the dead through the glory of the Father," "saluted of God a High Priest after the order of Melchizedek." And He had "ascended into Heaven, and sat down on the right hand of the throne of God." The contemplation and eager belief of these mighty facts were expected by God. How could it be otherwise?

These Hebrew Christians had heard this glorious gospel, and should have been *pressing on,* **leaving the word of the beginning of Christ.**

"Pressing on unto Full Growth" would be a good title for the Book of Hebrews!†

---

*Distinguish between Peter's using the key for the Gentiles in Cornelius' household, where *faith only* was a condition of "remission of sins" (Acts 10.43), and the key for the Jews in Acts 2.37, where the national sin of having rejected the Messiah being shown, not only *repentance concerning that* sin, but open confession of the rejected Christ in baptism, *preceded* remission of sins. With the Gentiles, water baptism *followed* faith and the remission of sins and the gift of the Holy Spirit (Acts 10.44-47). The door of faith was thus opened to the Gentiles by the sovereign God, but Peter, led of the Spirit, used the "key" Christ had given him, and opened the door of faith to the Gentiles, although Peter, Christ's apostle, said concerning Cornelius and his house, "Who can forbid the water that those should not be baptized, who have received the Holy Ghost as well as we?" (Acts 10.47, 48). *Bullinger* and his followers in our days "forbid the water" which Peter *commanded!*

†The great exhortation in Hebrews is to press on to "full growth." The danger connected

Let us press on unto full growth—The Greek word here, *teleiotêta,* signifies what we saw in Chapter 5.14: "*Strong meat belongeth to them that are of full-age.*" The process of the Holy Spirit within the believer will conform him to the image of Christ in faith, holiness, love, and knowledge, as we saw in Chapter 5. (See also Jas. 3.2; Col. 1.28.)

Let us note that **the word of the beginning of Christ*** having been accepted, there is to be a pressing on unto full growth. As Paul says in Ephesians 4.13-15.

"Till we all attain unto the unity of the faith, and of the knowledge of the Son of God, unto a fullgrown man, unto the measure of the stature of the fullness of Christ: that we be no longer children, tossed to and fro . . . but dealing truly in love, may grow up in all things into Him, Who is the Head, even Christ."

Not laying again a foundation—Here note three things:

1. That the foundation which these Hebrew believers had is about to be described.

2. That the laying of this "foundation" at the first was approved.

3. That the exhortation is, not to be occupied with *re*-laying the foundation, but to **press on unto full growth!**

We shall find in this passage, as we have said, describing the "foundation," six items. What are these six things?

The *first* one was, **repentance from dead works,** a remarkable expression. Now Gentiles were commanded to repent of *sins!* (Acts 8.22). You will find no Gentiles ever commanded to repent **from dead works.** Why? Because these "works" were such as people would be occupied with to whom "*works*" had been *pre-*

---

with "neglect," with sloth, non-use of spiritual faculties, accumulates before our minds. The infinitely loving God who has given His well-beloved Son for our sake warns of the danger of provoking His wrath by turning back from His revealed perfect work to religious forms or by choosing the sin which He died to save us from. These dangers are thoroughly warned against in Hebrews.

Meanwhile before the eyes of faith at God's right hand sits our great High Priest in the infinite value of His atoning work, also with all power in Heaven and on earth committed unto Him.

*Literal translation of the Greek for the first part of vs. 1. The R.V. has, "doctrine of the first principles of Christ"; the A.V., "principles of the doctrine of Christ." Neither is a satisfactory rendering. Darby well renders: "Leaving the word of the beginning of the Christ, let us go on [to what belongs to] full growth."

scribed. The Hebrews were the only people with whom this was the case. They had the Law—a yoke, indeed, which Peter declared neither their fathers nor they were able to bear (Acts 15.10). Nevertheless, there it was! The very first gospel announcement to the Hebrews would be something entirely new—repentance, an entire change of mind, as to "works" securing salvation—the announcement that such "works" were "dead," as regards obtaining eternal life, and were no longer to be trusted in, but wholly *left* as a ground of hope. There was to **be repentance from dead works.*** Their conscience was to be cleansed, by Christ's blood, **from dead** works (Ch. 9.14).

The Law given by Moses could *command:* "And Jehovah com-*manded* us to do all these statutes . . . and it shall be righteousness unto us" (Deut. 6.24-25). Alongside of this we must place the Spirit's word through Paul in Galatians 3.11-12:

"Now that no man is justified by the Law before God, is evi-dent: for the righteous shall live on the principle of *faith;* and the Law is not of faith; but, He that *doeth* them shall live in them."

Or, as Paul writes in Romans 10:2-4, concerning Israel,

"They have a zeal for God, but not according to knowledge. For being ignorant of God's righteousness, and seeking to establish their own, they did not subject themselves to the righteousness of God. For Christ is the end of the Law unto righteousness to every-one that believeth."

David also "pronounceth blessing upon the man unto whom God reckoneth righteousness apart from works" (Rom. 4.6).

The works of the Law (which cannot at all be kept by man, but is a "ministration of death") must be repented of just as sins must be—for to be occupied with our "works," which God has condemned as unclean, is, in effect, just the same as holding *sin.* With a wholly changed mind we must, we repeat, *repent* of, and turn from them, and find trust and rest in the work of *Another, even Christ,* Whose work God has *accepted!*

Therefore we find in Chapter 9.14, that from "dead works" the

---

*"Dead works" present the essential character of the works in themselves: "works of law"—present them in relation to an ideal, unattainable, standard! It follows therefore that repentance from dead works expresses that complete change of mind—of spiritual attitude—which leads the believer to abandon these works and seek some other support for life."— Westcott.

blood of Christ (and of course only that!) can relieve, "cleanse," the conscience. For no matter what efforts you put forth, your conscience tells you that you have not satisfied the infinitely holy God. But when, by His Spirit, the work of Christ on your behalf, and the infinite satisfaction of His blood for your sins, are seen, your conscience *rests*. There is no more driving the heart, which is thus "cleansed from dead works." It is delivered!

Second, **the word of the beginning of Christ** which they had heard and embraced, involved personal **faith toward** [or, *on*] **God.*** Strange though you and I may think it, the Hebrews (except such glorious witnesses as are exampled in Heb. 11) did not *trust* God. They regarded themselves as "the chosen people." But there were always Moses and the Law before them; the feasts and the ordinances, the sacrifices, the cleansing water (of the ashes of the red heifer). To turn away from all ordinances and works, and *rely directly* upon God, to them would have seemed presumption! Yet **the word of the beginning of Christ** had taught them just that! That on account of His sacrifice they had become as Peter described (I Pet. 1.18-21):

"Ye were redeemed, not with corruptible things, with silver or gold, from your vain manner of life handed down from your fathers; but with precious blood, as of a Lamb without blemish and without spot, even the blood of Christ: Who was foreknown indeed before the foundation of the world, but was manifested at the end of the times for your sake, who *through Him* are *believers* in God, that raised Him from the dead, and gave Him glory; so that your **faith** and hope might be **in God.**"†

---

*The Greek preposition *(epi)* means *upon*, in the sense of reliance upon, as in Acts 9.42; 16.31; Rom. 4.5, 24.

†Any Jew would have protested—nay, does protest—that his nation have been *the* believers in God. But note the sense of Peter's words, quoted above. He was writing to the Christian Jews (the Dispersion—the *Diaspora*), and he says that through Christ these very Jews had *become* believers in God, Who raised Him [Christ] from the dead . . . so that their *faith* and hope might be in God. No Jew could trust God in the gospel sense until he was sure that sin was put away. This was announced to him in the gospel, even in **the word of the beginning of Christ**. To believe there is a God is not necessarily to *have faith in* Him.

Furthermore, for a Jew to protest, "We are disciples of Moses: we know that God hath spoken unto Moses," and to rely upon performing Levitical duties, was faith in *his own works* only! Such an attitude brought forth our Lord's words, "There is one that accuseth you, even Moses, on whom ye have set your hope!" (Jno. 5.45). For, as He told them, "Did not Moses give you the Law? Yet none of you doeth the Law!" (Jno. 7.19).

Is it not remarkable that Abraham "rejoiced to see Christ's day; and he saw it, and was

The Jews nationally had no direct personal faith in God until, "enlightened," they had really "heard from the Father, and had learned" of Christ, as our Lord says in John 6.45.

Verse 2: *Third, the word of the beginning of Christ,* to these Hebrews, involved "the teaching of baptisms."* The word "baptisms" is plural, because unto the Jews God had prescribed (1) John the Baptist's baptism, and (2) Christian baptism. (Note at once that these two "baptisms" are the only ones connected with **the word of the beginning of Christ.**) We hear John say, "That He [Christ] should be made manifest *to Israel* . . . I came baptizing with water" (Jno. 1.31). And every one except the selfrighteous leaders had taken that (first) baptism:

"Then went out unto him Jerusalem, and Judea, and all the region round about the Jordan" (Matt. 3.5). "And all the people when they heard, and the publicans, justified God, being baptized with the baptism of John. But the Pharisees and the lawyers rejected for themselves the counsel of God, being not baptized of him" (Lk. 7.29, 30).

Thus by John's baptism a Jew confessed himself a *common sinner!*

As to (2) Christian baptism: upon the rejection, crucifixion and resurrection of the Lord Jesus, God prescribed by the mouth of Peter to the Jews on the day of Pentecost (Acts 2.5) repentance of their awful sin of rejecting their Messiah, and a public confession by water baptism "in the name of Jesus Christ" (Acts 2.38). These two "baptisms" were connected in the Hebrew believer's mind with **the word of the beginning of Christ.**

---

glad"? And Moses declared, "Jehovah thy God will raise up a Prophet from the midst of thee, of thy brethren, like unto me; unto Him ye shall hearken" (Deut. 18.15, 18). And again, David had the Messiah in view, for our Lord declares that "David in the Spirit called Him [Christ] Lord" (Matt. 22.41-45). And Isaiah said, "A virgin shall conceive, and bear a Son, and shall call His name Immanuel"; also, "The Lord hath laid on Him the iniquity of us all." Daniel saw "One like unto a Son of man, and He came even unto the Ancient of days, and dominion was given to Him." Even Abel, the first of the cloud of witnesses of Heb. 11, we find bringing death, not life, unto God!

In short, Divinely taught souls, knowing their own guilt, longed like Job for "a Daysman, to lay His hand upon them . . . both" . . . them and God! (Job 9.33). And such, like Job, found personal faith in God, confidence not in forms but in a Person.

So Peter witnessed to a great truth (I Pet. 1.21) in saying that through Christ and His precious blood the elect *Hebrews* of the Dispersion had *become* "believers *on God.*" Read also I Pet. 1.3: "God . ,, begat us again unto a *living hope* by the resurrection of Jesus Christ from the dead."

*See appendix B.

Fourth, of **laying on of hands**—This we find very frequently connected with the receiving of the Holy Spirit (Acts 8.17-19), and with the acknowledgment by the elderhood of those discerned by saints as chosen for special service (Acts 13.3; I Tim. 4.14; II Tim. 1.6); and also in connection with bodily healings (Acts 5.12; 9.41; 28.8). To the Hebrews the imposition of hands in association with their sacrifices as connecting them therewith had always been familiar.

Fifth, we may be surprised to find that the **word of the beginning of Christ** to these Hebrews included **the resurrection of the dead.** Edersheim says, "Even to the quotation of Isaiah 26.19, 'Thy dead shall live; My dead bodies shall arise. Awake and sing, ye that dwell in the dust; for thy dew is as the dew of herbs, and the earth shall cast forth the dead,' the Sadducees will answer that that promise must be understood spiritually like the resurrection of dry bones in Ezekiel." The resurrection of the body was believed in by orthodox Jews from such other passages as Daniel 12.2 and Job 19.25, though there was continual contention over the doctrine; and of course even orthodox Jews thought resurrection merely the bringing back into an earthly existence, such as our Lord gave to Lazarus. But **the word of the beginning of Christ** would include His resurrection by the glory of the Father, with a flesh and bones body indeed, but without blood, which He had poured out; and His becoming thus "the Firstborn from among the dead" in the sense of having received newness of life, a new kind of bodily existence.

The godly and scholarly Stuart says: "A general resurrection of the bodies of men is a doctrine which, if not left undecided by the Old Testament, is at least left in obscurity. The Jews of the apostles' time were divided in their opinion respecting it. Hence, it was insisted on with great earnestness by Christian preachers, as belonging to the peculiar and elementary doctrines of Christianity. It was connected, by them, with the account which every man is to render of himself to God; and such an accountability is a fundamental doctrine of the Christian religion."

Sixth, **the word of the beginning of Christ** included **eternal judgment.** There are some, yea many, so befooled by the devil as to hold that "all, even Satan himself, will finally be brought back to God." But there is no plainer teaching in God's holy Word than that the punishment of the damned will continue as long as God and His saints exist. The **eternal judgment** of men is a thing nearly connected with the resurrection of the dead. It is also linked closely with our Lord's resurrection from among the dead (Acts 17.31; 24.25).

Eternal judgment, we repeat, is constantly taught in the New Testament. Witness our Lord's words, "eternal fire prepared for the devil and his angels." And in Revelation 20.10, "unto the ages of the ages". This phrase is God's constant description of (1) the duration of *His own existence and glory:* (See Gal. 1.5; I Tim. 1.17; II Tim. 4.18; Heb. 13.21; I Pet. 4.11; 5.11; Jude 25; and fourteen times in the book of The Revelation!); (2) the duration of the existence and of the blessedness of the saints (Rev. 22.5).

We repeat, **eternal judgment** for the damned will continue as long as God and His saints exist—unendingly.

Verse 3: And this will we do, if God permit: In the word "we," Paul speaks generally, for all Christians. In the following verse he at once speaks of *"those,"* and proceeds to describe apostates— formerly professing Christians who had now inwardly "crucified the Son of God," and outwardly "put Him to an open shame" by sin, as we shall see. Therefore this word, Let us **press on unto full growth if permitted of God.** If permitted of *God?* say you. *Permitted* of the God Whose name is Love, Who gave His only begotten Son? The God Who saith, "As I live, I have no pleasure in the death of him that dieth"?

Yes, this same God! We are about to view certain souls to whom this God Whose name is Love will not vouchsafe blessing or grace from Him—certain whom He has "rejected." We must remember that no human being since Adam sinned has desired *in himself* to repent. Grace, uncaused in us, must effect repentance. At Jerusalem, upon Peter's report as to what had happened in the house of Cornelius the Gentile, they that heard of these things said with awe, "Then to the Gentiles also hath God *granted* repentance unto life." Therefore we must view those about to be described in verses 4-8 not at all as *willing, desiring, or longing to* be "renewed unto repentance" but on the contrary as having come to treat all the advances of Divine love and grace with inappreciation, and neglect; who had a steady disregard of their fruitless spiritual state toward God, and were fruitful in the thorns and thistles (vs. 8) of the evil heart. (Remember, "Thorns and thistles" came through *sin!* Gen. 3.18.)

There is no need to read the book of Hebrews beyond verse 3 of this chapter if you are not prepared to receive the exact intent of these words of Scripture, if God permit. And once again we beg you, guard your heart against that awful thought, that there are those truly seeking to get back to God, whom He will not receive!

4   For it is impossible as to those having been once enlightened, and having tasted, moreover, the heavenly gift, and partners of the Holy Spirit having become;
5   and furthermore having tasted as good the utterance of
6   God, and the powers of the coming age—and then having fallen away, to renew them again unto repentance: (they being such as) are crucifying for themselves the
7   Son of God and putting Him to an open shame. For the land which hath drunk the rain that cometh oft upon it, and bringeth forth herbs meet for them for whose sake
8   it is also tilled, receiveth blessing from God. But if it keeps bearing thorns and thistles, it is rejected and nigh unto a curse; whose end is for burning.

Verse 4: Note at the very beginning of our study of this passage, that the word once-for-all (Gr., *hapax*), *precedes and governs all the participles following:* having been enlightened, having tasted, having been made partakers, finally, having tasted the utterance of God to be good; and the powers of the coming age. These are all aorist participles, referring to an event definitely past; and they are all followed by the frightful words, having fallen away!

1.   Those who were once-for-all enlightened—They had that Divine illuminating involved in the first operation of the Holy Spirit upon the soul of man. The utter darkness and ignorance *of nature* was dispelled. We read in John 16.8: "He, when He is come, will convict the world"—not of their evil conduct, nor of each man's past guiltinesses, but of the sin of not believing on Christ: "in respect of sin, because they believe not on Me," and

"of righteousness," because Christ, adjudged of men a blasphemer, God received up to Heaven. And "of judgment," because the world's prince, Satan, was judged at the Cross.

This "enlightenment," then, about Christ, was the same which those finally saved received. To the mind of a Hebrew, it included complete persuasion by the Holy Spirit that Jesus of Nazareth was his Messiah. It is referred to again in Hebrews 10.32 in the words, "Call to remembrance the former days, in which, *after ye were enlightened,* ye endured a great conflict of sufferings." It is dealing lightly with Scripture to imagine that this "enlightenment" was merely some "intellectual illumination" and that of the "natural mind." R. A. Torrey's claim that "there is a quickening short of regeneration" is borne out by this, as well as other Scriptures, as e.g., Luke 8.13.

This enlightenment* was not merely intellectual, but embraced such a Spirit-wrought view of Christ, His earthly Messiahship, and His resurrection that those faithful Hebrews who received it and acted upon it, "continued steadfastly in the apostles' teaching and fellowship, in the breaking of bread and prayers . . . praising God and having favor with all the people" (Acts 2.42, 47).

This is the "enlightenment;" the miracle of the Holy Ghost from Heaven revealing a Risen, Living Christ—from which those of Hebrews 6.4 finally apostatized. For this is *apostasy*—willfully casting away known revealed truth! They *"rejected for themselves the*

---

*Mr. Darby says (Coll. Writings, Vol. XXVIII, p. 94): "It should be observed that there is nothing of *life* signified here. The expressions do not go beyond the indications of truth that might be received by the natural mind and the demonstrative power of the Holy Ghost which persons might partake, of, as Scripture shows, without being participators of eternal life."

We fully agree that these in Ch. 6.4-8 did not exhibit "the things pertaining to salvation" of vs. 9. Yet Mr. Darby's explanation, like that of all ultra-Calvinists, falls far short both of what is here revealed in Scripture, and of what has been fearfully illustrated in the experience of apostates. Remember that Paul denies the ability of the natural man to receive the things of the Spirit of God; and why? "For they are foolishness unto him; and he cannot know them, because they are spiritually judged" (I Cor. 2.14). Therefore in Mr. Darby's unfortunate words, "truth that might be received by the natural mind and the demonstrative power of the Holy Ghost," there is a departure from Scripture teaching. The wholly "natural" man can respond no more to the Holy Spirit's operations than a tree in the forest! But God says in Heb. 6.4 that those who become apostates were once enlightened. The Hebrews thus "enlightened" knew from God that Jesus of Nazareth was their Messiah! and further, that God had raised Him from the dead—that He was now living. Also, there was a 'tasting"—an experience such as "the natural mind" never could realize. *Tasting* was experienced by those of Ch. 6—but not drinking! Those of Ch. 10 tasted—and drank! *Both knew the taste.* Those who *drank* got *life* (Jno. 4.14).

counsel of God" (Lk. 7.30). We repeat, the word for "enlightened" in Hebrews 10.32 is the same Greek word as is used in Chapter 6.4: God can reveal only one Christ! The same Christ had been set before those of Chapter 10.32 as before the "tasters" of Chapter 6; and there was the same enlightening Agent, the blessed Holy Spirit. Beware lest you miss the message and power of the book of **Hebrews** by bringing in some "theological system" by which you judge all Scripture.

2. **And tasted of the heavenly gift**—Now what **heavenly gift** could be thus spoken of and known *without further definition?* What indeed but that described in Romans 6.23; "THE GIFT of God is eternal life through Jesus Christ our Lord." But our Lord's promise concerning "the gift of God" was not made to tasters, but to *drinkers;* as He said to the Samaritan woman:

"If thou knewest the gift of God, and Who it is that saith to thee, Give Me to drink; thou wouldest have asked of Him, and He would have given thee living water . . . Whosoever *drinketh* of the water that I shall give him shall never thirst; but the water that I shall give him shall become in him a well of water springing up unto eternal life" (Jno. 4.10, 14).

Thus all *drinkers* of the water of life are truly saved. But, you ask, Could a person *taste* of eternal life and yet be lost forever? Certainly! Tasting is not drinking! Drinkers are not mere tasters: there has been a consenting act of *the will.** They have committed themselves to what they drink. In tasting, the flavor and effect of the draught is discovered: the will thereupon must decide whether to drink or reject what has been tasted. The drinker commits the water to the man and the man to the water—a marvelous picture of saving faith! If it be the water of life, which Jesus gives, he has drunk of it; he has committed himself to it; his whole being is involved; his whole future is determined. Thousands today know the

*Because of their fear of "free will," many shut themselves out from honest interpretation of many a passage of Scripture, as here. Let me ask you about a word in another passage: Jude 12-13. No one denies that these are lost people—"The blackness of darkness" being for them "reserved forever." But what does the expression *"twice dead"* (vs. 12) mean? We profoundly believe that it can only indicate that there was in them "a quickening" connected with their being "enlightened." At first they were, as were we all once, "dead in trespasses and sins." But how *"twice* dead" unless there had been such a revelation of the Risen Christ as the "natural mind" knows nothing at all of, connected with their being "enlightened."?

taste of the heavenly gift, eternal life, who never did *drink that water!* who did not accept, receive, that gift in a saving sense. In this most solemn passage in the sixth of **Hebrews,** we find men who have tasted* and rejected—and *been* rejected by God.†

3. **And were made partakers** [partners] **of the Holy Spirit—** Note at once, it is *not* said that these were *sealed* with the Spirit, as were those at Pentecost (Acts 2), and in Samaria (Acts 8), and in Ephesus (Acts 19), who were "sealed unto the day of re- demption" (Eph. 4.30); as God says, concerning the Ephesian belivers:

"In Whom [Christ] ye also, having heard the word of truth, the good news of your salvation—in Whom, having also believed, *ye were sealed* with the Holy Spirit of promise, which is an earnest of our inheritance, *unto the redemption* of God's own possession" (Eph. 1.13-14).

Again, in Romans 8.9: "If any man *have* not the Spirit of Christ, he is none of His." And Jude describes the professing Christians as "mockers" of the last days, "walking after their own lusts of ungodliness, making separations [among the saints] *sensual, having not the Spirit.*"

---

*To insist that this "tasting" was simply an intellectual experience, is absurd. If you are a guest at a table, and there is before you some article of food, of which you taste but do not eat, you do not say that your tasting was an intellectual process!

Mr. R. A. Torrey's assertion, "There is a quickening short of regeneration," is the only explanation of this whole passage! God gave these Hebrews of Ch. 6.4-6 these experiences, having awakened them from the sleep of death sufficiently so that they experienced these things. They were "once *enlightened.*" They *"tasted."*

†In 1892 a company of us from the Gospel Tabernacle were holding a gospel service in one of the great corridors in Bellevue Hospital, New York. I was seated on a ledge in the corridor, expecting to give a testimony shortly. In front of me stood a company, singing a gospel hymn which repeated over and over the name of Jesus. Out from the patients seated beyond this singing company, and past the singers, dashed a man in terror. I was just able to seize and hold his arm, beseeching him to be seated. He turned a frightful look upon me, saying, *"I knew Him once!"*

I asked him what he meant.

"I mean Him they are singing about. I cannot bear to hear it. I really knew Him once— but I am *lost!"*

I turned to every passage of invitation. He simply shook his head in anguish. I said, "Christ will gladly receive any sinner."

"Look here," said he. Stooping to his left ankle, he began to unfasten safety pins. Turn- ing back the leg of his trousers—"Look at that," he said. I saw a hideous mass of syphi- litic sores. "I went back to *that,*" he said. Rapidly he replaced and fastened the bandage, and said, "Let me go! I *knew* Him *once!"*

I followed him down the corridor and held him as long as I could. Judas, on the way to hang himself, must have looked as did he. I went with him (in vain) as far as I could with- out his leaving the hospital (where he had a right, as an emergency patient, to be). But what a lesson he had taught me!

But that certain operations of the Spirit of God are "partaken of" both by the saved and by those that are finally lost, we know from the story of King Saul. We read of him, "The Spirit of Jehovah will come mightily upon thee, and thou shalt prophesy with them, and shalt be turned into another man" (I Sam. 10.6). This was fulfilled: "God *turned* him another heart" (vs. 9, R.V. marg., Heb.). And in the next verse, "The Spirit of God came mightily upon Saul." But alas, Saul departed into self-will, and so continued, until not only was he rejected as to the kingdom—"Now thy kingdom shall not continue" (I Sam. 13.14); "Jehovah . . . hath *rejected thee* from being king" (15.23); but also, —awful result of persistent self-will—"The Spirit of Jehovah *departed* from Saul, and an evil spirit from Jehovah troubled him" (16.14), to the day of his suicide! We read therefore in God's covenant with David, that although his son (Solomon) should be "chastened with the rod of men" upon disobedience, God prom- ised: "But My loving kindness shall not depart from him, *as I took it from Saul,* whom I put away before thee" (II Sam. 7.14-15).

Here then in Saul is one that was a "partaker" (partner) in the meaning of the word in Hebrews 6.4, **partakers of the Holy Spirit.** The Spirit came mightily on Saul, as we have seen; and Saul on his part at first acted with the Spirit, and was used of God. Thus was he a "partner" of the Spirit.* In like manner men are today **made partakers**—partners, **of the Holy Spirit,** who are *never sealed* by Him:

"And those on the rock are they who, when they have heard, receive the word *with joy;* and these have no root, who *for awhile believe,* and in time of temptation *fall away*" (Lk. 8.13. See also Mk. 4.16-17).

Judas Iscariot went with another disciple when the Lord sent them out two by two (Mk. 6.7-13) to preach "the kingdom of Heaven," and he did preach, and went on, and wrought miracles, without doubt (by the **partaking of the Holy Spirit,** in the sense

*Saul had fathomless ignorance of the things of God (I Sam. 9.5-10), no real faith (13.8, 9); no discernment as to what prayer is (vs. 12). He repeated the sin of Eli's sons in bringing the sacred ark into the midst of the profane host in battle (I Sam. 4.14-18). See also Saul's heartless giving over of Jonathan, the man of faith, to death. Saul *never really knew God.* How like Divine Grace, to choose *another Saul* from the same tribe, then "chief of sinners," the persecutor of His dear Church, through whom to reveal His utmost counsels and grace in the N.T.: "*Saul,* who was also called *Paul"!*

of our verse), unsuspected by the rest till the very Last Supper
of John 13! At first, doubtless, he deceived himself. Then, unwilling for the self-denial the path demanded, he yielded to his
inner greed, to his eternal ruin! And what about Demas, a companion and fellow-worker with Paul, saluting the saints in
Colossians 4.14, accounted a "fellow-worker" in Philemon 24?
But in Paul's last epistle, towards the end of his second imprisonment, Paul, nearing martyrdom, must dip his pen in bitter ink
indeed, and record, "Demas forsook me, *having loved this present
age.*" Let us be frank and honest despite all our feelings, false
traditions, and false hopes. There are those that *tasted* of life, so
that they knew what it was: and **were made partners** [*metachoi*]
of the Holy Spirit, so that they were conscious of Him and His
work, who are seen in this passage finally to fall away and be
eternally rejected of God.

4. **Verse 5: And tasted the good utterance of God**—This,
like the preceding statements, refers to experimental things. The
statement is not that the Word of God is good, which we all
know; but that an utterance *(hrēma)** of God's quickened to the
soul, has been found good by the spiritual sense of taste: "If ye
have *tasted* that the Lord is gracious" (I Pet. 2.3); see also Psalm
119.103, Ezekiel 3.3. These **who merely tasted the good utterance
of God,** in Hebrews 6.5, were "rocky ground hearers" of Luke
8.13, quoted above. They had attended and enjoyed Bible classes
and conferences. The word "taste" is often applied in Scripture
to that peculiar enjoyment of the living Word of God. John
(Rev. 10.10) said, "It was in my mouth sweet as honey." So
these "enlightened" souls who had "tasted" of the gift of life and
been made "partners" of the Holy Spirit in His presence and
operations, had also "tasted" of the quickened **Word of God**
which indeed is "good."

5. **And** [having tasted of] **the powers of the coming age**—
The explanation of this remarkable phrase, **the powers of the
age to come,** is clear in Scripture. In Exodus 15.26 we see a prom-

---

*Another Greek word—*logos,* means simply *word;* but here the **utterance of God is** expressed by the Greek word *hrema,* meaning *saying,* "that which has been uttered by the living voice," "things spoken." This is the *hrema* of the Spirit which is the sword of the
Spirit, of Eph. 6. Compare Matt. 4.4, 26.75; Lk. 2.51, Rom. 10.8 (twice), 17.

ise that upon diligent obedience, the Israelites would be exempt
from the diseases of Egypt, "For," God said, "I am Jehovah that
healeth thee." They were warned, also, in Leviticus 26.14-16, and
Deuteronomy 28.21, 22, 27, that among other judicial results
of disobedience would be diseases like "the boil of Egypt." We
know how they failed; here God's grace exceeded (Deut. 8.4).
Through disobedience they were smitten, and shall yet be smitten (until the Remnant of Israel turns to God) with these
various diseases. But in connection with the coming of "the King
in His beauty" to them, and the restoration of Zion, we find,
"The inhabitant shall not say, I am sick" (Isa. 33.24); and "The
eyes of the blind . . . opened, the ears of the deaf . . . unstopped";
"the lame man" leaping "as a hart," and "the tongue of the
dumb man singing" (Isa. 35.5-6).

Now when our Lord came with the gospel of the kingdom
(for He was the King of the Jews), offering to fulfill their
kingdom promises, He "healed all manner of diseases" (Matt.
4.23, 24). He fulfilled to Israel, His people, that which Isaiah had
prophesied (Matt. 8.14-7). At first, the healings were general,
numberless. Later, as official rejection developed, our Lord demanded personal *faith* of the sick. Finally, in Matthew 16.18, He
prophesies "I will build My Assembly" (the Church, an entirely
new thing! Eph. 2.15; Col. 3.10, 15). And then He forbids them
to tell the Jews that He *is* the Christ, the Jewish Messiah (Matt.
16.20). And He starts to Jerusalem to *die* (vs. 21). Thus those
"powers" of healing, of complete deliverance from disease, which
will be fully realized in the Millennium, **the coming age,** were
manifested to the Jews by our Lord.

Later, when the Holy Ghost came, and the building of the
Church was thus begun, we find on the day of Pentecost **the
powers of the age to come** manifested in the remarkable healings
of the book of Acts. So we have also present among the gifts
(*charismata,* I Cor. 1.7; 7.7 etc.) bestowed by the Holy Spirit, in
I Corinthians 12.4-11, one gift that directly touches the matter of
bodily healing (vss. 9, 28). But read carefully the footnote below.*

---

*We fully believe that these gifts belong to the Church throughout the dispensation:
first, because of Scripture; second, because of the history and teaching of these things; and
third, because of personal experience and observation. But we would have carefully noted
the peculiar form applied to that work of bodily healing which belongs to the Church time.

Now in the *age to come,* the Millennium, the Church will be with Christ in glorified, heavenly bodies; and Israel will be in their own land—not one of them, as we have seen, saying "I am sick," for they will be "forgiven their iniquity." Healing, then, is just one of the powers of the age to come, the manifestations of the power of God (I Cor. 12.4-11) of which these Hebrew believers had "tasted." For in the age to come, the Millennium, the glory of God is revealed at Jerusalem, and His mighty power publicly known, even upon other creatures than man (Isa. 40.5, Heb. 2.14). Christ will reign in personal Presence and power, Satan will be banished; peace will be enjoyed; ills will disappear. Every believer tastes even today something of that glory, however hindered through unbelief is its manifestation.

Verse 6: We come now to one of the two great crisis words of this most solemn passage of holy Scripture having fallen away: (Gr., *parapesontas*). This is the only occurrence of this word in Greek Scriptures. Its corresponding Old Testament word, *mahal,* is found, for example, in Ezekiel 14.13, Leviticus 5.14. This Hebrew word is defined by Gesenius: "To act covertly, treacherously, faith-lessly, as an adulterous woman against her husband" (Num. 5.12, 27); "to deal treacherously with Jehovah" (Deut. 32.51; II Chron. 12.2; 29.19; Job 21.34. See also Job 31.11, 26, 28). The same word is used concerning Achan's sin (Josh. 7.1). The inner meaning of the word translated "fallen away" in Hebrews 6.6 is that of secret departure from God: "apostasy gradually resolving into antipathy," as Saphir puts it.

Now *parapesontas,** having fallen away, is an aorist participle;

In I Cor. 12.8-10, it is a double plural: "To another, gifts *(charismata)* of *healings."* Just as in the following phrase: "To another, workings of miracles." As also, "To another, discernings of spirits" (I Cor. 12.9, 10, 28). Notice these plurals. The very expression, "gifts of healings," should guard us against the notion that to any person is given *a gift* of healing—that is, a gift of healing any and every one—as the Lord Jesus exercised the powers of the coming age at the beginning of His ministry. "Gifts of healings" is indeed a distinct bestowment by the Holy Spirit. But the very expression, a double plural, shows that the exercise of the power is directed by the Spirit in special cases: a different character of working from that of a gift like wisdom, or knowledge (vs. 8): or prophesying or teaching, vss. 10, 28. The unbelieving denial of these gifts as belonging to the Church is to be shunned. We recommend the reading of such books as Dr. A. J. Gordon's **Ministry of Healing,** and Nevius' **Demon Possession.**

*Two Greek words are used to denote that fatal spiritual state, falling away:
1. *Aphistemi,* which means primarily to separate from, either by one's own will (voluntarily), or by that of *another.* The four occurrences of this word in the Gospel of Luke will

the whole process is looked at as one event. And it is not a falling
into sin that is meant, but a falling away from God, from Christ,
from salvation, a renouncing the truth. The "once" *(hapax)* of
verse 4 governs all these verbs, as I have said, and looks at their
acts as of past time—done! This "falling away" is not I John 2.1,
"If any man sin, we have an Advocate." Nay, it is the abandonment of *desire for* the Advocate! Apostates are described here,
not backsliders; for to the latter God said:

"Return, thou backsliding Israel . . . I will not look in anger
upon you; for I am merciful, saith Jehovah, I will not keep anger
forever. Only acknowledge thine iniquity" (Jer. 3.12-13).

Even Webster defines apostasy as "Abandonment of what one
has voluntarily professed: total desertion of principles or faith."
The Greek word from which our word "apostasy" comes, stands
out in Hebrews 3.12: "Take heed, brethren, lest haply there shall
be in any one of you an evil heart of unbelief, in *falling away*
(Gr., *apostenai*) from the living God."

The noun *(apostasia)* of the same verb occurs twice in the New
Testament: in Acts 21.21, where Paul is accused of abandoning
Moses; and in II Thessalonians 2.3, where the general apostasy
from God to the Antichrist of Revelation 13 is described. Let
us put out of our thought, then, that those who in Hebrews 6.6
fell away merely through lack of faith honestly and earnestly
kept up Jewish practices; or that they are only in a fearful, un-

---

illustrate: Lk. 2.37: "Anna *departed* not from the temple"; "he (Satan) *departed* from
him [Jesus], until a fitting opportunity" (Lk. 4.13): The rocky ground hearers are said to
"fall away" in time of temptation, (by their own consent, clearly, even if unconsciously or
by degrees) (Lk. 8:13). Christ said He would say to the wicked "in that day" (as told
also in Matt. 7.22), *"Depart from Me,* all ye workers of iniquity" (Lk. 13.27). This will
be by the will of Another, the Judge.

This same word is used in Heb. 3.12, where the idea of *will* seems to prevail as in the
other cases cited.

Note also, Paul *"departed* from them [the Jews] and separated the disciples" (Act 19.9).
And "In later times some shall *fall away* from the faith." (I Tim. 4.1). In the same
epistle, "From such *withdraw* thyself" (I Tim. 6.5, A.V.). "Let every one that nameth
the name of the Lord *depart* from unrighteousness" (II Tim. 2.19).

2. The other Greek word, *parapipto,* is found in Heb. 6.6 only: . . . **and then fell
away.** *Parapipto* is compounded from *para,* alongside; and *piptein,* to fall—literally, to fall
alongside. "Hence, to deviate from the right path, to turn aside, to wander. In Scripture,
to fall away from the true faith, from Christianity."—Thayer.

Doubtless the thought of will is here also, but more that of delusion: so the Galatians
were said to be "bewitched" in turning from the way of simple faith back to Judaism. See
Gal. 3.1; 4.9-11.

In either case, certainly, only God's true saints, His elect, would be preserved, whether
from willful departure or from fatal bewitchment.

certain state. No, the verses following forbid any conclusion other than that they have turned back to the sin they have loved, away from the light they had seen (remember, they are **those who were once enlightened**) and had come to *hate the light!*

It is impossible to renew them again unto repentance—Note that in accordance with the whole present-day trend of false security, the impossibility of renewing such to repentance is placed in verse 6 in our Bibles, whereas in the Greek it belongs to verse 4, at the beginning, in the emphatic place: literally, **For impossible** (it is) **those once for all enlightened and having tasted . . . become partners . . . have tasted . . . and have fallen away to renew them again unto repentance.** In the awful word RE-JECTED of verse 8 lies the secret of the impossibility of renewing to repentance those that "fall away." For, (a) such do not themselves desire to repent! (b) No man or angel has power to bring about repentance. It is a granting, a gift, from God. (As see Acts 11.18; II Tim. 2.25.) Repentance in Scripture is shown to be a miracle, "about-mindedness"—what a man loved, he loathes; what he loathed, he is now drawn to. It is *not* that God is not able to renew them but—awful fact! that He is *unwilling;* that these are the "rejected." God rejected *them,* for there was no response, but the contrary, to His infinite love in the "heavenly gift" of Christ, which they had tasted.

And now for the summing up of their fearful sin: **Seeing they crucify to themselves the Son of God**—The word "afresh" is not in the text: it is with them (inwardly) to reject the Son of God for themselves, and (outwardly) **to put Him to an open shame**— or, to expose Him to public disgrace. No one but a professing Christian can put Christ **to an open shame.** An atheist, an infidel, a denier, puts Christ far from him. But a professing Christian has taken Christ's name upon himself. The world looks to him, and rightly, to exemplify in himself what they know the Son of God was and is. It is manifest that these who have fallen away have not only renounced their confession of Christ, but have also gone into open worldliness and sin.

Verse 7: We remember that in the parable of the Sower (the understanding of which our Lord indicated was fundamental to knowing all parabolic teaching—Mk. 4.13), it was the state of the ground in each case that decided the issue: the seed was the Word of God, the same in each case. So here in Hebrews 6.7, **the rain that cometh oft** upon the land, "the rain that cometh down from Heaven," was the same upon the ground **that bringeth forth herbs meet for them for whose sake it is also tilled,** and upon the ground **that beareth thorns and thistles,** the fruit of the curse. (Read Gen. 3.17.) Brethren, it is *always* herbs meet for the tiller, *or*—thorns and thistles. As for these "herbs," they are "things that accompany salvation" (vs. 9) to wit: work for God, and "love toward His name," shown in "ministering unto the saints"; and in *keeping on*—**still do minister.** It would not be *kindness* for God to give *assurance* to any saints but herb-growers. On the other hand, the thistle-growers have rejected all God's mercy, and choose to bear sins—**thorns and thistles** still. Therefore, they are right-eously *rejected*. Further grace and mercy would be inconsistent with the holiness and justice of God's throne. These, loving law-lessness, are allowed still to love it; and thus, finally, "fall into the hands," in judgment, of that "Living God" from Whom they "fell away" during their earth life. (See Ch. 10.31.)

Verse 8:   Now comes the awful final word of this passage, the second *crisis* word (the first was, "fell away": see comment on vs. 6). We now read: **IT IS REJECTED.** The natural results of re-jection follow: **nigh unto a curse; whose end is to be burned.*** God has exhausted with such apostates those means by which He reaches the hearts, consciences, faith, and affections of man; they having been "enlightened," having "tasted" of life, the heavenly gift, in Christ; and of the sweet goodness of the Word of God, and the blessed powers of the world to come, all to no effect. They have tasted Christianity and rejected it, **bearing thorns and thistles** despite God's blessing upon them. Having

---

*The Hebrews to whom Paul was writing, knew what their Scriptures spoke about God's using *fire* in judgment. "Abraham beheld, and lo, the *smoke* of the land went up as the smoke of a furnace" (Gen. 19.28). "Ye were as a brand plucked out of the *burning*, yet have ye not returned unto Me, said Jehovah" (concerning cities in Israel forward in sin, Amos 4.11).

Also Moses' warning prophecy in Deut. 29.22-28: "The whole land is brimstone, and salt, *and a burning.*"

So shall the final destruction of restored Babylon be: "Her high gates shall be *burned* with fire" (Jer. 51.58). "Every shipmaster, . . . and mariners, cried out as they looked upon the smoke of her *burning*" (Rev. 18.17-18).

rejected God, they are "rejected" of Him! Fearful state, fearful outlook!*

9   But, BELOVED, we are persuaded better things of you, and things that accompany SALVATION, though
10   we do thus speak. For God is not unrighteous to forget your work and the love which ye showed toward His name, in that ye ministered unto the saints, and still do
11   minister. And we desire that each of you may show the same diligence unto the fullness of hope even unto the
12   end: that ye be not sluggish, but imitators of them who through faith and patience inherit the promises.

We have studied three of the great warnings of Hebrews, which begin with (1) Chapter 2.1-4, and continue in due season throughout the epistle: (2) Chapters 3.7 to 4.13; (3) Chapter 5.11 through Chapter 6.8; (4) Chapter 10.36-9; (5) Chapter 12.14-17; (6) Chapter 12.25-29; and (7) Chapter 13.9.

Let us note at the beginning to whom these warnings are addressed. It is certain that they are not addressed to what Scripture calls "the world." In His great high-priestly prayer of John 17 our Lord said to the Father, "I pray not for the world." Christ on the Cross "tasted death for every man." "He gave Himself a ransom for all." "He is the propitiation for the whole world." The gospel is preached to the whole world, to all men; and Christ's atoning death, His burial, and His resurrection, is the gospel! But in Hebrews it is those who have confessed who are addressed. Even concerning the doom of the apostates, as in Chap-

---

*In connection with this we must remember Jno. 15.6; "If a man abide not in Me, he is cast forth as a branch, and is withered; and they gather them and cast them into the fire, and they are *burned.*"

There are those who would rob this verse of all meaning, by asserting that the ones spoken of here had never had Christian experiences.

Nor must we neglect the statement of Lk. 8.13, already quoted, concerning those who "for awhile believed." Believed what? Why, the word that they had "received with joy." It was the same word that the "good-ground" hearers received. The sole difference was in the *soil;* not in the seed—not in the Word preached! Our Lord emphasized that it was "upon the *rock*" that the shallow soil was, and we remember the Scripture, "Is not My word like a fire? saith Jehovah; and like a hammer that *breaketh the rock* to pieces?" Remember that *brokenness* shown by the publican, who "smote his breast, saying, God, be Thou merciful to me the *sinner!*"

Going back to Jno. 15.6: "If any man abide not in Me he is cast forth as a branch," indicates the very state described in Heb. 6.4-8, and 10.26-31. In no other way can the words, "tasted of the heavenly gift [eternal life]; and the blood . . . wherewith he was sanctified," be honestly explained. And the judgment of such is the same in Jno. 15.6 as in the Hebrews passages: "Cast forth as a branch . . . withered . . . cast into the fire . . . burned." *REJECTED . . . cursed . . . burned.* And Ch. 10.27: "A certain fearful expectation of *judgment,* and a fierceness of *fire* which shall devour the *adversaries.*"

ters 6 and 10, we have seen that it is those who had been "enlightened," had "tasted," had been "made partakers," or were
"sanctified," who are spoken of.

By misunderstanding the warnings of Hebrews, many true
believers have been cast down in spirit and filled with apprehen-
sions. But after the awful announcement concerning apostates,
there is the great passage, verses 9-20, which should give comfort and firmness of soul to such. For the Spirit has in mind true
believers, "saints," in Hebrews, as in all of the epistles. We see
this exemplified here: they are the *"beloved,"* of whom things
that accompany salvation are spoken. These two great words,
"Beloved" and "Salvation," are not used to and of apostates!
To them indeed Paul announces, "We are not of them that
shrink back unto perdition" (10.39), although he had been
warning them: for it is God's way with all those who confess
Him, to warn them of evil.

**Verse 9: But, beloved, we are persuaded better things of you,
and things that accompany salvation, though we thus speak:**
Vincent has an excellent word concerning **are persuaded** *(pepeismetha)*: "We are firmly convinced the verb indicates a past hesi-
tation overcome." Also Westcott: "The form implies that the
writer had felt misgivings and had overcome them." Alford says
here that the word is "stronger than *pepaithamen,* which would
express only a subjective confidence, whereas *pepeismetha* gives
the result of actual conviction by proof." Compare the remarkable
parallel in Romans 15.14, where the same word is used.

Paul said **though we do thus speak** (of the apostates of vss.
4-5), yet he now in contradistinction to these uses the precious
address "beloved" *(agapêtoi),* a word used sixty times in the New
Testament—the first nine times by God to Christ His beloved Son
(quoted thus by Peter in II Pet. 1.17); and then only of saints,
whether Gentiles ("To all that are in Rome, *beloved* of God"—
Rom. 1.7); or the Israelitish Remnant ("Touching the election,
they are *beloved* for the father's sake," Rom. 11.28).

In all Hebrews, Chapter 6.9 alone contains that precious word,
"beloved," which is always spoken of true believers. Take your
pencil and mark in I John, beginning with Chapter 3.2, *"Beloved,
now are we children of God,"* then verse 21; then Chapter

4.1, 7, 11; then III John 1, 2, 5, 11; ending with Jude 3, 17, 20.

And things accompanying* salvation—This whole verse turns on this word "salvation." There are described in the first part of Chapter 6, as we have noted, remarkable privileges, experiences, and professions; but the word "salvation" is *not connected with them*—not mentioned! Manifestly in the apostle's mind there were distinct and sure marks of those who are called, in Chapter 1.14, "heirs of *salvation*."

He does, indeed, "thus speak," as he puts it, *to* those of whom he is persuaded the **better things, the things connected with salvation.** For man is not an automaton. He is *told* of a *salvation* to be *received, by faith,* and of a *doom* to be *avoided.* All this, although "Salvation is of Jehovah" (Jonah 2.9; Ps. 3.8; 37.39; Lk. 3.6).

This great word SALVATION *(sōtēria)* is applied to actual deliverance over forty times in the New Testament (with its cognates, over fifty times) : and always meaning certain, eternal deliverance. For instance, we read, "Neither is there *salvation* in any other"; "The gospel is the power of God unto *salvation*"; "God chose you unto *salvation* in sanctification of the Spirit and belief of the truth"; "The *salvation* which is in Christ Jesus with eternal glory"; "The Author of eternal *salvation*" (Heb. 5.9). The word is used seven times in **Hebrews,** for instance Chapters 1.14; 2.3, 10; 5.9; 6.9; 9.28; 11.7.

So that while the Spirit **does thus speak** in Chapter 6.1-8 of the Divine rejection of those having fallen away, we may "rejoice with trembling" if we find the marks that **accompany salvation** with ourselves! For certain signs attend either *salvation,* or decay, and possible final damnation.

Verse 10: In this case, as verses 9 to 12 show, there was, **accompanying salvation,** certain spiritual activity which God calls **your work and the love which ye showed toward His Name.** Note that **love toward God's Name,** that *love which He treasures, is not a mere sentiment or ecstasy.* "Whosoever loveth Him that

---

*The Greek participle, *echomena,* is from the word *echō,* meaning "I have," "I hold." See Matt. 7.29; 8.9; 9.6. It is used over 600 times in N.T. and constantly concerning reality, possession, as in Jno. 3.15, 16, 36; never indicating a mere nighness to possession. Bloomfield renders it "connected with," as does Darby.

begat loveth him also that is begotten of Him" (I Jno. 5.1).
And what a word is this concerning our humble **ministering to
His saints**—that **God is not unrighteous to forget it!**

We may say that Hebrews 6.10 is a verse that we quote to
others very frequently. Living, as it has been our privilege to do
for many years, a life relying upon God, when one of His saints,
for example, as the Lord's steward, writes ministering to us, we
put in our reply, "Remember Hebrews 6.10!" Some of you have
been visiting and comforting the bereaved; others have helped
the weak, and visited the saints who are sick. Some of you have
that rare gift of discerning and relieving human loneliness, or
hidden sadness. Now, our Lord said even a cup of cold water
given in His name should in no wise lose its reward! Service
rendered to the Lord will not be forgotten! See Mark 9.41.*
God is not unrighteous. He hath said, "He that reapeth receiveth
wages," and He will be faithful to His Word.

There are terrible utterances in **Hebrews** concerning both
the unbelieving and the fearful, as well as the open rebels.
Also there is a consciousness developed here, as in all the epistles,
of genuineness, of sainthood, that is, of *being Christ's!* As John
says, "We know that *we* are of God, and the whole world lieth
in the evil one" (I Jno. 5.19). And Hebrews 6.10, "*Your* work
. . . ye . . . ye . . . the saints."

Verse 11: And we **desire that each one of you may keep on
showing the same diligence** (both in laying hold of the truth, and
putting it into service) **unto the full assurance** [same word as in
Col. 2.2; I Thess. 1.5, *et al.*] **of hope even to the end.** The words
mean, of course, the end of their pilgrimage through this world.

And Peter enjoins,

"Wherefore, brethren, give the more *diligence* to make your
calling and election sure" [not to God, but to yourselves]. "For if
ye do these things, ye shall never stumble: for thus shall be richly
supplied unto you the entrance into the eternal kingdom of our
Lord and Savior Jesus Christ."

Now what shall we say of those—yea, *to* those, willing to

---

*The R.V. gives the literal meaning, *"In name that ye are Christ's."* You may be
wrong concerning the person, but you did it *as unto Christ*, believing he was Christ's. That
renders the reward *certain!*

neglect this *diligence*, which adds grace upon grace—saying that they "believe in election," and straightway lapsing back into the slumber which they love? We would shout the word of warning! We would read this book of. Hebrews in the power of the Holy Spirit unto such, over and over. Three things we must emphasize then:

1.   That people may have experiences and Divine dealings, and yet fall away and be lost.

2.   That the word "salvation" is not in God's Word spoken of such, for "Salvation is *of Jehovah*," as we saw. And, as we read so clearly in II Corinthians 5.18: "But all things are *of God*, Who reconciled us to Himself through Christ"; or Romans 11.36: "For *of Him*, and through Him, and unto Him, are all things. To Him be the glory forever"! God's beloved are His elect* who will inherit *salvation* by His will—uncaused by them in any degree, for "the purpose of God according to election is *not of works*."

3. That God keeps His saints *by His Word*, as we saw anew in the words of Hebrews 6.9, "though we thus speak." "By which also [the gospel] ye are saved, *if* ye hold fast the word which I preached unto you," Paul wrote to the Corinthians (I Cor. 15.2). And,

"To present you holy and without blemish and unreprovable before Him: *if so be* that ye continue in the faith, grounded and steadfast, and not moved away from the hope of the gospel which ye heard" (Col. 1.22, 23).

It is no sign of the absence of faith to be concerned about our salvation, but rather the opposite. As Paul says to the Corinthians,

"Try your own selves, whether ye are in the faith; prove your

---

*Such have *passed through* the "Enchanted Land" of sluggishness ᴧᴧd drowsiness so ac-curately described by Bunyan in **The Pilgrim's Progress:**

"By this time they were got to the Enchanted Ground, where the air naturally tended to make one drowsy: . . . Then they came to an arbour, warm and promising much refreshing to the pilgrims, for it was finely wrought above head, beautified with greens, furnished with benches and settles. It had in it a soft couch where the weary might lean. This, you must think, all things considered, was tempting, for the pilgrims already began to be foiled with the badness of the way: but there was not one of them that made so much as a motion to stop there. Yea, for aught I could perceive, they continually gave so good heed to the ad-vice of their guide and he did so faithfully tell them of dangers, and of the nature of dan-gers when they were at them, that usually, when they were nearest to them, they did most pluck up their spirits and hearten one another to deny the flesh. The arbour was called the Slothful's Friend, on purpose to allure, if it might be, some of the pilgrims there to take up their rest when weary."

(Oh, get **Pilgrim's Progress,** and read this wonderful picture and warning!)

own selves. Or know ye not as to your own selves, that Jesus Christ is in you? unless ye be reprobate" (II Cor. 13.5).

It was no sign of the absence of faith that the disciples at the Last Supper asked with deep concern, "Lord, is it I?"

Hear Paul speak of himself:

"I fight, as not beating the air; but I buffet my body, and bring it into bondage: lest by any means, after that I have preached to others, I myself should be rejected"—reprobate, as "rejected" should read.*

It was not that Paul lived in uncertainty or terror, but that he knew and had accepted in his very soul the Christian path: and especially the path belonging to teachers of God's Word, who bear a heavy responsibility—James 3.1: "Be not *many* of you *teachers,* my brethren." "God *will keep* the feet of His *saints,*" but it has been His good pleasure to put red lights of warning at every "Bypath Meadow." And Christian may go on his way rejoicing, but those very Philippians who are told to rejoice evermore, are also told to work out their own salvation with fear and trembling: "For it is God Who worketh in you," says Paul, "both to will and to work, for His good pleasure." Or, see Hebrews 12.28, 29:

"Receiving a kingdom that cannot be shaken, let us have grace, whereby we may offer service well-pleasing to God with reverence and awe: for our God is a consuming fire."

Levity and lightness are as foreign to true faith as are unbelief and despair! Peter says:

"Receiving the end of your faith, even the salvation of your souls . . . Gird up the loins of your mind, *be sober,* and set your hope perfectly on the grace that is to be brought unto you at the revelation of Jesus Christ."

There is a false presentation of "eternal security" today that presumes that the believer is under eternal safety without taking heed to such warnings and exhortations to a holy walk as we find in **Hebrews** and indeed, throughout Scripture.†

*Paul does not here say, as in I Cor. 3.15, "If any man's *work* shall be burned, he shall suffer loss: but he himself shall be saved; yet so as through fire." But he says, "Lest I *myself*"—his person, "should be reprobate," the Greek word *adokimos.* The other occurrence of this word is in Heb. 6.8 concerning the ground: "If it beareth thorns and thistles, it is *rejected* and nigh unto a curse; whose end is to be burned."

†I was speaking at a Bible conference in Indiana several years ago. Near my table at lunch was a long special table set for a company. Soon they came in, a crowd of young

You say, There are those that are born again, and they are all safe; they are God's elect. We agree heartily that God's elect, the born-again ones, are sealed by the Spirit unto the day of redemption. Glorious fact! But, brother, it is in the eighth of Romans, the great citadel of the security of the saints, that God says to His saints, "If ye live after the flesh, ye must die [spiritual death]: but if by the Spirit ye put to death the deeds of the body, ye shall live." Romans 8 links up with **Hebrews**. "Give the more diligence to make your calling and election sure," says Peter— "sure" not to God, certainly, but to yourselves. And Peter insists that we *add* to our faith, virtue; to our virtue, knowledge; to our knowledge, self-control; to our self-control, patience—godliness . . . brotherly kindness . . . love.

But what about the passive, "sluggish," professing Christian, who claims he believes on the Lord Jesus Christ, but shows no spiritual life or activity? **Hebrews** tells him his danger! If neglect of "so great a salvation," or a spiritual slothfulness—that is, willingness to remain "babes" when "by reason of the time since we heard the truth" "we ought to be teachers" of others—if this is our state, let us read **Hebrews** and awake!

Those who rely on "security" apart from a holy life, and from that diligence enjoined in the book of **Hebrews**, either will find their sense of security bitterly attacked some day by the enemy (who will overwhelm them with a view of their unworthiness), or else will be let alone by the devil, to become companions of Mr. Vain Confidence.*

---

people, evidently enjoying a day's outing at the lake. They stood at attention behind their chairs around the table, and repeated three times in loud staccato tones, after the manner of a college football yell, the three letters,

"J! I! M!"

Then they seated themselves, and plunged immediately into vivacious conversation. Much perplexed, I called one of the waiters and asked, "What did those young people mean by shouting 'J.I.M.'?"

"That is *their* watchword," he replied. "It means, 'Jesus is mine.' "

Now there were doubtless, among those dear young people, many earnest ones. But can you imagine such a thing taking place on the day of Pentecost, or in Paul's great ministry at Ephesus? Persecution, death and dungeons were the lot of that early Church. Indeed, it is in the last chapter of **Hebrews** that we read of an imprisonment noted nowhere else: "Know ye that our brother Timothy hath been set at liberty." And Paul wrote of the wondrous heavenly calling of the Church, the Body of Christ, in the Epistles to the Ephesians and Colossians, with a Roman chain clanking on his wrist!

Has the world become "a friend of grace"?

*There are those (and they are sadly many) who are ready to cry, "Heb. 6 belongs only to

Ah, we could *cry out* because of these things! For have we not seen congregations dying before our faces? Have we not spoken to thousands to whom we knew our words were not welcome words (for fear that they would arouse them into real spiritual conscious-ness and activity)? Have we not cried, "Awake, thou that sleepest, and arise from among the dead ones, and Christ shall shine upon thee!" only to see most of the hearers passing out chattering about petty personal matters, or the crops, or the weather? Did not Christ say it is a "little flock" to whom the kingdom will be given? And un-to a hearer inquiring, "Lord, are there few that be saved?" He said:

"*Strive* [Gr.: *agonidzō, agonize,*] to enter in by the narrow door: for many, I say unto you, shall seek to enter in, and shall not be able" (Lk. 13.24).*

And, "For narrow is the gate and straightened† the way, that leadeth unto life, and *few* are they that find it" (Matt. 7.14).

These things being so, what mean ye by wondering at the mighty warnings of the Book of Exhortation, **Hebrews?**

Verse 12: That ye be not sluggish, but imitators of them who through faith and patience inherit the promises: Those in Chapter 5.12 were "sluggish," and became dull of hearing; be-came milk-users; and, awful thought! some of them became apostate! **But imitators of them** (that is, of the saints of old) **who through faith and patience inherit the promises**—Notice the connection with Abraham (vss. 13-15). His great example fol-lows: "Having patiently endured, he obtained the promise."

_____

the Hebrews!" Indeed, we have lately found those who claim that this entire passage "does not refer to Christians at all, but to the Hebrews as a nation, and to the way that God has led that nation for many centuries." But such teaching ignores the words of Heb. 3.1, where those addressed are "partakers of a heavenly calling": which the Hebrews as a nation never have become.

Instead of saying Heb. 6 belongs to the Jews, and dismissing its warnings, Christians should take just the opposite attitude: If *Hebrew* believers, with all *their* advantages, need warning, how much more we, branches of the wild olive tree, who have been grafted into the good olive tree, need to be warned! Read frequently Rom. 11, where Paul says:

"Be not high-minded, but fear: for if God spared not the natural branches, neither will He spare thee. Behold then the goodness and severity of God: toward them that fell, sever-ity; but toward thee, God's goodness, if thou continue in His goodness: otherwise thou also shalt be cut off" (Vss. 20b-22).

Agonidzō is the word of the *Greek games;* and means to use every energy in the face of difficulties and opponents. "Seek," represents mere desire, not contest!

†These city gates of the East admitted persons, *not baggage.* They were narrowed to admit the passage of a pilgrim at a time, if necessary!

13   For when God made promise to Abraham, since He
14   could swear by none greater, He sware by Himself, say-
     ing, Surely blessing I will bless thee, and multiplying I
15   will multiply thee. And thus, having patiently endured,
16   he obtained the promise. For men swear by the greater:
     and in every dispute of theirs the oath is final for con-
17   firmation. Wherein God, being minded to show more
     abundantly unto the heirs of the promise the unchange-
18   ableness of His counsel, interposed with an oath; that
     by two immutable things, in which it is impossible for
     God to lie, we may have a strong encouragement, who
     have fled for refuge to lay hold of the hope set before
19   us: which we have as an anchor of the soul, a hope both
     sure and steadfast and entering into that which is within
20   the veil; whither as a Forerunner Jesus entered for us,
     having become a High Priest for ever after the order of
     Melchizedek.

Verses 13, 14: You remember that the God of glory appeared
to Abraham (Acts 7.2) in the Chaldean land, and made him the
great seven-fold promise recorded in Genesis 12.1-3:

"Now Jehovah said unto Abram, Get thee out of thy country,
and from thy kindred, and from thy father's house, unto the land
that I will show thee: and I will make of thee a great nation, and
I will bless thee, and make thy name great; and be thou a
blessing: and I will bless them that bless thee, and him that
curseth thee will I curse; and in thee shall all the families of the
earth be blessed."

Verse 15: Abraham was seventy-five years old when he left
Haran.*

"After these things," came the great covenant of Genesis
15, and Abraham's believing in Jehovah, and God's "reckoning
it to him for righteousness" (Gen. 15.6). (Then came the birth
of Ishmael—an effort of Abraham's flesh to help God out! when
Abraham was eighty-six: Gen. 16.16.)

"Dwelling in *tents*," building *altars*, digging *wells*, in Canaan
(not asking yet to possess Canaan!), Abraham still believed God's
promise to him of the land! Then, when he was *ninety-nine*, comes

---

*How long he had "patiently endured" his father's fleshly effort to go along into the
land of Canaan or to hold Abraham back (Gen. 11.31, 32)—before that father's death, we
are not told.

the renewal of the promise, and the prophecy of the birth of Isaac. This, by the way, is the circumcision chapter, Genesis 17; and God's command was faithfully observed by Abraham, who commanded "his children and his household after him" (Gen. 18.19). Then came Isaac's birth and growth and the great testing from Jehovah of offering up Isaac a sacrifice! And God's *oath—spoken out from heaven* to His faithful servant:

"By Myself have I sworn, saith Jehovah, because thou hast done this thing, and hast not withheld thy son, thine only son, that in blessing I will bless thee, and in multiplying I will multiply thy seed as the stars of the heavens, and as the sand which is upon the seashore; and thy seed shall possess the gate of his enemies" (Gen. 22.16, 17).

And so, after Sarah's death, and the honor the Hittites paid to Abraham as "a prince of God among them," we come to the end of his life of faith: "Abraham died in a good old age, an old man, and full of years, and was gathered to his people" (Gen. 25.8).

Verse 15: Now the Spirit's comment upon all this in **Hebrews,** as we have seen is, **Having patiently endured, he obtained the promise.** We see that from Abraham's departure from *Haran* (Gen. 11.31, 32; 12.4) to his being "gathered to his people," was over a hundred years (from the promise made in Ur, it was more than that) of **patiently enduring.***

It is remarkable that after Jehovah's oath to Abraham when he was about to offer up Isaac (Gen. 22.15-18), there are no more recorded testings of his faith. He was now in such a deep rest of faith that he walked steadily therein, the remainder of his days. Indeed, he had said to his servants when on the way to offer up Isaac, "Abide ye here with the ass, and I *and the lad* will go yonder; and *we* will worship, and *come again* to you." And to Isaac he had said, "God will provide Himself the lamb!" (Read Gen. 22 *often!*)

Verse 16: **For men swear by the greater: and in every dispute of theirs the oath is final for confirmation:** Let us suppose that some king of England, renowned for uprightness, had promised

---

• *He failed in the matter of Egypt (Gen. 12); and in the matter of Hagar and Ishmael (Gen. 16); but did you ever observe this fact: NOT ONE SIN of an Old Testament saint is recorded in the New Testament?

one of his subjects he would raise him to a baronetcy. Doubts might arise in the subject's mind as to whether the king might forget his promise, or circumstances be allowed to interfere with its fulfillment. But if we may suppose further, that the King of England should humble himself to go before the Lord Chief Justice of the realm and *place himself under oath* that he would appoint the subject to a baronetcy; and that the king should give the subject *a record* of this royal oath, in addition to his promise—all room for uncertainty would be removed. How much more when God promises and takes His oath!

Verses 17, 18: God . . . pledged Himself with an oath that by two unchangeable things, (His word, and His oath; which is final for confirmation vs. 16; Ex. 22.11; Deut. 29.12) **in which it is impossible for God to lie, we may have a strong encouragement—** In a *promise,* the assertion of an intention is made; in an *oath,* the person's character is publicly and solemnly put behind the assertion! In a promise, we look at the *words;* in an oath, we look at who and what the promiser is!*

Now it is **to the heirs of the promise** that this assurance is made. You and I may ask, Are we such heirs? We dare not say so if we are careless and sluggish professors, instead of those of verse 12, "who through faith and patience inherit the promises." But of these, we have read further in verse 18, **By two unchangeable things** (the promise and the oath of God) **. . . we may have a strong encouragement, who have fled for refuge to lay hold of the hope set before us.†** Here, of course, the writer speaks of the

---

*"Had He sworn by Heaven and earth, I might have feared, lest, as they shall pass away, so His word might. But when the Most High swares by Himself Who abides forever, my fears are gone."—Govett.

And Andrew Murray: "God points to Himself, His Divine Being, His glory, His power, and pledges Himself, gives Himself as security, as hostage, that, as sure as He lives, He will fulfill His promise. Oh, if we would but take time to tarry in the presence of this God, and to listen to Him swearing to us that He will be faithful, surely we would fall down in confusion that we ever harboured for a moment the doubt, which thinks it possible that He may be untrue and not keep His word. And now let us pause and realize what all this argument about the blessing and the oath of God means. In the Christian life there is lack of steadfastness, of diligence, of perseverence. Of all, the cause is simply—lack of faith. And of this again the cause is—the lack of the knowledge of what God wills and is— of His purpose and power to bless most wonderfully, and of His faithfulness to carry out His purpose. It is to cure these evils; it is to tell His people that He will do anything to win their trust, and will do anything for them if they will trust Him, that God has taken His oath of faithfulness."—*The Holiest of All*, pp. 221-2.

†To how many of the professing Christians of your acquaintance would the word "ref-

"cities of refuge" to which a manslayer (who had killed someone "unwittingly" "unawares") might flee and be safe "till the death of the high priest." (See Ex. 21.13; Num. 35; Deut. 19; Josh. 20.) Three cities of refuge were appointed in Canaan on the west side of the Jordan, and three on the east side, whither the manslayer might flee "from the avenger of blood." Read carefully Numbers 35.9-15, and you will see that it was the business, the duty, of the manslayer to flee, "lest the avenger of blood pursue the manslayer, while his heart is hot" (Deut. 19.6). God would see to it that the man who fled for refuge "obtained that safe refuge" (Num. 35.28). What a picture, both of Hebrew sinners, to whom Paul was writing; yea, and of us all who have believed; and also of national Israel in the future! For they slew Him "unwittingly," "unawares"! So the Lord Jesus prayed, "Father, forgive them, for *they know not* what they do!" And Peter preached, "And now, brethren, I know that *in ignorance* ye did it, as did also your rulers" (Acts 3.17). But note that there was no ransom to be taken for the *murderer* (distinct in all the Law from the "manslayer"), just as no refuge from coming wrath is provided for the rejecter of Christ (Num. 35.31).

Verse 19: To a Hebrew believer, then, this **fleeing for refuge, to lay hold of the hope set before us** would be a vivid picture! Let it be so in our own hearts, for there is no other hope of rescue from judgment than "Christ Jesus our hope" (I Tim. 1.1); as Peter also says, "God . . . begat us again unto a *living hope* by the resurrection of Jesus Christ from the dead." CHRIST, in His work of putting away sin on the Cross, and now being our Great High Priest in Heaven, where the veil is rent, and access to God is absolutely free through Christ—*this* is the "hope" **we have fled to lay hold of . . . which (vs. 19) we have as an anchor of the soul** [a hope] **both sure and steadfast and entering into that which is within the veil.**

Note that while it is our **fleeing for refuge to lay hold** in verse 18: **the hope** we lay hold of in verse 19, becomes "an anchor" that holds us. "An anchor of the soul unfailing and firmly fixed," Stuart translates. It is well to reflect that **have fled for refuge is**

---

uge" and "fled" apply? They may have "joined the church," but have **they fled for refuge** [from coming judgment] **to lay hold of the hope set before them?**

in the perfect tense, while, **which we have as an anchor,** is present and continuous.* Mark this well. For in **Hebrews,** Christ is the Great High Priest, Who, by His present perfect knowledge of our needs, His sympathy with our path, and His intercession, perpetually keeps His own. It is not *our* holding fast, but His holding us fast. For note again the words of verses 19-20, **entering into that which is within the veil, whither as a Forerunner Jesus entered for us.** Notice that "within the veil" indicates Heaven itself, the very presence of God. It is that which is within the veil, and not the veil itself, which is in view. (As to "the veil," see comment on Chapter 10.20.)

Verse 20: Whither as a Forerunner Jesus entered for us, having become a High Priest forever after the order of Melchizedek. In Chapter 9.24 we read:

"Christ entered not into a holy place made with hands, like in pattern to the true; but into Heaven itself, now to appear before the face of God for us."

Vincent well says, " 'Forerunnner,' (a word used only here) expresses an entirely new idea, lying completely outside the Levitical system. The Levitical high priest did *not* enter the sanctuary as a forerunner, but only as the people's representative. He entered a place into which none might follow him, in the people's stead, and not as their pioneer. The peculiarity of the new economy is that Christ as High Priest goes nowhere that His people cannot follow Him. He introduces man into full fellowship with God."†

And now we return in Chapter 7 to the subject of the Melchizedek high priesthood of Christ; mentioned indeed in Chapters 5, 6 and 10, but (in 5.11 to 6.19) broken off by a prolonged parenthesis necessary on account of the "dullness of hearing," and lack of full growth of the hearers: for the apostle had "many things

---

*Some refer **sure and steadfast and entering into that which is within the veil** back to "refuge," of vs. 18 (which is grammatically possible); but to refer the words to "hope" is also grammatically possible, and is, we think, the meaning.

†To quote the saintly Andrew Murray, "He is a Priest forever, a Priest in the power of an endless life, a Priest Who opens to us the state of life to which He Himself has entered in, and brings us there to live here on earth with the life of eternity in our bosom."

"There is a sanctuary in which God dwells. There was a veil that separated man from God. Jesus came from within to live without the veil, and rend it, and open a way for us. He is now there for us as Forerunner. We may now enter in and dwell there, in the power of the Holy Ghost. This is the gospel according to the Epistle to the **Hebrews**."

to say" of Melchizedek, but they were hard to explain because of the hearers' low spiritual state. But in Chapter 6.9, as we have just seen, he calls them *"beloved,"* and is persuaded that "things that accompany *salvation"* are theirs—though he had thus spoken to arouse them out of sluggishness into diligence and imitation of the faith and patient endurance of such as Abraham.

Now we must consider this Melchizedek priesthood of Christ —a stupendous subject—and may God indeed assist us; for have we not all found ourselves to be "dull of hearing" as to many glorious truths spoken in Scripture?

CHAPTER SEVEN

1   FOR this Melchizedek, king of Salem, priest of God Most High, who met Abraham returning from the
2 slaughter of the kings and blessed him, to whom also Abraham divided a tenth part of all (being first, by interpretation, King of righteousness, and then also King
3 of Salem, which is King of peace; without father, without mother, without genealogy, having neither beginning of days nor end of life, but made like unto the Son of God), abideth a priest continually.
4   Now consider how great this man was, unto whom Abraham, the patriarch, gave a tenth out of the chief
5 spoils. And they indeed of the sons of Levi that receive the priest's office have commandment to take tithes of the people according to the Law, that is, of their brethren, though these have come out of the loins of Abraham:
6 but he whose genealogy is not counted from them hath taken tithes of Abraham, and hath blessed him that hath
7 the promises. But without any dispute the less is blessed
8 of the better. And here men that die receive tithes; but there one, of whom it is witnessed that he liveth. And,
9 so to say, through Abraham even Levi, who receiveth
10 tithes, hath paid tithes; for he was yet in the loins of his father, when Melchizedek met him.

WE MUST SAY EARNESTLY that in view of these words concerning Melchizedek in Chapter 5.11: "Of whom we have many things to say, and hard of interpretation," we need to approach this subject with earnest prayer for light and for wisdom from Heaven. For is it not true of practically the whole Church, at least in a sad degree, that we "are become dull of hearing . . . such as have need of milk"?

After the description of our Great High Priest, the Son of God (Ch. 1), and Son of Man (Ch. 2), Who, as such, is to have all things subjected to Him, it is emphasized at the close of Chapter

2, that, having suffered, having been tempted, "He is able to succor them that are tempted." Again at the end of Chapter 4 (vss. 14, 15) we read:

"Having then a Great High Priest, Who hath passed through the heavens, Jesus the Son of God, let us hold fast our confession. For we have not a high priest that cannot be touched with the feeling of our infirmities; but One that hath been in all points tempted like as we are, sin apart."

We should often reflect on these matters regarding Christ which lie at the beginning of the epistle, for they draw out our hearts toward Him Who partook of "blood and flesh . . . in like manner" with us. After setting forth these personal features which so endear our Lord to us, the Spirit immediately proceeds to bring before us two great facts, both of which must be laid hold of if we would understand either our present heavenly position and walk, or our future hopes in connection with our Great High Priest.

1. He is **a Priest forever after the order of Melchizedek** (5.6-10; 6.20; 7.17). His priesthood is, then, **after the order of Melchizedek**, not after the order of Aaron (7.11). After Melchizedek, "priest of God Most High, brought forth bread and wine" . . . and blessed Abram in Genesis 14, God waits *a thousand years,* and then Melchizedek appears in Psalm 110.4, where God says:

"Jehovah hath sworn, and will not repent:
Thou art a Priest forever
After the order of Melchizedek."

Therefore from eternity to eternity He is such!*

---

*"The whole place Melchizedek occupies in sacred history is one of the most remarkable proofs of the inspiration and the unity of Scripture, as written under the direct supernatural guidance of the Holy Spirit. In the book of Genesis all we know of him is told in three short, very simple verses. *A thousand years later* we find a psalm with just one single verse, in which God Himself is introduced, swearing to His Son that He is to be a High Priest after the order of Melchizedek. Another thousand years pass, and that single verse becomes the seed of the wondrous exposition, in this epistle, of the whole work of redemption as revealed in Christ Jesus. All its most remarkable characteristics are found enveloped in the wondrous type. . . . We see in it nothing less than a miracle of Divine wisdom, guiding Melchizedek and Abraham with a view to that which was to take place with the Son of God two thousand years later; revealing to the psalmist the secret purpose of the Divine mind in the promise made to the Son in Heaven; and then, by the same Holy Spirit, guiding the writer of our epistle to his Divinely-inspired exposition. It is indeed the Eternal Spirit, the Spirit of Christ Himself, through Whom all was wrought and in due time recorded. . . . So had God prepared in Melchizedek a wondrous prophecy of His Son, Whose right to the priesthood lay in no earthly birth, but in His being the Son of God from eternity to eternity.

We think of the word "order" as denoting inheritance, or succession; but here it denotes character of being, and office. This
"order" is *contrasted* in Chapter 7.11 with that of Aaron, as we
shall see. It becomes necessary, then, to the student of Hebrews
to inquire what this "order of Melchizedek" means, prophesies, and
anticipates; and none the less to inquire what is that priestly work
in which our Lord is now occupied which was set forth in type in
Aaron's priesthood.

To speak briefly: 1. Our Lord exercised priestly functions of care
and prayer for His own during His earthly life. Again, on the
Cross He "offered Himself" (Heb. 9.25, 28). Next, He was saluted
at resurrection by God as "Priest forever after the order of Melchizedek" (7.17).*

2. Aaron, on the other hand, is connected constantly with
sacrifices. He is traveling through the wilderness with the people
of God before they come into the land of their inheritance.

3. Melchizedek is revealed, in his person and ministry, to
Abraham, the great-grandfather of Levi, Aaron's ancestor. The
counsels of God revealed in Melchizedek, therefore, are prior to
those revealed in Aaron and his ministry.

The time and circumstances of Melchizedek's coming to meet
Abraham are most striking. Abraham is **returning from the
slaughter of the kings** (Heb. 7.1), the hosts of the Mesopota-
mian country that had overwhelmed Lot and the cities of the plain.
Abraham, the depositary of the Divine promises is *met* by Melchizedek, "king of Salem . . . priest of God Most High . . . Possessor
of Heaven and earth" (Gen. 14.18, 19). The king of Sodom is
about to offer Abraham of the spoils of the victory, saying, "Give
me the persons, and take the goods to thyself."

"May God teach us to know what it means that Christ is our Melchizedek, a Priest
forever. It is the spiritual apprehension of this everlasting priesthood . . . that lifts our
inner experience out of the region of effort and change, and failure, into the rest of God,
so that the immutability of His counsel is the measure of that of our faith and hope."—
The Holiest of All, An Exposition of Hebrews, Andrew Murray.

*It is idle to contend that Melchizedek was not connected with sacrifice but with
blessing only: Gen. 14 (quoted above), Heb. 7.15, 17, 24, and 27—"when He offered
up Himself": these verses concern Christ after the order of Melchizedek! He was not
"after the order of Aaron" at any time, though of course in the types such as the Day of
Atonement, blood sacrifice was set forth. But it was Christ *after the order of Melchizedek*
Who "offered up Himself," and thereafter appears in blessing, as did Melchizedek to
Abram in Gen. 14.

Melchizedek, we read, "brought forth bread and wine: and he was priest of God Most High" (Gen. 14.18). Now we read in the Psalms (104.15) of "wine that maketh glad the heart of man, and bread which strengtheneth man's heart"; and Jesse sent bread and wine to King Saul by David (I Sam. 16.20). The bread and wine Melchizedek brought forth would indeed refresh Abraham and his three hundred eighteen weary servants!

Now note again the *name of God* in connection with Melchizedek's priesthood: "He blessed him [Abraham], and said, Blessed be Abram of God Most High* [Heb., *El Elyon*], possessor of Heaven and earth" (Gen. 14.19). Melchizedek, as priest of God Most High, acts doubly: (1) He calls the blessing of God Most High upon Abraham; and then (2) he blesses God Most High. Thus he does in typology the very two things Christ will do: first, obtain blessing from God upon His people; second, lead their praise of God, as He says, "In the midst of the congregation [of 'My brethren'] will I sing Thy praise" (Ps. 22.22; Heb. 2.12).

Melchizedek, being priest of God Most High, "possessor of Heaven and earth," must represent Christ leading in worship, in Heaven as well as on earth! And here will be fulfilled in its time that "mystery of His will made known to us":

"According to His good pleasure which He purposed in Him [Christ] unto a dispensation of the fullness of the seasons, to sum up [gather together into one] all things in Christ, the things in the heavens, and the things upon the earth" (Eph. 1.9-10).

"For it was the good pleasure [of the Trinity] that in Him [Christ] should all the fullness dwell; and through Him to reconcile all things unto Himself, having made peace through the blood of His Cross . . . whether things upon the earth, or things in the heavens" (Col. 1.19-20).

We pause here in this great subject to sum up briefly in a footnote the teachings of our chapter in Hebrews concerning Melchizedek, under three heads: What he was, What he did, What the "order of Melchizedek" *means as to Christ.*†

---

*Read the footnote in the Scofield Bible (p. 23, a) concerning God Most High, *El Elyon*. It is most instructive.

†*I. What he was:*
 1. He was a *man* (Heb. 7.4), not Shem, as some contend, for the record of Shem's beginning of days and end of life is given to us.

What the "order of Melchizedek" means as to Christ: In our sad "dullness of hearing" the "many things" that we find concerning Melchizedek are indeed "hard of interpretation." He is, you may say, a type of Christ. Ah, but he is more than that! The Levitical priests were "after the order of Aaron." Aaron was thus not a mere type. We hear God say of Christ,

"Thou art a Priest forever

After the order of Melchizedek" (Chs. 5.6, 10; 6.20; 7.17). Christ is a Priest, and He is a Man. Mary was the mother of Jesus, but it is blasphemy to call her "the mother of God." Let us believe,

2. Named eight times in Hebrews (besides Gen. 14 and Ps. 110), superseding and preceding Aaron and all the Levitical economy, his place is exceeding high.

3. He was (vs. 1) King of Salem, priest of God Most High, a dignity high above that of Abraham the Patriarch.

4. His name means, King of righteousness (Calvary); his position, and then also King of Salem, means King of Peace (the result of Calvary). That is, he was King of righteousness as Christ first answered at the Cross all righteous claims against us; and second King of peace: Christ is our peace: "Being therefore justified by faith, we have peace with God." Melchizedek was king-priest: king before priest.

5. His father's name is not given, nor his mother's, though he had both father and mother, being a man.

6. The record is not that he was like the Son of God, but that (vs. 3) he was made like unto the Son of God, (in having no earthly origin given). He was made like (in his record) to the Son of God—evidently as to the facts of Heb. 7.1-3, of which note the last—abideth a priest continually.

7. Without father, without mother—revealed to us; without genealogy—revealed to us. The expression without genealogy simply means that his genealogy is not given, for from vs. 6 it is evident that he had genealogy: whose genealogy is not counted from them (the sons of Levi). Note especially without genealogy, for Jesus as Son of Man had genealogy: an official genealogy of the house of David (Matt. 1), and a maternal genealogy (Lk. 3). (Of course, as Son of God He had none! "I came forth and am come of God," He said. And, "Ye know neither Me, nor My father.")

8. Having neither beginning of days nor end of life—(vs. 3) revealed to us: no recorded time of birth, death, or age. We are not to draw from these remarkable words the inference some have drawn, that Melchizedek never was born, nor that he has not died. This is to misread the type. The conviction of Calvin and a host of careful commentators is a true one, that his having neither beginning of days nor end of life is a descriptive clause of the same character as without father, without mother, without genealogy.

9. No kingly line named, no "successor"; not as with the kings of Israel and Judah, a life with recorded beginning and end.

II. What he did:

1. He blessed Abraham, "who had the promises" (vss. 1, 6): so is greater "better," than Abraham.

2. He blessed God Most High on the occasion of Abraham's triumph over the kings (vs. 1), and his rescue of wretched Lot (type, perhaps of Israel's condition at Armageddon). This reminds us that throughout the New Testament, especially in Hebrews and the Revelation, we see that Christ's enemies are to be put beneath His feet as the first step in the establishment of the kingdom.

3. He received tithes of Abraham: unto whom Abraham, the patriarch, gave a tenth out of the chief spoils (vs. 4). Thus by tithes Abraham confessed Melchizedek's superiority, for (vs. 7): Without any dispute the less is blessed of the better.

III. See main text.

with hearts rejoicing, that there is a *Man* at God's right hand in the glory Who is our Great High Priest; and, that He is *God the Son,* through Whom the worlds were created! Let us not seek with our little minds to "reconcile" His humanity and deity, for God asks us to do no such thing, but to have the *faith* of *little children.*

Verse 2: **King of righteousness, and then also King of Salem, which is, King of peace:** Note carefully verses 17, 18, 27, where Christ, "after the order of Melchizedek," is seen as High Priest *offering Himself* for the sins of the people, once for all. Thus in type is set forth first, Christ's work on the Cross, where He met all the *righteous claims* of God against us victoriously, and from which death He was raised triumphantly. Then, the *result* of His work on the Cross:

"Being therefore justified by faith, we have *peace* with God through our Lord Jesus Christ" (Rom. 5.1).

"Through Him to reconcile all things unto Himself, having made *peace* through the blood of His Cross" (Col. 1.20).

Melchizedek was king, and that in a double sense: **King of righteousness,** as to character—no man like him on earth. His very name insists on this; and **King of Salem, which** (interpreted) **is, King of peace.**

Then this office of Melchizedek, **priest of God Most High,** must be meditated upon. We turn again to the story in Genesis 14—brief, but how significant! The eastern confederation of kings under Chedorlaomer has been victorious over the cities of the plain, where Lot dwells. Abraham and his three hundred eighteen trained servants pursues them, smites them by night unto complete victory, and rescues "his brother Lot." Then the king of Sodom comes out to meet the victor. What a place of temptation, for the king of Sodom will say, "Give me the persons, and take the goods to thyself."! But now comes Melchizedek, King of Salem. "And he was priest of God Most High."

Abram knew *El Shaddai,* the Almighty (Gen. 17.1); and God took the name of *Jehovah* toward the earthly nation of Israel; but *El Elyon,* God Most High, reaches everywhere and everything in Heaven and earth! It is a vaster name, all-inclusive, recognized, as we shall see, by Gentiles.

"And he blessed him, and said, Blessed be Abram of God Most High, Possessor of Heaven and earth: and blessed be God Most High, Who hath delivered thine enemies into thy hand."

Abraham entered readily into this new revelation of His God, so that his answer to the offer of the king of Sodom was,

"I have lifted up my hand unto Jehovah, *God Most High*, Possessor of Heaven and earth, that I will not take a thread nor a shoe-latchet nor aught that is thine, lest thou shouldest say, I have made Abram rich: let there be nothing for me [R.V., margin]; only that which the young men have eaten, and the portion of the men that went with me" (Gen. 14.22-24).

What deliverance this new revelation of his God wrought in Abraham's heart! So David speaks: "I will cry unto *God Most High*, unto God that performeth all things for me" (Ps. 57.2). And Moses:

"When the *Most High* gave to the nations their inheritance,
When He separated the children of men,
He set the bounds of the peoples
According to the number of the children of Israel.
For Jehovah's portion is His people;
Jacob is the lot of His inheritance" (Deut. 32.8, 9).

Here God is acting as the *Most High* (for He is that, as we shall see, to all nations and men), high over all earthly affairs, and arranging them in view of the children of Israel. For as we see from Deuteronomy 32.9, no other *nation* can say, "Jehovah is our God." But all nations and men must acknowledge Him as *God Most High (El Elyon)*. We see this first in the fourth of the remarkable prophecies of Balaam (unregenerate as he was, but under Divine control in these utterances):

"He saith, who heareth the words of God,
Who seeth the vision of the Almighty" (Num. 24.4).

Here we have God as God; as the *Most High*, above all; and as "the Almighty" *(El Shaddai)*, His name as revealed to the patriarchs (Ex. 6.2, 3).

Next we go to Daniel, where the first great king of the Gentiles, Nebuchadnezzar, is brought through seven years of humbling till he knew "that the *Most High* ruleth in the kingdom of men, and giveth it to whomsoever He will." Then he testified, "The *Most High* doeth according to His will in the army of Heaven, and among the inhabitants of the earth" (4.32, 35).

This brings us to "the army of Heaven," both holy and fallen angels. As to the latter, beginning with the "anointed cherub" (Ezek. 28.14), their prince, the highest being God ever made: God declares, "I said, Ye are gods, and all of you sons of the *Most High*. Nevertheless ye shall die like men, and fall like one of the princes" (Ps. 82.6-7). This "anointed cherub" in his hideous pur-pose said, "I will be like the *Most High*" (Isa. 14.14).

Even the demons, when our Lord came, cried out, "What have we to do with Thee, Jesus, Thou Son of the *Most High God?*" So also the cry of the poor demonized creature of Acts 16.17. It is precious to note in Gabriel's mission to Mary concerning the birth of Jesus, "He . . . shall be called the Son of the *Most High*," and "The power of the *Most High* shall overshadow thee." It is also most precious that our Lord promised to us, "Ye shall be sons of the *Most High:*" in doing good without hope of earthly reward, and in loving enemies.

We have spoken so fully of this great title of God, in order that our hearts may be drawn above all earthly and Jewish estimates of the priesthood of Christ. He is not to us the priest of *Jehovah;* but is, like Melchizedek, Priest of the Most High God, *El Elyon,* Possessor of Heaven and earth, above all national and dispensational considerations.*

Verse 3: Melchizedek did not belong to a royal line, as we have said: **without father, without mother, without genealogy.** Con-trast this with the records of the Kings of Judah and Israel. **Having neither beginning of days nor end of life**—as are recorded of those kings; **but made like unto the Son of God.** Note that it is not said that he is like the Son of *Man,* the Son of David, of Whose birth of the virgin, and of Whose death on the Cross Scripture is full: but **made like unto the Son of God.**

Now other Scriptures tell of our Lord's inheriting the "throne of His father David." But David was a man, not God. Christ

---

*If ye could but know and believe, O ye Jews, that we have a High Priest Who, while Man, is wholly heavenly; that all the Levitical things of your earthly tabernacle and temple were types that have vanished away; and the priesthood has been "changed" (Ch. 7.12), then you would cease naming your *Levis* and your *Cohens* (priests), for you would know that out of the royal tribe of Judah came the King-Priest Who shall sit upon His throne in Jerusalem—Who is now at the right hand of God; and that the veil, our Lord's flesh, has been rent, and that through His shed blood we come directly to God in Heaven, having a Great High Priest there, and the energy of the blessed Holy Spirit in our worship!

indeed is the Son of Man, but, as is brought out in Chapter 1, He is God's Son, addressed as God and as Lord—God Himself. Here then in Melchizedek stands before us one whom God made "like unto" His Son. No earthly things, no human things, are allowed to hinder. No royal heritage of earth, no record of parentage or birth or death; no account of derivation, office, or authority—simply the words, **made like unto the Son of God.**

Note further the word "made." It has to do with the description God uses in setting Melchizedek before us. As we have said, it was not that he was like the Son of God in essence, but made* like Him in description and consequent typical significance. Further, it is evident that the name **Son of God** here has reference to Christ's deity as the second Person of the Godhead, rather than to His Person as God-Man. For in contrast with the words **without father, without mother, having neither beginning of days nor end of life,** remember Gabriel's explanation to Mary: "The Holy Thing which is begotten shall be called the Son of God" (Lk. 1.35). Here the body that God "prepared" Christ is in view, and the Divine plan of securing its holiness, so that the Child being born, though partaking of blood and flesh, should be called "the Son of God."

But in our chapter in **Hebrews** the words **made like unto the Son of God** are preceded by the words **having neither beginning of days** (Christ, we have just seen and know, *had* "beginning of days"), **nor end of life**—which four latter words do not characterize the Melchizedek priesthood as consummated at Calvary, where our blessed Lord laid down His life. Yes, to "take it again," doubtless, but we are seeking for the significance of His Melchizedek priesthood.

---

*"The comparison is not between Christ and Melchizedek, but between Christ and the isolated portraiture of Melchizedek; and that in regard to the Divine Nature of the Incarnate Son, and not to His human Nature in which He both was born and died, nor even to His official dignity. It is not however implied that the record in Genesis was purposely designed to convey the meaning which is found in it, but that the history sketched by prophetic power has the meaning."—Westcott, **Epistle to the Hebrews,** p. 173.

"As to the import of these affirmations of vs. 3, they stand or fall together. If one may be taken to express the impression made by the silence of the historian, all may. That this latter is the correct view, I conceive to be beyond a doubt. What Christ is really, Melchizedek must be apparently; and this is all that is required. In a historical narration which makes in general great account of parentage, genealogy, and scrupulous record of ancestry and end—he, *the greatest of them all,* has no such mention. He stands, a solitary

In this connection also, we must go back to the first verse of Chapter 7, where Melchizedek is called "priest of God Most High," and to Genesis 14 where is added, "Possessor of Heaven and earth." For the first revelation concerning the Son in Hebrews is that He is "Heir of all things," and He must be remembered as such throughout the book. But we read in Chapter 2.7-8 that, although God "crowned [Him] with glory and honor," and "set Him over the works of His [God's] hands," and "left nothing that is not subject to Him," *yet now we see not yet all* things subjected to Him." In Chapter 10.12, 13, He is seen:

"He, when He had offered one sacrifice for sins forever, sat down on the right hand of God; henceforth *expecting till* His enemies be made the footstool of His feet."

And (Eph. 1.9-10) we find God

"making known unto us the mystery [secret] of His will, according to His good pleasure which He purposed in Him [looking forward] unto a dispensation of the fullness of the times, to sum up all things in Christ, the things upon the heavens, and the things upon the earth." Of course this last is not accomplished as yet.*

---

instance of a personage whose function transcends that of *every other* Scripture character . . . with not one word to shed light on his family or his nation, his reign, or his destiny. The inference is that the silence is intentional and significant."—A. C. Kendrick, **Commentary on The Hebrews**, p. 86.

*There is a recurring thought throughout **Hebrews** of a *future day* of manifestation of our Lord. Note the verses and portions quoted below:

Ch. 1.6: "When He [God] *again* bringeth in the Firstborn into the world.''

Ch. 2.5: "Not unto angels did He subject the *world to come,* whereof we speak."

Ch. 9.10: "Imposed *until* a time of rectification."

Ch. 9.11: "But Christ having come a High Priest of the good things *to come.''*

Ch. 9.28: "Christ . . . *shall appear a second time,* apart from sin, to them that wait for Him, unto salvation."

Ch. 10.36-7: "For ye have need of patience, that, having done the will of God, ye may receive *the promise.* For yet a very little while, *He that cometh shall come,* and shall not tarry."

Ch. 11.40: "God having provided *some better thing* concerning us, that apart from us they [the O.T. saints] should not be made perfect."

Ch. 12.26-28: "Yet once more will I make to tremble not the earth only, but also the Heaven . . . Wherefore, receiving *a kingdom that cannot be shaken,* let us have grace."

We see thus that in the book of **Hebrews** future things are constantly in view. And the Melchizedek priesthood of our Lord (which not only included His offering up Himself on the Cross (7.27), but a priesthood that lasts forever! looks forward to the day when His enemies have all been made "the footstool of His feet," and all things in the heavens and earth are beneath His hand.

We come now to the last clause in verse 3, [This Melchizedek] **abideth a priest continually:** There is no note of the beginning of his priesthood nor of its ending, but **made like unto the Son of God,** as we have seen, he comes on the scene as a *continual* priest, without earthly or human connection. And we note that the chief emphasis as to our Lord's Melchizedek priesthood is that it endureth "forever." Beginning at Chapter 5.6, "A Priest *forever* after the order of Melchizedek"; then Chapter 6.20: "Jesus . . . having become a High Priest *forever* after the order of Melchizedek," and so on, we find emphasized the last phrase of Chapter 7.3: **abideth a priest continually.** It was after the likeness of Melchizedek that Christ arose, "not after the law of a carnal commandment, but after the power of an *indissoluble life*" (vs. 16).

Again, verse 24: He "hath His priesthood *unchangeable*." And verse 25: "He *ever* liveth to make intercession for them."

Finally [Melchizedek] **abideth a priest continually** does not say that the man Melchizedek is a "continual priest" today, but simply that he appears on the scene as he does, and is made one, or rather, the only one, of the "order" of his name, fulfilling the great prophecy in Psalm 110.4. We find in him one who, while a man, yet stands alone as the head of an "order" of which Christ, *being* God (not, *made* to be God) is, and not of the order of Aaron, whose father and mother we know, and who was *not* **made like unto the Son of God.**

Verse 4: **Now consider how great this man was, unto whom Abraham, the Patriarch, gave a tenth out of the chief spoils:** Melchizedek comes into our view blessing Abraham, the depositary of God's promises, the father of the household of faith, and progenitor of Israel. Concerning no other man are we told, **Consider how great this man was.** For it is not the custom of Holy Scripture to set forth the greatness of man—but the contrary. Man is less than nothing, and vanity. Yet Melchizedek is pronounced "great"; Abraham recognized his greatness; we are told to "consider" it. Though a man, he is looked at as in that dignity in which the Most High God has set him, a dignity beyond that conferred on any other human being: for if we regard Moses as the great revelator of the Old Testament (and he is), and if we regard Paul as God's great herald and revelator of the New Testament (as he is), we come to this: That all Mosaic revelations are set aside in view of that priesthood set forth in Melchizedek, and that Paul is the one who narrates this great- ness. Therefore, we need hardly say, it is the position of Melchize- dek, the dignity conferred by God upon him, and not natural human greatness, that is in view. Tithes are paid to him, subject- ing to him Abraham, Aaron, and Levi, and all his descendants. And he blessed Abraham: **But without any dispute the less is blessed of the better (Vs. 7).** It is as if the Scripture had hasted to speak of Melchizedek as the priest after which order our Lord Jesus is. Eight times, we repeat, his name occurs in Chapters 5 to 7, God delighting to say concerning Christ, "Thou art a Priest forever after the order of Melchizedek" (7.17).

How great this man was is shown also in his having the offices of both priest and king. He was **King of Salem, which is, King of Peace.** But Salem, which Psalm 76.2 identifies with Zion, is agreed by very many to be Jerusalem (which means, Foundation of Peace). For we must remember God's word concerning the place of Israel's sanctuary: "A glorious throne, set on high from the beginning, is the place of our sanctuary" (Jer. 17.12). "The beginning" evidently goes back to Creation itself. It was shown to Abraham when he offered up Isaac, wonderful picture of Christ! (Gen. 22.2ff.)*

---

*There are two elevations in Jerusalem: the lower, Moriah, where God had Abraham offer up Isaac, and where God indicated to David the temple site (I Chron. 21.15 to 22.1). The other and higher elevation was Mount Zion, where David's throne was set. Indeed, the whole city and land became known by that name. This hill of Zion is the place beloved of God on this earth, for the typical services in the old temple were to pass away, and that temple be destroyed, but of Mount Zion God says,

"Jehovah hath chosen Zion:

He hath desired it for His habitation.

This is My resting-place forever:

Here will I dwell; for I have desired it" (Ps. 132.13, 14).
And,

"It shall come to pass in the latter days, that the mountain of Jehovah's house shall be established on the top of the mountains, and shall be exalted above the hills; and all na- tions shall flow unto it, and many people shall go and say, Come ye, and let us go up to the mountain of Jehovah, to the house of the God of Jacob; and He will teach us of His ways, and we will walk in His paths: for *out of Zion* shall go forth the Law, and the word of Jehovah from Jerusalem" (Isa. 2.2-3).

You may say, How could the infinite God desire a habitation, a resting place, upon this earth? I reply, You were made in God's image, and while you may enjoy many other

We are not told that Melchizedek reigned over a large part of Palestine—possibly only over the locality where God's sanctuary afterwards was erected. This will be no surprise to them that know God and His ways. Nor did Salem need to be a "great" city in the eyes of men, nor its king a "great" earthly potentate.* For men were blind then, and are today, to true greatness, which has to do only with God.

We must beware of slight thoughts of Melchizedek because he is mentioned but once in history (Gen. 14), once in prophecy (Ps. 110.4), and now finally here in **Hebrews,** while Levi and Aaron and Aaron's priesthood have many chapters devoted to them and to their service. It is God Who says Melchizedek was greater than even Abraham. It is God Who declares that His dear Son as Priest is **after the order of Melchizedek**—not Aaron!

It is evident from these scriptures that royalty is connected with priesthood, for David thereafter sacrificed at Moriah. Now David was of the tribe of Judah, not of Levi. He acted, then, in what we find in **Hebrews** to be a kingpriest function, and thereafter the priest was subject to the Judaic royalty.

Here then is Melchizedek, no Canaanite, but priest of *El Elyon,* God Most High—not of one nation, as was Aaron afterwards of Israel; and he is also king of the place that Jehovah delighted in and chose above all others in which to dwell. And this is as we find it in **Hebrews.** Our Lord is a King; He is also Priest: but King first, shall we not say? as we read in Zech. 6.13: "He shall *sit and rule* upon His throne; and He shall be a Priest upon His throne."

Verse 5: Reread this verse, and compare Numbers 18.21, 26; II Chronicles 31.4 ff. Tithes belong to God: Leviticus 27.30; Proverbs 3.9; Malachi 3.8. We saw Abraham in Genesis 14.20 giving a tenth to Melchizedek; and Jacob, years afterwards, promised, if

---

places, you love your own home. Mount Zion, in Jerusalem, is God's earthly home. In the Millennium this "mountain of Jehovah's house" shall be exalted at the head of all the nations: Isa. 2.2, 3; Ps. 78.68; 87.2; Zech. 8.3; 2.10; 9.9—quoted in Matt. 21.5. Thither must all nations of the earth "go up year after year to worship the King, Jehovah of hosts" (Zech. 14.16).

*This word "great"—to how few of the human race has *God* ever applied it! To Abraham (Gen. 12.2): "And I will bless thee and make thy name *great";* to David (II Sam. 7.9): "I will make thee a *great* name"; the Shunammite was called "a *great* woman" (II Kings 4.8); and the angel of the Lord said of John the Baptist, "He shall be *great* in the sight of the Lord" (Lu. 1.15). Other than these, I find none except Melchizedek called "great" by God.

God would bless him, to give God "a tenth of all." The Levites, then, in receiving and using the tenth, were blessed as the servants of God. Tithes were given by the Israelites to the priests of Aaron's house because those priests represented Jehovah to Israel. But Abraham recognized at once in Melchizedek the priest of God Most High, and honored him with "a tenth of all," thus subjecting himself and also Levi to the Melchizedek priesthood.

Verse 6: **But he whose genealogy is not counted from them hath taken tithes of Abraham, and hath blessed him that hath the promises:** Here disappear all Jewish claims! The Jews are nothing in religious matters except as connected with Levi and his priesthood. But here Abraham (Jacob, his grandson from whom Israel's tribes sprung, being not yet born) is acknowledging and paying tithes to one that has no connection with himself or his seed after the flesh. We know that Paul says our Lord was of Israel "as concerning the flesh" (Rom. 9.5). But here we are dealing with counsels of God which regard the Son of God as "Heir of all things." From and through Him will come Israel's blessing, certainly, in the Millennial days. But the attitude of most Jews is that Divine blessing sprung from them; whereas the truth is that God's counsels, in infinite mercy and grace, brought this about: that our blessed Lord had a body "prepared" for Him, and was granted in sovereign grace, not by natural claims, to Israel as their Messiah.*

Verse 7: The apostle now brings out as regards Melchizedek, that **the less is blessed of the better.** So that despite the fact that the promises had begun to be given to Abraham (Gen. 12; Acts 7.2-3), and were, after Melchizedek's appearance and blessing, to be spoken more distinctly, with enlargement and detail (Gen.

---

*Judaism is of course supplanted by the introduction of this Melchizedek priesthood with which Levi and Aaron had no connection. But not in the same language or manner as that of the vehement denunciation by the apostle of the Galatian believers who were desiring to take over Jewish things to which they had never had a title, does the apostle deal with these Hebrew believers who had had that title directly from God. It is striking, for example, and it has been to me a key in discerning the attitude of God toward the Hebrew believers to whom this epistle is directed, that the author of Hebrews does not charge home upon them the national sin of the rejection and crucifixion of their Messiah (as does Peter, and as do the apostles in the book of Acts). Instead, there is loving but firm instruction of these Hebrew believers that the day of Judaism, of the Levitical economy, of the temple with its visible services so attractive to the flesh, was over; that these things had all been superseded, as see further in Chs. 8 to 10.

15.17-21): we see, and must keep in mind, that Melchizedek is greater than Aaron—inexpressibly greater: blessing, as we have just seen, "him that had the promises," and taking tithes not, as the priests of Aaron's house, representing Jehovah; but from Abraham, the ancestor of the priests of Aaron's house, as representing "God Most High."

Verse 8: **And here, dying men** [thus the Greek, emphasizing *dying*]* **receive tithes; but there one, of whom it is witnessed that he liveth:** That is, his human, earthly life was viewed as perpetuated; his priesthood, yes, and his kingship of Salem must also be so viewed.† But, contrary to this, in that very city, Jerusalem, upon Mount Zion, God will set His King upon "the throne of Jehovah," on which David and Solomon sat (I Chron. 29.23), now disappeared, then to be re-established. This king, Christ, shall be "a Priest upon His throne," where, doubtless, then, will be the thought of Melchizedek, who once occupied the kingship and priestly function, at Salem evidently, as we see connected in Psalm 76.2, with Zion.

Verses 9, 10: **Levi,** [Abraham's grandson, not yet born] **Levi,**

---

*"The Levites are dying men, who pass away in due course, and are succeeded by others. But there [in the case of Melchizedek] (He receiveth them of whom) it is witnessed that he liveth. The Greek is very condensed: lit.: being attested that he liveth. The A.V. fills it out correctly. Melchizedek does not appear in Scripture as one who dies, and whose office passes to another."

"Under the Mosaic Law, dying men, men who were not only liable to death, mortal, but men who were actually seen to die from generation to generation, enjoyed the rights of priests. For such an order there is not only the contingency but the fact of succession. While Melchizedek was one to whom witness is borne that he liveth. The writer, recurring to the exact form of the record in Genesis, on which he dwelt before, emphasizes the fact that M. appears here simply in the power of life. So far he does not die: the witness of Scripture is to his living. What he does is in virtue of what he is."—Westcott.

†If one should insist that the expression he liveth refers to life in the flesh, he would have to maintain that M. is still exercising priesthood. But the book of Hebrews sets forth CHRIST as the Great Priest of His people. True, John and Peter testify:

Christ "loosed us from our sins by His blood, and He made us a kingdom, *priests* unto His God and Father" (Rev. 1.5, 6).

"Ye also, as living stones, are built up a spiritual house, to be a holy priesthood, to offer up spiritual sacrifices, acceptable to God through Jesus Christ" (I Pet. 2.5).

But it is only by the *death* of our one Great High Priest that believers are constituted a priesthood. Remember, however, that all believers are equally priests in this priesthood.

"*Through Him* then let us offer up a sacrifice of praise to God continually, that is, the fruit of lips which make confession to His name" (Heb. 13.15).

There is therefore no place now for a priest who has not been made so after and through the shedding of Christ's blood.

who receiveth tithes, paid tithes, subjecting forever any Levitical priesthood to the higher Melchizedek priesthood.*

Of course in the Levitical arrangements Melchizedek was not mentioned, so that we have a new paragraph beginning with verse 11:

11 Now if there was perfection through the Levitical priesthood (for under it hath the people received the Law), what further need was there that another priest should arise after the order of Melchizedek, and not be
12 reckoned after the order of Aaron? For the priesthood being changed, there is made of necessity a change also
13 of the Law. For he of whom these things are said belong-eth to another tribe, from which no man hath given at-
14 tendance at the altar. For it is evident that our Lord hath sprung out of Judah; as to which tribe Moses
15 spake nothing concerning priests. And what we say is yet more abundantly evident, if after the likeness of
16 Melchizedek there ariseth Another Priest, Who hath been made, not after the Law of a carnal commandment, but
17 after the power of an endless life: for it is witnessed of Him,

> Thou art a Priest forever
> After the order of Melchizedek.

One of the most difficult spiritual tasks is to read the types of Exodus and Leviticus, and be prepared in and through those types to see the pattern of priestly intercession—and yet hold fast the truth that our Lord does not belong to the Levitical order. For we see in Hebrews that the Levitical things were shadows, and the contrast is constantly drawn between the incessant activities of Israel's priests and the once-for-all work of the Lord Jesus on the Cross. Unless we are careful we shall, in reading the Scrip-tures, drift into that wrong regard of the high priest to whom all Israel looked, and whose prominence in New Testament days in procuring the death of our Lord, and acting proudly toward His

---

*Compare the author's Romans Verse by Verse, p. 179:
"We did not have to wait to be born, or to have a sinful nature; but when Adam, our representative, acted, we acted (Rom. 5.19).
"The same Divine principle is illustrated in the fact that through Abraham even Levi [Abraham's great-grandson], who receiveth tithes, hath paid tithes; for he was yet in the loins of his father when Melchizedek met him (Heb. 7.9, 10). God says of Levi, who was not yet born, whose father was not yet born, whose grandfather (Isaac) was not yet born: LEVI PAID TITHES!"

disciples in judgment after the resurrection (Acts 5.17 ff), made these high priests the chief tools of Satan on earth.*

Verse 11: It will not do to say, as do some beloved brethren, that Christ's priesthood is **after the order of Melchizedek** but is exercised **after the order of Aaron.** Let us beware lest we forget His words, "All things have been delivered unto Me of My Father"; and, after His resurrection, "All authority hath been given unto Me in Heaven and on earth." Nothing of this sort was in Aaron's hands! The Father hath indeed "set within His own authority" times and seasons, so that our Lord said concerning His coming again,

"Of that day and hour knoweth no one, not even the angels of Heaven, neither the Son, but the Father only" (Matt. 24.36). Therefore even now we find our blessed Lord waiting, though invested with all authority, till the hour and the moment come when the Father will say to the Son,

"Ask of Me, and I will give Thee the nations for Thine inheritance,

And the uttermost parts of the earth for Thy possession.

Thou shalt break them with a rod of iron;

Thou shalt dash them in pieces like a potter's vessel"
(Ps. 2.8, 9).

Thereafter will He "sit and rule upon His throne" (Zech. 6.13)—a manifest reign of righteousness and peace; "and He shall be a Priest upon His throne;" in His earthly, millennial Melchizedek priesthood—"King of Righteousness, and King of Peace."

But He must be viewed now as that same King-Priest, though not yet in the full exercise of His King-Priest office (because it is now the time of God's long-suffering, the iniquity of the earth being not yet full).

We see then that Christ is set forth in **Hebrews** as a priest **after the order of Melchizedek,** not an Aaronic priest. He is of the royal *tribe* of Judah, and Aaron's work is *contrasted* with

---

*The same deluded dependence in human priesthood among those who do not know the gospel of Grace, makes possible the blasphemous fable of "the vicar of Christ," the pope of Rome. If the book of Hebrews sets aside the Levitical priesthood which God established, and sets before us the *one* "Great Priest over the House of God," the Son of God, how would this same book of Hebrews deal with Rome's man-appointed system of priests?

Christ's. All the things of the first tabernacle show that the way into the Holies was not yet manifest.

No, we must not be drawn into any notion of perfection (lit., full attainment of a designed end) through the Levitical priesthood under which Israel received the Law. But we must become subject in our very hearts to this astonishing passage which sets aside not only the Levitical priesthood but the Law itself, in order that Another Priest may be set before us—**after the order of Melchizedek, and not . . . reckoned after the order of Aaron.**

Verses 12-14: **The priesthood being changed**—Let us hold to this word, for, however the Levitical priesthood might shadow forth the heavenly things, that priesthood has been "changed," withdrawn, so that there is no vital connection between it and the heavenly worship the book of **Hebrews** sets before us. **For . . . our Lord hath sprung out of Judah, as to which tribe Moses spake nothing concerning priests:** the Aaronic order giving way to the Melchizedek order: Levi to Judah, the royal tribe, out of whom by Divine election, **our Lord hath sprung.***

Now come verses 15 and 16 pointing to the One Who should **arise after the likeness of Melchizedek, Who hath been made, not after the law of a carnal commandment** (as the Levitical priests were), **but after the power of an indissoluble life.** We say "indissoluble" because "endless" does not express the thought of the Greek word here.† It is the undying character of the risen life of our Great High Priest that is here before us, rather than its mere endlessness. "According to the power of a life not subject to destruction" describes that priesthood after the order of which Christ is, of which Melchizedek was the earthly type.

---

*Of King Uzziah II Chron. 26.16 ff. tells us the tragic story: "When he was strong, his heart was lifted up . . . and he trespassed against Jehovah his God; for he went into the temple of Jehovah to burn incense upon the altar of incense." Uzziah was indeed of the tribe of Judah, but when he attempted to offer incense in the temple, the priests then rightly contended that he was intruding upon the work of the sons of Aaron. But the anger of God and the judgment of leprosy that fell on him may well be regarded as God's jealousy for that true Son of David, of the house of Judah, the Son of God, yet to be born, of Whom Melchizedek was a prophecy.

†The Greek word is *akataluthos*. This negative form of the word occurs but this once. "If the earthly house of our tabernacle be *dissolved—*" (II Cor. 5.1) is the same word, except that "alpha privative" (the letter *a* signifying negation) precedes the word in Heb. 7.16, making it mean, *unable* to be dissolved. "Incapable of dissolution," is the excellent translation of the word in Bagster's **Analytical Lexicon**; and Thayer translates: "Not subject to destruction."

Compare the last word of verse 24, *aparabaton,* which means in-violable, not transient, unchangeable.

Verse 17: We now have the final reference to Christ's eternal, Melchizedek priesthood: **For it is witnessed of Him,**

Thou art a Priest forever,

After the order of Melchizedek.

The *contrast* of this priesthood with mortal Levitical priests must ever lie in our minds, rather than the comparison:

With the Levitical priesthood, many priests; with our Great High Priest—One.

With those priests, continual yearly offerings; oft-repeated sacrifices; with Christ, one, on the Cross, accomplishing eternal redemption.

With human priests, sin, failure, and final death; Christ, sin-less, and through suffering "perfected for evermore."

Those priests, after the order of Aaron; Christ, the Son of God, **after the order of Melchizedek.**

Those priests, connected with the Mosiac Law; with Christ, (vs. 18) **a disannulling of a foregoing commandment,** and be-lievers told that they are not under Law but under Grace, dead to the Law and discharged therefrom (Rom. 6.14; 7.4, 6); **because of its weakness and unprofitableness (for the Law made nothing perfect) (vs. 19),** for man had no strength, and the Law conferred none on him; Grace, by Christ, **bringing in a better hope, through which we draw nigh unto God.**

Those priests had no power in themselves; our Great High Priest has all authority (Matt. 28.18, R.V.).

Those priests were not kings; Christ was born a King, and is typified by Melchizedek, who, as we have seen, was doubly a king—of righteousness and of peace.

Finally, earthly high priests lacked full sympathy and under-standing, as we have said; but our Great High Priest is able to be "touched with the feeling of our infirmities; One that hath been in all points tempted like as we are, sin apart"; "A merciful and faithful High Priest."

And keep remembering that while those priests were daily occupied with sacrifices and offerings, their work never done, sin was not put away; our blessed Lord, "having offered up one sacrifice for sins forever, *sat down*."* Unless we are constantly watchful, the idea of priesthood and of an active priest brings before our mind sacrifice, placating God. The thought that our sins were forever put away at Calvary, and that Christ not only exercises His priestly work on the sole basis of His work on the Cross, but that He Himself entered in through His own blood into the Holies above (9.12)—this remembrance, we repeat, must be held fast; otherwise ignorance, or unbelief, or a bad conscience will send the believer, when he prays, to calling upon Christ to propitiate God on His behalf, instead of coming to God as directed here in Hebrews. Propitiation *has been made,* once for all (Rom. 3.25, R.V.).

As to the place of Christ's priesthood, it is Heaven itself, where He now appears "before the face of God for us" (9.24). There is no place of worship on earth since our Lord's ascension. The saints, not the earthly building, are the Church of God (Acts 7.48; 17.24; I Cor. 6.19; II Cor. 6.16).

To sum up what we have learned about Christ's priesthood thus far:

1.   Our Great High Priest has gone up on high and is seated on the right hand of God.

2.   He is a Priest forever after the order of Melchizedek, "and *not . . .* after the order of Aaron." Yet the priestly *functions* are set forth in the ministry of Aaron: (a) the necessity and Divine appointment of priesthood; (b) its being based upon the death of victims for sacrifice, and (c) its continual existence for the people of God.

3.   It was not until Christ had "made purification of sins" that He "sat down on the right hand of the Majesty on High" (Ch. 1.3): this was after He became a sin-offering at Calvary, where He had as a Priest after the order of Melchizedek offered up Him-

---

*"The Lord Jesus went up to Heaven and took His place at the right hand of God, to enter on a new kind of action there, which was founded on the purgation of our sins by the sacrifice of Himself. Christ's priesthood supposes that the great and absolutely necessary work of grace on their [our] behalf has been accomplished."—Kelly.

self (7.17-27), as said John the Baptist, "Behold the Lamb of God that taketh away the sin of the world." We find in the book of Hebrews a marvelous unfolding, generally by *contrast* with the Levitical offerings and Aaronic priesthood, of the necessity, nature, and results of this great offering up of Himself.

4. Studying the Old Testament types in the light of the utterances of the Spirit in the epistle to the Hebrews, we should fervently look forward to the "good things that are to come" in that day when Our Lord, the Melchizedek Priest, shall return and be a Priest upon His throne,* whereas He now sits upon His Father's throne, "expecting" (Heb. 10.13).

Some Christians (and it is tragic to say it!) have never seen Christ as their present and eternal Priest. This very week a godly, earnest Christian man said to me, "I never knew that I had Christ as my Priest!"

A godly woman, also, came to the altar recently, saying with tear-brimmed eyes, "I did not know till tonight that I had a Priest in Heaven, Jesus!"

Alas, there are so many beloved Christians who do not "Seek out of the book of the LORD, and *read*"! They are content with those verses they have already known. Oh, that they would give themselves to the Word of God—even for a brief time *daily!*

We have asked one earnest Christian after another these questions: "Are you a born-again child of God?" "Yes." "You are a member of Christ's Body?" "Yes." "Why then do you need a priest?"

---

*That this is at the Millennial time is evident from the context and from comparison with other Scriptures, for we read:

"Thus speaketh Jehovah of hosts saying, Behold the Man Whose name is the Branch" (Zech. 6.12).

"And there shall come forth a shoot out of the stock of Jesse, and a Branch out of his roots shall bear fruit. And the Spirit of Jehovah shall rest upon Him, the spirit of wisdom and understanding . . . with righteousness shall He judge the poor, and decide with equity for the meek of the earth; and He shall smite the earth with the rod of His mouth; and with the breath of His lips shall He slay the wicked . . . And the wolf shall dwell with the lamb, and the leopard shall lie down with the kid; and the calf and the young lion and the fatling together; and a little child shall lead them" (Isa. 11.1-6).

"Behold, I will bring forth my Servant the Branch" (Zech. 3.8).

"Behold, the days come, saith Jehovah, that I will raise unto David a righteous Branch, and He shall reign as King and deal wisely, and shall execute justice and righteousness in the land. In his days Judah shall be saved, and Israel shall dwell safely; and this is the name whereby He shall be called: Jehovah our righteousness" (Jer. 23.5, 6).

And they do not know! For they have been taught in their "standards" that Christ's priestly work was done upon the Cross, which means He *was* their Priest; but as to having Christ as their *present* Priest, they know nothing of it. Of course, they pray, "For Jesus' sake," or, "In the name of the Lord Jesus." But the priestly work of Christ to them is connected with putting away sin, nothing more.

But the astonishing word of God is, that He saluted Christ as a *Priest forever* upon His resurrection and ascension. So we may ask these dear Christians further questions:

"You believe, then, that priesthood belonged to and pertained to the Hebrew nation?"

"Well, yes."

"Why then **a Priest forever after the order of Melchizedek**, who is set forth as before Abraham, and thus before Levi, Aaron, or even Israel? Why is the Son of God addressed as a Priest forever?"

And why, indeed, "forever"?*

In answer, we say:

1. That Christ is declared **a Priest forever after the order of Melchizedek.**

2. That the intercessory work of Christ as pertaining particularly to our needs as we traverse this world must continue for the Church, that is to say, present-day believers, until all are brought safely home to Heaven. For any believers thereafter, He must keep succoring them; "He must reign, till He hath put all His enemies under His feet" (I Cor. 15.25), thus fulfilling the Melchizedek priesthood. Even when God takes His great power and reigns (Rev. 11.17), it is Christ Who is exercising the royal authority, as we know, for "great voices in Heaven" say,

"The kingdom of the world is become the kingdom of our Lord, and of His Christ: and He shall reign forever and ever" (vs. 15).

---

*The Westminster standards say, "Christ executeth the office of a priest, in once offering up of Himself a sacrifice, to satisfy Divine justice and reconcile us to God, and in making continual intercession for us." But this, excellent as it is! makes no provision for the word "forever." The day will come when all that are saved have been brought home to the presence of God, and do not need that care and intercession so necessary when they are on earth. The word still remains, **Thou art a Priest forever.**

3. As to the words of Revelation 22.5, "They shall reign for-ever and ever," we ask, How could this be apart from Christ? For our Lord said, "All authority" was given unto Him (Matt. 28.18, quoted above); and, "Neither doth the Father judge any man, but He hath given all judgment unto the Son" (Jno. 5.22).

4. And in the matter of worship, which shall be eternal, who will be the leader if not Christ? Psalm 22 must continue to be ful-filled: how long, if not forever? Incentives to worship will be eternal, for God is infinite. How easily in this life on earth do we settle down into a ritual: certain thoughts about God, certain forms of worship—very much as we go about our daily round of business. But it will not be so in the ages to come. A billion, yea, a trillion ages after the saints enter glory, they shall find them-selves as it were beginning to know their God, to Whose endless glories it will ever be the delight of the Lord Jesus to open the door to us. And, He being Man as well as God, it will be His eternal delight to lead our praises.

5. We have only to study the Gospels and the epistles to see how wholly both God the Father and God the Holy Spirit delight to make Christ the Center of affection as well as the Fullness of all the saints. During our Lord's earthly ministry, for the disciples, all centered in Christ. The Bridegroom was with them: they had no cares. And after His death how desolate they were until, upon His resurrection, Jesus again "stood in the midst of them, and saith unto them, Peace be unto you." God will have it so for all eternity.

6. Our Lord's priestly work may be said to be threefold: (1) Offering Himself up a Sacrifice once for all for our sins, on the Cross, where He "put away sin by the sacrifice of Himself"; (2) making continual intercession for us as we pass through the wilderness of this world on our way to glory; and (3) ever lead-ing the praises of those redeemed, on through eternity into deeper, ever deeper knowledge of the infinite blessedness of God, unto Whom Christ has devoted Himself forever as Servant. (See the type of Ex. 21.2-6 quoted in Ps. 40 and in Heb. 10.5—and com-ment there.)*

---

*As Priest, Christ in Heaven is in full, constant sympathy with our needs, trials, and temptations down here; but He leads the praises of the saints, whether individually or as they are gathered together: Peter and John (Act 4.23, ff.) "being let go" from imprison-

For God is the only good. Whatever His blessings, including
life itself, the only good is God. When a human being leaves this
earth, he takes nothing; and, if a saved one, enters Heaven, where
God is all in all.* How slowly do our hearts come to realize that
there is no good but God Himself!

> **18** For there is a DISANNULLING OF A FOREGOING
> COMMANDMENT because of its WEAKNESS AND
> **19** UNPROFITABLENESS (for the Law MADE NOTH-
> ING PERFECT), and a bringing in thereupon of a bet-
> ter hope, through which we DRAW NIGH unto God.

Here we must enumerate again several forgotten facts which
need to be held in mind in the study of **Hebrews:**

1.   The Law (meaning the Ten Commandments with all the
ordinances—see Lk. 10.26, Dt. 6.5, Lev. 18.19) was never given
to the human race.

2.   The Law was given to Israel at Sinai, and to *no other nation!*
—Psalm 147.19-20.

3.   The object of the Law was to reveal sin, and not to secure
holiness: for fallen men had no strength.

4.   There is a disannulling of a foregoing commandment, the
Law, Hebrews 7.18 says, **(for the Law made nothing perfect).**
You ask at once, How can God control His creatures except by
legal enactment?

5.   We answer that there is another principle, infinitely and
eternally stronger than Law. We read in Ephesians 1.4 that God
"Chose us in Him before the foundation of the world, that we
should be holy and without blemish before Him in LOVE."

---

ment by the persecuting chief priests and rulers, "came to their own company, and re-
ported all that the chief priests and the elders had said unto them." The whole company
of saints "when they heard it, lifted up their voice to God with one accord, and said,
O Lord, (Gr., *Despotēs*, Master) Thou that didst make the Heaven and the earth and
the sea, and all that in them is: Who by the Holy Spirit, by the mouth of our father
David Thy servant, didst say,
Why did the Gentiles rage,
And the peoples imagine vain things?
The kings of the earth set themselves in array,
And the rulers were gathered together,
Against the Lord, and against His Anointed."
So goes on this rapture of united praise. Then they pray, the place is shaken, and they
are all filled with the Holy Spirit. Such praises most certainly come up to God *through
Christ.* That was a company of "priests unto God" crying this praise, and they went di-
rectly to God because their Great High Priest was in glory, at the Father's right hand. This
holy character of our worship cannot be overemphasized.

*Or will be, when Christ shall have put down every foe, after the rebellion at the close
of the thousand years.

And in I John 4.16 "For God is love; and he that abideth in love abideth in God, and God abideth in him."

Christ obeyed the Father because He *loved* Him!

God calls the Law "a ministration of *death,* written and engraven on stones" (II Cor. 3.7). And again He calls it "the ministration of condemnation" (vs. 9). God tells us that the Law "came in besides [or, *alongside*], that the trespass might abound." The Law demanded what fallen man could not supply (righteousness, holiness, obedience to God), and in undertaking to supply which, he would discover his lost condition (Rom. 7.22-24). Now if God says that the Law "came in besides" (as an *added* thing after God's plan of salvation by Christ was revealed—as in Romans 5.8: "God commendeth His own love toward us, in that, while we were yet sinners, Christ died for us") and deluded, self-confident man seized upon it in the false hope of achieving righteousness and acceptance thereby, then no matter how such a false hope has been wrought falsely into the creeds of men, we stand by this Word of God: that the Law came in as an added thing, "that the *trespass* [*not* the obedience] might abound." Sin was already there, but Law having been laid down, sin became known trespass.

You ask, Why, then, was the Law given? It was given that by breaking it man might discover what God knew all the time—his utter sinfulness and weakness. While the Law could do nothing for us, but only demand of us, by the transgression of it, or breaking through its bounds, men would discover what already existed. For sin was there by Adam (Rom. 5.12-21). But sin does not break forth into conscious trespass until there is a Divine enactment against it: "The POWER OF SIN is the LAW" (I Cor. 15.56). "I HAD NOT KNOWN SIN except through the LAW" (Rom. 7.7). This explains why a God of love who delighted in mercy would give His chosen people (the Hebrew nation) that which would "bring iniquity to remembrance"—make them know it.

6. Now if God tells the Hebrews that **there is a disannulling of a foregoing commandment because of its weakness and unprofitableness . . . and a bringing in instead of a better hope** (the work of Christ), **through which we draw nigh unto God—** let not you or me dare to mix the two. God says concerning those under Law (especially Hebrew believers), that they died

unto the Law, that they were discharged from the Law, "so that we serve in newness of the spirit, and not in oldness of the letter" (Rom. 7.6). They are to "bring forth fruit unto God," and *fruit* is the result of life through Jesus Christ by the operation of the blessed Holy Spirit dwelling in them: "Being filled with the *fruits* of righteousness, which are through Christ Jesus, unto the glory and praise of God" (Phil. 1.11).

The Geek word translated disannulling, *athetêsis,* is the same as appears in Hebrews 9.26 for the *putting away* of sin "by the sacrifice of Himself." *The disappearance of the Law is as absolute, therefore, as the putting away of sin!* The order in time here is marked by the quotation from Psalm 110.4, a psalm by David, therefore upwards of 500 years after the Law: that is why the Law is spoken of as **a foregoing commandment,** or that which antedated God's recorded oath.

(If you have hopes in the Law, note here in verse 18 that both the Law and Levitical relationships are gone! Christ only and His work are left as any hope for you or anyone now!)

The reason the **foregoing commandment,** the Law, with all its "ten thousand things," (Hos. 8.12) has been annulled, put away, is, we repeat, **because of its weakness and unprofitableness.** It was "weak" in that it was unable to obtain obedience in those over whom it was placed. It was "holy, just and good," but men were carnal, "sold under sin." Even the good that they would, they did not. And it was "unprofitable" because by it thousands, yea, millions of hours of human life must be occupied in ordinances concerning the cleanness of the flesh, in sacrifices, in pilgrimages, in purifications. And even if all things were accomplished, the conscience was not fully relieved, for the same sacrifices must be made the next year or upon any personal trespass.*

---

*Alas, today it is the same: tens of thousands of those whom we believe truly converted, born of God, pass numberless hours, days, in ceremonies God did not command, but the contrary! (Gal. 4.10). Whence came Lent? Who commanded Good Friday? As it goes into deeper darkness, Christendom is practicing more and more such things as the celebration of "holy week." You know the so-called Plymouth Brethren do not; you know the early "holiness people," filled with the Spirit, did not. You know that, though legal in many ways, the Puritans did not, nor the persecuted Covenanters. No one does who knows and walks with and talks with God and knows His Word! For all such observances are not of Him during this dispensation of grace.

7. Therefore we who are Gentiles after the flesh, as we sit and listen to God's Word to that nation with whom He had relationship formerly, are not to try to imitate that relationship, but to recognize that God was not in relationship with Gentiles, and that now, we having believed on the Lord Jesus Christ, along with true Hebrew believers, are "partakers of the heavenly calling," whose life-practice and wondrous privilege it is daily, hourly, to "come boldly to the throne of *grace*," having a *Great High Priest* in Heaven! Let us beware lest we be found trusting in "religion" or "church membership" or "ordinances" or "activities." In the book of Hebrews godliness, and to be perfected therein, is the walk of the true believer.

A godly and dearly beloved theologian says, "God has authority to address the human conscience only in His Law," giving this as the conclusion of some forty or fifty passages. But what about the words before us: **disannulling of a foregoing commandment . . . weakness . . . unprofitableness (for the Law made nothing perfect)?** What about that? What about Galatians 2.19, 20, where Paul says, "I through Law *died to Law,* that I might live unto God. I have been crucified with Christ; and it is no longer I that live, but Christ liveth in me"?*

---

*Several years ago in my teaching, by earnest request, in a Southern city, the Book of Romans, great interest was shown by a large company of young people who would gather about me after each meeting asking questions. There were two fine young men who earnestly protested that the words, "Ye were made dead to the Law," (Rom. 7.4), could not mean exactly that—that the Law was the only means God had of preserving our obedience. So for a number of evenings they made their plea to keep Moses and Elijah on the Mount of Transfiguration, though God left "Jesus only" there!

I learned incidentally that one of these young men had recently been married. Therefore, in the course of the lesson the next evening, I went right down to him, for he and his wife were sitting in the second row of seats, and said,

"I understand you have lately been married."

He began to redden up with embarrassment, but said, "Yes."

", said, "Does your wife obey you?"

"Certainly," he said.

I said, "Have you kitchen rules posted up for your wife's behavior in the kitchen? Have you dining-room rules?"

"None," he said.

"Have you parlor rules?"

"None."

"Have you any rules at all posted up in the house?"

"None."

"And yet you claim that your wife obeys you," I said. "Why does she?"

And he said, "She loves me," which was a happy solution of our question.

Alas for the pride of the creature's heart! When God asked
Israel, through Moses, if they would allow their relationship to Him
to be dependent upon their obedience to His statutes, their instant
reply was, "All that Jehovah hath spoken we will do." Here is
perfect self-confidence, which the Law was given to destroy. It
matters not to you, dear friends, that Israel then made a
calf and worshiped it, and broke all the Commandments. You
still teach that the Law is the rule of life. The moment the Law
was promulgated, trust was placed therein as if the conditions of
obedience were already fulfilled! And those to whom the Law was
given—the "ministration of death" and of condemnation, gloried
in having it! Their attitude became summed up in that of the
Pharisees and scribes toward the common people of the Jewish
nation: "This multitude that knoweth not the Law is accursed."
Yet our Lord could say, "Did not Moses give you the Law, yet
none of you keepeth the Law?"

So, brethren, I beseech you, when you hear, as Hebrews is read,
God not only taking away from those Hebrews (to whom alone
He gave the Ten Commandments), the whole Levitical system,
but also disannulling the Law, hearken to God, not to man. To
God, Christ is all in all, and so He is to every Pauline believer.

You answer, It is not so written in my church doctrine. Very
well, it is so in Heaven. Do you not believe Paul's words in
Galatians 3.11, 12, "The righteous shall live by faith; and the Law
is not of faith"? To take away the Law utterly from the ordinary
Christian leaves him in a state of panic, which shows that his hopes
have really been in his own efforts rather than in the grace of God,
all along. You say, Do away with the Law, and what have you left?
Ah, you have thus revealed yourself: "For Christ is the end of
the Law for righteousness to every one that believeth" (Rom. 10.4).
And as regards life: "If there had been a law given which could
make alive, verily righteousness would have been of the Law"
(Gal. 3.21).*

---

*David permitted the Law he had broken to judge him:

"For Thou delightest not in sacrifice; else would I give it: Thou hast no pleasure in
burnt offering. The sacrifices of God are a broken spirit: A broken and a contrite heart, O
God, Thou wilt not despise." (Ps. 51.16, 17).

Here is a complete renunciation of self-effort, of Law help. Consequently David came
into a deeper acquaintance with God than perhaps any other O. T. saint.

In Ephesians 5 we find Christ presenting the Church to Himself "a glorious Church, not having spot or wrinkle, or any such thing." Will the Church in eternity be under that temporary dispensation under which God put Israel at Sinai? Nay, verily! and never was. But she having died with Christ and·been raised with Him, and in the beauty of the presence of her eternal Bridegroom delighting, that word of Ephesians 1.4 will be brought to pass, "holy and without blame before Him in love." God's name is Love; and those who come into the infinite felicity of dwelling in the Father's house where the many abiding places are, will find that the principle there is not Law, but Love. One principle will rule—devotion to God. "Only love seeks love, and only love satisfies love," says someone; and this will be constant for all eternity.

Verse 19: And all is summed up in the words, **for the Law made nothing perfect.** This is a parenthesis, but a powerful one. Let us simply believe it. It is one more reason why we should have no hope in the Law principle. David cried in the 119th Psalm.

"I have seen an end of all perfection;
Thy commandment is exceeding broad."

Let all legalists mark this: **The Law made nothing perfect.**

Let the Seventh Day Adventists mark: **The Law made nothing perfect.**

Let all those who dream of the Law as a rule of life remember: **The Law made nothing perfect.**

Let all believers remember: **The Law made nothing perfect.** The God of truth says those in Christ "are not in the flesh" (Rom. 8.9), and that when, before believing, they were in the flesh, "the passions of sins, which were THROUGH THE LAW, wrought in our members to bring forth fruit unto *death*" (Rom. 7.5). These are *God's* words, not ours. What God has brought in for you in Christ is not to "live a Christian life," but for *Christ to live in you* by simple faith (Gal. 2.19, 20; Col. 1.27; Phil. 1.21). "Ye are not under Law, but under Grace," distinct, opposite states of being (Rom. 6.14). Do not forget the word "hath" in Romans 13.8, and "fulfillment," in Romans 13.10. One walking in love, bearing "fruit" against which "there is no Law" (Gal. 5.18, 22, 23), is "not under Law," not under that principle. Such a one hath fulfilled, without being under it, what the Law asked.

We must hold fast these words, **the Law made nothing perfect,** as well as "weakness" and "unprofitableness", when we read the account of the glory and majesty of the giving of the Law upon Sinai; and also when we study the particular directions the Law prescribed for every phase of human life.

This attitude will not be dishonoring to God, but the exact opposite. "For the Law was given through Moses; grace and truth came through Jesus Christ." In the book of **Hebrews** God announces the setting aside of the whole Levitical code as a system of "shadows," not indeed setting forth God's real High Priest at all, for Jesus Christ was of another order: that of Melchizedek, not of Aaron. And God announces the Law as "disannulled."

If we do not humbly, but jealously and zealously, hold fast these facts, we shall not be able to give true place to our blessed Lord and His ministry.

For after saying that **the Law made nothing perfect,** God says there was brought in (in Christ) **a better hope, through which we draw nigh unto God,** adding (vs. 22): "By so much also hath Jesus become the Surety of a *better covenant*"—than the Law.

In Colossians 2.16, 17, we are told:

"Let no man therefore judge you in meat, or in drink, or in respect of a feast day or a new moon *or a sabbath day:* which are a *shadow* of the things to come; but the body *is Christ's.*"

Those obeying God (and not tradition) will find themselves in a freedom—hated and persecuted of course by the "religionists"— a freedom that only true *faith* finds. There is plenty of Grace to keep you from judging your Law-bound brother. But be *you free,* yourself, walking in the blessed place of freedom into which "Another Priest," "after the power of an endless life," **a Priest forever after the order of Melchizedek,** has brought His saints to **draw nigh unto God.**

The Law is *man's* work: we mean, it commanded *man* to do this or to abstain from that. The Law was consequently "weak through the flesh," for man's sinful flesh controlled him.

Christ's work, though on behalf of man, was *wholly His:* glorious and perfect, yet to be received by man in its blessed results of eternal pardon, peace and blessing. To be received, we say, by simple *Faith,* unmixed with human effort. A humbling process, indeed! For man must go out of the righteousness-producing business, and rest wholly and forever on the work of Another, even *Christ.*

And a bringing in thereupon of a better hope, through which we draw nigh unto God: Mark that there is no mixture. For the Hebrews, the Law, with all its ordinances and its spirit, was *"disannulled."* For Gentile believers who were at liberty to **draw nigh unto God,** there is no thought of Law (which never was given to Gentiles); but to *Christ only.* No one whose conscience still holds him under Law can with full freedom **draw nigh unto God.** In the first tabernacle there was no drawing nigh, but a standing without the veil. There was Jehovah's presence, but not drawing nigh. Even the high priest was to "come *not* at all times into the holy place within the veil . . . that he die not." Once a year, only, could he come, and that with a sin-offering for himself before he dared offer one for the people (Lev. 16). Then the veil was closed against the high priest and all the priests for another year; while two veils kept back the people. God's *presence,* with the people *shut out,* described the situation.

But as we shall see in Chapters 9 and 10, Christ has now entered in "with His own blood"; the veil, that is to say, His flesh, is rent. We have "a Great Priest over the house of God"; and we are told to draw near with boldness to God Himself. This is not mere justification and regeneration: it is the action of justified, born-again ones, toward Him Whom they have come to know. The book of **Hebrews** takes justification for granted, but deals with drawing nigh, coming unto. (The Greek word in this verse comes from *eggus,* which means near, close up. In verse 25 a different word for "come unto" is used, as in Chapters 4.16; 10.1, 22. See also Jas. 4.8). Oh, that all believers would hearken to the book of **Hebrews** daily, hourly, and *draw nigh* to their God, for this is the constant desire of His infinite love. But legalists, of whatever stripe, never learn the blessed connection between these two phrases of verses 18 and 19: **DISANNULLING of a foregoing commandment . . . We DRAW NIGH unto God.***

---

*It will be a sad day for those who cling to "traditions", church "standards," and "articles" when their lives will be examined not by those, but by the living Word of God.

When the Pharisees and scribes asked our Lord, "Why do Thy disciples transgress the tradition of the elders?" He asked them,

"Why do ye also transgress the commandment of God because of your tradition? . . .

Ye have made void the Word of GOD because of your tradition. Ye hypocrites, well did Isaiah prophesy of you, saying,

This people honoreth Me with their lips;
But their heart is far from Me.
But in vain do they worship Me,
Teaching as their doctrines the precepts of men." (Matt. 15.2-9).

When our Lord Jesus did not keep the Sabbath according to the Jewish doctors' traditions, they "went about to kill Him"—Who was the Lord of the Sabbath. God speaks over and over of *changing* His methods of dealing with men; but people will not hear of it. When the Scripture says, *"At the end* of these days," in which He had "spoken of old time unto the fathers in the prophets" (Heb. 1.1, 2), plainly the Old Testament days, God *means* the end! To have the Church begin with Abraham, despite our Lord's word in Matt. 16.18 that the Church was in that day future, is to ignore Heb. 1.1, 2, and to ignore God's saying in Heb. 7.18-9: There is a DISANNULLING OF A FOREGOING COMMANDMENT . . . WEAK . . . UNPROFITABLE . . . THE LAW MADE NOTHING PERFECT. But will "church members" today part with Moses and the Law? Nay, they cannot, because the Law "hath dominion over a man for so long time as he liveth" (Rom. 7.1), and they do not know or believe that we *died* with Christ unto sin, and unto the Law that gave sin its power (Rom. 6.1-14; 7.1-6); and that therefore the Cross ended our history in the first Adam before God.

What do such words mean as "Christ *abolished* in His flesh the enmity, even the Law of commandments contained in ordinances; that He might create in Himself of the two [Gentiles and Israel] one new man"? (Eph. 2.15). Or, "Having *blotted out* the bond written in ordinances that was against us, which was contrary to us: and He hath *taken it out of the way, nailing it* to the Cross"? (Col. 2.14).

Now to call this "bond," this "Law of commandments in ordinances" the "ceremonial law," and to say that the "moral law" is still binding upon us, is ignorance, traditionalism, and even wickedness. For the "ceremonial law," so-called, prescribing days, seasons, months, years, sacrifices, washings, *could* be kept, and *was* kept. (Many a traditionalist is keeping a ceremonial law today!). But the moral law, prescribing a heart condition of entire love to God, and to our neighbors as ourselves, was impossible of fulfillment by man in the flesh—which God says is just what the Law was given to bring out and make plain! "The Law came in besides, that *the trespass* might abound" (Rom. 5.20)—*not* that *sin* might abound. Sin was there already, had been there 2500 years. But the mind of the flesh, being enmity to the Law of God, not subject to it, nor possible to be subject, according to God's holy Word (Rom. 8.7), the Law was given to bring out this fact; as Paul said, "I had not known sin except through Law, for I had not known coveting except the Law had said, Thou shalt not covet" (Rom. 7.7). Mark you, "Thou shalt not covet" is no "ceremonial" commandment. It is a moral obligation, a heart condition forbidden.

But Reformed Theology puts man right back under the Law as a "rule of life," not knowing or believing that believers, in the eyes of the Law, are *not living.* They have been "made dead to the Law through the body of Christ" (Rom. 7.4)—of Christ-made-sin for us; and "our old man crucified with Him"; and now we have been "annulled from the Law" (Rom. 7.6), that is, the Law knows nothing of us, we are put out of business (by death with Christ) from the Law as a ruler, and from Law as a principle: "Ye are not under Law, but under Grace" (Rom. 6.14). (Note the absence of the article, the. *The* Law means the code; Law, means the principle.)

Now you may know by your response to this truth whether you are a religionist or Christ's freedman; whether you are an ABC believer, or an adult. Paul in Gal. 4, 1-3 describes the ABC believer: "So long as the heir is a minor, he differeth nothing from a bondservant." "So *we* also, when we were *infants* (or under age), were *held in bondage* under the religious principles of the world." (See the two words for minor and adult contrasted in Heb. 5.13, 14: Greek, *nēpioi,* babes; opposed to *teleioi,* fullgrown men). Note three things in Gal. 4.3: (1) In using the word "we" Paul is speaking of Hebrew believers before Christ came, before the bond was taken out of the way. (2) At that time they were in a period of infancy as over against adulthood, in spiritual things. (3) They were "held in bondage" under what the Holy Spirit now calls even Judaism: "religious principles of the world." But Paul says in Col. 2.20-22, *"We died with Christ* from the religious principles of the world," and asks, "Why, as though living in the world, do you subject yourselves to ordinances? [such as] Handle not, nor taste, nor touch (all which things are to perish with the using), after the precepts and doctrines of men?"—remember what we saw our Lord said of these, in Matt. 15.2-9.

Ah, legalists, of whatever stripe, never learn the infinitely blessed connection of these two phrases of verses 18 and 19: DISANNULLING of a foregoing commandment ... We DRAW NIGH unto God!

20 And inasmuch as it is not without the taking of an
21 oath (for they indeed have been made priests without an oath; but He with an oath by Him that saith of Him,

> The Lord sware and will not repent Himself,
> Thou art a Priest forever);

Note in verses 20-22 the place God gives His *oath* in connection with the Melchizedek priesthood. The Levitical priests, many in number, became such by natural descent. But those priests "were made without an oath. The solemnity of the oath with which this priesthood was inaugurated, is the measure of its superiority and existence." God's word to Christ is, (Ps. 110.4, quoted in Heb. 7.21):

> The Lord sware and will not repent Himself,
> Thou art a Priest forever.

"The value of the covenant is determined in this passage by the presence or absence of the oath of God. The Levitical priests were made without an oath, for they attended a transitory office of imperfection and decay. But an oath is something final and determinative in its nature. In *Jesus* God has won the end of all His counsel. Therefore, by all the value of that oath of God, is the covenant which is now administered by His Son of greater sanction and of better trust than that which Aaron served."*

In my university days we had as the director of the music department Prof. Carl Merz, a remarkable teacher, filled with the spirit of the old musicians, and withal a true Christian. We loved him much. Every year we gave an oratorio. I have seen him mount on a chair in the music hall, and with tears streaming down his cheeks lead Handel's "Hallelujah Chorus" in *The Messiah*, while the whole great chorus of singers he was leading was thrilled through and through with the magnificent words and music of praise.

But there were pupils in that town in the first grade of the public schools, who would not have known how to pronounce the word, "Hallelujah"! They were occupied with their ABC's. For century after century the professing church has settled down in this world as an earth religion. People "hope to go to Heaven when they die." The thought of being *now* a heavenly people with a heavenly calling, and with a High Priest in Heaven conducting heavenly worship, has never entered their mind. We say this with firmness, because it is true; but we speak not with arrogance, but with deep humiliation.

*Pridham, On the Hebrews, p. 178.

How different from God's oath to Abraham, "Surely blessing I
will bless thee" (Ch. 6.4), is God's oath to Christ! The promise
of blessing to Abraham was of course, to and through Abraham's
Seed, "which is *Christ*" (Gal. 3.16). But now is revealed to us
in Him, in and *through* Whom all blessings are as **Priest forever,**
God's *oath,* from which **He will not repent.***

We see here also that the Levitical priests, though many in
number, never had a man to whom God committed Himself
thus—"forever." By death they were "hindered from continuing" (Vs. 23). God's purposes of blessing are all connected
with Christ, the Second Man, the Last Adam. And how good
it is to hear God say to our Lord, **Thou art a Priest forever.**
Remember Christ as a Priest went into God's presence *on our side,
committed to our cause.* All that God's nature, His holiness, His
righteousness, His truth, His majesty, could demand against us,
had been once for all and forever met, at the Cross. Oh, that all
our hearts might really rest upon this: that God's Word, which
He has magnified above all His name, is pledged that the One Who
bore our sins in His own body on the Tree is pronounced a **priest
forever,** our Priest.† But how infrequently do either our hearts
or our lips claim Him as our Priest, our Great High Priest!

20 And inasmuch as it is not without the taking of an oath

22 . . . by so much also hath Jesus became the Surety of a

---

*It is very touching to the heart that knows the God Whose name is Love to note how
often God *did* repent concerning deserved and threatened judgment. The following are the
references: do not let the study of them cause you to forget that there will be, must be,
eternal judgment against the impenitent, for "The Strength of Israel will not lie nor repent" (I Sam. 15.29). But let us note the following: it makes a wonderful Bible reading:

Ps. 90.13, 106.45; 135.14; Jon. 3.9,10; 4.2; Ex. 32.12, 14; Jud. 2.18; II Sam. 24.16;
(I Chr. 21.15); Jer. 26.19; Joel 2.13, 14.

These are moving words concerning a merciful God, the while we do not forget such
verses as Jer. 15.6, 18.10; Zech. 8.14; Ezk. 24.14. Let us believe such passages with child-
like hearts, and not let them lose their power upon us through idle theological arguments;
God's purpose is eternal, is fixed, so that He will not be moved by any attitude of man.

†We have heard earnest saints speak of His as "our Christ." No, He is *God's* Christ,
for God sent Him and anointed Him. He is God's Son, and concerning the future, God says
to Him that He will set Him as His King upon His holy hill of Zion (Ps. 2). But we
freely say of Him, "Our Saviour," "Our Redeemer." And, as His redeemed ones, loving
and serving Him, we call Him our Lord. We even hear people earnestly speak of Him as
"Our coming King"—although to a bride, as a Bridegroom, He is Head over all things
to the church which is His Body, rather than a king! He is indeed King over Israel, *God's*
King! But the Church, His Bride, shall reign *with* Him!

23 better covenant: And they indeed have been made
priests many in number, because that by death they are
24 hindered from continuing: but He, because He abideth
25 forever, hath His priesthood unchangeable. Wherefore
also He is able to save to the uttermost them that draw
near unto God through Him, seeing He ever liveth to
make intercession for them.

Verse 22: Here we find the familiar words, **by so much,** the
measure of infinity, once again. How else, indeed, could Christ's
blessed Person and work be described than by such an appeal to
our judgment, contrasting them with the feeble, incomplete
shadowing in the Levitical ordinances,* as is constantly done in
Hebrews. Let not ceremonies of the former tabernacle, however
interesting in narration and detail here in **Hebrews,** intrigue the
mind: for CHRIST is before us. God is speaking to us in a SON.
It is not the time, the Spirit tells us in Chapter 9.5, to speak of
these earthly types in detail. Let these repeated words of infinite
contrast, "by so much" as to His Person (1.4); "by so much"
as Son, not Servant, over the house of God (3.3); **"by so much"**
as our **Surety of a better covenant** (7.22); "by so much" as to
His mediatorship of a better covenant (8.6); and "how much
more" as to the value of the blood of Christ compared to that of
goats and bulls (9.14)—let these repeated words of infinite
contrast, we say, cause all to fade from our eyes and thoughts
but Christ, and His work and glorious ministry.

**By so much also . . . JESUS . . . the Surety of a better cov-
enant:**† The Greek is beautiful here, placing our Lord's name at

---

*By so much also hath Jesus become the Surety of a better covenant: Here the measure
of difference is between the weak and unprofitable "foregoing commandment" (with its
perishing, passing priests, with whom no Divine oath of continuance was connected), and
Christ, of Whom "The Lord sware . . . Thou art a Priest forever." Infinite is the distance
between the Old Covenant, and Christ as the Surety of a better covenant.

"But now hath He obtained a ministry the more excellent, *by so much* as He is also the
Mediator of a better covenant" (Ch. 8.6). Again, *"by so much"* is a measure of measure-
lessness! All things of the Levitical economy have passed away from God's sight, but the
Risen Christ is a Minister of the sanctuary, and of the true tabernacle, in the presence of
God forever.

†"Here, first in this Epistle, occurs the word covenant (*diathēkē*). In 9.16 the versions
slide over into *testament;* here such a rendering seems without reason. A 'surety' belongs
rather to a covenant than to a will. Of this better covenant, Jesus is surety, not as *sealing*
it with his death and resurrection (as Alford, Lunemann), for these *created* it and could
scarcely therefore, be its guarantee; but as High Priest in the heavenly sanctuary, perpetual
and unfailing, in emboldening His people to draw near to God, assured that the throne of
justice has become a throne of grace."—A. C. Kendrick, **Commentary on The Hebrews,**
p. 93.

the very end of the sentence—the emphatic place, and naming Him from our human side, the Bethlehem name, JESUS. That our blessed Lord, the Son of God, was born down here, among us, in that "prepared body" described in Chapter 10.5-6, is indeed a very *surety* from God, the beginning of assured blessing! The Law had nothing to do with all this, except dimly to shadow forth in the Levitical types the manner of approach, based on shed blood —while God remained *behind the veil*. How wondrous were Christ's words, "Destroy this temple, and in three days I will raise it up"—the temple of His *body*. For *Jesus* was *God's temple*. Hear it, my brother, the tabernacle in the wilderness, and the temple thereafter were, after all, mere buildings. So that if we have discerning eyes and hearing hearts, we read the four "Gospels" with this before us. The Holy Ghost descended as a dove and abode upon Him, and He kept saying, "The Father abiding in Me doeth His works"; and, "By the Spirit of God I cast out demons." God dwelt and walked during those three and a half years, in *Christ!* And then, at Calvary, God laid on Him our sin, and judged it according to His own being as the Holy One, and thus Christ cried, "It is finished!" The third day God raised Him from the dead, and shortly received Him in glory.

But He had, at the Last Supper (after the Passover) passed to the disciples the broken bread, instituting a new feast, and saying concerning the cup, "This is My blood of the covenant, which is poured out for many, unto remission of sins."

Ah, we know these things, but let us repeat them more and more. On Calvary that blood was shed, and into the infinite benefits of it, all believers alike enter. And Jesus is **THE SURETY,** now, at God's right hand, of this **better covenant.** We repeat that this is the blood of the *"eternal covenant"* between "the God of peace" and "the Great Shepherd of the sheep," (as we see in Ch. 13.20), in which we are not the actors but the beneficiaries. And the witnesses: "For as often as ye eat this bread, and drink the cup, ye proclaim the Lord's death till He come" (I Cor. 11.26).

In verses 23-5, the perpetuity of *Christ's* priesthood, **because He abideth forever,** is set over against that of the Levitical priests, **made priests many in number, because that by death they are**

hindered from continuing. Out of this intransmissible priesthood of the Risen Christ comes the blessed assurance that is in all the most familiar passages of this great epistle. Verses 24-5 might well be a text to characterize a whole commentary on **Hebrews.** Literally:

But He, on account of continuing forever, the priesthood intransmissible has. Wherefore also to save completely He is able those coming through Him to God: always living to intercede in behalf of them.

In the study of this great utterance, let us anew lay to our hearts the difference between intercession and reconciliation. Our blessed Lord is interceding for us, but He is in no sense appeasing God. All that God's holy Being and righteous government could demand was once for all, completely and forever, satisfied at the Cross. As we read in Chapter 9.26: "Now *once* at the consummation of the ages hath He been manifested to put away sin by the sacrifice of Himself." In that "once for all" sin-bearing, God is forever resting and delighting. But, you ask, Does not the text say, **He is able** (now, at God's right hand) **to save to the completion* those that come unto God through Him?** Yes, those are the words. But that word "save," please mark, has a three-fold application, we may say: past, present, and future.†

---

*This, Newberry's rendering, is the best we have seen. It is not that Christ is able to reach utterly bad cases, although that is true; but that He is able to carry the believer right through all trials, temptations and infirmities, unto the completion of his pilgrimage, and present him faultless in the day of His coming again.

†*Past:* In Tit. 2.11 we read, "For the grace of God *hath* appeared, bringing salvation to all men." This was the gift of Christ, as Simeon discerned, and said, holding The Babe in His arms, "Mine eyes have seen Thy Salvation" (Lk. 2.30). So Christ went on to Gethsemane and Calvary, and drank the cup of wrath for our sins; and there went forth the glad message of *Salvation* through faith in Him—the gospel which Paul calls "the power of God unto salvation" (Rom. 1.16). So every believer looks back to the time when he obtained this salvation (II Tim. 1.9, 2.10), as the Lord Jesus Christ said in Zacchaeus' home, "Today is salvation come to this house." (See also Tit. 3.5).

2. *Present:* Those who have obtained this salvation are spoken of as those "who are being saved." (I Cor. 1.18, R.V., marg.). See also Acts 2.47, marg.; I Cor. 15.2, II Cor. 2.15.

3. *Future:* The word is also used concerning the future; Paul said, "In hope were we saved" (Rom. 8.24)—i.e., placed in expectation of future deliverance; and Peter, in the council, Acts 15.11: "We believe that we shall be saved through the grace of the Lord Jesus, in like manner as they." Thus we *have* salvation; also we *are* being saved by the constant grace of God; and we look *forward* to the consummation of this salvation (the redemption of our bodies, when our Lord returns), as Paul says: "Now is our salvation nearer than when we first believed" (Rom. 13.11). And, "So Christ also, having been once offered to bear the sins of many, shall appear a second time, apart from sin, to them that wait for Him, unto *salvation*" (Heb. 9.28).

Therefore every preacher of the gospel and teacher of souls should always first point out that our blessed Lord Jesus Christ has forever met all Divine claims against sinners:

"God was in Christ reconciling the world unto Himself; *not* reckoning to them their trespasses." "He that believeth *hath* eternal life." "He that believeth on Him is not judged . . . cometh not into judgment, but *hath* passed out of death into life." "Through this Man is proclaimed unto you remission of sins . . . By Him every one that believeth *is* justified from all things from which ye could not be justified by the Law of Moses."

And what shall we say further to them? That they have peace with God, that they are now under grace and have hope of glory (Rom. 5.1-2)? But is this enough? There lies before each of them a pilgrim path, "babes in Christ" as they are; with the enmity of God's great foe, Satan; and the hatred of that world which is controlled by him. They must be told two great things:

1. That when they believed, the blessed Holy Spirit sealed them; that having received the Lord Jesus, they have the right to call God Father (Jno. 1.12), and the Spirit will bear witness to them in this, Romans 8.16; also that He was sent to guide them into all truth and be within them "the Comforter": taking the things of the Risen Christ and manifesting them unto them.

2. That they have a Great High Priest on high; that their pathway through this world is being cared for, planned, and protected by Him; that He is infinitely sympathetic, and **able to save completely, ever living to make intercession for them.**

For remember that in the least spiritual exercise, in any turning of the mind toward Divine things, we are approaching a court of infinite greatness and glory. To favor at this court, the shed blood of the Son of God, and His presence there, entitle us. But how constant is our need of a Priest to carry on matters with the King of glory, the Creator of all things! Think of "coming boldly" into the Holy Place of the presence of God Almighty; Jehovah, the Most High!

Now it is necessary again to specify those in whose interests our Lord's priestly work is being carried on—it is for believers: "I pray *not* for the world, but for those whom thou has given me out of the world, for they are thine" (John 17.9). It is for those who come through Him to God.* Carrying His own, bought by His blood, through their pilgrim journey, is included in the words **able to save completely.**† The only other occurrence of the phrase is in Luke 13.11, concerning the woman who "was bowed together, and could in no wise lift herself up *unto completion*"— that is, as we would say, straighten up. So in our **Hebrews** verse, it indicates Christ's readiness and sufficiency in whatever need we may have, in whatever adverse circumstances. The true be-

---

*We are again confronted by the great and constant question (raised by so many in these very days), as to whether the coming to God in **Hebrews** is the same exactly as that described in Paul's Epistles before **Hebrews**. For example, in Eph. 2.18: "Through Him [Christ] we both [Jew and Gentile believers] have our access by one Spirit unto the Father." And again, in Rom. 5.11: "We also rejoice in God through our Lord Jesus Christ, through Whom we have now received the reconciliation"; or in Rom. 8.15-16: "Ye received the spirit of adoption, whereby we cry, Abba, Father. The Spirit himself beareth witness with our spirit, that we are born-ones of God."

Now in **Hebrews** there is described no such inner witness. Also, we come *to God* as God, rather than intimately to Him as Father.

But it must be remembered that there was a people of God whom He brought out of Egypt and among whom He dwelt, both in the wilderness and afterwards in the temple. And there was a complete system of shadows by which they were taught to approach God.

Now here we find an epistle addressed to these **Hebrews** as having possessed (which the Gentiles did not at all), this system of approach to God through an earthly high priest, with days and ordinances—"the ten thousand things of the law" (Hos. 8.12).

The question, therefore, in **Hebrews** is not God's fatherhood, but the method of approach to Him as *God*.

Nor is **Hebrews**, therefore, the book wherein we shall find described those inner operations of the blessed Spirit of God set forth in those epistles which define the calling and character of the saints of this Church age.

Again, we do not find the Church described in **Hebrews** at all, but individual saints are addressed, partaking indeed of a heavenly calling (Ch. 3.1) but addressed as those with whom the true God has been in relation in the past. Indeed, what makes it especially difficult for Gentiles to understand **Hebrews** is the very fact that God was in relation with the Hebrew people and with no other people at all, as we read in Ps. 147.19-20:

"He showeth his word unto Jacob,
His statutes and his ordinances unto Israel.
He hath not dealt so with *any* nation;
And as for his ordinances, *they* have not known them."

It is largely because the Gentile professing Christians have conjured up a "religion" called "the Christian religion", that they do not readily grasp **Hebrews!** Therefore, let us keep before us the fact that those with whom God had been in relationship are being exhorted to desert all things that belong to the Divinely given Levitical system, and go forth to a rejected and crucified Son of God "without the camp"—without any earthly religious connections whatever, and join in that heavenly worship which pertains to all who partake of the heavenly calling: having Christ now appearing before the face of God for them.

Therefore, instead of asserting (as do the Bullingerites, etc.) that the other Pauline Epistles are on higher ground than **Hebrews**, let us rather adore the graciousness and tenderness of God in giving patient instruction in new things to those to whom He had given a former religion now to be abandoned.

†Both the King James and the Revised read, **to the uttermost.** If their meaning is set forth literally the Greek phrase, *eis to panteles,* well and good. It translates literally, **to the all [or entire] end.**

liever early finds self-confidence to be his snare: he has in himself neither wisdom nor strength. The mature believer is one who
has realized his weakness, ceased to strive for strength, and rests
in Christ for every need. From their spiritual infancy unto full
growth, from the beginning of their pilgrim path to the completion thereof, they have always One **Who ever liveth,** of
Whom it is the constant, unvarying purpose **to make intercession
for them.** Whether therefore it be a sinner, a publican who has
cast himself upon the mercy of God and gone down to his house
justified; or whether it be a Paul, finishing his course, and standing before the mouth of the lion, it is always, "The Lord stood
by me and strengthened me." He ever looks after His own.

"What then shall we say to these things? If God is for us, who
is against us? He that spared not His own Son, but delivered Him
up for us all, HOW SHALL HE NOT also with Him freely give
us all things?" (Rom. 8.31 ff).

Then follow the words that comfort me in the preparation of
this commentary on **Hebrews:**

"Who shall lay anything to the charge of God's elect? Shall
God that justifieth? Who is he that condemneth? Shall Christ
Jesus that died, yea, rather, that was raised from the dead?"
Of course these court room truths belong to Romans, but note
how the following words of Romans (8.34) join it to **Hebrews:**
"Who is at the right hand of God, Who also is *making intercession
for us.*" This is the only direct assertion of such intercession outside of **Hebrews.** Bullinger, of the "Companion Bible," (whose
falsehoods are followed today by so many), says: "God has put
asunder the epistle to the Romans and the epistle to the **Hebrews**"
—taking away any direct application of **Hebrews** truth to us
today. To prove his position, he goes to Romans 8, which he says is
directly about us, where "There is no condemnation to them that
are in Christ Jesus," and "no separation from the love of God,
which is in Christ Jesus." He is offended by the warnings of
Hebrews 6 and 10, whereas in Romans 8 we have exactly the
same warning (vss. 12, 13) as in **Hebrews,** and, in what we have
quoted, the very same priestly intercession* of Christ at the right

---

*Christ's intercessory work:
1. Not at all, atoning: propitiation was once for all accomplished at the Cross.

hand of God! (vs. 34).

Not as a prophet, telling us our duty, but as a Priest, represent-ing not God but us, is Christ set forth in **Hebrews**. Reverently we say, He is not on God's side but on our side! He is called *our* Great High Priest; prophets were called *God's* prophets.

The king in Israel, was God's "power." He represented God's authority. So David (and Saul before him) was anointed "king over Israel." Our Lord Jesus is coming back as King of kings, and Lord of lords (Rev. 19.16), as the Seed of David (Isa. 11.1, 10; Lk. 1.32). "Behold A KING shall reign in righteousness" (Isa 32.1). See also Zechariah 14.9, 16 ff; and all the prophets. He is to reign as we have seen, as "a Priest upon His throne" (Zech. 6.13). "Of the increase of His government and of peace there shall be no end, upon the throne of David" (Isa. 9.7).

Even now, He has "all authority in Heaven and on earth," as He had not on earth. We are looking daily for His return, when the full glory of His Melchizedek priesthood will be revealed. As one has said, "Our Lord is the manifested One at last, through Whom men come to God. He is a manifest Priest reigning there."

---

2. Therefore His intercession is not to turn God away from wrath against believers. It was GOD Who loved the world. It was GOD Who gave His only begotten Son for us. And it is God Who is delighting in the finished work of Christ on our behalf.

3. We can conceive that God, to Whom all things are possible, could have wrought directly upon us, and brought us home to Heaven. But He chose to set Jesus as our High Priest at His right hand, and He has given us marvelous encouragement: for we find Him in Hebrews "a merciful and faithful High Priest," "made in all things like unto His brethren"; "not a high priest that cannot be touched with the feeling of our infirmities; but One that hath been in all points tempted like as we are, sin apart."

Here then is the wonderful love of God toward us displayed afresh, in His not only giv-ing His Son, but having Him pass through all temptations and trials in order, when exalted, to keep sympathizing with us in understanding tenderness that knows no bounds.

4. Christ's intercession also *precedes* our temptations and trials. He warned Peter of a coming attack by Satan: "I *have prayed* for thee that thy faith fail not." Peter disregarded the warning, and fell into the devil's trap, denying the Lord he loved. But when "the Lord turned, and looked upon Peter" (not a look of fault-finding, but of tenderest love), Peter went out to burst into bitter tears.

5. Remember, it is "the *Man*, Christ Jesus," that is our High Priest. Yes, He *is* God also; but He has forever taken the place of subjection, "the form of a servant, . . . in the likeness of men." He entered into the Holies above through His own blood, keeping the fashion of a man, and the form of a servant. And thus will He be forever; for He Himself shall at last be "subjected" to God the Father. Eternally, then, He has the place of Priest and Intercessor. It is God the Father's yearning not only that we have, certainly, assurance of our eternal safety, as we find in Romans; not only that we have a heavenly calling and are members of the Body of Christ Himself; but that we come into an unbroken experience of the daily, hourly, tenderness of infinite Divine love: and this is brought about, is fitted to our poor capacities, by the work of Him Who **ever liveth to make intercession for us.**

Verse 26: **For such a High Priest became us: holy, guileless, undefiled, separated from sinners, and become** [made] **higher than the heavens;** Humbly we would call attention to the emphatic place in this sentence of the word "us." For here we have the "partakers of a heavenly calling" in plain view.

Study the beautiful progress in the words of verse 26. First, the High Priest Who **became us,** even Christ, is called "Holy." "Holy" has reference to nature. Gabriel's announcement of our Lord's birth was, "That which is to be born shall be called *holy*, the Son of God." Twice the word is used in Acts (2.27, 13.35): "Thy holy One"; Christ as we have seen, "through the eternal Spirit offered Himself without blemish unto God" (Heb. 9.14). When it came to Calvary, the end of His earthly life, He was still the Holy One; and in Revelation 15.4, "Thou only art holy."

The next word is "guileless." It means, without an evil thought —like an innocent little child. Such was Christ! This word is very difficult for us, because, since Adam sinned, this world is crowded with a race none other than guile*ful*. Peter tells us (I Pet. 2.1, 2): "Putting away therefore all wickedness, and *all guile*, and all hypocrisies, and envies, and all evil speakings" (what a heart full of guile this list reveals!) "as new born babes, long for the spiritual milk which is *without guile*, that ye may grow thereby unto salvation." The only human beings we know who are naturally without guile are utter babes and very young children.

Now in Christ there was no guile whatever. He said, "I came not to judge the world, but to save the world" (John 12.47). This was the reason publicans and sinners crowded around Him. Unconsciously, they found One Who was guileless as any child! He spoke words which, because He was The Light, discovered indeed their sins to them,—but, all the while, they knew He was the *Friend of sinners!* Gently and guilelessly He could say to the Samaritan woman who had had five husbands, and was then living with a man not her husband, "Thou saidst well, I have no husband."

Our Lord is still the "guileless" One, "the same yesterday and today, and forever." He is not today a judge, a severe inspector. Think not of Him so! The day of His judging (Acts 17.31) is not come. Rely on Him as your Friend. It is impossible, except by

God's help, to conceive of this guilelessness in the One Who knew all things, Who "knew what was in man" (Jno. 2.25). But it is of inestimable comfort to our hearts, this fact of guilelessness in our Great High Priest! of utter absence of evil thoughts concerning us.*

The next word concerning the Great High Priest Who "became us," is "Undefiled," or unsoiled. Literally it means unstained, undyed by foreign color; consequently, uncontaminated. (The word without the negative is used in Ch. 12.15). Such was our Lord that though passing through the midst of and thronged by publicans and harlots, and ecclesiastics full of Satanic pride, of sin and stain of every sort and degree, He remained unsullied, undefiled. This affords our hearts measureless comfort and confidence. It is such a high priest, unstained by the sin and sinful scenes that confront us daily, Who is at the right hand of God, ever keeping His own.

Necessarily we have the next descriptive word, **Separated from sinners.** No Pharisee would understand this. Look at Luke 15.1, 2 for example: "All the publicans and sinners were drawing near unto Him to hear Him. And both the Pharisees and the scribes murmured, saying, This man receiveth sinners, and eateth with them." See also Matthew 9.10-13. But you say, Publicans and sinners drew near to Him in perfect liberty, for was He not everywhere known as a friend of publicans and sinners (Matt. 11.19; Lk. 7.34), "eating and drinking" with them? He was! praise God for it! And yet all the while this astonishing, to us impossible, but glorious *fact* remained: **separated from sinners.**

This separation does not mean as Alford contends that He was "void of all contact and commerce with sinners, removed far away

---

*Years ago I brought from Edinburgh, Scotland, along with many theological books, a history of Roman Catholicism in which, at the foot of the page, were printed in Latin questions priests were compelled to ask their confessors. These questions were so indescribably vile, even unnaturally indecent, that I destroyed two volumes, lest my sons, who were young, might grow up to even read these unutterably filthy imaginings of the worse than pagan priests of this false religion. The whole occupation of the priest in the so-called confessional was (and is) to conceive evil, imagine evil, draw out from the confessor expressions of evil, and place in the imagination even of young confessors evil as yet unthought of, and often never to be thought of, except as put into the mind by the foul questions of the inquisitor.

This alone is an excellent illustration *by contrast*, of our Great Priest, Who is guileless. This Greek word, *akakos*, which we translate guileless, could be literally translated evil-less. Its only other occurrence is in Rom. 16.18, where saints are warned against certain insidious, false teachers: "By their smooth and fair speech they beguile the hearts of the *innocent*," in this case, wholly unsuspecting, guileless hearers.

in His glorified state and body, into God's holy place" (Alford, *en loc.*). This idea defeats any true understanding of this won-drous expression. For if Christ must be carried up to Heaven to be **separated from sinners,** all the four blessed things already af-firmed of Him are defeated. Note that "separated" is the parti-ciple in the passive voice, aorist. I am thankful that the passive voice is used, for our blessed Lord did not say, Behold Me: I have separated Myself from sinners. (Although He did say, with the calmness of Deity, "Which of you accuseth Me of sin?" And there was no answer to that!) His was not such a physical with-drawal from the world as that which the monks and nuns and all the hermits (Prov. 18.1) follow—taking their sin with them into their self-deceiving seclusion! But it was as the Sinless One: "I came out from the Father, and am come into the world: again, I leave the world, and go unto the Father." "I am not of the world." What a strengthening of heart to us to know that this Jesus, the **holy, guileless, undefiled One, separated from sinners,** has passed through this earthly scene!

By His whole history among us there unfolds before us the holy flower of Deity—of "God manifested in the flesh." **Sep-arated from sinners** indeed was He, yet did the publicans and sinners draw near to Him, for here was a Teacher such as they had never heard, Who spoke with the authority of Heaven, Whom yet in their hearts they knew for a friend! Thus was fulfilled in Him this blessed passive voice, **separated from sinners.**

In the next words, we follow Him into Heaven as our Great High Priest: **and made higher than the heavens.** Now in Ephesians 1.20 and 21 we read:

"God wrought in Christ, when He raised Him from the dead, and made Him to sit at His right hand in the heavenlies, far above all rule, and authority and power, and dominion, and every name that is named, not only in this world, but also in that which is to come."

In Ephesians 4.10 we see Him as "ascended far above all the heavens." And in Hebrews 4.14: "Having been a Great High Priest Who hath passed through the heavens, Jesus the Son of God;" and in Chapter 8.1:

"Now in the things which we are saying the chief point is this: We have such a High Priest, Who sat down on the right hand of the throne of the Majesty in the heavens."

Here then is the High Priest that became us, who in the infinite wisdom and grace of God are partakers of a heavenly calling. Are we born again *(anothen,* literally, *down from above)?* We have a *High Priest above.* Is our citizenship in Heaven? Our representative, our "Forerunner" and Great High Priest is already there, a Man in the glory. Has God,

"being rich in mercy, for His great love wherewith He loved us, even when we were dead through our trespasses, enlifed us together with Christ . . . and raised us up with Him, and made us to sit with Him in the heavenlies"?

Even so! And although we ourselves are yet traveling through the world in our unredeemed bodies, the earthly tabernacle in which we groan, being burdened, yet Christ, the Firstfruits of the resurrection, the First-born from the dead, has already ascended up on high, and been greeted by God as High Priest forever! And to Him has been given the place of honor at the right hand of God.*

There used to be a teaching that Heaven was at the center of the created universe, which revolved around it! Not so. The throne of God is far above all the heavens, far above His created universe. Our Great High Priest was **made higher than the heavens.** But His position "far above all" does not change His affections, His sympathy. How humbling it is to us who "look to the hole of the pit whence we have been digged" by sovereign Divine mercy and grace, we who have received a heavenly calling, with such a High Priest as this!

---

*The heavens, of which three are mentioned in Scripture (II Cor. 12.2), were created by Christ. Solomon at the dedication of the temple said:

"But will God in very deed dwell with men on the earth? behold, heaven and the heaven of heavens cannot contain Thee; how much less this house which I have builded!" (II Chron. 6.18).

The third heaven is evidently synonymous with Paradise, (for Paul says he was "Caught up to the third heaven . . . into Paradise, and heard unspeakable words, which it is not lawful for a man to utter"), the abode of the spirits of the blessed, doubtless. Our Lord indeed said, "In my Father's house there are many abiding places"—of various orders of heavenly beings. But he "ascended 'far above all'," even of these heavenly dwelling places, when He took His seat at the right hand of the throne of God.

Indeed, this one blessed verse, Chapter 7.26, could afford an excuse to that great man of God, John Owen, the Puritan, to write his commentary of nine volumes on this wondrous epistle to the **Hebrews!**

To proceed:

27 **Who does not day by day need, as those high priests, first for His own sins to offer sacrifices—then for those of the people. For this** [whole matter of sacrifice for sins] **He attended to once for all when He offered up Him-**
28 **self. For the Law constitutes men high priests, having infirmity; but the Word of the oath, which was after the Law*** [in time], **a Son, perfected for evermore.**

Verses 27, 28: **He offered up Himself:** The objection of some, that our Lord was not acting as a priest when **He offered up Himself** upon the Cross, is baseless and harmful. How foolish so to misinterpret a verse that positively says, **He offered up Himself.** And again, "I lay down My life for the sheep"—commanded of the Father so to do (See Jno. 10). Our Great High Priest now is in the glory at God's right hand, fulfilling His blessed heavenly priesthood. And He will be back *upon earth*, "a Priest upon His throne," in the one thousand years.

It is as a Priest after the order of Melchizedek that He thus "offered Himself" here in Hebrews 7.27. This must not be forgotten, as some seem to forget it, who insist that, as Melchizedek Priest, He only blesses. Read the chapter from verse 11: no other conclusion can be arrived at than that the words **He offered up Himself** refer to our blessed Lord as Priest after the order of Melchizedek. Priesthood is based upon sacrifice, and Christ's priesthood perhaps most of all, for He is Himself the great Antitype of all priesthood! Therefore **He offered up Himself,** and that when He was upon earth, not as connected with the Levitical system, but laying down His life of Himself, as we have seen, by the direct command of the Father. Remember also that He suffered without the gate, despised and rejected by the earthly priesthood!

---

*"It happens in this case, as in all others of a like nature which occur in our epistle, that the deep and accurate knowledge of the writer, in respect to everything which concerned the Jewish dispensation, becomes apparent, just in proportion to our knowledge of the usages which really existed under that dispensation."—Moses Stuart, *in loc.*

He offered up Himself! This no Levitical priest was asked to do. Therefore the Levitical priesthood could only "shadow" here and there the things belonging to those heavenly realities brought in by Christ, when **He offered up Himself,** and "entered once and for all into the holies [in Heaven] through His own blood."

We see from Chapter 5.2 that the high priests taken from among men were to bear gently with the ignorant and erring because they themselves were "compassed with infirmity; and by reason thereof were bound, as for the people, so also for themselves, to offer for sins." And because the way into the holiest was not made manifest as yet, and God had not come out to them as He did to the nation when He was presented as the Messiah, their King, they could have **high priests having infirmity,** one of themselves, Aaron, (and after him his sons) subject himself to death and **needing daily** (vs. 27) **to offer up sacrifices, first for his own sins, and then for the sins of the people.**

But we see the *utter absence of infirmity* in our Great High Priest, in verse 28: **For the Law constituted men high priests, having infirmity; but the word of the oath, which was after the Law, constituteth a Son, perfected for evermore.**

However much we may see our Lord when on earth, compassed by trial, temptation, difficulty, *we never see infirmity in Him.* For He always does the will of the Father, and is now doing that will in the Glory, and will be accomplishing it for evermore!

CHAPTER EIGHT

1   Now the chief point in the things being said is this: Such an One we have as High Priest, Who sat down on the right hand of the throne of the Majesty in the
2   heavens, a Minister of the holy things, and of the true tabernacle, which the Lord pitched, not man.

CHRIST, AS OUR HIGH PRIEST, is a Minister of the holy things of God's actual, glorious presence in Heaven! For in the words **which the Lord pitched, not man,** we observe at once that the evident meaning is a contrast of **the true tabernacle,** the reality, in Heaven, with that which God commanded Moses to "pitch" in the wilderness days of Israel. The Levitical tabernacle, (full of types and lessons, doubtless), *disappears utterly* in the book of **Hebrews,** together with all jealous thought for it, on the part of those willing to enter the *heavenly worship,* and, as regards earthly religion, to go forth unto Jesus "without the camp, bearing His reproach." Such have no "holy temple" on earth, nor sacred buildings of any sort, knowing that now "the Most High dwelleth not in temples made with hands" as said Stephen (Acts 7.48) and later Paul (Acts 17.24). Paul had heard Stephen say it.

But *now,* in the words of verse 3: **For every high priest is appointed to offer both gifts and sacrifices: wherefore it is necessary that this High Priest also have somewhat to offer.**
Let us leave for a moment the question of the **gifts and sacrifices** He is to offer, and proceed to the great lesson of this Chapter.

We have, then, the hypothetical statement (vss. 4, 5) that:
4   **If He were on earth, He would not be a priest at all, seeing there are [in the as yet undestroyed Jewish temple, when Hebrews was written] those who keep offering**
5   **the gifts according to the Law; who serve a copy and shadow of the heavenly things, even as Moses is warned of God when he is about to make the tabernacle: for, See, saith He, that thou make all things according to the pattern that was shown thee in the mount.**

The contention of some that verse 4: **If He were on earth, He would not be a priest at all,** sets forth that Christ's priesthood began only after resurrection and the Lord's ascension, is strange indeed. For in this verse the apostle is speaking of Christ risen from the dead and now in glory, Who had **sat down on the right hand of the throne of the Majesty in the heavens, a Minister of the sanctuary.** It is of this One in that ministry that it is affirmed, **If He were on earth, He would not be a priest at all.** For there were at that moment those of the Aaronic order, in the temple which was then standing, carrying on the service which the Law, **the copy and shadow of heavenly things,** prescribed. To affirm that Chapter 4 excludes the propitiation by blood made on the Cross from priestly functions is utterly to obscure this passage. Our Lord in His earthly ministry, though so often speaking and working in the temple itself, never assayed to *its* priesthood!

But Christ is God, God manifest in the flesh. "God in very deed" (II Chron. 6.18) had come to dwell in the tabernacle and afterwards in the temple. It was "zeal for God's house," as such, that ate Him up. (Ps. 69.9, Jno. 2.17). The morning and evening sacrifices, the Day of Atonement, the Passover Lamb, and all the sacrifices as ministered by dying, ever-changing Levitical priests, all this was a "shadow" of Christ's priestly work.*

But now we come to better words:

6 But now hath He obtained a ministry the more excellent, by so much as He is also the Mediator of a better covenant, which hath been enacted upon better promises.
7 For if that first covenant had been faultless, then would
8 no place have been sought for a second. For finding fault with them, He saith,
    Behold, the days come, saith the Lord,
    That I will make a new covenant with the house of
        Israel and with the house of Judah;
9 Not according to the covenant that I made with their fathers
    In the day that I took them by the hand to lead them
        forth out of the land of Egypt;

---

*Next in sadness to the words, "They that dwell at Jerusalem, and their rulers, because they knew Him not, nor the voices of the prophets . . . fulfilled them by condemning Him," is the fact that they went about their sacrifices, Passover and all, with the Great Priest of Whom all these sacrifices spoke, before their eyes—and they blind—as unto this day.

For they continued not in My covenant,
And I regarded them not, saith the Lord.

Verse 6: A ministry the more excellent—Now if we can only step out from the shadows (vs. 5) and behold the substance! Christ's one offering would have been complete if there had been no shadows or types whatever. And we must be so delivered in spirit that our conception of our Lord's ministry shall not be governed by types and shadows: but the types by the reality. The measure of the difference between the old Levitical ministry and that of Christ is again the blessed phrase, A ministry the more excellent by so much—And what is the measure? By so much as He is also the Mediator of a better covenant, which hath been enacted upon better promises.

Here the words a better covenant are contrasted with the first, or legal covenant. Now, what covenant is this "better covenant"? And what are these "better promises"?

First, it is not the covenant of Hebrews 13.20, for that was not between creatures, but between "the God of peace" and "the Lord Jesus," and the condition was the obedience unto death of Christ to the Father; its ground, the shed blood of Christ; and its issue, "an eternal covenant." This is the great fundamental transaction between God and Christ: no creature is seen; but, ah! believers become—apart from works—beneficiaries! So that God can go on and make (in the Millennial future) a second (or "new") covenant with Israel, who "continued not" (vs. 9) in the Sinaitic or "first" covenant.

But not two things about this new covenant (vs. 8): a. It is based, as we have intimated, on the "eternal covenant" of Hebrews 13.20.

b. God does everything in this "new covenant." There is no "If ye—" as at Sinai; but it is all "I will:" I will make a new covenant (vs. 8).

"I will put My laws into their mind—" constant remembrance—not on external stone tables.

"I will write them also on their heart"—supreme affection.

"And I will be to them a God, and they shall be to Me a people" (vs. 10). "All shall know Me . . . (vs. 11). "I will be merciful to their iniquities, and their sins I will remember no more."

Now you see this is all Grace and flows freely from the "eternal covenant" in Christ's blood of Chapter 13.20. But the great word as to the former covenant is: "He hath made the first old . . . nigh unto vanishing away." It vanished indeed in A.D. 70, when the temple was sacked and burned, and Jerusalem destroyed by Titus. While place is foretold for "the house of Israel and the house of Judah" in this epistle to the Hebrews, yet lay this to heart: *the old covenant is gone* (vs. 9, 13); and the new not yet come. Paul is writing to Hebrew believers with whose fathers God had made a "covenant," and with which nation God will, by and by, at the Messiah's return to Israel, make a "new" covenant, saying, "And this is the covenant from Me unto them, when I shall take away their sins"—Romans 11.27. These Hebrew believers were called, then, to face the fact that the old covenant, with the Law principle of blessing, had been set aside. We behold national Israel today without a covenant, "regarded not" by Jehovah! And so we turn to Hebrews 13.20, and "in the blood of an *eternal* covenant" between the God of peace and the Lord Jesus, we find ourselves, with true Hebrew believers, all "partakers of a heavenly calling"—we all find ourselves blessed indeed! And it is the blood of that covenant which we celebrate when we gather at the Lord's table; so that all hope in man has passed away forever; and so has all hope in Divine Law to be fulfilled by man as the "condition of blessing."

To return to verse 6, our Lord **hath obtained a ministry the more excellent BY SO MUCH AS** (who can measure this Divine comparison?) **He is also the MEDIATOR of a better covenant.** Now that "better covenant" is not made with us, but like the "old" covenant of Sinai, pertains to national Israel; and the blessings of the **better promises** will be lavished upon them.

Verse 7: **For if that first (covenant) had been faultless, then would no place have been sought for a second:** Here it is most evident that the two covenants, the legal one at Sinai, and the "new covenant" which God will make "with the house of Israel and with the house of Judah" (vs. 8) are before us. Look down to verse 13 and you get the lesson:

"In that He saith, A new covenant, He hath made the first old. But that which is becoming old and waxeth aged, is nigh unto vanishing away."

It is quite striking that in verse 7 the word "faultless" refers to the covenant; while in verse 8 we read:

8   For finding fault with them He saith,
    Behold the days come, saith the Lord,
    That I will make a new covenant with the house of
    Israel and with the house of Judah.

Anything resting upon man's faithfulness goes down. Hear Jehovah's own word by Moses when He gave the Sinai covenant:

"For when I shall have brought them into the land which I sware unto their fathers, flowing with milk and honey, and they shall have eaten and filled themselves, and waxed fat; then will they turn unto other gods, and serve them, and despise Me, and break My covenant" (Dt. 31.20).

Salvation is of GOD, my brother! and not in any sense of man. The Law, "written . . . in tables of stone," the letter, killed (II Cor. 3.3-9). It is Divinely *contrasted* with Salvation by Grace through the shed blood of Christ. Believers were so identified in Christ's death that "our old man was crucified with Him" (Rom. 6.6) so that we are "dead to the Law" and "discharged from the Law" (Rom. 7.4, 6).*

It is of great importance for us to note concerning the "covenants" of whom they are spoken, and with whom they are connected. To apply verse 8, **I will make † a new covenant with the house of Israel and with the house of Judah,** to Christians today, is blank ignorance, or presumptuous folly. Indeed, the very next verse compels us to know with whom the new covenant will be made, for we read it will *not* be:

---

*If you have been taught "theology" before you were taught to study the Scripture itself (and therefore never learned to read and believe Scripture freely), read Rom. 6 and 7. Look at the phrases:

"Not under Law but under Grace" (6.14). "Free from the Law" (7.3). "Dead to the Law through the body of Christ" (7.4). "Discharged from the Law" (7.6). "Not through the Law was the promise made to Abram or to his seed" (4.14). "The Law worketh wrath; but where there is no Law, neither is there transgression" (4.15). (*We* did not write Romans, brother!). "I through the Law died unto the Law, that I might live unto God. I have been crucified with Christ; and it is no longer I that live, but Christ liveth in me: and that life which I now live in the flesh I live in faith, the faith which is in the Son of God, Who loved me, and gave Himself up for me" (Gal. 2.19, 20). To me the greatest proof of human self-righteousness and unbelief in Grace is this contention for the Law by those of the Reformed Theology. A good question to ask them is, *"Are you* the righteousness of God in Christ?"* (II Cor. 5.21).

†Note the R.V. margin in vss. 8 and 10: **I will accomplish** (Gr.) a new covenant with the house of Israel; and, This is the covenant that I will covenant with the house of Israel. This corresponds to Rom. 11.27, "And this is My covenant [or, margin: the covenant *from Me*] unto them, when I shall take away their sins."

Verse 9—According to the covenant that I made with their fathers in the day that I took them by the hand to lead them forth out of the land of Egypt.

(Of course, the next words, **They continued not in My covenant, and I regarded them not, saith the Lord,** everyone has willingly consigned to calf-worshipping Israel!)

Neither the first covenant, at all, or ever, nor the new covenant, as yet to be made with Israel and Judah, relates to Christians. Believers today must avoid the bondage of the first; and the false hopes aroused by misapplication of the promises of the second. To be particular:

The old, or first, covenant, does not apply to Christians for:

1. It was made with national Israel, not with Christians, as see, (besides Ch. 8.8 and 9 above) Exodus 19.3-6; Deuteronomy 4.31; 7.6-16; read and believe Psalm 147.19-20; Exodus 31.16; 34.27; Nehemiah 9.14.

2. At the first Church council in Jerusalem (Acts 15), this very question, as to whether the legal covenant with Israel applied to Gentile believers, was thoroughly entered upon, Peter asking:

"Why make ye trial of God, that ye should put a yoke upon the neck of the disciples which neither our fathers nor we were able to bear?"

And declaring:

"But we believe that we shall be saved through the GRACE of the Lord Jesus, in like manner as *they*" (Gentile believers—Acts 15.10, 11).

Then James utters the dispensational explanation of verse 14, that God *first* (i.e., before the restoration of Israel to their land) "visited the Gentiles, to take out of them a people for His name." Read also the verses following.

3. God's awful word through Paul concerning anyone preaching "another gospel" was that he was *accursed* (Gal. 1.8). As Paul further explains, "Ye are severed from Christ, ye who would be justified by the Law; ye are fallen away from *Grace*" (Gal. 5.4). For

Paul classes Judaism with Paganism in this present time when God has set aside the Jewish religion and is occupied with *mercy* apart from works of Law—that is, the first covenant—to both Jewish and Gentile sinners. "How turn ye back again to the weak and beggarly elements?"* asks Paul of the Galatians (See Gal. 4.8-11).

God has repeatedly declared the day of the first covenant is done. So we see in Chapter 7.18: "A disannulling of a foregoing commandment . . . a bringing in thereupon of a better hope, through which we draw nigh unto God"—which they were never allowed to do under the first covenant. And as to Israel, we have just seen Chapter 8.8, 9. And again, "In that He saith, A new covenant, He hath made the first old" (vs. 13). But the Jews know not this. They sit in four-fold pride: (a) that of nature; (b) that of a past real relationship with Jehovah; (c) that of having despised and rejected their own Messiah Who was sent in lowliness; (d) that of carrying on synagogue services with "cantors" and "rabbis", in complete spiritual blindness. *Instructed Christians* are the only real friends of the Jew. The modernist preacher, denying the virgin birth, the blood atonement, and the bodily resurrection, and inviting a Jewish rabbi to his platform, is the chief murderer of Jews—worse than Hitler, Himmler and Streicher themselves. For a Jewish rabbi invited to a "Christian pulpit" which is not Christian, but infidel, is thereby mollified, flattered, and deceived; and confirmed in his rejection of the only Saviour of either Jew or Gentile.†

---

*The word elements, or (R. V.) rudiments, is Greek *stoicheia,* first principles. Paul uses the term in Col. 2.8, 20, as in Galatians, to describe the religion of the world, the religious principles in which people walked who "observe *days.*" God had once prescribed them to Israel, but He having finished with them, and Christ being rejected, Christ went out from the temple saying it was left unto them, (the Jews), "desolate". At His crucifixion the veil of the temple was rent in twain and all religious performances completely ended. Man's business, inspired by the devil, is to build up what God has destroyed. There is no religious observance whatever left. Paul said to the Galatians, "Ye observe days, and months, and seasons, and years. *I am afraid of you,* lest by any means I have bestowed labor upon you in vain." The saints at Pentecost had no *stoicheia:* nor desired any, for they had God's own presence, and Christ was before their eyes. Religious observances are to hide the living, Risen Christ.

Remember that the Lord's Supper is a *remembering* Christ Himself, just as water baptism, after faith, is a personal confession of identification with Christ Himself. There are no *stoicheia.*

†To claim that Lk. 23.48 teaches that the Jewish nation repented at the Cross is simply high folly. Christ indeed prayed on the Cross, "Father, forgive them; for they know not what they do." This prayer will in due season be answered. But whatever the effect of the stupendous impression made by the three hours' darkness, the earthquake and the cry, the

Israel then is at present out of covenant with God entirely. In the first, the legal covenant, **they continued not,** and God **regarded them not.** There is therefore no standing for Israel before God under the Mosiac covenant. As to the Law, they have not "continued" in any real regard thereto; and as to the promises made to Abraham, they have fallen short completely of those promises. They regard themselves today as "chosen people," but God says, **I regarded them not.** Into the new covenant, the people of Israel have not yet entered, and indeed its blessings are based on the Person and work of the Messiah Whom they rejected and crucified.

So that Peter on the day of Pentecost cried to the "men of Israel,"

"Repent [of the fearful sin of Calvary] and be baptized every one of you in the name of Jesus Christ, unto the remission of your sins; and ye shall receive the gift of the Holy Spirit . . . and with many other words he testified and exhorted them, saying, Save yourselves from this crooked generation" (Acts 2.38-40).

Salvation for a Jew involves a complete breaking with his unbelieving nation! We find the obedient Jews who were "enlightened" (Heb. 10.32),

"Endured a great conflict of sufferings; being made a gazing stock both by reproaches and afflictions; . . . becoming partakers with them that were so used . . . bonds . . . spoiling of their possessions" (vss. 32-4).

This is not often found today, and is an awful proof of existing spiritual conditions, both among the Jews and Gentiles, called "professing Christians." As for Christendom today, it has become so Judaized, with its forms and ceremonies, "Sabbath" and "moral Law," worldly respectability and property, and its emasculated gospel, as to give slight offense to many Jews.

Israel then, while "an elect race . . . a holy nation," have not obtained that eternal mercy which is future, and by virtue of which they will be an "all righteous" nation; just as any individual, being

---

nation as such remained not only impenitent, but under bondage to the Sadducean priesthood (Acts 5.17). They imprisoned the apostles, and stoned Stephen. The truth concerning the Jewish nation is told by the Holy Ghost in I Thess. 2.15, 16: "—the Jews, who both killed the Lord Jesus and the prophets, and drove out us, and please not God, and are contrary to all men; forbidding us to speak to the Gentiles that they may be saved; to fill up their sins always: but the wrath [which will end in 'Jacob's trouble'] is come upon them to the uttermost."

one of God's elect, is not actually pardoned, justified, and regenerated till *"faith cometh"* (Rom. 10.17). Israel's hopes are *legal:*
"Being ignorant of God's righteousness, and seeking to establish
their own, they did not subject themselves to the righteousness of
God" (Rom. 10.3). Ignorant of mercy and of Grace; unconscious of
sinnerhood; glorying in the Law which they do not, cannot keep;
trusting in Moses, who will condemn them (Jno. 5.45), they are
actually today the worst off, the farthest from God, of any nation.
"To the Jew first," has long ago been fulfilled, and "there is no difference" between Jew and Greek as to sinnerhood and need. Paul
shut the door upon them nationally as regards the gospel, in Acts
13.46, and 28.28:

"And Paul and Barnabas spake out boldly, and said, It was necessary that the word of God should first be spoken to you. Seeing ye
thrust it from you, and judge yourselves unworthy of eternal life,
lo, we turn to the Gentiles" (Acts 13.46).

"They departed after that Paul had spoken one word . . . Be it
known therefore unto you, that this salvation of God is sent unto
the *Gentiles:* they will also hear" (Acts 28.25, 28).

We speak these truths because we love the souls of Jews.

Our present verse keeps making the simple statement concerning
Israel, **They continued not in My covenant, and I regarded them
not, saith the Lord.** They obtained then, no ground of recognition
through their promised obedience. "The Law made nothing perfect." But how slow are men who have faith in their own spirituality
(rather than in the indwelling Christ, which faith Paul had), to
acknowledge as Paul did, "In me, that is in my flesh, dwelleth no
good thing." The legal covenant, in any form, brings only into
bondage. Pope's lines,

"Hope springs eternal in the human breast:
Man never is, but always to be, blest,"

are true in general; the first line is absolutely true concerning legal
hope—unless God in sovereign grace removes all hope from man's
heart, so that man discovers himself guilty, lost, helpless and hope-
less: *then* the gospel may be preached to him!

But you say, There is a new covenant, the spiritual blessing of
which we partake of, and unto which national Israel in due season
shall be brought. Why, you ask, does God still use this word,

"covenant" concerning relationship to Him through what Christ did?

You have asked a good question. May God reveal its answer to us. Let us consider:

1. This new covenant, as regards its principals, is between the Father and the Son. We are not participants, as Israel was asked to become in the legal covenant. Let us turn to Chapter 13.20-21. Inasmuch as here in Chapter 8 we are dealing with both these covenants, it may be well to consider the great word in Chapter 13 at this point:

"Now the God of Peace, Who brought again from the dead the great Shepherd of the sheep in the blood of an eternal covenant, even our Lord Jesus, make you perfect in every good thing to do His will, working in us that which is well-pleasing in His sight, through Jesus Christ; to Whom be the glory for ever and ever. Amen."

As we have said, in this "everlasting covenant" (for on the ground of it we have *eternal* redemption, an *eternal* inheritance, an *eternal* peace from the "God of Peace"), the party of the first part is God, the party of the second part, our Lord Jesus. As to God, the very name "the God of Peace," involves His so dealing that the saints are set before Him in quietness and confidence forever.

2. Let us consider further, that it was "in [Gr. *en,* because of, in view of] the blood of the eternal covenant" that "the God of peace brought again from the dead our Lord Jesus, the great Shepherd of the sheep." Here the contracting parties are plainly seen to be God and Christ. The "sheep" will receive the blessing, but they are not actors. "The God of peace" promised that if the Great Shepherd, the Lord Jesus, would lay down His life for the sheep, He, God, would raise Him from the dead. Our Lord Jesus relied wholly upon His word: which the God of peace indeed fulfilled.

3. Finally, consider that measureless rest of heart comes to the believer who sees something of what our Lord meant in the words, "It is finished," and, "I glorified Thee on the earth, having accomplished the work which Thou hast given Me to do." How wonderful that God calls this work of Christ a covenant! What rest of heart in contrasting Christ's perfect finished work with the feeble efforts of fallen man under the legal covenant.

4. Chapter 13.21 follows as a matter of course. When the heart comes to rest where God rests, in the shed blood of Christ, then is God enabled to "perfect us in every good work to do His will"; for "*God worketh* in us [*not* sets *us* to do a work!] that which is well-pleasing in His sight"; and it is all "*through Jesus Christ.*" How gladly then, the saints ascribe to Him the glory forever and ever! How precious to them becomes that memorial supper (celebrated at least weekly by the early saints—Acts 20.7), where our Lord says, "This cup is the new covenant in My blood, even that which is poured out for you."

This covenant, we repeat, was between "the God of peace" and "the Great Shepherd of the sheep, our Lord Jesus Christ," the terms of which are evident here: that if the Great Shepherd would (as the "Good Shepherd" of Jno. 10) lay His life down for the sheep, God would bring Him again from the dead. So that even when forsaken on the Cross, Christ held fast the word "My", saying: "My God," claiming God's faithfulness. (See entire Ps. 22.) But in Psalm 16, quoted by Peter at Pentecost (Acts 2), and by Paul at Antioch of Pisidia (Acts 13.35ff), we find Him saying "Thou wilt not leave my soul in Sheol [whither He went during the three days and nights], neither wilt Thou suffer thy Holy One to see corruption" (corruption, that is, of His body in Joseph's tomb). "Thou wilt show Me the path of life" (newness of life in resurrection); In thy presence [whither He would return] is fullness of joy; In thy right hand [where He would be seated], there are pleasures for evermore."

> 10 For this is the covenant that I will make with the house
>   of Israel
>   After those days, saith the Lord;
>   I will put My laws into their mind,
>   And on their heart also will I write them:
>   And I will be to them a God,
>   And they shall be to Me a people:
> 11 And they shall not teach every man his fellow-citizen,
>   And every man his brother, saying, Know the Lord:
>   For all shall know Me,
>   From the least to the greatest of them.
> 12 For I will be merciful to their iniquities,
>   And their sins will I remember no more.

13 In that He saith, A new covenant, He hath made the
first old. But that which is becoming old and waxeth aged
is nigh unto vanishing away.

Verse 10: Going back to the "new covenant" of verses 8-13,
we wish to press upon the reader's attention not only the people
with whom this covenant is to be made, but also its particulars—
just what God will do in the future:

**For this is the covenant that I will make with the house of
Israel
After those days, saith the Lord.**

Here we see three things: (1) It is a *future* covenant; (2) It is
made with the *house of Israel;* (3) It will be **after those days** (that
is, when the present dispensation has passed and other circumstances have come in)—the "good things that are to come" (9.11;
10.1).

Note also: (1) This is an unconditional covenant. (2) Its announced result is the removal of transgressions and iniquities from
Israel (vs. 12). (3) It takes for granted that while individuals
from a nation have obtained eternal mercy, yet the nation as such
has not yet obtained mercy; for the new covenant does not appeal to Israel's will, but announces God's sovereign action. That is,
blessing is not conditioned upon obedience, but on uncaused
mercy, as in the case of the Gentiles (Rom. 11.27). Resulting
from this covenant, God announces, **I will be merciful to their
iniquities . . . their sins will I remember no more.** Therefore, this
covenant is to be consummated after the "time of Jacob's trouble"
(Jer. 30.7; Dan. 12; I Thess. 2.15-16).

Jehovah will indeed "be inquired of by the house of Israel, to
do it for them" (Ezek. 36.37): but this prayer is the result of the
pouring out from God of "the spirit of grace and of supplication"
(Zech. 12), and is therefore all of grace, to be fulfilled "in its
time."

Finally, the results of this new covenant are eternal. The nation
will never again be put on trial, but will be eternally the object of
God's mercy and grace.

Verse 11: And now, concerning the particular acts of God
upon those with whom He makes the new covenant: His Laws
are put **into their mind,** written **on their heart.** They shall be to
God "a people:" "a nation"—of course in every land; "all shall

know Him" . . . their sins remembered no more (vs. 12). We are quoting from Jeremiah 31.31 ff which agrees with Isaiah 60.21, where we are told that in that millennial day the Israelitish people "shall be all righteous."*

All the arrangements of the New Covenant are to be carried out with them, God's elect, royal nation.†

Nor will the new covenant be made with what our Lord calls "*this* generation,"—that is, the present generation of unbelieving Jews; as He said to them in Matthew 21.43: "The Kingdom of God shall be taken away from you [it has been], and shall be given to a nation bringing forth the fruits thereof." Indeed, it will be on an altogether different principle—that of sight, that the nation will be born in a day when "They shall *look* unto Him Whom they have pierced" (Zech. 12.10; 13.1). Remember Thomas: "Because thou hast *seen* Me, thou hast believed" (Jno. 20.29).

Meanwhile let us not forget the words of Romans 11.28, 29: "As touching the Gospel they are enemies for your sake: but as touching the election, they are beloved for the fathers' sake. For the gifts and the calling of God are not repented of."

Behold, then, a people not in present covenant relation with God. Behold, one of that nation, seeing this terrible fact, enlightened as to the Person and work of the Lord Jesus, their rejected Messiah. Behold, next, the miracle of grace in such a one, by which he renounces the false claim that by nature he is one of the chosen people; and lo, he finds himself trusting "the blood of the covenant which was poured out for many for the remission of sins," and such a one finds himself truly one of Abraham's seed. For does it not read, "Know therefore that they that are of faith, the same are sons of Abraham"? And again, "If ye are Christ's then are ye Abraham's seed, heirs according to promise" (Gal. 3.7, 29). He who has re-

---

*See also the "very small Remnant" of Isa. 1.9; also, "He that is *left* in Zion, and he that *remaineth* in Jerusalem" (4.2, 3); "the *Remnant* of Israel and they that are escaped of the house of Jacob, shall no more lean upon him that smote them, but shall lean upon Jehovah, the Holy One of Israel, in truth" (10.20); "A *Remnant* shall return, even the Remnant of Jacob, unto the Mighty God" (10.21).

†It is evidently for this reason that at the very close of the Millennium, when Satan is loosed from his prison, the unregenerate of the nations, the great majority, flock to his banner to go up against the camp of the heavenly saints over Jerusalem, the beloved city itself. Inexorable hatred toward Divine sovereign arrangements is found in the unregenerate human heart. The mind of the flesh is enmity against God, not able to be subject to Him. This is the reason that Satan so easily controls the human race. They hate a benefactor.

nounced his fleshly hopes in Abraham has become a true child of Abraham, an heir of God, "where there cannot be Greek and Jew, circumcision and uncircumcision, barbarian, Scythian, bondman, freeman; but Christ is all, and in all" (Col. 3.11). As for Christians, as seen in Scripture, they are not "covenanters" at all: but the *objects* of *Grace*. They are of those "sheep" of which the Lord Jesus is "The Great Shepherd."*

---

*The Church has a heavenly calling; Israel, an earthly. The Church is Christ's Body; Israel, while in the future to be His nation on earth, is never called Christ's Body. Believers today are created in Christ—in a heavenly, Risen Christ (Eph. 2.10), and are the righteousness of God in Christ (II Cor. 5.21). While the Remnant of Israel which will enter the Millennium are to be an "all righteous" nation, they have not this marvelous relation which belongs by sovereign grace to believers during this time when God is taking out from the Gentiles [with elect Hebrews, as in Heb. 3.1] "a people for His name" (Acts 15.14).

Again, believers now, being "joined unto the Lord, one spirit" with Him, as one with Christ, and charged to have "love out of a pure heart and a good conscience and faith unfeigned" (I Tim. 1.5), still dwell (until Christ's coming) in bodies—"tabernacles" in which they groan, "being burdened." It is not said to believers now that God "takes away the stony heart out of the flesh." But, being indwelt by the Holy Spirit, and walking by Him, they have victory.

But it is said of Israel that God will "take away the stony heart out of their flesh." This can only be construed as that the disposition to sin will be removed from them. God will put within them "a heart of flesh," contrasted with the "stony heart" of unbelief, disobedience, idolatry, tendency to evil, which they before had and chose to have (Zech. 7.12). "Heart of flesh" has not the meaning of "flesh" (Gr. *sarks*), the moral sense of "flesh" in the Pauline epistles; but means a tender heart, responsive to all God's injunctions (Ezek. 11.19-20, and 36.25-27).

God's word concerning believers today is that they have been made "dead to the Law through the body of Christ [made sin for us] that we should be joined to Another, even to Him Who was raised from the dead." So that they are not under Law as a principle, but under Grace (Rom. 6.14; 7.4). On the other hand, it hath pleased God "to magnify His Law and make it honorable," not only in that our Lord Jesus walked perfectly as an Israelite under Law; but also that when in the future God makes His New Covenant after those days—the present days, He will put His laws into their mind, He says; so that they will no longer forget even the least detail; and on their heart also He will write them, so that all will truly say, "Oh how *love* I Thy Law! It is my meditation all the day" (Ps. 119.97).

Here at last will be a whole nation that are regenerate. Today, Israel are *Lo Ammi, not* God's acknowledged people; and are *Lo-ruhamah,* that is, "That hath not obtained mercy," (Hos. 1.6, 9, and margin). But remember Hos. 1.10 to 2.1, connecting this with Heb. 8.12, For I will be merciful to their iniquities. And their sins will I remember no more. Mercy in this sense has never yet been Israel's portion from God. As Moses said to them at the end of the forty years, "Ye have seen all that Jehovah did before your eyes in the land of Egypt . . . but Jehovah hath not given you a heart to know, and eyes to see, and ears to hear, unto this day" (Deut. 29.2, 4). But read Isa. 6.10, and our Lord's final message on Israel, Jno. 12.35-40. And again, Acts 28.25-28, closing, "Be it known therefore unto you, that this salvation of God is sent unto the *Gentiles: they* will also hear."

We call attention to these things about Israel, because of the confused mind of today concerning Israel nationally. It will be as those utterly lost and undone, and as if they had never had a law, that "by the [example of] *mercy* shown to you" (Gentiles) they will also then obtain mercy. Individual Israelites to whom God has revealed Himself have indeed cried, "Who shall deliver me?" with Paul, or, "Woe is me! for I am undone; because I am a man of unclean lips," with Isaiah; but in the terrible days to come, the

The gospel is *not a* covenant, but the proclamation of news of the finished work of Christ. God has never made any covenant with Gentiles, nationally, or individually. What have Gentiles to do with covenants? We go back through church history and find Gentiles—uncircumcised—calling themselves "Covenanters." But God says in Romans 9.4, 5, that certain things pertain to Paul's kinsmen according to the flesh: "Who are Israelites; whose is the adoption, and the glory, and the COVENANTS, and the giving of the law, and the service [religious forms and ordinances] of God, and the promises; whose are the fathers, and of whom is Christ as concerning the flesh, Who is over all, God blessed for ever."

Now why should God make covenant arrangements and agreements with His creatures? Why should not all God's blessings be directly, unconditionally—yes, even unconsciously to him, bestowed on man? It will appear immediately upon reflection, that this would be to treat man practically as the vegetable kingdom, which receives rain and sunshine without consciousness of relationship to the Giver.

Verse 12: The last statement of verse 10: **And I will be to them a God, and they shall be to me a people,** is the fulfillment of the six great material blessings promised to Israel in Daniel 9.24*.

---

time of Jacob's trouble, the Great Tribulation, with the God-hating, Israel-hating nations beleaguering Jerusalem, to "cut them [Israel] off from being a nation," (Ps. 83.4), there will be poured upon them "the spirit of grace and supplication," and they "will look upon Him Whom THEY pierced," and thus, as from Saul of Tarsus in his three days of darkness, everything but the hope of mercy will be removed. That God should remember sins no more will be their only way out.

What a glorious day it will be when Israel is pardoned, all iniquity forever forgotten, become the joy of the earth, a nation of priests, of Jehovah, "the seed which Jehovah hath blessed" (Isa. 61.6-9). Then shall be fulfilled the great statements of the Millennial psalm (48.2, 11):

Beautiful in elevation, the joy of the whole earth,
Is Mount Zion, on the sides of the north,
The city of the Great King.
Let Mount Zion be glad,
Let the daughters of Judah rejoice,
Because of Thy judgments.

*As students of prophecy all know, the 69 (62 plus 7) of these heptads or periods of seven years of Dan. 9, beginning with Neh. 2.6, 8 (the command to rebuild Jerusalem) and ending with our Lord's death, have already passed. We are now in the long interval before the coming of the seventieth heptad. Mark: these seventy *heptads* (weeks) were decreed "upon thy [Daniel's] people and upon thy holy city" (Jerusalem). They have nothing to do with the Church, with the times of the Gentiles. Let no man deceive you here, saying that believers must pass into at least the first part of the seventieth week. For God tells us that He did *not* appoint *us* unto wrath, and in the same epistle tells us that the measured (or appointed) wrath is come on them (the Jews) to the uttermost. (Cf. I Thess. 5.9 with I Thess. 2.15-16).

Daniel's great prophecy goes even to the establishing of the Holy of Holies, the millennial temple of Ezekiel 40-48. The closing statement in Hebrews 8.12 does not go on to the millennial temple, but does make this remarkable promise: **I will be merciful to their iniquities, and their sins will I remember no more.** Please distinguish carefully this wonderful word here: **I will remember them no more,** from "remembering *against*." The conclusion drawn by the apostle from **I will remember them no more,** is given in Chapter 10.18, and exactly befits the object of the epistle here: "Now where *remission* of these is, there is no more offering for sin." We fear the consciousness of even intelligent believers generally is somewhat like this: "God will forgive me; I believe He has forgiven me, but He can never forget what I have done." Does not this lie in the basement, so to speak, of many a Christian heart? But this is not what God says. On the contrary, there is remission for sin, wholly on the ground of the one great Sacrifice that put sin away. This is New Testament truth; this is the *gospel*. In the word "atonement" (Heb. *kaphar,* to cover) of the Old Testament, there was a covering, temporarily, from God's sight by the shed blood of offerings, of that which still was there. In those sacrifices there was a "*remembrance* made of sins year by year" on the great Day of Atonement (Heb. 10.3), while verse 4 says, "It is impossible that the blood of bulls and goats should take away sins."* But as we have seen in Hebrews 13.20, an eternal covenant is found, and the contracting parties are "the God of peace" on the one hand, and "the Great

---

*There is a common expression today, "My sins are under the blood." This is not Christian truth. This is a mixture, and results in a state of mind scarcely able to understand God when He says, "Their sins will I remember no more." How could God remember sins which Christ has put completely and forever away by His sacrifice? In pardoning and justifying a sinner, God reckons to the sinner the whole, undiminished value of the work of Christ on the Cross, although justified ones may not fully realize what has been done.

Sad to say, for centuries, beginning with the so-called Christian Fathers themselves, in one way or another, the effect both upon God and upon the believing sinner, of the shedding of Christ's blood, has been perverted. For instance, a phrase has been current among some, which, (never dreamed of by them) defeats grace. I refer to the shallow, thoughtless rendering of "justified" by the words "just-as-if-I'd never sinned." This would merely seek to view the pardoned sinner as being restored to the position in which Adam was before he sinned. It comes infinitely short of the truth. Thus one has said of the word "at-one-ment," that it is a "babyish" interpretation of *atonement*. Now "just-as-if-I'd never sinned" not only looks at our escape from punishment as the chief object to be attained at the Cross, but minimizes that Divine forsaking and judgment, sparing not of His own Son, as well as the unutterable glory of being placed in that Son and one with Him. It falls so far short of the work Christ did and of the place the believer is in, that I am ashamed to speak of it further.

Shepherd of the sheep" on the other. None but God is speaking here, in His sovereignty and in His grace.

Verse 13 is in two parts: the first is a statement about the old covenant: (literally) **In the saying, new, He has made old the first.** The second part is a general observation: **that which grows old and aged is near unto disappearing.** Conybeare remarks concerning the two parts of this sentence, "The first refers to time, the second to the weakness of old age." Rotherham's rendering is striking also: **By saying: 'Of a new sort', He has made obsolete the first. But the thing that is becoming obsolete and aged, is near disappearing.**

Verse 13 is a comment upon verses 8 to 12, which set forth three great facts: (1) That Israel **continued not** in the first legal covenant (vs. 9b) from Kadesh-Barnea on, through the wilderness history and in Canaan. (2) That God **regarded them not.** Note this past tense. From the time Israel disregarded His covenant, Jehovah really disregarded *them*—that is, as to any genuine relationship to Himself under that first legal covenant. (His counsels of blessing were not affected, for these counsels preceded the legal covenant and were according to promise to Abraham). (3) That God will make in the future a new covenant **with the house of Israel** (vs. 10): **This is the covenant that I will make.** Though the conditions were all met at the Cross, the covenant is not yet made with Israel.

Verse 13 follows naturally from the past tense of verse 9, **I regarded them not,** and from the words, **I will make a new covenant,** verse 8. These Hebrew believers of Paul's day, therefore, would naturally and rightly read verse 13 as if dating back not only to the days of Jeremiah, who uttered the preceding prophecy, but also and really to the time when God **regarded** not the old covenant.

No doubt Jehovah permitted Israel to go on under the old forms even until their temple was destroyed, and after that in the restored temple in the days of Ezekiel and Nehemiah; and after that in the "four hundred years of silence" between Malachi and Matthew. But we can ourselves easily see how God had **made the first** covenant old, and that it had **waxed aged** as the years passed on.*

The great desire of the writer in Hebrews 8. 13 is to impress upon these Hebrew believers that away back in the days of Jeremiah the legal covenant had been pronounced old, and the prophesied bringing-in of a new covenant in due season made the other covenant "old" and **nigh unto vanishing away** even in the prophet's days. The figure is that of an old man who is **waxing aged** and is ready to pass from the scene. This would shake to the foundations of his soul any Hebrew that heard it. What! Be without a temple? (For the temple was yet standing in Jerusalem.) Have no morning and evening sacrifice? No earthly priests and high priests to carry on the worship of Jehovah? Abandon the hopes wrapped up in the Mosaic institutions held for fifteen hundred years? Yea, said the Apostle, These things **are nigh unto vanishing away.** (Hebrews was written shortly before the destruction of Jerusalem by Titus, A. D. 70, and the dispersion of the Jews). Yea, said Paul, true believers have not here an abiding continuing city—what a shock beyond description to an Israelite who knew that Jehovah had set His name in His temple there in the Holy City!

So the believing Hebrew was asked to turn from all hope in the

---

*The history of national Israel with Jehovah may be roughly divided into five sections:

(1) The deliverance from Divine judgment by the passover blood in Egypt, and the deliverance from Egypt and her bondage at the Red Sea by God's gracious intervention on their behalf, *before the Law was given* or any "covenant" had been made with the nation.

(2) The proposal at Sinai by Jehovah to make their obedience the condition and ground of their national relationship to Him, which their ignorant self-confidence immediately seized upon: "All that Jehovah hath spoken we will do." Upon this, Jehovah announced Himself and the great "ten words." Under this "ministration of death and condemnation" (II Cor. 3) Israel now was.

(3) The breakdown of the priesthood in the days of Eli; with even the ark of God taken by the Philistines, and the rejection by Jehovah of that priestly branch.

(4) The renewal in Divine grace of relationship with Israel under David and his house (prophetic of future blessing under David's Son). God did not abandon the priesthood, neither did David usurp that office, although, like Moses, who offered sacrifices on behalf of Aaron and his sons, David acted at the altar he had erected, and God's accepting fire fell upon his offerings.

(5) The restoration "for a little moment a little reviving in our bondage" (Ezra 9.8). But again there is selfishness, sin, neglect of God, and the refusal to confess, saying: "Wherein have we robbed God?" (Note the "wherein's," the "wherefore's," and the "what's" of Malachi, their last prophet: Chs. 1.2, 7; 2.14, 17; 3.7, 8, 13—defiant denials instead of humiliation.)

Then the four hundred years of silence, in which the Gentile rules and only a few "that know their God" are "strong" (Dan. 11.32); the coming of the forerunner, and the advent of their Messiah in their midst,—only to be despised, rejected, crucified, His apostles and disciples denounced and persecuted. This is the unbelieving "generation" that we see today. This is the nation from which the Kingdom of God has been taken away to be given in the future to that nation formed that day when a "very small Remnant," they actually look on Him Whom they pierced.

former legal covenant and set all his hopes in Heaven itself whither the Priest after the order of Melchizedek had gone.

Therefore every instructed Hebrew believer saw that the Old Covenant had already passed away, that the blood of the New Covenant had been shed, and that they enjoyed its benefits. They saw that God would in the future deal with "Israel and Judah" in blessing, bringing them together and making them as a nation partake of all the things joined to the New Covenant, which God would then extend to them nationally. To sum up verses 9-13:

The Law was "holy, just, and good": but its blessing was conditioned on obedience.

But God had made *un*conditional promise to Abraham!

Israel, trusting in themselves, promised obedience.

But they practiced disobedience—"they continued not" in God's covenant.

God, consequently, did not "regard" them, but let them go into captivity—as at this day.

Neither the first nor the second covenant is God's covenant with Abraham: though both are based on that.

The first covenant's blessings were *conditional*: man must do his "part."

The blessings of the second covenant will be wholly God's: "And this is the covenant *from Me* unto them, when I shall take away their sins" (Rom. 11.27).

CHAPTER NINE

THIS CHAPTER IS a chapter of contrasts. We have in it the great contrasts between:

1. The two tabernacles: (a) one earthly, way to God *veiled;* (b) the other in Heaven itself—no veil there! the one "made by hands"; the other, "not of this creation."

2. The two priesthoods: (a) Levitical priests, and (b) CHRIST, our one Great High Priest.

3. Their offerings: (a) The Levitical priests' *continued* sacrifices, and Day of Atonement every year; and (b) Christ's *one sacrifice of Himself* at the Cross.

4. The results: (a) Of their sacrifices of animals, "goats and bulls"; could not atone for sin or relieve the conscience of the sinner. (b) Christ offered up Himself, through the Eternal Spirit, which "cleansed the conscience to serve the Living God": Christ's one offering obtaining "eternal redemption," and an "eternal inheritance."

5. (a) The earthly sacrifices, mere "copies of things in the heavens," sanctifying "unto the cleanness of the flesh." (b) Christ's sacrifice, which brought Him "not into a holy place made with hands, like in pattern to the true; but into Heaven itself, now to appear before the face of God for us" not once a year, but constantly!

6. (a) The sacrifices of the Levitical priests constantly repeated; (b) Christ's, once for all: "Now ONCE at the consummation of the ages hath He been manifested to put away sin by the sacrifice of Himself."

7. (a) The universal appointment unto men "once to die, and after this, judgment" (vs. 27). (b) Christ, "having been once offered to bear the sins of many [which included death and judgment] shall appear a second time, apart from sin, to them that wait for Him, unto salvation" (which includes our bodies).

1   NOW even the first covenant had ordinances of Di-
     vine service, and its sanctuary, a sanctuary of this world.
2   For there was a tabernacle prepared, the first, wherein
     were the candlestick, and the table, and the showbread;
3   which is called the Holy Place. And after the second
     veil, the tabernacle which is called the Holy of Holies;
4   having a golden altar of incense and the ark of the cove-
     nant overlaid round about with gold, wherein was a
     golden pot holding the manna, and Aaron's rod that
5   budded, and the tables of the covenant; and above it
     cherubim of glory overshadowing the mercy-seat; of
     which things we cannot now speak severally.

In the opening words of Chapter 9, **Even the first covenant—**
we see to what degree that covenant, with the ordinances of
which, the unbelieving Hebrew nation were occupied, had disappeared; or, rather, been fully discerned in its shadow character by
the writer of **Hebrews.** Contrast **Even the first covenant had
ordinances,** with the Jews' words: "We are disciples of Moses
. . . but as for this man [Jesus] we know not whence he is." To
one, therefore, taught by the Spirit, it was clear that the first
covenant was "becoming old and waxing aged, and nigh unto
vanishing away" (8.13).

Now as to the Levitical ordinances of Divine service, we have
the following description of the tabernacle and the furnishing
thereof:

1.   The tabernacle containing (a) **the candlestick,** and **(b)
the table, and the showbread,** all these pertaining to what was
called **the Holy Place. And after the second veil, the tabernacle
. . . called the Holy of Holies, having (vs. 4)** (a) **a golden altar of
incense;** * (b) **the ark of the covenant overlaid . . . with gold,** . . .

---

*The statement in vs. 4 that the Holy of Holies had a **golden altar of incense,** together
with **the ark of the covenant,** has been attacked by shallow infidel criticism as ignorance and
inaccuracy on the part of the author. This is just another example of the inventive reck-
lessness of unbelief. In I Kings 6.19-22 we read that Solomon, in preparing the temple,
(the furniture of which was arranged exactly as was that of the tabernacle), "prepared an
oracle in the midst of the house within, to set there the ark of the covenant of Jehovah";
and, "the whole altar that *belonged to the oracle,* he overlaid with gold." Here in the Holy
Place, close to the second veil, therefore near the ark of the covenant, was this golden altar
for incense. It, therefore, is regarded by the Spirit of God, in Heb. 9.4, as *belonging* to
the Holy of Holies, although placed in the Holy Place, that incense might be offered up

holding the manna, and Aaron's rod that budded,* and the tables
of the covenant; (c) and above it [golden] cherubim of glory,
overshadowing the mercy-seat (vs. 5).

Verse 1: At the beginning, we find two firsts. For verse 1

---

daily. We read also in Ex. 30.1, 6, 10:

"Thou shalt make an altar to burn incense upon . . . thou shalt put it before the veil
that is by the ark of the testimony, where I will meet with thee . . . And Aaron shall
make atonement upon the horns of it once in the year; with the blood of the sin-offering of
atonement once in the year shall he make atonement for it throughout your generations: it is
most holy unto Jehovah."

And, "Thou shalt set the golden altar for incense before the ark of the testimony"
(Ex. 40.5).

These passages clearly show that the golden altar for incense "belonged to the oracle,"
that is, to the ark, although placed where it was available at other times than on the Great
Day of Atonement.

*Take heed to *Scripture's attitude towards Scripture!*
O.T.: "God said, Let there be light: and there was light." (Gen. 1.3).
N.T.: "God commanded the light to shine out of DARKNESS." (II Cor. 4.6).
O.T.: "Yet shall his days be a hundred and twenty years" (Gen. 6.3).
N.T.: "The days . . . before the Flood—" (Matt. 24.38).
O.T.: Elijah's prayer for rain (I K. 18.41-5).
N.T.: Elijah *"prayed* . . . and the heaven *gave* rain" (Jas. 5.18).
O.T.: Elisha's cleansing Naaman, the Syrian leper (II K. 5.7).
N.T.: To "Naaman, the Syrian," was Elisha sent (Lk. 4.27).
O.T.: "My God hath sent His angel and hath shut the lions' mouths" (Dan. 6.22).
N.T.: "By faith . . . stopped the mouths of lions" (Heb. 11.33).
O.T.: "And Jonah was in the belly of the fish three days and three nights" (Jon. 1.17).
N.T.: "For as Jonah *was* three days and three nights in the belly of the whale—"
(Matt. 12.40).
O.T.: "His [Lot's] wife . . . became a pillar of salt" (Gen. 19.26).
N.T.: *"Remember* Lot's wife" (Lu. 17.32).
O.T.: "Moses made a serpent of brass, and set it upon the standard" (Num. 21.9).
N.T.: "As Moses lifted up the serpent in the wilderness—" (Jno. 3.14).
See also Rev. 2.14, 20, where our Lord mentions two O.T. characters.

When God's Word says, "The sun stood still" at Joshua's word to Jehovah: or, "The
iron did swim", at the prayer or will of "the man of God," (Elisha); and here (Heb.
9.4), Aaron's rod that budded—(O.T.: "The rod of Aaron . . . was *budded*, and put
forth buds, and produced blossoms, and bare ripe almonds" (Num. 17.8), simple faith delights in the showing of the majesty of God.

Christ, walking on the water, commanding the tempest to be still; feeding thousands
from a few loaves and fishes; saying "Cast the net on the right side of the boat and ye
shall find," or telling Peter how to find the coin in the mouth of a fish—little things, all,
but "to be explained by natural processes," say the infidel-modernists, with the smile of
superiority and tolerance: (which smiling is on this earth only: "Woe unto you that laugh
now, for ye shall weep; whose weeping shall be forever!")

Know ye not that this book called the Bible is the Word of the Living God Who has
spoken it and Who lives therein? How can He, being the Mighty One, keep His might
forever concealed? How can He, being the King, never display His royal robe? Miracles are
manifestations of Majesty.

"The haughtiness which excludes God, because it is incompetent to discover Him, and
then talks of His work, and meddles with His weapons, according to the measure of its own
strength, can prove nothing but its own contemptible folly. Ignorance is generally confident
because it is ignorant; and such is the mind of man in dealing with the things of God."
These words from J. N. Darby's Synopsis of the Books of the Bible, (Vol. I, preface,
p.xi) are very truth.

sets forth the first tabernacle as a whole, which **had ordinances of Divine service, and its sanctuary, . . . of this world.** This evidently refers to the wilderness tabernacle as a whole, called in verse 8, "*the first* tabernacle."

Verse 2: Then immediately this tabernacle is divided up. For in verse 2 we read, **There was a tabernacle prepared, the first**—and in verse 3, **And after the second veil** [the second division] **the tabernacle which is called the Holy of Holies.** Here, then, two divisions, or parts, of the whole tabernacle are before us: the one called **the first . . . the Holy Place** (into which the priests went continually—vs. 6); **and after the second veil, (vs. 3)** the second, **called the Holy of Holies** into which went "the high priest alone, once in the year, not without blood" (vs. 7). We may remark that together they are called "the Holies."

Now concerning the some ten articles in the two parts forming this **sanctuary of this world,** we have this surprising yet comforting statement at the end of verse 5: **of which things* we cannot now speak in detail.** I say, this is a surprising statement, when we see the aweinspiring particularity of directions for both the making and the use of these various articles by Israel of old. We see at once that something new has taken the place of all these oldtime things, types though they doubtless were, of which the author of **Hebrews cannot now speak in detail.** (It is not the time nor the place to do so, else we would become absorbed in the details† and miss the lesson of the great contrast.) But it is the

---

*The R.V. correctly renders **of which things**—that is, of all the things of this tabernacle, indeed, of the whole tabernacle itself. The word is plural in the Greek.

I may say here, that in **Hebrews,** the *tabernacle* worship, and *not* the temple services as instituted by David, are always in view. The tabernacle worship typically sets forth the work of Christ in redemption, whereas the temple service pictures the millennial kingdom worship, when Christ "shall sit . . . a Priest upon His throne" (Zech. 6.13).

†Is it not true that in some meetings God's people have pondered over the measurements, furniture, colors, and materials of the tabernacle, and been occupied with its shadowy worship, while the Son of God, of whom all these things are a mere shadowy picture, was by His Spirit present, and ready to reveal *Himself?* I would prefer an old-fashioned "holiness meeting," where people dealt directly with God, and became devoted to Christ and filled with the Holy Spirit; though they would not have been able to answer many of the questions that these students of a model of the tabernacle might have asked them!

It is the worship, and not the furniture, of which God is speaking here. (Paul carried no model of the tabernacle about with him!)

Kelly well says: "The aim of the Holy Spirit, in referring to the first covenant with its ordinances, and especially its sanctuary, becomes now apparent. It was not to speak in de-

disposition of "religionists" to go deeper and deeper into the bondage of the forms and ceremonies of their "religion." The Gospel, believed, delivers the heart, and enables the mind to view types and shadows with profit, but not be enslaved by them.

Now we are prepared for what we find in verses 6 and 7:

6 Now these things having been thus prepared, the priests go in continually into the first tabernacle, accomplishing
7 the services; but into the second the high priest alone, once in the year, not without blood, which he offereth for himself, and for the errors* of the people.

The high priest alone—These statements concerning the high priest have power over a legal heart. Be watchful here! For we are going to read the contrast of all this: for, first, the high priest of Israel himself dared not go in "at all times" (Lev. 16.2); second, he went in only **once in the year**; third, he went (not through his own blood), but **not without blood** — (that of appointed animals); fourth, he had to repeat the sacrifice each year: it was never finished, witnessing that sin was not put away forever; fifth, he had to pass through a veil that shut out all the people; sixth, the high priest himself was subject to death, and his office passed to another; seventh, the sacrifices of the high priest made "a *remembrance* of sins" (Heb. 10.3), but could not remove them. No Levitical high priest even remotely thought of his own blood being offered up! Therefore his sacrifices *could* not set forth the great coming *fact* of redemption by Christ.†

---

tail of the contents of the tabernacle exterior or interior, however symbolically instructive, but [to speak] of its distinctive contrast as a whole with Christianity."—W. Kelly, p. 161.

*Literally, "ignorances," or sins committed in ignorance: Lev. 5.17-9.

†The high priest of Israel on the Day of Atonement entered the presence of God, the Holy of Holies on earth.
   Contrast, Christ after His death, "entered into Heaven itself," (called the Holies), "before the face of God" (vs. 24).
   2. The high priest had no personal right to be there: he was a sinner.
   Contrast, Christ *had* a personal right to return to "the glory" which He had with the Father "before the world was" (Jno. 17.5).
   3. The high priest had to have the blood of a bullock poured out for him before he dared enter the Holy of Holies.
   Contrast, Christ through the eternal Spirit offered Himself without blemish [at the Cross] unto God.
   4. The high priest carried the blood of the slain goat ("blood not his own"—vs. 25). for the sins of the people.
   Contrast, Christ, through His own blood (shed for the sinners) entered in.
   5. The high priest did this "year by year" (10.1).

We must see that Christ's work in Heaven governs all previous
Levitical "shadows"; not the Levitical "shadows," Christ's work in
Heaven! The very thought of the high priest entering, and the
people left outside, is to be put away in **Hebrews!** Do we not read
at the beginning (2.11), "He that sanctifieth [Christ] and they
that are sanctified are all OF ONE"? The very opposite was true
in the Old Testament arrangements. For there we read (as in
Ch. 9.7) **the high priest alone** entered within the veil. Further,
only a special class, "the priests," went into the first part of the
tabernacle, while the people stood *without.*

Keep these contrasts in mind. Study the lesson of the "shadows,"
or types, but do not be brought into bondage under their influence—Romanists are, and most Protestants. To find one reading
the types of Leviticus with a spirit set free by the blood of our
Great High Priest, once-for-all shed, is rare. And now mark most
carefully:

Verse 8: **The Holy Spirit this signifying**—*not* that you are to
get a model of the tabernacle and spend hours and days upon it,
however helpful a simple review of the tabernacle might be, but,
**The Holy Spirit this signifying, that the way into the Holy Place
hath not yet been made manifest, while the first tabernacle is yet
standing.** The great message of Chapters 9 and 10 is of *a closed
way,* and then of *an open way.* God here emphasizes that **the first
tabernacle** constantly said to the nation of Israel, God is here, but
you cannot come to Him. That is what the veils meant, and
especially, of course, the second veil. That word "not," **NOT yet
. . . made manifest,** should be emphasized constantly. Otherwise,
the human heart being what it is, those Levitical forms and ceremonies which made up Judaism, will secure an almost unshakable
power over the conscience and heart. If you do not go to the
Cross and get deliverance from all "religion," and find yourself
in the presence of God, with all claims met, these Levitical things

---

Contrast, Christ . . . **entered in once for all into the holies, having obtained eternal
redemption.**

6. The Levitical high priests "by death were hindered from continuing" (7.23).
Contrast, Christ "abideth a Priest forever" (7.24), having "a priesthood that doth not
pass to another" (7.24, R. V. Margin).

7. The Levitical high priest was "after the order of Aaron." (7.11).
Contrast, Christ was after another order, "**the order of Melchizedek**" (7.11), one
greater and "**better**" than Abraham (7.6, 7).

will have a subtle hold upon you, like the Cross on top of a
Romish cathedral—while the "Word of the Cross" (I Cor. 1.18),
the "power of God" which sets people free, is wholly unknown
to that monstrous pagan system. In the Levitical things, you are
to see the *contrast* to what you now enjoy, *not* the very example
of it.

This way into the Holiest in Heaven, our access thither, yea, unto
the continual access and worship described in **Hebrews** as full
growth, is the great distinction of the work of Christ. Under the
old legal Levitical offerings and gifts the veil was never done
away with. There was no access, there was no *coming nigh* to God.
The way into the holy place now has been *opened,* as we are to see,
and a mighty invitation and exhortation—the great, central exhortation of **Hebrews** (10.19), sounds out, to enter into it with *boldness.*
(See 10.19 ff.)

Verse 9: **Which** (the first tabernacle with its worship) **is a figure**
(Gr.: *parabole,* parable) **for the time present; according to which**
(parable or temple worship) **are** (constantly being) **offered both
gifts and sacrifices which cannot, as touching and conscience, perfect the** (one serving, or) **worshiper.**

As touching the conscience—now what is "conscience?" It is
commonly said to be that by which we distinguish good and evil.
Yet, like Paul, a man may live mistaken "in all good conscience:"
"I verily thought with myself that I ought to do many things contrary to the name of Jesus of Nazareth"—really opposing God.
Conscience, therefore, is not a complete guide to conduct, but is
subject to instruction. So we have the presence with us of the inspired Word of God, which sets forth our path. Revelation of
Scripture's meaning, by the Holy Spirit to the human spirit will
therefore govern conscience.

The human spirit is controlled by what is believed, and the seat
of believing, the throne room of the being, is the heart. "As a man
thinketh *in his heart,* so is he." In this throne room we live and
make our decisions, for, *"Out of the heart** are the issues of life."

---

*Man, as we have before said. is a spirit, living in a bodily tabernacle, and possessing a
soul. So God says, "My son, give me *thine heart*"—not, thy conscience. And, "Keep thy
heart with all diligence, for out of it are the issues of life." Concerning David's desire to
build God a temple, Jehovah said to him, "Thou didst well that it was in thy *heart.*"

When the heart seeks refuge from conscience, it may so harden itself against light and truth as to "sear" or "brand" the conscience "as with a hot iron" (I Tim. 4.2). In this case a course of sin may be followed without feeling (Eph. 4.19).

Or, the heart may so rest in the shed blood of Christ (by Whom sin was once for all and forever put away) as to be wholly relieved from all accusation by conscience, and so cease from all religious self-efforts—"dead works" (Heb. 9.14). This is what is meant by "a cleansed conscience" (vs. 14), or, "hearts sprinkled from an evil [or accusing] conscience" (10.22). For the conscience of a true believer may be weak and therefore easily "defiled"—that is, rendered accusatory.*

Paul says, "My conscience bearing witness with me in the Holy Spirit," not that every moral choice of a believer is to have the conscious inner witness of the Holy Spirit, but that the indwelling Spirit guiding us into all truth may be relied upon to warn against an evil path, and check by inward darkness or trouble in experience, any false step; for "the mystery of the faith" is held "in a pure conscience" (I Tim. 3.9).

Our Saviour has rendered our conscience perfect, so that we can go into the sanctuary without an idea of fear, without one question as to sin arising in our minds. A "perfect" conscience is not an innocent conscience, which, happy in its unconsciousness, does not know evil and does not know God revealed in holiness. A perfect con-

---

To Ananias, Peter said, "Why hath Satan filled *thy heart?* . . . How is it that thou hast conceived this thing *in thy heart?*" And to Simon Magus, *"Thy heart* is not right before God . . . Pray the Lord if perhaps the thought *of thy heart* shall be forgiven thee."

Paul wrote of the gospel, "The word is nigh thee, in thy mouth and *in thy heart:* . . . if thou shalt confess with thy mouth Jesus as Lord, and shalt believe *in thy heart* that God hath raised Him from the dead, thou shalt be saved." Read also Ex. 35.29 concerning those whose *hearts* "made them willing." Finally, Christ would "dwell *in our hearts* by faith." (Eph. 3.17).

*We are to "hold faith and a good conscience," (I Tim. 1.19), which is further associated in vs. 5 with "love out of a pure heart, and faith unfeigned." Paul exercised himself to have "a conscience void of offence." (Acts 24.16). The conscience is seen in I Cor. 10.29 discerning or judging actions in other persons as good or evil: "Conscience, I say, not thine own, but the other's; for why is my liberty judged by another conscience?"

The fact that the conscience "of a believer" looks morally Godward is seen in I Pet. 2.15: "For so is the will of *God*, that by well-doing ye should put to silence the ignorance of foolish men." The conscience of all men is seen in Rom. 2.15 as "bearing witness," testifying within: "In that they show the work of the Law written in their hearts, their conscience bearing witness therewith, and their thoughts one with another accusing or else excusing them."

science knows God; it is cleansed, and, having the knowledge of good and evil according to the light of God Himself, it knows that it is purified from all evil according to His purity. Adam in inno- cence, not knowing good or evil, needed not and had not conscience. But when Adam sinned, God said, "Behold, the man is become as one of Us, to know good and evil." (Gen. 3.22.) This, then, can be the basic definition of conscience.

To continue: Vincent's rendering of the latter part of verse 9, and verse 10, is striking: **according to which are offered gifts and sacrifices which cannot perfect the worshipper as touching the conscience, (10) being mere ordinances of the flesh on the ground of** (resting upon) **meats**—etc. Or, we may render verse 10 again, **Being ONLY (with meats and drinks and divers washings*) ordinances of flesh** (i.e., to be performed by bodily, not necessarily spiritual exercises **which until a season of rectifying** (when Christ should come) **are IMPOSED.**†

Only carnal ordinances—Let those occupied with forms and ceremonies pay heed, whether Jewish, Romanists, or pagans. God brands "ordinances" of men *carnal,* of the flesh. Here perish be- fore Him all "observings" of days, seasons, months, years; all "un- bloody" sacrifices of the Mass; all demon-taught forbiddings of meats (I Tim. 4.1-3); all rushings to dying bedsides with "holy water"; and a thousand other inventions of ignorant presumption! If God has set aside as "carnal", ordinances which He Himself had imposed, how much more doth He now abhor the thrice carnal ly- ing forms and "observances" that men have brought in to hide the perfect finished work of His Blessed Son?‡

Imposed until a time of rectification:§ We may ask, What was to be rectified? And answer:

1. The old worship and its **meats and drinks and divers wash-**

---

*See Appendix B.

†"The gifts and offerings of that time were only provisional, to tide the people over to a better time."—Vincent, p. 480.

‡"The services of that tabernacle were only meats and drinks and divers washings. Not one sin did they actually take away; no nearer to God did they bring the offerers. They were but shadows, pointing onward to the substance."—William Lincoln.

§Setting things right, Gr. *diorthoscos:* "A complete rectification."—Bagster's Analytical Greek Lexicon.

ings called **carnal ordinances,** the indefinite continuation of which would shut out spiritual realities.

2. The entire Levitical system, called "a copy and shadow of the heavenly things" (8.5). A time must come when the reality of which they were a shadow would be revealed, which was done, of course, by Christ, in His Person and work.

3. The veil shutting the worshipers out from God. This was *rectified* when the veil was rent by our Lord's death, so that we now come, by "a new and living way, through the veil, that is to say, His flesh" (10.20) and by His blood, and having Him as our Great High Priest in Heaven, directly to God. The **time of rectification** has come!

Let every Gentile believer be therefore encouraged—not to remain in ignorance of the things of the first tabernacle, but joyfully to reflect that all those things are in contrast to what we now enjoy, a contrast as to the very thing which the book of **Hebrews** especially enjoins, that is, *drawing near to God.*

For however closely the student of the old tabernacle may consider it, however distinctively and accurately he has its form and furniture in his view, he comes always to the UNRENT VEIL. There he is shut out, as was the Hebrew nation, from entering into the very presence of God; whereas now, drawing near is commanded: "Let us draw *near*"; "Come with boldness," since the veil was rent at the Cross when Christ was "put to death in the flesh." (Compare Heb. 10.20 and I Pet. 3.18.) This mighty contrast must be constantly borne in mind by the reader of the Levitical ordinances. We repeat Hebrews 7.12, 18, 19, for we dare not forget these verses:

"For the priesthood being changed, there is made of necessity a change also of the Law . . . For there is a *disannulling* of a foregoing commandment because of its weakness and unprofitableness (for the Law made nothing perfect) and a bringing in thereupon of a *better hope,* through which we *draw nigh* unto God."

This "better hope", as we know, is *Christ:* His work on the Cross in putting away our sin, and His priesthood in Heaven, in leading our worship and interceding for us. We dare not confuse the two (Law and Grace). That which God put asunder let not man join together. The fact that our Lord's heavenly priesthood, while after the Melchizedek order, is typified in Aaronic and Levitical things, that is, the things of the tabernacle worship, being compared, or mostly contrasted therewith, does not warrant for one moment our forgetting that the "heavenly calling" (of which these Hebrew believers are said in Chapter 3.1 to be partakers) was given to Paul to set forth in detail in his epistles, from Romans to Philemon. We remind the reader again that **Hebrews** does not set forth Church truth,* never reaching what we might call the corporate calling of believers as the Body of Christ; nor does it describe our individual position as enlifed with Christ, raised up with Him, and made to sit with Him in the heavenlies (Eph. 2.5-6). Indeed, it does not go back to the great fundamental thing, our identification in death and resurrection with Christ.

There is a danger therefore in the study of this great book of **Hebrews** (which takes us back to the whole sweep of Old Testament history, type, and prophecy), that we become occupied with our journey "through this world," and are ready to set up the "tabernacle in the wilderness" again, as it were, and spend our time in religious forms, and man-invented ceremonial worship; whereas the apostle tells us that even the tabernacle forms afore prescribed by God have now passed away.

Let the preacher and teacher of the Word of God be occupied with the doctrines belonging to the Assembly of God today, and the exhortations connected therewith, as seen in the epistles of Paul. Let him make them constantly live before those to whom he speaks. Thus will be evident perpetually the facts and duties of our walk in the Spirit as dead and risen with Christ; and thus only shall we hold in proper proportion this mighty truth of the heavenly priesthood of Christ, referred to in Romans 8.34, and set forth fully in **Hebrews,** as contrasted with the former earthly worship.

11   **But Christ having come a High Priest of the good things to come, through the greater and more perfect tabernacle, not made with hands, that is to say, not of this**
12   **creation, nor yet through the blood of goats and calves, but through His own blood, entered in once for all into**
13   **the Holy Place, having obtained eternal redemption. For**

---

*See Appendix C.

if the blood of goats and bulls, and the ashes of a heifer
sprinkling them that have been defiled, sanctify unto the
14 cleanness of the flesh; how much more shall the blood of
Christ, Who through the eternal Spirit offered Himself
without blemish unto God, cleanse your conscience from
dead works to serve the Living God?

In Chapter 9, attention should be fixed on five subjects:

1.   The tabernacle in the wilderness, with its furniture, and its
ordinances of Divine service, (vss. 1-7).

2.   The emphasis thus by the Holy Spirit upon the fact that "the
way into the Holy Place was NOT made manifest while the first
tabernacle was yet standing" (vs. 8).

3.   The fact that this tabernacle economy provides a parable
"for the time present," (i.e., for the present dispensation).

4.   The fact that the **time of rectifying** was at the Cross, where
there was "a disannulling of a foregoing commandment"—the
Law (which "made nothing perfect'), and the disappearance
therefore, from God's sight and consideration, of all the typical
ordinances of the old tabernacle, because Christ fulfilled all by
His one offering at the Cross, and by means thereof brought in
"a better hope, by which we draw nigh unto God." Thus the
temporary things (the Law, tabernacle, and priesthood), gave
way to eternal things: (a) eternal redemption, verse 12; (b)
eternal inheritance, verse 15; (c) eternal salvation, Ch. 5.9. Note
also the precious name, "eternal Spirit," (vs. 14); and "eternal
covenant" (between the Father and the Son: 13.20).

5.   The good things to come, that is, when our Lord shall return, which is "*the* promise," the spirit of which runs all through
Hebrews:

"For yet a very little while,
He that cometh shall come, and shall not tarry" (10.37).

Verse 11: **But Christ having come**—Christ Himself appears,
having nothing to do with carnal ordinances or Levitical forms;
but, **a High Priest of good things to come:** "to come" contrasted
with all old things. First let us observe that it is as High Priest
that our Lord is spoken of here, not primarily as Redeemer from
the penalty of sin, but as in verse 14, where we see His blood
cleansing the conscience "from dead works to serve the Living

God." He is viewed as *having* obtained eternal redemption, not as in the process of obtaining it. Human priests are always occupied with the business (as they say) of obtaining Divine favor. Our High Priest has obtained that infinite boon forever!

Further, the **good things to come** of which He is High Priest are those good things brought by His **having obtained eternal redemption** at the Cross: pardon, justification, reconciliation, association with Him as His brethren; "access with confidence," "drawing near" to God in Heaven through Him; and, of course, all future blessings connected with "the promise" of His coming again (10.36-7). *Of course* the good things connected with Christ's priesthood are on *now,* and must be, ever since He **obtained eternal redemption.**

Next note the words: **Through the greater and more perfect tabernacle, not made with hands** (as was the tabernacle in the wilderness). There are two tabernacles in this chapter: the one, "of this world," (Gr., *skēnē*), verse 1. But the other, **the greater and more perfect tabernacle, not made with hands . . . not of this creation,** in Heaven itself!

In the tabernacle in the wilderness, God was indeed present, in infinite condescension, between the cherubim, upon the mercy seat, behind the veil. But the **greater and more perfect** one is Heaven itself. (Compare Revelation 11.19, 15.5, and see Appendix D.) Moses was told to make all things "after the pattern of the things in the heavens," and here are the things in the heavens! If we make this "temple of God that is in Heaven" a mere idea, that is, make it into a phrase describing in general God's presence, we do violence to our reason, for God speaks even more definitely concerning "the temple of God that is in Heaven" in Revelation 11.19, and 15.5, 8. Now we know (unless we are ignorant modernists, idly denying God's Word), that angels are realities. And these angels "come out of the temple." There is, therefore, *in Heaven now,* what God calls His "temple," as we read also in Revelation 14.17, 16.1. It is an evidence of the inconsistency of unbelieving hearts that people can believe that the earthly tabernacle, when reared up and dedicated, saw the glory described in Exodus 40.34-5; and that when the earthly temple was dedicated, "the glory of Jehovah filled Jehovah's house," as de-

scribed in II Chronicles 5.13-4; 7.2; and these same people doubt
the reality of the heavenly temple.*

To conceive of a tabernacle-temple on high, "made without
hands," is Scriptural. Otherwise, we should have a type typifying
a type—as those must do who say that the patterns of the things
in the heavens were real, but that the heavenly things themselves
were not real!

Also, the words, **not of this creation**, while not asserting that
the temple-tabernacle in Heaven was created, intimate that it was
so: when, we know not. But from what we see therein (Rev.
11.19), we at once associate it with the Ark of the Covenant on
earth, which was patterned after that in Heaven and had to do
with it. The Ark, as the Ark of the Covenant, was the symbol of the
absolute faithfulness of God, and marvelously set forth Christ, in
both His Person and His work.

The Levitical system was a series of "shadows" of heavenly
things, giving the earthly nation of Hebrews a hint of possible
future earthly fellowship with God, but not setting forth to that
nation as such even a suggestion of entering Heaven, or of the
glorious sanctuary prepared by the Risen Christ. For the Hebrew
nation had and has an earthly calling. Their future blessing, even
in the Millennium, is earthly and is to be connected indeed with
the glorious temple at Jerusalem.

However, the Hebrews to whom this esistle was addressed,
were partakers of the heavenly calling. Crucified, risen, and glorified, He had sent forth the Holy Spirit, baptizing believers into
Him, into actual sharing of His heavenly life and place.

No more shadows! Did the Levitical Day of Atonement demand
the sprinkling of blood on and before the mercy seat? Yes, every
year.

The blood of Christ was shed once for all; all Levitical shadows

---

*It is indeed true that we, the Assembly of God, "worship by the Spirit of God and
glory in Christ Jesus"; that "by one Spirit we have our access unto the Father," because
we have been directly created by God "the firstfruits of His creatures," of the New
Creation; and "are the righteousness of God in Him," and belong to that place which our
Lord is preparing which when revealed as the New Jerusalem ("which is our mother"—
Gal. 4.26), will be found to have no temple. "I saw *no temple* therein; they shall see His
face; and His name shall be on their foreheads" (Rev. 21.22; 22.4). Then shall be realized
in every outward sense what is true today of every believer.

disappeared to the eyes of faith—disappeared as fulfilled, and therefore done.

While into Heaven itself the Risen Christ had gone, and all believers with Him, they were now wholly heavenly: not Jewish, Israelitish, or even Hebrew; not Gentile, but a new creation, new creatures in Christ.

And their worship, that of these new creatures, was wholly heavenly. The blood of Christ was their right; the Holy Spirit of God was their power. They had "eternal redemption," we shall see; and an "eternal inheritance." **The greater and more perfect tabernacle, not made with hands . . . not of this creation, is,** therefore, the tabernacle with which the Risen Christ is connected.

Verse 12: **Nor yet through the blood of goats and calves—the** means by which Israel's high priest came before Jehovah, even into His presence, on the Great Day of Atonement. But such blood was a typical, temporary shadow, of what was to be done. Such offerings could not maintain man, nor even his representative, the high priest, in Jehovah's presence; nor, indeed, give him liberty to open his mouth from behind the veil in Jehovah's presence, the Holy of Holies. All he could do was to swing a censer of incense which spoke of that "sweet savor" which Christ's sacrifice was one day to be before God; and then sprinkle the blood, the laid-down life of the sacrifice, upon the mercy seat, then seven times before the mercy seat, and then withdraw.*

But through His own blood, entered in once for all into the Holies—Here we learn several astonishing things.

First, these words, **through** *(dia)* **His own blood,** reveal that Christ entered Heaven with a memorial of His own sacrifice. "Named of God [a High Priest] forever after the order of Melchizedek," He comes back to Heaven in that character! Not merely as Son of God, Creator of all things; not as Heir, nor as the sinless Man, returning (as in Ch. 7.26), "holy, guileless, undefiled,

---

*Mark well, however (Lev. 16), that the high priest was also to cleanse, to "make atonement for the holy place" (vs. 16), "because of the uncleannesses of the children of Israel, and because of their transgressions, even all their sins," AND "go out unto the altar . . . and make atonement for it . . . and cleanse it, and hallow it from all the uncleannesses of the children of Israel" (vss. 18, 19). The holiness of God's being and the effect of the blood in Heaven, was the primary consideration in the Great Day of Atonement, as afterwards on the Cross.

separated from sinners, and made higher than the heavens." (He could indeed say to the Jews, "Which of you convicteth Me of sin?") But it was not on that ground or in that capacity that He sat down on the right hand of the Majesty on high. He entered in **by virtue of His blood.** He might have entered Heaven at any moment during His perfect life here. But He would have gone alone as He came alone. But He has not entered Heaven in that way. Always pleasing unto the Father, **through the eternal Spirit He offered Himself without blemish** [at the Cross] **unto God (vs. 14).** We glory in Him as the sinless One, but as such our sins were laid upon Him, with the guilt thereof. So they became His, on the Cross. Indeed, He was "made *to be sin* on our behalf." He was forsaken of God. He cried:

"For innumerable evils have compassed Me about;
Mine iniquities have overtaken Me, so that I am not able to look up;
They are more than the hairs of My head;
And My heart hath failed Me" (Ps. 40.12).
We had committed those sins, of which He said again,
"Mine iniquities are gone over My head:
As a heavy burden they are too heavy for Me" (Ps. 38.4).
He said, "That which I took *not* away" (man's standing with God) "I have to restore" (Ps. 69.4). He recognized our iniquities now as His. Hear Psalm 22:

"Forsaken . . . groaning . . . My heart is like wax; it is melted within Me . . . My strength is dried up . . . My tongue cleaveth to My jaws . . . brought into the dust of death."

Such words were His in the day that your load of guilt and mine lay upon Him! Then after He had said, "It is finished," there came the piercing spear, and the outflowing blood and water.

He was buried. But according to His frequent words to His disciples concerning His death, that the third day He would be raised up, He was "raised from the dead by the glory of the Father." Forty days He spent with His beloved disciples, "showing Himself alive after His passion by many proofs." Then He ascended on high, saluted by God as a High Priest "after the order of Melchizedek," as we have seen.

He *was* the Creator—"All things have been created through Him and unto Him." But not as the Creator did He enter Heaven, "now to appear before the face of God for us." He kept the Law perfectly, as Israel had not; but He did not go back to Heaven as one who had kept that Law. He was the Son of God, but He did not return to Heaven merely as the Son.

Nor is it as though He came to the earth and did something for us and then went back to Heaven, leaving us to get there if we could; but, contrariwise, having entered **through His own blood,** He has us there already potentially; and to simple faith, actually.*

Behold, then, the Son of God, the Man also, without blemish, returning whence He came: and entering God's presence **through His own blood.** He must enter thus or leave the redeemed behind forever. But His character now forever was that of a Redeemer. For did He not **enter in . . . having obtained eternal redemption?** He must be forever before God as One Who "bare our sins in His own body on the Tree." Ours was the sin and guilt; His was the finished sacrifice of the Cross. *That* work was done. But He returns gladly in the character God gave Him: "Thou art a *Priest*

---

*Inasmuch as this wonderful phrase, **through His own blood,** is such a vital one, upon the proper understanding of which so much depends, we think it well to subjoin a brief extract from each of several comments thereupon, to set before the reader's mind the judgment of these godly saints whose aim has been to make plain God's truth as it has appeared to them:

Ridout well says: "Christ might have entered Heaven at any moment during His perfect life here, but He would have gone alone, as He came alone; there would not have been a single one to share His glory with Him. But He has not entered Heaven in that way. He has entered by, or, in virtue of His blood—not by His perfect character, not by His keeping the Law of God, not by His personal worthiness, even; but He has entered by His own blood, after having accomplished redemption: and because of that work He is there before God." Pp. 164-5.

And J. N. Darby: "Not, He got in by that means, even as to us, but He went in *in that way.*"—XIII, p. 193.

And in his Synopsis: "He has gone into the heavenly sanctuary *by virtue of* an *eternal* redemption, of blood, that has everlasting validity. The work is completely done, and can never change in value . . . The blood shed once for all is ever efficacious.

"Here then are the three aspects of the result of the work of Christ: immediate access to God; a purged conscience; an eternal redemption."—Pp. 288-9.

"The worshiper, under the former tabernacle, did not come into the presence of God; he stayed outside the unrent veil. He sinned—a sacrifice was offered: he sinned again— a sacrifice was offered. *Now* the veil is rent. We are always in the presence of God without a veil. Happen what may, He always sees us—sees us in His presence—according to the efficacy of Christ's perfect sacrifice. We are there now, by virtue of a perfect sacrifice . . . He has opened an access for us, even now, to God in the light, having cleansed our consciences once for all—for He dwells on high continuously—that we may enter in, and that we may serve God here below.

"God has established and revealed the Mediator, Who has accomplished the work in an eternal way . . . The Mediator has paid the ransom. Sin has no more right over us."— Pp. 293-5.

forever."* He would forever be connected with those whom He had redeemed.

Christ went into God's presence for us with only one claim on our behalf: His shed blood! That blood was the witness that in the person of our Substitute, Divine wrath and judgment had been endured. That blood witnessed that we who believe dared not in ourselves approach God, that we abandoned all hopes in ourselves, and were "made nigh in the blood of Christ." There is nothing that should bring men to despair of self-righteousness like the story of the Cross, for *all we can do* is to sit there in the darkness and let Another be judged in our place!

As Priest, that is, as representing us, *not* God: God's claims against us having all been satisfied at the Cross, forever—as Priest He is committed to our interests. (For, we repeat, a prophet came out from God, representing God to the people; while a priest went in to God, representing the people to Him.†) Indeed, having borne our sin with the guilt thereof, Christ entered in above as our Substitute and Representative, not alone, but taking us with Him, in the right and power of His infinite sacrifice. Thus He is before God, and thus, as to fact and standing, are all those in Him. Is Christ there? Then we are there in Him, blessed be God.

When the redeemed are in the glory above, there will be this consciousness: Christ, the Son of God, became what I was. I committed the sin; He bore the sin. He even became sin on my behalf, and here I am, *the righteousness of God in Him!* I am not only righteous now before God, but I *am* the righteousness of God!

---

*It behooves us to know in what attitude to God our Lord returned on high—in what old and new respects He came there: for we enter with Him! He re-entered indeed as Deity, that "glory He had with the Father before the world was." Into that place He alone could enter. To speak reverently, He could give to no creature to be Deity! God is God; creatures, creatures—forever!

But Christ re-entered Heaven as Man, also. And do not be led into that source of error—seeking to distinguish between "natures": He was ONE PERSON. Let Jno. 3.13 suffice: *"The Son of Man Who is* in Heaven." Do not reason here, for reason *fails;* but *believe.* Our Lord spoke so to Nicodemus—"the Son of Man Who is in Heaven"—for He is ONE PERSON: and, "God was manifest *in the flesh,"* and thus speaks, to the great comfort of faith, the element in which the just *live!*

†Hebrews, presenting access and worship, does not take up the question of an individual Christian's sin. We find this dealt with in I Jno. 2.1, 2, where "any man" means of course, any believer. If believers sin, fellowship is interrupted, but the attitude of the Advocate changes not!

(II Cor. 5.21). Therefore, to bring me here, Christ exchanged places with me. My Lord, Himself, became so completely my sin, that when He returned to the glory there, He entered in **through His own blood.** Therefore, when I look at my righteousness, my heart turns with unspeakable love back to where He put away my sin, and when I look at the Cross and its finished work I look at this, that I am now forever more "the righteousness of God in Him." Unspeakable Grace surrounds me, whichever way I turn. I am overwhelmed with the Grace of God that brought this salvation.*

So if He, our Sin-Bearer, entered the **Holies** above **through His own blood,** we whose sins He bore find a glad welcome there also. A sense of eternal unchanging welcome at the throne of grace possesses our hearts. Oh, if we could always abide in this, that God is evermore delighting in Christ, that dear Son Who, after finishing the work of redemption the Father had given Him to do, entered the Holies above **through His own blood,** and now "appears before the face of God for us." What a rest of heart would be ours!

Here then, let our conception of the priesthood of Christ find its eternal foundation. He entered into Heaven itself, **through His own blood,** as having borne our sins, having been once offered to bear the sins of many.† If Christ, Who did no sin, yet bore mine, entered into the Holies "before the face of God" **through His own blood,** shed at Calvary, how shall I, being invited through that blood also to enter with boldness—how *can* I shrink back?

---

*If our blessed Lord had reversed His work; if He had renounced us, for whom His blood was shed; He would have had to put off manhood, the form of man, and return as the Second Person of the Diety only. But this was impossible—although it had been possible: for even in Gethsemane He said He could make request of the Father and He would even then send Him more than twelve legions of angels.

But He went on to the Cross, and the Cross became a fact. That day was "the consummation of the ages" (9.26) we read. It could not now be reversed, that He had "put away sin by the sacrifice of Himself"! Forever before God, Christ is in the character of having been the Sin-Bearer. That is why "There is life for a look at the Crucified One"—a look of faith!

†The hideous paganism of Roman Catholicism glares here with the eyes of the serpent it is! The man-appointed, therefore pagan, priest, undertakes to offer in the Mass, over and over, what he calls "the sacrifice," and promises the poor dupes that he will obtain them Divine pardon and favor by his lying performances. Rescue all the Romanists you possibly can, showing them the great words of Heb. 9.12, 14, 24-28: Christ *"once* offered to bear the sins of many." And, the *one* Mediator: "There is one God, one Mediator also between God and men, Himself man, Christ Jesus" (I Tim. 2.5).

It is not (far, far be the thought!) that we sinners learn that our sins have been borne, that the work is finished, and we can forget that, and pass on to something beyond and deeper. THERE IS NOTHING DEEPER, for all eternity! The gift of God was infinite: His only begotten Son. The devotion of Christ was infinite: "The cup My Father hath given Me, shall I not drink it?" The devotion of God to His Son (always unmeasured) is now communicated to creatures, yea, sinful creatures. It is beheld by the holy beings of Heaven with endless marvel!

But some say they are on a higher level than those newly pardoned through Christ's blood, because they are now new creatures and are seated in heavenly places. But in Whom were they created? The only answer is, In the Risen Christ: the Christ of the wounds; the Christ Who entered Heaven **through His own blood.** It is a fearful undertaking to try, as some (like Bullinger)* do, to describe a condition beyond and above being redeemed by the shed blood of Christ, Who Himself sits at God's right hand, through His **own blood!**

It will be found in eternity that the endless love of an infinite God was expressed at Calvary; also the quenchless affection of our Great High Priest, even Jesus. Get beyond that, you never will!

To have been redeemed will be the highest place in glory, because God is most revealed by the sacrifice of His Son, and the Son most revealed by His offering of Himself! And mark this, it is not as having left the shedding of that blood behind as a past event, merely, that He enters into the glory above, but it is strictly in the character of One Who has shed His blood, which character He will retain for all eternity.

Should He, my friend, He the Holy One, enter God's presence **through His own blood,** and you dare dream of entering in apart from that blood? Would you as a sinner (and you know you are that) pass right by the blessed Son of God, Who entered God's presence **through His own blood,** and present yourself to that

---

*"I am dealing with a book—with principles and with minds that may be affected by it. I believe it is a dishonour to yourself; but as regards your book, you are but a name attached to the moral condition of mind contained in it, and there represented to the public. I am not dealing with you about it, but with it before God and my reader."—J. N. Darby, Vol. 6, p. 3.

Holy God as one who had "done his best"; who had "tried to keep the Law"; one who "had been a 'church member', and recognized on earth as 'good' "? I say, would you *dare,* you who have never as a guilty sinner fled to Him for refuge, thus enter God's holy presence?

There could be no more absolute and eternal insult to the God Who gave His Son, and Whose Son entered His presence **through His own blood,** than for you to undertake to come to God apart from the blood of Christ.

Hear the description of the saints in **Hebrews:**

Those "that draw near unto God through Him" (Christ).

Those that "enter into the holy place by the blood of Jesus, . . . by a freshly-slain and living way, through the veil, that is to say, His flesh."

Those who, "having a Great Priest over the house of God, . . . draw near with a true heart in fullness of faith, having our hearts sprinkled from an evil conscience."

Those who "have grace, whereby we may offer service well-pleasing to God with reverence and awe."

Those who "offer up a sacrifice of praise to God continually, that is, the fruit of lips which make confession to His name."

Those who "endured a great conflict of sufferings," for their faith's sake; being "in subjection" [as sons] under their Father's chastening hand.

Those who "bear the reproach" of Jesus, Who "suffered without the gate"; "laying aside every weight" and besetting sin; "running with patience the race that is set before us."

Those who refuse to "cast away their boldness" toward God, despite all obstacles and temptations; looking for THE PROMISE: "He that cometh shall come"—"shall appear a second time, apart from sin, to them that wait for Him, unto salvation."

If you and I find ourselves among this company, blessed are we! But take heed: the Divine elevator is about to start for Heaven, but there is a great sign above its door, "FOR SINNERS ONLY." Paul is in it, who of sinners is the chief. Peter is there, who swore he did not know Christ. Jerry McAuley, "the river rat," is there; and John Newton, "once a libertine and infidel, a servant of slaves in Africa," as reads his epitaph written by himself and a great multitude of others.

(Tertia, who is writing this dictation, says that readers will object, saying, "These men are already in Heaven." It is not my
thought *when* they go there, but *how* they go there. This I am
illustrating by the elevator.)

"FOR SINNERS ONLY": Here comes a Jew, saying, "I belong
to the Chosen People." Paul's answer is ready, "He is not a Jew who
is one outwardly." Nobody gets on the elevator for Heaven because
of racial descent.

But now comes a Presbyterian, and the keeper of the door (a
faithful pastor or teacher of the word of God), says "Do you see
the sign above the door, 'For Sinners Only'? Will you step in as a
sinner only?" The reply of this estimable person is, "I am a Presbyterian!"

"Keep back, then, with the Jew."

Then comes the great roll of "church people": Episcopalians,
Methodists, Baptists, Congregationalists, Lutherans, Christians. The
question of the faithful man who keeps the door always is, "Do
you enter only as a sinner?" How evasive are the replies! Once in a
while, one, like the publican, says, "Indeed, yes! Nothing but a sinner, thanking God for the news that Jesus died for me!"

"Step right in!"

Dear friends, pardon this crude illustration. It is for your soul's
sake, and we hope it is spoken in tender love. No one will get to
Heaven as a Presbyterian, as a Baptist, as a Congregationalist, as a
Lutheran, as a Plymouth Brother, for they all are sinners only! But
we ask you solemnly to consider: Is *your* hope that of a sinner only?
No righteousness of yours, whether personal, or attained (in your
imagination) through "church work," or denominational "membership," has anything whatever to do with your entering the heavenlies above. Christ Himself entered there **through His own blood.**
Have you given His shed blood that absolute place God has given it?
We do not now pray, "God be merciful to me a sinner" for since
Christ spoke those words, God *has* been merciful, and has transferred the sin of the world to the Substitute, even Christ, Who *put
away* sin by the sacrifice of Himself. Is that *your* only hope?

O "professing Christians," "church members," down here on
earth—whether "active" in "church work" or not, hearken! Where-

on are your hopes of Heaven built? What right have you, who committed the sins Christ bore, what possible right have *you* to Heaven?
None whatever! If He **entered through His own blood,** how do
you expect to enter? God has shut out all "good works." I beg you,
trust not in "confirmation," or "baptism," or in any *ordinance*
whatever; or in your "church duties," or generous giving, or "regular attendance," or zeal in "Christian activities", whether at home
or abroad, and however approved by men. Nay more, trust not in
your fancied "spirituality," your "prayer-life," your separation from
the world, your being persecuted, even.

For Christ Himself *entered in through His own blood.* And what
do you mean, you poor sinner? Do you dream that God will look
at your "works"? Why then did not Christ return to Heaven in
view of *His* works? He was sinless, and His life, perfect. You are a
poor sinner, nothing else: "All have sinned"! hear it; and, "There
is no difference": God, Who cannot lie, says that! You, a sinner,
thinking to enter Heaven by works, while Christ the Holy One
entered **through His own blood**—though he had never sinned,
entered with blood—not works! Oh, the damning delusions under
which many so-called "Christians" walk! Never having known
their guilty, lost, state; never told by their preachers that guilty
men can be made nigh to a holy God only by shed blood; that
"apart from shedding of blood there is no remission": that Christ
has entered Heaven and God's presence **through His own blood;**
that He is there representing only sinners, who, as guilty sinners,
have seen their guilt put away by the shedding of Christ's blood—
that alone!

Oh, the vast multitude of so-called "Christians" relying on their
own profession, and not upon the blood of Christ!

And what about your "moralists," your "evolutionists," your
"worldlings," your careless crowds (for whom, all, the undertaker
is patiently waiting: for, "It is appointed unto men once to die,
and after this cometh judgment")—what about these? "Modern
education," and "modern life," leave the Bible out; these millions,
God will leave without! For Christ entered Heaven **through His
own blood,** and these know nothing, willingly know nothing, of
the way to God, of pardon through Christ's blood.

Nay, do not begin to say that you "believe in a God too merciful to shut out forever these creatures—who were ignorant of His salvation." Ignorance! You say you believe in such and such a God—a god made in your own sin-darkened imagination; a God that does not exist! You will find this to be true at "the revelation of the Lord Jesus from Heaven."

All sinners who enter God's presence enter by the shed blood of Jesus.

Tell me, sinner, Do you desire to spend eternity in Heaven, like the elect angels whom God's power *kept from* all transgression? Or do you desire, yea, long, to be eternally on exhibition as one toward whom the unaccountable love of God was extended in pardon, wholly on the ground of the shed blood of his Creator-Redeemer?

Christ in Heaven can only say to any human being, that He is forever in the character of One Who has borne sin. On earth He said, "NO man cometh unto the Father but by Me." Now in Heaven, having entered **through His own blood,** He is infinitely ready to receive any sinners who rely on the blood He shed on the Cross as having put away their guilt. Read in the first two chapters of the **Hebrews,** of Who He is. Then read in the ninth of **Hebrews** of how He put away human sin by the sacrifice of Himself. And now and forever He is the Lamb that hath been slain. He can receive only sinners! If you can, as nothing but a sinner, rely on Him, He is your Great High Priest in Heaven. You need not fear: He bore your sin for you.

For us who have sinned, have been guilty, to be able to have rest of conscience, is a miracle, an operation of God within the soul. But Christ is seated in Heaven (and will be eternally so) as having put our guilt away. Meditate upon that. For no half-measures are possible: our sin has either been put away, or it has not. And God says it *has!*

Remember always to distinguish between that **eternal redemption** which Christ purchased upon the Cross, and His entering into the Holies **through His own blood.** People say, I thought Christ's work was finished at the Cross. It was, as bearing wrath and judgment for our sin, as you read in Chapter 9.26: "Now once at the consummation of the ages hath He been manifested to *put away sin* by the sacrifice of Himself." Therefore it is not in any sense an *atoning* work that Christ as Priest is carrying on in Heaven.

But notice once more, and finally, lay to heart with all your being, that Christ is eternally in the Holies on the basis of having been the Sin-offering. He entered Heaven not, as He came, as One that *had* no sin; but as One that had *borne* sin, and put sin away by the pouring out of His blood on the Cross. That was the character in which He entered, and continually abides, a High Priest forever! The Cross was primarily *atoning;* our Lord's place in Heaven is primarily *positional.*

Thus are we in Christ brought *to God.* God extends to the believing sinner all the benefits of Christ's death, resurrection, ascension to Heaven, and place at God's right hand! The believer is in exactly the same infinite love and favor as His Redeemer!

Then the last words of this great twelfth verse, **eternal redemption**—how they rest the heart! An Israelite who had sinned brought a sin offering, and placed his hand upon its head, confessing his sins. The victim was then slain, its blood presented before God, its body burned without the camp. The priest could then say to him, Jehovah's word is, You are forgiven.

Nevertheless, on the yearly Day of Atonement, the whole sin question is up again for all Israel. No Israelite could leave that great concourse rejoicing in heart, saying, My sins have been put away forever from Jehovah's sight. I have *eternal* redemption. He knew the Great Day of Atonement would come again in another year. Nay, Moses, their leader, lamented,

"Thou hast set our iniquities before Thee,
Our secret sins in the light of Thy countenance" (Ps. 90.8).

That was the design and proper effect of the Law, which was a ministration of condemnation and death, a stern conductor of the soul to Christ and His salvation. "The Law is become our tutor to bring us unto Christ, that we might be justified by faith. But now that faith is come, we are no longer under a tutor" (Gal. 3.24-5).

To the Jews under Law, therefore, there was no consciousness of the putting away of sin, for sin was *not put away* until it was done once for all by Christ at the Cross.

Eternal redemption* in Hebrews 9.12 signifies everlasting freedom from the penalty of sin, Christ having borne it at the Cross;

*Redemption: See Ex. 21.30; Lev. 25.24, 51; Num. 3.46, Ps. 49.8, etc.

and includes also complete and eternal deliverance from the power of sin; not only from spiritual death. It also includes the redemption of the body, for which believers are waiting; and finally, praise God, complete deliverance from the power of the devil, who had the power of death over the race (2.14) from the time that Adam fell. Such glorious words as those of our verse should be kept in the heart and repeated over and over: **Having obtained eternal redemption.** The opening word, "For," of verse 13, has in view this complete and eternal separation from the very presence of sin which is the hope of the instructed believer.

Verse 13: **For if the blood of goats and bulls, and the ashes of a heifer sprinkling them that have been defiled, sanctify unto the cleanness of the flesh:** In the earthly tabernacle, in which, behind the veil, God dwelt, there was indeed prescribed the blood of designated animals,* **of goats and bulls.**

We remember that the sin-offering was to be burned entirely without the camp. The water of sprinkling which was poured upon the ashes of the red heifer was prescribed as a simple, constantly available means of that ceremonial **cleanness of the flesh** demanded by Jehovah, Who dwelt among the Hebrews. Doubtless to many of them God opened the truth that the blood of this creature had been shed under His direction, that the body had been burnt in a clean, holy place which belonged entirely to God, and that the application of the ashes meant self-judgment and reliance upon the death of the substitute. But we know that all these types pointed to Christ. The **cleanness of the flesh** was all that any of them ever accomplished, however much they exercised the conscience, and however fully the Israelite might cast himself

---

*In the ordinance of the red heifer (Num. 19.2), the high priest took the ashes of an heifer "without spot, wherein was no blemish," the blood of which had been sprinkled toward the front of the tent of meeting seven times, and then the entire body burnt, along with cedar wood (representing power), and hyssop (faith), and scarlet (royalty). Then the high priest washed his clothes, and bathed his flesh in water, and afterward came into the camp and was unclean "until the evening." The man that burnt the heifer had to do and be likewise.

Then we read,

"A man that is clean, [that is, ceremonially, outwardly,] shall gather up the ashes of the heifer, and lay them up without the camp in a clean place; and it shall be kept for the congregation of the children of Israel for a water for impurity: it is a sin-offering" (Num. 19.9). This "water for impurity" was to be sprinkled on anyone who touched a dead body (Vss. 11, 12). Read Num. 19 carefully: it is a commentary on our present verse, Heb. 9.13, sanctifying unto the cleanness of the flesh.

upon the mercy of God, as, for example, David did (Ps. 51). There never was the consciousness that sin had been removed, had been put away out of God's sight forever. And why? Because, we repeat, sin had NOT been removed until Christ put it away by His one sacrifice.

Verse 14: **How much more shall the blood of Christ, Who through the eternal Spirit offered Himself without blemish unto God, cleanse your conscience from dead works to serve the living God?** We enter here upon one of the great verses of Scripture. **How much more** or, **How much rather?** As much more as Christ the Creator is greater than the creatures He created. Again we have an infinite chasm between two contrasted persons or things, as in Chapters 1.4 (see footnote there), 3.3; 7.22; 8.6. **Shall the blood of Christ**—perhaps in Chapters 9 and 10, which form one passage, blood is more frequently mentioned (15 times) than in any other equal portion of Scripture. **The blood of Christ, Who through the eternal Spirit offered Himself without blemish unto God**—We knew that each Person of the blessed Trinity was equally eternal, but it is sustaining to the heart to have the fact noted here that it was **through the eternal Spirit** that Christ **offered Himself without blemish unto God.** It is beyond measure blessed that we find here all three Persons of the Godhead occupied in our salvation! First, it is *God* to Whom the atoning sacrifice for our sin is to be made; second, it is **Christ Who offers Himself** to this end; third, it is **through the eternal Spirit** that He offered Himself without blemish.

Always the Levitical offerings were to be **without blemish,** as in the case cited in verse 13, from Numbers 19.2. But that was mere freedom from outward blemishes; whereas we know that Christ walked all of His life, from Bethlehem to Calvary, without moral or spiritual blemish before the all-seeing eye of God the Father. It is to be marked that again and again our Lord disclaimed working by His *own* power: "I live because of *the Father*"; "The Son can do nothing of Himself but what He seeth *the Father* doing"; "*The Father* abiding in Me doeth His works." The *Holy Spirit* descended upon Him at the Jordan; He was driven *by the Spirit* into the wilderness at the time of temptation. When He began to preach in Galilee, He announced, "*The Spirit of the Lord is* upon Me, because He anointed Me to preach good tidings." And again, "I by the Spirit of God cast out demons." But here in Hebrews 9.14 we find that it was **through the eternal Spirit** that He walked and wrought, and thus by that Spirit at Gethsemane and on Calvary, **offered Himself without blemish unto God,** as the Great Sin-Offering for us.

It is most natural that those directly serving **the Living God** must have their conscience cleansed from condemnation and defilement.* But lo, and behold, **the blood of Christ** is here regarded as cleansing the conscience, not from consciousness of sin and guilt, but from something entirely different: **from dead works.** What a strange expression! Generally we connect works with life, but here, the opposite—**dead works,** appears. What can this mean?

We read in II Corinthians 3.7, 9 that the Law written "in tables of stone" was "a ministration of death . . . of condemnation"; and in Galatians 3.10, "As many as are of the works of the Law are under a curse: for it is written, Cursed is every one who continueth not in all things that are written in the book of the Law, to do them." The conscience drives the heart of one who knows his sin, to get relief. **Dead works,** therefore, become the vain effort to relieve a troubled conscience by legal obedience.

---

*The conscience is never said to be cleansed from *sin*. Believers are, and so are believers' hearts. See Acts 15.8-9, where Peter, referring to the filling of believing Cornelius and his household with the Holy Spirit, said,

"God, Who knoweth the heart, bare them witness, giving them the Holy Spirit, even as He did to us; and He made no distinction between us and them, *cleansing their hearts* by faith."

The word "cleansing" here is in the aorist (definite past tense). After that experience, Cornelius had what Scripture calls "a clean heart," the heart of a little child toward God, even as the Lord said, "Except ye become *as little children.*"

If it be objected that "The heart is deceitful above all things, exceedingly corrupt," and, "He that trusteth in his own heart is a fool"—certainly! And in the natural state, "evil thoughts," "evil things" (Mk. 7.21-2), "proceed out of the heart of men." But Christ came, and on the Cross all these evil things were dealt with. And when He entered into the Holies above, in virtue of, by power of His own blood, all these sins were as if they had never been. The blood of Christ met not only all that man had done but all that man was, so that we read: "The blood of Jesus Christ His Son cleanses us from all sin."

Sin does not reside in the conscience, but the *consciousness* of sin, does. Therefore the conscience, knowing good and evil, accuses the heart (the throne room of the being, "out of which are the issues of life"), until the heart is cleansed by faith.

The body, of course, remains unredeemed until Christ comes, and even though Christ be in us, "is dead because of sin." It is the tabernacle in which we groan, "longing to be clothed upon with our habitation which is from Heaven," our new bodies.

But we are not our bodies, nor our souls; we possess both. We are *spirits:* "That which is born of the Spirit is *spirit,*" the new creature called into being by God's creative act in the Risen Christ, the last Adam (II Cor. 5.17).

With the Hebrews, of course, it was efforts through the works prescribed by the Law. With the sincere Gentile, like Cornelius, the action of the conscience* was the same. Not only Hebrew believers, but Gentile believers also, burden themselves with **dead works.** They become occupied with "duties," with "church work," even with "Christian service." They are not **serving the Living God.**

But Moses endured "as seeing Him Who is invisible." David danced before the ark of God because he knew the God of the ark. Paul cried, "God is my witness, Whom I serve *in my spirit*": Jude exhorts us to build up ourselves on our most holy faith, "praying in the Holy Spirit." John on Patmos, after he saw the glorified Christ, feared not, though taken up to Heaven, and seeing the throne of the Triune God, the wonderful living creatures, the elders, the innumerable host of angels. Why? He served **the Living God.**

Four times in **Hebrews** is this great name, **the Living God,** written: twice concerning the saved, twice concerning the lost. Here in Chapter 9.14 believers, their conscience cleansed **from dead works,** delivered from self-effort and all fear, serve with gladness One Whom they know, the Living One, God. So that we find them in Chapter 12.22 arriving at the "city of the Living God, the heavenly Jerusalem," for an eternity of untold delight with Him Whose service "is perfect freedom."

---

*We repeat, conscience involves the knowledge of good and evil. Before man sinned, he was in innocency. But when he had sinned, Jehovah God spoke a solemn word: "Behold, the man is become as one of us, to know good and evil." Here is the basis, the beginning, of human conscience, literally joint-knowledge. God knew good and evil, and chose holiness and good, absolutely and forever. However, knowing all things, He discerned both the character of and all the operations of, evil. Nothing was hid from Him. Evil was by Him known but rejected, and its power never felt.

Not so with fallen creatures, whom man had now joined. To the sinning creature, evil became a master, and good, a memory. There was the knowledge of good and evil, but no power in himself to extricate him from either the guilt or defilement. If God redeem him not, he goes into eternity unredeemed. But Christ having come, in the mercy of God, and at Calvary having borne sin for the whole world, the cleansing of the conscience became possible. For conscience deals directly with God, and, Gospel enlightened, is set free.

Note the following Scriptures: "Conscience toward God," (lit., of God—I Pet. 2.19); "a good conscience," (I Tim. 1.5; Heb. 13.18); "a pure conscience," (I Tim. 3.9; II Tim. 1.3); a "conscience . . . defiled," (Tit. 1.15); a "conscience weak . . . defiled," (I Cor. 8.7, 12); "a conscience void of offense," (Acts 24.16); conscience "branded", or seared—disregarded; no longer able to function (I Tim. 4.2); "No more consciousness [conscience, same Greek word] of sins," because conscience cleansed by the blood of Christ (Heb. 10.2).

To serve the Living God: Elijah's voice on Carmel to the gathered nation of Israel, was, "If Jehovah be God, follow Him." You say, What has that to do with the words, **the Living God?** it has this: Christendom today, (like Israel when Elijah spoke), is not serving a Living God. If it were, it would allow all its service to be judged by the consciousness of God's presence, of His infinite, intimate knowledge of us, of our hearts and motives. This would be worshiping "in spirit and in truth" (and God accepts no other worship); not by mere "church membership," by forms warned against in God's Word; by ceremonies, days, months, years; even in idolatrous, blasphemous caricatures of true worship and service in the Spirit. It would be judging everything by the question, What does God, Who is *living,* think of this? You have heard earnest preachers say, "You cannot fool God." Yet how many professing Christians (and this may mean you), expect to do so.*

Note that **A LIVING GOD** is one of the great key words of this great epistle. The modernist talks about a "God of love," "the universal fatherhood of God," etc. But alas, the modernist has never met a living God! God is *living, before* He is loving. All His motions toward guilty sinners, whether pardon, justification, or (here in Heb. 9.14) service, are based on the shed blood of Christ. Yet the false prophets of Christendom proclaim neither guilt of lost sinners, nor transference of their sin and guilt to the head of a Substitute. Avoid them, flee them, unless you court your doom! Read Jeremiah 23 about the false shepherds and prophets.† There is peace

---

*The words **a Living God,** (28 times in Scripture), are not a title of God, but a definition of His being. A Living God takes no interest in "church attendance" as such. How would you like people to drive up to your residence, seat themselves in your house, and by and by depart—without ever speaking to you, or recognizing your presence? And how would you like it if before departing one of them should arise and say, "We will now take up a collection for the running expenses of this establishment"—all without speaking to you or recognizing you as head and master of the establishment?

†"Concerning the prophets. My heart within me is broken, all my bones shake; I am like a drunken man . . . whom wine hath overcome, because of Jehovah, and because of His holy words. For the land is full of adulterers; for because of swearing the land mourneth; the pastures of the wilderness are dried up. And their course is evil, and their might is not right; for both prophet and priest are profane; yea, in My house have I found their wickedness, saith Jehovah. Wherefore their way shall be unto them as slippery places in the darkness: they shall be driven on, and fall therein; for I will bring evil upon them, even the year of their visitation, saith Jehovah.

"And I have seen folly in the prophets of Samaria; they prophesied by Baal, and caused My people Israel to err. In the prophets of Jerusalem also I have seen a horrible thing: they commit adultery, and walk in lies; and they strengthen the hands of evil-doers, so that

through faith in the shed blood of Christ, and there is no other peace. And lying Modernists will learn it.

Has the blood of Christ so cleansed **your conscience from dead works**—all "religious" forms whatever, that you are consciously in the presence of God? Or, if walking in darkness, having no light, are you yet able to stay upon His Word, and occupy yourself with a "sacrifice of praise to God continually, that is, the fruit of lips which make confession to His name," even though you are in the midst of trial? So did Christ: "Hold not Thy peace, O God *of My praise:*" so the 109th Psalm, in which He continues, "They have compassed Me about with words of hatred, and fought against Me without a cause." So Jeremiah: "Heal me, O Jehovah, and I shall be healed; save me, and I shall be saved; for Thou art *my praise.*"

To serve the Living God includes, besides a cleansed, freed conscience, a heart believing God's love, and acceptance of Christ's easy yoke in the knowledge of being *in* Him (having died with Him to sin and to the Law, having been enlifed with Him, and raised up with Him, and made to sit with Him in the heavenlies— the "heavenly calling" of which these Hebrew believers were partakers, though the details of it are not given in **Hebrews**). Last, in patiently "doing the will of God," in view of the promise,

"Yet a very little while,

He that cometh shall come, and shall not tarry" (10.36-7), and the *sure* realization of the "good things to come," at His coming.

15   And for this cause He is the Mediator of a new covenant, that a death having taken place for the redemption of the transgressions that were under the first covenant, they that have been called may receive the promise of

16   the eternal inheritance. For where a covenant is, there

17   must of necessity be the death of him that made it. For a covenant is of force where there hath been death: for

18   it doth never avail while he that made it liveth. Wherefore even the first covenant hath not been dedicated with-

---

none doth return from his wickedness: they are all of them become unto Me as Sodom, and the inhabitants thereof as Gomorrah. Therefore thus saith Jehovah of hosts concerning the prophets: Behold, I will feed them with wormwood, and make them drink the water of gall; for from the prophets of Jerusalem is ungodliness gone forth into all the land" (Jer. 23.9-15).

See also vss. 16 to end of chapter; and Ezek. 13.10 ff.

19 out blood. For when every commandment had been
   spoken by Moses unto all the people according to the
   Law, he took the blood of the calves and the goats, with
   water and scarlet wool and hyssop, and sprinkled both
20 the book itself and all the people, saying, This is the
   blood of the covenant which God commanded to you-
21 ward. Moreover the tabernacle and all the vessels of the
22 ministry he sprinkled in like manner with the blood. And
   according to the Law, I may almost say, all things are
   cleansed with blood, and apart from shedding of blood
   there is no remission.

Verse 15: And for this cause He is the Mediator of a new
covenant—In these words (and the same words in Ch. 12.24),
there is no infraction of the statement of Galatians 3.20: "Now a
mediator is not a mediator of one; but God is One." Both Stephen
(Acts 7.53) and Paul (Gal. 3.19) declare that the Law at Sinai
was "ordained through angels." The meaning of this statement
we do not find amplified in Scripture; the fact alone is revealed.
In the next verse, Galatians 3.20, Paul adds to the words "ordained
through angels," the additional phrase, "by the hand of a mediator" (of course, Moses): and he explains, as just quoted, "Now a
mediator is not (a mediator) of one; but God is One"; that is, the
contrast is drawn between God's promises made unconditionally
and directly by God to Abraham "and to his Seed . . . Christ,"
Galatians 3.16, (which promise needed no mediator!) and the
Law afterwards "added" till the Seed should come, of Whom the
promise had been made.

For this cause He (Christ) is the Mediator of a new covenant—
That is, Christ has taken the place of Moses, a mediator of the
first covenant. We have all heard the fatuous expression, "Christ,
when on earth, re-affirmed the Ten Commandments." No one who
has brought God's truth to human souls will deny that the last
fortress of unbelief to be overthrown in man's heart is his persuasion that God is requiring righteousness of him. But the mediatorship of a new covenant spoken of in our verse (9.15) passes over
all man's works and duties and ability to the words, a death having taken place. Christ's mediatorship dates after His death, not to
his life and preaching.

For example, our Lord in Matthew 5 to 7, the so-called "Sermon on the Mount," was bound to back up God's legal covenant to Moses, giving also His own commands as the great Prophet Whom God had raised up to Israel (foretold by Moses, Deut. 18.15, 18), and announcing the kingdom. Then in Matthew 8 to 15 the unbelief and rejection of the Jews is brought out; and in Chapter 16.18 the Lord prophesies that He will build (what was not yet built) the Assembly, His Body, the Church; and the disciples are commanded to publish no further the Gospel that Christ is the Messiah of Israel. He must go and die, and be three days and three nights in the heart of the earth (Matt. 12.40).

The Gospel Paul preached to Jews and Gentiles begins with Christ's death, not with His virgin birth, or His spotless life: "I delivered unto you first of all that which also I received: that Christ died for our sins according to the Scriptures" (I Cor. 15.1, 3). Therefore Hebrews 9.15 sets Him forth as **the Mediator of a new covenant,** in view of the fact of **a death having taken place,** (on account of which only) **they that have been called may receive the promise of the eternal inheritance.** Note that **they that have been called*** have this relationship to the new covenant, that its conditions have been fulfilled, and that on the basis of this death of Christ, the new covenant is in operation, Christ being its Mediator. Moses in his day was "mediator" to bring the Law with its commands, its demands, its threatenings, and its blessing conditioned on obedience, into the camp. But do not dare to make Christ a second Moses because the word **Mediator of a new covenant** is used concerning Him.† For this new covenant is that of Hebrews 13.20, in which the parties are the two Persons of the Godhead. Our blessed Lord did not come as Moses, bringing conditions for man to fulfill. But He said, "The words that I say unto you, I speak not from Myself: but the Father abiding in Me doeth His works" (Jno. 14.10); "I and the Father are One" (Jno. 10.30). God was manifested in the flesh. Therefore, when our Lord is called **the Mediator of a new covenant,** it is of the new covenant

---

*John MacNeil used to say, when questioned about election, "Preach the Gospel to all sinners, and if you get somebody into Heaven that God didn't elect, He'll forgive you, for He loves sinners!"

†"Our Lord Jesus was made a curse for us, became the great Sin-Offering, and now has become the Mediator of a better covenant, in which all the promise is on God's part, and man receives every blessing as pure grace."—Ironside, **Studies in the Epistle to the Hebrews,** p. 97.

in His blood (Lk. 22.20, I Cor. 11.25). So that, Christ being God,
Galatians 3.20 is fulfilled. And when we come to the name
"mediator" in I Timothy 2.5: "For there is one God, one Mediator
also between God and men, Himself Man, Christ Jesus," we find
the word "Mediator" having the meaning of Galatians 3.20—the
other side of that verse: "A mediator is not a mediator of one."
Christ is seen here between God and men: blessed fact! But let
not this truth disturb in our minds the blessed words, **Mediator
of a new covenant,** in which the parties are God and Jesus Christ,
and we the beneficiaries. We are receivers, not contracting parties,
not actors. God and Christ are the contracting parties in that
eternal covenant (13.20) by which we **receive the promise of the
eternal inheritance.**

Luther used to say, "Christ is no Moses! Take heed lest thou
set Christ upon the rainbow, with a stern countenance, as of a
judge." No! God has made no legal covenant with men, that if
they will do and be so and so, He will "save them at last." What a
blessed place have we, the beneficiaries of an eternal covenant the
conditions of which have already been fulfilled! "It is finished,"
Christ said; and the God of peace raised Him from the dead in
view of that covenant.* (13.20).

One more point as to Hebrews 9.15: Reading this verse carefully, we see that if those **that were called,** God's elect, were to
receive the promise of the eternal inheritance, there must be **the
redemption of the transgressions that were under the first covenant.** Strictly speaking, this limits the application of this verse to
those who were under the Law: for Gentiles were never in cove-

---

*The words, **a death having taken place,** involve,

First, The putting away of all sins (Ch. 9.26, I Pet. 2.24).

Second, The identification of Christ with sin, with our old man as connected with Adam,
so that it was written (Rom. 6.6): "Our old man was crucified with Him"; "We died
with Christ" (Rom. 6.8).

Third, Our relationship to sin broken, for (Rom. 6.10, 11): "The death that He died,
He died unto sin once; but the life that He liveth, He liveth unto God. Even so reckon ye
also yourselves to be dead unto sin, but alive unto God in Christ Jesus." In view of the
death of Christ (in Whom we now are) unto sin, our relationship to sin becomes that of
the Risen Christ to sin.

Fourth, Death to Law (which gave sin its power—I Cor. 15.56; as was manifest in the
commandments of the Mosaic Law), meaning the legal principle upon which God demanded
righteousness of the creature; and the believer's complete discharge therefrom. Mark the
correct translation of Rom. 7.6: "But now we have been *discharged* from the Law, HAV-
ING DIED to that wherein we were held"; instead of the A.V. translation, which mistak-
enly makes the Law die, whereas the believer dies unto the Law and the legal principle.

nant with God. To every sincere Hebrew believer, this "redemption" or removal from before God of their former transgressions
under Law, came as a welcome thing. The Law with its "ten
thousand things" (Hos. 8.12), is no longer between the Hebrew
believer and the eternal inheritance. Indeed, the Law had nothing
to do with this inheritance, "For the Law made nothing perfect"
(Heb. 7.18); bringing neither life nor righteousness nor peace, not
to speak of hope.

Peter thus describes the eternal inheritance:

"An inheritance incorruptible, and undefiled, and that fadeth
not away, reserved in Heaven for you, who by the power of God
are guarded through faith unto a salvation ready to be revealed
in the last time" (I Pet. 1.4-5).

Paul calls this "the recompense of the inheritance" (Col. 3.24),
and declares (Rom. 8.17) that believers are "heirs of God [mar-
velous words!] and joint-heirs with Christ; if so be [or since] we
suffer with Him, that we may be also glorified with Him"—more
marvelous words! The inheritance of these Hebrew believers had
formerly been earthly, the land of Israel, with millennial blessings to come. But the eternal inheritance* goes infinitely beyond
that!

Verse 16: For where [there is a] covenant, there must of necessity be brought the death of† the one covenanting. (17) For a
covenant has force over dead [persons or things], since it in no
way has power when he is living who covenanted. The opening
word, "For," of verse 16 must be governed, we see at once, by
the "death" spoken of in verse 15: A death having taken place.
Any reader of this page who is familiar with the King James,
or Authorized Version of the New Testament, has also noticed
that we are translating the Greek word diathēkē, covenant,

---

*It has often been remarked in this passage how God delights to dwell upon the word
"eternal":

1. "Eternal salvation" (Ch. 5.9): Christ the Cause, obedience the condition.

2. "Eternal redemption" (9.12): By the blood of Christ, Who "THROUGH THE
ETERNAL SPIRIT offered Himself . . . unto God" (vs. 14).

3. Eternal inheritance (9.15): Compare, "the *inheritance* among all them that are sanctified," Acts 20.32; "an *inheritance* among them that are sanctified by faith in Me" [Jesus],
Acts 26.18; "The Father made us meet to be partakers of the inheritance of the saints in
light," Col. 1.12; "an inheritance incorruptible, undefiled, that fadeth not away, reserved
in Heaven" for us—I Pet. 1.4, as we have quoted above.

†Or, death proceeding from one covenanting—genitive of definition. Winer (Ed.
VI, p. 198.)

and not "testament" as does the Authorized Version. This we shall now explain and consider.

Two facts must be borne in mind in our examination of this word *diathēkē,* covenant. (1) The word "covenant" is confined, as are all other quotations and references in the book of **Hebrews,** to the definition and use already made of them by God in the Word of God. Therefore arguments concerning the use of *diathēkē* in Greek or Roman literature have no bearing whatever.

2. The word "covenant," or *diathēkē* in Chapter 9.15-17 is evidently spoken of those covenants that have to do with relationships, communication, and dealings with the holy God, which of course are confirmed by shed blood: and therefore is the use of blood emphasized.

We are persuaded, therefore, that the change in translation of the Greek word *diathēkē from* "covenant" (vss. 15, 20) to "testament" (vss. 16, 17), in the Authorized Version, is both incorrect and confusing. For the expression **the first (covenant)** of verse 18 simply continues the argument **(the first covenant)** of verse 15. We would commend to the student the unanswerable comment by Westcott **(Hebrews,** p. 298 ff.) We quote from this in the footnote below:*

Nor am I at all persuaded that verses 16-17 constitute a parenthesis, as some say. For,

1. The argument of verses 15 to 20 is continuous: the word *diathēkē* being translated "covenant" in vs. 15, is called "the first" (covenant understood), in verse 18; and verse 18 begins with the word "Wherefore," or "Whence," and the word *diathēkē* is translated "covenant" consequently in verse 20.

---

*"The Biblical evidence then, so far as it is clear, is wholly in favour of the sense of 'covenant,' with the necessary limitation of the sense of the word in connection with a Divine covenant . . . The mention of the 'Inheritance' in vs. 15 does not appear to furnish any adequate explanation of a transition from the idea of 'Covenant' to that of 'Testament.' It is true that Christ has obtained an inheritance (1.4); and it is also true that He entered on the possession of it through death. But it cannot be said that He 'bequeathed' it to His people . . . By union with Him they enjoy together with Him what is His. But He does not give them anything apart from Himself. It is also important in this respect to notice that the thought of the bequeathal of an inheritance by Christ to His people is not supported by any other passage of Scripture (not by Lk. 22.20) . . . The conceptions of Christ as the 'Mediator of a Covenant,' and as a 'Testator,' the 'framer of a will,' are essentially distinct. A covenant is the disposition of things determined by God for man and brought about through Christ; a Testament would be the expression of Christ's own will as to what should be after His death. *The thoughts are wholly different;* and the idea of death is unable in itself to combine them."—Westcott *in loc.*

Note that "For" in both verses 16 and 17, like "Wherefore" in verse 18 and "For" in verse 19, closely connect the argument of the whole paragraph about a *covenant*. These verses *cannot be set asunder*.

2. It is inconceivable that only the Epistle to the Hebrews should depart from the Old Testament use and meaning of the word "covenant" (used 17 times in **Hebrews** and 17 times in the rest of the New Testament), to a new and entirely different meaning of the word—a Graeco-Roman use, not a Biblical!

3. Moreover, it is a "Mediator of a new *covenant*" the passage has been speaking of, and a "testament" (vs. 17) or "will" does not need a "mediator." A *covenant* in Scripture has a mediator, as Moses, the mediator of "the first" (vs. 18); and Christ, **the Mediator of a new covenant.*** A man who makes a will does not perforce execute its provisions!

The great Bible illustration of the word "covenant" is given in Exodus 24.

"[Moses] sent young men of the children of Israel, who offered burnt-offerings and sacrificed peace-offerings of oxen unto Jehovah. And Moses took half of the blood, and put it in basins; and half of the blood he sprinkled on the altar. And he took the book of the covenant, and read in the audience of the people: and they said, All that Jehovah hath spoken will we do, and be obedient. And Moses took the blood, and sprinkled it on the people, and said, Behold, the blood of the covenant, which Jehovah hath made with you concerning all these words" (Ex. 24.5-8).

---

*"With the utmost decision must we continue to protest against the introduction of 'testament' as the meaning of *diathēkē* in verses 16, 17. It is needless, and it does violence to the continuity of our Author's argument. It is needless, as a patient consideration of Gen. 15.7-21, and Jer. 34.18-9, might have shown, where both parties to the Covenant are represented as dead to all change of mind; and it does violence to the argument of the present passage as the sudden jerk back to the covenant idea, which in that case is felt in vs. 18, all sufficiently shows: Whence **not even the first apart from blood hath been consecrated. The first**—what? 'Testament'? Nay! *the first* (that at Sinai) was *not* a testament but a covenant. Besides, as well said by the 'Speaker's Commentary' on Ch. 7.22, 'A testament no more requires a surety than it does a *mediator*' and on Ch. 9.15, 'The use of the term 'Mediator' shows that we have here to do with the *Hebrew* idea of a *covenant*, not with a *Roman* idea of a 'testament.' A mediator is the proper guardian of a *covenant* (see Gal. 3.15-20), but has no place in regard to a testament. Neither, again, does the death of a testator possess any of the sacrificial character which is referred to in vss. 15-22."—Rotherham, pp. 138-9.

"There is not a trace of the meaning *testament* in the Greek O.T."—Vincent.

See also the able and searching rejection of the word "testament" in Kendrick's edition of Olshausen, pp. 512-7.

This, mark, is the example of the inauguration of a Biblical covenant, and it is a Biblical covenant only which is before us throughout Hebrews 9 and 10.*

Note that it was the blood, not of the Israelites, who were entering into the covenant; nor of Moses, a Mediator of that covenant, but of appointed animals, that was shed: **death proceeding from the covenanting one.** The one great point is that a covenant with Jehovah could not be dedicated or inaugurated apart from blood-shedding.

Verse 17: For a covenant is of force where there hath been death: [or, Over dead persons or things]: **since it in no way has power when he who covenanted is living:** Why death, blood-shedding, in pledge or "ratification" of God's "covenant"? First, God could have dealings with fallen man only on the ground of death. "Thou shalt surely die," God had said to Adam—if he should sin. And when he did sin, and God sent him and Eve from Eden, He "made for Adam and for his wife coats of skins" (obtained after death) "and clothed them." Also when Abel learned (as Cain never did) the way of approach to God, it was by blood— the blood of a firstling lamb.

Again, when God desired to confer upon Abram's seed the land of promise, He directed Abram to place on the right hand and on the left the divided carcasses of appointed victims, symbols of the death of Christ by means of which alone He can bestow promised blessing upon His own:

"And it came to pass, that when the sun went down, and it was dark, behold a smoking furnace, and a flaming torch that passed between these pieces. In that day Jehovah made a covenant with Abram, saying, Unto thy seed I have given this land, from the river of Egypt unto the great river, the river Euphrates" (Gen. 15.17-8).

Here Abram, with whom Jehovah was covenanting, did *not* die, but appointed sacrifices died *in his stead.* It was a covenant of promise, an announced purpose of God to bless him, and—through his Seed, Christ—all nations. The fact, however, that it was a

---

*A covenant is between two or more parties.

A covenant states the conditions of relationship or action.

The Old Covenant made Divine blessing dependent upon human obedience. The New Covenant proceeds wholly from God, and is based entirely upon Christ's work.

Note, "the blood of the covenant," Heb. 9.20; and "The Lord Jesus . . . said. . . . This cup is the new covenant *in My blood*" (I Cor. 11.23-5).

mutual agreement between God and Abram, each fulfilling pre-scribed conditions, is brought out in Nehemiah 9.7-8:

"Thou art Jehovah the God, Who didst choose Abram, and broughtest him forth out of Ur of the Chaldees, and gavest him the name of Abraham, and foundest his heart faithful before Thee, and *madest a covenant* with him to give the land of the Canaanite, the Hittite, the Amorite, and the Perizzite, and the Jebusite, and the Girgashite, to give it unto his seed, and hast performed Thy words; for Thou art righteous."

Second, This ratification by blood-shedding certainly indicates the solemnity, "even unto *death*," of undertakings between God and men. Even men thus ratify their statements and promises: "I hope to *die*, if I don't do it!"

Third, To go further, there is the *sanction of death* in these Old Testament covenants, especially in that of Exodus 24. Why should not the Law, which was a "ministration of death," have the sanction of death? As our next verse reads,

Verse 18: **Wherefore even the first covenant hath not been dedicated without blood.** We repeat, the word "Wherefore" open-ing this verse connects it directly with what is said in verses 16 and 17. Verse 18 ff. is an illustration of the ratification of a *cove-nant, not* the announcement of a will or testament.

It must be constantly remembered that in verses 11 to 28 there are two tabernacles and two covenants before us. In verse 11 Christ is seen "having come a High Priest of the good things to come, through the greater and more perfect tabernacle, not made with hands, that is to say, not of this creation"; and in verse 12, entering into the holy place—Heaven itself, "through His own blood." The infinite efficacy of this blood is contrasted with that of animals, in verses 13 and 14. Then (vs. 15) because of this efficacy He is **the Mediator of a new covenant, a death having taken place, for There must of necessity be the death of the one covenanting (vs. 16).** Then in verse 18 the comparison is carried on: **Where-fore even the first [covenant] hath not been dedicated without blood . . . The tabernacle and all the vessels of the ministry (vs. 21) [Moses] sprinkled in like manner with the blood . . . all things . . . cleansed with blood and apart from shedding of blood . . . no remission [dismissal] of sins (22).**

Verse 23: We find the comparison still carried on: **The copies of the things in the heavens . . . cleansed with these; but the heavenly things themselves with better sacrifices than these.** *The whole thought so far* has been that of *a ratification by death* of a Divine covenant.

We must go back now for a longer look at the remarkable scene of verses 18-22, reported from Exodus 24, to which we have already referred. Let us remember that it is to a people that have been re-deemed from Egypt that this solemn covenant was given; and that this covenant of Exodus 24, under which Israel passed after the Law had been proclaimed from Sinai, leaves blessing dependent upon *man's* faithfulness, *man's* responsibilty. There are several ele-ments in the striking scene:

1. Aaron and his two eldest sons and seventy of the elders (representatives of Israel) are called up and worship afar off.

2. Moses, a type of Christ the Mediator, alone comes near.

3. The people are forbidden to come up (for God is preparing for a priesthood to intervene between Him and them).

4. Moses reports to the people Jehovah's words, the ordinances of Chapters 22 and 23.

5. The second time, the people solemnly promise, "All the words which Jehovah hath spoken will we do" (vs. 3). They repeat this promise (vs. 7) after burnt-offerings and peace-offerings are offered by "young men of the children of Israel" (vss. 4-5).

6. Moses sprinkles half the blood upon the altar.

7. Then he takes the book of the covenant, that is, the Law with the ordinances of Exodus 22 and 23, and reads it in the audience of the people: upon which they promise to do "all that Jehovah hath spoken, and be obedient."

8. Moses then takes the other half of the blood and **sprinkles all the people,** after having **sprinkled the book itself (Heb. 9.19) saying, This is the blood of the covenant which God commanded to you-ward (20).**

9. Note that no man was ever saved by keeping this Law. This sprinkled blood of course pointed to Christ's shed blood; yet here emphasizes that sanction of death which the legal covenant had.

Verse 22: **And according to the Law, I may almost say, all things**

**are cleansed with blood, and apart from shedding of blood there
is no remission.** To grasp the deep import of this most important
verse, we must turn to that instructive, and, alas, neglected, book,
Leviticus:

1. "The life of the flesh is in the blood": (Lev. 17.11, 14).

2. God commanded Israel that blood, whether of sacrifices
(Ex. 29.12; Lev. 4.7, 18, 25), or of that which was taken in hunting (Deut. 12.16, 24; 15.23), was to be "poured out upon the
earth."

3. Blood was not to be eaten, forbidden even to Noah: this is
one of the conditions of the everlasting covenant: "But flesh with
the life thereof, which is the blood thereof, shall ye not eat"
(Gen. 9.4). This prohibition was repeated under the Law to
Israel (Lev. 7.26; 17.10-13). It was one of the four directions sent
to the Gentile churches from the council at Jerusalem: ". . . That
we write unto them, that they abstain . . . from what is strangled,
and from blood" (Acts 15.19-20).*

4. The essence of any of the offerings was the *pouring out* of
its *blood*: whether of the burnt offering (Lev. 1), the peace offering
(Lev. 3), the sin offering (Lev. 5), or the trespass offering (Lev.
6); or the morning and evening sacrifice of the lamb, or the slaying
of the goat for Jehovah's lot on the Great Day of Atonement. The
essence of all was the pouring out of the blood, this being the laying
down of the life: for *the blood was the life.*

Doubtless in the burnt offering there was the sweet savor in the
burning of the whole body upon the altar, representing Christ giving
Himself up for us, "an offering and a sacrifice to God for an odor
of a sweet smell" (Eph. 5.2). There was also the fellowship of the
priests with Jehovah in those parts of the various sacrifices assigned
to them to eat. But, we repeat, in every offering where death took
place, it was the pouring out of the blood, the laying down of the
life, that was the essential thing.

5. It is of the utmost importance, then, to remember that the
shedding the blood, the pouring it out upon the ground, meant
laying down what God calls "the life of the flesh": "As to the

---

*It is to this day a mark of inherent savagery and infidel brutality to consume "blood
puddings."

life of all flesh, the blood thereof is all one with the life thereof
. . . the life of all flesh is the blood thereof" (Lev. 17.14,
and see vs. 11, quoted above.) The great point in our minds
here should not yet be *why* the shedding of the blood of the
offering was demanded, but the fact that it *was* so. The shed
blood was an open witness that the life with which it was connected, which life indeed it *was,* had been laid down. See Jehovah's
word concerning the Passover blood sprinkled upon the doors in
Egypt: "When I see *the blood* I will pass over you." All Egypt,
including the Israelites, was under Divine judgment, but the outpoured blood of the Passover lamb protected the houses of Israel
from the judgment that fell upon those not having the sprinkled
blood. And remember that Paul wrote, "For our passover also hath
been sacrificed, even Christ" (I Cor. 5.7). His poured-out blood,
which was "the life of the flesh" which He laid down, protects us
from Divine judgment, as Israel was protected in Egypt.

6.   If we inquire now, *Why* **shedding of blood?** Why must life
be laid down? Scripture answers, It is demanded by the *being* of
God: "Thou art of purer eyes than to behold evil" (Hab. 1.13);
"Holy, holy, holy, is the Lord God, the Almighty" (Rev. 4.8); and
by the *government* of God: "Righteousness and justice are the
foundation of His throne" (Ps. 97.2). Every sin defies the majesty
of the infinite God. Therefore, however measureless His love to man
may be, man's sin must be taken away ere he can stand for an
instant before God.

But taken away—how? In **Hebrews** here we read, **Apart from
shedding of blood there is no remission.** This statement arouses
the venom of a serpent-taught, human, shallow "theology" to cry,
"We do not believe in a God like that, Who must have His anger
appeased by the blood of a victim!" What sheer, blind folly such
utterances show! What ignorance of Scripture! What fancied security of the speakers in *their* lives of sin and guilt!

Have they never considered that the shed blood witnessed to a
life laid down, ended? Not only has the God of this universe risen
in judgment, but in the shed, outpoured blood of Christ, the great
Sin Offering, man *disappeared!* his human standing was ended.
When the Jewish high priest took the blood of the slain goat into
the Holy of Holies on the Great Day of Atonement, with the whole
congregation of Israel assembled without, he spake no word, uttered

no confession, made no plea. Going to the mercy seat, the top of the ark of the covenant, he sprinkled the blood upon it, and before it, seven times, then went out. That *blood* witnessed that the goat which was "Jehovah's lot" had died; its life was poured out, ended. When the high priest went forth from the tabernacle and, laying his hands upon the head of the other goat (for the people), confessed all their sins and iniquities, it was as a result of the laying down of the life of the first goat, for the two together constituted one type of Christ's death, Christ's shedding His blood for sin, and the result. This second goat was sent away into the wilderness, not to be found.

Remember, Christ did not resume the flesh and blood life that He had before dying. That life was laid down, ended. We are so accustomed to associate resurrection with sin bearing, that Christ's resurrection becomes in our mind a resuming of the life that He laid down. We forget that the blood poured out ended the life in the flesh. The blood of the Cross takes away all man's possible standing before God forever and ever. It brought it to an end. The Cross brought man to an end.

We know that God did raise up Christ, but as The Firstborn from among the dead, in newness of life of which mankind knows nothing until saving faith comes. And saving faith, Divinely given, includes despair in consciousness of unremovable sin and guilt, with a resting upon the shed blood of Christ as removing personal sin and guilt (as human means could not) and a claiming of the Risen Christ by faith.

23 It was necessary therefore that the copies of the things in the heavens should be cleansed with these; but the heavenly things themselves with better sacrifices than
24 these. For Christ entered not into a holy place made with hands, like in pattern to the true; but into Heaven itself,
25 now to appear before the face of God for us: nor yet that He should offer Himself often, as the high priest entereth into the holy place year by year with blood not His own;
26 else must He often have suffered since the foundation of the world: but now once at the end [or, consummation] of the ages hath He been manifested to put away sin by
27 the sacrifice of Himself. And inasmuch as it is appointed
28 unto men once to die, and after this cometh judgment; so Christ also, having been once offered to bear the sins

of many, shall appear a second time, apart from sin, to them that wait for Him, unto salvation.

Verse 23: **It was necessary therefore that the copies of things in the heavens should be cleansed with these; but the heavenly things themselves with better sacrifices than these:** Both in Hebrews and in The Revelation we find that there is a temple at present in Heaven. This word "temple" means sanctuary, or place of worship of God as He shall prescribe. In The Revelation, such words as these occur:

"There was opened the temple of God that is in Heaven; and there was seen in His temple the ark of His covenant" (Rev. 11.19).

"And after these things I saw, and the temple of the tabernacle of the testimony in Heaven was opened: and there came out from the temple the seven angels, that had the seven plagues, arrayed with precious stone, pure and bright, and girt about their breasts with golden girdles . . . And the temple was filled with smoke from the glory of God, and from His power; and none was able to enter into the temple, till the seven plagues of the seven angels should be finished . . . And I heard a great voice out of the temple, saying to the seven angels, Go ye, and pour out the seven bowls of the wrath of God into the earth" (Rev. 15.5-6, 8; 16.1).

We find then that there is a temple in Heaven. Moses was told to make the tabernacle "according to the pattern shown him in the mount"; and in Hebrews 9.23 we find that those tabernacle and temple forms were **copies of the things in the heavens;** and in the following verse that **Christ entered not into (lit.) Holies made with hands, like in pattern to the true; but into Heaven itself,* now to appear before the face of God for us.**

Now you may ask, why must **the copies of the things in the heavens be cleansed?** Scripture answers,

"Behold, He putteth no trust in His holy ones;
Yea, the heavens are not clean in His sight.
The stars are not pure in His sight" (Job. 15.15; 25.5).

Also, it was in Heaven that Satan, the "day-star, son of the morning" sinned, said his fivefold "I will" in his heart, and was "cast out as profane" (Isa. 14.12-15; Ezek. 28.14-16). Again, the record of man's sin existed in Heaven. But when the great Sin-

---

*"Heaven itself, the heaven of heavens, the place of the glorious residence of the presence or majesty of God, is that whereinto He entered."—Owen, Vol. 6, p. 278.

Bearer entered . . . into Heaven itself, "through His own blood,
once for all . . . having obtained eternal redemption," as we have
seen, sin had been put away from God's sight through the value
and power of that infinite sacrifice of Himself, the laying down of
His own life. Then were the heavens "cleansed," potentially and
eternally cleansed; and then indeed were the sins of all believers,
all who would risk themselves upon the sin-bearing, the blood-
shedding of this infinite Sin Bearer,—then were their sins actually
put away from God's sight forever.

Verse 24: **For Christ entered not into holies made with hands
(the Levitical tabernacle), like in pattern to the true; but into
Heaven itself, now to appear before the face of God for us:** But
many object, We died with Christ and have been created in the
Risen Christ, enlifed together with Him, and raised up with Him,
and made to sit in the heavenlies in Him; if we are the very Body
of Christ, why should we need that **Christ now appear before the
face of God for us?*** This is a natural question, but it shows utter
ignorance of the place of priesthood. We must learn what that is.
For there are matters revealed pertaining to the priesthood of
Christ, that are not touched even by the fact of our union with
Him as His Body.

Alas for those who are told in gospel meetings simply to believe
in Christ and His finished work, and are not told of His present
priestly work of keeping and caring for His own. If they are indeed Christ's own whom the Father has given Him, they will indeed be brought safely through. But let all true preachers and
teachers of the Word be careful to speak of this work of intercession in which our blessed Lord is *continually occupied* on behalf
of His saints! God has chosen that believers be "sojourners and
pilgrims" here. If Israel needed a priesthood in connection with their
earthly worship, how much more do we need one! For Israel was
journeying from one earthly country to another not far distant.
But we are journeying to the heavenly city that has no connection

---

*If there be any question who is meant by this word "us", we would say, it must be the
"us" of Rom. 8.34; "maketh intercession for *us*"—Jewish and Gentile believers alike; and
the "us" of Heb. 10.19, 20, 22: "the way which He dedicated for *us* . . . Let *us* draw
near."

Furthermore, the "us" in Rom. 8.31, "If God is for *us*, who is against *us*?" connects with
the same word in Heb. 6.19-20: "—within the veil; whither as a Forerunner Jesus entered
for *us*, having become a High Priest forever after the order of Melchizedek."

whatever with this world. Moreover, our Lord has been rejected
and crucified by this world, and has passed, by resurrection, into a
new state of being, in a realm called "the heavenlies" (Eph. 1.3 etc.),
and while we as belonging in the heavenlies with Christ, are travelling thither, all is by faith: as see the great faith Chapter, 11.14-16.
"We walk by faith, not by appearance." Besides, we face deadly
foes—Satan and his hosts; and have a warfare appointed unto us.

So we need a priest, and thank God! we have a priest—"a Great
Priest over the house of God," that is, all believers.* May God give
us open eyes, and the humility to recognize our great need—our
daily need, our hourly need, of His blessed, glorious, and intercessory work.

One more thing: "Christ suffered for sins once . . . that He
might bring us to God" (I Pet. 3.18). We are told to come boldly
unto the *throne* of grace. Now our Lord is not upon His own throne
yet, as He will be when He returns and the Lord God gives unto
Him the throne of His Father, David, in Jerusalem. He is on His
Father's throne, and it is *unto God, by* Christ that we are to come,
rather than *to Christ.* Some one has said, "Most Christians connect
Christ with love, and God with judgment." But this is to forget that
"God so loved the world that He gave." This attitude of heart
imagines Christ doing atoning work in Heaven, propitiating an
angry God. No wonder such a state of heart does not understand
Hebrews!

Christ died for us, did He not? Was not that a priestly work?
Did not God have all salvation depend on His sacrifice? Even so,
now, in Heaven He "appears before the face of God for us.†

---

*Heb. 9 presents Christ as a High Priest—for whom?
  1. Not to the Jewish nation, for He is of another order than Aaron and the
Levitical system.
  2. Not of unbelievers, Jews or Gentiles. Note His high priestly prayer of John 17: "I
pray not for the world, but for those whom Thou hast given Me; for they are Thine."
What unbelievers must do is appropriate Christ, believe in Him, and receive the right
thus to become sons of God.
  They then become (Jno. 1.12) "children of God," and the objects of His priestly prayer.
It is for believers passing through the world to their eternal home in glory, that Christ is "a
Great Priest over the house of God." He "maketh intercession for us" with infinite
watchfulness and marvelous sympathy.

†You may say, "Christ finished His work for me, on the Cross."
Scripture answers, "He ever liveth to make intercession for us."
You may say, "I read in Ephesians 2 that we have been 'made alive together with
Christ and raised up with Him and made to sit with Him in the heavenly places.' "

Oh, if young believers were but instructed in these things—their own weakness; the untrustworthiness of their own hearts, even in the best frames and feelings; the deadly enmity of Satan, and his planned wiles against all Christ's own; together with the fact that the world through which he journeys is "lying in the evil one"!

Then too we need a priest because we are going on into eternity. How wonderful it is to know that we are in One Who is both God and Man. As God, He sits upon the throne, "the throne of God and of the Lamb" (Rev. 22.1). The Lamb, Christ, is God the Son; yet, having become man, He can say, "My Father and your Father, and My God and your God." This does not argue distance, how-ever. We are already addressed as those "in God the Father and the Lord Jesus Christ" (I Thess. 1.1; II Thess. 1.1).

But God is infinite in all His attributes; and we shall be learning, and adoring, forever! A great part of the Levitical priest's work was to instruct the people in the word and ways of Jehovah, their God. So will it be with Christ. The question of sin will not come up, for that was forever settled; but the remembrance of the love that put sin away will be eternal.

How wonderful, then, is the eternal scene! Christ not ashamed to call the redeemed ones "brethren"; Christ declaring the name of God the Father unto His brethren—ever with fresh knowledge; finally, Christ in the midst of the great Assembly of His saints, singing, along with them, the praise of God! To contemplate an eternity

---

Scripture also says, "He ever liveth to make intercession for us," and He appears "before the face of God for us."

You say, "I am complete in Him" (Christ).

Scripture says, "He (Christ) ever liveth to make intercession for us."

You may say, "Christ offered up one sacrifice for sins forever and sat down at the right hand of God."

Scripture still says, "He ever liveth to make intercession for us."

You may say, "Christ acted as our Great High Priest when He offered up Himself on the Cross, putting away our sin from God's sight forever."

True, He certainly did. Yet Scripture says, God saluted Him, as risen from the dead, "Thou art a Priest forever after the order of Melchizedek."

You may say, as did Peter, "Lord . . . I will lay down my life for Thee"—"And in like manner also said they all" (Mk. 14.31; Jno. 13.37). But Scripture says, "Simon, Simon, behold, Satan asked to have you [plural], that he might sift you as wheat: but I made supplication for thee [sing.] that thy faith fail not; and do thou, when once thou hast turned again, establish thy brethren" (Lk. 22.31-2).

These disciples were honest and earnest; they had faith in their Lord, but they did not know their own hearts nor the journey they had to make through this world, nor their need of a priest.

with such an outlook is to have a heart filled with holy and heavenly expectations, even on the way to Heaven.

Verses 25, 26: **Nor yet that He should offer Himself often, as the high priest entereth into the holy place year by year with blood not his own; (26) else must He often have suffered since the foundation of the world:** These verses emphasize still further the contrast between the things of the Levitical economy, with its oft-repeated sacrifices, and Christ's offering Himself once, **to put away sin by the sacrifice of Himself.** Here again permit the Word of God to relieve your inmost heart and conscience of the thought that Jesus Christ is now making sacrifice for you in Heaven. He is *not* now offering Himself in sacrifice for our sins, for this was done **ONCE at the consummation of the ages,** at the Cross, as we read in verse 26.

Beginning with the words **(1) the foundation of the world,** we have next to look **(2)** at the "ages" or *aions* of the world's existence; then **(3)** at the remarkable phrase **the consummation of the ages**—at which time Christ was manifested; and finally **(4)** at the meaning of the words **to put away sin by the sacrifice of Himself.**

1.   **The foundation of the world**—We look back to Chapter 1.10 when God addresses Christ thus: "Thou, Lord, in the beginning didst lay the foundation of the earth." How far back in years Genesis 1.1 and John 1.3 take us, God has not revealed. But when it came to creation by the Father's will and the Son's word, "It was very good."

2.   **Ages** (Heb., *olams,* Gr. *aions*), succeeded. Again, God does not say how many. The term "ages" denotes lapses of time during each of which was being accomplished some phase of the Divine purpose. There came the invasion of sin into the world—nay, into the universe. Although we cannot here go thoroughly into the passages concerning sin's history, we repeat that sin is *anomia,* lawlessness (I Jno. 3.4) : that it is the rising into independency of the will of the creature. We may also repeat Romans 5.12, "Through *one man* sin entered into the world"; and recall our Lord's words concerning the tempter of Eve, "He was a murderer from the beginning" (Jno. 8.44); and I John 3.8, "The devil sinneth from the beginning."

3.   We come next to the astonishing phrase, **the consummation**

of the ages. To explain these words, demands a Divine plan. We read in Galatians 1 of "this present evil age" out of which Christ will deliver His saints. Our Lord spoke also when on earth of "this age", and "that which is to come." To set forth the meaning of the consummation of the ages, then, let us first look at the end of the verse:

4.   (Christ) hath been manifested to put away sin by the sacrifice of Himself: Recall to mind the wounds in the hands and feet and side of the Son of God's love Who is at His right hand. In Romans it is, "justified *in His blood*": in Ephesians, "made nigh *in the blood* of Christ"; in Hebrews, Christ entered into the holies "*through His own blood,*" and our entering "into the holy place *by the blood* of Jesus."

Thus He **put away sin,** and this putting away sin was **at the consummation of the ages.** All previous ages led up to this; all succeeding ages are governed by this! It seems necessary, therefore, to believe that each *aiōn* had to do with this stupendous thing, Christ's being **manifested to put away sin by the sacrifice of Himself.**

As to the devil, for example, whatever the history of the past, the consummation is seen at the Cross (Ch. 2.14): "That *through death* He might bring to naught him that had the power of death, that is, the devil." Again, as to Adam, upon his sinning, "Jehovah God made for Adam and for his wife coats of skins," as a result of a death first inflicted on substitutes by God, "and clothed them." So that, outside of Eden, they began a fallen race, each individual of whose millions is dependent upon that manifestation of Christ **at the consummation of the ages** to put away his sin,—dependent if ever to be saved!

Again, on Sinai, Jehovah spoke awful earth-shaking words to Israel. For what purpose? That the Law might "become our tutor" (Gr., *paidagōgus*) to bring unto Christ those who had been kept in ward under the Law (Gal. 3.24), that is, Israel; that they "might be justified by faith." But faith in what? In His blood Who was **manifested to put away sin.** Whether therefore we look at man's fearful need, or at the display of the infinite mercy and love of

God; or whether we look at the ages past or at the ages to come, that manifestation of Christ **to put away sin by the sacrifice of Himself** will be the theme forever.

Verses 27-8: And inasmuch as it is appointed unto men once to die, and after this cometh judgment; so Christ also, having been once offered to bear the sins of many, shall appear a second time, APART FROM SIN, to them that wait for Him, unto salvation: There could not be a greater contrast than this. We see on every hand unsaved men and women to whom two things are **appointed; (1) death, (2) judgment.** So Christ on the Cross met the double appointment: not only physical death, but death under Divine judgment, for He cried that He had been forsaken of God.

But when we see a believer, one of **those who are waiting for Him,** we see one for whom death and judgment are gone! If physical death comes, the Lord calls it "falling asleep," or "departing to be with Christ." And John 5.24 will be literally fulfilled at our Lord's second coming: the believer "entereth not into judgment, but hath passed out of death into life." If the Lord should come today, believers would be "caught up to meet Him in the air," to "see Him as He is," to enter into His glory. Neither death nor judgment is "appointed" unto believers.

But in Hebrews 9.28 we have in the words: **Christ . . . offered to bear the sins of many,** what Peter wrote of: "Who His own self bare our sins in His own body on the tree" (I Pet. 2.24). Or Paul, "Christ died for our sins" (I Cor. 15.3). It is the actual bearing of sins by the Substitute that is looked at here. Notice also the word "many":* as Paul writes in I Tim. 2.5-6, "Christ Jesus, Who gave Himself a ransom for all"; and as our Lord said in Matthew 26.28, "This is My blood of the covenant, which is poured out for *many* unto remission of sins."

Shall appear a second time, apart from sin (Gr., *choris hamartias,* "sin apart," as in Ch. 4.15) **unto salvation:** Compare Romans 13.11: "Now is our *salvation* nearer to us than when we first believed."† **Sin apart**—The sin question will not be brought up at

---

*"Solely His own [people] and not mankind indiscrimnately."—Kelly

" 'Many' is opposed here not to *all* but to *few*"—: Schlichting, from Alford.

†Not that we do not now possess *salvation:* we do: as see Lk. 1.77, Eph. 1.13, Phil. 1.28 and many other verses. Nor is it that our salvation is not being carried on: it *is:* I Cor. 1.18, margin; Phil. 3.20, 21. But our *salvation* will be consummated at the coming of the Lord Jesus and the redemption of our bodies.

Christ's second coming, any more than it is now being brought up by Christ, our Great High Priest, at God's right hand. He bare sin "once for all"!

To them that wait for Him—(A.V., "look for Him"): The verb in the Greek is a very intensive one:* meaning to wait eagerly or ardently. Let me here emphasize the fact that *all* whom our Lord has redeemed, *all* "they that are Christ's" are raised or raptured at His appearing. It is not a question here of those having "dispensa‧tional" instruction concerning our Lord's coming, concerning the distinction between the Rapture and the Revelation, known now by thousands of believers. Some "groaning" ones (Rom. 8.23) have not much knowledge of prophecy, yet they have the "firstfruits of the Spirit," and they are waiting for the glorious day of their adop‧tion, even the redemption of their bodies; and of course, being born again, their faith and hope are all in Christ. These all **wait for him** in the sense of Hebrews 9.28.

There are, sad to say, many thousands of true believers who have not yet fully entered into the great fact that their own sins are forever gone in Christ's death. Yet they once learned their lost, guilty condition; and threw themselves, like the publican of Luke 18, upon the mercy of God; and their hope is in Christ, though that hope be not yet blossomed out into confident assurance. So they are Christ's, and in the sweep of Divine grace, they are included. There are those also who, through personal failure, or from listening to weak, ignorant preaching, are spirit‧ually poor and wretched: yet their hope is in Christ. Thousands of backslidden ones, too, belong to Christ. Think of him of I Corinthians 5.1, and I Corinthians 11.21!

In I Corinthians 1.7, just quoted in the footnote, to those "wait‧ing for the revelation of our Lord Jesus Christ", there follows the promise, "Who shall also confirm you unto the end, that ye may be unreprovable in the day of our Lord Jesus Christ." But though they would be finally unreprovable," Paul at once sets out to reprove them! Yet these members of Christ's Body, of the "church of God," (1.2), called "babes in Christ" (3.1), are said to be *"wait‧ing for Christ,"* for His coming again.

---

*This word "wait" *apekdechomai* is found in Rom. 8.19, 23, 25, which verses set forth the spirit of the meaning, which is, "desired anticipation": "The earnest expectation

We do not say these things to excuse ignorance, spiritual poverty, backsliding, or sin of any kind, but the contrary. Nothing but grace could write the Corinthian epistles! *Grace is for those who need it,* as did they—and as do we, both in our walk, and in our judgment of others. Remember, you who deem that only a peculiar, "consecrated", "overcoming", "devoted" few are meant in Hebrews 9.28, that Paul did not threaten these carnal babes in Christ in Corinth with exclusion from the Rapture. He said,

"We all shall not sleep, but WE shall ALL be changed . . . The dead shall be raised incorruptible, and WE shall be changed . . . Thanks be to God, Who GIVETH US the victory through our Lord Jesus Christ. Wherefore, my beloved brethren, be ye steadfast" (I Cor. 15.52-58).

Blessed are they that are saying with Paul, "I know that in me, that is, in my flesh, dwelleth no good thing"; who have found that the law of life makes free from the law of sin and death. These, if true, are tender, and ready to weep over others, as was Paul.

Christ shall appear a second time . . . to them that wait for Him —that is, then, to *all* His own.*

In a sense, Chapter 9.24-28 sums up the whole book of **Hebrews.** For we have here first, the Person of Christ, entered into the Holy Place above. Then, His priesthood, "now to appear before the face of God for us." Then, the finality of His one offering: **Once at the consummation of the ages hath He been manifested to put away sin by the sacrifice of Himself.** And lastly, His second coming, **apart from sin.** These are the great themes of the exhortation TO THE HEBREWS.

---

of the creation *waiteth* for the revealing of the sons of God . . . We with patience *wait* for it." And in I Cor. 1.7: "Ye . . . *waiting* for the revelation of our Lord Jesus Christ."

See also Phil. 3.20, Gal 5.5. Thayer's definition of this word is, "assiduously and patiently to *wait*" for Him. Compare English, to *"wait out."* Liddell and Scott give, "expect anxiously."

*The "partial rapture" people refer to the "overcomers" of Rev. 2 and 3 as the only ones to be raptured. But God sets forth who are the overcomers, when the New Creation comes: Rev. 21.6, 7: "I will give unto him that is athirst of the fountain of the water of life freely. *He that overcometh* shall inherit these things; and I will be his God, and he shall be My son." It is plain that all that are born of God "overcome," for the following verse says, "But for the fearful, and unbelieving, and abominable, and murderers, and fornicators, and sorcerers, and idolaters, and all liars, *their* part shall be in the lake that burneth with fire and brimstone; which is the second death." Only two classes: those who have God and are His children; and, on the other hand, the eight-fold list of the eternally lost!

Erewhile I reasoned of Thy truth,
  I searched with toil and care;
From morn to night I tilled my field,
  And yet my field was bare.
There lie my books—for all I sought
  My heart possesses now.
The words are sweet that tell Thy love,
  The love itself art Thou.
One line I read—and then no more—
  I close the book to see
No more the symbol and the sign,
  But Christ revealed to me.
And thus my worship is, delight—
  My work, to see His Face,
With folded hands and silent lips
  Within His Holy place.
I sit an infant at His feet
  Where moments teach me more
Than all the toil, and all the books
  Of all the ages hoar.
I sought the truth, and found but doubt—
I wandered far abroad;
I hail the truth already found
  Within the heart of God.

                                        Ter Steegen

Chapter Ten

1   FOR THE LAW having a shadow of the good things
     to come, not the very image of the things, can never with
     the same sacrifices year by year, which they offer con-
     tinually, make perfect [in standing] them that draw nigh.
2   Else would they not have ceased to be offered? because
     the worshipers, having been once cleansed, would have
3   no more consciousness of sins. But in those sacrifices there
4   is a remembrance made of sins year by year. For it is
     impossible that the blood of bulls and goats should take
     away sins.

MANY DEAR SAINTS who delight in the Word of God insist on the study of the Old Testament types as setting forth fully
and accurately the things of Grace we are now enjoying, and the
good things to come when the Lord returns. Indeed, we have
known some beloved teachers so governed by Old Testament
typology as to permit no entrance of New Testament truth except
as explained and defined by Old Testament types.

But the first verse of Chapter 10 flatly denies to the types the
very thing that these people would give them: the Law (and its
entire economy) had a shadow of the good things to come, but
not the very image. The Greek word for "image" is *eikōn*. An
image, or *eikōn*, like a good statue or photograph, reveals features
and facts accurately. This a shadow cannot do. A tree casts its
shadow on the ground: you see its general shape; but you cannot
tell the kind of tree, or discern foliage, blossom, fruit. Now The Law
had *only* shadows. One who tries to turn these shadows into
images finds himself presently under their spell. Reversing things,
he judges facts by shadows.

Before we leave verse 1, let us remark that "image" *(eikōn)* sets
forth the substance, as in Matthew 22 (also Mk. 12, and Lk. 20)
our Lord asks concerning the denarius, a Roman coin, "Whose
image *(eikōn)* and superscription" (Caesar's name) "hath it?" This

image was no shadow of Caesar, no mere hint that such a being existed, but the man's very features portrayed on the metal.

But God says in Hosea 8.12, "I wrote for him the ten thousand things of My Law; but they are counted as a strange thing." The "things" here are the ordinances, precepts, judgments, sacrifices, ceremonies; but "My Law" lies in God's mind as one Law. Again, what about John 1.17: "For the Law was given through Moses; grace and truth came through Jesus Christ"? Can you maintain that the "ceremonial law" is referred to here, while God still holds over the believer what you call the "moral law," with its blessing conditioned on your obedience instead of on Christ's work?

Finally, what will you say, with your manmade distinction between what you call "ceremonial law" and what you really trust in, "the moral law," to the distinction God makes in II Corinthians 3 between lawkeeping and that blessed operation of the Spirit here described?

"Now the Lord is the Spirit; and where the Spirit of the Lord is, there is liberty. But we all, with unveiled face beholding as in a mirror the glory of the Lord, are transformed into the same image from glory to glory, even as from the Lord the Spirit" (Vss. 1718). Will you retain your "moral law" claim here? Very well, compare that to the contrast in that Chapter, verse 3. A Christian, as an epistle of Christ, is said to be "written *not* with ink, but with the Spirit of the living God," and further, "*not* in tables of stone, but in tables that are hearts of flesh." Now let your tables of stone go! There are your ten words, including the fourth commandment about the Sabbath, given to Israel as a token of God's relation to them (Ex. 31.13, 17; Neh. 9.1314). Let it go, for Christ (II Cor. 3.6) "made us [the apostles] sufficient as ministers of a *new* covenant; *not of the letter,* but of the spirit: for the letter killeth, but the spirit giveth life"! Mark, finally, that the Law, the Law given on stones, the ten words, is called in verse 7 (same chapter) "the ministration of death," and described as a passing thing: and in verse 9 as "the ministration of condemnation." You are a sinner, and the Law can for all eternity do nothing for you but condemn you. The Law did not even have **the very image of the** [heavenly] **things.** There had to be a *rectification* (Heb. 9.10, last word), a "vanishing away" of "that which is becoming old and waxeth aged."

But you cry, What shall take the place of the Law? We have believed that God forever controls His creatures by Law!

What do you do with "He chose us in Him before the foundation of the world, that we should be holy and without blemish before Him in love" (Eph. 1.4)? Do you still believe that the bending of your will to Divine enactments is a stronger method?

Take the great truth next set forth: **The Law can never with the same sacrifices . . . make perfect [in standing] them that draw nigh. Else (verse 2) would they not have ceased to be offered? because the worshipers, having once been cleansed, would have had no more conscience of sins:** If the Israelitish worshiper had known that his sins were all put away forever—which the instructed Christian knows *his* sins are, by the one offering of Christ —he would have had no more conscience of sins. (The A.V. reads, "conscience of sins".) Doubtless all the Levitical sacrifices pointed to Christ's sacrifice: but they effected *nothing* in the way of putting away sin. *Cleansing* is an *application,* connected with and following Divine forgiveness in Heaven. Cleansing is the removal of sins from the person justified! See Acts 22.16: "Arise, and be baptized, and *wash away thy sins,* calling on His name." (We shall return to this matter of cleansing in a moment.)

Again, Hebrews 10.3 says, **But in those [Levitical] sacrifices there is a remembrance made of sins year by year.** Let us at once put far from our thought that the Levitical sacrifices ever *removed* sins. God, in pardoning any sinner, in the Old Testament, looked forward to the work of His dear Son on the Cross. Conceive, therefore, of the true meaning and effect of those Levitical sacrifices: **a remembrance [not a removal] of sins year by year.**

To return to the word *cleansed.* This is not pardon, but the result of pardon. Scripture teaches that sins are *things;* that they are attached to the person, yea, to the very body of the sinner. Certain unpardoned sinners are thus described in Ezekiel 32.27: "They are gone down to Sheol . . . and their iniquities are *upon their bones.*" As we read in Psalm 109.18 of a wicked enemy of David (a prophecy of Judas Iscariot—vs. 8 and Acts 1.20),

"He clothed himself also with cursing as with his garment,
And it came into his inward parts like water,
And like oil *into his bones.*"

The pardoned man is described in Hebrews 10.2 as *cleansed*. Sins are removed from his person—literally! Christ bare our sins in His body on the tree. He was "delivered up for our trespasses, and raised for our justification." (Rom. 4.25). "So Christ also was once offered to bear the sins of many."

This being so, and God reckoning the atoning work of Christ to a believing sinner, his sins are removed forever from him, from his *person*. Thus is he, according to God's word in Hebrews 10.2, *"cleansed"*. Looking back at Calvary, he sees the removal of his sins by the shed blood of Christ, and is filled with peace and joy. But the very continuance of the Levitical offerings was proof of their ineffectiveness and "shadow" character.

The conscience of a devout Jew resembled the conscience of a devout Roman Catholic today. The Catholic must go to his "priest," to the "confessional," telling this man-made priest his sins; and the promise is, that the "priest" will get him forgiveness. The "priest" resorts to the figment of the "unbloody sacrifice" of "the Mass," for he knows not the finished work of Christ, by Whose blood sin was *put away* once for all, on the Cross. What the Romish "priest" finds and the Jew of old found, is **a remembrance of sins.***

Did a Hebrew sin? Had he committed a trespass? Let him bring the trespass offering according to Leviticus 4 to 6. But why, since on the Great Day of Atonement once a year (Lev. 16) the high priest carried the blood of the slain goat within the veil, then confessed all the transgressions and sins of the children of Israel upon the head of the live goat, and sent it away, bearing upon him "all their iniquities unto a solitary land"—why, when the high priest had done all this, should not a sinning Israelite later simply say, I will confess this trespass unto Jehovah, and rely upon the blood of the slain goat of the Day of Atonement?

He could not do that for two reasons: first, because the blood of the slain goat of Leviticus 16 did not put away all his sins forever,†

---

*Of course this is an illustration, and we shall not at heart compare the Divinely appointed Levitical system of sacrifices with the blasphemous performances of Rome's self-appointed priests. For to the pope's puppets, with whom He has nothing to do, God makes no promise of forgiveness of sins at all, which He did make to the Hebrew bringing the appointed offering under the Levitical system. (Lev. 4.20, 26, 28; 5.10, 13, 16, 18; 6.7).

†Note the seven cases of forgiveness: (1) "The whole congregation": Ch. 4.13, 20. (2)

as Christ's one Sacrifice has availed to do for us; second, because each worshiper was commanded to bring a trespass offering *each time* he sinned; and he also knew that the high priest must again offer the blood of a goat before Jehovah, and again confess the sins of the children of Israel over another living goat, and send it away, at the next yearly Atonement, and the next—the same forms year after year. For **in these sacrifices there is a remembrance** [not a removal], **made of sins year by year.** As we read:

Verse 4: **For it is impossible that the blood of bulls and goats should take away sins.** Therefore the Israelitish worshiper, be he ever so sincere, would only know that by his trespass offering he was forgiven up to date, but must be ready to offer another tres-pass offering upon another failure.* We repeat, the *removal* of sins, not the *reminding* the worshipper of them ("remembrance"), was the way in which the conscience was "cleansed." Sins must be "*taken away.*" If that were done, conscience would no longer accuse, there would be "no more consciousness [or conscience] of sins." "Cleansed," therefore, refers not at all to something done to the per-son of the worshiper, but to his sins' having been once for all re-moved or *taken away.*†

"A ruler": Ch. 4.22, 26. (3) "Anyone of the common people": Ch. 4.27, 31, 35. (4) "Any one": Ch. 5.1, 10, 13. (5) "If anyone commit a trespass and sin *unwittingly*": Ch. 5.15, 16. (6) "If any one sin and do" what "Jehovah commanded *not* to be done": Ch. 5.17, 18. (7) "If any one . . . deal falsely with his neighbor": Ch. 6.1, 7.

*Alas, many earnest professing Christians are practically upon Levitical ground as con-cerning Christ's sacrifice. They say, "I am saved if I hold out. And each time there is a failure, there must be a new application of the blood." *God* says, "If any man sin, we have an Advocate with the Father, Jesus Christ the Righteous: and He is the propitiation [on the ground of His once-for-all putting away sins] for our sins." A believer's sin does not come in before God as Judge, at all. It was *all* dealt with on Calvary!

†Note the recurrence in Scripture of this thought, to take away sins:
"He hath given it [the sin-offering] to you to *take away* [R.V., margin] the iniquity of the congregation, to make atonement for them before Jehovah" (Lev. 10.17).
"On this day [the Great Day of Atonement] shall atonement be made for you, to cleanse you: from all your sins shall ye be clean before Jehovah" (Lev. 16.30).
"And why dost Thou not pardon my transgression, and *take away* mine iniquity?" (Job 7.21).
"Therefore by this shall the iniquity of Jacob be forgiven [margin, *expiated*], and this is all the fruit of *taking away* his sins (Isa. 27.9).
"Take with you words and return unto Jehovah: say unto Him, *Take away* all iniquity" (Hos. 14.2).
(Jeremiah speaking of those that "contended with" him): "*Forgive not* their iniquity, *neither blot out* their sin from Thy sight" (Jer. 18.19, 23).
"Then flew one of the seraphim unto me, having a live coal in his hand, which he had taken with the tongs from off the altar: and he touched my mouth with it, and said, Lo, this hath touched thy lips, and *thine iniquity is taken away, and thy sin forgiven*" (margin,

But because the once for all putting away of sin forever from God's sight (see Ch. 9.26) is so seldom and so feebly grasped by Christian believers, these Levitical oft-repeated sacrifices are taken as setting forth Christian experience. Thus, even our Lord's priesthood is, in the heart of hearts of most believers, somehow connected with atonement. If it were told to the average real Christian, "Jesus in Heaven will never put away another sin for you," it would strike him with real terror: for he has not rested in that once for all putting away sin at the Cross concerning which Christ said, "It is finished."*

That it is **impossible that the blood of bulls and goats should take away sin** is at once apparent: compare in your mind the pre-

---

expiated.) Isa. 6.6, 7).

"And I will *cleanse* them from all their *iniquity*, whereby they have sinned against Me; and I will *pardon* all their iniquities, whereby they have sinned . . . and transgressed against Me" (Jer. 33.8).

"In those days, and in that time, saith Jehovah, the iniquity of Israel shall be sought for, and there shall be none; and the sins of Judah, and they shall not be found: for I will pardon them whom I leave as a remnant" (Jer. 50.20). Note pardon connected with the removal of iniquity.

"I, even I, am He that blotteth out thy transgressions for Mine own sake: and I will not remember thy sins" (Isa. 43.25).

"I will save [the children of Israel] from all their backslidings [margin] wherein they have sinned, and will *cleanse* them" (Ezek. 37.23).

"And I will *cleanse* [hold as innocent, margin] their blood, that I have not cleansed: for Jehovah dwelleth in Zion" (Joel 3.21).

"According to the multitude of Thy tender mercies blot out my transgressions.

Wash me thoroughly from mine *iniquity*,

And *cleanse* me from my sin" (Ps. 51.1, 2).

"As far as the east is from the west,

So far hath He removed our transgressions from us" (Ps. 103.12).

"Jesus seeing their faith said to the sick of the palsy, Son, be of good cheer; thy sins are *forgiven*" (Matt. 9.2).

"John . . . seeth Jesus coming unto him, and saith, Behold, the Lamb of God, that *taketh away* the sin of the world" (Jno. 1.29).

"Ye know that He was manifested to *take away* sins" (I Jno. 3.5).

Ananias said unto Saul, "Why tarriest thou? arise, and be baptized, and *wash away* thy sins" (Acts 22.16).

"And this is My covenant unto them, when I shall *take away* their sins" (Rom. 11.27).

"If we confess our sins, He is faithful and righteous to *forgive us our sins*, and to *cleanse us from all unrighteousness*" (I Jno. 1.9).

---

*This leads us to say, Most Christians *do not have peace*. If my house is mortgaged, and I am in daily expectation of foreclosure, what can give me rest? One thing: for some one to pay off the mortgage, and let me behold it cancelled: then I can rest. In Heaven now, at God's right hand, He is not atoning for sin! That would make Him simply the equal of one of the Levitical priests who kept standing, offering up sacrifices for sin daily. This, Christ is *not* now doing. Why? This He did as Priest, once for all and forever, on the Cross.

Every Christian uncertain whether all his sins have been put away forever, needs to look to God's words about the Cross and the death of Christ, not to His priestly work on high. The mortgage on your soul has been paid off: "One sacrifice for sins forever"! Oh, read Ch. 10.12 over and over, repeat it daily, hourly, if need be; and say, It was for me!

cious blood of Him Who did put away sins, with the blood of these animals! You may ask then, Why did God prescribe sin and trespass offerings of their blood? Well, first, to bring sin to the remembrance, to consideration, by the trespasser; (2) to make him see that the Divine sentence upon his sin was death; (3) to make him see that God had a way and plan of mercy, for the trespasser was to be forgiven—till he should trespass again; (4) to bring some apprehension of substitutionary atonement to the offender's mind. Read most carefully Leviticus 4.1-12—better still, Chapters 4 to 6. From the Cross we look back and understand as the Israel-ites of old could not; and yet they could see even then that sin was to be forgiven on the ground of substitutionary sacrifice, that is, through blood shedding, or through blood.

Nevertheless, no offerer under the Levitical system ever went away with a conscience "cleansed" forever.*

5   Wherefore when He cometh into the world, He saith,
         Sacrifice and offering Thou wouldest not,
         But a body didst Thou prepare for Me;
6   In whole burnt offerings and sacrifices for sin Thou
         hadst no pleasure:
7 Then said I, Lo, I am come
         (In the roll of the book it is written of Me)
         To do Thy will, O God.
8   Saying above, Sacrifices and offerings and whole burnt
         offerings and sacrifices for sin Thou wouldest not, neither
         hadst pleasure therein (the which are offered according
9   to the Law), then hath He said, Lo, I am come to do
         Thy will. He taketh away the first, that He may establish
10   the second. By which will we have been sanctified through
         the offering of the body of Jesus Christ once for all.

Verses 5, 6: There is a perfect illustration of a saint's appre-hension of the truth that God **had no pleasure** in the death of the sacrificial animals; and that these had no efficacy in *putting away* sin, in David's prayer in Psalm 51. Adultery; murder to hide it; re-fusal to judge himself; impenitence and guile till Bathsheba's child was born and had become dear to David—all this had come in when the prophet Nathan charged home his sin upon him (II Sam. 12); yet told him that God had put away his sin, and he should not

---
*See Appendix E.

die. Read this 51st psalm: you say, Was not David under the Law? Outwardly, yes. That is, the Law was the external method of a gracious God in dealing with the Jewish nation. You say, Were not sin-offerings and trespass-offerings prescribed? Yes, as you read in Leviticus 4.22 ff:

"When a ruler sinneth, and doeth unwittingly any one of all the things which Jehovah His God hath commanded not to be done, and is guilty; if his sin, wherein he hath sinned, be made known to him, he shall bring for his oblation a goat, a male without blemish. And he shall lay his hand upon the head of the goat, and kill it . . . it is a sin-offering."

But David did not do this; instead he went directly to God:

"Have mercy upon me, O God," he asked, "according to Thy loving-kindness:"

(Not according to the principles of the Law, but according to the realities of His own Being).

"According to the multitude of Thy tender mercies blot out my transgressions." (Ps. 51.1).

Then he said,

"For Thou delightest not in sacrifice; else would I give it:
Thou hast *no pleasure* in burnt-offering.
The sacrifices of God are a broken spirit:
A broken and a contrite heart, O God, Thou wilt not despise."
(Ps. 51.16-17).

This we find revealed in Psalm 40.6-8, quoted in Hebrews 10.5-7:

5   Wherefore when He cometh into the world, He saith,
     Sacrifice and offering Thou wouldest not,
        But a body didst Thou prepare for Me;*

---

*There is something exquisitely beautiful in this quotation in Hebrew:
"Sacrifice and offering Thou hast no delight in;
Ears hast Thou pierced for Me;" (R. V., margin.)
This is the fulfillment by our blessed Lord of Ex. 21.6, the very first "ordinance" after the Law was given; where the "Hebrew bondman" so delights in his master that he says, "I love my master, my wife, and my children; I will not go out free"—when he *might* go out free at the seventh year.

"Then his master shall bring him unto God [or, the judges] and shall bring him to the door, or unto the door-post; and his master shall bore his ear through with an awl; and he shall serve him forever" (Ex. 21.5, 6).

This is the very spirit of what our Lord chose to do, and wonderful to relate, in passing out Ps. 40 into the Greek language, reaching all the earth (the Septuagint was translated about 270-285 B.C.—Angus), the Spirit of God, Who watched over His Word (Jer. 1.12), saw to it that the type was here set before us in its fulfillment, so that Christ's prophetic word, "Ears hast Thou digged for Me," becomes in the book of Hebrews, translated into Greek (quoting the Septuagint), "A body didst Thou prepare for Me."

6   In whole burnt offerings and sacrifices for sin Thou hadst
     no pleasure:
7   Then said I, Lo, I am come
     (In the roll of the book it is written of Me)
     To do Thy will, O God.

What a discovery David made! This was not David's "breaking
the Law." It was his going to the very spirit of God's will, casting
himself as guilty on a God of mercy. David knew *grace* perhaps
better than any Old Testament saint. You remember how the Lord
Jesus referred the legalistic Jews to his (David's) eating the showbread which our Lord said was "not lawful for him to eat, neither
for them that were with him, but only for the priests" (Matt.
12.1-4).

This brings us face to face with an overwhelming fact: that the
Law was not that in the fulfillment of which God trusted; nor in the
sacrifices of which *as such* (but only as types of Christ) He delighted.* It will *not be under Law* that His saints will be before Him
in the New Jerusalem, in eternity! But "They shall see His face; and
His name shall be on their foreheads." We were "chosen in Him
before the foundation of the world that we should be holy and without blemish before Him IN LOVE"—not under Law!†

Let us be instructed: If David, who was outwardly under Law,
discerned that animal sacrifice did not delight God; if he threw himself upon the mercy of God, what shall be said about us, if we do

---

(Nearly all godly and scholarly commentators on Hebrews state that Paul invariably, in
quoting O.T., used the Septuagint. See Angus, Alford, Stuart, etc.)

*How frightful is the wickedness of those who speak of Jehovah as "delighting in the
slaughterhouse," and thus reject the sacrifice of Christ for their sins! These will shortly
answer direct to Him Who said, He "delighteth not in sacrifice" (Ps. 51.16); and Heb.
10.5, Sacrifice and offering Thou wouldest not. Blood sacrifices were necessary, we repeat.
But how hateful for men, creatures to whom God gives life and breath and all things, walking through a world of beauty created by a loving God Who cares daily for all His
creatures,—how hideous that bits of selfish, guilty, condemned dust, should call true Christianity "a slaughterhouse religion"!

†But there seems no hope of turning Christendom back from the "other gospel" (Gal.
1.8) which has brought in the Law as a "rule of life," daring to rob it of its power to
curse, but professing that its enactments are God's final method of governing His people:
"giving them power through the Spirit to keep it." But all this is a falsehood. God says
that even those who were under the Law were made dead to it by the body of Christ-made-
sin (on the Cross) that they might be "joined to Another, even to Him Who was raised
from the dead"—with what effect? "that we might bring forth fruit unto God . . . So that
we serve in newness of the Spirit," in happy freedom, "and *not* in oldness of the letter"
(Rom. 7.4-6). "A *new* covenant, *not* of the letter, but of the Spirit: for the letter killeth,
but the Spirit giveth life" (II Cor. 3.6).

not obey the "Let us draw near" of **Hebrews** (4.16, 7.19, 10.22)
since Christ the Son of God has come and put away sin by His
infinite sacrifice, and God commands us to *draw near,* relying
upon His shed blood, because the veil is rent, and Christ our Great
High Priest is there? Dare you say, I am not worthy? Was Christ
offered for *worthy* people? A thousand shames upon such nigh-
blasphemous unbelief!

Verse 7: **Then said I, Lo, I am come**
            (In the roll of the book it is written of Me)
            To do Thy will, O God.
Here is summed up our Lord's blessed work.

First, **Then said I, Lo, I am come**—Here is the Creator entering
the world, as Gabriel said to Mary,

"The Holy Spirit shall come upon thee, and the power of the
Most High shall keep overshadowing thee."

God the Father prepared our Lord a body by the Holy Spirit's
power. Nonetheless Deity, He is there in the manger, having entered the creation He created. And His eye is ever toward the
Father Who sent Him. These words, **Lo, I am come,** are addressed
after His birth to His Father.

Second, **In the roll of the book it is written of Me**—Ah, that
Scripture! How infinitely dear to our blessed Lord! Unto this
blessed "roll of the book" God wakened Him "morning by morning . . . to hear" (Isa. 50.4-6). Even at last, on the Cross, "Jesus
knowing that all things are now finished, *that the Scripture might
be accomplished,* saith, I thirst" (Jno. 19.28).

Third, **To do Thy will, O God:** Take the four Gospels, upon
your first opportunity, and find and mark our Lord's constantly re-
peated testimony that He "came to do the will of Him that sent
Him." Over and over He told His disciples that He was going up to
Jerusalem to be crucified and the third day be raised from the dead.
Triumphantly, just before His ascension He said,

"These are My words which I spake unto you, while I was yet
with you, that all things must needs be fulfilled, *which are written*
in the Law of Moses, and the prophets, and the psalms, concerning
Me" (Lk. 24.44).

Had He not said as He was going up to Jerusalem, "I have meat to
eat that ye know not . . . My meat is to *do the will* of Him that
sent Me, and to accomplish His work"? (Jno. 4.32, 34).

Verses 8-9: Now comes the Divine application of this precious passage: **Saying above, Sacrifices and offerings and whole burnt offerings and sacrifices for sin Thou wouldst not, neither hadst pleasure therein (the which are offered according to the Law), then hath He said, Lo, I am come to do Thy will.** Here are the four classes of offerings enumerated, with the amazing statement that God did not desire them or have pleasure in them: though from Moses to Christ they were offered **according to the Law.** However much God might delight in the loving subjection of the offerer, yet no offering whatever was in itself His delight, except as pointing to Calvary.*

Verse 9, contd.: **He taketh away the first, that He may establish the second:** Note here that "the first," the sacrifices "offered according to the Law," must be "taken away," before "the second," Christ's infinite sacrifice, can be "established," for God Himself gave the Law and the Levitical code, with its sacrifices. Now if Christ is to come with His one infinite sacrifice for sin—if that be God's will, then the other, the multiplied sacrifices, must disappear. "The first" must here mean all the Law economy, as we read in Chapter 7.18-9, "A disannulling of a foregoing commandment [the Law] . . . and a bringing in thereupon of a better hope." For Christ, and Christ alone, must perform God's will. His work is, therefore, the "second" thing of the verse we are studying, Chapter 10.9.

Therefore, to sum up this most important verse, two matters stand out: first, as over against the oft-repeated sacrifices of verse

---

*For example, you need a load of wood: you go to your wood man, and he takes you to a large oak tree in the far corner of the lot. Pointing to the long shadow it casts, he offers to sell you this *shadow*. Will you take it? Now, if God says that in the Law there was a *shadow*, not even the very image of the things—and, of course, not the things themselves, why will you hold to the shadow? Yet Reformation theology does so, alas!

How wonderfully clear in this epistle is God's repeated declaration that the old Levitical things, yea, the whole Law, had been supplanted:

In Ch. 7.18, 19 it is, "There is a *disannulling* of a foregoing commandment . . . (for the Law made nothing perfect)."

In Ch. 8.6 it is, "He is also the Mediator of a better covenant, which hath been enacted upon better promises." In verse 13: "In that He saith, A new covenant, He hath made the first old. But that which is becoming old and waxeth aged is nigh unto vanishing away."

In Chapter 9.9-10, "gifts and sacrifices" offered according to the first tabernacle, "cannot, as touching the conscience, make the worshiper perfect, being . . . carnal ordinances, imposed until a time of rectification."

8, *Christ* had come **to do God's will**—in this place, as to sacrifice. Second, that **the first** (Levitical system of sacrifices) was **taken away, that He may establish the second.**

Note then that it is not the devotion to God's will, abstractly considered, blessed as that is, that is here in view; but that express will of God by which Christ was offered up on the Cross. Consequently, we come to verse 10, which (along with verse 14), must be studied by us with the greatest attention:

Verse 10: **By which will we have been sanctified through the offering of the body of Jesus Christ once for all:** The moment we come to the word "sanctified," the holy life of the believer comes to mind. But this meaning is not possible here. For, the statement is, **We have been sanctified through the offering of the body of Jesus Christ once for all**—not through the operation of the Holy Spirit, nor through consecration or devotion,* but as the result of Christ's work for us. Christ will need to make no further offering! We are completely, eternally, gloriously *separated to* God. This peculiar result of Christ's one offering should be emphasized to every believer at the very beginning, as Paul says to the Corinthians, "Ye are *not your own; for ye were bought with a price:*

---

*Concerning the word for "sanctify" *(hagiadzein)*, Thayer well says: "Since the stamp of sacredness passes over from the holiness of God to whatever has any connection with God, *hagiadzein* denotes to *separate* from things profane, and dedicate to God."

The word is even twice used in I Cor. 7.14 concerning the unbelieving husband "sanctified" by the wife—and the unbelieving wife "sanctified" in the husband. That is, God regards the home of such ones as—as we would say—"Christian,"—entirely different from a wholly unbelieving home. This was not, of course, because of any operation of the Spirit in either the unbelieving husband or unbelieving wife.

"Sanctified," then, in Hebrews means *set apart to God* wholly, not referring to our "surrender" or "consecration" or action of the Holy Spirit within us, I Thess. 5.23, II Thess. 2.13; and I Pet. 1.2, where believers are seen as "elect . . . according to the foreknowledge of God the Father, in *sanctification* of the Spirit, unto obedience and sprinkling of the blood of Jesus Christ."

We see in these words of I Pet. 1.2, that the blood of sprinkling and the sanctifying of the Spirit are distinct, connected with different persons of the Trinity. We are born of the Spirit; baptized by the Spirit into the Body of Christ; indwelt by the Spirit; filled with the Spirit, and are to walk by the Spirit, Who by His indwelling power "cleanses our hearts by faith." But sanctification in Hebrews is looked at as the effect of Christ's death, on account of which God counts anyone believing the gospel and confessing Christ's name as cut off from the world, separated to Him.

This (as compare Thayer, above) was what was meant of old when God said, "Whatsoever *toucheth the altar* shall be holy." The character of the object was not changed, but its relation to God was changed.

(Alas, people thus professing and confessing *may* afterward turn their back, indeed, as do those in Heb. 10.29, rejecting the Christian position, and refusing to regard longer as of infinite worth, the blood of Christ, "the blood of the covenant wherewith they were *sanctified*," as the one thing that separates to God).

glorify God therefore in your body" (I Cor. 6.19, 20). The recognition of this separating to God not only brings rest and untold blessing to the believer, but is the only attitude of soul consistent with the facts. For Christ said, "They are *not of the world,* even as I am not of the world." **Through the offering of the body of Jesus Christ once for all,** we were, then, "sanctified," or separated to God: for, the shedding of His blood took away all our sin and guilt; and, being identified with Him, Who was made *to be sin* on our behalf, we died with Him; and since He died *unto* sin and now lives to God, we also are commanded to do so, since He is our Adam, and what happened to Him belongs to us: "Reckon ye also yourselves to be dead unto sin, but alive unto God in Christ Jesus" (Rom. 6.2, 6, 10, 11). For we were cut off from the human race in Adam, at the Cross; and created in Christ Risen, the Second Man, the Last Adam. This is true of all believers and of all those who are in Christ.

We shall see that in verse 14, which is plainly to be connected with verse 10, it is emphasized further that **by one offering He hath perfected forever them that are sanctified**—separated unto God. This can have no reference to our "growth in grace," which belongs, as we have seen, to the operation of the blessed Spirit. **Perfected forever** must therefore refer to the absoluteness of the effect of Christ's work on the Cross: both in respect of the putting away of our guilt and defilement through His blood; and the removal of sins from our persons forever, in His death, which separated us unto God. That work has *"perfected"* us forever, inasmuch as we are one with Christ before God, as we have seen. There is no difference in this respect between one saint and another: there cannot be, since all are in Christ.

11 **And every priest indeed standeth day by day ministering and offering oftentimes the same sacrifices, the which can**
12 **never take away sins: but He, when He had offered one sacrifice for sins forever, sat down on the right hand of**
13 **God; henceforth expecting till His enemies be made the**
14 **footstool of His feet. For by one offering He hath perfected forever them that are sanctified.**

In this passage we have seven elements: (1) The *standing* priests. (2) The **day-by-day** repeated sacrifices, utterly unable to **take** away sins. (3) Christ's offering one sacrifice for sins forever. (4) His sitting down on the right hand of God. (5) His *"expecting"* His coming triumph over His foes in His millennial kingdom. (6) The inspired witness of the Holy Spirit to Christ's blessed work, No more offering for sin (vs. 18). (7) His one offering perfected the saints forever!

The central words in all this passage are one sacrifice, expecting, perfected, sat down. We draw especial attention to the words sat down. A seated priest argues a *completed* work.*

Verse 12: But He when He had offered one sacrifice for sins forever, sat down on the right hand of God—It is offering up *once for all* that is of eternal consequence. It is important to trans-late this central verse as do both the King James and the Revised Version, that is, the Greek words meaning "for ever" *(eis to diēnekēs),* are to be taken with the preceding verb, "offered," rather than with the following verb, "sat down."

But on the other hand, if we allow the phrase translated "for ever"† to modify offered one sacrifice, and read offered one sacrifice for ever, all is clear. Christ sat down on the right hand of God. Why? Read godly Andrew Murray's note (and others), quoted below; and mark its spiritual understanding.‡

---

*Contrast the blasphemous performances of the Romish "priests": you never heard one of them preaching on the finished work of Christ, the One Sacrifice, and our Lord's session at God's right hand in view of it. But there is always some so-called "priestly" activity on the part of these Judaeo-pagan pope-appointed "priests." They are always *standing* gabbing in Latin, an unknown tongue; or fiddling about their Satanic invention of the "unbloody sacrifice of the Mass."

Scripture (Rev. 1.5) gives glory unto our blessed Lord thus: "Unto Him that loved us, and loosed us from our sins by His blood; and He made us to be a kingdom, to be *priests* unto His God and Father; to Him be the glory and the dominion for ever and ever. Amen."

Yea, all believers are priests, and this only is Scriptural.

The pope-appointed "priests" make "signs" of the Cross, but never preach the work of Christ finished there!

†We have in this tenth chapter three of the four occurrences in N. T. of this remarkable phrase, eis to diēnekēs: vss. 1, 12, 14. The fourth in Ch. 7.3.

‡By one offering He hath perfected forever them that are sanctified (vs. 14). The *once* of Christ's work is the secret of its being *forever:* the more clear the acceptance of that Divine once-for-all, the more sure the experience of that Divine *forever,* the continually abiding working of the power of the endless life.

"*Once* and *forever:* see how the two go together in the work of Christ in its two principal manifestations. In His death, His sacrifice, His bloodshedding, it is once for all. The propitiation for sin, the bearing and the putting away of it, was so complete that of His suffering again, or offering Himself again, there can never be any thought. God now remembers the sin no more forever."—Murray.

"The sacrifice was efficacious forever, through all time, being appropriated by each be-

In verse 13, we find Him **henceforth expecting till His enemies be made the footstool of His feet.** But this, according to all prophecy, was to follow His one sacrificial work—as it will indeed—and, we today believe, follow swiftly.

Verse 14: **For by one offering He hath perfected** [in standing] **forever them that are sanctified** [made to be saints]: When the heart realizes that sin has all been put away forever, the conscience becomes "perfected,"* in the language of **Hebrews** (10.1, 14), and then, and not until then, does the thought of an ever-continuing High Priest become a delight. (See again comment on vs. 14 under vs. 10).

15 And the Holy Spirit also beareth witness to us; for after He hath said,

16   This is the covenant that I will make with them after those days, saith the Lord:

    I will put My laws on their heart,

    And upon their mind also will I write them;

    then saith He,

17   And their sins and their iniquities will I remember no more.

18   Now where remission of these is, there is no more offering for sin.

In verses 15-17 above we find again the verses from Jeremiah quoted in Chapter 8.10-12. They are quoted also as the direct inspiration of the Holy Spirit to Hebrew believers: **The Holy Spirit also beareth witness to us.** (This word "witness," by the way, is the most direct reference to the work of the Holy Spirit in the believer in all **Hebrews).**

---

liever (vs. 14). The connection of *eis to diēnekēs* with the following *ekathisen* (forever sat down), is contrary to the usage of the Epistle; it obscures the idea of the perpetual efficacy of Christ's one sacrifice; it weakens the contrast with *esteken;* and it imports a foreign idea into the image of the assumption *(ekathisen)* of royal dignity by Christ."—Westcott.

" 'Forever'; construe with 'offered'. The reason appears in vs. 14. It is according to the usage of the epistle to place this phrase *after* that which it qualifies. Thus **one sacrifice forever** is contrasted with the same sacrifices often. This agrees also with what follows. He offered one sacrifice forever, and then sat down awaiting its eternal result."—Vincent.

*A "perfect" conscience in **Hebrews** does not mean that of a perfected, or fullgrown, believer. A babe in Christ might learn that his sins had been put forever away: he might believe the Word of God in I Pet. 2.24: "Who His own self bare our sins in His body upon the Tree"; he would have many things to learn, and indeed he might be at that time in ignorance doing that with which God was not pleased. But that is not the question. The minute he should see that Christ bore his sins and by His blood put them away before God, his *conscience* would be at rest.

Verse 16: **This is the covenant that I will make with them—**
See Chapter 8 for comment on the covenants.

Verse 17: The application that is made of Jeremiah's prophecy
in this connection is, to insist that since God said: **And their sins
and their iniquities will I remember no more,** therefore, **(vs. 18)
Where remission of these is, there is no more offering for sin.**
How utterly wonderful are these words! The infinitely holy God,
Who knows all about all human sins and iniquities, Who alone
saith of man, "I know their thoughts," declares to His saints, **I
will remember (your) sins and iniquities no more!** Surely *all* things
are possible with God! Certainly, then, **There is no more offering
for sin!** Sins have been remitted, remembered no more forever!

Verse 18: In the words, **No more offering for sin,** we reach the
conclusion of the doctrinal part of this great epistle to the
Hebrews. Would it might sink into the heart of every reader that
the only offering for sin that will ever be made *has* been made on
the Cross, and can be rested in by any willing heart! From the "Now
once at the consummation of the ages hath He been manifested to
put away sin by the sacrifice of Himself" (Ch. 9.26) follow on to
the *"Once* offered to bear the sins of many" (Ch. 9.28), and to
"The offering of the body of Jesus Christ *once for all"* (Ch. 10.10),
"One Sacrifice for sins forever" (10.12), "By *one offering* He hath
perfected forever them that are sanctified" (vs. 14), down to verse
18, **There is no more offering for sin!** The soul that leans or rests
on that **ONE OFFERING** will spend eternity in the delights of
Heaven!

Since **Hebrews** is an epistle of exhortation, and in verses 19-25 of
this chapter we have the great central exhortation, the consideration of this next passage becomes most important:

19   **Having therefore, brethren, boldness to enter into the**
20   **Holiest by the blood of Jesus, by the way which He**
      dedicated for us, a freshly-slain and living way, through
21   **the veil, that is to say, His flesh; and having a Great Priest**
22   **over the house of God; let us draw near with a true heart**
      in fullness of faith, having our hearts sprinkled from an
      evil conscience: and having our body washed with pure
23   **water, let us hold fast the confession of our hope that it**
24   **waver not; for He is faithful that promised: and let us**
      consider one another to provoke unto love and good

25 works; not forsaking our own assembling together, as the custom of some is, but exhorting one another; and so much the more, as ye see the day drawing nigh.

I

Three things we have: (1) **Boldness to enter into the Holiest by the blood of Jesus (vs. 19);** (2) **A freshly-slain and living way through the veil, that is to say, His flesh (vs. 20);** (3) **A Great Priest over the House of God (vs. 21).**

II

Five things we are to do: **(1) Draw near, (2) Hold fast confession, (3) Consider one another, (4) Assemble together, (5) Exhort one another (vss. 22-25).**

III

Having a Great Priest over the house of God, LET US DRAW NEAR—
It is into the presence of God, as God, that believers are invited to come with boldness. Our own salvation is, of course, the first thing; and next come love and service toward Him Who saved us: publishing the good tidings to all whom we should reach. Third, we become occupied with God's plan of salvation, doctrinally; and if we are instructed aright, we learn to expect the coming again of the Lord from Heaven, to rapture His Body, the Church, and to sit upon His millennial throne in Jerusalem.

But all these things may be true of us without our entering into that worship into which Hebrews introduces us. **To have boldness to enter into the Holiest . . . draw near with a true heart in fullness of faith,** involves an active godliness which superficial study of the Scriptures may not beget in us. How many saints do we know, who, when they pray, carry us with them into the very presence of God? But Christ is there, maintaining forever that character set forth in verse 20: **the Way which He dedicated for us, a FRESHLY-SLAIN* AND LIVING WAY.** It is eternally as if *just now* He had borne our sins in His own body on the Tree, as if *just now* He had said, "It is finished," and the soldier had pierced His side and there had come forth blood and water. He is

---

***Freshly-slain,** R.V.: "new": (Gr., *prosphatos*): "Properly, lately slaughtered." (Thayer.) "The original sense would be, 'newly slain.' . . . Later the word was weakened into 'new.' " —(Vincent).

evermore freshly-slain. Not, mark it, slain anew, but there before God Who inhabiteth eternity, as His Lamb, provided in His infinite love, and just now slain! How shall a sinner then dare be filled longer with terror of God? God's eyes are on His Son perpetually as upon a Lamb just slain, Who has just now put away sin.

"My God is reconciled,
His pardoning voice I hear.
He claims me as His child,
    I can no longer fear.
With confidence I now draw nigh,
    And Father, Abba, Father, cry."

It will not do for us to *stop* at the Cross where Christ shed His blood for our sins, and where we have peace through that blood, security from Divine judgment. For the blood of Christ has a heavenly ever-present power and efficacy connected with our acceptance and worship, and this is the peculiar message of **Hebrews**. If we do not become worshipers, really occupied with the things of God, with the praises as well as prayers which the blood of Christ has made a delight to God, at which Heaven wonders and worships, this great Epistle to the Hebrews has failed to reach our hearts. For the immediate presence of the all-holy God, Whose Name is LOVE, is where Christ is now sitting; whither every true believer is going; and into which, by the principle of faith, every believer is exhorted to **enter with boldness.***

---

*I have frequently asked an audience of believers, "How many of you want to go to Heaven?"

All hands go up. Then I put another question: "How many of you want to go to Heaven *today*?" A silence falls, and then here and there goes up a hand of some one whose earthly hopes have died out, and to whom the world has become weary. *They* want to go to Heaven, for they are through with earth. The rest want to go eventually, but as I have often said to Florida audiences, "You want to go to Heaven when you have to, but you want to stay in Florida as long as you can!"

But is this to be the spirit of the saints in the book of Hebrews? No, a thousand times No! On the contrary, God says, Come near, enter boldly, now, today! And not as with Levitical priests of old, for a brief tarrying for prescribed worship, but to abide forever. For we read in the last chapter, "Through Him [Jesus] let us offer up a sacrifice of praise to God *continually*" (13. 15).

And if people "neglect," or "doubt," or "refuse," to draw nigh to God in Heaven, into the presence of God, as a worshiper now—what is that? It is an insult against God Himself, against His holy Being (which was satisfied by the blood of His Son); against His infinite love (which was shown in the free gift of that Son to die); against His righteousness, against His majesty—as the Judge of all; against His truth—for unbelief makes Him a liar! Unbelief is the root sin.

Since the death of the Son of God, which in its value utterly put away sin before God, there have been no degrees of standing for those who rely on Christ's shed blood. It is not, as in the old tabernacle, a place into which the people can come, and then the priests, and

Through the veil, that is to say, His flesh—"The Word was made flesh, and tabernacled among us," wrote John. But no one as yet came in before God in Heaven. "The way into the holiest was not yet made manifest" (Heb. 9.8). But when our Lord was pierced, when He poured out His blood, laid down that life (which was indeed His blood—Lev. 17.11), and was raised up, through and in that pierced flesh—behold! the veil was gone! Was not sin gone? Yes, **by the blood of Jesus.** Was not He the Son of God? Yea, indeed, yet He was man: "See My hands and My feet, that it is I Myself." Were we "made nigh unto God"? Yes, in Christ's blood. And His pierced flesh proves all this to our hearts, and lo: we are before the throne of grace in Heaven! So we **enter into the Holies (1) by the blood of Jesus, (2) by the newly slain and living way*, (3) through the veil†** . . . **His flesh, and (4) we have Him as our Great Priest over the house of God.**

Therefore all human "religion" has become an insult to God, a denial of Christ's finished work, a turning away from grace back to legal things, a refusal to **draw near with a true heart,** relying on the shed blood of Christ and on His presence as our Great High Priest. God's dear Son is seated at His right hand in all the acceptance of His perfect sacrifice. There is no cessation, day or night, in the delight God has in Christ and His work. But down on earth, people are "observing sabbaths" (despite Col. 2.17); abstaining from certain meats, or from all meats on certain days;

---

finally, the high priest, once a year, into the Holy of Holies, the very presence of God. Whether believers realize it or not, the full value of the blood of Christ is reckoned to them by God. They are invited to come into God's immediate presence. All believers are so, here in **Hebrews.**

*"The Way must be opened, for every other way is closed. Through the veil: the veil of the Holy of Holies is rent. Christ's work does not stop short of the believer's complete access to God Himself, **through the veil,** which consisted in **His flesh.** His flesh was the state through which He had to pass before He entered Heaven for us. The veil of the temple was rent. He passed through humanity to glory as the Forerunner of His people."— Vincent, **Word Studies in the N. T.,** pp. 499-0, Vol. IV.

†On the Cross, upon our Lord's death, the veil of the temple, we know, was rent in two from the top (God's side) to the bottom. This was the veil within which the high priest of Israel was permitted to enter once a year on the Great Day of Atonement. It witnessed this: that Israel, by the whole Levitical ceremony, was shut out from God's immediate presence. But what was signified by the rending of it? First, that which separated man from God's immediate presence was gone. Second, any religious rites, ceremonies, observances, would constitute a rebuilding of the barrier between man and God, and therefore a denial of the rent veil, and a rejection of our Lord's word, "It is finished." Third, all official priesthood is by the rent veil denied. There is no such thing! All believers are alike priests, and our Lord is the one Great High Priest above.

"going to church" as a "religious" duty; even going to "the confessional," to a "priest." Others are glorying in men, in "Doctor"
this or that, in "my church"—all which things are contrary to
Scripture, subversive of the truth, and dishonoring to God. For
they ignore the Great High Priest and the heavenly worship being
carried on in the Spirit, and the "access" to God's throne which is
continually exhorted in this great book of Hebrews.

But there came a time in A.D. 70 when God had Titus burn the
temple of the Jews and destroy Jerusalem, having warned the
saints to flee the city (Lk. 21.20-24)—a warning which history
tells us they obeyed. So also will it be with those today who
either indifferently or presumptuously keep on with things God
says are done away. He will by and by deal with such inattention
and disobedience.* Of course, God looks at the heart: where there
is true grace and devotion to Himself, He puts up with "religious"
performances, though an abhorrence to Him. God is patient and
loving, but He is a God Who can say even yet, "Ephraim is joined
to His idols; let him alone." Thus it seems to be with most of
Laodicean Christendom. How awful to step into eternity self-
deluded!

And having a Great Priest over the house of God—Let us remember that in our worship, we being the **house of God** over
which Christ our **Great Priest** now is, we do not pray to the priest,
but instead, He leads our worship to God as God.† How foreign
to all things, on the Day of Atonement when Israel gathered about
the tabernacle, would have been a prayer to the priest! The great
fact that their priest had gone in beyond the second veil, representing them, was before their mind. To begin to pray to the priest
would have been to indict his fidelity to the people.

A prophet came from God to the people: he represented God;
he was on God's side. Contrariwise, a priest went in for the people

---

*It may be in such a manner as will leave the objects of His dealings quite unconscious of
it! We have seen people deeply exercised for awhile by some spiritual question, only to have
that exercise fade away: an awful state!

†It is not true to say, as do some, that Christ's work as Priest in Heaven did not begin
until after His resurrection, for it includes (1) His praying for His own before His death,
as the wondrous prayer of Jno. 17; and the particular watching of Lk. 22.31: "Simon,
Simon, I have made supplication for thee." (2) the "offering up of Himself once for
all"; (3) His intercessory work in Heaven for those who are passing through this world;
and (4) His leading the praises of God's people, and declaring God's Name, for all eternity.

to God. He was on the people's side; he represented the people. So Christ also, having "obtained eternal redemption," is now **a Great Priest over the house of God.** As we have seen, it is by the will of God that He came to offer Himself: therefore we trust God, and know that Christ is on our side, appointed so by God. He is committed to our case; He is *our* Priest. As Son He is God; as man, He is Priest. We beseech you, receive this glorious fact, and walk in it by simple faith. He will not cease from being God, and High Priest, forever.* Get this great matter firmly established in your conscience, laying hold of it for yourself. Then follows fellow-ship, as it is written, "We have fellowship one with another, and the blood of Jesus Christ cleanses us from all sin." There is no fel-lowship, we believe, in this universe, such as is enjoyed by be-lievers who are resting, individually and thus as a company, upon the Person and work of our **Great Priest over the house of God.**

Now, *why* a Priest? Let me ask in answer, Would you like to go into the presence of God as an independent one—redeemed indeed by the blood of Christ, but set free to go on your own way forever? You know you would not if you are one of God's own. Your union with Christ forbids such a thought. And His revealed priestly work draws the heart. Weaklings are we, passing through a world over which Satan is still the prince, and living in an age of which he is the god—in a world that has not changed since it joined in the cry against Christ: "Crucify Him!" Do we not need help? Ah, we need nothing else! "I can do nothing of *myself,*" cries the apostle; "I glory in my *weaknesses,* that the power of Christ may rest upon me" (II Cor. 12.9). Yes, we need a Priest, and we have a Priest, thank God, **a Great Priest over the house of God**† (vs. 21). Let us mark, however, that *we* do not serve *Him* as Priest: He serves *us.* We are not directed to come to Him as Priest, but to God's

---

*He is *God's* Christ (not *our* Christ, as I have heard excellent saints, in testimony or prayer, speak of Him); He is our Saviour, our Lord, and in His full name, He is our Lord Jesus Christ (in which, *Lord* governs the expression.)

†We might do well to sum up here Christ's varied relations to us: (1) Redeemer (Sin-Bearer); (2) Life (Risen) we have in Him; (3) Our membership in His Body, of which He is the Head, our being "built up" in Him; (4) He is the Giver of the Holy Spirit, and through Him Bestower of "gifts" (as, evangelists, pastors, teachers, apostles, prophets) to His Church: Eph. 4.8-12; compare I Cor. 12.4, 28. (5) LORD: Rom. 14.9, Jno. 13.13, 14, Col. 3.24, Eph. 6.6, 7. This includes His Lordship over each individual believer, and also His direction of the service and affairs of the Assembly. (6) Great High Priest in Heaven; (7) The coming King according to Heb. 10.13.

throne of grace, relying on Christ's shed blood, and having Him as **Great Priest over the house of God.**

You and I do not need to "get God on our side." He is already on our side! We may say boldly with Paul, "God is *for* us." He spared not His own Son: "how shall He not with Him freely give us all things?" So we come directly to the throne of God, **having a Great Priest over the house of God.** In "things pertaining to God" He still "appears before the face of God for us."

> "There is an eye that never sleeps
> Beneath the wing of night;
> There is an ear that never shuts
> When sink the beams of light."

II

Now the five things we are to do, as outlined on page 344:

1. Verse 22: Let us draw near:

(a) With a true heart—"The heart is deceitful above all things." Millions pray, even using the Name of the Lord Jesus and speaking of His sacrifice, whose hearts are not true. Repentance of sin has not broken them up. "A broken and a contrite heart, O God, Thou wilt not despise." **A true heart** does not mean a heart that trusts in itself, but one which genuinely comes to a holy God.

(b) In full assurance of faith—This does not mean that there will be no consciousness of unworthiness, but rather, a confidence in a faithful God, Who is sure to bless one who is trusting in the shed blood of Christ.

(c) Having our hearts sprinkled from an evil conscience—This is a beautiful picture of the same deliverance as in Chapter 9.14: "The blood of Christ, Who through the eternal Spirit offered Himself without blemish unto God, cleanseth our conscience from dead works to serve the Living God." And we are told in Chapter 12.24 that "we are come to the blood of *sprinkling* that speaketh better than Abel." True faith brings about this Divine action of "sprinkling," that is, of so appropriating the effect of the blood of Christ shed on our behalf as to relieve our burdened consciences because we see that our sins have been laid on our Substitute. There is no other deliverance from an evil conscience (that is, a conscience that is accusing us). God "sprinkles" such believing hearts by reckoning to them the value and power of Christ's shed blood; and the heart has *rest*.

Nearly forty times, beginning with Exodus 29.16: "Thou shalt slay the ram, and thou shalt take its blood, and *sprinkle it* round about upon the altar," this word "sprinkle" in the Old Testament describes the application of the blood of the typical sacrifice. Writing as he was to Hebrews, Paul addressed their vivid consciousness of the meaning of "sprinkle"—to *apply* "the blood of sprinkling," with faith, in obedience to God's directions. This faith is illustrated in Hebrews 11.28:

"By faith he [Moses] kept the passover, and the sprinkling of the blood, that the destroyer of the firstborn should not touch them."

Peter illustrates the use of the word in **Hebrews** in the expression:

"Unto obedience and sprinkling of the blood of Jesus Christ" (I Pet. 1.2).*

Thus are fulfilled the types of Leviticus 4 and the Great Day of Atonement (Lev. 16), which spoke of the sprinkling of the blood—though of course repeated then, time after time. Both sprinkling and washing with water are illustrated in the consecration of Aaron and his sons (Lev. 8.6, 24).

And having our body washed with pure water—We believe that I Peter 3.21, as well as the necessary spiritual application of **washed with pure water,** forbids the interpretation of this expression as water baptism. The water washing of the body is *not* "baptism," for Peter, as noted above, says, "Which after a true likeness doth now save you, even baptism, *not* the putting away of the filth of the flesh, but the answer of a good conscience toward God." Also, the baptism of a believer is just as real when he is immersed in muddy water in a stream or pool, as when the water is clear!

Ridout well says:

"The **body washed with pure water** speaks of the sanctifying work of the Spirit in the new birth; and also, of the practical cleansing in connection with the daily life of the priests."— Ridout, page 204.

---

*Note that Paul, in his epistles to the Gentiles, does not use this word.

2. **Verse 23: Let us hold fast* the confession of our hope—** Here we have again what is constantly urged upon believers—the public confession of our hope in our Lord. This was set forth in Luke 12.8:

"Every one who shall confess Me before men, him shall the Son of Man also confess before the angels of God"; and in Romans 10.9, 10:

"If thou shalt confess with thy mouth Jesus as Lord, and shalt believe in thy heart that God raised Him from the dead, thou shalt be saved: for with the heart man believeth unto righteousness; and with the mouth confession is made unto salvation."

It is especially emphasized in Hebrews 13.15: "Let us offer up a sacrifice of praise to God continually, that is, the fruit of lips which make confession to His Name."

That it waver not—How wonderful has been the constancy and boldness of the many saints recorded in Scripture: Abraham, Moses, Samuel, David, Daniel and the prophets, and the apostles in the Acts!

For He is faithful that promised: The great preventive of wavering is remembering that **He is faithful that promised.** Our hope is built upon the faithfulness of God, and not in any wise upon anything in ourselves.

3. **Verse 24: Let us consider one another to provoke unto love and good works:** You say, **Consider one another to provoke,** is strange language for Christian guidance. Yes, brother, if we turn to human reasoning and practice, there is plenty of considering others—their faults, their failures, in merciless criticism, which provokes. But this passage reads, **To provoke unto love and good works.** How can we provoke one another unto love? By loving others, constantly and tenderly. They will find it out, and will be provoked to return love! The same is true concerning good works. We provoke others to good works by constant good works toward

---

*The Greek word here, *krateo*, built from the word meaning force, strength, indicates a *holding fast* against foes, a fight of faith on earth. For there were many indeed that would rob the Hebrew believer of his heavenly faith and hope, and destroy his confession of them; just as indeed with all believers: such foes as Satan, the world, worldly Christians, the earthly church-system, false friends. So Paul says to us:

"If ye then were raised together with Christ, seek the things that are above, where Christ is, seated on the right hand of God. Set your mind on the things that are above, not on the things that are upon the earth" (Col. 3.1, 2).

The beginning of Christian warfare, indeed, the essence of it, we have here!

them. As I look back through the years, my heart lights upon one and another, and another, whose tender love and constant goodness "provoked" me, "provoked" everyone to imitate them.

4. **Verse 25:** **Not forsaking the assembling of ourselves—as Christians**—This speaks of an **assembling together** which is remarkably designated as **our own** (R.V.), or that peculiar to us, Greek *heautōn**— an assembling belonging to our very own selves. Since there is a real presence of the Spirit in the whole Body of Christ, as well as His individual indwelling of each believer, this assembling of themselves as believers becomes both the channel of blessing and the protection against apostasy.

The custom of some was to "forsake" this Christian gathering, whether from indifference, fear, ignorance, or self-centeredness. **Our own assembling together** does not demand a large or outwardly important company: "Where two or three are gathered together in My Name"—we know the promise. The Name in which and unto which we gather characterizes **our own assembling.** The book of **Hebrews** does not enter upon what the Assembly of God is, as over against what the Hebrew nation was—and some day will be, except to say that those written of were "partakers of the heavenly calling." And it is remarkable that even here the gathering together of believers should thus be insisted upon.

Note how continual it was in the early Church, as the quotations from Acts in the footnote† show. It does *not* mean turning on

---

**Heauton:* This is an emphatic word in this verse. It is thus used in Matt. 8.22, "Let the dead bury their *own (heauton)* dead." So Christians have their *own* assembling. There is no thought in Scripture of an assembly of "Hebrew-Christians," as some have dreamed. Such an assembling would build up again the "middle wall of partition" (Eph. 2.14) which Christ "brake down," fill Hebrew believers with legal pride, and end in the rejection of all Paul's gospel.

†"And they continued steadfastly in the apostles' teaching and fellowship, in the breaking of bread and the prayers" (2.42).
"And all that believed were *together* . . . and day by day, continuing steadfastly *with one accord* in the temple" (2.44, 46).
"Being let go, they came to *their own company*" (4.23).
"The multitude of them that believed were of *one* heart and soul" (4.32).
"They were all with *one accord* in Solomon's porch. But of the rest [outsiders] durst no man join himself to them: howbeit the people magnified them; and believers were the more added to the Lord" (5.12-14).
"For a whole year they [Paul and Barnabas] *gathered together with the assembly* . . . and the disciples were called Christians first in Antioch" (11.26).
"Peter, therefore was kept in the prison: but prayer was made earnestly of the Church unto God for him . . . He came to the house of Mary, the mother of John . . . where many were *gathered together* and were praying" (12.12).

the radio! Much as that has been blessed, it is, we are sure, often made an excuse for not going to the trouble of **gathering ourselves together.** You may say, There is no "denomination" in our community where the Truth is set forth as I know it. That may be so, but if you prayerfully seek, you will find at least two or three who will gather in the Name of the Lord in the simple Christian **gathering together** meant in the passage here in **Hebrews.**

5. **Exhorting one another**—Our "own gathering together" gives an opportunity to fulfill this word, **Exhorting one another;** especially in view of the coming of the Lord—**so much the more, as ye see the day drawing nigh.** Christian exhortation means the expression of our hearts to others to urge them to continue on the Christian path. It may include testimony, and often will necessitate warning. May God make us faithful, not only in our gathering as Christians, but also **in exhorting one another,** for **the day draweth nigh,** indeed!

One further remark here: May I say that there is a deadly danger to us in this verse, unless we have this whole hortatory passage, verses 19-25, before us? When we come to the words, **Not forsaking our own** (Christian) **assembling,** we may say, "Well, I certainly fulfill *this* condition, for I assemble with Christians, as a believer, every Lord's Day." And there will be those who may say, "I have given especial attention to this very matter of assembling. I have abandoned all divisions and sects, which I see are contrary to Scripture; I gather only with separated believers who meet to remember the Lord in the breaking of bread, as He instructed us."

But listen again: **Having a Great Priest over the house of God, let us draw near**—For the worship of God is carried on by the Church of God, by those who, having been cut off from the human race in the death of Christ, are called by Paul in Philippians 3, "*The* circumcision, who *worship in the Spirit of God,* and have no confidence in the flesh." This worship is defined in Ephesians 2.18: "Through Him [Christ] we both have our access *in one Spirit* unto the Father." I do not say this to judge my brethren, but I profoundly fear, alas, that there are many who take heed **not to forsake the assembling of themselves together** after the letter, concerning whom it could not be said that they have **drawn** near . . . into the holy place by the blood of Jesus, and by Christ Himself as their **Great Priest,** and are worshiping "in the Spirit of God." Is it not so?

Have I made it plain that even "Brethren," gathering in the most careful (and some in the most "exclusive" manner), could miss the great exhortations of this passage to **draw near with a true heart,** into God's very presence, and really *worship* "in one Spirit"? If I have not made this plain, sad indeed is my failure.

26   **For if we sin willfully after that we have received the knowledge of the truth, there remaineth no more a sacri-**
27   **fice for sins, but a certain fearful expectation of judg-ment, and a fierceness [Margin, jealousy] of fire which**
28   **shall devour the adversaries. A man that hath set at nought Moses' Law dieth without compassion on the word**
29   **of two or three witnesses: of how much sorer punish-ment, think ye, shall he be judged worthy, who hath trodden under foot the Son of God, and hath counted the blood of the covenant wherewith he was sanctified an unholy [Margin, common] thing, and hath done de-**
30   **spite unto the Spirit of grace? For we know Him that hath said, Vengeance belongeth unto Me, I will recom-**
31   **pense. And again, The Lord shall judge His people. It is a fearful thing to fall into the hands of the Living God.**

In these verses we have a passage which, like Chapter 6.4-8, views apostates from that faith which they once professed. No true exposition can account for either Hebrews 6 or Hebrews 10 on any other ground.* You will notice that just as in Chapter 6.4-8 there occur the "better things" people, with the "things that accompany salvation"—though Paul did "thus speak"; so in Chapter 10.32-35, there is the same sharp distinction. There are those who "endured a great conflict of sufferings" for Christ's sake, who were "made a gazing-stock by reproachers and afflic-tions," and had fellowship "with them that were so used" (vs.

---

*The danger is that this great warning in Heb. 10 shall be handed over in our minds to outrageous blasphemers, publicly declared apostates; whereas, all three attitudes here spoken of: toward (a) **the Son of God,** (b) His **sanctifying blood,** (c) the blessed **Spirit of grace,** may be *drifted* into by those who simply "forsake" Christian assembling. They gradually but really desert and reject Christ within, as did those of Ch. 6 who "crucified to themselves the Son of God." Such will indeed, by their return to the world, out of which their tempo-rary faith in the word of a kingdom delivered them, go on, though not perhaps boisterously, to put Christ "to an open shame." (6.6).

33). They "had compassion on believers that were in bonds," and "took joyfully the spoiling of their possessions," in the knowledge that they had a "better and abiding possession" (vs. 34). They had "boldness" of faith (vs. 35).

But those in view in Chapter 10.26-31 were those who, after receiving **the knowledge of the truth** (vs. 26), and being "enlightened" (compare 6.4 and 10.32), sinned *hatefully*. For the Greek word for "willfully," *ekousios*, Thayer defines: "Voluntarily, willingly, of one's own accord: tacitly opposed to sins committed inconsiderately and from ignorance or from weakness." The other occurrence of the word (I Pet. 5.2) translated "willingly" as over against under constraint, illustrates the situation also. In Hebrews 10.26 there is the absence of that holy "seed" which does not *consent* to sin, which we see in I John 3.9: "Whosoever is begotten of God does not practice sin, because His [God's] seed abideth in him; and he cannot sin, because he is begotten of God."*

Vs. 26-7: There remaineth no more a sacrifice for sins, but a certain fearful expectation of judgment, and a fierceness [Margin, jealousy] of fire which shall devour the adversaries: There is no "adversary" equal to a traitor—one who has enjoyed the privileges he now forsakes and betrays. Nor are we at all questioning the blessed doctrine of the security of Christ's sheep in what we say. Remember that in John's Gospel, both those eternally given by the Father to Christ (17.6, 12), and those who were His disciples for awhile and then "went back and walked no more with Him" (6.66) are seen. There is then a "choosing" by Christ, and an association with Him, which may not mean eternally abiding in Him. So John 6.70 sets forth: "Jesus answered them, Did not I *choose you the twelve*, and one of you is a devil?"

---

*There is reference here to that holy nature which true believers have—they having "become partakers of the Divine nature, having escaped from the corruption that is in the world by lust" (II Pet. 1.4). In I Jno. 2.1, "These things write I unto you that you *may not* sin . . . we have an Advocate"—we see the possibility of a true believer's sinning, and the benefit of the Advocate. But the case in I Jno. 3 is quite different, as vs. 4 reads: "Every one that *practiceth (poiōn)* sin" makes sin his business. This is also the statement of vs. 9, which reads literally, "Every one that has been begotten of God, sin does not *practice*" (poiei).

As Dr. Charles F. Deems used to say: "The unregenerate man lives in sin and loves it; the regenerate man may lapse into sin, but he loathes it."

The primary meaning of this verb *poieō* is "to make, to produce, to form or construct." The *producing of sin* is not the work of the *nature* (seed) *born of God!*

The *eternal* choosing is set forth in John 13.18: "I know whom I have *chosen*: but that the Scripture may be fulfilled. He that eateth My bread lifted up His heel against Me." As He says in His great prayer of John 17.12, "While I was with them, I kept them in Thy name which Thou hast given Me: and I guarded them, and not one of them perished, but the son of perdition; that the Scripture might be fulfilled"—which unutterably solemn necessity is set forth by Peter in Acts 1.15-20. Meditate deeply on this:* for inexpressibly solemn are the words, "That he [Judas] might go *to his own place*" (Acts 1.25). The simpler the protection of your own heart here, the better: remember, "Him that cometh to Me, I will in no wise cast out" (Jno. 6.37).

We know well that the thought of anyone's "tasting" that eternal life that is in Christ and then *falling away,* as we saw in Hebrews 6.4-6, is alarming and repugnant to the mind of those who have been accustomed to lax or false teaching of the words of God on the subject of apostasy. It is customary often to dismiss these Hebrews passages with a gesture, saying, "That belongs to the Jews." But indeed it does not: certainly it is spoken directly to Hebrew believers, but the truth taught concerns every believer.

Verses 28, 29: A man that hath set at nought Moses' Law. dieth without compassion on the word of two or three witnesses: of how much sorer punishment, think ye, shall he be judged worthy, who hath trodden under foot the Son of God, and hath counted the blood of the covenant wherewith he was sanctified an unholy thing, and hath done despite unto the Spirit of grace? Here there is a complete setting at naught. This comes out further in the words of verse 29, **accounted the blood of the covenant a comon thing**—the true rendering of the Greek word, *koinos*.†

---

*The distinction to be noted in Jno. 15 between the two branches, is, the branch that did not bear fruit is "taken away," while the fruit-bearing branch is cleansed "that it may bear more fruit." "Taken away"—whither? To Heaven, certainly, for this one was "taken away," but remained a branch in Christ; while the one in vs. 6 refused to abide in Christ, and therefore "as a branch is cast forth, and is withered," and finally "cast into the fire, and . . . burned."

†Note the use of *common* in Acts 2.44, 4.32; and of "common and unclean" (Acts 10.14, 28). This ceremonial use of the word "common" occurs, for example, three times in Rom. 14.14. The translation "unholy," occurring in both the King James and the Revised, is incorrect, as "unholy" is understood today. *Not holy,* or, not sacred, would be nearer the thought. To a Hebrew, things and acts were either clean or unclean, ceremonially; unclean meaning "common"—not sacred. (See Heb. 10.29, R.V., margin.)

Westcott well says, "The offence (against Moses' Law) is regarded in its isolated completeness: the culprit set at nought Moses' Law. His act was final and decisive."

The King James translation falls so wide of the truth as to be dangerous. For this culprit counted the blood of the covenant wherewith He was sanctified not as an "unclean" thing, but just a common thing, to be disregarded, or forgotten. It is implied that he had had this revelation of truth, that he knew about the covenant. He had "tasted of the heavenly gift" as in Chapter 6.4. There is no separation from this world, no life apart from the world, except through faith in Christ. They of Hebrews 10.29, therefore, are they of whom our Lord spake, who "for awhile believe, and in time of temptation fall away" (Lk. 8.13). In connection with such apostates neither is the word "salvation" used, nor "sanctification of the Spirit": salvation is rooted in grace; and the Spirit seals and sanctifies God's elect.

The last clause in verse 29 is, hath done despite unto the Spirit of grace—This word done despite, used only here, is an intensified form of the word translated to treat shamefully in Matthew 22.6; to insult in Luke 18.32, Acts 14.5, I Thessalonians 2.2. Bagster's Interlinear renders "insulted"; Thayer, "treated with contumely." Now we may agree that perhaps no form of insult is quite equal to that of ignoring one's presence. Yet considering that these in Hebrews 10 as in Chapter 6, were "enlightened," and were made "companions" of the Holy Spirit (not sealed as born of God; but companions of His presence and operations, intelligently recognized by them); there must have been non-co-operation with the Spirit's influences; then such inward resistance as to render His voice less and less audible; and at last so to make the Spirit's voice entirely unheard that they counted as a common thing the blood of the covenant wherewith, in their previous "enlightenment" and "tasting" and so in their Christian confession, and consequent public setting apart as the Lord's, these persons were sanctified.*

---

*As regards the danger of seeking to solve by our puny minds the mystery of the incarnate Christ—Son of God, Son of Man—we will simply quote a few passages:
"The blood of Jesus" (Heb. 10.19); "The blood of Christ" (Heb. 9.14); "The blood of Jesus Christ" (I Pet. 1.2); "The precious blood of Christ" (I Pet. 1.19); "The blood of Jesus His Son" (I Jno. 1.7, R.V.); "White in the blood of the Lamb" (Rev. 7.14).
But the Lamb is worshiped as God, in Rev. 5.11-14!

And finally, in verse 29, we must ponder deeply the solemn question, **Of how much sorer punishment, think ye, shall he be judged worthy** who hath done the things just enumerated, and which we have just studied? Here is a question submitted to our judgment: **How much sorer punishment, think ye?** In the case of Moses' Law the glorious appearing and authority on Sinai of Jehovah, "Whose voice then shook the earth," are set at naught. But *there was no revelation at Sinai of the heart of God.* Yet the commandments were righteous, and the creature knew his obligation, and, **setting it at naught, died without compassion.**

How much sorer punishment? This one has despised the infinite love of God, Who gave His Son; and **hath trodden under foot** this Son. A bit of rebel dust has **counted the blood of the covenant** which he once confessed, **a common thing**—the blood by which he was numbered among the Christians—and hath **insulted the Spirit of grace Himself!** Remember, "The Father hath given all judgment unto the Son," and this bit of creature dust has despised the bleeding wounds of the Son of God, the Creator! **HOW MUCH SORER PUNISHMENT?** Who can answer!

Verse 30: For we know Him that said, Vengeance belongeth unto Me, I will recompense. And again, The Lord shall judge His people: The judgments recounted in the Book of The Revelation are awful in character and solemnity; but in the book of **Hebrews** judicial visitation has a peculiarly personal character, because in **Hebrews** God is speaking in tenderness "in a Son," and woe to them that will not hear! This personal element in God's punishment of Christ-rejecters you hardly hear mentioned in these days. Even earnest preachers, who do show the danger of "losing the soul," rarely describe the far more fearful thing of meeting an infinite God full of eternal jealousy. But what will it be to face the offended Majesty of the blessed and only Potentate, the King of

---

Christ is ONE PERSON. He is as truly man as any of us! God prepared for Him a body (Heb. 10.5); but it is "the blood of Jesus His Son" that "cleanseth us from all sin." See prayerfully these words in I Jno. 1.7.

It is *God become man* with a body of blood and flesh. He poured out that blood to redeem us! Let your faith rejoice in this.

But woe to those who undertake to explain through their foolish *reasoning* how this could be! Christ, we repeat, is one Person, both God and man. Here let our hearts rejoice!

It is significant that those in Heb. 10.29 who have **trodden under foot the Son of God,** have therewith counted the blood of the covenant . . . a common thing. Here the Son of God and His shed blood are indissolubly connected!

kings? To feel the jealousy of love despised?* The penalty of contempt of a court where God is Judge of all? To meet the fury that
comes upon patience finally exhausted—the infinite hatred of God
towards rebels who have finally allied themselves with the sin that
God hates? To feel the terrible impotence of finite rebels against
infinite aroused wrath? To know the meaning of that word
"vengeance" when a Being of infinite power arises bent at last upon
revenge?

Those who are forever seeking to do away with a God Who is
capable of wrath, and to make void His words, are ready to quote
the last part of verse 30, **The Lord shall judge His people,** and
claim that the expression **His people** must make the verse mean
that here God is dealing in "chastening" with His own children.
But let us turn to the Old Testament passage (Deut. 32.35, 36)
from which the words are quoted:

> **"Vengeance is Mine, and recompense,**
> At the time when their foot shall slide:
> For the day of their calamity is at hand,
> And the things that are to come upon them shall make haste.
> **For Jehovah will judge His people,**
> And repent Himself for His servants."

No one with Scripture open before him will deny that in dealing
with **His people** *(Israel),* God has done "terrible things in righteousness." Korah, Dathan and Abiram, "these wicked men"
(Num. 16.26), were "swallowed up" by the earth, and "went
down alive into Sheol." "They *perished* in the gainsaying of Korah"
(Jude 11). Thus God **judged His people!** Will any claim that those
whom the fiery serpents slew (Num. 21.6), or the idolaters who
fell by the sword (Ex. 32.28), or the 70,000 who died by the
plague when David numbered Israel (II Sam. 24)—will any claim
that these were true children of God, dealt with in *chastening?*
Nay, the wicked of whom we read in the Psalms are, in general,
the wicked of Israel. And the very first Psalm says, they

> " . . . are like the chaff which the wind driveth away.
> Therefore the wicked shall not stand in the judgment,
> Nor sinners in the congregation of the righteous."

---

*"Love is strong as death;
Jealousy is cruel as Sheol;
The flashes thereof are flashes of fire,
A most vehement flame of Jehovah!" (S.S. 8.6, R.V., margin).

"The righteous," of course, are *saved* Israelites. Every Israelite "written in the book" (Dan. 12.1); "even every one that is written *unto life* [R. V., margin] in Jerusalem" (Is. 4.3), by Divine grace, will be among the Remnant that are saved even amid the judgment which then is, raised up to salvation along with the preserved Remnant of Daniel 12.1, which we repeat in full: "At that time thy people [Daniel's people, Israel] shall be delivered, every one that shall be found written in the book."

Therefore the word, **The Lord shall judge His people,** involves the culling out from His people by His judicial action, in any age, those who profess, but who depart from their confession, even to viewing lightly the salvation purchased by **the blood of the covenant, of the Son of God.*** For, alas, there are those who "neglect so great a salvation," which means that they do not *care.* There are those whose souls were never really roused, who, while they professed, remained "sluggish," became "disobedient," and "hardened by the deceitfulness of sin"; who forsook Christian assembling; who became unconcerned that God had made an infinite sacrifice for them. Their lives of sin put "to an open shame" Him they had once confessed. They did not care! (Hush! The streets of Christendom are crowded today with those who do not care! though many of them have heard the story of God's love, all their lives.) But their personal rejection of **the Living God** will bring on the Personal dealing **of the Living God.** And what will that be? And for how long?

Verse 31 : It is a fearful thing to fall into the hands of the Living God: In Chapter 3.12 we saw him with "an evil heart of unbelief" "falling away from the Living God"—that is, from all His gracious offers and operations, but not getting away from His jurisdiction. But here, the apostate **falls into the hands**—frightful thought! of

---

*"The more we examine the cross, the more we shall find how all good and evil found its issue, and how it connects together the consummated evil of man in hatred against God, manifested in Christ in love, the full power of Satan as prince of this world, his hatred against goodness, and audacity against the Lord. Then perfection in man in Christ, and love to the Father, and obedience (and we may thankfully add to us), the double character of love to God: as man upward, and divinely to us. And all this in the very place of sin where it was needed, Christ being made sin. Then in God, perfect righteousness against sin, and perfect love to sinners. All was concentrated in the cross."—J. N. Darby, Vol. XXVI, p. 175.

the same **Living God,** now unappeased, unpropitiated, forever! "Be silent, all flesh before Jehovah and hear." "What if God, willing to show His wrath and to make His power known, endured with much long-suffering vessels of wrath fitted [not by God, but by themselves] unto destruction?" We repeat, four times in **Hebrews, THE LIVING GOD** appears: twice with reference to the saved, who, with conscience cleansed by Christ's blood, serve Him (9.14); and who are thus come to "the city of the Living God" (12.22). And twice as to the lost, who fall away in unbelief *from* the Living God (3.12), and who here (10.31), unsaved and unsavable, lost and damned, **FALL INTO THE HANDS OF THE LIVING GOD.**

We may say regarding these eight words:

1. All men are in the hands of God (a) as the Author of their being: "Of Him are all things"; (b) as the Upholder and universal Provider (see Belshazzar, Dan. 5.23: "In Whose hand thy breath is"; the God-forgetters on Mars Hill: Acts 17.25-28; and Rev. 14.7, the God that made all things); (c) as the Judge, Who has pronounced all men "sinners."

2. But all are, potentially, placed in the protection, in this life, of Christ's sacrifice: "God was in Christ reconciling the world unto Himself, not reckoning unto them their trespasses" (II Cor. 5.19).

3. To **fall into the hands of the Living God** is, therefore, to have resisted His love, refused His salvation, despised the warnings of His Spirit, and to have persisted thus past the point where God can consistently show further grace.

4. It is to fall, therefore, into the hands of Infinite Power, moved by naught but wrath, vengeance, and eternal indignation, into the hands of **the LIVING GOD;** into the hands of unpropitiated holiness, loaded with unexpiated guilt. Vessels of wrath are they which became fitted for destruction only, upon whom shall be poured out forever and ever infinite, continual vengeance.*

---

*Those vacillating in mind concerning eternal punishment should read some of the great sermons of Jonathan Edwards, probably the greatest mind, and one of the most devoted saints God has given America. (May be obtained from Grace Publications, Inc., 100 West Chicago Ave., Chicago.) God greatly used him around the eighteenth century to arouse this nation to a sense of sin, and to the salvation of untold thousands: we quote:

"But know, thou stupid, blind, hardened wretch, that God doth not see, as thou seest

"Jehovah is slow to anger, and abundant in loving-kindness, for-giving iniquity and transgression; and that will *by no means clear the guilty*" (Num. 14.18).

As the Holy Spirit saith in Nahum 1.2, 6, 7:

"Jehovah is a jealous God, *and 'avengeth;* Jehovah avengeth and is full of wrath; Jehovah taketh vengeance on His adversaries, and He preserveth wrath for *His enemies.* Who can stand before His indignation? and who can abide the fierceness of His anger? His wrath is poured out like fire, and the rocks are broken asunder by Him. Jehovah is good, a stronghold in the day of trouble; and He knoweth them that take refuge in Him."*

---

with thy polluted eyes: thy sins in His sight are infinitely abominable. Thou knowest that thou hast a thousand and a thousand times made light of the majesty of God. And why should not that majesty, which thou hast thus despised, be manifested in the greatness of thy punishment? Thou hast often heard what a great and dreadful God Jehovah is: but thou hast made so light of it, that thou hast not been afraid of Him. Thou hast not been afraid to sin against Him, not afraid to go on day after day, by thy sins, to provoke Him to wrath, nor to cast His commands under foot, and trample on them. Now why may not God, in the greatness of thy destruction, justly vindicate and manifest the greatness of that majesty which thou hast despised?

"Thou hast despised the mighty power of God; thou hast not been afraid of it. Now why is it not fit that God should show the greatness of His power in thy ruin? What king is there who will not show his authority in the punishment of those subjects that despise it? and who will not vindicate his royal majesty in executing vengeance on those that rise in rebellion? And art thou such a fool as to think that the great King of Heaven and earth, before Whom all other kings are so many grasshoppers, will not vindicate His kingly majesty on such contemptuous rebels as thou art? Thou art very much mistaken if thou thinkest so. If thou be regardless of God's majesty, be it known to thee, God is not re-gardless of His own majesty; He taketh care of its honor, and He will vindicate it."

*We must be careful to define God's enemies as Scripture defines them. There is much looseness in sermons, hymns, and testimonials concerning these things. Recently we were in an assembly of devoted believers who were singing a hymn in which the line occurred:

"That I, a child of hell, should in His image shine."

Now, all called the children of hell in Scripture will *go* to hell. Scripture does not call the children of men, by nature children of hell, but calls them "children of *wrath*" (Eph. 2.4), that is, possessed of a nature against which God's wrath must arise. But Eph. 2.5 is, "But God, being rich in mercy—"! There is hope for the children of wrath. To them the gospel is preached. David was born a being who would excite the wrath of God: he said:

"Behold, I was brought forth in iniquity;
And in sin did my mother conceive me."

But this does not touch *the will.* Paul (Rom. 7.7-24) mourned the presence of such a nature in himself, but finally found deliverance from its power (as he had from its guilt) "through Jesus Christ our Lord."

In Matt. 23.15 we read our Lord's words,

"Woe unto you, Scribes and Pharisees, hypocrites! for ye compass sea and land to make one proselyte; and when he is become so, ye make him twofold more a child of hell (Gr., *Gehenna*) than yourselves."

In Jno. 5.39-40, we find these Jews refusing, as a matter of *will,* to hear the "witness" the Scriptures bear of Christ:

"Ye *will not* come to Me [Gr., Ye do *not will* to come] that ye may have life," and, "Ye are of your father the devil, and the lusts of your father it is your will to do" (R.V.).

32 But call to remembrance the former days, in which,
    after ye were enlightened, ye endured a great conflict of
33 sufferings; partly, being made a gazing-stock both by re-
    proaches and afflictions; and partly, becoming partakers
34 with them that were so used. For ye both had compassion
    on them that were in bonds, and took joyfully the spoiling
    of your possessions, knowing that ye have for yourselves
35 a better possession and an abiding one. Cast not away
    therefore your boldness, which hath great recompense of
36 reward. For ye have need of patience, that, having done
    the will of God, ye may receive the promise.
37   For yet a very little while,
        He that cometh shall come, and shall not tarry.
38   But My righteous one shall live by faith:
        And if he shrink back, My soul hath no pleasure in him.
39 But we are not of them that shrink back unto perdition;
    but of them that have faith unto the saving of the soul.

Verses 32-4: These Hebrew believers, in their earlier experience
—the former days after they were enlightened, had endured a
great conflict of sufferings . . . had had compassion on them that
were in bonds, and took joyfully the spoiling of their possessions.
Here is constancy in suffering and trial. They had come to the
Cross; they had believed on the Son of God Who had borne
their sins there and had returned to Heaven in resurrection blessing. Their unbelieving countrymen treated them as they had
treated Christ Himself. Look at the words, gazing-stock, reproaches, afflictions, bonds, spoiling of possessions!

And how did they endure? In the knowledge that they had for
themselves an abiding possession on high! Look again at several
other words now: partakers, compassion, joyfully, confidence of
a better possession and an abiding one.

"Ye are actuated by him (the devil) of your own freedom, lusts and choice" (Thayer).

Thus do men by resisting the truth *become* "Satan's children," as Paul, filled with the
Holy Spirit, said to Elymas the sorcerer,

"O full of all guile and all villany, thou *son of the devil,* thou enemy of all righteousness,
wilt thou not cease to pervert the right ways of the Lord?" (Acts 13.9-10).

Our Saviour called the Scribes and the Pharisees and their dupes "sons of *Gehenna,*" for
they then belonged there, having rejected the only Redeemer: He said, "Depart from Me, ye
cursed, into the eternal fire which is prepared for the devil and his angels."

We have then the fact that the children of men are *by nature* "children of wrath," but
by the mercy of God may become *children of God* in accepting Christ; and we have other
children of men who, rejecting Christ, become such sharers of Satan's attitude as to be
called "children of the devil," "sons of *Gehenna.*" Awful thought!

Verses 35-36: Cast not away therefore your boldness, which hath great recompense of reward. For ye have need of patience, that, having done the will of God, ye may receive the promise: The temptation, ever present with all of us, was to grow weary in welldoing, which in their case was to **cast away their boldness,** that is, to leave the path of simple faith. This path of faith was "bold" indeed to a Hebrew who had been taught from his youth to stand back from the presence of God; that he could not enter: only priests could; that his path was to fulfil religious obligations, only; never come boldly* to God! To Hebrew believers of those days, such "outspokenness" toward God, such consciousness of the absence of any condemnation, or of any conditions, was unheard of. Had not Moses himself said, "Thou hast set our iniquities before Thee, our secret sins in the light of Thy countenance"? And had not even David, who danced before the ark in his love for Jehovah, yet been "afraid of Jehovah on that very day"? **(II Sam. 6.9, 14).**

If this boldness toward God be entered upon, then the devil's constant threat is, You are in presumption: cast away this boldness and return to religion. But God says it **hath great recompense of reward . . . Cast it not away.** Witness the apostles in the Acts, and Paul (who says, "In Whom we have *boldness* and access in confidence through our faith in Him," Eph. 3.12; and John, who having once seen the glorified Christ (Rev. 1), goes in vision to Heaven and speaks with elders and angels, and at last says, "Amen: come, Lord Jesus!"

Verse 36: And so we see what we might call the gap which *patience* is quietly, firmly, even ploddingly, to bridge: **For ye have need of patience, that, having done the will of God**—that is, in our own way of speaking, one bridgehead of the gap; and (that) **ye may receive the promise** is the other. "Patience" is one of those

---

*The Greek word for "boldness" is a combination of the Greek word *pan,* all; and *brema,* spokenness—giving *parrēsia,* all-spokenness, boldness. Ponder and appropriate this great word. The verbal form means "To bear oneself boldly or confidently, to be free-spoken" (Thayer). See I Tim. 3.13; II Cor. 3.12. "Speaking out every word, as opposed to fear, ambiguity, or reserve" (Vincent).

The boldness toward God of Heb. 10.19 rested on consciousness of sin "remembered no more"—remitted; "no more offering for sin" going on (10.17, 18). See Chs. 3.6, "If we hold fast our boldness"; and 4.16, "Let us draw near with boldness," and read the comment at these places.

deep, quiet words of Scripture (Gr., *hypomonē*), which means literally to remain down under; so, not to fly up, or be disturbed, either by the afflictions from man's hand, or from the enemy (Jas. 1.12); or by chastening from God's hand, as see Hebrews 12.7. We are to abide steadily in the path despite all opposing temptations from without, or, still more subtly, from within our own fickle, naturally fearful hearts.

Doing the will of God, to these Hebrew believers, meant believing the testimony concerning Jesus as their Messiah, crucified, dead, risen; and their sin put away, and their worship a heavenly one, their High Priest being now at the right hand of God. Then, of course, would follow the afflictions and persecutions; and the temptations to return to Judaism and earthly worship, and to peace with unbelieving Israel.

Having done the will of God, they would be ready to **receive the promise:** What promise?

Verse 37: For yet a very little while,

He that cometh shall come, and shall not tarry.

Throughout **Hebrews** is this great return of the Lord for His millennial reign in view: see Chapter 1.6: "When He *again* bringeth in the Firstborn into the world He saith, And let all the angels of God worship Him." Compare The Revelation 5.11, 12. Again in Hebrews 2.5: "Not unto angels did He subject the inhabited earth *to come:*" this is the millennial earth, not, of course, any mere condition of things.

Then Christ is "named of God a High Priest after the order of Melchizedek" (5.10), and finally to fill that name, must be "a Priest upon His throne"—the throne of David in Jerusalem (Lk. 1.32, 33). Again, our Lord is seen in Hebrews 9.11 as "a High Priest of the *good things to come*," which we believe must be interpreted in the light of the passage just quoted. See also Chapter 9.15, "A death having taken place . . . they that have been called may receive *the promise of the eternal inheritance.*" What then is **THE PROMISE** of Chapter 10.36? The coming of the Lord! *He'll* bring the inheritance. Look also ahead to Chapter 11.39: "The PROMISE": they "received it not" as yet.

We repeat verse 37 and ask you to study it phrase by phrase with profound attention:

For yet 'a little while,' how short! how short!
The Coming One will be here, and will not delay.—
                                        Rotherham's translation.

First, **He that cometh**—This, believer, is the definition of Christ which God desires to print on your soul. You are not looking for death: like those at Thessalonica, we "wait for His Son from Heaven"; or like the Philippians,

"Our citizenship is in Heaven, whence also we wait for a Saviour, the Lord Jesus Christ: Who shall fashion anew the body of our humiliation, that it may be conformed to the body of His glory." (Phil. 3.20, 21).

The Christian who is looking for death is already, as it were, sitting in the cemetery! But, "*He* is not here, but is risen!" Get your eyes upon this mighty hope: **He that cometh** is the definition of your Saviour! Let it be in all our hearts, and remember that He said, "Watch," as well as "Wait." See Hebrews 9.28.

Second, **He that cometh shall come**—As Peter says,

"In the last days mockers shall come with mockery, walking after their own lusts, and saying, Where is the promise of His coming? for, from the day that the fathers fell asleep, all things continue as they were from the beginning of the creation" (II Pet. 3.3-4).

Loathe, abhor, fear, utterly avoid *such* wickedness! Did not two witnesses from Heaven tell the apostles at His ascension,

"This same Jesus, Who was received up from you into Heaven, SHALL SO COME in like manner as ye beheld Him going into Heaven"? Did not Paul in the Holy Spirit write:

"The Lord Himself SHALL DESCEND from Heaven, with a shout, with the voice of the archangel, and with the trump of God: and the dead in Christ shall rise first: then we that are alive, that are left, shall together with them be caught up in the clouds, to meet the Lord in the air"?

There must be no uncertainty of this coming mighty event. It is **THE PROMISE** before us now. "The promise" to Israel of old was the Messiah: He came. Then He Himself called "the promise" the coming of the Holy Spirit which He would send (Lk. 24.49; Acts 1.4). Now the Holy Spirit has come, and lo, the expression **THE PROMISE** is transferred to the Person of our Lord in the matter of expectation of His arrival on earth again. This is "the lodestar of the Church."

THE Promise of Hebrews 10.36 is the "blessed hope" of our faith. When our Lord said, "Take ye heed, watch and pray: for ye know not when the time is" (Mk. 13.33), He based His warning on our ignorance, I say, our *utter* ignorance of the time. Nay, He had just said that neither the angels, nor Himself, the Son, knew of that day and hour, "but the Father" alone (Mk. 13.32). Therefore when the opponents of the doctrine of the imminent coming of our Lord begin to point to any event which *they say* must come *first,* such as the evangelization of the world, in the very face of Christ's words, "But watch ye at *every* season . . . in an hour that ye think *not* the Son of man cometh"; "Take ye heed: . . . *ye know not when* the time is" (Lk. 21.36; 12.40; Mk. 13.33), they are placing their own judgment about facts or conditions *before* our Lord's warning to "watch."

Suppose I am a servant, sent to the railway station to meet my master's guest. I go at noon. But I hear the reports of the movements of trains, and judge by them that the guest will not arrive for several hours. I may *await,* from then on, the guest's arrival; but I cannot *watch* for him, for I no longer believe he is coming soon: I have so judged from official reports. But if my master has specifically said to me, "You go to the station and *watch* for my friend's arrival," these directions take precedence of all else. If I am a faithful servant, I will allow nothing to turn me from obeying the command of my master to *watch.*

Dr. I. M. Haldeman, in His sermon, "The Imminent Coming of Christ," says that the Christian's attitude towards our Lord's coming should be "to be ready for that event—which is *not in the sequences of time,* nor bound by its laws!" to which we heartily agree. The Christian is to be ready for the "unknown" hour in which our Lord may come.

Someone may object that *all* events are "in the sequences of time." This we flatly deny! Did not our Lord Jesus Christ, being God the Son, know the "sequences"—the before-during-and-after, of all events? *You* say, Of course He did—using your reason rather than believing *His word,* which is, we repeat: "Of that day or that hour *knoweth no one,* not even the angels in Heaven, *neither the Son, but the Father!*" And again, in Acts 1.7, "It is not for you to know times or seasons, which *the Father* hath set within His own authority." Nor does this knowledge, exclusive to the Father, detract in the least from the Deity of the Son, Whom our book of **Hebrews** in one chapter alone calls Son, Creator, Heir, Upholder, God, Lord! (1.2, 5, 8).*

Third, **And shall not tarry:** Remember, it is the wicked servant that said, "My Lord tarrieth," and he said so *"in his heart."* He did not want Him to come.† This, by the way, has been the history of ecclesiastical Christendom. Has it not given up really looking for our Lord's return?

Alas and alas, it is not only Christendom in general, that has said, "My Lord delayeth His coming," but those who have been taught prophetic truth, only to turn aside from the plain teaching of the imminent coming of the Lord and the command to watch daily for Him, with some vain—always "religious" excuse! Perhaps the latest one, and that which is deceiving many excellent Christians,

---

*Some 44 years ago, when, although a "church member," I had never heard a sermon on the coming of our Lord, I came down very early in the morning, long before breakfast, from my room in the Alliance House in New York, and heard voices talking eagerly and earnestly. Looking into the front parlor, I saw a circle of perhaps ten or a dozen Christians, and to my complete amazement, they were speaking intimately of the arrival of the Lord Jesus from Heaven as if it might really occur that very day! HE THAT COMETH SHALL COME had filled their hearts and governed their thoughts!

†Of course I recognize that the quotation is from Hab. 2.3 ff, where the prophet is agonized by the coming of the Chaldeans against Israel, yea, looking further, to the awful last wicked one (Chaldean, Babylonian, as well as Roman). In Ch. 2.1 he stands upon his watch to see what Jehovah will say to him. The answer is,

"Write the vision, and make it plain upon tablets, that *he may run* [the godly remnant from Babylon, the Chaldean land: Jer. 50.8, 28; 51.6, 45, 50] that readeth it.

"For the vision is yet for the appointed time, and it hasteth toward the end, and shall not lie: though it tarry, wait for it; because it will surely come, it will not delay" (vs. 3).

But again the prophet's anguished eyes are upon him that hath "plundered many nations" (2.8; Rev. 13, etc.), he knowing all the while (vss. 13, 14) that,

"The peoples labor for the fire, and the nations weary themselves for vanity. For the earth shall be filled with the knowledge of the glory of Jehovah, as the waters cover the sea."

But yet, as he is in anguish with the vision in answer to the prayer of Ch. 3.1, there is shown to him the glorious coming of Jehovah at Armageddon, when He rides upon His horses and "chariots of salvation," to fulfill "the oaths to the tribes" (8, 9), and the sun and moon shall stand still, and He "wounds the head out of the house of the wicked man" —i.e., Antichrist: vs. 13.

The prophet hears, and his body trembles (vs. 16) in his place: "Because I must wait quietly for the day of trouble" (the time of Jacob's trouble), "for the coming up of the people that invadeth us" (Zech. 14—all nations against Jerusalem).

Then the glorious trump of faith of the Remnant:

"Yet I will rejoice in Jehovah,

I will joy in the God of my salvation" (vs. 18).

All this is rendered in the Septuagint *as of the coming of the Messiah;* the Coming One of Hab. 2 is made the Messiah in the LXX.

is the claim, that the Church has not yet brought the gospel to the whole inhabited earth.

Now the Holy Spirit by Paul in Colossians 1.23 says the gospel in Paul's day was "preached in all creation under Heaven."* This affirmation is very positive, the form of language, the aorist participle, indicating what has taken place, not what should or will do so. To call this passage hyperbole is therefore impossible—except we reject the accuracy of Scripture statement. Again, in Romans 1.8, the apostle declares, "Your faith is proclaimed [or better, announced, talked about] throughout *the whole world*." In Colossians 1.23, it was the whole *creation;* in Romans 1.8, it is the *cosmos,* the ordered world. And note I Thessalonians 1.8: concerning this remarkable assembly Paul says, "From you . . . *in every place your* faith to God-ward is gone forth." Again, Acts 17.6: "These that have turned the world [Gr., *oikoumenê,* inhabited earth] upside down are come hither also," said the jealous Jews to the rulers of the city of Thessalonica.†

Verse 38: But My righteous one by [*ek,* "along the line of"] faith [or, along the line of believing] shall keep living, [or, be living],

And if he should shrink back, My soul delights not in him.‡

---

*"By 'was preached' he means not merely 'is being preached, but *has been actually, as an accomplished fact, preached.*' Pliny, not many years subsequently, in his famous letter to the Emperor Trajan (B.X., Ep. 97), writes, 'Many of every age, rank, and sex, are being brought to trial. For the contagion of that superstition (Christianity) has spread over not only cities, but villages, and the country.' "—Fausett. J.F.B. Commentary, Col. 1.23.

†See Appendix F, "Delayers of Our Lord's Coming."

‡The three N. T. occurrences of this quotation from Hab. 2.3, 4, "The just shall live by faith," are, Rom. 1.17; Gal. 3.11 and Heb. 10.38, our text. Proper emphasis in each case brings out the special meaning.

In Romans, the question is one of righteousness before God, so that we read there, "Therein [in the Gospel] is revealed a righteousness of God on the principle of faith, [where faith exists] as it is written, The righteous shall live by faith." Here the emphasis is on the *just,* or the righteous.

In Galatians, it is the subject of being perfected. They were "foolish." Having "begun in the Spirit," they were now seeking to be "perfected in the flesh" (3.3). So the question is about living, and the answer, "The righteous shall *live* by faith."

In Heb. 10.38 the emphasis is on the word "faith." The "great conflict of sufferings" of "former days after they were enlightened" has been brought up. They were not to "cast away their boldness . . . For they had need of patience, that, having done the will of God [which may involve suffering and trial], they might receive THE PROMISE," the great promise of our Lord's coming again—His absence being for "a very little while." Meanwhile, God directs, My righteous one shall live by faith, faith being his spirit's constant attitude God-ward—the vital air of all the hosts of witnesses who are about to be set before us in the great eleventh chapter!

Here, of course, not only the first step of faith, but a vital con‑
tinuing on the path of faith, is set before us as a way of life: not
only the obtaining of life, but the manner of life of the true be‑
liever—one of whom God says, **My righteous one**. Then the con‑
trast: one of the most solemn and awakening warnings in all the
book of **Hebrews**: the one who **shrinks back** from the path of
faith, through fear, through weariness, through influence of mere
religionists about him; or through neglect of the means of living
(the Word of God, and constant contemplation of the great salva‑
tion); or through unjudged thorns and thistles of the old life
(Ch. 6); but most particularly through that unreadiness of the
human heart to "endure as seeing Him Who is invisible" (Ch.
11.27).*

God has sent Christ; Christ has been here; Christ has "obtained
eternal redemption" for us at the Cross; but Christ has gone up
out of sight. Yet the living Word is in our hands, and the blessed
Holy Spirit Who inspired it is in our midst, and the command is
to **live by faith**, that God's justified ones, having believed, *keep
on* believing. To give up faith, is the greatest of all snares. "We
walk," says Paul, "by faith, not by *appearance*," (II Cor. 5.7,
R.V., margin). It seems a little thing to yield to this fearfulness
of the path of faith, to shrink back. But how terrible really are the
results: God **takes no pleasure** in such a one, for he has turned
back from God's path; he is no longer conscious of a Living God.
He turns back to "dead works" (6.1; 9.14), from which the shed
blood of Christ has set him forever free. The next verse will set
forth the end of each path, the one to doom; the other to glory:

Verse 39: But we are not of shrinking back [of those who do

---

*The father and mother were out for the evening, and had left little Mary for the first
time, in the sole care of her grandmother. By and by, the grandmother took the little girl
upstairs, heard her "say her prayers," and covered her up in bed. Then she turned out the
light.

"O Grandma, Mother always leaves a light burning till I go to sleep!"

"Oh," said the old grandmother, "God is up here with you. He is in the darkness as well
as in the light. Don't forget, He is here with you."

Then she went down to the living room below. After a while there was the patter of little
feet and a tremulous voice, "Grandma, please turn on the light for me till I get to sleep."

"Oh, my dear, God is there with you! Go back to bed!"

Reluctantly the little one obeyed, but by and by again came the pleading voice down the
stairs:

"Grandma, O Grandma, please come up here and stay with God, while I go down where
the light is!"

shrink back] unto perdition; but on the contrary [we are] those
of faith unto the preservation of the soul (a preservation [or
preserving] of the soul, of course, which has been purchased by
the blood of Christ). Here we have the same stepping into the
circle—shall we say?—of true believers, as in Chapter 6.9. There,
it was "Beloved, we are persuaded better things of you, and things
that accompany salvation"—though he had just spoken most solemnly of those who merely taste, and fall away. Here, we have in the
"we" the same circle, and the same blessed consciousness of perse-
vering in that living faith which in the preceding verse was the faith
in which God's justified ones were living; the faith is viewed as that
which operates to preserve the soul from that perdition* unto
which go those that shrink back from the path of faith.

Thus in Chapter 10 is prepared the way for those great examples of faith, living faith, set forth in the following chapter,
"the Westminster Abbey of Scripture."

---

*Remember that in Rev. 21.8 "the fearful" head the list of all who go into the lake that
burneth with fire and brimstone, which is the second death; the fearful who shrank back
from resting upon the work done by any other than themselves—by Another at the Cross.
   Once more we shall see them in Ch. 12.15 in the words, "Looking carefully lest there be
any man [that is, any professed believer] that falleth short of the grace of God."
   Unto perdition—(eis apôleian) sets forth damnation, especially as the destination and condition of those who have left this world under judgment, as in Rev. 17.11 of the Antichrist:
"He goeth into perdition;" and in II Thess. 2.3, same word concerning the same being.
The wicked, in Rom. 9.22, are called "vessels of wrath fitted unto destruction." Judas is
called "the son of perdition." Destruction (Gr., olethron), and perdition, are named together in I Tim. 6.9. Destruction, I suggest, indicated the ruin that accompanies their
earthly overthrow: compare I Cor. 5.5, "the destruction of the flesh," even in the case of
this man whose spirit was to be "saved in the day of the Lord Jesus."

CHAPTER ELEVEN

1 NOW FAITH IS a confidence [giving-substance-to]
2 things hoped for, a conviction [putting-to-the-test] of
things not seen. For therein the elders had witness borne
to them.

A DEFINITION AND A DESCRIPTION of faith, with an
illustration of its action, is contained in these first two verses of
Chapter Eleven. To repeat, **Faith is a giving-substance-to, [making
real] hoped-for things, a test (R. V., margin) of things when they
are not yet seen.***

Hoping for something is not yet *faith!* Faith says, "I *have* it!"
Things not seen shows there is no consulting of human faculties
or "feelings." The ark is the *test* of faith. When Noah entered the
ark, there was the same conviction of the fact of the coming flood
that he had during the years of building the ark. *God* had spoken!
That was all that was before his mind. He never looked at the
sky. **Faith is a conviction of things when they are not seen! a
giving-substance-to** [Greek, *hypostasis*] **things hoped for.**

This Greek word for confidence, *hypostasis,* is used only five times
in the New Testament, three of them in **Hebrews:** Chapters 1.3;
3.14; 11.1. That in Chapter 3.14 we remember, reads, "If we hold
fast the begining of our *confidence* firm unto the end," and
indicates the same exercise of the soul as set forth in our text
in Chapter 11.1; and the third is in Chapter 1.3: "the very image
of His *substance (hypostasis).*"† This is the correct reading (R.V.).

We speak thus in particular because of the ever-present tempta-

---

*"By *faith* we are sure of eternal things that they *are;* by *hope* we are confident that
we shall have them." J.F.B. **Commentary,** *in loc.*

†Thayer remarks concerning *hypostasis,* "It is very common in Greek authors in widely
different senses:
"1. A setting or placing under, that is, a *foundation.*
"2. That which has *foundation,* is firm. Hence, (a) that which has *actual existence.*
(b) *The substantial quality or nature* of any person or thing, as *of God* (Heb. 1.3). (c)
Steadiness of mind, firmness, resolution, confidence, firm trust, assurance." (Here we may
class 3.14, and 11.1.)

tion to confuse *faith* with *feeling*—trusting God's Word, with look-ing for signs. But Paul says, "We walk by faith, not by sight." And our Lord's words in Mark 11.23, following His command, "Have faith in God," vividly illustrate this **giving substance to things hoped for:**

"Verily I say unto you, Whosoever shall say unto this mountain, Be thou taken up and cast into the sea; and shall not doubt in his heart, but shall *believe* that what he saith cometh to pass; he shall have it. Therefore I say unto you, All things whatsoever ye pray and ask for, *believe* that ye *received* them, and ye shall have them."

"Believe that ye *received*" (aorist tense), that is, received them when asking! Faith therefore becomes *a power;* as Jehovah said through Isaiah, "Concerning the works of My hands, *command* ye Me" (Isa. 45.11). Westcott well says, "Faith essentially deals with the future and with the unseen; the regions not entered by direct physical experience." Rotherham's happy translation is, "But faith is of things hoped for, a confidence, of facts a conviction, when they are not seen."

Let us remark that it is the subjective state and attitude of the human heart that is in view in these first verses, and indeed right through this chapter. That is, it is not here faith as a "gift from God" that is in view. That true faith is a gift from God, a blessed gift, we fully recognize. But we find on the other hand that doubt, distrust, unbelief, are *sins.* No man has a right to doubt God for one moment! Our Lord's great command which we have quoted, *"Have faith* in God," and His questions, such as "O thou of little faith, wherefore didst thou doubt?" show that there is a positive sense in which faith *may* be, *should* be, exercised by us!

And this human side (if I may call it that) is before us in Hebrews 11. Here in verse 1 there are certain blessings **hoped for,** but **Faith is the substantiating,** or **giving-substance-to** these **hoped-for things.*** Again, in the second statement of verse 1, [Faith is] **a conviction of things not seen,** "conviction" (Gr.,

---

*The King James rendering, "Faith is the substance of things hoped for," is devoid of meaning, and disregards the other occurrences of the Greek word *hypostasis,* which we have listed. We love the King James Version, but we must speak plainly here. For instance, how absurd it would be to render Heb. 3.14, "If we hold fast the beginning of our sub-stance"! Therefore, Chapter 11.1 should be rendered, **Faith is the confidence of things hoped for, the sure expectation of these things**—arising from a spiritual realization of the things: **a giving substance to things hoped for!**

elengchos) means not merely a "conviction," but a putting that conviction to the test, as we have noted in Noah's building the ark.

We must reflect deeply upon God's order in this matter of faith, for no plague of our hearts is more pernicious than the placing "feeling" before *faith*.

Verse 2: For therein the elders had witness borne to them: The term "the elders" has in view the Old Testament saints, especially those pointed to in this chapter as prominent in the activity of faith. The assertion is not that they "obtained a *good report*" in this world; nor does it refer to their reputation among the saints; but rather to that *inner "witnessing"* of I John 5.10, "He that believeth on the Son of God *hath the witness in himself."*

The Authorized ("King James") Version of verse 2, **by it** [faith] **the elders obtained a good report,** is very unfortunate. The Greek word translated "obtained a good report," is *martureō*, used eight times in Hebrews (7.8, 17; 10.15; 11.2, 4 [twice], 5, 39). We read in verse 4 that Abel through his **more excellent sacrifice than Cain, had witness borne to him that he was righteous, God bearing witness in respect of his gifts.** The same word in verse 2 is wrongfully rendered in the Authorized Version "obtained a good report." The word here used in Chapter 11 as connected with personal faith expresses the approval by God of that faith *to the consciousness of him exercising it.* The "elders" obtained from the Divine side a conscious inner testimony. The word has absolutely nothing to do with any "good report" to those outside! In fact, "the elders" of verse 2, and those associated with them, so far from having from the world "a good report," are described in verses 35-38 as "tortured," "mocked," "scourged," "imprisoned;" "stoned," "tempted," "slain with the sword," "going about in sheepskins, in goatskins," "destitute," "afflicted," "illtreated," "wandering in deserts and mountains and caves, and the holes of the earth"!

And now notice another mistranslation in the Authorized Version, verse 39. The Revised translation, **These all, having had witness borne to them through their faith,** is correct. They had indeed "a good report" (Authorized Version) in glory, but you see how they were named and treated in this wicked world!

Get a Revised Version New Testament, for although it is **not** perfect, very many such mistranslations are corrected in it, and you should always seek to know *just what God* has said.

We shall note this in the various cases following. For example, **Abel had witness borne to him that he was righteous . . . Enoch had witness borne to him that . . . he had been wellpleasing to God** (verses 4, 5).

Keep this in mind as we begin the marvelous rehearsal of the deeds of men of faith of the Old Testament. But first, to begin at the beginning, we see:

Verse 3: By faith we understand that the ages (aiōnas) have been framed by the word of God [the *uttered* word, Gr. *hrēma*]: **so that what is seen** [the visible universe] **hath not been made out of things which appear** [visible matter.].

Yea, indeed, the Word begins at the beginning—at the first of Genesis, for "the beginning" in Scripture narration refers to the creation of the "Heavens and the earth." The ages date from that creation. We know from such a passage as Ephesians 1.4, concerning those now in the Risen Christ, that God chose them in Him "before the foundation of the world"; as also in II Timothy 1.9: "God saved us, and called us with a holy calling, not according to our works, but according to His own purpose and grace, which was given us in Christ Jesus before the times of ages." See also Titus 1.2, "In hope of eternal life, which God, Who cannot lie, promised before the times of *ages*"—same Greek word, *aiōn*.

Now faith is the laying hold of God's revealed Word. But this necessitates an understanding of the facts revealed. So that we turn to Genesis 1.1 and read: "In the beginning God created the heavens and the earth." Here the word "create" is the Hebrew word *barah*. This word is used three times in Genesis 1: in verse 1 as quoted; in verse 21 concerning the "great sea monsters"; and in verse 27, concerning men. It means, to call into existence out of nothing! The other word used is *asah*, and concerns the framing what has already been called into existence.

It is evident that there is a great gap between verses 1 and 2 of Genesis One. For, in Isaiah 45.18, God says of the original creation of the earth that He "created it not a waste" (Heb., *tohu*), but "formed it to be inhabited," whereas the next verse declares: "And the earth was [or became] waste," (a desolation) *tohu;* and adds, "and void"—*bohu;* that is *void of inhabitants!*

"And the Spirit of God moved [or, was brooding] upon the face of the waters. And God said, Let there be light! And there was light" (Gen. 1.2, 3). As Paul says, "God said, Let light shine *out of darkness*" (II Cor. 4.6) : that is, by creative *fiat*—not light reflected from some other region where it already existed!

Then follows the "framing" of the six days in which the earth was made habitable for man; and those conditions and creatures which should accompany man's history on earth, were brought into being. Men do not like to study these things. Find the reason, in II Peter 3.5-7.

But it is blessed to know that this faith of which Hebrews 11 is speaking fears not to go back to the beginning, and find not only created beings, called into existence by God, but *the ages framed by Him!* So that "evolution" does not lift its head in the presence of true *faith*, which, having Divine light shed upon the Divine Word, perceives Divine truth—and *knows* it is truth!

4 By faith Abel offered unto God a more excellent sacrifice than Cain, through which he had witness borne to him that he was righteous, God bearing witness in respect of
5 his gifts: and through it he being dead yet speaketh. By faith Enoch was translated that he should not see death; and he was not found, because God translated him: for he hath had witness borne to him that before his trans-
6 lation he had been well-pleasing unto God: and without faith it is impossible to be wellpleasing unto Him; for he that cometh to God must believe that He is, and that He
7 is a rewarder of them that seek after Him. By faith Noah, being warned of God concerning things not seen as yet, moved with godly fear, prepared an ark to the saving of his house; through which he condemned the world, and became heir of the righteousness which is according to
8 faith. By faith Abraham, when he was called, obeyed to go out unto a place which he was to receive for an inheritance; and he went out, not knowing whither he went.
9 By faith he became a sojourner in the land of promise, as in a land not his own, dwelling in tents, with Isaac and
10 Jacob, the heirs with him of the same promise: for he looked for the city which hath the foundations, whose
11 builder and maker is God. By faith even Sarah herself

received power to conceive seed when she was past age, since she counted Him faithful Who had promised:
12 wherefore also there sprang of one, and him as good as dead, so many as the stars in Heaven in multitude, and as the sand, which is by the sea shore, innumerable.

We come now to *four great men of faith*: ABEL, ENOCH, NOAH, ABRAHAM; and *one woman of faith*, SARAH; each illustrating a special phase of the operation of faith, and its fruit. (Note the "these all" of verse 13, summing up those who have been mentioned; and the "these all" of verse 39, gathering up all those of faith of "old time.")

ABEL. We read that **By faith Abel offered unto God a more excellent sacrifice than Cain.**

1.   Mark immediately that Abel and Cain came to worship the same God—the true God! In Genesis 4.2 we read, "Abel was a keeper of sheep, but Cain was a tiller of the ground" (as God sent the race out of Eden to be).

But Cain forgot the ground was *cursed;* he came to God with some of his crop, as a *patronizer,* acknowledging God's existence, desirous of His favor, but *not* acknowledging himself a *sinner,* and that "the wages of sin is *death";* he refused responsibility; went out from the presence of Jehovah; dwelt in the land of Nod (Wandering); begat children and built himself a city—the first city of man; gave it his son's name; and began a line and a civilization, without God—the beginning of the world, with its "lust of the flesh, lust of the eyes, and vain glory of life."

God had brought in *death,* when He "made coats of skins, and clothed" Adam and Eve; so that they had taught their children that death must come—the death of a substitute, if they were to stand before God!

Verse 4: By faith Abel offered unto God a more excellent sacrifice than Cain—(1) Abel recognized his sinnerhood, his guilt, his inability to approach God.* This is the first step toward salvation!

---

*It seems that until the Flood the cherubim stood with "the flame of a sword" at the gate of Eden. And while there is no mention in Genesis of Jehovah's being there in any direct manifestation, yet He is spoken of over and over as seated "above the cherubim." His throne is always connected with them. From Gen. 3.24: "He placed at the east of the garden of Eden the cherubim, and the flame of a sword which turned every way, to keep the way of the tree of life," we are compelled to deduce that worship was carried on there. So we read, "Cain went out from the *presence* of Jehovah" (Gen. 4.16). Even Cain and his descendants knew where the worship of the true God should be carried on!

2. Abel was a keeper of sheep, and brought "of the firstlings of his flock," that is, a *lamb,* when he came to worship God. This lamb he *slew:* he poured out the life-blood. Marvelously had God taught man, both as to his own guilt, and as to the offering of a substitute, the poured out life-blood of which should take the place of his own death. Abel brought death to God, instead of life, as Cain had brazenly done.

3. We see that Abel's sacrifice was accepted. Doubtless the fire of Jehovah fell upon it, visibly, as at the tabernacle (Lev. 9.24) and at the temple in Israel's time (II Chron. 7.1); and upon David's and Elijah's offerings (I Chron. 21.26; I Kings 18.39).

4. Next we read that **Abel had witness borne to him that he was righteous,** that is, righteous before God. Abel was just as truly a sinner as Cain, for God says, "There is no distinction; for all have sinned"; and "There is none righteous, no, not one." **God bore witness in respect of Abel's gifts,** not his character! God did not need anything, as Cain's contribution seemed to indicate that He did. But that a sinner should judge himself to be a sinner, worthy of death, and also at the same moment dare to exercise faith in a holy God, on the ground of a sin-offering alone, a substitute, pouring out its life-blood in the sinner's place—this double thing God could with joy accept. This was *faith;* this was God's way. Cain lacked *self-*judgment as a sinner, and, consequently, did not have *faith;* for none but self-condemned sinners can really trust a holy God! Cain was "of the evil one," we read in I John 3.12.

What a precious witness Abel carried around in his bosom: "I am righteous, I who have no righteousness! I have been accepted on the ground of poured-out blood!"

5. Finally, **he being dead yet speaketh.** How? **through it,** on account of it—that is, his faith. Not only shall the righteous "be held in everlasting remembrance," but their faith *speaks* with a living voice down through the centuries.

Verse 5: By faith Enoch was translated that he should not see death; and he was not found, because God translated him: for he hath had witness borne to him that before his translation he had been wellpleasing unto God:—As we have seen, ABEL represents the path of *salvation by faith* in the blood of a substitute. ENOCH is the next step: one who is declared righteous is seen *walking with*

God; NOAH represents the next result of faith—testimony of coming judgment. And ABRAHAM, a tent-dwelling *pilgrim,* living
on Divine *promises.*

**Verse 6: And without faith it is impossible to be wellpleasing
unto Him; for he that cometh to God must believe that He is,
and that He is a Rewarder of them that seek after Him:** God having made faith the condition of relation with Himself, and
being the very God of truth, can be pleased with nothing else
than faith. In this verse faith is resolved into its two great primary
elements or characteristics: (a) There must be **belief that the living God exists:** and (b) **that He is a Rewarder of them that seek
after Him.** These elements of faith had Enoch, "the seventh from
Adam," who "prophesied" (Jude 14), walked habitually with
God, "begat sons and daughters . . . and was not; for God took
him" (Gen. 5.22, 24). These two elements seem most simple, but,
alas, how many professing Christians act as if God were not living;
and how many others, though seeking after Him, are not *expecting from Him* as Rewarder!

**Verse 7: By faith NOAH, being warned concerning things not
seen as yet, moved with godly fear, prepared an ark to the saving
of his house; through which he condemned the world, and became
heir of the righteousness which is according to faith.** Here is a perfect example of the two elements of faith of the preceding verse.
We find NOAH in living knowledge and communication with
God; and second, we see him building the great ark, expecting to
be preserved through it. And so we read that this faith of his
had the double effect of **condemning the world**—which heard
Noah's warning as preacher of righteousness, and saw the mighty
ark preparing—and, second, the effect of making Noah "heir of
the righteousness which is according to faith."

**Verse 8: By faith Abraham, when he was called, obeyed to go
out unto a place which he was to receive for an inheritance; and
he went out, not knowing whither he went.**—ABRAHAM is the
next step, the *pilgrim* character. The world has been judged by the
Flood, and as soon as possible set out to build the tower of Babel!
Led by Nimrod, idolatry and deification of man set in. Abraham
represents separation, pilgrimhood. He is called to leave everything, his country, his kin, even his father's house, going out **not**

knowing whither he went, and, with Isaac and Jacob later, called **strangers and pilgrims** (vs. 13).* So here we have a precious element of the believer's life: he is a *pilgrim* out from his land, his city, and, if need be, his father's house, his relatives. On what principle? That of simple faith!

If we had stopped Abraham's caravan to question him, some' thing like this would have been heard:

"Whence do you come?" "From the land of Shinar." "Where are you going?" "I do not know, but I am going to a land that I am to receive for an inheritance." "Who told you that you would find such a land?" "The God Whose I am." At these replies, the world would shake its head and say, "This man has lost his mind!"

But so it is with every obedient Christian. He has come out from the world, for His Lord has said, "Ye are not of the world, even as I am not of the world" (Jno. 15.18-9; 17.16). The Christian is journeying on to the City that hath foundations—that glorious City of the last two chapters of the Bible. He has not seen it, but he reads, and believes! **Faith is the conviction of things not seen.**

Verse 9: By faith he became a sojourner in the land of promise, as in a land not his own, dwelling in tents, with Isaac and Jacob, the heirs with him of the same promise. Round about him were the high-walled cities of the Canaanite nations, yet this land now belonged in *promise,* which was in *fact,* to *Abraham.* But he accepted the principle voiced by David, when he said, "We are strangers before Thee, and sojourners, as all our fathers were" (I Chron. 29.15). And he *waited* for the realization of the promise. Meditate on these verses. It is great food for faith! God says, "The meek shall inherit the earth." And they certainly will! But if they are walking as their father Abraham, they are not seeking *now* to inherit it, nor are they striving to accumulate as much of its goods as they can!

---

*Adam represents federal, racial headship—and failure through sin.

2. Noah represents God's gracious preservation of His own from the utter destruction of the Flood (Gen. 6.6-8, 13; 7.1).

3. Abraham reveals God's counsels of salvation and mercy: "To Abraham were the promises spoken, and to his Seed . . . which is Christ" (Gal. 3.16). God promised: (1) To be a God to Abraham and his seed. (2) To bless the world through him.

4. But now, also in Abraham, the principle of strangerhood is first seen: Abraham is *called out;* for the world had left God. So God's people are to leave it today.

5. Abraham **obeyed . . . not knowing.** So should Christians!

What an example Abraham set! First, see his *family:* Isaac, his son, devoted himself to his father's will *even unto death* (Gen. 22). Had not God said, "Shall I hide from Abraham the thing that I do? . . . I have known him to the end that he may command his children and his household after him" (Gen. 18.17, 19). And his grandson, ambitious Jacob, humbled by God, saying, at last, "I have *waited* for Thy salvation, O Jehovah" (Gen. 49.18), and they were laid to rest in the only "real estate" that Abraham had— Machpelah (Gen. 23). Even the Hittites said to Abraham, "Thou art a prince of God among us." What a blessed testimony! And lastly, Abraham got God's vision of the glorious coming *city!*

Verse 10: For he looked for the city which hath the foundations, whose Architect and Maker is God: What a vision of truth God gave this pilgrim! Our Lord said of him, "Your father Abraham rejoiced to see My day; and he saw it, and was glad" (Jno. 8.56). And now this second revelation, of **the city which hath the foundations.** Read Revelation 21.19-20.

Verse 11: By faith even Sarah herself received power to conceive seed when she was past age, since she counted Him faithful Who had promised: Dear Sarah! Always admirable in that subjection to Abraham which is true queenliness in God's sight. For does not Peter thus commend her: "As Sarah obeyed Abraham, calling him lord"? And self-sacrificing: see the story of Hagar, Genesis.16. But God waits thirteen years between Genesis 16 and 17, and then changes the names of both Abram (17.5) and Sarai (vs. 15), Abraham, ninety-nine; Sarah, ninety. Abraham laughs, not in derision, at the thought of his begetting and Sarah's bearing, a child. Sarai's new name, Sarah, is *Princess!* And she had herself laughed (Gen. 18.9-15). Scores of years before, she had given up "hope." But the record now is, **By faith even Sarah herself received power to conceive seed when she was past age.** For we read, **She counted Him faithful Who had promised.** Ye Christian women, let 90-year-old, wrinkled Sarah, teach you: For she laughed at first in unbelief, and then learned to laugh in faith (Gen. 21.6), saying, "*God* hath made me *to laugh;* everyone that heareth will laugh with me."

Verse 12: Wherefore also there sprang of one, and him as good as dead . . . as the stars . . . and as the sand—uncounted multitudes. Even Sarah, to whom the promise had not been made directly, entered into the blessing of it. She therefore shows in a remarkable way the power of the principle of faith in bringing blessing from God. **By faith Sarah . . . wherefore also there sprang** of Abraham—multitudes! **She counted Him faithful:** There is no more complete definition of the power of faith than these simple words: "she counted Him faithful Who had promised."

Life in ABEL, walk in ENOCH, witness in NOAH, pilgrimhood in ABRAHAM, and the power of faith to bring blessing to the *weakest,* in SARAH.

13   **These all died in faith, not having received the promises, but having seen them and greeted them from afar, and having confessed that they were strangers and pil-**
14   **grims on the earth. For they that say such things make it manifest that they are seeking after a country of their**
15.   **own. And if indeed they had been mindful of that country from which they went out, they would have had op-**
16   **portunity to return. But now they desire a better country, that is, a heavenly: wherefore God is not ashamed of them, to be called their God; for He hath prepared for them a city.**

Note the words **These all,** of verses 13 and 39. Verse 13, speaking of the saints of the Old Testament, says, **These all died in faith.** Now the Greek of the word in *(kata)* here means according to: or, as we might say, in the line of, in the *path* of, the *way* of. They believed the promises, and kept believing, and died believing: though what was promised had not yet come. Note, in verse 13, that the words **not having received the promises,** do not at all mean that the promises failed, or that they lost them! A promise depends on the faithfulness and ability of the person promising!

The second thing noted concerning them is that the promises were ever in their delighted view: **Having seen them and greeted them from afar!**

The third thing which is noted is that they **confessed that they were strangers and pilgrims on the earth,** and any real trust in God's Word makes a **stranger and pilgrim** on this earth out of any one!

The fourth blessed word is **(vs. 16), Now they desire a better**

country, that is, a heavenly. This marvelous mark on the brow of those bound for Heaven, *only enlightened eyes see!*

We could almost *expect* the next words of verse 16: **Wherefore God is not ashamed of them to be called their God!** We cannot shrink from saying, that of many whose faith is not real, God is ashamed. But think of the King of the universe saying of poor us, "I am not ashamed of him"!

Lastly, **He hath prepared for them a City.** This City was described in verse 10 as looked for by the patriarchs, Abraham, Isaac, and Jacob. Our thoughts are instantly drawn to Revelation 21.1-4, which I have no doubt was in Abraham's vision expectantly. Furthermore, we must not forget the Jerusalem millennial city and temple, with its mountain foundations, yet to appear (Isa. 2.2, 4; Ezek. chaps. 40-48, etc.).

17 By faith Abraham, being tried, offered up Isaac: yea he that had gladly received the promises was offering up
18 his only begotten son; even he to whom it was said, In
19 Isaac shall thy seed be called: accounting that God is able to raise up, even from the dead; from whence he did also
20 in a figure receive him back. By faith Isaac blessed Jacob
21 and Esau, even concerning things to come. By faith Jacob, when he was dying, blessed each of the sons of Joseph;
22 and worshiped, leaning upon the top of his staff. By faith Joseph, when his end was nigh, made mention of the departure of the children of Israel; and gave command-
23 ment concerning his bones. By faith Moses, when he was born, was hid three months by his parents, because they saw he was a goodly child; and they were not afraid of
24 the king's commandment. By faith Moses, when he was grown up, refused to be called the son of Pharoah's
25 daughter; choosing rather to share ill treatment with the people of God, than to enjoy the pleasures of sin for a
26 season; accounting the reproach of Christ greater riches than the treasures of Egypt; for he looked unto the rec-
27 ompense of reward. By faith he forsook Egypt, not fearing the wrath of the king; for he endured, as seeing Him
28 Who is invisible. By faith he kept the passover, and the sprinkling of the blood, that the destroyer of the first-
29 born should not touch them. By faith they passed through the Red Sea as by dry land: which the Egyptians assaying
30 to do were swallowed up. By faith the walls of Jericho

fell down, after they had been compassed about for seven
31 days. By faith Rahab the harlot perished not with them
that were disobedient, having received the spies with
peace.

**Verse 17: By faith Abraham, being tried, hath offered up
Isaac**—the verb reads thus in the Greek, and should be thus
translated. God on His side, when a man believes Him, reckons
that faith's account is closed. Abraham took the knife to slay his
son, the final action of a completed faith—a faith under extremest
trial. God reckoned it *done!*   ..

Verses 18-19: Note the double action of faith within Abraham's
heart: first, he remembered that God had said, **In Isaac shall thy
seed be called**—that Isaac would be the father of the coming,
promised seed. Second, he remembered that **God was able to raise
up, even from the dead**—for he did expect to slay Isaac. This
was indeed to give "substance" to "things hoped for." The result?
He did also in a figure receive him back . . . from the dead (vs.
19).

Trial comes in the pathway of faith, and trial often touches our
affections—what is nearest and dearest to us. God does not delight to deprive us of what we treasure. On the contrary, Paul
tells us to have our hope "set on God, Who giveth us richly all
things to enjoy." So to prevent His saints from forgetting the only
Giver of good things—and thus passing into a life of selfishness,
leading on to death, He is continually saying to His own, "Put
back into My hands what I have given you." Blessed are they who,
like Abraham, prove to God their love for Him above all, by sur-
rendering all. The words of God out of Heaven when Abraham
had offered Isaac, are most touching!

"Lay not thy hand upon the lad, neither do thou anything unto
him, for now I know that thou fearest God, seeing thou hast not
withheld thy son, thine only son, from Me . . . And the angel of
Jehovah called unto Abraham a second time out of Heaven, and
said, by Myself have I sworn, said Jehovah, because thou hast
done this thing, and hast not withheld thy son, thine only son:
that in blessing I will bless thee, and in multiplying, I will multiply
thy seed as the stars of the Heaven . . . and in thy Seed shall all
the nations of the earth be blessed, because thou hast obeyed My
voice" (Gen. 22.12-18).

When God tries faith, it is to give still greater blessing. Let us not fear, let us not fail God, but as at the beginning of the life of faith, so in the trial of it, be like our father Abraham.

Verse 20: By faith Isaac blessed Jacob and Esau, even concerning things to come: Read Genesis 27.27-9; 39-40 (in R. V. if possible, for it is more accurate, and also gives the verses in the poetical form in which they are in the Hebrew). Despite Isaac's craving a venison dinner, there was in him that living faith that spoke the very words God desired. This is proved by his subsequent refusal to change the blessing of the firstborn back to Esau, as he said, "I . . . have blessed him, yea, and he shall be blessed" (Gen. 27.33).

Verse 21: By faith Jacob, when he was dying, blessed each of the sons of Joseph; and worshiped, leaning upon the top of his staff. What a beautiful picture! Jacob dying, blessing, worshiping, leaning! It had taken many years for Jacob, by nature so strong and self-sufficient, to sit for this photograph! Years afterward in Egypt we read (Gen. 49.18) his words, "I have waited for Thy salvation, O Jehovah!"*

Verse 22: By faith Joseph, when his end was nigh, made mention of the departure of the children of Israel; and gave commandment concerning his bones: Like his father Jacob, Joseph when his end was nigh had clear vision and excellent choice. In Isaac's, Jacob's and Joseph's cases, there was the prophetic vision, and the knowledge of what God desired done. But mark this: there was also the essential element of *faith* in their utterances. It was by *faith* that Jacob claimed Ephraim and Manasseh as his own (Gen. 48.5). It was by faith that he placed Ephraim before Manasseh (Gen. 48.14, 19, ff). Neither Isaac nor Jacob nor Joseph was an automaton. Each saw God's mind for the future, and said it would be so. Each had a "confidence of things hoped for, a conviction of facts not seen."

---

*The God of all grace calls Himself "the God of Jacob" more often than "the God of Abraham"—over 70 times, in fact: hunt them out in your concordance. So we read in Mic. 7.20:

"Thou wilt perform the truth to Jacob, and the lovingkindness to Abraham, which Thou hast sworn unto our fathers from the days of old." It was "loving-kindness" to Abraham, all undeserved; it was "truth" to Jacob, so ill-deserved! Because our God "delighteth in mercy" (Heb., lovingkindness), God's grace, in which He delights, extends to Jacob. Not that Jacob is the cause: *God* is the cause, and Jacob the object.

How beautiful was the choice by Joseph, the lord of all Egypt, land of magnificent monuments to the dead, to be carried up to humble Shechem for burial in the land of Canaan! "He was put in a coffin in Egypt" (the last words of Genesis). But Joseph was not of Egypt. He had *faith*, and wanted to be where the people of God were! "A coffin in Egypt" is all any of us will finally hold in *this* world! It was all Joseph got! But his bones were carried up to be buried in the piece of ground bought by Abraham when Sarah died (Gen. 23.1-20). Moses remembered to carry them up (Ex. 13.19).

Verses 23-8: By faith MOSES—(1) When born, "fair unto God" (Acts 7.20, R. V., margin)* (2) **grown up**, refusing royalty, (3) **choosing ill-treatment with the people of God**, (4) **rejecting the pleasures of sin, the treasures of Egypt,** for **the reproach of Christ,** (5) **eyes fixed on the (Divine) recompense of the reward,** (6) **he forsook Egypt:** the people with him, but *he* having the God-given faith. (7) **He endured, as seeing Him Who is invisible:** FAITH defined in a phrase! (8) **He hath kept the passover.** The people went through the form, but the faith that preserved the nation Jehovah gave to His servant Moses! Note that verse 28 begins, **By faith he has kept**—and ends, **that the destroyer of the firstborn should not touch them.**

Verse 29: By faith they passed through the Red Sea as by dry land: which the Egyptians assaying to do were swallowed up: At last we come to **By faith they!** I Corinthians 10.1-2 was fulfilled: "Our fathers . . . were all baptized *into* (Gr., *eis*) Moses in the cloud and in the sea." Remember Exodus 14.27 to 15.1:

"And Moses stretched forth his hand over the sea, and the sea returned to its strength when the morning appeared; and the Egyptians fled against it; and Jehovah overthrew the Egyptians in the midst of the sea . . . all the host of Pharaoh . . . there remained not so much as one of them. But the children of Israel walked upon dry land in the midst of the sea . . . Thus Jehovah saved Israel that day out of the hand of the Egyptians; and Israel saw the Egyptians dead upon the seashore. And Israel saw the great work which Jehovah did upon the Egyptians, and the people feared Jehovah: and

*"I am persuaded, from that expression of Stephen, 'fair unto God,' that there was an appearance somewhat Divine and supernatural, which drew the thought and minds of the parents unto a deep consideration of the child." With these words from John Owen we fully agree. Later Moses' face was so bright that the children of Israel could not look upon him!

they believed in Jehovah, and in His servant Moses. Then *sang* Moses and the children of Israel . . . unto Jehovah."

Verse 30: By faith the walls of Jericho fell down, after they had been compassed about seven days: It seemed the quintessence of weakness just to go around blowing horns! But it was what God had commanded, and they by faith obeyed. Believer, keep on blowing the horn of faith. No matter how high the walls about you and before you, keep praying and praising! The walls will fall in due season.

Verse 31: By faith Rahab the harlot perished not with them that were disobedient, having received the spies with peace. Note the following seven points about Rahab:

1.   Rahab was a common sinner, even a harlot. God says as to all of us, "There is no difference; for *all* have *sinned*."

2.   Rahab's faith (Josh. 2.8-11) was confessed by her in the words, "*I know* that Jehovah hath given you the land, and that the fear of you is fallen upon us, and that all the inhabitants of the land melt away before you."

3.   This belief meant complete turning against her own people, just as a believer now comes out from, and is no longer of, the world.

4.   It included belief that Jericho would be *destroyed* (2.13); and it brought concern for her own kin.

5.   It brought about the beautiful typical picture of the scarlet cord, tied up in her window, by which the spies also escaped (2.15-21). How that cord reminds us of the shed blood of Christ!

6.   By her faith she, her father, her mother, her brethren, and all her kindred—"*Whosoever* shall be with thee in the house"— (2.19), were preserved (6.22-23, 25).

7.   She became the mother of *Boaz* (Matt. 1.5), great-grand-father of David the king! (Ruth 4.21-2).

Now let us go back and run over the names—familiar, blessed, sweet names they—of the "witnesses" of verses 4 to 31, who "had witness borne to them."

BY FAITH—

ABEL learned—and offered a blood sacrifice; **ENOCH** was told —and believed; **NOAH** was warned—and took warning; **ABRA-HAM** was called—and obeyed; was tried, and **offered up Isaac. ISAAC** saw **things to come; JACOB** blessed each of the sons of

JOSEPH and worshiped; JOSEPH (though exalted) clung at his end to Israel and their departure from Egypt; MOSES was hid . . . by his parents,* refused royalty, chose ill-treatment, rejected sin's pleasures and Egypt's treasures, looking unto the recompense of the reward: forsook Egypt, endured, kept the passover.

BY FAITH Israel passed through the Red Sea, the walls of Jericho fell down, Rahab perished not.

32 And what shall I more say? for the time will fail me if I tell of Gideon, Barak, Samson, Jephthah; of David and

33 Samuel and the prophets: who through faith subdued kingdoms, wrought righteousness, obtained promises,

34 stopped the mouths of lions, quenched the power of fire, escaped the edge of the sword, from weakness were made strong, waxed mighty in war, turned to flight armies of

35 aliens. Women received their dead by a resurrection: and others were tortured, not accepting their deliverance; that

36 they might obtain a better resurrection: and others had trial of mockings and scourgings, yea, moreover, of bonds

37 and imprisonment: they were stoned, they were sawn asunder, they were tempted, they were slain with the sword: they went about in sheepskins, in goatskins; being

38 destitute, afflicted, ill-treated (of whom the world was not worthy), wandering in deserts and mountains and caves, and the holes of the earth.

Right through this great eleventh of Hebrews these men and women of God act in *reliance upon Him or His stated Word, wholly apart from their own feelings.*

Take Gideon (vs. 32): Go to the book of Judges and read his record: how he trembled and shrank at the thought of taking a step in leadership of God's hosts. God met his trembling heart, of course, not only twice in the matter of fleece, but afterwards in the dream his servant was given to hear (Jud. 7.9-15). And that trembling heart became strong so that he was able to say to the

---

*Moses' parents discerned that God would use him, and were filled with faith. Cf. Hannah, I Sam. 1; and John the Baptist, Lk. 1.13-17, where Zacharias displayed unbelief concerning God's purposes for John the Baptist.

people of Israel: "Jehovah HATH delivered into your hand the host of Midian." This is Mark 11.24 again, "a conviction of things not seen."*

Verse 32: Then **Barak, Samson, Jephthah, David and Samuel and the prophets,** of whom the apostle writes: **What shall I more say? for the time will fail me!** What a history of triumph he does crowd into the next words:

Verse 33: Who through faith subdued kingdoms—David is chief here, though Joshua preceded him, and Asa, Jehoshaphat, Hezekiah, Josiah, yea, and the Maccabaean brethren, faithfully followed him. **Wrought righteousness**—Elijah, Elisha, and "all the prophets" come in here; and along with them we must not forget King Josiah—read his story: II Kings 22.1 to 23.30. **Obtained promises**—here comes Caleb, claiming and receiving a promise of God given forty years before (Josh. 14.6-14). Find the promises Gideon and Barak claimed and received. **Stopped the mouths of lions**—Daniel shines here: "My God hath sent His angel, and hath shut the lions' mouths." Remember also David's victory over the lion and the bear (I Sam. 17.34), and forget not Samson (Jud. 14), nor David's mighty man, Benaiah (I Chron. 11.22),

---

*The proper place of what we call "feeling" is perfectly illustrated in the case of the woman who "heard the things concerning Jesus, came in the crowd behind, and touched His garment" (Mk. 5.25-34).

First, we read of her wretchedness: she "had suffered many things of many physicians, and had spent all that she had, and was nothing bettered, but rather grew worse."

Second, observe she had "heard the things concerning Jesus." Now we know that "faith cometh by hearing, and hearing by the word of Christ," so we saw she "came in the crowd . . . and touched His garment. For she said, If I but touch His garments, I *shall* be made whole." There was no maybe-so about it: her faith gave substance to the thing she hoped for.

Third, we have the miracle: "And straightway the fountain of her blood was dried up." God answers faith! Oh, that we all might touch HIM with the finger of faith!

Fourth, we have the proper place of *feeling:* "She *felt* in her body that she was healed of her plague."

And before we pass, note two more points, vitally connected:

Our Lord said, "Who touched My garments?" calling her out to testify before all. "The woman . . . fell down before Him, and told Him all the truth," as Luke says (8.47), "in the presence of all the people."

The last thing Jesus said unto her was, "Daughter, thy *faith* hath made thee whole." Here we have grounds for assurance. No matter how she felt the next day or any other day, she could say, "The Lord, Who healed me, said I was made whole, and I am."

I am convinced that many, because of an unwillingness to come out openly and confess all that the Lord hath done for them (whether they be men or women) are robbed of the assurance that belongs to them.

who "went down also and slew a lion in the midst of a pit in time of snow"—"a difficult thing in a difficult place at a difficult time."

Verse 34: Quenched the power of fire—Here we think of Shadrach, Meshach, and Abednego in Babylon, who said to the king, "Our God Whom we serve is able to deliver us from the burning fiery furnace; and He will deliver us out of Thy hand, O king. *But if not,* be it known unto thee, O king, that we will not serve thy gods, nor worship the golden image which thou hast set up." "And the satraps, the deputies, and the governors, and the king's counsellors [after the furnace] saw these men, that the fire had no power upon their bodies" (Dan. 3.17-18, 27). And why? They trusted God!

Escaped the edge of the sword—Whether it be King Saul's sword or Goliath's, beloved David speaks again: "Jehovah, that delivered me out of the paw of the lion, and out of the paw of the bear, He will deliver me out of the hand of this Philistine." Jeremiah, also, blessed man, who for Jehovah's sake made countless hating foes,* **escaped the edge of the sword.**

From weakness were made strong—Remember weak Sarah, who "By faith . . . received power"; and Gideon (of whom we have spoken above), who when Jehovah said to him, "Go in this thy *might*" answered, "My family is the poorest in Manasseh, and I am the least in my father's house." Then the trembling faith that put out the fleece, and the sending Gideon forth against the mighty host of the Midianites with only three hundred men! as Abraham, with only eighteen more men, conquered all the kings of Mesopotamia (Gen. 14).

Isaiah as he began his service said, "Woe is me! for I am undone, because I am a man of unclean lips." And Jeremiah, "Ah, Lord Jehovah! I know not how to speak, for I am a child." (If you are a lonely witness amid hostile surroundings, I beg you, read and re-read Jeremiah.) And how *weak* was Job made: "I abhor myself, and repent in dust and ashes." **But from weakness he was made**

---

*"Now the word of Jehovah came unto Jeremiah, while he was shut up in the court of the guard, saying . . . I will deliver thee in that day, saith Jehovah; and thou shalt not be given into the hand of the men of whom thou art afraid. For I will surely save thee, and *thou shalt not fall by the sword* . . . because thou hast put thy trust in Me." (Read Jer. 39.)

strong, an intercessor, mighty with God, listed in His Word as one of "*these three men,* Noah, Daniel, and Job" (Ezek. 1414).

Waxed mighty in war—Hear David again: "By my God do I leap over a wall." "Jehovah my rock, Who teacheth my hands to war, and my fingers to fight." Or take the thrilling tale of David's mighty men, in I Chronicles 11 and 12; or King Asa against a million, in II Chronicles 14; or Jehoshaphat's great prayer of faith in II Chronicles 20.12:

"O our God, wilt Thou not judge them? For we have *no might* against this great company that cometh against us; neither *know* we what to do: but *our eyes are upon Thee!*"
Someone has well called this "a prayer of the irresistible might of weakness."

Turned to flight armies of aliens: This, as we have said, did Abraham; also Moses' mighty praying; Joshua's fighting against Amalek (Ex. 17); and Joshua's obeying with power the Divine command, "Concerning the work of My hands, command *ye Me*" (Isa. 45.11). For we read:

"Then spake Joshua to Jehovah in the day when Jehovah delivered up the Amorites before the children of Israel; and he said in the sight of Israel,

"Sun, stand thou still upon Gibeon;

And thou, moon, in the valley of Aijalon.

And the sun stood still, and the moon stayed,

Until the nation had avenged themselves of their enemies" (Josh. 10.12‑13).

The **armies of aliens** were those who refused the royal govern‑ment of the earth through Israel, Jehovah's elect nation.

Verse 35: Women received their dead by a resurrection:—So it was with the widow who sustained Elijah, and still more strik‑ingly with the Shunammite, who, leaving her dead child upon Elisha's bed in the prophet's chamber of her home, replied to his question, "Is it well with the child?" "It is well" (II Ki. 4). Blessed faith, here!

And others were tortured, not accepting their deliverance; (lit. the redemption: they *could* have escaped!) **that they might obtain a better resurrection:**—Eleazer says in II Maccabees 6:30,

"Whereas I might have been delivered from death, I now endure sore pain." "The people that know their God shall be strong, and do exploits" (Dan. 11.32) refers to, and was fulfilled also in, the noble Maccabeans and their followers.*

Verse 36: And others had trial of mockings and scourgings, yea, moreover of bonds and imprisonment: Sometimes God tries faith *directly,* as in verses 17 ff. Only God and Abraham were—privately, so to speak—in such a trial. **The trial of mockings and scourgings** from the world is of a different character. Observe this carefully, dear saints: God may take *you,* as He took Abraham, into trial that will bring the way of God Himself into question, to the very foundations of your own soul. Be not dismayed! Be like Abraham when God called for *Isaac;* or like the Shunammite woman, whose trial was not from the world, but from God's loving ways with *her;* or like Ezekiel (Ch. 24) when God took away his wife "with a stroke" for a *parable* to those to whom Ezekiel must minister. Or like John Bunyan, who testified that he walked in despair for seven years, yet called God "The God of my salvation," as in Psalm 88.1 and 18:

---

*While the Apochrypha, in which the books of the Maccabees are found, is not inspired, and was never a part of the Bible, it has been very useful as history of the "four hundred silent years" between the Old and New Testaments. The Maccabees, Books I and II, are, on the whole, godly, earnest, historically accurate, and especially valuable. We here quote portions of II Mac.: Ch. VII:

"The constancy and cruel death of seven brethren and their mother in one day, because they would not eat swine's flesh at the king's commandment:

"And when he (the first brother) was at his last gasp, he said, 'Thou like a fury takest us out of this present life, but the King of the world shall raise us up, who have died for His laws, unto everlasting life!' " (vs. 9).

"So when he (the fourth brother) was ready to die, he said thus, 'It is good, being put to death by men, to look for hope from God to be raised up again by Him: as for thee, thou shalt have no resurrection to life' " (vs. 14).

"But the mother was marvelous above all, and worthy of honorable memory: for when she saw her seven sons slain within the space of one day, she bare it with a good courage, because of the hope that she had in the Lord. Yea, she exhorted every one of them in her own language, and . . . said unto them:

" 'Doubtless the Creator of the world, Who formed the generation of man, and found out the beginning of all things, will also of His own mercy give you breath and life again, as ye now regard not yourselves for His law's sake.'

"Now Antiochus, whilst the youngest was yet alive, assured him with oaths that he would make him both a rich and happy man if he would turn from the laws of his fathers (that is, apostatize) . . . But the young man said,

" 'Whom wait ye for? I will not obey the king's commandment: but I will obey the commandment of the Law that was given unto our fathers by Moses . . . Then the king, being in a rage, handled him worse than all the rest, and took it grievously that he was mocked. So this man died undefiled, and put his whole trust in the Lord. Last of all, after the sons, the mother died" (vss. 20-41).

"O Jehovah, *the God of my salvation,*
I have cried day and night before Thee.

. . . .

Lover and friend hast Thou put far from me,
And mine acquaintance into darkness."

When we reflect that Paul is writing to earnest Hebrew believers, and that most, if not all, the "witnesses" of Chapter 11,
from Abraham on, were connected with the Hebrew nation, we
see how weightily this history would affect them! Such a mighty
influence has been exercised upon the soul of Gentile Christians
by Fox's **Book of Martyrs.**

Verse 37: They were stoned—This was peculiarly by Israelitish method of execution. "Stoning was the ordinary mode of
Hebrew execution," says the **National Encyclopedia** (Vol. 4,
pp. 250-5, *in loc.*). (See Ex. 19.13; Josh. 7.25; II Chron. 24.21.)
Zachariah, son of Barachiah, whom our Lord mentioned in Matthew
23.35, was thus stoned. He in the Old Testament and Stephen in
the New, are the most prominent examples of martyrdom by this
means. **They were sawn asunder**—There is a tradition that Jeremiah suffered thus under King Manasseh. (See Jewish **Mishna.**)
Justin Martyr also (158 A.D.) reproached the Jews with this awful
accusation concerning Isaiah: "Whom ye sawed asunder with a
wooden saw." But these were one or two of many, according to the
spirit of this passage in Hebrews 11.

They were tempted—Always, of course, by Satan; but here,
probably, especially by those who sought to turn them back from
the faithful confession. The word "tempted," standing as it does
between the more terrible (physically) sufferings of being "stoned"
and "sawn asunder" on the one hand and **slain with the sword** on
the other, has perplexed many; so that some have sought to discover
if some other word were not meant. But this will not be entered into
by any who have **suffered being tempted** directly by Satan's guile
and power. Do not think that Luther in Wartburg was deceived
when he threw the inkstand at Satan! Remember that Peter in his
first epistle, the subject of which is suffering, says to saints, "Now
for a little while, if need be, ye have been put to grief in manifold
trials" (1.6). And Paul speaks of our wrestling as having its "evil
day" (Eph. 6.13). There are times and occasions when God permits

Satan to assault the spirit directly, as we have said; and the anguish of such hours is greater than any other. It is not so much an allure-ment to evil, as a direct assault. Bunyan knew it, or he could never have written of the fight with Apollyon. To quote Peter again: "Be sober, be watchful: your adversary the devil, as a roaring lion, walketh about, seeking whom he may devour" (I Pet. 5.8). (Thank God for the "*may*"! Satan must have Divine permission for any-thing he does!)

They were slain with the sword: So in Acts 12 Herod slew the Apostle James. Millions of God's faithful ones have dyed red with their life-blood the swords of persecutors! **They went about in sheepskins, in goatskins.** Here were "the excellent of the earth, in whom," God says, "is all My delight." Be ready, O believer, to follow such a path of banishment from man as this indicates! **Being destitute, afflicted, ill-treated**—there is somehow in our very soul as we look at these words the prophecy that some, prob-ably many, reading them, will experience them.

Verse 38: (Of whom the world was not worthy)—What a glory it would be to have it written thus of us by the Holy Spirit, as He writes it of those who suffered of old as God's own! And now see how ends this great passage descriptive of God's saints: **Wander-ing in deserts and mountains and caves, and the holes of the earth:** We know how this continued. These Hebrew saints of old have their counterpart in the Covenanters of Scotland, the Vaudois of France, the Albigenses, the Waldensians; remembering always the persecuted Puritans; and, we may add, every *real* Protestant. For the Roman Catholic harlot (Rev. 17.1-6, 18), seated on her seven-hilled city (vs. 9), is still "drunken with the blood of the saints, and with the blood of the martyrs of Jesus" (vs. 6).

But now, we beg you, hearken to what we are more and more convinced will happen before our eyes, in our days. There is much talk of prayer for a great revival, a world-wide revival, as they call it. But John says, "Ye have heard that Antichrist cometh" (I Jno. 4.3). Let me say boldly, I profoundly fear that in the hearts of many who pray for world-wide revival, there is that unconscious desire: that we may be delivered back into a time of reverence for God's Word, such as the Puritans brought to these shores; into a time of deliverance from the hideous scandal of Sodomite indecency that flaunts itself more and more before our eyes every day; into an old-fashioned revival in-gathering of thousands into respectable, God-fearing churches; into a condition of things where godly preachers and Bible teachers will be subjects of the old-time regard from men of the world; and their sermons and teachings be welcomed by the public press and read by hundreds of thousands, as Spurgeon's and Talmadge's sermons used to be.

But what if these closing verses of Hebrews 11 should be *prophetic* of the world's attitude toward true Christians—true men of faith, as of old? Are we ready for this in our prayer? Suppose that our prayer for revival should result in such a quickening of faith and entering into complete separation from the world, that the world would turn upon us in *persecution?* Are we not praying for a respectable, nay, a regenerate and yet bearable condition, rather than our becoming "the scum and offscouring of all things" with Paul? Will you let your prayer include *that?* **Destitute . . . afflicted . . . ill-treated! Deserts . . . mountains . . . holes of the earth!** Suppose God should choose to have His Church, before its rapture, as separate as it was on the day of Pentecost? Or suppose, the Church having given its testimony, a "great persecution" should arise against it, such as followed the death of Stephen?

May God in mercy search us all out, making us as sincere as was Paul, who was ready to say at any time, "God is my witness."

God in His wisdom has already permitted His dear saints in many lands to suffer at the hands of their enemies. Devoted missionaries tell of the horrors inflicted upon Christians in many lands; and there come trustworthy reports of believers lying in prison, or starved in concentration camps, in many parts of the earth. The temptation of the devil is for Christians in such trials to question God's kindness or justice. But we learn in this very epistle that God's own dear Son was *perfected through the things which He suffered!*

The Divine movement in this age is *not* that righteousness shall triumph, but on the contrary, that human wickedness shall have full headway and come to its climax, before being visited by the Great Day of Wrath preceding the Millennium, and be finally judged at the Great White Throne at the Millennium's close. Even during the Millennium it will be *peace by compulsion.*

In the Hebrews narrative of triumphs, pursuits, and escapes on the one hand, and captivity, torment, pursuits and death on the other, we have been seeing that *FAITH* is victorious under all circumstances. But let us beware of falling into the Delilah arms of a Philistine world. For this world is an *armed camp against God, against Christ,* and *against all operations of the Holy Spirit!* Does not Peter warn us, "Forasmuch then as Christ suffered in the flesh, arm ye yourselves also with the *same* mind" (i.e., same expectancy)? It were kinder to young converts to warn them from the first of the deadly foes in the heavenly places and among men, through whom the life of faith takes us, than to let them, unwarned, choose that life—only to "shrink back."

39 **And these all, having had witness borne to them through**
40 **their faith, received not* the promise, God having provided some better thing concerning us, that apart from us they should not be made perfect.**

Verse 39: Having had witness borne to them—This precious word "witness" accompanies this "so great cloud of witnesses" from Hebrews 11.2 to Chapter 12.1. God spoke to them, and they knew it; their hearts were filled with an expectancy—of what? Paul's great general definition of the saints in Romans 2.7 will give the answer: "Them that by 'patience in well-doing seek for glory" (that is, connected with the presence of God) "and honor" (the opposite of the guilt, disgrace, and uncleanness of sin) "and incorruption" (that is, a state of bodily deliverance).

Through their faith—Their faith brought the witness and the expectation, but not yet the realization. **Received not the promise** —As Joseph said down in Egypt as he lay dying, "God will surely visit you"; and he asked that his bones be carried up to Canaan, the land of promise, for burial. There they lie yet—waiting.†

---

*Rotherham's rendering, "Bare not away the promise" is good here.

†We beg you, go through the Word of God studying the word "wait," as toward God. It is one of the great words of Scripture. Jacob said, "I have waited for Thy salvation, O Jehovah."
Isaiah:
"They that *wait* for Jehovah shall renew their strength" (40.31).
"They that *wait* for Me shall not be put to shame" (49.23).
"For from of old men have not heard, nor perceived by the ear, neither hath the eye seen a God besides Thee, Who worketh for him that *waiteth* for Him" (64.4).
Jeremiah:
"Jehovah is good unto them that *wait* for Him, to the soul that seeketh Him.
It is good that a man should hope and *quietly wait* for the salvation of Jehovah"

Verse 40: God having provided some better thing for us, that apart from us they should not be made perfect: First, here, who are the "us"? They are Hebrew believers spoken to and of, as "partakers of a heavenly calling." (This the Israelites, the "these all" of verse 39, never were and never will be. "Us" discriminates between *them* and all believers on an exalted, *heavenly* Christ.) What is the "better thing"? We believe that our heavenly calling, our membership in the Body of Christ, is that "better thing." Oh, let us cherish it! Since the lives of these great believers in Chapter 11, Christ the Son of God has come, has died and been raised; and we died with Him, and were raised with Him into "heavenly places" and "seated" there with Him.*

They of the Old Testament were continually conscious of the great *veil* that hung between them and the ark of God's presence. How infinitely "better" it is to be invited "by a new and living way," by the blood of Christ and with Christ, to enter into the presence of God, by the Spirit! They of the Old Testament had a legal yoke which Peter said neither their fathers nor they "were able to bear"—the "ten thousand things" of God's Law. We have fellowship in the Spirit, He dwelling in each believer and, in a peculiar way, in the Assembly of believers. We have the Lord's

---

(Lam. 3.25, 26).
　　And David:
　　"I *waited* patiently for Jehovah,
And He inclined unto me and heard my cry" (Ps. 40.1).
　　"Rest in Jehovah and *wait* patiently for Him" (Ps. 37.7).
In waiting, the saints give God His place. Blessed is the man who finds himself taken by sovereign grace into His plans of infinite wisdom. God says to the Hebrew believers and to us, "Ye have need of patience, that, having done the will of God, ye may receive the promise" (Ch. 10.36-37).

*"This better thing" than the O. T. saints had, is not explicitly described in Hebrews, for the great message of Hebrews is to a religious nation to whom Jehovah had spoken, and given a "religion." But now that God had "spoken in His Son," former things—temple, sacrifices, days, seasons—were done away. The constant temptation of these Jews was to go back to this Judaism. But the only Priest God now recognized, having been offered for sin on earth—yea, "outside the gate" of Jerusalem itself, was at God's right hand in Heaven.

Infinite love had given Christ to die for sin. But, as today, and ever with wretched man, there was a turning to "religion," from which GOD had turned away! Man said, "*I am a Jew*"—just as today they say "*I* am a Presbyterian," "*I* am a Methodist," "*I* am a Baptist"—and so on. (And this despite specific forbidding in I Cor. 1.12-13.) But Christ died for *sinners!* Whether Jewish, Protestant, Catholic, infidel or atheist, or idolator, Christ died only for the LOST!

And He is the Great High Priest in Heaven of *sinners*, who as *sinners*, helpless, lost, and undone, have come to faith in a God Who "so loved" sinners, and in a Saviour to Whom alone at God's right hand is given the blessed work of maintaining believers on the way and bringing them where He is, in Glory!

Supper by which to keep in vivid memory that He has finished,
Himself, the work He did at the Cross; and by which we show His
death "till He come." And we have the blessed hope of our blessed
Lord's return, looking for Him "so much the more, as we see the
day drawing nigh" (10.25).

That apart from us they should not be made perfect: Here
indeed is a glorious unity of all God's people: Israel with the
earthly calling, and the saints now with the heavenly calling, looking
forward to that day when shall be consummated in them and for
them all their desire, yea, "exceeding abundantly above all they
have asked or thought." Concerning the patriarchs our Lord Jesus
told the Pharisees: "Ye shall see Abraham, and Isaac, and Jacob,
and all the prophets, in the kingdom of God, and yourselves cast
forth without" (Lk. 13.28). And as to the antediluvian saints,
Enoch, for example, has been in Heaven between three and four
thousand years. What it will be for Enoch to be "made perfect"
must, we believe, concern bodily things; for we read in Chapter
12.23, "Ye are come unto the *spirits* of just men made perfect."
The spirits of these saints, now in heaven, had already been made
"perfect." The "perfecting" of verse 40 looks forward to that
"salvation" consummated at the coming of Christ (9.28), which
includes the redemption of *the body*. Compare Romans 13.11.

The same Greek word is used in Chapter 6.1, where the exhortation is to "press on unto full growth." This "full growth," "no
longer babes," is seen in Philippians 3.15, and I Corinthians 2.6.
That such an adult spiritual condition is attainable in this life is
manifest. It corresponds to "him that is spiritual" of I Corinthians
2.15: that is, controlled by and walking in the Spirit. May it be the
condition of all of us!

CHAPTER TWELVE

1   THEREFORE LET US ALSO, seeing we are compassed about with so great a cloud of witnesses, lay aside every weight, and the sin which doth so easily beset us, and let us run with patience the race that is set before

2   us, looking unto Jesus the File-Leader and Perfecter of faith, Who for the joy that was set before Him endured the Cross, despising shame, and hath sat down at the

3   right hand of the throne of God. For consider Him that hath endured such gainsaying of sinners against Himself,

4   that ye wax not weary, fainting in your souls. Ye have

5   not yet resisted unto blood, striving against sin: and ye have forgotten the exhortation which reasoneth with you as with sons,

      My son, regard not lightly the chastening of the Lord,
      Nor faint when thou art reproved of Him;

6   For whom the Lord loveth He chasteneth,
      And scourgeth every son whom He receiveth.

7   It is for chastening that ye are enduring; God dealeth with you as with sons; for what son is there whom his

8   father chasteneth not? But if ye are without chastening, whereof all have been made partakers, then are ye

9   bastards, and not sons. Furthermore, we had the fathers of our flesh to chasten us, and we gave them reverence: shall we not much rather be in subjection unto the Father

10   of spirits, and live? For they indeed for a few days chastened us as seemed good to them; but He for our

11   profit, that we may be partakers of His holiness. All chastening seemeth for the present to be not joyous but grievous; yet afterward it yieldeth peaceable fruit unto them that have been exercised thereby, even the fruit of

12   righteousness. Wherefore lift up the hands that hang

13   down, and the palsied knees; and make straight paths for your feet, that that which is lame be not turned out of the way, but rather be healed.

THE ELEVENTH OF HEBREWS has been called "God's Westminster Abbey," in which He puts up monuments to the saints of the past. Rather, it is the heavenly amphitheater from which those who have gone before, the **so great cloud of wit-nesses,** are viewed as looking upon the race that you and I are running, down in the arena right now!

Therefore let us also, seeing we are compassed about with so great a cloud of witnesses, lay aside every weight, and the sin which does so easily beset us, and let us run with patience the race that is set before us—
Notice first the distinction between "weight" and "sin." How runners strip themselves of every weight possible, wearing the lightest clothing, the lightest shoes!* Many a weight carrier who may eventually get to Heaven, will be passed on the way by those who have laid *weights* aside.

Now as to **the sin which doth so easily beset us**—some make this *the flesh,* which is with the believer, although he is not *"in* the flesh" but *"in* the *Spirit,"* Who gives him the victory. Others regard **the sin which so easily besets** as *unbelief,* that terrible temp-tation which these Hebrew believers were ever beset with, of letting go heavenly things for an earthly worship. "Easily" is a Greek word often translated *plausibly,* and meaning literally, "well-standing-around." **The sin easily besets us.** One well says, "Let us never for-get that; nor think for a moment that we can get in a position in which sin will not be natural to the flesh, or where we do not need to be on our guard. Sin is as natural to the flesh as it is for an animal to breathe. And the moment the eye is taken off Christ, you have the certainty of the sin besetting you."

Next we have, **And let us run with patience the race that is set before us**—This "patience" is illustrated in Abraham in Chapter 6.15: "And thus, having *patiently* endured, he obtained the prom-ise." God *could* take each believer up to Heaven as soon as he be-lieves. But then all would be babes, would they not? God sets be-

---

*Mr. Ridout well says here:
"We often hear, alas, the question: What is the harm or the sin in my doing this or that thing; engaging in this business, or indulging in that pleasure? The question is answered just here. Is the thing a weight, or is it a wing? Is it that which speeds you on your course or does it hold you back? . . . Weights are not necessarily external: they are first of all in the *heart.* Duties are never weights. But the moment a thing gets a place in my heart and mind which is not in God's mind for me, it becomes a *weight,* no matter what it is."

fore each of us *a course, a race*. It is not carried on in Heaven, but *here*, where is only *the wilderness*, with its constant trials of faith, the patient endurance of which is the only way to perfecting. So indeed it was with the Lord Himself, Who was "made perfect through sufferings" (2.10), "learned obedience by the things which He *suffered*," and thus was *"made perfect"* (5.8, 9).

Lay aside every weight, and the sin . . . let us run with patience the race—First we have the preparation for the race, then the running. This running our course* is in view, as we have said, of the great examples of faith of the preceding chapter. Paul said to the Ephesian elders, "I hold not my life of any account as dear unto myself, so that I may accomplish *my course*" (Acts 20.24).

And again,

"Know ye not that they that run in a race run all, but one receiveth the prize? Even so run; that ye may attain. And every man that striveth in the games exerciseth self-control in all things. Now they do it to receive a corruptible crown; but we an incorruptible. I therefore so run, as not uncertainly; so fight I, as not beating the air" (I Cor. 9.24-6).

Later, writing from prison in Rome, he says he has not yet finished his course, but:

"I am pressing on, if so be that I may lay hold on that for which also I was laid hold on by Christ Jesus . . . I count not myself yet to have laid hold: but one thing I do, forgetting the things which are behind, and stretching forward to the things which are before, I press on toward the goal unto the prize of the high calling of God in Christ Jesus" (Phil. 3.12-14).

And finally, just before Nero set his spirit free to go to be with Christ, which is "very far better," he writes,

"I *have* fought the good fight, I have *finished the course*, I *have* kept the faith: hencefore *there is* laid up for me *the crown*" (II Tim. 4.7-8).

Verse 2: And now comes the great positive attitude in this conflict: **Looking steadfastly on Jesus, the Leader and Completer of faith: Who, in view of the joy lying before Him, endured the Cross, having despised the shame, and is set down at the right**

---

*How dare you or how dare I count ourselves exempt from this race? Christendom is full of professing Christians who are not running this race, but are weighted down, and have never even considered laying aside cares, riches, pleasures, and "lusts of other things," as our Lord puts it in Mk. 4.19—"weights," all of them. Let us not dare to be like these!

hand of the throne of God! Our Lord is here made the *Archēgos,* the Author and Captain or Perfecter *of faith* (not for all of *"our* faith," as the A. V. and also unfortunately the R. V. render, interpolating the word "our" which is not in the Greek). Jesus is the One Who *Himself* had *perfect* faith! Thayer well translates *Archēgos,* "One who takes the lead in anything, and thus affords an example, a predecessor in the matter," adding of Christ, "Who in the pre-eminence of *His* faith far surpassed the examples commemorated in Chapter 11." Our directions here are, to look objectively at our Lord Jesus, the File-Leader of the column of believers, those who had perfect faith to look at Him just as objectively as we would look at Abel, Enoch, Noah, Abraham, or any of the other great cloud of witnesses.

Mr. Darby's words are illuminative: "When **looking at Jesus**" (which is here enjoined as the positive engagement of the soul, **laying aside** being negative) "the new man is active; there is a new object, which unburdens and detaches us from every other by means of a new affection, which has its place in the new nature: and in Jesus Himself, to Whom we look, there is a positive power which sets us free." And Grant: "To get on in the road is the way to escape entanglements and the need of a battle. Christ is the goal; and if our eyes are upon Him, we find at once the perfect example and the energy for the way."

Jesus endured the Cross, despising shame, to reach that place of eternal joy at the Father's right hand set before us as an example of faith. Even His enemies confessed, as they saw Him on the Cross, "He *trusted* on God!" What a wonderful thing, then, to **be compassed about with so great a cloud of witnesses** as we find in Chapter 11! Yea, and to be *among* those witnesses ourselves, traveling through this wilderness, remembering always to look upon* the great Chief Witness, the **Archēgos—the File-Leader** *of all who have trusted God—even upon Jesus!*

The One leading the column of witnesses was He who **in view of the joy that was set before Him endured the Cross**—For Jesus knew—had set before Him by the Father, in all its Divine fullness,

---

*The Greek verb *aphoraō* translated "looking unto" (Thayer) means, "to turn eyes away from other things, and fix them on something"—in this case, a Person. The meaning here is not to look to Him for help, but to *consider* Him.

the reward, and that eternal, that awaited Him risen from the dead and re-entering the glory which He had with the Father. There was no joy in all eternity like that of our Lord's meeting the Father after Calvary—meeting His Father's infinite delight in His Son's absolute obedience—"unto death, yea, the death of the Cross"!

There is no joy like the accomplishment of a noble task: and of the noblest task of all eternity, Christ was to say, "I have finished it."

There is among us on earth no joy like that of rescuing a fellow-creature from ruin. But Christ had **the joy set before Him** of rescuing and redeeming from endless woe so many that He would "see the travail of His soul and *be satisfied*"!

There was no joy like that of lavishing His infinite love on those eternally lost and undone without it and Him: for, being God, He is Love: and now it became possible to let love freely out, fully and forever.

There was no joy like unselfish love receiving, without stint or limit, that love for which true love longs: "Only love seeks love, and only love satisfies love."

There was no joy like looking forward, after the ages of sin, to a New Creation, based on His sacrifice, "where righteousness is *at home.*"

There is no earthly delight like that of doing the will of, perfectly pleasing, another to whom our will is properly subjected. How infinitely more with Christ, Who said:
"I delight to do Thy will, O My God;
    Yea, Thy Law is within My heart."
And, "My meat is to do the will of Him that sent Me, and to accomplish His work." "The cup which the Father hath given Me, shall I not drink it?"

The joy of being the means of *letting out the heart of God* toward His creatures was **set before** Christ! When He bare men's sins and put them away, then the mighty river of *grace, pure grace,* from the *heart* of God, Who *delighteth in mercy,* could *pour forth!* "God was in Christ reconciling the world unto Himself, not reckoning unto them their trespasses." "God *so loved* the world that He gave His only begotten Son." Or, "Herein is love, not that we loved God, but that He loved us, and sent His Son to be the Propitiation for our sins." Or, "We know and have believed *the love* which God hath in our case."

Finally, there is the joy of the Victor: "I also *overcame,* and sat down with My Father in His throne" (Rev. 3.21). God the Father eternally speaks to Him: "Thou hast loved righteousness and hated iniquity" . . . "Thou didst resist unto blood, striving against sin." And now, "Judgment has returned unto righteousness, and all the upright in heart rejoice with Thee and with Me forever."

Verse 3: For consider Him that hath endured such gainsaying of sinners against Himself, that ye wax not weary, fainting in your souls: When this we do, our strength to endure is uncon-sciously recovered, just as it is in lesser measure when we con-template any of the heroes of faith of the Bible or of history. MacArthur and Wainwright and their brave men, in their heroic stand in the Pacific, roused the patriotism of all lovers of liberty, and strengthened those who were beginning to **wax weary . . . in their souls.** We are not instructed, when being chastened or in time of distress, to cry unto the Lord only—excellent as that is—but to *run* with patience the race set before *us,* considering con-stantly our Lord; **to consider Him in His enduring!** It is God's plan that we shall *keep* considering Him, follow His path in "the days of His flesh," study His attitude in every trial—for He had *all* the trials! Such contemplation will deliver us from **fainting in our souls.**

Verse 4: Then these believers are told, **Ye have not yet resisted unto blood, striving against sin:** Your strife* against sin has not entailed the shedding of your blood, as it did that of many of the Old Testament worthies, and of Jesus Himself! To "strive" here is literally, in the Greek, *antagonizing.* In fact the two strongest words for *conflict* occur here in Hebrews 12.4 within five Greek words! Blessed is the man that has made no inner truce with sin! **And ye have forgotten the exhortation which reasoneth with you as with sons,**

---

*Striving against sin: "Sin is personified"—Vincent.
"The personification of sin is natural and common: Jas. 1.15; Rom. 6.12 ff. Sin is *one,* whether it show itself within, in the Christian himself (vs. 1), or without, as here, in his adversaries."—Westcott.

Verses 5-6: My son, regard not lightly the chastening of the Lord,

> **Nor faint when Thou art reproved of Him;**
> **For whom the Lord loveth He chasteneth,**
> **And scourgeth every son whom He receiveth.**

In these verses the Greek word for *son* is *huios,* adult-son, son come-of-age. Five times is this word used in verses 5-8!

(See the author's note on the Greek words *tekna* and *huioi,* in Romans Verse by Verse, p. 312-316.)

Infants (Gr., *tekna,*) we cannot **reason with.** Little children in the family may not understand the parents; but as they grow up and become adult-sons, **huioi,** it is our delight to see them entering into and hearkening to our parental counsels. Here in verse 5 **the parental reasoning** is called **the exhortation,** the word that characterizes the **Hebrews** epistle (13.22). Beautiful expression, **the exhortation which reasoneth with you as with adult-sons!**

Then we have the two attitudes toward God's dealing with us, which we must guard against: (a) **regarding lightly His chastening hand;** or (b) **fainting:** saying, "My trouble is greater than I can bear." (a) Many and many a believer, when God brings chastening, refuses to consider the matter as from God, forgetting that in His hand our breath is, and His are all our ways (Dan. 5.23), forgetting that nothing merely "happens" to us. Are *you* **regarding lightly** some chastening of His?

(b) **Nor faint when thou art reproved of Him:** We are told by the Spirit through Paul that "God is faithful, Who will not suffer you to be tempted above that ye are able" (I Cor. 10.13); that "all things work together for good" (Rom. 8.28); that our Lord's "grace is sufficient" (II Cor. 12.9).

And now look at the word "chasten." Mr. James McConkey emphasized the fact that the word for a child-at-school, or under discipline, the Greek word *pais,* is here formed into a verb, *paideuō,* which one may translate, as he does, to "child-train."*

---

*This word in vs. 5, as well as the verb in vss. 5, 7, 8; and 6, 7, 9, 10, indicates a child in relation to parents, from infancy to young manhood. Springing from this word are:

Paideia, meaning education, training and nurture of children (Eph. 6.4); instruction, discipline (II Tim. 3.16); and here in **Hebrews,** corrective chastisement: Ch. 12.5, 7, 8, 11.

Paideuo (12.5-13) to give admonition, training, chastening. This verb is frequently used: II Tim. 2.25; Tit. 2.12; I Cor. 11.32; II Cor. 6.9. See Rev. 3.19: *"As many as I love,* I reprove and *chasten":* the very words of Heb. 12.5, and vs. 6: **Whom the Lord loveth He chasteneth.**

Verse 7: It is for chastening that ye endure; God dealeth with you as with sons; for what son is there whom his father chasteneth not? Alford says, It is "not for punishment, not for any evil purpose. You are beneath the attention and affectionate superintendence of the Father." (So, if a real *son!*)

Verse 8: But if ye are without chastening, whereof all (sons) have been made partakers, then are ye bastards, and not sons— Of chastening and its place, note here beloved King David's treatment of Adonijah, the son who rose up to kill his father: it is written, "His father had *not displeased* him at any time in saying, Why hast thou done so?" No chastening, ever!* (I Kings 1.5, 6.) But from another son of David, Solomon, to whom God gave wisdom concerning human life as to no other man, we quote from his Book of Proverbs as follows: and how we *beseech* parents to read these passages! In these wretched days, when children are *not chastened,* hear what God says:

"He that spareth his rod hateth his son;
But he that loveth him chasteneth him betimes" (Prov. 13.24).
"Chasten thy son, seeing there is hope;
And set not thy heart on his *destruction*" (19.18).
"Foolishness is bound up in the heart of a child;
But the rod of correction shall drive it far from him" (22.15).
"Withhold not correction from the child;
For if thou beat him with the rod, he will not die.
Thou shalt beat him with the rod,
And shalt deliver his soul from Sheol" (23.13, 14).
"The rod and reproof give wisdom;
But a child left to himself causeth shame to his mother" (29.15).

Let no shallow wickedness of a teaching developing in these Sodom days deceive you, O parent! But literally obey—always prayerfully and with love—these Divine directions for bringing up your children, and God will reward you.

---

*"The meaning of vs. 8 is, If ye are not dealt with as all legitimate children are, it would follow that ye are considered as not belonging to them." (Stuart.)

Calvin says, "the profession of Christ would be false and deceitful if they withdrew themselves from the discipline of the Father, and they would thus become bastards, and be no more children."

And Owen: "Those who have only the name of Christians are called bastards or spurious or illegitimate children, because they are not born of God, being only children of the flesh—not Isaacs, but Ishmaels, whatever their profession."

A "bastard" bears the family name—but does not *belong!* Of all dooms, to bear the *name* of a child of God, and not *be* a child, is worst!

Verse 9: Furthermore, we had the fathers of our flesh to chasten us, and we give them reverence: shall we not much rather be in subjection unto the Father of our spirits, and live? We gave them reverence—Note this, ye parents. A child's "reverence" for a parent springs from proper "chastening." **Shall we not much rather be in subjection unto the Father of spirits, and live?**—How unutterably solemn these words! For life, and that *eternal,* is involved! In God's providence the fathers of our flesh did not have our *spirits* in their hands. Man is essentially *a spirit,* living in *a body,* possessed of *a soul.* Here again God is seen as "the God of *the spirits* of all flesh" (Num. 16.22; 27.16). Compare *"The spirit* returneth unto God Who gave it" (Eccl. 12.7); "And her *spirit* returned" (Lk. 8.55). **And live?**—"Living" is dependent on being **in subjection unto the Father of our spirits.** *As Paul said, "God is my witness, Whom I serve *in my spirit* in the gospel of His Son." Compare also John 3.6: "That which is born of the Spirit *is spirit,"* without which birth a man cannot even see the kingdom of God. Note that this verse does *not* teach annihilation—that those who refuse to be subject to the Father of spirits cease to exist. On the contrary, it teaches the regeneration, and the *life* thereafter, both in this world and that to come, of those who **become in subjection to the Father of spirits.** We are constantly taught that those are saved who become *obedient* to the word of truth, the gospel (Acts 6.7; Rom. 15.18).

Verse 10: For they indeed for a few days chastened us as seemed good to them; but He for our profit, that we may be partakers of His holiness: Here temporary parental chastening is contrasted with the loving Divine discipline of verse 6. How long it takes us to learn this! How blessed it would be if at the very beginning of the believer's life he were taught to surrender himself into a loving Father's hands for whatever discipline necessary, looking to the glorious goal-partaking of God's own "holiness." Everyone begotten of God has tasted this holiness, but the full bliss of it lies in the future, when His servants *"shall see His face* and *His name* shall be in their foreheads."

Verse 11: All chastening seemeth for the present to be not

---

*Alford well says here, "Your *endurance,* like Christ's endurance, will not be thrown away. He had *joy before Him,* you have a *life* before you."

joyous but grievous; yet afterward it yieldeth peaceable fruit unto them that have been exercised thereby, even the fruit of right-eousness: Let this verse speak for itself! Note the yet afterward—and the other word, exercised thereby. To be exercised thereby is neither to "lightly regard it," nor to "harden" oneself to it, not seeing the Father's hand but to *enter into its meaning with sur-render and joy.*

Verses 12, 13: Wherefore lift up the hands that hang down, and the palsied knees; and make straight paths for your feet, that that which is lame be not turned out of the way, but rather be healed—These verses contain quotations from the Old Testament in the Septuagint Version (as are all O. T. quotations in **Hebrews**). Verse 12 quotes Isaiah 35.3, "Strengthen ye the weak hands, and confirm the feeble knees." Verse 13 quotes Proverbs 4.26: "Make level the path of thy feet, and let all thy ways be established." (See Conybeare and Howson here.)

The exhortations turn upon the word **"wherefore."** Hands that hang down have ceased glad service; **palsied knees** are not joyfully walking! The limping limb **(that which is lame)** is in danger of being permanently so; whereas God desires to have it **healed!** These exhortations are that we may not misunderstand the blessed end of God's fatherly chastening and discipline. Mark Paul's ex-perience when, after *the great revelation,* the catching up to Heaven of II Corinthians 12, there was given to him a thorn in the flesh! He went to the Lord three times regarding it, begging its removal. When, behold, his Lord says to him, "My grace is sufficient for thee: for My power is made perfect *IN weakness"!* And now note, and let us all remember, Paul's glorious response: "Most gladly therefore will I rather *glory in my weaknesses,* that the power of Christ may rest upon me! Wherefore I take pleasure in weak-nesses, in injuries, in necessities, in persecutions, in distresses, for Christ's sake: for when I am weak, then am I strong!"

And look at God's saints of old: At David, when God's hand fell upon him regarding the child by Uriah's wife (II Sam. 12.1-23), or when Absalom drove him out (II Sam. 16.9-14).

Or at Job, declared by Jehovah to be the best man on earth, yet everything taken from him! He moaned, protested, but *always prayed.* And at last Jehovah said to Eliphaz and the three friends:

"My wrath is kindled against thee; for ye have not spoken of Me the thing that is right, as My servant Job hath. Now therefore, take unto you seven bullocks and seven rams, and go to My servant Job, and offer up for yourselves a burnt-offering; and My servant Job shall pray for you; for him will I accept" (Job 42.7-8).

Or look at such a saint as Frances Ridley Havergal, who never saw a well day, but the fragrance of whose devotion to the Lord has filled the Church! We had just such a woman in Chicago—Mrs. Fred Soukup, now with Christ. Many, many years she lay on her bed, unable even to lift a hand to feed herself! But saints came from all about to hear her words of praise, and see her heavenly face!

This is the experience of all who learn from the *heart*, the blessed words, "whom the Lord loveth he chasteneth"! Oh, let us believe it, and be ready to rejoice in tribulation as it comes. And meditate often on such verses as Paul sets before us, and Peter.*

We have in verses 5-13, here in Chapter 12 the clearest teaching of the relationship of children with God the Father that is found in Hebrews.

14 Follow after peace with all men, and the sanctification
15 without which no man shall see the Lord: looking carefully lest there be any man that falleth short of the grace of God; lest any root of bitterness springing up trouble
16 you, and thereby the many be defiled; lest there be any fornicator, or profane person, as Esau, who for one mess
17 of meat sold his own birthright. For ye know that even when he afterward desired to inherit the blessing, he was rejected; for he found no place for a change of mind in

---

*"We also rejoice in our tribulations: knowing that tribulation worketh steadfastness" (Rom. 5.3).

"Patient in tribulation" (Rom. 12.12).

"I am filled with comfort, I overflow with joy in all our affliction" (II Cor. 7.4).

"Insomuch as ye are partakers of Christ's sufferings, rejoice" (I Pet. 4.13).

"Wherefore I ask that ye may not faint at my tribulations for you, which are your glory" (Eph. 3.13).

"Let them also that suffer according to the will of God commit their souls in well-doing unto a faithful Creator" (I Pet. 4.19).

"The discipline of the human father is regulated 'according to his pleasure.' Even when his purpose is best, he may fail as to the method; and also his purpose may be selfish. But with God, for His part, purpose and accomplishment are identical; and His aim is the advantage of His children. The spiritual son then may be sure both as to the will and as to the wisdom of his Father."—Westcott, p. 403.

his father, though he sought it diligently with tears.

In these verses we have another solemn exhortation and warning. First, verse 14, **Follow after peace with all men:** The words **Follow after** translate a Greek word meaning *to pursue,* as in a chase or battle. Paul frequently uses the word, as "Follow after love" (I Cor. 14.1). Peace, in a world like this, and especially **peace with all men,** will not just come our way. It must be *pursued* by us. We may well remember that the Greek word is used often to denote *persecution,* in which the persecuted were followed, hunted, sought out. Let us examine ourselves as to whether we are thus diligently seeking **peace with all men.**

And the sanctification without which no man shall see the Lord. Here is at once an excuse for all "holiness" conventions and camp meetings that ever took place! Remembering that this whole verse is governed by the word "follow" in the sense of "pursue," we find, **Follow on after . . . the sanctification** *(hagiasmos)*—This word is used ten times in the New Testament, all but once by Paul; the other use, I Peter 1.2, "sanctification* of the Spirit," even emphasizing and defining its other occurrences.

Howbeit, in I Corinthians 1.30, it is used in its fundamental sense, which must be attended to by all who would receive the gospel as

---

*Many earnest believers are very poorly instructed as to scriptural "sanctification." Let us note:

1. All those who are *in Christ* are "sanctified." This is seen from I Cor. 1.2, "the Church of God which is at Corinth, even them that are *sanctified in Christ Jesus.*" This cannot refer to their "experience," for we see from Ch. 3.1-3 that they were "babes" and "carnal." But they were no longer in Adam, but in the Second Man, Christ, and II Cor. 5.17 was true of them—they were "new creatures."

2. Sanctification in Hebrews has this meaning, *separated to God.* It does not refer to our experience or feelings. "We have been sanctified through the offering of the body of Jesus Christ once for all" (10.10). It was brought about through the blood of Christ—Who, "that He might sanctify the people through His own blood, suffered without the gate" (13.12). Christ's shed blood is called "the blood of the covenant wherewith one was sanctified." In Ch. 10.29, we see that this separation to God could wholly be abandoned by apostasy—by "counting the blood a 'common thing.' " In Ch. 12.14 we see that this separation to God, accomplished by the blood shed for us, and trusted in, was to be persisted in, not apostatized from.

3. In I Thess. 5.23 we read, "And the God of peace Himself *sanctify you wholly.*" This refers to the work of the Holy Spirit in a believer, by which the life and walk become *separated and devoted to God.* It is this passage that "Holiness" people constantly emphasize, and rightly! But we must not be ignorant of that sanctification which is true of *all believers,* of all "in Christ," that of I Cor. 1.2. Nor must we be intolerant of degrees of devotion short of I Thess. 5.23. Let us not, also, base our assurance of "holiness" upon some "experience" we have had, but rather upon the *fact* that all in Christ were sanctified (as said in paragraph No. 2), and *have* the Holy Spirit, and are asked to *yield* to Him! to be "filled" by Him!

given by God: "Of Him [God] are ye who are in Christ Jesus, Who was made unto us wisdom from God: [which included three things:] righteousness and sanctification, and redemption.

We must remember our Lord's prayer in John 17.19: "For their sakes I sanctify Myself, that they themselves also may be sanctified in truth." It is evident that our Lord's "sanctifying" Himself could not signify any moral or spiritual change in Himself, *but rather* a setting Himself apart to the task that was before His mind, even the procuring of our being separated, handed over, to God, through Christ's sacrifice. God made Christ "*to be sin* on our behalf; that we might become *the righteousness of God* in Him." In Christ we have been *cut off* (at the Cross) *from the world,* and belong *in Heaven!* He said, "They are not of the world, *even as I* am not of the world."

Again, let us observe, that "sanctification" or holiness in such texts as Romans 6.19, 22; I Thessalonians 4.3, 4, 7; I Timothy 2.15, does not refer to making the believer any more a "new creature" than when he first believed, when he was "sanctified in Christ Jesus." But it does refer to that result of *surrender to the operation of the indwelling Spirit* by which He takes charge of our conscious faculties. It is written to believers, "Ye are not in the flesh, but in the Spirit, if so be the Spirit of God dwelleth in you." For upon and in connection with this marvelous operation called "sanctification of the Spirit" (II Thess. 2.13), the Spirit Himself indwells those "created in Christ Jesus" (Eph. 2.10). This "sanctification of the Spirit" refers to *the whole work of the Holy Spirit in us,* in accordance with the fact that *we died* with Christ, and are *now in the Risen Christ* (Rom. 6.8-11). It is the "renewing" referred to in such passages in Romans 12.2; Ephesians 4.23; Colossians 3.10; Titus 3.5. It is accomplished by the Spirit through the Word, Ephesians 5.26: "That He might *sanctify it* [the Church, vs. 25], having cleansed it by the washing of water with the Word." "Sanctification" in this aspect becomes a conscious state in the believer, a complete change in our conscious faculties, as is described in Philippians 4.7: "The peace of God, which passeth all understanding, shall guard your hearts and your thoughts in Christ Jesus"; or Colossians 3.17: "Whatsoever ye do, in word or in deed, do all in the name of the Lord Jesus, giving thanks to God the Father through Him."*

---

*While on the one hand we must guard against any thought that the flesh is changed, or

—**Sanctification, without which no man shall see the Lord:** We are made to tremble (as we ought to tremble) many times in this book of **Hebrews;** and here again. Shall we say that none but those who have followed on unto entire control by the Spirit of God shall **see the Lord?** No, for although this warning is most solemn, connected as it is with the exhortation to **look carefully** **(vs. 15)** concerning some who might come eternally short of salvation, yet it must be connected with those Scriptures which reveal the infinite reach of Divine grace! As, for example, the passage about the incestuous man of I Corinthians 5; or those of I Corinthians 11 who, partaking of the Lord's Supper in carelessness or ignorance, had been chastened unto physical illness and even death (I Cor. 11.30), that they might *not* "be condemned with the world"! (vs. 32).

Yet on the other hand, we must not miss the truth that there is that sanctification which all true saints yearn after, and in their measure "pursue." John in his first epistle says, "Whosoever is begotten of God doth not practice sin, because His [God's] seed abideth in Him; and he cannot practice sin, because he is begotten of God."

Again, in Hebrews 12.14, do not confuse the sanctification with our pursuing it. God does not say that no man shall see the Lord except those who have pursued sanctification (do we not all feel that we have pursued it too feebly?) But He does say **that no man without that sanctification shall see the Lord.**

Verses 15, 16: looking carefully lest there be any man that falleth short of the grace of God; lest any root of bitterness springing up trouble you, and thereby the many be defiled; lest there be any fornicator, or profane person, as Esau, who for one mess of meat sold his own birthright. These verses are directed to all the Assembly, but especially to those, as in Chapter 13.17, who

---

that our bodies are to be trusted; yet, on the other hand, we must either accept the fact that God takes complete charge of us, or deny these, His plain words, and such testimonies as Paul's: "To me to live is Christ." How sane is his word, also: "For I know nothing against myself; yet am I not hereby justified: but He that judgeth me is the Lord."

The "Holiness" people (dear saints, and *none* of them modernists!) make "a clean heart," which as we have seen, is taught in the N. T. (I Tim. 1.5; Acts 15.8-9), to be "eradication of the sinful principle from *the flesh*"—which is *tragic error.*

The "flesh" will be with us till we get our new bodies. Paul could have "walked after the flesh," for the flesh was present with him; but he did not! Instead, he says, "Thanks be unto God, who *always leadeth us in triumph in Christ*" (II Cor. 2.14).

"had the rule over them," and "watched in behalf of their souls." These were to watch for four kinds of troublers:

1. **Lest (there should be) any man that falleth short of the grace of God.**
2. **Lest any root of bitterness springing up trouble you.**
3. **Lest (there should be) any fornicator.**
4. **Lest there be any profane person.**

On reading this, our hearts sink within us as we contemplate the churches today, for who is ready to observe these so searching directions of the holy apostle?

1. First, then, **Lest there be any man** among professed believers that really was **falling short** of or (literally in the Greek) **falling back from the grace of God.** What sort of person is this, and how does he fall short of the grace of God? Westcott insists, "The construction marks a falling back from that with which some connection exists, implying a moral separation. The present participle describes a continuous state and not a single defection." This agrees with that fatal "falling away" of Chapter 6.6—after "tasting." Is it not also suggested in Paul's plea in II Corinthians 6.1: "And working together with God we entreat also that ye receive not the grace of God in vain"—through neglect or sloth falling back from it? Chrysostom says, "The image is taken from a company of travelers, one of whom lags behind, and so never reaches the end of the long and laborious journey."

We remember how the rocky-ground hearers of our Lord's parable at first eagerly responded. The seed sprang immediately up, but there was little soil and unbroken rock beneath; and the Lord said, "These have no root, who for awhile believe, and in time of temptation fall away" (Lk. 8.13). How solemn is the use of this word "fall" in the book of **Hebrews!** First, Chapter 3.12, "Take heed, brethren, lest haply there shall be in any one of you an evil heart of unbelief, in *falling away* from the Living God." Then Chapter 6.6: "tasting," and then "falling away"—impossible to "renew," because "rejected" of God!

Then Chapter 4.11 "Give diligence to enter into that rest, that no man *fall* after the same example of disobedience."

Next, Chapter 10.31, "It is a fearful thing to *fall into the hands of* the Living God"!

And now, Chapter 12.15, **To fall back from [or fall short of]
the grace of God!** Compare I Timothy 4.1; Galatians 5.4; remember Revelation 2.5!

2.   **Lest any root of bitterness springing up trouble you**—This
is a quotation from Moses' terrible warning to some presumptuous
hearer of the Law, who, listening to the warnings, "blesses himself in his heart, saying, I shall have peace, though I do walk in
the stubbornness of my heart" (Deut. 29.18-21). Such a one was
called "a root that beareth gall and wormwood." Now such may be
in the Assembly undiscovered, until they **spring up and trouble**—
by evil doctrine or practice. For if not dealt with, such will **defile
the many.*** Is there anyone reading this who knows himself to
have been the cause of "bitterness" and trouble among the saints?
Let him beware!

3.   **Lest there be any fornicator**—In Chapter 13.4 we read, "for
fornicators and adulterers God will judge"—that is, in the future;
but the leaders of the Assembly, and in fact all in the Assembly of
God, are to watch that fornicators are not tolerated. There are also
warnings in I Corinthians 5.9-11 and 6.9 against such toleration;
for Corinth was notorious throughout the world for its extreme
looseness in this thing. The immoral men of the world in England
in the eighteenth century called themselves "Corinthians." Indeed,
this sin was so universal in the Greek world as not to be a matter of
conscience at all; and the council at Jerusalem of Acts 15 decided
to lay upon the Gentiles "no greater burden than these necessary
things: that ye abstain from things sacrifice to idols, and from
blood, and from things strangled, *and from fornication.*"

4.   **Lest there be [in the Christian Assembly] any profane
person, as Esau, who for one mess of food sold his own birthright:**
Note how the example of what is here **called a profane person is**
set forth in Genesis 25: Esau came in from his hunting (for he was
a "sporting man," taking life as a thing of enjoyment, with no ap-
preciation of the God with Whom his father Isaac and his grand-

---

*Alas, how frequently has a whole assembly of saints been "defiled" by such a **root of
bitterness** permitted after it **springs up,** and is plainly evident. Time after time we have
ourselves seen it, and Church history is full of such instances. The time the leaders in an
Assembly (the *episkopoi,* I Tim. 3.1) should deal with such an one, is immediately upon
his "springing up," that is, manifesting himself. Thus Paul directs the Corinthians: I
Cor. 5.13.

father Abraham had dealt) faint with hunger. His brother Jacob, we read, was "a perfect man" ("a quiet man," A.R.V.). Not perfect morally, but appreciating what human life means, and giving himself to its tasks. We find him attending to the family needs, boiling pottage of red lentils. Esau, the "man of the field" points to the pot of red lentils Jacob's industry has prepared, and then to his own red beard, and utters one of the very few "jokes" the Bible records, saying (literally), "Feed *that* red to *this* red." Jacob, without yet fully comprehending the vastness of blessing which the Divine Abrahamic covenant conveyed, yet rightly valuing it above all else, meets his elder brother's jesting but selfish demand with a shrewd request of his own: "Sell me first thy birthright." Out blurts from Esau's "profane" mouth: "Behold, I am about to die!" (ridiculous falsehood!) "and what profit shall the birthright do to me?" Jacob, not trusting him, puts him under oath, then feeds him his fill of red lentil pottage. And off he goes, having "despised his birthright" (Gen. 25.34).

Now, God did not forget this profane despising of Himself and His covenant promises. Esau knew no more of God than did the beasts he hunted! He was godless in the sense that God was not "in all his thought." As the psalmist says, "Man being in honor abideth not: he is like the beasts that perish" (49.12). So here in **Hebrews** he is called a **profane person.*** And why do we quote all this? **Lest there be any** professing Christian or known professor, who becomes like Esau, **a profane person,** no real godliness about him; no sense of the infinite value of eternal things; for whom the devil has probably already laid the trap to sell out eternity for one mess of meat in this passing, dying world. Unbelievable as it may seem, you know such people! Alas, how many thousands does this describe, for the Hebrew believers in this passage are being exhorted concerning their own company—**Lest there be** *among them* **a profane person!** Alas for the day when, like Esau, such as have despised spiritual privilege will **desire to inherit the blessing of** eternal bliss and be rejected! For there follows verse 17:

---

*The Greek word *bebēlos* translated here profane, has no necessary reference to blasphemy or violent wickedness, but, almost, if one might say so, the opposite. It denotes literally "a threshold that anyone and every one may trample over." It refers to something in which there is no special consciousness (I Tim. 1.9; 4.7; 6.20; II Tim. 2.16). We must gather that a *profane* man, then, is one in whom there is *no thought of God!*

For ye know that even when he afterward desired to inherit the blessing, he was rejected; for he found no place for a change of mind *in his father* (Gen. 27:33, 40), though he sought it (the despised blessing) diligently with tears. This Revised Version change from the King James reading is correct. It is strange that some excellent commentators have translated *metanora,* change of mind, as "repentance," and made it mean a spiritual state which Esau strove to attain and could not. No doubt the will of God, which Isaac clearly knew, was behind his words to Esau: "I have blessed him [Jacob] . . . yea, and he shall be blessed . . . I have made him thy lord . . . Thou shalt serve thy brother" (Gen. 27.33, 37, 40). But Esau was *not* seeking God, or repentance from sin, but a lost birth-right, and the blessing it would have brought.

18 For ye are not come unto a mount that might be touched,
     and that burned with fire, and unto blackness, and dark-
19 ness, and tempest, and the sound of a trumpet, and the
     voice of words; which voice they that heard entreated that
20 no word more should be spoken unto them! For they could
     not endure that which was enjoined, If even a beast touch
21 the mountain, it shall be stoned! And so fearful was the
     appearance, that Moses said, I exceedingly fear and
22 quake! But ye are come unto Mount Zion; and unto the
     city of the Living God, the heavenly Jerusalem; and to
23 innumerable hosts of angels, the general assembly; and
     to the Church of the firstborn who are enrolled in
     Heaven; and to God the Judge of all; and to the spirits
24 of just men made perfect; and to Jesus the Mediator of a
     new covenant; and to the blood of sprinkling that speak-
     eth better than that of Abel.

In this great passage we have before us the marvelous contrast between the position of those under Law and that of those under Grace, set forth in an overwhelming manner. The infinite moral distance between the holy God and sinful man is the foundation. It is not a setting forth of man's inability to carry out the instruc-tions of the Law that is here before us, but the presence of the Lawgiver. God is present, and at the foot of the mountain sinful man is present. And what is the effect on man? Terror! Inability to endure the consciousness that no one—not even a beast—should touch the mountain. Here is guilt unexpiated, and God's presence inescapable! Therefore they cried out to Moses, "Go *thou* near, and hear all that Jehovah our God shall say: and speak *thou* unto us all that Jehovah our God shall speak unto thee; and we will hear it, and do it" (Deut. 5.27).*

Verse 18: For ye are not come—(The word "For," in this place is not specially to be connected with its immediate context, but with the whole preceding part of the epistle.) Contrast **Ye are not come,** with verse 22, **But ye are come.** Now follow some eight things which the Holy Spirit of God declares Christians— Christian believers, whether Hebrews as here, or any who get under Judaizing influences—are not come to:

1. **For ye are not come unto a mount that might be touched**— This at once sets forth the walk of faith which is ours, in contrast to the visible, earthly things the Hebrews had. "We walk by faith, not by appearance" (II Cor. 5.7, R.V., margin).† It is a strange, but almost universal tendency of the human heart when seeking to deal with God, to try to find some *sacred place*. But our Lord said to the Samaritan woman, "The hour cometh, when neither in this mountain, nor in Jerusalem, shall ye worship the Father"

---

*In Romans and Galatians Paul shows that even this promise was vain, if sincere. Yet until the Lord Jesus came and put away sin at Calvary, God suffered Israel to have the Law and the Levitical code, with its sin-offerings on its Day of Atonement, all prophetical and typical, of course.

†God speaks in vs. 22 of the heavenly Jerusalem to which we have come. We shall find in Rev. 21 that this is *a literal city,* whose streets of gold will indeed be "touched" by the feet of the risen bodies of the saints. But the description here of Mount Sinai sets forth the fact that God came down to a nation in the flesh—came demanding holiness and righteousness, and He was entirely too near! If He had spoken from Heaven, they would have promised themselves obedience, and peace thereby—promised in the self-delusion of sinners, certainly, but cherishing their delusion.

But when God came down to a mount at the foot of which they were, **unto a mount that might be touched,** it was terrible to them. While it **might be touched,** their touching it would cost them death. (Sinai was a tangible mountain. It could be touched by fingers of flesh. God's commanding is *not* to be touched by unholy man is another thing altogether.)

Read Ex. 19.11-13. "Jehovah will come down in the sight of all the people upon Mount Sinai. And thou shalt set bounds unto the people round about, saying, Take heed to yourselves, that ye go not up into the mount, or touch the border of it: whosoever toucheth the mount shall be surely put to death; no hand shall touch him, but he shall surely be stoned, or shot through; whether it be beast or man, he shall not live."

No wonder we read in vss. 16-18: "And it came to pass on the third day, when it was morning, that there were thunders and lightnings, and a thick cloud upon the mount, and the voice of a trumpet exceeding loud; and all the people that were in the camp trembled. And Moses brought forth the people out of the camp to meet God; and they stood at the nether part of the mount. And Mount Sinai, the whole of it, smoked, because Jehovah descended upon it in fire; and the smoke thereof ascended as the smoke of a furnace, and the whole mount quaked greatly."

(Jno. 4.21). Let all legalists assemble and hearken to the thunders, and the trumpet "exceeding loud"! If they must have Moses' Law, let them go and stand beneath *Sinai*. There is no other place from which God declares it.

But let the Seventh-Day people of all sorts (whether or not they mix Adventism with it); the "under-the-law-as-a-rule-of-life" people, proud with Reformed orthodoxy; also those who would abstain from meats forbidden to the Jews; and those who "observe days, and months, and seasons, and years" (of whom Paul was "afraid"); yea, all whose conscience accuses them because of trespasses done, or duties undone: let all these hearken well to this word of verse 18: **YE ARE NOT COME!** and to that of verse 22, **But ye ARE come!** Mount Sinai must disappear, O Hebrew believer, for God hath said, **Ye are NOT come there!** (And God never brought a Gentile believer there!) For hear further:

2.   **And that burned with fire**—There is no approach here, but death only! In Deuteronomy 4.11 we read, "Ye came near and stood under the mountain; and the mountain *burned with fire* unto the heart of Heaven." And Moses repeated to Israel in Chapter 5.4, 5: "Jehovah spake with you face to face in the mount out of the midst of the fire (I stood between Jehovah and you at that time, to show you the word of Jehovah: for ye were *afraid because of the fire,* and went not up into the mount)."

Remember that disobedient sinners will one day find the realization of Hebrews 12.29, "Our God is a consuming fire." He had taught Moses at the burning bush that the bush burned with fire and not a leaf withered! Moses saw the great sight: "The bush burned with fire, and the bush was not consumed" (Ex. 3.2). So is God with His people: it is *our* God Who is a consuming fire, and yet His name is Love, and He delighteth in mercy!

Then why the scene at Sinai? Let us proceed with the description and then seek to answer.

And unto blackness and darkness—(The third and fourth things **Ye are NOT come** unto.) Here was no real revelation of God, except of His infinite distance from sinful man. That there should have been "fire to the heart of Heaven," as we quoted above, and yet "thick darkness" as the people looked, seems impossible. But there could not be a truer description of what the Law does spiritually for sinners. There is the awful energy of fire, and yet no revelation of light, but instead, *darkness*. There is the mountain "quaking"—irresistible power, but no means of approach- ing or appeasing God. The people showed fear, indeed, of the majesty displayed, but no such self-judgment as was in the publican who "smote his breast, saying, God be Thou merciful [lit., 'propi- tiated'] to me a sinner." Let those mark well who would come the Sinai-route to God, by "good works" that they do, or think they have done: He is a consuming fire, but there is no revelation of *Himself*: fire, but **blackness and darkness**. God's name is LOVE, we repeat, but He is also infinitely holy and righteous.

5.   **And tempest**—Again there is the sense of terrible power, but no hint of a way of approach for a sinner. God's power, but not Himself. "Tempest" is the exhibition of Divine energy in judgment, the very opposite of peace, which we have found in Christ. Even when Elijah "stood upon the mount before Jehovah" (I Ki. 19.11-12): "Behold, Jehovah passed by, and a great and strong wind rent the mountains, and brake in pieces the rocks before Jehovah; but Jehovah was not in the wind: and after the wind an earthquake; but Jehovah was not in the earthquake: and after the earthquake a fire; but Jehovah was not in the fire; and after the fire a sound of gentle stillness" (R. V., margin, Heb.).

These first three manifestations were what Elijah expected God to show. ("Wilt Thou that we bid *fire* to come down from Heaven, and consume them, even as Elijah did?" asked James and John. They are not the only ones who have had that desire!)

Now God is ever the same, and you ask, Can **blackness, and darkness, and tempest** be of Him Who took up little children in His arms, and laid His hand on the leper, and said to the wretched woman, "Neither do I condemn thee"? Yes, the very same! And this was why the Law was given on Sinai: that it might be "the ministration of *death*," "the ministration of *condemnation*" (II Cor. 3.7, 9) which God calls it. Let us not dare to think of it differently. "The Law came in alongside, *that the trespass* might abound" (Rom. 5.20). Sin was there before, but when the Law was given to Israel, they *knew* the mind of Jehovah! What was sin, now became *trespass*—which means, *breaking through bounds*. See the effect of

the Law on the meekest and best servant of God then on earth:
Moses said, "All our days are passed away in Thy wrath . . . Thou
hast set all our iniquities before Thee, our secret sins in the light of
Thy countenance" (Ps. 90.9, 8).

Compare that with John 1.17: "*The Law* was *given* through
Moses; *Grace and Truth came* through Jesus Christ . . . " And in
that first of John, God the Father is a Bosom (vs. 18), Christ a
Lamb (vs. 29), and the Holy Spirit, a Dove (vs. 32). God is not
angry with us, but God is God—infinitely loving, or He would not
have given His Son; but absolutely holy, for when our sin was placed
on this Son, God did not spare Him, but delivered Him up. Friend,
it is because of that hatred of God for sin, and His having at the
Cross dealt with sin, forsaking His own Son, that we can trust God!
If the judgment against sin at the Cross had not been complete, we
could but fear that at some time in the future God would bring up
our sins again. He *never* changes: but **we are not come unto a
mount** where His presence in fiery judgment is being exhibited.*

6. (Verse 19) **And the sound of a trumpet**—Here is authority;
here is the awakening, awful command of Divine Majesty, from
Sinai, covered with blackness and darkness.† How different the
gentle words of the gospel of Grace! "the illumination of the gospel
of the glory of Christ, Who is the image of God" (II Cor. 4.4,
margin). A trumpet of awful warning and alarm—**we are not come
to that.**

---

*The obstinate perversity of man is not more clearly shown than in his attitudes toward
Law and Grace. The Jews gloried in the Law that cursed them, yet turned back to their
lusts which the Law forbade. The Gentiles, to whom are given the good things of Grace, instead of Law, habitually turn back to the Law. See their "Standards" and "Creeds". Their
"services" sometimes hear the Ten Commandments read several times on a single occasion!
Yet they pass by God's Word, that affirms, over and over, that the believer, being *not*
under Law, but Grace, shall be delivered from sin's bondage.

†"On the third day . . . thunders . . . lightnings . . . a thick cloud . . . and the
voice of a trumpet exceeding loud; and all the people that were in the camp trembled . . .
When the voice of the trumpet waxed louder and louder, Moses spake, and God answered
him by a voice . . ." (Ex. 19.16, 19).
Again, a trumpet called Israel into assembly or into marching order:
"And Jehovah spake unto Moses saying, Make thee two trumpets of silver . . . and
thou shalt use them for the calling of the congregation, and . . . they shall blow an alarm
for their journeys . . . and when ye go to war . . . ye shall sound an alarm with the
trumpets" (Num. 10.2, 6, 9).
So much for trumpets used by man. In The Revelation you remember the seven trumpets
(8.1 ff). We read also of a trumpet in connection with the Rapture of the Church, when:
"The Lord Himself shall descend from Heaven, with a shout, with the voice of the
archangel, and with *the trump of God*" (I Thess. 4.16).
See also I Cor. 15.52, where that trumpet is again connected with the resurrection of the
just.

7. **And the voice of words**—Remember verse 26 of our chapter, "Whose voice then shook the earth"!* There are those today who would seek for visions and voices to arouse their faith. Dear friend, we are not come to that, but rather, "These things" are "*written* unto you, that ye may know that ye have eternal life, even unto you that believe on the name of the Son of God" (I Jno. 5.13). Our Lord said, "*The words* that I have spoken unto you are spirit, and are life" (Jno. 6.63). Yet you want to go to Sinai. Are you prepared to hear the voice that shook the earth? Do you prefer that to the sweet tidings of a finished work of Christ on the Cross? God has chosen to give us the gospel by written words. I beg you, learn to rest in these, asking no sign.

See the effect upon those at Sinai who heard **the voice of words**: it was, **which voice they that heard entreated that no word more should be spoken unto them.** If only those who trust in their law-keeping could go where the Law was given, and hear that voice, they would do as Israel did—at that time—flee as far from Sinai as they could, and beg for a mediator.

Verse 20: For they could not endure that which was enjoined, If even a beast touch the mountain, it shall be stoned—At last man was made conscious of the immeasurable distance, the awful gap, that sin had made between himself and God. It made the place untenable: **If even a beast touch the mountain, it shall be stoned:** Here was a mount that "might be touched," but it was death to touch it, death to approach that mount. Man and the creation over which he has been placed, and which had been "subjected to vanity" in

---

*Now you may say, Such a display of glorious majesty and power would certainly bring about in the very hearts of those who heard, godliness. Friend, you are utterly astray! The Law written on tables is said to be "a ministration of condemnation and death" (II Cor. 3.7, 9). God says the Law was given that the trespass thereof (*paraptoma*, the breaking through its commands) might *abound* (Rom. 5.20). What are you going to believe: your own "reason" or God's repeated statements? Christendom has what it calls "the Christian religion," but remember that God gave *one* religion, *Judaism*—which has passed away; and that "Christian," as we said, is a Gentile, ignorant name for *believers*, a name of contempt (Acts 11.26), like the name "Jesus-men," as the Oriental called believers. God may and does say that believers are not under Law, having died unto the Law principle: and are now "annulled" (*katergeo*) from that principle (Rom. 7.6). God may devote an epistle of burning, loving remonstrance against any Gentiles even looking toward Sinai, warning, "You are annulled from Christ, ye who would be justified by the Law" (Gal. 5.4): and again, "The Law is not of Grace." God may, and does, in Heb. 7.18, say, "There is a disannulling of a foregoing commandment because of its weakness and unprofitableness; (for the Law made nothing perfect)"; and may follow with the setting forth of a better hope, even Christ and His work, "through which (Christ) we *draw nigh unto God.*" What will men do? They will mix Law and Grace! Every so-called "great" denomination *holds fast to Moses.*

man's fall, are shown lost, undone, hopeless, in the presence of the Holy One demanding a righteousness and a holiness which the fallen creature can never produce. Here is shown the bridgeless moral distance between man and God.

Just now, for your comfort *and relief,* behold Jesus, taking up the children into His arms and laying His hands upon them and blessing them. That is not Law: we repeat, "The Law was given through Moses; grace and truth came through Jesus Christ." And yonder comes a leper: the Law sternly said, "Stand off and cry, Unclean, unclean." But Jesus, when the leper, bowing at His feet, pleads, "If Thou wilt, Thou canst make me clean," moved with compassion, stretches forth His hand and touches him, and saith unto him, "I will, be thou made clean."

"Yes," you say, "It is well to heal a leper, but why *touch* him?"

Grace, I reply; grace unmixed with Law or human religion, has touched him! Let us bow and give thanks to God!

Verse 21: And so fearful was the appearance, that Moses said, I exceedingly fear and quake: In order to lead us into that fear of Jehovah which is the beginning of wisdom (Prov. 1.7), God must reveal His holiness: "Thus saith the high and lofty One that inhabiteth eternity, *Whose name is holy*" (Isa. 57.15). Therefore Jehovah, Who had spoken out of the bush to Moses, Who had "caused His glorious arm to go at the right hand of Moses" (Isa. 63.12) in the miracles of Egypt, and afterwards; and with Whom Moses was (as we would say) acquainted, now comes down upon Sinai with so fearful an appearance as to cause Moses to say, I **exceedingly fear and quake.**

O my friends, if we do not learn a lesson here, where then shall we learn it? How shall we ever again put our faith in works? How shall we ever again go back to Sinai?

Fear and quake? That is just what the twentieth century does *not* do. It will not hear preachers that speak of this God. Not because they have "fled for refuge to the hope set before them" in judgment that fell on Christ are they free from fearing and quaking but because they are sin-hardened, sin-blinded, and know not God, Whom they will shortly meet.

Oh, that day, that day! when the Law-trusters of every stripe and degree shall stand in the presence of this same unchangeable,

holy God! "Our God is [*not was*] a consuming fire"! Happy those
who know His grace! Moses had indeed seen Him in the burning
bush, where fire was, yet life was. No green leaf was withered. That
same fire in tongues of flame sat upon the heads of those in the
upper room at Pentecost while they were filled with joy unutterable. And why? Let us see unto what these Hebrew believers in the
Lord Jesus had come, instead of unto Sinai.

Verse 22: But on the contrary ye are come—In these words
there is truly awful import. These Hebrews addressed had heard
the gospel concerning Jesus the Son of God and had accepted or
professed to accept that gospel. Now their whole position was
changed. Into new spheres *of blessing,* new relationships and re-
sponsibilities they had never known, they were come!* Before
hearing and believing they had indeed known that to their nation
God had spoken by Moses at Sinai, and by the prophets; whereas
the Gentiles knew nothing of the true God, being, as Paul said to
Peter, mere "sinners of the Gentiles." Now, however, all was
changed. The meaning of the stupendous fact of the Cross, the
"consummation of the ages" (9.26), God had shown them—which
changed everything for the one learning it. The Temple left by
Christ "desolate," Judaism as God's way *gone*—but *Heaven opened!*
Oh, that all believers might hear these solemn words, **Ye are come!**
Redeemed ones, *justified, reconciled,* dead and risen with Christ;
raised of Him to "heavenly places," "citizens of Heaven," they were
to walk in *the consciousness of all these new relationships.* They now
belonged in Heaven!

Therefore, when God says to these Hebrew believers, **Ye are
come**—He is describing facts into which they by simple faith
have entered. Hence it follows, in verses 22-24† that these believers
are told the things to which they are come:

---

*Let us remember that while we are members of the Body of Christ, even as were these
Hebrew believers: "partakers of a heavenly calling"; nevertheless the great fundamental attitude and acts of the life of faith are the same in every age. This makes the O. T. a *mine
of gold.* What believer has not been thrilled with encouragement and renewal of heart when
reading of those great O. T. men and women of faith in Heb. 11?

And so here we have the great contrast between those at the foot of Sinai and Hebrew
believers today! We, if wise and willing, will here learn much. Not following the folly of
so many readers of this passage, we shall not say, "Oh, that belongs to the *Jews!*" My
friend, those whom the Spirit is addressing here are on their way to the heavenly Jerusalem,
the city of the Living God! To what city are *you* journeying?

†Note carefully that it is absolutely necessary in the understanding of vss. 22-24 to
adhere *to the Greek text.* After opening up the subject with the words, *But on the contrary*

1. **To Mount Zion.**
2. **To the city of the Living God, the heavenly Jerusalem.**
3. **To myriads of angels, the general [heavenly] gathering.**
4. **To the Assembly of the firstborn who are enrolled in Heaven [the Church of God].**
5. **To God the Judge of all.**
6. **To the spirits of just men made perfect.**
7. **To Jesus, Mediator of a new covenant.**
8. **To the blood of sprinkling that speaketh better than Abel.**

1. A believing Hebrew has come, in God's sight, **to Mount Zion.** If God's purposes of forgiveness for national Israel, for all connected with the promises by natural birth (Hebrew believers), if God's future blessing is connected with Mount Zion, what more natural, indeed, necessary, than that these Hebrews, who had heard the gospel and believed, should be told, **Ye are come to Mount Zion?** Certainly they are immediately instructed about heavenly things, the heavenly Jerusalem, the Church of the Firstborn on high, as we shall see. But God's purposes of grace upon Israel are connected with Mount Zion.

Three mountains an Israelite would remember: first, Mount Sinai, of which we have spoken: God's majesty, power, holiness and righteousness, and yet requiring righteousness from Israel, with what results we know!

Second, Mount Moriah, which God pointed out to Abraham upon which to offer up Isaac his son, wonderful type of a Redeemer! (Gen. 22.2). And after Israel's utter failure in the land—

(Gr., *alla*) ye are come to Mount Zion, God's Word opens each following particular with the word *"and"* (Gr., *kai*). This careful arrangement connects heavenly Jerusalem with city of the Living God. Next, "and [*kai*] to myriads of angels, the universal assembling." Only note that it is in apposition with myriads of angels—such a "gathering" as appears in Rev. 5.8, 11, or Rev. 19.4, 6; it should read, therefore, and [*kai*] to innumerable hosts of angels—the general [heavenly] assembly."

Literally the Greek of verses 22-24 reads, But on the contrary ye are come to Mount Zion and [*kai*] to the city of the Living God, the heavenly Jerusalem; and [*kai*] to myriads of angels—*panegyric* and [*kai*] to the assembly of firstborn ones enrolled in Heaven and [*kai*] to God Judge of all and [*kai*] to spirits of righteous ones perfected and [*kai*] to Mediator of New Covenant, Jesus and [*kai*] to blood of sprinkling speaking better than [the blood of] Abel.

No one has any right to use the words, the "general assembly" *with* "the Church" (*Ekklesia*); for *God* connects it with the "myriads of angels," just preceding the words "the Church."

the breakdown of the priesthood under Eli and the King in Saul—yea, and the pride of His chosen King David in numbering the people, bringing judgment upon seventy thousand of Israel, and sackcloth and ashes upon the King, Moriah again is pointed out as the place where sacrifice turned away wrath (I Chron. 22.1), and which became the site of the temple of Jerusalem (II Chron. 3.1). There were offered the typical sacrifices, for there the Shekinah glory dwelt till Ezekiel saw it return to Heaven (Ezek. 8-11). And yet after seventy years the restoration temple was built, by God's direction, under Zerubbabel—relatively insignificant—yet acknowledged, and greatly enlarged (after the flesh) by Herod. But types are not actual blessings.

Unto this Moriah temple our Lord Jesus came, and every type and sacrifice spoke of Him; yet He, as we shall see in Chapter 13, "suffered without the gate."

Third, Mount Zion, connected in Scripture with actual blessing upon Israel. It was the other hill, the higher in Jerusalem (Moriah being the lower), where David finally overthrew the Jebusites (II Sam. 5.6-9): "David took the stronghold of Zion; the same is the city of David . . . And David dwelt in the stronghold, and called it the city of David." Mount Zion stands in Scripture for grace, the opposite of Sinai, which was Law, and judgment for disobedience. We all know that in the future, when the Lord Jesus returns, "He will build again the tabernacle of David, which is fallen" (Acts 15.16). That will be the millennial temple, and that mountain will be "exalted above all the hills" (Isa. 2.2, 3). See the last nine chapters of Ezekiel for the description of that beautiful temple. **Mount Zion**, therefore, to Hebrew believers, represents final pardon and blessing for the Remnant—those "that are escaped" (Isa. 10.20). Inasmuch, therefore, as pardoning grace was to be given to the nation from **Mount Zion** under the new covenant, it was most fitting that these Hebrew believers should be told that they were "*already* **come unto Mount Zion.**" The great spiritual realities of mercy and pardon, theirs already, would belong to the nation in the future. Meanwhile, the calling of the Hebrews of our epistle was *heavenly.*

It would not do for a Gentile to say that he had come unto **Mount Zion,** for he had never been of the nation to which **Mount**

Zion was to be the place of great blessing. If a believer, his calling, with that of all true believers, was immeasurably higher than that of the earthly nation, Israel. **Mount Zion,** then, is the chosen scene and source of future saving blessing for Israel.* But as Paul says, "The Jerusalem that is above is free, which is our mother" (Gal. 4.26). Their hearts and thoughts are set upon that city, being upon Christ, as Paul directs: "Set *your mind* on the things that are above, not on the things that are upon the earth" (Col. 3.2).

2. **Unto the city of the Living God, the heavenly Jerusalem—** This city is described in Revelation 21.9-27; 22.1-5. It is a literal city† of which the description is given (dimensions, materials, walls, gates), together with the fact that there is "no temple therein" (Rev. 21.22).

In the expression—**Ye are come unto**—we find the sphere of relationships entered, whether by Israel at Sinai, or by the Hebrew believers on the Lord Jesus. Wherefore we understand that in applying the expression, for example, to the heavenly city, the New Jerusalem, we are to remember of course that our bodies are not yet redeemed, and we are on earth. Yet read in Ephesians 2.5 ff, that we were "Made alive together with Christ, and raised up with Him,

---

*In Ps. 78.68-70 we find that God
"Chose the tribe of Judah,
The **Mount Zion** *which he loved!*"
See also Ps. 132.13, 14:
"For Jehovah hath chosen **Zion**;
He hath desired it for His habitation.
This is My resting-place forever:
Here will I dwell; for I have desired it."
Such words from God should overwhelm us! Yet, speaking with reverence and humility we may say, God made man "in His image, after His likeness," and at the right hand of God in glory there is a MAN, concerning Whom God has said,
"Yet I have set My King
Upon My holy hill of Zion" (Ps. 2.6).
If God has set His affection upon a certain place in His earthly creation, **Mount Zion,** shall we who love *our* homes *wonder?*
We can but refer here to the 144,000 of Rev. 14: "And I saw, and behold, the Lamb standing on the **Mount Zion,** and with Him a hundred and forty and four thousand, having His name, and the name of His Father, written on their foreheads." That is the place of Israelitish blessing (Rev. 7.4). They are seen there in millennial victory and song. What a place to be standing, "on the Mount Zion" that God has loved and chosen of all places on earth!

†Read the author's book, **The Revelation** (pp. 348-9), or any work that does not "spiritualize" these heavenly things, but takes them in their reality, thus honoring God, instead of man's ingenuity. Abraham *looked for a city,* and he will see one. God "hath prepared for them a city" (Heb. 11.16).

and made to sit with Him in the heavenly places, in Christ Jesus."
The facts about us, therefore, are that we who are in Christ are
"not of the world, even as He is not of the world"; that we have "a
heavenly calling" (See Heb. 3.1) : even as Paul declares:

God "made us meet to be partakers of the inheritance of the saints
in light; Who delivered us out of the power of darkness, and translated us into the kingdom of the Son of His love" (Col. 1.12-13).

3. **And to innumerable hosts of angels—the general** [heaven-
ly] **gathering—***

It is unto this heavenly host that the Hebrew believers (and, of
course, all believers, for all now partake of this heavenly calling)
are come. Since we are exhorted to "come boldly to the throne of
grace" above, where the Son of God Himself is our Great High
Priest, it is no marvel that we **are come** to those thus naturally
belonging to Heaven! But it is well and blessed that we are reminded
of this. (Note, however, that "our fellowship is with the Father and
with His Son Jesus Christ" by the Spirit. Though **we are come to**
this **heavenly** *panegyris,* we are not to seek fellowship with these
heavenly beings, or become "worshipers of angels" [Col. 2.18].
Indeed, to be *in Christ,* one with Him, is a higher calling than
angels have!)

4. **Verse 23: to the church of the firstborn who are enrolled
in Heaven.**

The Church (better translation, **Assembly**): This is the Greek
word *Ekklesia,* used over 100 times for the Church of God. (Literally it is "called-out-assembly.")

The firstborn [ones]—The Apostle James, speaking of those who
hold the faith of our Lord Jesus Christ, the Lord of glory,

---

*See Greek of Rev. 5.11: "I saw, and I heard a voice of many angels round about the
throne and the living creatures and the elders; and the number of them was myriads of
myriads *(myriades, myriadōn),* and thousands of thousands" *(chiliades chiliadon).* Note the
other heavenly beings here; also include the six-winged seraphim of Isa. 6, and the four-
winged cherubim of Ezek. 1.6, 26, who support the throne (which is *above* them),
and the four six-winged living beings of Rev. 4 and 19: "In the midst of the throne, and
round about the throne, four *living creatures* . . . the voice of a great multitude . . . of
many waters . . . of mighty thunders, saying, Hallelujah: for the Lord our God, the
Almighty, reigneth"—(Rev. 4.6; 19.6).

Remember also, the "principalities and powers in the heavenlies" of Eph. 3.10, primarily
indicate servants of God.

The word *panēgyris* includes the "myriads of angels," and all heavenly beings. As Alford
happily puts it, "A complete, multitudinous, above all, jubilant, festal and blissful
assembly."[1]

says, "Of His own will He brought us forth by the word of truth, that we should be a kind of *first-fruits* of His creatures" (1.18). Not for the *seraphim* (Isa. 6) nor the *cherubim* (Ezek. 1 to 11), nor the *four living ones* (Rev. 4 and 5), nor the *myriads of angels,* was the blood of the Son of God shed; nor have these been "created in Christ Jesus," "members of His Body."

Because they were "born *from above*" (see Jno. 3.3, 7; and verse 31, "from above," of Christ; Jas. 1.17; 3.15, 17), our Lord said of His disciples, "They are not of the world, even as I am not of the world." Believers, therefore, since our Lord ascended, since Pente-cost, when the gospel was first announced, have been the *first beings** to enter the new creation. Christ Himself having been raised from among the dead, is named "The Head of the Body, the Church [*Ekklesia*]: Who is the Beginning, the Firstborn from among the dead ones" (Col. 1.17-9).†

Jehovah said by Moses to Pharaoh, "Thus said Jehovah, Israel is *My son, My firstborn*" (Ex. 4.22). Israel is the firstborn of *earth* —as if there had been no other nation, and should be no other. The Church is enrolled in Heaven as "firstborn" *there,* "the first-fruits of God's creatures" in this *new creation,* sharing Christ's risen life (II Cor. 5.17; Eph. 2.10; 4.24; Col. 3.10).

Enrolled in Heaven—When the disciples came back to Jesus rejoicing that the demons were subject to them, He said, "In this rejoice not, that the spirits are subject unto you; but rejoice that your names are *written in Heaven*" (Lk. 10.20). God is acting now wholly according to Himself, which the Cross set Him free to do; and He can place these *redeemed, blood-bought* creatures as the "Firstborn"—those through whom He reveals Himself *fully,* as He could not by mere creation. There is no limit, therefore, to the

---

*"Those who compose it (the Assembly of firstborn ones enrolled in Heaven) are here characterized: (1) in relation to Him Who was carefully shown us in Chapter 1 to be the Firstborn . . . (2) in relation, by Grace, to our proper and destined sphere of glory, Heaven, and not earth, where Israel as such look for their blessedness and triumph under Messiah's reign."—Wm. Kelly.

†The word "Firstborn" is in Rom. 8.29 a title: "The Firstborn among many brethren"; in Col. 1.15, Christ is called "The Firstborn of all Creation," in view of the fact that all things were created "through Him and unto Him" (Col. 1.16). But in Col. 1.18-19, where He is seen as "The Head of the Body, the Church," we read the wonderful words, "Who is the Beginning, the Firstborn from the dead; that in all things He might have the pre-eminence," because in Him "was pleased to dwell the whole fullness of God" (R. V., margin).

favor in which God in sovereignty, in uncaused grace, places redeemed man. Could any other creature than man say as said Paul,
"To me to live is *Christ*"? It is not a question of our deserts or
attainments or service. It is a question of where God in His sovereign
will *placed us!* "That in the ages to come He might show the exceeding riches of His grace in [showing] kindness toward us in
Christ Jesus" (Eph. 2.7). The last thing we wretched humans desire
and learn is to be the recipients of unearned, undeserved, unat-
tained, bloodbought Divine *favor,* through the sovereign *will* of
God: objects merely of *grace!*

5.   **And to God the Judge of all**—What a place for sinners!
But what an eternal place of blessing for believers! They have heard
and believed the gospel, telling how Christ drank the cup to the
full, that God, the Righteous Judge, in unspeakable love to sinners,
had given to Him, His only begotten Son! How He forsook Him
instead of us, the sinners, and how Christ finished the work of our
redemption and brought us to God, "through His own blood."

God is in Heaven, and is **Judge of all**. But the Lord Jesus said
concerning believers, "He that believeth on Him is *not* judged"
(John 3.18); and,

"He that heareth My word, and believeth Him that sent Me,
hath eternal life, and cometh *not* into judgment, but hath passed out
of death into life" (Jno. 5.24).

So that these solemn words, **God the Judge of all**, do not mean
that God is judging *you,* believer! *That* judgment is *past!* So that
you need not fear this **Judge of all**—among the eight things unto
which "Ye are come." Unless we think carefully here, we would expect God to be named as Father, for we have just seen the word
"firstborn." But the words are even more wonderful than that. It is
God as God Whom we meet in this Epistle to the Hebrews. Consistent with this are the words, **God, Judge of all** (for there is no
article in the Greek). The name of Him Who certainly is Judge
of all His creatures is not placed before us here as One actively
judging, but in His Person only. Again, note that these Hebrew
believers had been brought to Him Whose voice at Sinai, in giving
the Ten Commandments of the Law covenant, had shaken the
earth; which covenant their nation had broken. But Another had
borne the judgment of it all, and here they are come, unafraid,
to God the Judge of all!

Even to Moses, though on Sinai "fearing and quaking" (Ex. 33.11), "Jehovah spake face to face, as a man speaketh unto his friend." And God testified to Miriam and Aaron in Numbers 12.8, "With him will I speak mouth to mouth, even manifestly, and not in dark speeches; and the form of Jehovah shall he behold." And this before Christ had come; before sin was put away by the blood of the Cross; before the Lord had been raised from the dead and hailed as Priest forever; before He had entered into the Holies above through His own blood and sat down on the right hand of the Majesty on high, there "to appear before the face of God for us"!

You may say, I can enter into such a verse as I John 3.1:

"Behold, what manner of love the Father hath bestowed upon us, that we should be called children of God; and such we are."

But is not *this* God, Who in the new birth has become your Father indeed, yet in very truth **Judge of all?** It is told of Emperor William I of Germany, that as he sat at the head of a great table surrounded by his lords and counselors, his little son, a mere child, got into the room, and, running to his father, pulled down his head to speak something into his ear. The father put his arms around him lovingly, and hearkened. Then, patting him gently, sent him quietly out, and turned again to the affairs of state.

O saints of God, what a company is this to which **ye are come! Innumerable hosts of angels, the general assembly of heavenly beings; the Church of the Firstborn enrolled in Heaven!** And behold, we are come to **God, Judge of all**—not, as we have said, judging *us*, but **Judge of all** is His eternal place. Let us meditate upon it, with faith indeed, but with applied hearts, for such is the company into which we have come! That God, **Judge of all**, should be one of this company, puts us in the very dust of humble gladness, brings rest beyond measure! If He Who is **Judge of all** saith to us poor sinners who know that our judgment was finished at Calvary—if *He* saith, **Ye are come to the Judge of all**, there is peace without end, *rest!*

Nevertheless, although God's saints, those who are born again, know God as their Father, and have the sweet witness of that fact by the Holy Spirit in their hearts, saying, Abba, Father; yet **Hebrews** sets forth God as God, "not in His relationships." When the blood of Christ is spoken of, it is with reference to the approach to the holy God, rather than as redeeming us. For example, *Jesus* is spoken of in the next verse (12.24), but not as "our Saviour," or "our Redeemer," but as **Mediator of a new covenant,** and His blood not as procuring our forgiveness, but as **the blood of sprinkling.** It is most conducive to true godliness to remember that we are come, as pardoned and cleansed, **to God the Judge of all.***

6.   **And to the spirits of just men made perfect**—In Chapter 11.39, reading of the Old Testament saints, we found that these saints had as yet "received not the promise," that is, the full realization of what God had revealed they were going to have; and the explanation there is, "that apart from us they should not be made perfect."

But now, Christ having died and been raised and glorified, it is freely said that **we are come to . . . the spirits of just men made perfect.** The future program for each of these saints has not yet been realized (for example, Dan. 12.13), yet as to their spirits they have been "made perfect" by the sacrifice of Christ. They were **"just men,"** justified by faith while still on earth, as was Abraham.† It should move us unto a profound unworldliness and holy reverence to remember that God's word is that we **are come . . . to the spirits of just men made perfect.** What a revelation! But remember that this does not mean that we are to endeavor to communicate with these spirits of just men made perfect, any more than with angels, as we noted. It refers to our heavenly *position:* we belong among *them,* and not to this world!

As to what companies of saints are already in Heaven: first, there are the Old Testament saints, called **the spirits of just men**

---

*The extent to which the fact reaches, that our judgment was borne by Another at the Cross, is magnified in our minds when we reflect that God will, by-and-by, commit judgment, both of men and of angels, to His Church saints! "Know ye not that the saints shall judge the world? . . . Know ye not that we shall judge angels?" (I Cor. 6.2, 3). "And I saw thrones, and they sat upon them, and judgment was given unto them" (Rev. 20.4). God does not cease here as **the Judge of all.** But that He should commit to redeemed creatures the position and qualification of judge of other creatures, shows how complete was Christ's work for us: not only "no condemnation," but made judges!

†I have often wondered in what state Moses and Elijah were when they "appeared in glory" with our Lord on the Transfiguration Mount. We know they had not their bodies, for Christ is the firstfruits of the resurrection. But they appeared "in glory," and when the bright cloud came, disappeared, going back into Heaven, evidently. If this could be written of them before our Lord's death and glorification, what God now means by their being made perfect, we must humbly and reverently leave to Him.

made perfect, as we have seen. Second, those of the Church of God who have "departed to be with Christ," which is "far better."* Evidently made perfect does not include that glorification for which all the saints are waiting, sharing Christ's manifested glory at His second coming (I Jno. 3.2; Rom. 8.19; Col. 3.4; Heb. 11.40); but rectifying in the sense of completing any deficiency of development. Delivered from all presence and effects of sin, in the full value of Christ's atoning work, they are in the presence of God, the Judge of all, up yonder, resting and waiting there for Christ's manifestation when they shall "see Him as He is," and "be like Him," be glorified!

We are of course not to hold communication with these spirits of just men made perfect; or have any consciousness of them; but only that we are come into the same sphere and stage as they! Such is the measureless power of the blood of Christ! Are they—these spirits—now fit to be in Heaven? So are we. Are they made perfect? So are we, in this epistle, while exhorted to go on unto full growth, told that we are come, already, to these made perfect.

7. And to Jesus, the Mediator of a new covenant—Sweet name, Jesus! as over against "Judge!" Now what new covenant is here meant? Matthew Henry well says: "Christ is the Mediator of this new covenant; He is the middle Person that goes between both parties, God and man, to bring them together in this cove-nant . . . to offer up our prayers to God, and to bring down the favors of God to us; to plead with God for us, and to plead with us for God; and at length to bring God and His people together in Heaven, and to be a Mediator and fruition between them for-ever; they beholding and enjoying God in Christ, and God behold-ing and blessing them in Christ." These Hebrew believers had "come" to Jesus, not in the sense necessarily that they had heard Him personally, as did the disciples, and received Him. They are

---

*Respecting the Church, the Assembly of the firstborn enrolled on high, whatever their place as members of Christ (unspeakable marvel!) they have not yet been glorified with us who are still on earth. They are fulfilling Heb. 9.28, for they with us await His coming Who "shall appear a second time, apart from sin, to them that wait for Him, unto salva-tion." "Apart from sin" does not mean that they are not now in Heaven, delivered from sin: they certainly are. But as we have noticed elsewhere, it means that His second coming, for which we wait, will be apart from all question of sin. "Salvation" here in Hebrews 9.28 is the consummation of that wonderful work, in the redemption of our bodies. He will in that day "present the Church to Himself a glorious Church, not having spot or wrinkle or any such thing; but that it should be holy and without blemish" (Eph. 5.27).

"come" here refers, as in all this remarkable series, to that spiritual sphere with its relationships into which, by faith in the gospel of Christ they had entered. Further, they had found in Jesus a **Mediator of a new covenant**—not referring, of course, to the new covenant of Chapter 8.8, which will be brought in "after those days" (that is, this present dispensation), and will be made "with the house of Israel and with the house of Judah" as we saw, at Christ's second coming. This new covenant with Israel, we repeat, lies yet in the future, in the Millennium. Nevertheless, in Chapter 8.6 we saw that Christ "obtained a ministry the more excellent, by so much as He is also the Mediator of a better covenant, which had been enacted upon better promises." Do you ask, Of what covenant is our Lord the Mediator? We rejoice to say, Of the *new covenant* of which He speaks in Luke 22.19, 20—and in Hebrews 13.20 (see below). After the last Passover Feast, closing Jewish matters, He brings in the Lord's Supper, which belongs to believers now, whether Hebrew or Gentile. "And He took bread, and when He had given thanks, He brake it, and gave to them, saying, This is My body which is given for you. This do in remembrance of Me. And the cup in like manner after supper, saying, This cup is the new covenant in My blood, even that which is poured out for you."

Now we turn to Hebrews 13.20, 21, the great Christian benediction of this whole epistle: "Now the God of peace, Who brought again from the dead, the Great Shepherd of the sheep, with the blood of an eternal covenant, even our Lord Jesus, make you perfect in every good work to do His will."

As we have said in connection with this passage, it is necessary to view the blood of this "eternal covenant" between "the God of peace" and "our Lord Jesus," as the source, cause and means of all blessing to us sinners, Jew or Gentile. We know that Israel and Judah will be blessed *as such* in the future; but they are not yet so blessed. And when the new arrangements with them shall be entered into (as we see in Ch. 8), it will be on the ground of "the blood of an eternal covenant," the one we are speaking of here, in Luke 22.20, and in Hebrews 13.20-21.

In our present verse, then (Chapter 12.24), Jesus is spoken of as **Mediator of a new covenant.** His blood having been shed as the means and fulfillment of this *eternal agreement between the God of peace and our Lord Jesus,* He naturally and necessarily becomes the Mediator of this covenant, of which the cup at the Lord's Supper is a constant reminder.

For there is one God, one Mediator also between God and man, Himself man, Christ Jesus. Thayer well remarks, "A mediator does not belong *to one party,* but to two or more." "Christ is God's," I Corinthians 3.23 says; but in Chapter 1.2 of that same epistle, the saints are told that the Lord Jesus Christ is "ours"! It is not only of blessing but of necessity that we remember that God has given His beloved Son not only *for* us, but *to* us! This draws us immediately close to God. We are Christ's and Christ is God's. God has His Mediator, and is satisfied; we have *our* Mediator!

To be the Mediator of this new, eternal covenant, our blessed Lord receives all whom the Father has given Him (Jno. 17.12), "keeps" them, perfects them, and presents them before God (Jude 24; II Cor. 4.11; Eph. 5.2; Col. 1.22; Heb. 12.2). You will ask, What, then, is our part? To hear the good news—yea, to hearken, and believe (as we shall see in vs. 25)!

8. **And to the blood of sprinkling that speaketh better [things] than Abel:** We have come now to the most solemn thing of all. We remember that in Exodus 24, in connection with the legal covenant, Moses "sprinkled both the book itself and all the people" with the blood of that covenant (Hebrews 9.19-20). "The tabernacle and all the vessels of the ministry" were also sprinkled (Heb. 9.21), and thus set apart to God.* The ordinance also of the sprinkling with "the water for impurity," made from the ashes of the red heifer and "living water" (Num. 19.1-9, 13, 17-9), comes to mind. The *blood* of this heifer had been shed, and the heifer was to be *burned,* and the *ashes* with "living water" made it an application of sacrificial death readily available to anyone defiled!

Again, in Leviticus 8, we find Aaron and his sons, when they are consecrated, sprinkled with the blood, and thus set apart to the priesthood. It is striking also that in Leviticus 14.7 when the leper

---

*We recall that the sprinkling of the blood upon the people, in connection with the Law covenant, brought to the front the liability to death upon any who disobeyed. God, however, acted in great mercy and patience.

was cleansed, he was sprinkled with the blood, indicating his entire *freedom* from defilement, before God. Compare Hebrews 9.13, 14, 19; 10.22, and 11.28, where Moses "By faith kept the passover, and the sprinkling of the blood," when God said (Ex. 12.13), "When I see *the blood* I will pass over you." It protected them from the judgment of death which was falling upon all Egypt.

But as we examine the other passages named above, we find the "sprinkling" to be connected with *cleansing*—and that of the *conscience*—as in Hebrews 9.14: "the blood of Christ" *cleansing* the *conscience* "from dead works to serve the Living God." This refers to the individual's receiving and understanding, by his cleansed conscience, the power and effect of the shed blood, rather than to God's apprehension of it. In Hebrews 9.22, both God's side and the effect upon us are seen in, "all are cleansed with *blood,* and apart from shedding of *blood* there is no remission."

The blood of sprinkling that speaketh better than Abel, then, points not only to the shedding of Christ's blood, but to the personal application of it to an individual's heart; so that peace, which Christ "made through the blood of His Cross," is *spoken unto the heart* of believing souls. No amount of prayer, no resolve of consecration, will relieve a burdened conscience, which keeps accusing the heart. The conscience keeps saying "Oh my sin!" (and won't say anything else!) The Holy Spirit says, "It was borne by Christ, and His blood put it away on the Cross." Then conscience is robbed of its power to affect the heart. **This blood of sprinkling** is not an *experience,* but is a view of what happened at the Cross, and what was done for us there. We read in Genesis 4.10-11 God's words to Cain:

"What hast thou done? The voice of thy brother's blood crieth unto Me from the ground! And now cursed art thou from the ground, which hath opened its mouth to receive thy brother's blood from thy hand!"

Thus the blood of Abel called for judgment. But the blood of sprinkling—that is, the application by faith of the shed blood of Christ—speaks of judgment past forever, and of *eternal peace with God Himself!* No wonder, then, that the next verse reads as it does:

25   See that ye refuse not Him that speaketh! For if they escaped not when they refused Him that warned them on

earth, much more shall not we escape who turn away
26 from Him that warneth from Heaven: Whose voice then
shook the earth: but now He hath promised, saying, Yet
once more will I make to tremble not the earth only, but
27 also the Heaven. And this word, yet once more, signifieth
the removing of those things that are shaken, as of things
that have been made, that those things which are not
28 shaken may remain. Wherefore, receiving a kingdom that
cannot be shaken, let us have grace, whereby we may
offer service wellpleasing to God, with reverence and
29 awe: for our God is a consuming fire.

Verse 25: Him that speaketh, as we learn at the beginning of
this great book of **Hebrews** (1.1-2), is GOD. The eight marvelous
contrasts with the Mount Sinai revelation have just been set before us in verses 22-24 ending with, **The blood of sprinkling that
speaketh better things than Abel.** The overwhelming possibility
of refusing such a God meets us first of all with the warning,
See that ye refuse not. Mark, it is **God the Judge of all** (vs. 23)
Who is speaking. Beside Him is **Jesus the Mediator** (vs. 25).
Before Him, and us, is **the blood of sprinkling:** Limitless, uncaused, Divine love—unutterable sacrifice! It is thus the Voice
cometh!

Friend, *see* to this! How personal, how definite, how distinct,
this word, "See!" All about you, people are "seeing to" this and
that: occupied therewith; most, seeing to business; many, to pleasure;
many, to bodily health. But how many are *seeing to* this one great
call to the creature from His Creator?

See that ye refuse not! Oh, that awful word, "refuse"! Can it
be that the God to Whom "the nations are as a drop of a bucket,
and are accounted as the small dust of the balance," can mean
that one of these infinitesimal bits of dust can refuse HIM? It
means just that. Oh, that our hearts, our very beings, might be
overwhelmed with a sense of values! These creatures of dust are
rushing forward to meet Him, the infinite, almighty One, Who
speaks here! **See that ye refuse not Him that speaketh!***

---

*The reader's attention is solemnly called to Deut. 29.18-21, where there was no outward
denial of Jehovah's testimony, but an inner heart-excusal. The Greek word for "refuse"
used as we see in verse 25, and in verse 19 (literally "excused themselves, asking that the
word be not addressed to them any more,") primarily means to *excuse oneself*. See it in
Lk. 14.18, translated, "began to *make* excuse."

O friend, I shout at you, **See that ye refuse not!** I cry unto you! You have a *will*. This is the most solemn, awful thing about the bits of dust you and I are: we have *wills*, we can *refuse* (for the brief life) the Almighty!

Now mark what follows: **For if they escaped not when they refused Him that warned them on earth,** that is, at Mount Sinai and onward in Israel's history. For however terrible were the warn- ings of the Law (Heb. 2.2; 10.28; Deut. 17.2-7; Num. 15.32-36) and its accompaniments, they concerned a *God*, not revealed fully, but hidden behind the tabernacle veil.

Verse 26: It was one thing for Jehovah to descend to Mount Sinai and speak to an earthly nation, Israel, about morality on earth—the Ten Commandments: **His voice then shook the earth** (Ex. 19.17-8).But it was quite another thing when in His infinite love God sent His Son to be born of a humble human virgin; and to walk the path of loving care and tenderness for men, and sub- mission to the Father's will at every step; having "no place to lay His head": traveling on to Gethsemane and the Cross; to "bear our sins in His body on the Tree."

Thus God spake from Heaven, opening out His whole heart and holy being to sinful man!

In view of God's revealing thus from Heaven in His own Son His righteousness and love at Calvary, the uttermost is uttered regarding coming judgment: **Now He hath promised, saying, yet once more will I make to tremble not the earth only, but also the Heaven!**

Verse 27: Then comes the Divine interpretation: **And this, Yet once more, signifieth the removing of those things that are shaken, as of things that have been made, that those things which are not shaken may remain:** Three great facts are to be noted here.

First, The earth and the Heaven are to be utterly *done away!* Such words as Revelation 20.11 cannot be avoided: there are many Scriptures corresponding:

"I saw a great white throne, and Him that sat upon it, from Whose face the earth and the Heaven *fled away!* and there was *found no place* for them!"

As our Lord often said, "Heaven and earth shall *pass away!* But My words shall not pass away!" To teach, as do many, that these

words refer merely to a "change" in the present creation, is to take
a stand beside the modernists, who do not believe the *words* of God!
Sin began in Heaven with the anointed one of the cherubim (Ezek.
28.11-18; Job 15.15; 25.5); and all things of the present creation
have been defiled. The New Creation is founded upon the redemption of Christ! *This only is eternal!** There are two spheres of
eternal duration of God's creatures: The Saved: "New heavens
and a new earth, wherein righteousness shall be at home" (II Pet.
3.13). The Lost: "The eternal fire prepared for the devil and his
angels . . . eternal punishment" (Matt. 25.41, 46; "eternal fire,"
Jude 7). Of course, there will be *no annihilation of lost beings*:
their destiny is plainly affirmed again and again (Rev. 20.10).†

Second: The reason: their *end* is accomplished! It is **as of things
that have been made** that these words are spoken. These shall be
shaken and done away. There was object in their creation: that
object was fulfilled, and they are *gone!* They were of the first, the
"former" creation: not of the second, which is wholly based on
Christ's redeeming work!

Third: **That those things which are not shaken may remain:**
God's uttered Word will abide forever; every one who has in
heart received and believed that word will remain forever! You
cannot say of one who has by God's direct miracle been "created
in Christ" that he is one of **the things that have been made.**

**Verse 28: Wherefore, receiving a kingdom that cannot be
shaken, let us have grace, whereby we may offer service well-
pleasing to God with reverence and awe:** How blessed, being
"new creatures in Christ," to be part of that **kingdom that cannot be shaken.** Believers belong to that New Creation which is so

---

*"The scope of creation has been the establishing of the kingdom of redemption that it,
the transitory and baseless, may pass away when its work is fulfilled, and give place to
that which shall never pass away. This view is strongly taken by Delitzsch, after Grotius
Bengel, Tholuck, and others."—Alford. This view is Scriptural. See Isa. 65.17; 34.4;
II Pet. 3.13; Rev. 21.1.

†Three realities (none of which modern "theology" grasps) are then before us here:
1. The blotting out of the present creation.
2. The fact that those saved are new creatures in the Risen Christ: of whom it is already
said, "He that is joined to the Lord is one spirit"; and to whom will shortly be given
bodies "like unto the body of His glory."
3. The existence and eternal duration of a literal hell of literal fire into which go not
only Satan and his angels, but also (Rev. 20.15) "any not found written in the Book of
Life."

marvelously set forth in the last two chapters of The Revelation! Knowing and believing this, fills saints with that blessed grace [or thankfulness] **whereby, with godly fear** [R.V., margin] **and awe, we are able to offer service well-pleasing to God.**

And now for **verse 29: For our God is a consuming fire.** The comparison here is to Sinai. See Exodus 19.17, 18; Deuteronomy 4.11: *God changes not.* This last verse of Hebrews 12 is literally true: it terrifies not His saints, but ministers to *godly* fear. But it should terrify His enemies, or any careless-hearted ones reading the words. What will *you* do with it? Will you relegate the book of *Hebrews* to the days of Moses, when the whole voice of this epistle *contrasts* it with those old days? These Hebrew believers were told they were "NOT come unto a mount that burned with fire," and yet the solemn warning with which this chapter closes declares that now **our God is a consuming fire.** Of course, this announcement is drawn forth by the possibility of some refusing to hear, **turning away from Him that warned from Heaven.** But what about His words concerning those who come up in judg- ment before a holy God, having chosen to retain their sins, with iniquity unpardoned? O modernist, O trifler, remember there is no preacher who spake so much, proportionately, of the doom of the damned, as did our blessed, loving Lord Himself! He announces that He, the Judge, will say to you:

"Depart from Me, ye cursed, into the *eternal fire* which is pre- pared for the devil and his angels" (Matt. 25.41).

And again,

"Neither doth the Father judge any man, but He hath given all judgment unto the Son; that all may honor the Son, even as they honor the Father. He that honoreth not the Son, honoreth not the Father that sent Him . . . And He gave Him authority to execute judgment, because He is a Son of man" (Jno. 5.22-3, 27).

This marks Christ as the Sitter on The Great White Throne of Revelation 20, "from Whose face the earth and the Heaven flee away." (See author's **Revelation,** pp. 327-334.)

Through simple faith only we reconcile Hebrews 12.29 with "God is Love," and "God so loved the world." Let no one yield to the delusion that "God *out of Christ* is a consuming fire"! Mr. Darby well says, "This expression, **Our God is a consuming fire,** they say, is spoken of God out of Christ. We know nothing of God out of Christ! We may be out of Christ ourselves, and then indeed as a consuming fire the presence of God would be destructive to us. But, as known to those who are in Christ, He is a GOD *intolerant of evil,* of all that is *inconsistent with Himself.*"

Let us hold fast by faith to the blessed words that begin this last verse, **Our God!** And let *Him* open it to us! There will be a day when the infinite holiness of God will become an indescribably blessed delight and joy, as His saints look forward to the ages to come!

CHAPTER THIRTEEN

1-2 LET LOVE OF THE BRETHREN continue. Forget not to show love unto strangers: for thereby some have
3 entertained angels unawares. Remember them that are in bonds, as bound with them; them that are ill-treated,
4 as being yourselves also in the body. Let marriage be had in honor among all, and let the bed be undefiled: for
5 fornicators and adulterers God will judge. Be ye free from the love of money; content with such things as ye have: for Himself hath said, I will in no wise fail thee, neither
6 will I in any wise forsake thee. So that with good courage we say,

> The Lord is my Helper; I will not fear:
> What shall man do unto me?

THE EXHORTATIONS for practical daily living in this closing chapter are strikingly befitting. The first is:

Verse 1: Let love of the brethren continue. There would be a natural attraction to others, especially to prominent and wealthy ones of their own race; but these were not the brethren. Most of the brethren were classified by God in I Corinthians 1.26-28: "foolish," "weak," "base," "despised," zeros—"the things that are not"! The word for love-of-the-brethren is *philadelphia*, love of the brotherhood. It should be the determination of the very heart and soul of every believer that nothing should interrupt or mar this love for the precious brotherhood, that is, *for those in Christ*. But by all means let him "continue" it, at any cost of self-sacrifice! For as we find it in Chapter 10.24, "Let us consider one another to provoke [by our own kindnesses and example] unto love and good works."

Paul thus commends a beloved household, that of Stephanas: "Ye know the house of Stephanas . . . that they have set themselves to minister unto the saints, . . . I beseech you, brethren, that ye also be in subjection unto such, and to everyone that helpeth in the work and laboreth." There is no ministry that brings such a response in a heart subjection of love!*

Verse 2: Forget not to show love unto strangers: for thereby some have entertained angels unawares: The old version renders this precious word, "entertain strangers," but God did not say "entertain," but show love unto strangers. (See Revised Version.) And "hospitality" is but a weak rendering of this word. **Love to strangers** is possible perhaps only to believers, for in them the Holy Spirit lives and exercises the very emotions of God. How often have we heard someone say, "I attended such and such a church for weeks and no one spoke to me." Or, "I was a stranger, and the only ones these Christians seemed to recognize were their own company and friends."

These Hebrew believers, "partakers of a heavenly calling," have only *Christ,* and Him in the glory. They are relieved from earthly, "religious" things and can let their love, or rather His love through them, be extended to "strangers."

The personal attitude of Christians toward strangers, who are not of their own regular assembly, particularly, is in view here, as well as the truly Christian attitude toward just common "strangers." There is to be love shown *such.* It is not duty, formality, nor in any wise pretense: it is allowing the love of God in Christ to go through us toward them, without seeking some reward from their side. We verily believe that an assembly of saints showing love to strangers will soon have plenty of strangers to love. The expression **some have entertained angels** doubtless has included, through the centuries, many who still remained unaware of their heavenly visitants. Therefore let us not forget **to show love unto strangers.** Visit them—especially if sick! Look after them—even to loaning, or giving them money! "Love is *love!*"

Verse 3: Next, an equally beautiful exhortation: **Remember**

---

*The author's book, **Romans Verse by Verse** (p. 471-2), makes this comment on Heb. 13.1-5:

We have in Heb. 13 three uses of the Greek root *phil*—meaning love: (1) "Let love of the brethren *(philadelphia)* continue"; (2) "Forget not to show love unto strangers" *(philoxenia)*; and, (3) in verse 5, "Be free from silver-loving" *(philarguros)*. If you are tempted to *philarguros, philadelphia* and *philoxenia* will cure you! . . . Let us make "Strangers' Inns" of our homes. We are not staying here long. And the Lord may send "angels" around when we least expect! . . . Even if the reference in "unawares" is not to Abraham in Gen. 18 (for he at once recognized the Lord, and knew His attendants), yet the statement seems rather an absolute one of inspiration, suggesting such a possibility for any of us! See also the case of Gideon in Jud. 6; and Manoah, Jud. 13.

them that are in bonds, as bound with them.* Beloved Paul yearns for such fellowship: "Remember my bonds" (Col. 4.18). This takes peculiar grace, but grace can do peculiar things! It enables one in freedom, even in ease, to enter the deepest dungeons of saints in affliction, and the Holy Spirit, in both this praying saint and that bound one, working in both, administers comfort. Blessed is the saint gladly entering into these sufferings!

(Remember) them that are ill-treated, as being yourselves also in the body: These are no common directions to "pity" those suffering bonds and ill-treatment, but to enter by the Holy Spirit, in love and prayer, into their condition with them, *visiting* them when possible.

Verse 4: And now such a needed exhortation: (If needed then, how vastly more in these days hurrying on toward Sodom!) **Let marriage be had in honor in all things† and let the bed be undefiled: for fornicators and adulterers God will judge:** The entire conduct of married people as such toward each other is looked at here. (See Eph. 5.25-28; I Cor. 7.1-5; Mk. 10.2-12; I Pet. 3.1-7).

Verse 5: Be ye free from the love of money, content with such things as ye have! Money—and the love‡ and pursuit of it, has ever been a snare to the Hebrews (as Gentiles constantly mark and *re*-mark: though with no less covetous hearts, and probably less acquisitive ability!) But mark the great word *"content,"* that God uses to describe that state of heart pleasing to Him in His people. **Content with such things as ye have.** Would that these words described all Christians!

Verse 6: Loving trust in the Lord banishes all fear, so that the psalmist here quoted writes,

> **The Lord is my helper; I will not fear:**
> **What shall man do unto me?**

Surely he had entered into the truth of the *"in no wise fail . . . in no wise forsake thee."* How blessed this life of simple *faith!*

---

*Excellent commentators refuse to confine these counsels of mercy regarding the stranger, prisoners, and the "ill-treated," to Christians only; but make them include all, as Conybeare: "Remember the prisoners, as though ye shared their prison."

†"In all things: Greek, *en pasim:* 'In all respects and circumstances.' *Pasin* is neuter as in verse 18, 'all things'; I Tim. 3.11, etc."—Westcott.

‡See note on verse 1.

7   Remember them that had the rule over you, men that
       spake unto you the word of God; and considering the
       issue of their life, imitate their faith.

8   Jesus Christ is the same yesterday and today, yea and
9   forever! [Therefore] be not carried away by divers and
       strange teachings: for it is good that the heart be estab-
       lished by grace; not by meats, wherein they that occupied
10   themselves were not profited. We have an altar, whereof
11   they have no right to eat that serve the tabernacle. For
       the bodies of those beasts whose blood is brought into
       the holy place by the high priest as an offering for sin,
12   are burned without the camp. Wherefore Jesus also, that
       He might sanctify the people through His own blood,
13   suffered without the gate. Let us therefore go forth unto
14   Him without the camp, bearing His reproach; for we have
       not here an abiding city, but we seek after the city which
15   is to come. Through Him then let us offer up a sacrifice
       of praise to God continually, that is, the fruit of lips
16   which make confession to His name. But to do good and
       to communicate forget not: for with such sacrifices God is
17   well pleased. Obey them that have the rule over you, and
       submit to them: for they watch in behalf of your souls,
       as they that shall give account; that they may do this
       with joy, and not with grief: for this were unprofitable
       for you.

Verse 7:   Remember those leading you—In three verses (7,
17, 24) these "leaders" (them that had the rule over you) in the
assemblies which these saints had known, are set before us, always
in Hebrews, with a lesson to all believers.

   1. They were leaders (lit., those leading).* God raises up by

---

*It is very instructive that in the New Testament this Greek word, *hēgeomai*, meaning
to go before, to be a leader, etc., is used only in the participliar form, which indicates that
it was their work, and not an office, to which God is calling attention. There are no popes,
no bosses, in the early Church; and there is no other church than after this pattern.
"Judas called Barsabas, and Silas," in Acts 15.22, are called "Leading men among the
brethren." In rendering this word "have the *rule* over you," both the Authorized and
the Revised Version show the relics of popery. The Assembly of God has no earthly popes,
though it does have Divinely appointed and therefore Divinely annointed brethren upon
whom God has placed the burden of the care of the Assembly. These are elders (*presbuteroi*)
to care for the Assembly spiritually and to defend it from error; and deacons (*diakonoi*)
to care for the temporal matters, such as looking out for the poor, as did the seven of Acts
6. Both elders and deacons are to be clearly distinguished from those who are gifted by the
Spirit in any of the nine or ten ways spoken of in I Cor. 12: "apostles, prophets, teachers,"
etc., for example. Leadership involved responsibility for the condition of the Assembly;

His Spirit in each assembly of saints those whom He fits to care
for it. They are *not* rulers as "bosses."

2. These leaders **spake the word of God** unto the saints. This
is illustrated in Acts 14.12, where Paul was the chief speaker,
literally, took the lead in speaking: the same Greek verb, *hegeomai,*
as Hebrews 13.7. (This is the very opposite of the Satanic tyranny
over the Roman Catholics, in which the "priests" do not even
permit the people to read the Scriptures for themselves!) These
Scriptural leaders were, of course, by no means the only ones in
the assemblies of saints who **spake the word of God,** for there is
wondrous freedom in a Scriptural assembling of the saints. As
Paul says, "When ye come together, *each one* hath a psalm, hath a
teaching, hath a revelation, hath a tongue, hath an interpretation.
Let all things be done unto edifying" (I Cor. 14.26). Here was
no one-man ministry!

But the "leaders," while including the God-appointed elders or
overseers, especially taught the Word of God, as an excellent commentator translates I Timothy 5.17: "Let the elders who *take the
lead* well [among the saints] be esteemed worthy of double honor."
In each assembly there would be those fitted by God to do as Paul
exhorts the elders of the Ephesian assembly to do: "Take heed
unto yourselves, and to all the flock, in which the Holy Spirit hath
made you overseers,* to feed the Church of the Lord which He
purchased with His own blood . . . Wherefore watch ye" (Acts
20.28-31).

---

whereas a teacher would "give himself to his teaching." One of the supreme needs of the
hour now is for Christians to find out from God exactly what He has fitted them for.

*Greek, *episkopoi.* Note two things about these overseers here: (1) There were not one
but several in each Assembly. Compare with Phil. 1.1, addressed to "all the saints in Christ
Jesus at Philippi, with the overseers *(episkopoi)* and deacons." How eagerly the human heart
seizes the least excuse for self-exaltation, and for aloneness and aloofness of power, is seen
in the sad misapplication of the term "overseer" (used always in Scripture, we repeat, of
several in each assembly) as arrogating to itself the title of "Bishop" and even of "Arch-
bishop" of *many* assemblies—such a person to be addressed as "My Lord Bishop"!

2. Note again in Acts 20 that those addressed as overseers *(episkopoi)* are simply "the
elders" of the assembly (vs. 17): Paul "sent to Ephesus, and called to him the elders
(presbuterio) of the assembly."

Note also that Scripture confines eldership to a local assembly. In Acts 11.30 the elders
are those of the assembly at Jerusalem. In Acts 14.23, Paul and Barnabas "ordained elders
in every assembly." Compare 21.18; and Tit. 1.5: "ordained elders in every city." Again,
Jas. 5.14: "Let him call for the elders of the assembly."

An elder, therefore, was such in the assembly where he was. There was no hint by the
Holy Spirit of a confederating of various assemblies into what is now called a "Presbytery,"
"Conference," an "Association," or a "Convention," any more than there is Scripture for
denominations.

3. The saints were to **imitate their faith**—the faith of such leaders, and to be especially drawn to this imitation by **considering the issue of their life.** The word "issue" has special reference to the character of their closing testimony, "Considering *what kind of an end** they made."—Vincent. So we do well to remember the leaders, and to **consider the end of their kind of life.** Thus are our hearts drawn out to imitate, not them, but *"their faith";* not their mannerisms, but their methods with God; their separation unto Him; their reliance upon Him; the boldness and confidence in their *trusting* Him.

Verse 8: Jesus Christ is the same yesterday and today, yea and forever!†—Let this mighty verse grasp our hearts, for it is spoken of our Saviour, Jesus Christ. Out of past eternity, never having had a beginning—for is He not God the Son—He comes to us.

Yesterday—Oh, what a word! Remember out of this eternal "yesterday" He comes to do the Father's will and also to let His infinite love work for us.

And to-day—His obedience to His blessed Father and His infinite devotion to us, we see in the choice of the cup of Divine forsaking, and the drinking of it to the finish on the Cross. When

---

*For myself, for instance, I look back first to my father, a godly minister, who lived to within three years of a century, in whose life I cannot remember the least dishonorable or unchristian act, and whose end was perfect quiet and very peace!

Then I think of R. A. Torrey, in the Moody Institute in Chicago, whom Mr. Moody had appointed superintendent. When I consider Mr. Torrey's manner of life, and the ending thereof, my heart is peculiarly filled with tenderness. Once, in his praying with me and for me, I happened to glance at his face, and tears were running down. So I remember *that* leader!

As for Mr. Moody, he came to the Chicago Auditorium Theatre, and held two meetings a day, morning and afternoon. In that last series in Chicago, how he preached! One day, for instance, on Elisha's receiving Elijah's mantle, when you could fairly see that old camel's hair garment drop from the skies, and Elisha rending his own clothes, taking Elijah's mantle, and smiting the waters with the words, "Where is Jehovah, the God of Elijah?"—and the Jordan dividing!

Mr. Moody went from Chicago to Kansas City, to a great audience in Convention Hall, where he was stricken, and went home to Northfield to go to be with the Lord on what he called his "Coronation Day," saying just before he went home:

"Earth is receding and Heaven is opening; God is calling me."

†Sapphir well says, "All their departed teachers and elders had shown them in life and death what they had declared: The just shall live by *faith*. They had passed away; but the Great Prophet, the Great Apostle and High Priest, the true Shepherd, remained—**Jesus Christ, the same yesterday, today, and forever** . . . His yesterday has no beginning but it ends with His burial in that new tomb. His today commences with His resurrection, and is even now the 'today' while we hear the voice of grace. His 'forever' commences with His second advent. His incarnation is only the manifestation of the mind that was in Him from all eternity."

does this blessed word "to-day" begin? I beg you to consider if its meaning be not *since His* resurrection; since He sent the message to His disciples on that resurrection day, "Go to My brethren"; since He appeared that night to them saying, "See My hands and My feet"; and He ate with them, and "showed Himself alive . . . by the space of forty days." Then He ascended to the right hand of Him Who said, "Thou art a priest forever, after the order of Melchize-dek," and, "Sit Thou at My right hand until I make Thine enemies Thy footstool." Then in ten days He sent forth the blessed Spirit upon His beloved believers, and lo, the Church, the Body of Christ is found! All this—and how much more is included in the blessed words "and to-day!"

What an unspeakable marvel! There is One Who changeth not. Our God changes not and in the blessed quotation from Psalm 102.27, we find these words applied to the Lord Jesus:

"But Thou art the same,
And Thy years shall have no end."

And unto the ages* (Gr., *eis tous aiōnas*)—This is, of course, for the eternity to come! But in the mind of the Spirit, "eternity" is looked at as a succession—endless, of course—of periods during each of which some purpose of God is fulfilled, for example, the age *(aiōn)* succeeding the present one is called the age to come.

Change with us is constant, universal. How unspeakably blessed that the Christ to Whom we have transferred our life and hopes is the same unto the ages, **yesterday and today, and forever!** Of no one but Deity could this be spoken. Even of angels it is writ-ten, that they "desire to look into" certain things. And so with all creatures: how blessed that we know One Who changeth not! The love that redeemed us was in His bosom from all eternity. We therefore wholly reject **divers and strange teachings (vs. 9).**

---

*The meaning of *aiōn* must be understood despite man's dispensational ignorance or prejudice, if we would understand what the Word of God says to us in this word: It means a duration of time during which God is accomplishing certain things. It never means the created world itself.

How tragic it is that even the Revised Version banishes to the "margin," the word *age,* substituting the word *world* as for example in Matthew 24.3: "Thy coming, and of the end of the *world.*" The disciples asked literally, "What shall be the sign of Thy coming and the consummation of the *age?*" In Matthew 13.39, 40, 49 and 28.20 also the word age *(aiōn)* is banished. What right has anyone to substitute the word *cosmos* (world), God's word to denote the *earth* (Matt. 13.35; John 21.25; Acts 17.24; I John 3.17), that is a *material* creation, for the characteristic *operation* of God in that created world? His creation is *cosmos* (world). His operation is age *(aiōn)*.

Verse 9: Be not carried away by divers and strange doctrines—
"Strange teachings": Look at them today! Buchmanism, Bullingerism, Unity, Christian Science, Seventh Day Adventism, Rus-
sellism, British Israelism, Psychianna, and many more! God may
bring back to truth and soberness some of these foolish folk, who
have been carried away by them, but the real apostate has
turned his back on Christian things and Divine mercy forever.
**For it is good that the heart be established by grace; not by meats,
wherein they that occupied themselves were not profited:** Here
you must turn to Leviticus 11. We beg you, go read this chapter.
The conscientious Israelite was occupied with *meats!* But the Law
"made nothing perfect," as we found in Hebrews 7, so that there
was "a disannulling of a foregoing commandment," and now comes
GRACE, through our Lord Jesus Christ.*

Verses 10-11: We have [that is, in Levitical things, especially
on the Great Day of Atonement] **an altar, whereof they have no
right to eat who serve the tabernacle. For the bodies of those living creatures whose blood is brought into the holies by the high
priest as an offering for sin, are burned without the camp:** The
opening word in the Greek, **We have,** is merely a verb making a
statement, referring to Old Testament things, and not a statement
of any distinction between Jews and Gentiles. In **We have, the**
writer is speaking as a Hebrew, and the emphatic words are
"have," and *"altar."* This "altar" is the one that was in the taber-
nacle† of old. The altar was not the offerer, much less the victim.
It was the place where the victim was presented, slain. Christ is nowhere called an altar, nor is the Cross.‡ Indeed, verse 11, the chief

---

*"Nothing is plainer proof that the heart is not practically in possession of that which
gives rest in Christ, that it does not realize what Christ is, than the restless search after
something new—divers and strange doctrines. To grow in the knowledge of Christ is our
life and our privilege. The search after novelties which are foreign to Him, is a proof of
not being satisfied with Him."—Darby, Syn., p. 346.

†Note that it is the "tabernacle"; not the temple as existing when this epistle was written. This use of "tabernacle," instead of temple, is consistent throughout Hebrews, for the
temple looked forward to kingdom times; the tabernacle in the wilderness, meant atonement
and worship. We expect, therefore, to hear of some ordinance or ceremony connected with
that tabernacle, and we have this in verse 11.

‡To make the altar Christ, now in Heaven, is to pass by the work done at the Cross, and
pass on to the worship in Heaven—which cannot be carried on except in view of the perfect
sacrifice on earth. To make Christ in Heaven the altar would be to set up in Heaven what

point of the passage, does not support this. It carried on the explanation concerning the altar *in the tabernacle*. Of that altar those who
served the tabernacle were indeed to eat: but *not* of **the bodies of
those living creatures whose blood is brought into the holies by
the high priest as an offering for sin.** (See Lev. 6.26, 30; 4.7, 12,
18, 21; 16.15, 27, 28.) We see in these passages that when the
blood of the sin-offering on the Great Day of Atonement was
presented in the Holy of Holies (in the immediate presence of God,
as most precious to Him), **the bodies of those living creatures** of
which the blood had been shed were **burned without the camp.**
So Christ suffered the wrath of God **without the gate** (vs. 12),
and entered into the presence of God "within the veil" (Heb.
6.19; 10.20).

Going back for a minute to verse 10, we must see what truths
are set forth by this burning **without the camp:**

1.   The fire represents God's wrath upon Christ-made-sin at
the Cross.

2.   This took place **without the camp,** showing Him becoming
a curse and forsaken of God.

3.   The burning of these bodies had nothing to do with atonement for sin, because "it is *the blood* that maketh atonement," and
the blood of these beasts had been poured out, and taken into the
holy place as an offering for sin, not only on the Great Day of
Atonement, but also whenever sin had been committed, as we saw
in Leviticus 4, cited above.

From man's side, carrying out the type, Christ should have died
in the temple at the altar. But human religion was on the throne
there, and human religion has no place for atoning blood. Men give
up hope in "religion" when they transfer their trust to the poured-
out blood of the Son of God! Jerusalem was the "holy city": "religious" sinners are out for His blood, but will not have it shed
there. So they take Him to Golgotha, outside the whole religious

---

He finished on earth; for the altar was not the place of worship, but of sacrifice.

The altar was standing in front of the temple at Jerusalem when the Apostle was writing;
and on it was the sacrifice, the sin-offering (vs. 11) of which none were permitted to eat.
It was of course afterwards destroyed by the Romans.

To suppose this altar to be what we today call "the Lord's table," will not do; for all
partake of that table; but no one partook of the sin-offering, which was burned without the
camp, symbolizing God's wrath against sin.

camp. And that day saw a world of sin with the Redeemer cast out
by them!

Note now that verse 11 connects itself with verse 10 by the word
"For," and verse 12 opens out the new subject with the words
Wherefore Jesus also. (Vs. 11 refers to and depends on vs. 10.)*

Verse 12: Here we have the object of this burning **without the
camp,** fulfilled by our Lord's suffering **without the gate.** (Remember the brazen altar was inside, not without!) It was **that He
might sanctify the people through His own blood.** Here the meaning of the word sanctify as it is generally found in **Hebrews** prevails.
It is, to separate unto. (See comment on 10.14, 29; 12.14). When
our blessed Lord died, outside the gate, outside all "religious"
connection, despised and rejected of men, the way was laid for
Him, risen from the dead, to give us His own life and place.
Joined to Him (for "Both He that sanctifieth and they that are
sanctified are all of one") they are, and are worshiping. There
is no other worship. The world, even the religious world, has been
left behind by a Risen Christ, and so by all His own. The saints,
believers, are sanctified, separated, unto God. "They are not of
the world even as I am not of the world," our Lord said (Jno.
17.14). Was He despised? Was His place **without the gate,
without the camp?** Then the place of all His own is there. The
world despises them, knows them not, as it knew not and despised
the Lord. The world is a black ball doomed, rolling on to judgment!

**Verse 13: Let us therefore go forth unto Him without the camp,
bearing His reproach:** Inasmuch as Jesus had **suffered without the
gate** down here, "a reproach of men, and despised of the people"
(Ps. 22.6), believers were now to **go forth unto Him without the
camp.** It is a blessed thing that in thus going forth **without the
camp** we go forth **UNTO HIM.** For Christ is known only by and
in the Holy Spirit, and true worship is that of Ephesians 2.18:
"Through Him we both [Jew and Gentile believers] have our access by one Spirit unto the Father."†

---

*Vss. 10 and 11 refer to *the type*, vs. 12 is *the application* of it, vs. 13 is the *exhortation*
in view of it, vs. 14, our *expectation*, and vs. 15 our *true sacrifice* in praise to God.

†Our Lord's suffering is **without the gate,** while we are exhorted to go forth unto Him
without the camp. The types of Hebrews are those of the tabernacle in the wilderness, but
by the Spirit of prophecy (Rev. 19.10) the word "gate" is used, referring to our Lord's
going forth through the gate of Jerusalem to the hill of Calvary.

"The camp" to those Hebrew believers whom Paul is addressing, of course meant apostate Judaism that had crucified their Messiah. But the term "camp" includes all those "religious" developments, by whatever name called, which, though professing to be Christian, are Judeo-pagan.* You must choose between earthly "religion" and heavenly reality. You must know a heavenly Christ or not know Christ at all. Your worship must be by the Spirit, or be worse than paganism.

Six words might sum up the believing Hebrew's position: "Within the veil" (6.19; 10.20); **without the camp.** "Within the veil" is the heavenly position: Christ is there, and believers in fact are there in Him, and are to be there in constant entrance (10.19 ff). **Without the camp** reveals where Christ is and His followers are, as to this world and its "religion." If God takes Judaism away from the Hebrews, and commands them to "draw near with boldness unto the throne of grace," having "no continuing city" on earth, no temple, ceremonies, special days†—no religious camp, but Christ in the glory only—let us beware of any "religious" things man sets up on earth! All earthly *religious* things are of the flesh, which has been forever rejected of God. Let no man build it up by religious forms, lest it prove his doom.

Again and again we say, since their "religion" is taken away from the Hebrews (to whom God gave it), let no Gentile (to whom religion was never given) dare to claim to have it! You—who are you? A publican, we trust, who has smitten his breast, saying, "God be merciful to me, a sinner" (Lk. 18.9-14). Otherwise, you are a Pharisee!

---

*This refers not only to Roman Catholicism, which openly claims temporal power, holding not one Christian truth in purity, and having an order of "priests" who blasphemously undertake to do that work for men which our Great High Priest has done on the Cross, and now is accomplishing in Heaven. It refers also to all who, despite God's Word to the contrary, disobey God's command not to "divide Christ" by sectarianism. Thus we see what is called Christendom, where Christ is named, but which believes in human righteousness, hates grace for the guilty, and thinks of itself as having "the Christian religion": people not born again, not having the Holy Spirit, never having been convicted of their lost state "joining" what are called "churches."

† "It [the kingdom of Christ] has no sacred days or seasons, no special sanctuaries, because every time and every place are alike holy. Above all, it has no sacerdotal system. It interposes no sacrificial tribe or class between God and man. The only priests under the Gospel, designated as such in the New Testament, are the saints, the members of the Christian brotherhood. As individuals all Christians are priests alike."—Bishop Lightfoot, of Durham.

Bearing His reproach: For if there is anyone despised or re-proached on earth, it is one openly holding a hope of Heaven, yet having no connection with human "religion." Let such an one love fellow Christians, and unsaved people too, howevermuch; and let him testify ever so faithfully of God's infinite gift of love, even Christ, dying for our sins—yet the question the world will ask will be, "What *religion* do you profess?" or, "What *denomination* do you belong to?"

And if he says, "To none: I belong to Christ," they cast him out. Yea, the "denominations" themselves will persecute him. And why all this? Hearken:

Because the sins of such a one were put away by the blood of Christ, and he knows it.

Because he died with Christ and is a new creature in a Risen Christ, and he knows it.

Because, wonder of wonders!—he is a member of the Body of Christ; and the Spirit, Who baptized him into that Body, indwells him—and he knows it.

Because he finds in the Cross the end of all human religions, the end of all man's hopes of whatever sort.

Because he is not of the world even as Christ was not of the world; and he is hated because Christ is hated—and he knows it.

Of course all this makes him "different" from the world. Unless *your* only hope is not "religion," not being a "church member," not so-called Christian activity, but—the blood of Christ Who entered Heaven "through His own blood," having shed it on the Cross, for-saken of God for your sins—your hope is a damning delusion, what-ever your "priest," "pastor," or "spiritual adviser" may tell you.

So any man or woman who knows the true gospel is in a world where he will **bear His reproach.** "All that would live godly in Christ Jesus shall suffer persecution" (II Tim. 3.12).* Let it be known that you believe the *mere profession* of "the Christian religion" to be a delusion, and you will at once find yourself bear-

---

*The world *will not* have *Christ Himself* set before them: as their only hope of escape from hell; as having immediate claims upon them as their Creator God, as the Redeemer at the cost of His own blood; as their appointed Judge. Let these claims of Christ be set forth in the power of the Holy Spirit, and you will find the wrath of this Satan-ruled world to be just what it was when they spat in the face of the Son of God, and nailed Him to the Tree!

ing His reproach. "Religion" is a false hope. Christendom has put on this garment and goes right on sinning. Salvation, on the other hand, involves men's knowledge of and acquaintance with Jesus Christ in Heaven Who bore their sins in His own body on the Tree. *Saved* people have HIM. They have deserted "religion" for a Person—a Divine Person—and are waiting for Him from Heaven. The nation that had "religion," blind to their sins, crucified their Messiah. So religion's day was done.*

Verse 14: For we have not here an abiding city, but we seek after the city which is to come: Thus did Abraham, as we have said (see Ch. 11.10); and all the patriarchs (11.13-16). They "confessed they were strangers and pilgrims on the earth" . . . that they were "seeking after a country of their own . . . that they desire a better country, that is, a heavenly."

Thus these Hebrew believers not only were "partakers of a heavenly calling," but saw they had a heavenly destiny. Those whose consciences have been cleansed by the blood of Christ (9.14) "to serve the Living God," come to the city of the Living God (12.22)—not only in expectation now, but in realization shortly!

Verse 15: Through Him then let us offer up a sacrifice of praise to God continually, that is, the fruit of lips which make confession to His name: Friend, this exhortation of Hebrews takes you into heavenly worship. The subject of **Hebrews** is *not* our justification, *not* our being delivered from condemnation: but our being brought into the glad company who are worshiping and praising God, Christ leading this worship.† As He said concerning us, in the won-

---

*In the Millennium to come, as shown in the prophets (see Ezek. 40-48) there will be a temple, with memorial sacrifices. But this will be only after the Remnant of Israel have "looked unto Him Whom they have pierced," and "mourned for Him," and have rested upon His sacrifice.

†One Sunday night, many years ago, the writer was preaching in the old Moody Church building in Chicago, on the finished work of Christ on the Cross, and His present priesthood in Heaven. As usual on Sunday nights, the song service led by beloved D .B. Towner had crowded the auditorium. All seats were full, and people standing against the walls, both upstairs and down.

A little Irish woman, a Roman Catholic, who was unattractive in appearance and had lost one eye, hearing the great volume of song, came to the entrance, could not get in on the first floor, and went to the gallery. There too she found people standing, but pressed on to the aisle which led down through the gallery to a point opposite the pulpit. There she took a stand, looking right down at the pulpit.

At that moment the speaker was saying, "Let this Bible in my left hand represent the

derful Twenty-second Psalm (vss. 22 ff—the *Risen* Christ),

"I will declare Thy name unto My brethren:

In the midst of the Assembly will I praise Thee."

But you say, My time is occupied with getting a livelihood! I hope to get to Heaven by the blood of Christ shed for me on the Cross. But as to my occupation now, I am a practical man. I attend church faithfully, but when Monday morning comes, it is out in the world for me, to make my way. This absorbs my thoughts.

Nay, you are wrong, you are tragically wrong! You can "praise the Lord in *all* things"! See Psalm 145.2-3; 146.2; Lamentations 3.22-3; Acts 5.42; and Psalm 55.17, as wrote David with the un-

---

world's sin, your sin and mine. I now transfer this book to my right hand" (and he did). "Thus God transferred the sin of the world, your sin and mine, to Christ, and now says to us, 'Behold the Lamb of God, that taketh away the sin of the world!' God forsook Christ on the Cross, instead of forsaking us; for there the judgment of human sin was being held, held ahead of time, that we sinners might not be judged, but our Substitute judged in our place!

"And now God has raised Him from the dead, and He has entered Heaven 'through His own blood,' and in the value and power of that shed blood He is at God's right hand just now. Believe on Him, believe that He has put away *your* sins by His blood on the Cross, and lo, you have Him as your Great High Priest in Heaven, in things pertaining to God, making intercession for you, sympathizing with your every need. Your conscience is then forever free as regards guilt and judgment, for the Lord Jesus has said,

" 'He that heareth My word, and believeth Him that sent Me, *hath* eternal life, and cometh not into judgment, but hath passed out of death into life.' "

That little Irish Catholic woman, just as she heard, believed—believed God's Word, believed on the Lord Jesus Christ. She left that gallery, that building, and went home to the convent where she was a servant, and began to pack up her belongings to remove from there.

They said, "What do you mean? You cannot leave us!" She answered, "I *must* leave you, and I will, tonight! For I have heard tonight that Jesus Himself put away my sin forever, and is my Great High Priest in Heaven!"

And she did leave that convent! She went to live in a humble rented room, and began to publish in every spare moment the good news of salvation she had heard and believed.

What a straight course in the truth she held! She testified to everybody, on the streets, everywhere. Soon all the policemen in the "Loop" knew her, and let her alone, for they knew that her message of salvation helped, rather than hindered, good government.

One night about 11 o'clock I was on a State Street car coming from a meeting on the South side. The snow lay many inches deep. What was my astonishment, as the car stopped opposite a vacant lot surrounded by illuminated billboards, to see standing in the snow 75 or 100 men, and, on a box, "Sister" Duffy, telling those men the good news, from her very soul.

What had happened to her? That night in the old Moody church, the swelling song of 2,000 voices had drawn her in, and she had joined—what? Through simply believing the blessed message of Christ's work on Calvary, and His present priesthood on high, she had joined the great company of adoring *worshipers* who through Christ have become real believers in God Who raised Him from the dead!

So may this book of **Hebrews** I pray, draw any who have not yet believed, who have not yet rested on the transferring of their guilt to the head of Christ on the Cross, and the putting away forever of their sin from God's sight by the offering of Himself! May this book of **Hebrews** lead us to join the glad song of worship which the Risen Christ, Himself the High Priest, leads, the heavenly worship of His saints, those who have believed!

counted burdens of the whole kingdom on his shoulders! Do you not remember that the Lord Jesus said, "The Father seeketh worshipers"—in spirit and in truth? What does your little earth life amount to? As James says, "What is your life? For ye are a vapor that appeareth for a little time, and then vanisheth away" (4.14). And you say, I have not time to be a worshiper. Is not that tempting God? "The God in Whose hand thy breath is, and whose are all thy ways, hast thou not glorified," as said Daniel to Belshazzar (Dan. 5.23). And a creature depending on God for breath "has not time" to use that breath to praise him!

What is *time* compared with *eternity*—endlessness of being? We can believe nothing else than this: that the vast majority of professed Christians refuse to become worshipers, want to do as the world does as far as they safely can; place their little earth affairs before the heavenly Father's desire for worshipers—those who **offer up a sacrifice of praise* to God continually.** The hope of most Christians is "to go to Heaven when they die." Meanwhile, they are to pray for grace to "live the Christian life." But believers are to *enter into Heaven,* where Christ is, NOW.

In **Hebrews** as in no other book, is set forth a believing human being left here for a few years of pilgrim existence as to earth, but really occupied with Heaven, with the throne there, the throne of grace; with the Great High Priest there, Jesus, the Son of God. As regards the earth, the world, and all human religion, believers have gone forth unto Christ "without the camp, bearing His reproach." But, as to Heaven, they enter into "that which is within the veil." Nor is their entrance there to be spasmodic or temporary, but habitual and permanent. The "heavenly minded" saints we all have read of or perhaps blessedly known, are simply those

---

*Vincent well observes that this **sacrifice of praise** "was the Levitical term for a thank-offering," quoting the LXX, Lev. 7.2, 35, etc. Various commentators also quote an ancient saying of the Jewish rabbins: "In the future time all sacrifices shall cease; but praises shall not cease." Philo says, "They offer the best sacrifice who glorify with hymns the Saviour and Benefactor, God." Oh, that this might have been entered into by the whole Hebrew nation! Instead, alas, the nation, with no Messiah, no blessed Holy Spirit to guide and fill their hearts with worship in the name of the Great High Priest appointed for believers, build synagogues, and observe "feasts" at which there can be no festivity, for *God* is not in it!

Most of Christendom, imitating the poor Jews, has "Christian" synagogues and forms of worship. But on how many lips is there the **sacrifice of praise to God continually**, open **confession to His name**, which should be the true "fruit" of Christian lips? Instead, alas, a printed form of "service," a one man ministry, a paid choir, and the lips of the saints silent. It was not so in the early assemblies of the saints (I Cor. 12, 14).

who had exercised the rights, yea, obeyed the invitation God had given them and us, through the blood of Christ. Indeed, the book of **Hebrews** sets before us the Christian life as something that *absorbs the whole attention* of the believer. This fifteenth verse of Chapter 13 is its great message.

And wherefore? We are to draw near to God in the holiest above, are we not? Suppose any other creatures in God's presence should undertake to live the low, casual, absent-minded, interested-in-other-things life that most professing believers engage in. What would all Heaven think of *that*? Suppose cherubim, seraphim, or angels, undertook to engage in an occasional worship or service of God; prayed to be "excused": that they had other interests, not connected with God's service? What would God think of *that*?

If God's creatures in Heaven constantly, gladly, serve and worship, His saints on earth, for whom He gave His Son, should respond to His unspeakable kindness with the utter devotion which befits it, devotion to God such as no other beings have!

But we "go to church" for an hour, and go home and go about other things with no thought of that constant worship which is being carried on in Heaven. Ah, this is not **Hebrews**! For in this great epistle there is no thought of our withdrawing from nearness, from worship. There is *constant* spiritual activity, **praise continually.** We have elsewhere noted that forever and ever in eternity new discoveries of the infinite glories of God will be revealed to His saints; and evermore the Leader of their praises is Christ. **Through Him**, then, here and now, and by His blessed indwelling Spirit, yea, by Christ formed within us by that Spirit (Rom. 8.2, 11; II Cor. 3.17, 18), **let us offer up a sacrifice of praise to God continually.** There is nothing occasional about the true Christian life. It is continual! Against spiritual sluggishness, now-and-then-ness, indifference, unbelief, we are warned in **Hebrews.** It is *neglecting* "so great a salvation"!

Beloved, we are in a world rapidly rushing to judgment. At the bottom of the heart of every unsaved "religious" one today lies the perhaps unexpressed, even unconscious, word of the high priest and his company to Peter and the apostles: "Ye have filled Jerusalem with your teaching, and intend to bring this Man's blood upon *us!*" (Acts 5.28). Jesus said of the world, "Me it hateth, because I testify of it that its works are evil." Despite all its dreams and delusions about a "lasting peace," iniquity is increasing—every honest, unbiased observer knows this. The earth is daily becoming more godless, getting ready, and fast, for the Great Tribulation and the worship of the Antichrist: these are dead ahead. As our Lord said, "I am come in My Father's name and ye receive Me not: if *another* [Antichrist] shall come in his own name, him ye will receive." (Thank God, the Church will be raptured away from that hour of trial! Rev. 3.10).*

We need, as never since our Lord ascended, to *leave* this world; to "set our mind on the things that are above, where Christ is, seated on the right hand of God"; to become such as are **offering up a sacrifice of praise to God continually, that is, the fruit of lips which make confession to His name.** Finally note, that those who **make confession to His name** continually, will be finding out what being His representative means. The world wants to salve its conscience with "religion," but the world hated and crucified the Christ of God, and that is its attitude still. We beg you, believe it, and keep making **confession to His name!** This should describe your constant occupation perhaps more simply and understandably than any other verse in this great book of exhortation.

Verse 16, the verse that follows: **To keep doing good, and communicating** [to others] **of your substance forget not,** comes naturally with a life of continual praise. See Romans 12.13, and Galatians 6.6. God says He is "not unrighteous to forget your work and the love which ye showed toward His Name, in that ye ministered unto the saints" (6.10). Nothing is easier for us to forget! How blessed to read that **with such sacrifices God is well pleased!** We have known, even we ourselves, a few such praisers and givers. Aunt Sarah Cooke was one of the two sainted women who fasted and prayed for D. L. Moody till he received a mighty anointing of the Holy Ghost. Clad in a quiet dress and little black bonnet she would come into my Bible classes in Chicago, and I always thanked God for her presence. She sat well to the front. Her face was heavenly. When she quietly raised her right hand

---

*Be not deceived: today men are seeking to unite the nations in a perpetual bond of peace, with their "post-war planning" for a "new and better world"! But Scripture, which cannot lie, says that until the very end there shall be wars and rumors of wars; and that only when our Lord returns as High Priest for His Melchizedek reign, will He "make wars to cease to the end of the earth."ⁿ

with her eyes closed (for I watched her), I knew that her soul was full of rapture. She was always praying and praising, and often I knew God was answering her prayer just then with power in the meeting.

God had such a handmaiden also in St. Louis. In an afternoon Bible reading on prayer in the old Dr. Brookes church there, I said, "If *one person* in this audience today yields his or her life up to praying, God will not only transform such a one, but will reach hundreds, perhaps thousands, through those prayers." I saw to my left in the back, a woman bow upon the pew in front of her, for she was doing the very thing I spoke of. She was a widow whose son, a doctor, had an office downtown, and she, alone at home, had hours which she gave over daily to prayer and praise. Soon requests began to come for her to remember, not only in St. Louis, but from hundreds, then thousands of miles away. She became known as "Mother" Hopkins. After some years she went to Heaven, but what a funeral! There was such consciousness of her entering victoriously into the presence of the Lord, that it was a triumph, melting everyone with very joy.

John S. Inskip, whose life was spent praying and praising God, shouted as his last words, "Victory! triumph! triumph!"

Susanna Wesley, John Wesley's mother, was the mother of old-time Methodism. Her last uttered request was, "Children, as soon as I am released, sing a psalm of praise to God."

"Who offereth the sacrifice of thanksgiving glorifieth Me," saith our God (Ps. 50.23).

Verse 17: Obey them that are leaders over you, and be submissive: for they watch in behalf of your souls, as they that shall give account; that they may do this with joy and not with grief: for this were unprofitable for you: Paul having urged upon these Hebrew believers (vs. 7) loving remembrance of "them that had the rule over you" (now passed away), urges next, **Listen to those leading you** [at present] **and do not be resisting them** (literal rendering). Let us at once lay to heart that no matter how marvelously the Spirit of God may be operating in our midst, "God is not a God of confusion, but of peace" (I Cor. 14.33). So that we are to be guided both by this passage in Corinthians, which tells each believer to be subject to the Spirit in the way of order in the Assembly, and also by Hebrews 13.17, which commands obedience, rather than rebellion and strife, to those God-appointed leaders among us; and this because they are **watching in behalf of our souls, as they that shall give account.**

We see here the work of one truly leading God's saints, whether elder, deacon, or bishop. They are such as are watching over others' souls in view of Christ's coming. We are not claiming that all elders—those today leading the saints—are here described; but such is the pattern. As Paul told the Ephesian elders, "After my departing grievous wolves shall enter in among you, not sparing the flock; . . . Wherefore *watch ye.*" So it is now. It is not a sign of spirituality to be stubborn and resisting, brother (I Sam. 15.23). Help these leaders to give an account of their leadership (as they shortly must) **with joy, and not with grief** (literally, the word is, *groaning*), both in prayer here, and in loving regret at the judg-ment seat of Christ.

18   **Pray for us: for we are persuaded that we have a good**
19   **conscience, desiring to live honorably in all things. And I exhort you the more exceedingly to do this, that I may be restored to you the sooner.**

In verse 18 we have Paul's common plea, **Pray for us,*** with his reasons therefor, in verses 18 and 19. And then the next words, Chapter 13.20, are, **Now the God of peace.**

20   **Now the God of peace, who brought again from the dead the Great Shepherd of the sheep with the blood of**
21   **an eternal covenant, even our Lord Jesus, make you per-fect in every good thing to do His will, working in us that which is wellpleasing in His sight, through Jesus Christ; to whom be the glory for ever and ever. Amen.**

Here we have a *Christian* address (using the word Christian to set forth the whole company of the saved, Hebrew and Gentile).

First, the Name of God, **the God of Peace,** used only by Paul,†

---

*"Praying at all seasons . . . and on my behalf" (Eph. 6.18, 19); "Brethren, pray for us" (I Thess. 5.25); "Finally, brethren, pray for us" (II Thess. 3.1); "Now I beseech you, brethren . . . strive together with me in your prayers to God for me" (Rom. 15.30); "Ye also helping together on our behalf by your supplication" (II Cor. 1.11); "I hope that through your prayers I shall be granted unto you" (Philem. 22).

†Six other occurrences of this precious name of God are: Phil. 4.9: "The God of peace shall be with you." II Cor. 13.11: "Finally, brethren, farewell. Be perfected; be com-forted; be of the same mind; live in peace: and the God of love and peace shall be with you."

is before our eyes here; and the Name given to Christ—**Our Lord Jesus.** He is called "Lord Jesus" nearly forty times, and "Our Lord Jesus" here and in the following passages, all in Paul's epistles: I Corinthians 5.4 (twice); II Corinthians 1.14; I Thessalonians 2.19; 3.11, 13; II Thessalonians 1.8.*

Then the Name, **The Great Shepherd of the sheep,** takes us to John 10, the "sheep chapter," when among the "poor of the flock" who believed on Him when He was on earth, we hear our Lord speak of "My sheep," and say they were "given Him of the Father," and that "they shall never perish," and that "none shall pluck them out of His hand." Further, "Other sheep I have, not of this [Jewish] fold: them also must I bring . . . and they shall become one flock, one Shepherd." (The fold was Jewish, but the "other sheep" are here included—all the saved.)†

Next in Hebrews 13.20 we have the word "covenant" (which we saw so frequently in Chs. 8, 9, 10, 12) and an **eternal covenant;** and its character and meaning unfold before our wondering eyes like the opening of a great rose—yea, and our beings are filled with the fragrance thereof! For here we find **The God of peace bringing again from the dead our Lord Jesus, the Great Shepherd of the sheep—how? with the blood of an eternal covenant.** That is, in accordance with the terms of an agreement between the Father and the Son, which terms are seen to be a promise from the Father that if the Son would become "a little lower than the

---

I Cor. 14.33: "For God is not a God of confusion, but of peace."ⁱ

I Thess. 5.23: "And the God of peace Himself sanctify you wholly,; and may your spirit and soul and body be preserved entire, without blame at the coming of our Lord Jesus Christ."

Rom. 15.33: "Now the God of peace be with you all. Amen."

Rom. 16.20: "And the God of peace shall bruise Satan under your feet shortly."ⁱ

(We have sought to place these Scriptures in their *spiritual* order.)

Paul only uses the words **Our Lord Jesus.** And of the nearly 30 times the Name "Lord Jesus Christ" is used, Peter uses it twice (Acts 10.37; II Pet. 2.20); James once (1.1); and Paul all the other times.

†As has been so often said, as the *Good* Shepherd, Christ "lays down His life for the sheep"; as **the Great Shepherd,** He is **brought again from the dead;** and as the *Chief* Shepherd He will shortly be manifested, and reward those who have cared for the sheep and lambs in His absence (I Pet. 5.4).

Dear friend, do you have a sheep's attitude towards your Lord? David, the shepherd, said it so well: "The Lord is my Shepherd." Did you ever notice the last verse of Psalm 119: "I have gone astray like a lost sheep: *seek Thy servant;* for I do not forget Thy commandments"? He prays, "Seek Thy servant," not, I will seek Thee. Remember the two things the sheep is without: first, it has no *wisdom:* if it starts wandering, it must be recovered by the shepherd. Second, it has no *weapons.* It cannot defend itself, but must be protected by the shepherd. So with *you* and *me!*

angels for the suffering of death," shedding His blood for us, the Father would bring Him again from among the dead. (Here is the only assertion of the resurrection of Christ in the book of **Hebrews.**)

The Son came to earth, and became "obedient even unto death," and the Father indeed **brought Him again from among the dead. The eternal covenant** was kept.

Before we go farther, it will be well to look back over Scripture teaching as to covenants. To make a covenant effective, the parties thereto must be able to fulfill the conditions undertaken. But with fallen man, such fulfillment is unthinkable, impossible. For,

(a) Man is a creature, and all the ability must be supplied by God.

(b) Man is a *fallen* creature, and unable to put away his guilt.

Therefore the legal covenant of Sinai was, as II Corinthians 3.7, 9 says, a "ministration of death . . . of condemnation." It revealed to man his helplessness, but it supplied no strength. We are removed, then, in our consideration of Hebrews 13.20, both from the legal covenant of Chapters 8 and 9, and from the future "new covenant with the house of Israel and with the house of Judah" (8.8) because:

(a) "The Law [with its covenant] made nothing perfect" (7.19), and was "disannulled" "because of its weakness and un-profitableness" (7.18-19). (b) The "new covenant" to be made with Israel and Judah at our Lord's return to that nation, we have seen is all grace—God's operation instead of their response (Jer. 31.31-34; Ezek. 37.12-14, 21-23, 25-28). Therefore the "new covenant" which the Hebrew believers to whom Paul was writing had had explained to them, was not yet on, nor will be till Christ's return; and then it will apply to "the house of Israel and the house of Judah," as God says, in the land of Palestine, with the peculiar blessings described in Scripture.

But—there is yet **an eternal covenant,*** detailed in Hebrews 13.20, in which and according to which Paul knows that all believers may be made **perfect in every good work.** This eternal covenant, in which **the God of Peace** and **our Lord Jesus** are the actors, and the sheep are the beneficiaries—this covenant, I say, is the only

---

*To sum up, for we must repeat these great truths till they are clearly in mind:

1. There was the old covenant with Israel, called in Heb. 9.1 "The first covenant"; THIS IS OFF.

covenant which believers, whether Hebrews or Gentiles, should keep in mind as already and eternally fulfilled in its conditions, and available to all.

Remember, God never made a covenant with the human race: they are not under any covenant. He made, as we have seen, a covenant with His Son, that if He would bear sin unto death, He would raise Him up. So, **The God of Peace brought** (Him) **again from the dead . . . in the blood of an eternal covenant.** If the word were *dia*, through, instead of *en*, in,* it would mean that it was *through* the blood that God brought Christ **again from the dead.** He did not do that. Christ had committed no sin. The word is *en*, in—in agreement with, in accordance with the terms of the covenant. This is the **eternal covenant** of which the Lord Jesus is said **(9.15)** to be the Mediator, and which is celebrated in the Lord's Supper, in view of His death, by those benefited forever thereby!

This was revealed to Paul: "The Lord Jesus in the night in which He was betrayed took bread . . . in like manner also the cup, after supper, saying, This cup is the new covenant in My blood: this do, as often as ye drink it, in remembrance of Me." And II Corinthians 3.6: (God) "Who made us sufficient as ministers of a new covenant; not of the letter, but of the spirit." Note also Luke 22.20: "And the cup in like manner after supper, saying, This cup is the new covenant *in My blood,* even that which is poured out for you." This is the covenant of Hebrews 13.20.†

2. There is to be made "a New Covenant with the house of Israel and with the house of Judah" (Ch. 8.8-12). THIS IS NOT YET ON.
Therefore Israel and Judah are *out of all* covenant relationship with Jehovah at present. (And remember God was *never* in covenant with Gentiles.)

3. There is the everlasting covenant of Ch. 13.20. THIS IS ON FOREVER. The parties in this covenant are: (a) **The God of Peace,** and (b) **The Great Shepherd of the sheep . . . our Lord Jesus.**
The terms of the covenant were: (a) God—**The God of Peace** (for all things are of God), requested the Son to come to earth to "give His life a ransom for many." (b) The Divine promise was made to Him that, He having done so, God would **bring Him again from among the dead.**
See comment also on Ch. 8.9.

*Alford well says, "The expression itself **(in the blood of an eternal covenant),** can hardly but be a reminiscence of Zech. 9.11: and if so, the import of the preposition here will be at least indicated by its import there. And there, it is, 'by virtue of (in the power of) the blood of the covenant' entered into with Thee. By virtue of that blood also He was raised up as The Great Shepherd, out of the dead, and to God's right hand."

†This **eternal covenant** did not have an external mediator (as Moses). Gal. 3.20 must be fulfilled: "Now a mediator is not a mediator of one; but God is One." No external mediator is needed here. The covenant of Heb. 13.20 has, indeed, Christ as "Mediator." But this covenant being between two Persons of the Godhead; and all conditions fulfilled (Christ's

Let us meditate yet a little farther on this wonderful **eternal covenant.** We repeat, the parties to it are not man, nor any creature! It is an agreement between God and His Son. It antedated creation, for we read in Eph. 1.4 that we were chosen in Christ "before the foundation of the world," that is, before anything was created. And further, Paul writes that God "saved us . . . according to His own purpose and grace, which was given us in Christ Jesus before times of ages" (II Tim. 1.9).

In fulfillment of this covenant, the Son, the Lord Jesus, came to earth subject to all the arrangements directed by God (Heb. 10.5-7), and became obedient even unto . . . the "death of the Cross" (Phil. 2.8). He went to death in the unwavering attitude of faith. "When the days were well nigh come that He should be received up, He steadfastly set His face to go to Jerusalem" (Lk. 9.51). From the time His journey to Jerusalem began we read, as in Matthew 16.20, 21: "From that time began Jesus to show unto His disciples, that He must go unto Jerusalem, and . . . be killed, and the third day be *raised up.*"

Compare Luke 9.20-22; Mark 8.31; "the third day *rise again,*" Luke 18.33. Read "with hearing" all these verses, and you will marvel anew at Christ's perfect confidence in God's raising Him up according to the **eternal covenant**—which He trusted!

God the Father, accordingly, faithful to the terms of the covenant, **brought Him again from the dead.** For we read, "He was raised from the dead through the glory of the Father" (Rom. 6.4). "But God raised Him from the dead" (Acts 13.30). We are giving in a footnote some of the O. T. Scriptures which were fulfilled.*

---

death and God's raising Him **from the dead**), the term "Mediator" must no longer demand conditions to be fulfilled. There is peculiar blessing in seeing clearly that an **eternal covenant** or agreement exists between God the Father and God the Son—one God.

*See the psalms and the prophets: Ps. 16.10, 11:
"Thou wilt not leave My soul to *Sheol.* [Gr., Hades; see Acts 2.27]
Neither wilt Thou suffer Thy Holy One to see corruption.
Thou wilt show Me [even though My body lie in the tomb, and My spirit descend into the heart of the earth] the path of life [resurrection life]:"
And further:
"In Thy presence [whither Thou wilt receive Me] is fullness of joy;
In Thy right hand there are pleasures forevermore."
Peter at Pentecost, and later Paul, call this wondrous psalm of trust to remembrance (Acts 2.25-28; 13.35).
Abundant also are the prophecies that the Son would "give His back to the smiters, and

We have another wonderful view of the blood of the **eternal covenant** in Zechariah 9. The ninth verse, with which everyone is familiar, identifies Christ:

"Thy King cometh unto thee; He is just, and having salvation; lowly, and riding upon an ass, even upon a colt, the foal of an ass" (this is the Triumphal Entry).

Then follows verse 10, in which, passing over the time of Christ's rejection, God declares that Christ

" . . . shall speak peace unto the nations: and His dominion shall be from sea to sea, and from the River [the Euphrates] to the ends of the earth."

Then comes the further reach of this covenant, which evidently here covers all those God ever gave to Christ:

"As for Thee also, because of the *blood of Thy covenant* I have set free Thy prisoners from the pit wherein is no water" (vs. 11). Note the word "also": Not only will Christ ride into Jerusalem, as we see in verse 9, but at His future coming "His dominion shall be from sea to sea" (vs. 10). "Also" speaks of something more and different.

It is "because of the blood of His covenant" that what God here says He will do, has to be done. Prisoners were not "set free" through the Mosaic covenant. Indeed, we saw in Hebrews 8.9 that Israel continued not in God's covenant, and God "regarded them not." But because of the **eternal covenant** in Christ's blood, God can do anything for His dear Son. That is, it was wholly and solely because of Christ's shedding His blood, and not for their own goodness, that God, in the Old Testament days, delivered Christ's prisoners from going to the compartment of *Sheol* (Gr., *Hades*), where lost spirits go, the place of torment into which the rich man of Luke 16 went: "In Hades he lifted up his eyes, being in torments." This place was separated by "a great gulf fixed" from the place where the "prisoners of hope," the Old Testament

---

His cheeks to them that plucked off the hair." That He would "hide not His face from shame and spitting" (Isa. 50.6).

So it was done!

"Awake, O sword, against My Shepherd, and against the Man that is My Fellow, saith Jehovah of hosts; smite the Shepherd" (Zech. 13.7).

And Christ returned answer to God,

"Thou, Who hast showed me many and sore troubles, wilt quicken me again, and wilt bring Me up again from the depths" (Ps. 71.20, R.V., margin).

saints, were at rest with Abraham, which is called "the strong-hold" (vs. 12), the place of security and rest they were in until Christ visited them during the three days when He was "in the heart of the earth" (Matt. 12.40).

Not only are Christ's "prisoners"—His dear saints whom His blood has bought—"set free" from the pit of torment, but the additional word is spoken,

"Turn you to the stronghold, ye prisoners of hope."

Now, while these disembodied spirits were still prisoners, they were "prisoners *of hope*." (Dives was hope-less!) The blood of the covenant which would free them and open Heaven to them had not yet been shed, but they were "comforted," as Abraham said of Lazarus, upon his bosom, while those "in the pit wherein is no water," were in anguish. It was because of simple faith in the Word of God on the ground of sacrifice, that they had their place of protection.

The prophetic Word, after addressing Christ's "prisoners of hope," turns again to Christ:

"Even today do I declare that I will render double unto *Thee*" (vs. 12). "Rendering double" signifies first, God's delivering the "prisoners of hope" from the pit, on account of the blood not then shed; and second, Christ's going down into "the lower parts of the earth" (Ps. 68.18 as opened to us in Eph. 4.8-10), when the blood had been shed, and bringing up those prisoners from the stronghold—"leading captivity captive," upon His ascension.

Finally turn to Zechariah 9.14-17, and read of the wondrous triumph He gives the Jews over their enemies in establishing them in the land He promised Abraham: "For how great is His goodness, and how great is His beauty!" (vs. 17).

Verse 21: Now the apostle's benedictive prayer that **the God of peace will make them perfect in every good thing to do His will, working in them that which is wellpleasing in His sight, through Jesus Christ; to Whom be the glory unto the ages of the ages. Amen.** Now this is Christian language: this is Pauline. Here, as we said above, we step out into Christian truth. Not that the words of Peter, John, James, and Jude are not Christian. But God now has, in this marvelous **Hebrews** epistle, brought out from their former religion these Hebrew believers, these "other sheep,"

to where they can forget former legal things, have their hope set
on Christ in glory, call their God **the God of peace**, and speak
of the Son of God as **our Lord Jesus!**

We know that "the Lord gave" Paul "authority for building up"
the saints (II Cor. 10.8); let us regard, then, as authoritative and
effectual, this confident, apostolic committal of the saints to God.
Let us receive to our very hearts, if we are of the sheep, this
great and blessed word of comfort, for it **is the God of peace**
Who undertakes a work *within* believers, those sheep. This working
within us is nowhere else found in **Hebrews**. It is, we repeat,
Christian truth in Christian terms as direct and simple as any
epistle of Paul, involving the indwelling and operation of the Holy
Spirit, and His undertaking to perfect us in the Divine will.*

The blessed Spirit Who inspired this epistle does not here name
His own inworking in us. All attention is drawn to Him Whom,
one with and equal to God, both the Father and the Spirit delight
to honor, He of Whom "Moses in the Law, and the prophets wrote,"
as He Himself, to the two walking to Emmaus, opened out "in all
the Scriptures the things concerning Himself."

At the close of this epistle, from Chapter 13.20 on, these Hebrews addressed are simply believers, as the word is, on "Christian" ground. Their intelligent consent to the teaching of the preceding chapters of the epistle is presumed. How different from the
Judaism under which *they* did the working, is **the God of peace
. . . working in us that which is wellpleasing in His sight through
Jesus Christ!** To have entered into a spiritual state in which they
consented to these words—how different from that state of even
earnest Jews described by Paul to Agrippa: "Our twelve tribes,

---

*It is to be noted, and with awe, that the Lord Jesus is so set before us in **Hebrews**
that the Holy Spirit's working in us is not described unless it be in Chapter 9.8 and 10.15,
where He is opening the *written Word*. The reason for this is readily seen from the contents of **Hebrews**: it is all CHRIST. Not, as we have said, Christ speaking, but God
speaking in the Person, work, and present position of the Son, Who was to fulfill all O.T.
Scriptures concerning Himself.

Today "modernism" (which is the name of Satan-deluded man for the last days), walks
with blinded eyes right past the whole book of **Hebrews**, on down to the Apocalypse, the
book of judgment. "Modernism" does not hear God speaking in this Son "Whom He appointed Heir of all things," the Great High Priest Who shed His blood for all sinners, and
entered Heaven through that blood.

We remind you again that He is the Great High Priest there only for those who have
believed on Him. "I pray *not* for the world," He said (Jno. 17.9). If you are not a believer, Christ is not your Priest, but He will be your Judge! (Jno. 5.22). Hasten to find
Him, "while it is called *Today*."

earnestly serving God night and day, *hope* to attain"! (Acts 26.6).

It is Hebrews who are "partakers of a heavenly calling," and in Christ are "holy" and "beloved" (3.1, 6.9), whom we joyfully meet here at the end of **Hebrews.** Along with them, all believers join in ascription of praise to our blessed **God of peace.**

22   But, I exhort you, brethren, bear with the word of exhortation: for I have written unto you in few words.
23   Know ye that our brother Timothy hath been set at liberty; with whom, if he come shortly, I will see you.
24   Salute all them that have the rule over you, and all the saints. They of Italy salute you.
25   Grace be with you all. Amen.

Verse 22: **Word of exhortation**—Exhortation is not doctrine; these believers knew Christian doctrine, even concerning the "heavenly calling" (3.1). Doctrine is received, believed; exhortation is to be followed, obeyed. In **Hebrews,** since "God, having of old time spoken unto the fathers in the prophets by divers portions and manners, hath at the end of these days spoken unto us in His Son" (1.1), exhortation will concern our attitude toward His Son. Since He "became unto all that obey Him the Author of eternal salvation" (5.9), exhortation will persuade to obedience to *Him.* This obedience will not in **Hebrews** be so much to Christ as Lord, or as Head of the Body, as to Him as Great High Priest, appearing "before the face of God for us" (9.24), leading our worship and praises, as well as taking care of our needs.* The chief disobedience in **Hebrews** will be to stay out of that worship, whether through neglect, unbelief, slothfulness of spirit, or (deadly danger!) shrinking from bearing Christ's reproach, and so living in compromise with the religion of earth, with its "great" divisions, and "established" institutions, carried on not in the Holy Spirit, but by human means, measures and movements—in short, to stay *in* "the camp."

Thus the great exhortation which this book of **Hebrews** is, becomes the supreme safeguard to the believer against that religionism which was found in Israel, which crucified† the Lord of glory.

---

*Priesthood has to do with maintaining before God the position, privileges, worship, warfare, and progress through temptations and trials, of God's saints; just as Christ's sacrifice had to do with putting away forever of their sins, and the bringing them into God's presence in resurrection, and in the full value of His blood.

†It *is*, in view of other Scriptures, astonishing to read the book of **Hebrews** through and

Man, uneasy in conscience, desires relief from that uneasiness, but he does not desire to draw near to God *now*. But *this* the book of **Hebrews** proposes: for we are exhorted to "come boldly to the throne of grace." And where is that throne? In Heaven, where Christ is our Great High Priest, and where we are to offer up sacrifices of praise continually, as we saw in verse 15. Such a life is a *heavenly* life. It is not the mere apprehension of the doctrines of justification or of "Church truth"*—of our position, by God's infinite grace: created in Christ and seated with Him in the heav-

---

not find in it any accusation such as those which fill the mouths of Peter, Stephen and Paul in the book of Acts:

"Ye by the hands of lawless men did *crucify* and slay" (Acts 2.23). "Ye *denied* the holy and righteous One, and asked for a murderer to be granted unto you" (3.14). "In the Name of Jesus of Nazareth, Whom ye *crucified*, Whom God raised from the dead, even in Him doth this man stand here before you whole" (4.10).

And Paul in Thessalonians: "—the Jews, who both *killed* the Lord Jesus, and the prophets and drove out us" (I Thess. 2.15).

You ask, Why was not this fearful fact emphasized in the Epistle to the Hebrews? Because, first, the Word of God is one: *all preceding utterances are taken for granted*. The great national crime of Calvary is not stated, though all knew it had been the nation's act, as it is their attitude today.

But consider further that each book has its special object, and the object in Hebrews is to call believers away from earth and its religion "the camp," to Heaven, to the throne of grace, where alone true worship of God is being carried on. The epistle is addressed to Hebrews who had professed faith in this rejected Christ; who had been "enlightened" (6.3); and knew that God had raised Jesus from the dead. Lovingly, therefore, the Holy Spirit in this epistle will woo such believers, presenting Christ as Deity, as well as man, crowned now with glory and honor as our Great High Priest, having entered Heaven "through His own blood," and interceding there for all that come to God by Him.

Of course He will also *warn*. But it will be the danger of neglecting "so great salvation," of hardness of heart, of unbelief; of refusing God's speaking "in His Son," so marvelously set forth in Hebrews.

*We might here summarize what Hebrews does *not* teach:

1. *Church truth:* The Risen Christ, the Head of the Body; saints heavenly, raised with Him. Believers are not in Hebrews seen as seated with Christ in the heavenlies, but as making their pilgrimage through this world. Christ is seen as coming, but not definitely as the Bridegroom of the Church as in Ephesians 5, or even as Lord of the service of individual believers. True and wonderful as these things are, they are not the lines of truth brought out in Hebrews.

The second coming of Christ, and the "good things to come" therewith, constantly in view; but *not* the Rapture, or the catching up of the Church as in I Thess. 4.16, 17; I Cor. 15.52, etc., although these Hebrew believers are "partakers of a heavenly calling."

2. In Hebrews, Christ is the High Priest in Heaven. Worship is being carried on there, "within the veil." The whole Levitical economy, and all man-made forms and ceremonies, done away. No "holy place" left on earth, no tabernacle, temple, or "continuing city." "Christianity" as a "religion" unknown; instead, the living confession of a heavenly hope. Believers not to "forsake their peculiar assembling together" (10.25), but the Church as seen in Ephesians, Colossians, and other epistles, *not found* in Hebrews.

3. Neither God the Father as such (nor the indwelling Holy Spirit, the Comforter, evoking the "Abba, Father," cry) is revealed, except in Ch. 12.5-11, where the Father is spoken of in connection with chastening.

enlies: but it is the actual realization through faith of this heavenly place with all its privileges, and the obedient entering on a life of heavenly worship "by the blood of Jesus, by the freshly-slain and living way, *through the veil* . . . His [pierced] flesh;" and having Him as our "Great High Priest over the house of God" (10.19-21), drawing near "with a true heart in full assurance of faith," because our hearts are fully delivered—"sprinkled from an evil conscience."

My brother, Church "membership" and "Christian service" will not do in **Hebrews. WITHIN THE VEIL . . . WITHOUT THE CAMP**, describes, almost *defines* God's saints here. Does it describe *you*? **Hebrews** constantly exhorts believers to come in, to draw nigh to God with boldness, which of course means to come boldly into the presence of God Himself. The sacrifice has been made; our Great High Priest has gone in through His blood and sat down, and God waits for those who have heard and believe to press in boldly. Our Great High Priest is there, filled with sympathy, for He passed through this world, and tasted to the full its trials, temptations, and sufferings. Our welcome to Heaven is as great and actual as the gift of God of His Son for us, and as intimate and blessed as He upon Whose breast John laid his head at the supper, can make it.

Oh, let us take heed that we are not deceived into a "Christian" life which yet makes excuse, which does not "press on unto full growth" (6.1); which does not "draw *near* with *boldness* unto the throne of grace" (4.16); which pursues not "the sanctification without which no man shall see the Lord" (12.14), and finally avoids the great exhortation of Chapter 13.15, to continual praise. Of course, the world and worldliness will shun you, if you press on "within the veil . . . without the camp." Are you afraid of that? What a state for one professing to be redeemed by the shed blood of the Son of God!

Is our High Priest living? Is He "the same yesterday, and today, yea and forever"? Has His sacrifice availed to put away sin? Are you invited? Yea, indeed! And note again Paul's words, **I exhort you brethren, bear with the word of exhortation.**

And oh, how *simple* the path! Bear with the word of exhortation: Why? For I have written unto you in few words—roughly estimated, less than ten thousand words! Compare "the *ten thou-*

sand things" of the Law (Hos. 8.12) : days, seasons, months, years; daily offerings unceasing; watchings against many, many forbidden things; repeated cleansings against defilement—as Peter called it all (and thus it was meant to be), "a *yoke* . . . which neither our fathers nor we were able to bear." Compare, I say, the manifold directions for conduct from Exodus 19 on, with the great word of Hebrews 11: FAITH. Christ has *finished* the work that opens Heaven! We have only to come, "Come for all things are now ready." Are you the Spirit-filled, constantly praying person in your Christian company? *Are you?*

It is not easy to the flesh—this life of constant access to God in Heaven:

> "The way of faith is hard to flesh;
>   It is not hard to love;
>
> If thou wert sick for want of God,
>   How quickly wouldst thou move!"

Verse 24: Salute all them that have the leadership over you, and all the saints: All the saints are equal, certainly; but recognizing the established order, he mentions leaders first. As to the rest of the verse, a word farther on.

Now why should Paul urge upon the Hebrew believers three times over (vss. 7, 17, 24), that they remember, obey, and salute, those who were, by Divine appointment, leaders among them? We beg you, consider how different from that of the Gentile believer, the Hebrew believer's position would be. The Gentiles would come into the faith from raw paganism; the Hebrew believer had known and worshiped the true God according to His revealed oracles, in His temple at Jerusalem. He had known nothing from his babyhood but a Levitically descended priesthood; ordinances, days, feasts, abstainings. He had indeed known a "religious" leadership which belonged to his religious system.

But now the Hebrew believers were in an assembly where the Holy Spirit controlled, where He engifted whom He would, independently of any religious system. Therefore the temptation would be strong to ignore such leadership, or to fear it as not connected with what they and their fathers had known in Judaism.

Verses 23-5: It is agreed among commentators that this very unusual epistle, TO THE HEBREWS, called by many a treatise, seems to end (vss. 18-25), in Paul's usual epistolary manner, both in the reference to Timothy, and in the author's expectation of traveling again with Timothy: **with whom, if he come shortly, I will see you.** It includes, as we have seen, the great prayer of bene-diction (vss. 20-21); and the final urging to **bear with the word of exhortation** (the whole epistle).

Then come the last salutations. Do you not recognize the hand that writes, **Our brother Timothy hath been set at liberty; with whom, if he come shortly, I will see you** (vs. 23)? And, **They of Italy salute you** (vs. 24)?

And finally comes "the token in every epistle" (II Thess. 3.17) **Grace† be with you all. Amen.** Only Paul ends thus.

---

*See Appendix G, "Authorship of Hebrews."

†The grace of our Lord Jesus Christ be with you" (Rom. 16.20).

"The grace of the Lord Jesus Christ be with you" (I Cor. 16.23).

"The grace of the Lord Jesus Christ, and the love of God, and the communion of the Holy Spirit, be with you all" (II Cor. 13.14).

"The grace of our Lord Jesus Christ be with your spirit" (Gal. 6.18).

"Grace be with all them that love our Lord Jesus Christ with a love incorruptible" (Eph. 6.24).

"The grace of our Lord Jesus Christ be with your spirit" (Phil. 4.23).

"Grace be with you" (Col. 4.18).

"The grace of our Lord Jesus Christ be with you" (I Thess. 5.28).

"The salutation of Me Paul with mine own hand, which is the *token* in every epistle: *so I write:* The grace of our Lord Jesus Christ be with you all" (II Thess. 3.17, 18).

"Grace be with you" (I Tim. 6.21).

"The Lord be with thy Spirit. Grace be with you" (II Tim. 4.22).

"Grace be with you all" (Tit. 3.15).

"The grace of our Lord Jesus Christ be with your spirit" (Philem. 1.25).

"He closes every epistle by praying for GRACE to those whom he addresses . . . Paul's characteristic salutation, known to be his badge, not used by others in his lifetime."— **Fausset.**

No more veil! God bids me enter
  By the new and living way—
Not in trembling hope I venture,
  Boldly I His call obey;
There, with Him, My God, I meet
God upon the mercy-seat!

One with Him, O Lord, before Thee,
  There I live, and yet not I;
Christ it is Who there adores Thee
  Who more dear, or who more nigh?
All the Father's heart mine own—
Mine—and yet His Son's alone.

All the worth I have before Him
  Is the value of His Blood;
I present, when I adore Him,
  Christ, the First-fruits, unto God!
Him with joy doth God behold,
Thus is my acceptance told.

                        —Ter Steegen

APPENDIX A
WHY "TO HEBREWS"

This book is addressed to HEBREWS.

What had the Hebrews that others had not, and that rendered it necessary to address an epistle in particular to them?

God had revealed Himself to that people. Over 2,000 years before Christ, God having called Abraham in Mesopotamia, brought him to the land of Canaan, and covenanted with him to give it to him and his seed. His son Isaac followed, bestowing upon Jacob his son the blessing of Jehovah.

Twelve sons of Jacob (then Israel), headed the twelve tribes of Israel, whom Moses led forth from Egypt through the wilderness: Jehovah their God revealing Himself to the nation in a marvelous way at Mount Sinai, and there announcing a Law-Covenant with the nation. God gave Moses specific directions concerning the construction of the tabernacle in the wilderness, in the Holy of Holies of which, when completed, Jehovah manifested His presence.

By a pillar of cloud by day and fire by night He led them on, Joshua, Moses' minister, finally bringing them into Canaan. Their history under the judges and the kings has been referred to in the main body of this commentary on Hebrews.

After their being captives for seventy years on account of disobedience, God restored them from Babylon, more than five hundred years before Christ, when they rebuilt, humbly, their temple.

Mark this: To no other nation did God ever give a *religion*. Romans 9.4, 5 is literally true:—"Israelites, whose is the adoption [as God's earthly nation], and the glory, and the covenants, and the giving of the Law, and the [religious] service, and the promises; whose are the fathers, and of whom is Christ as concerning the flesh, Who is over all, God blessed forever. Amen."

Of course, God's coming to them brought about the religion, with its sacrifices, laws, feasts, and directions for everyday life, as to worship, meats, and the many ordinances which ruled the Hebrew's life.

Now we find the book of **Hebrews** taking these things away and setting before them the Melchizedek priesthood (not at all after Aaron's order), which involved the disannulling of the Law and of the whole manner of life of the Hebrew, setting before them CHRIST, Risen from the dead, the Great High Priest at the right hand of God, in whom all his hopes are. It is no longer *religion*, but simple faith in the accomplished work of Christ the Son of God.

You ask, What about "Church truth"? What about the glorious revelations of the believer's place *in* Christ, members of His Body, seated with Him in the heavenlies, having died with Him and been raised in identification with Him? Also, what about the glorious privileges of the believer (sealed by and indwelt with the Spirit of God, as he is), the privileges of being filled with that Spirit and being able to say with Paul, "To me to live is *Christ*"?

Well, you will find in the book of **Hebrews** but one hint of the glorious truth God gave to Paul to unfold concerning the Church of God.*

That hint, as we shall see, is in Chapter 3.1: "partakers of the heavenly calling." But not a word as to *union* with *Christ*, unless indeed it be at the very end:

"The God of peace, Who brought again from the dead the Great Shepherd of the sheep with the blood of an eternal covenant, even our Lord Jesus, make you perfect in every good thing to do His will, working in you that which is well-pleasing in His sight, *through Jesus Christ!*"

This is of course not because Hebrew believers had no share in this glorious heavenly truth: by no means! They certainly had that share. But they had already a God-given *religion*. This would ever be coming between them and the blessed, glorious finished work of Christ.

So the book of **Hebrews** takes that religion from the Hebrews, leaving them only *Christ*.

---

*Distinguish in **Hebrews** things which concern:
1. CHRIST.
2. The saints.
3. Apostates.
4. The world.
5. Unbelieving national Israel in the past.
6. Believing national Israel of the future.
7. The author of the exhortation and those with him, especially in Chapter 13.

APPENDIX B

THE TEACHING OF BAPTISMS (CHAPTER 6:2)

The Greek word is *baptismos,* meaning baptisms, or washings. The Jews had many of these. It is to deliver saints from such religious performances, evidently, that Paul refers to the *"one baptism"* of Ephesians 4.5, although the Spirit of God looked forward, as always, foreseeing such heresies as horrid Bullingerism, which in England denies both the Lord's Supper and baptism, and in America denies baptism, saying that only the baptism with the Spirit is meant. This is presumptuous ignorance, and confuses many saints. For they twist the meaning of Paul's saying to the Corinthians, "For Christ sent me not to baptize, but to preach the gospel" (I Cor. 1.17), ignoring verse 14, where Paul says *he* baptized Crispus. Now who was Crispus? We read in Acts 18.8 concerning him,

"And Crispus, the ruler of the synagogue, believed in the Lord with all his house; and many of the Corinthians hearing, believed, and were baptized."

Any believer in those happy, tradition-less days, could baptize another who desired it. But Paul evidently said of Crispus, I will myself baptize this synagogue ruler in water, that all may connect water baptism with faith and confession of Christ, as the Risen One commanded:

"Go ye therefore and disciple all the nations, *baptizing them* into the name of the Father, and of the Son, and of the Holy Spirit" (Matt. 28.19).

And again, "He that believeth and is *baptized* shall be saved" (Mk. 16.16). Note two things in this verse: first, baptism connected with faith as the first step in the confession of faith; second, no mention of baptism when the *opposite* of salvation is described: "He that *dis*believeth shall be condemned"; for salvation is by *faith,* not by baptism. The thief on the cross was not baptized!

Nonetheless, the Lord prescribed water baptism, as the whole Church has confessed, however much they have differed as to its meaning and mode.

Note again in I Corinthians 1.14, 16: "Gaius . . . also the household of Stephanas," were baptized in water by Paul himself, for Gaius was known everywhere: he was the host "of the whole Church" (Rom. 16.23); and of the household of Stephanas, the first converts in Greece (I Cor. 15.16), Paul evidently said, "Let me baptize them by my own hands, for they are the first converts in Greece, and I wish everyone to connect confession by water baptism with identification with Christ by faith in Him."

Thus Paul sets before the Roman believers in Romans 6.3 the real teaching of that water baptism which they had all taken: namely, that it involved association with Christ both in His death to sin (vs. 10), and in His burial (vs. 4), and life unto God in resurrection (vss. 10, 11). Compare with Colossians 2.12, where burial with Christ as pictured in the ordinance of water baptism is so vividly set forth. No reasonable person can connect the word "burial" with the work of the Holy Spirit. The Bullingerites have no answer to this! Our burial with Christ is wonderfully set forth in Romans 6 and remarkably illustrated in water baptism.

Water baptism, then, is commanded by our Lord; is connected always with present faith; was practiced as a matter of course by the early believers; and was administered in special cases by Paul himself to emphasize these facts, and also that, although he did not himself often baptize, he left that work to others.

So did Peter (Acts 10.47) with Cornelius' household, when he said, *after* the hearers had believed and been baptized by the Holy Ghost into the Body of Christ, "Can any man forbid water, that these should not be baptized, who have received the Holy Spirit as well as we?"

Peter adds his solemn testimony here in the remarkable passage in his first epistle, which is simple, if we remember that water is a symbol of judgment:

"God waited in the days of Noah, while the ark was a preparing, wherein few, that is, eight souls, were saved through water: which also after a true *likeness* doth now save you, even baptism, not the putting away of the filth of the flesh, but the interrogation of a good conscience toward God, through the resurrection of Jesus Christ" (I Pet. 3.20-1).

Water was ruin and death, and they were saved *through* it. The ark is a type of Christ; eight is the resurrection number; the waters that judged the earth, the ark passed safely through. (Note the word "*likeness,*" vs. 21. Baptism in itself is nothing. It is a *figure* of Christ's passing through the judgment of death, bringing us safely through.)

APPENDIX C

THE NATURE OF THE CHURCH

Concerning the nature, character, calling, and walk of the Church, the *Ekklesia* of God, the epistles of Paul, and (especially to the circumcision) those of James and Peter, constitute a complete revelation. And the book of Acts sets forth the example of assembly life.

Two things may be said about our position now: First, the Gentiles as such will be cut off from the place of blessing now enjoyed, when the real Church is raptured to Heaven, and Israel received again as "life from the dead." Second, we cannot change the state of things we see about us—all kinds of divisions, and those even gloried in. But we need not be conformed thereto. Mr. Moody used to say, "If I thought there was a drop of sectarian blood in my body, I'd open my veins and let it run out before night!"

Let us search our hearts, or ask God to do so. Here and there on earth even now are saints who can say with Paul, "To me to live is *Christ*"—Christ alone: saints who have no sectarian consciousness whatever: for *Christ* has none.

We trust we love our brethren, whatever their position, and we purpose by God's permission and grace to keep on ministering wherever the Lord opens the door.

Here is a paragraph from Mr. Turner's biography of J. N. Darby which refreshed me:

"His largeness of heart, for one of strong convictions and of practical consistency, showed itself in many ways. After he left the Anglican Establishment he preached occasionally at the call of godly clergymen who urged it; but he only appeared for the discourse and was not present at the previous service. So in France afterwards he preached for pious ministers of the Reformed Church; nor did he refuse the black gown as an academical dress; but when they brought the bands, 'Oh, no,' said he: 'I put on no more.' Again, he did not spare, but warmly rebuked the zealots among half-fledged brothers, who were so ignorantly bitter as to apply what the Apostle said of heathen tables to those of the various denominations. It was only fundamental error which roused his deepest grief and indignation. Then, as one of these (a heterodox teacher) said to me, 'J.N.D. writes with a pen in one hand and a thunderbolt in the other.' "

Our beloved and honored brother, A. C. Gaebelein, followed a like path. In his **Half a Century** (pp. 84-5), he says:

"Through these brethren beloved I had become acquainted with the works of those able and godly men who were used in the great spiritual movement of the Brethren in the early part of the nineteenth century, John Nelson Darby and others. I found in his writings, in the works of William Kelly, F. W. Grant, Bellett and others, the soul-food I needed. I esteem these men next to the Apostles in their sound and spiritual teaching. But as for an actual affiliation with any of the numerous parties of Brethrenism I could not consent to this, for I found that the party spirit among these different divisions was even more sectarian than the sectarianism of the larger denominations. Nor did I feel that it was my commission to denounce denominations, as is so often done. Denominationalism exists, and there is nothing that will change it. But my commission was to go and minister the truth wherever the Lord would open a door for His servant. Invitations to hold Bible Conferences came from many states, in increasing numbers, and with the year 1900 began that nation-wide ministry which it has been my privilege to follow these many years."

Appendix D

Three Greek Words for "Place"

We have in John 14.2 three words to be distinguished and re-membered. The first is *oikia,* dwelling, used here to indicate the abode of God's throne, as He says: "I dwell in the high and holy place, with him also that is of a contrite and humble spirit, to revive the spirit of the humble, and to revive the heart of the contrite" (Isa. 57.15). And as Paul says (I Tim. 6.15, 16), "The blessed and only Potentate, the King of kings, and Lord of lords; Who only hath immortality, dwelling in light unapproachable."

The fundamental thought in *oikia* (a dwelling) and its cognates is a fixed dwelling place in the sense of a house.

The second word is *monē* (pl. *monai*). The Revised Version margin, "abiding places," is quite good if we admit the sense of permanency of "abiding," and read further into the words, *appointed* abiding places. Of what "abiding places" is our Lord speaking? He cannot be referring to the home of the Bride, the Church, the New Jerusalem, for this clearly is indicated by the *third* word, *topos:* "I go to prepare a place [*topos*] for you." This *topos* was evidently not then prepared.

(By the way, this, John 14.2, is the first hint by our Lord that His Church will be in Heaven. He had already shown in Matthew 16.18 that the saints of the Assembly of God, the Church, would not, as were the Old Testament saints, be required to go down to the stronghold in Hades and await the death and resurrection of our Lord. See Zechariah 9.12, "stronghold"; and Luke 16.)

To be absent from the body is to be present with the Lord for the saints now, we know. But this *topos*, this abiding place, might be translated *special place,* that is, one designed and appointed.

The "many abiding places" are evidently for other orders of heavenly beings. Concerning only the four living ones of Revelation 4.6-8 is it said that "they have no rest day and night, saying, Holy, holy, holy, is the Lord God, the Almighty, Who was and Who is and Who is to come." That is their constant and evidently their eternal occupation, and that is their bliss, in which the infinite power of God sustains them. The twenty-four elders also (which belong to Heaven by creation, as do the four living ones) join perpetually in the worship of which the four living ones are the perpetual leaders (Rev. 4.4, 9-11: for "and when" of verse 9 read *whensoever*). As to other heavenly beings, whether angels, principalities, or powers, known or unknown to us, the "many abiding places," we believe, are theirs. Their service unto and delight in God is nonetheless real and perpetual in that they are not the leaders of Heaven's adoration as are the four living ones and the elders. Those certain angels, as Gabriel, who stands "in the presence of God," (Lk. 1.19) and the seven angels that "stand before God" (Rev. 8.2) are always at God's command to "fly swiftly" on His errands (Dan. 9.21).

APPENDIX E

THREE ELEMENTS OF DIVINE FORGIVENESS

The three differing elements of Divine forgiveness should be taught to every believer. These are, (1) The once-for-all pardon of the Judge, (2) the daily renewed forgiveness of the Father, (3) the governmental action of God toward His children.

1. In Romans we see the whole world brought in guilty before God, not one righteous, all mouths stopped. Then, God setting forth Christ as a Propitiation "through faith in His blood," and those believing, written down righteous in Heaven. All the atoning work of Christ is reckoned to them; yea, they are even "the righteousness of God in Christ" (II Cor. 5.21). David celebrates this in Psalm 32, quoted in Romans 4.7-8. It was after his great sin of adultery, murder, and prolonged "keeping silence" impenitently. The prophet Nathan was sent to him with the story of the rich man who took the one ewe lamb of a poor man, instead of from his own flocks and herds, and made a feast from it for a visitor (II Sam. 11, 12).

David was very angry. (It is remarkable how indignant we can get over other people's sin!) He said, "The man that hath done this is a son of death [margin]; he shall restore the lamb fourfold." Then the long finger of the prophet points to the guilty king, fixing the parable upon *him*: "*Thou* art the man!" David breaks down, saying, "I have sinned against Jehovah!" Instantly Nathan says, "Jehovah also hath put away thy sin; thou shalt not die." It was not David's penitence, but God's purpose, that Nathan here announced, for in the quotation concerning this scene from Psalm 32 we have not only "iniquities forgiven" and "sins covered," but the words, "Blessed is the man to whom the Lord will not reckon sin." This is the *once-for-all pardon of the Judge*.

You remember that Balaam, at the request of Balak, king of Moab, tried four times to curse Israel (Num. 22 to 24), but blessed them each time, because the Spirit of God took hold on this prophet, wicked as he was, and made him utter these words:

"He hath blessed, and I cannot reverse it.

He hath not beheld iniquity in Jacob;

Neither hath He seen perverseness in Israel:

Jehovah his God is with him."

God has told us that there had been both iniquity and perverseness in that nation; how they had murmured from Egypt on, how the bones of the first generation fell in the wilderness. But when it came to the enemy and his accusation, the word was, "He hath not seen perverseness in Israel."

Nor does this wonderful fact of an eternal pardon, truly received in faith, make for a life of looseness; but rather one of devotion to such a God of grace!

2. *The daily renewed forgiveness of the Father:* Turn to I John 1: we are told that this epistle has to do with fellowship: "That ye also may have fellowship with us: yea, and our fellowship is with the Father, and with His Son Jesus Christ: and these things we write, that your joy may be made full" (vss. 3, 4). Then our walking in the light, not in darkness, is seen as a condition of this fellowship, in which "the blood of Jesus His Son cleanseth us from all sin"; and the warnings to be tender of conscience concerning sin, neither saying that we have no sin, nor that we have no sins, in any particular matter. Then the blessed verse 9: "If we confess our sins, He is faithful and righteous to forgive us our sins, and to cleanse us from all unrighteousness." That this is the forgiveness of the Father rather than of the Judge at the first, we see from Chapter 2.1, 2: "If any man [a believer] sin, we have an Advocate with the Father, Jesus Christ the righteous: and He is the propitiation for our sins; and not for ours only, but also for the whole world."

Now, only those who distinguish between the once-for-all pardon of the Judge, and this forgiveness by the Father in the matter of fellowship, escape confusion. As to the first, God's judicial action was based wholly upon the shed blood of Christ at the Cross. Sin had been judged there fully and forever—put away. Those who believed entered into the benefit of this.

As to the second, the forgiveness of the Father to His confessing children, there is the double fact: first, that God "is faithful [to His Word] and righteous [to Christ Who bore our sins] to forgive us our sins"; and second, if a believer sin, "We have an advocate with the Father"—not to make the Father willing to forgive us, for that willingness is shown (vs. 9): but who is this Advocate? "Jesus Christ the righteous," Who put away our sin forever, so that it cannot come in before God judicially again. Moreover, Christ is called the Propitiation for our sins.

3. *The governmental action of God toward His children:* This also is wonderfully set forth in the story of David's sin, for Nathan, after saying, "Jehovah also hath put away thy sin; thou shalt not die," proceeds: "Howbeit, because by this deed thou hast given great occasion to the enemies of Jehovah to blaspheme, the child also that is born unto thee shall surely die." It died, and David bowed, and worshiped Jehovah. But the very next chapter (II Sam. 13) shows a second son, the eldest, Amnon, killed by Absalom, for David had said to Nathan of the rich man, "He shall restore the lamb *fourfold.*" Then Absalom becomes the third; and Adonijah, I Kings 2.25, the fourth to die. You ask, If God had forgiven David, and held nothing against him judicially, why should four of his sons die in the sight of Israel, three under such public dishonor? Because David had "given great occasion to the enemies of Jehovah to blaspheme," and God must deal with him publicly, for His own glory in the sight of Israel, that His holiness and justice be not beclouded, nor David regarded as a favorite to whose failures and sins Jehovah paid no attention.

All God's saints should walk softly: it is "whom the Lord loveth He chasteneth."

We quote from Owen on Hebrews 10:12:

"Howbeit in these words, thus transiently mentioned, He judgeth and condemneth the two grand oppositions that at this day are made against that one sacrifice of Christ, and efficacy of it. The first is that of the Papists, who in the Mass pretend to multiply the sacrifices of Him every day, whereas He offered but "once"; so as that the repetition of it is destructive unto it. The other is that of the Socinians, who would have the offering and sacrifice of Christ to be only His appearance before God to receive power to keep us from the punishment of sin, upon His doing of the will of God in the world. But the words are express as unto the order of these things, namely, that He offered His sacrifice for sins before His exaltation in glory, or His sitting down on the right hand of God. And herein doth the apostle give glory unto that offering of Christ for sins, in that it perfectly accomplished what all legal sacrifices could not effect. This, therefore, is the only repose of troubled souls."

APPENDIX F

DELAYERS OF OUR LORD'S COMING (CHAPTER 10:37)

The delayers of our Lord's coming continually quote our Lord's words,

"This gospel of the kingdom shall be preached in the whole world [inhabited earth] for a testimony unto all the nations; and then shall the end come" (Matt. 24.14).

This verse, they say, must be fulfilled by an ever-failing Church whose earnest ones are always pleading for revival of it. Their argument is that there yet remains a work to be done by such a Church, the horrors of whose history stain its pages red with blood, black with heresy, and green with jealousy. So they say, While we wait for Him, we must not *expect* Him! that is, must *not watch* for Him, as He commanded!

The answer to all their claims is: (1) According to the Scriptures quoted above, the gospel had been already in the apostolic age, preached to all the world; witnesses had gone with the message of Christ to every part of the inhabited earth.

2.   The gospel of the kingdom, spoken of in Matthew 24.14, is "THIS gospel of the kingdom." So we turn back, in this very book of Matthew, to find the Messiah, the virgin-born King of the Jews (Chs. 1, 2), "teaching in their synagogues, and preaching *the gospel of the kingdom,* and healing all manner of disease and all manner of sickness among the people, speaking of the "kingdom of the heavens" (the Greek is plural), directly from Daniel 4.26, where Nebuchadnezzar found that "the heavens do rule," and that "the Most High . . . doeth according to His will in the army of Heaven." In the "blesseds" of what we call "the Sermon on the Mount," note Matthew 5.3, 10; 7.21; 10.5, 7 ff, in the commission of the Twelve (*heavens,* each time); and Matthew 15.24, to the Canaanitish woman.

Now what does the context of Matthew 24 teach us? The Lord is answering the three questions in verse 3 concerning (1) the overthrow of Jerusalem and the temple; and (2) what would be the sign of His coming; and together with these two, as to (3) the sign of the consummation of the age. Now we all know that Titus took Jerusalem and burned the Temple in A. D. 70; but how about this word, "sign"? "The *Jews* ask *signs*"—this was just what these apostles were doing. It was a Jewish question, and will have a Jewish answer. See Matthew 24.29:

"Immediately after the tribulation of those days the sun shall be darkened, and the moon shall not give her light, and the stars shall fall from Heaven, and the powers of the heavens shall be shaken"—as in the trumpets and vials of Revelation 8, 9, 16, and in Joel 2.31, 3.15. And note:

"And then shall appear the SIGN of the Son of man in Heaven" (vs. 30). Now what possible reference to the Church of God could the "SIGN of the *Son of man in Heaven,*" preceding the Rapture of the Church, have? None whatever, none possible. At the Rapture of the Church it will be

"In a moment, in the twinkling of an eye, at the last trump": for "the trumpet shall sound, and the dead shall be raised incorruptible, and we shall be changed"—we living souls—and caught up in the clouds to meet the Lord in the air. But what do we read further in Matthew 24?

"And then shall all the tribes of the land [or earth] mourn" (vs. 30). Does this describe the Rapture? Nay, verily, but it describes what Zechariah tells us concerning the Remnant of Israel, the elect, those "written in the book" (Dan. 12.1):

"And I will pour upon the house of David, and upon the inhabitants of Jerusalem, the spirit of grace and of supplication; and they shall look unto Him Whom they have pierced; and they shall *mourn* for Him, as one mourneth for his only son" (Zech. 12.10).

As when Joseph, revealing himself unto his brethren who had delivered him to death and sold him into the hands of the Midianites so many years before, said, "I am Joseph," thus it will be in that day. The mourning in Jerusalem will be great:

"And the land shall mourn, every family apart; the family of the house of David apart, and their wives apart; . . . all the families that remain, every family apart, and their wives apart" (Zech. 12.12).

What a weeping that will be! And then the blessed next verse:

"In that day there shall be a fountain opened to the house of David and to the inhabitants of Jerusalem, for sin and for unclean-ness" (13.1).

The Jews will be beleaguered by the nations, ready to be cut off by their enemies, with sun and moon darkened, the stars falling from Heaven, the powers of the heavens shaken (Ps. 46, and the upheavals under the vials of Rev. 16). Then suddenly the SIGN is seen!

I am inclined to believe that "the sign of the Son of man in Heaven" may be a luminous cross! On earth is blackness of dark-ness, sun, moon, stars, gone; Rome, the harlot (Roman Catholicism), which had abused, even to idolatry, the mark of the Cross, having now been completely wiped out by the Antichrist and his ten kings (Rev. 17.16-18) several years before, so that both Rome's "religion" and her misuse of the sign of the Cross have been forgotten; it might well be that God would set in the heavens the sign of that Tree upon which the nation of Israel had nailed their Messiah! At all events, it is some "sign of the Son of man" readily interpreted and under-stood by the godly Remnant of Israel who see it. John says,

"Behold He cometh with the clouds; and every eye shall see Him and they that pierced Him; and all the tribes of the earth shall mourn over Him" (Rev. 1.7; Dan. 7.13).

The human mind cannot conceive the awful collapse of the Jews in that day. A remnant will be spared; the unbelieving will be done away in slaughter. There will be a mourning such as this world has never seen. *Their Messiah! Their King!* They have slain Him! And what is there for them? Nothing but mercy, sovereign mercy, what Zacharias called "the heart of mercy of our God" (Lk. 1.78).

Wherefore be blind to that blessed parenthesis which God has revealed by Paul and the other apostles, hid in God from both the ages and the generations—the Church of God—which is being "taken out from the nations" (Acts 15.14) now? Why confuse the blessed counsels of Divine grace which will catch this completed company up to meet the Lord in the air, with the things of Matthew 24, in which this great mystery of the Church is not revealed at all? Note our Lord in Matthew 24.15 says,

"When therefore ye see the abomination of desolation, which was spoken of through Daniel the prophet, standing in the holy place" ("where he ought not," Mark adds; that is, in the restored Jewish temple), "then let them that are IN JUDEA flee unto the mountains: . . . And pray ye that your flight be not in the winter, neither on a sabbath."

Does that sound like Paul:

"Let *no* man judge *you* in meat, or in drink, or in respect of a feast day or a new moon or a sabbath day"?

Nay, verily, but it sounds exactly like Israel when the Church has been caught away, yea, THE CHURCH, ALL of it, brother: not "overcomers" only, but "*they that are Christ's.*" Why confound the blessed grace shown unto us, with God's ways with Israel, who must pass through "the time of *Jacob's* trouble" (Jer. 30.7, Matt. 24-21, the Great Tribulation)?

So then this "gospel of the kingdom," which must be "preached in the whole world" before "the end" can come, has *nothing to do* with the Church and its blessed gospel. The Church is not of this age or world. Nor has the Church to do with the time of the end, or with the end, as does Israel. For the end cannot come till the Tribulation is over; and "God appointed *us*," the saints of the Church, in His infinite grace, "NOT UNTO WRATH" (I Thess. 5.9), as said our Lord:

"Because thou didst keep the word of My patience, I also will keep thee from the *hour of trial,* that hour which is to come upon the whole world *(oikoumenē,* inhabited earth), to try them that dwell upon the earth" (Rev. 3.10).

No, none of God's counsels are left to depend upon the fulfillment of conditions by *man!* At a moment known to the Father only, He will send our blessed Lord, first *for* the Church; and afterwards, *with* the Church and angels, to come and establish the Millennium. But remember, He has said the gospel *has been* preached (even if that were, which it is *not,* a condition of Christ's coming) to the whole creation, and "spoken of by the whole world," so that the whole inhabited world *(oikoumenē)* was "turned upside down." Of course the gospel has been proclaimed! Brother, in your town, no matter how small, only a few understand and have received the gospel. But tell me, how is it that under the sixth seal they cry,

"Fall on us and hide us from the face of Him that sitteth on the throne, AND from the wrath of *the Lamb:* for the great day of their wrath is come; and who is able to stand?" (Rev. 6.16, 17).
Where did they find out about *this?* Again, in Revelation 14, the Church will at that time have been raptured, as Revelation 4.1 proves; but earth's multitudes *know* God sitteth on the throne, and they have heard about the Lamb.

It is intensely interesting, and should be finally significant, that in the very last chapter of the Bible our blessed Lord repeats thrice His familiar word to His own, "Behold I come *quickly.*" The word translated "quickly" means without delay, and is intended to arouse expectancy. When John says to the Lord, "Amen: come, Lord Jesus"; it is in answer to our Lord's third and final form of "Behold I come quickly," in which He exchanges the word *idou,* behold, for the word *nai,* which is the most emphatic Greek form of as-surance, as, *truly, assuredly,* for a *fact,* I am coming quickly! May the response of the beloved John, "Amen: come!" be the expression of our own hearts, yea, of our expectation.

While believers delight in and urge the evangelization of all men, our expectation of Christ's coming is not governed or limited by the completion of any of our own or human conditions. Our expecta-tion is of Christ Himself. "And what I say unto you," He said, "I say unto all, Watch."

There must come into our hearts a faith that holds fast the words, "In such an hour as ye think *not,*" "Of that day knoweth not *the Son.*" Is it not said that a crown of righteousness, like Paul's, awaits those that *love* Christ's appearing? Let those who point to this and that, rather than to His *actual coming* beware! "Lest coming sud-denly He find you sleeping" (Mk. 13.36). Of our Great High Priest, the Holy Spirit saith, He "sat down on the right hand of God; henceforth *expecting till* His enemies be made the footstool of His feet" (10.12-13). Whatever *you* are *expecting,* you who call your-self a Christian, *Christ your Lord is expecting* to return to this earth as King! If *you* are not expecting what *He* is expecting, you are out of line with His plans and thoughts!

Why do you call yourself a Christian and yet reject Christian revelation? Our Lord was constantly speaking of His own return, and all the epistles hold it before us. One of the great tragedies of all history, if not the greatest, is the casting away by the Church of the great and mighty sustaining hope which first the Lord Himself, and then His apostles in the Acts and epistles, urged upon the Church as not only the great path of separation from the world— "Every one that hath this hope set on Him"—when He appears— "purifieth himself, even as He is pure" (I Jno. 3.3) but the thought sustaining the Christian soul through every adversity and trial:

"If I go and prepare a place for you, I come again, and will receive you unto Myself" (Jno. 14.3).

"For the Lord Himself shall descend from Heaven, with a shout, with the voice of the archangel, and with the trump of God: and the dead in Christ shall rise first; then we that are alive, that are left, shall together with them be caught up in the clouds, to meet the Lord in the air" (I Thess. 4.16-17).

Indeed, Paul's description of the Thessalonians to whom he wrote the above is,

"Ye turned unto God from idols, to serve a Living and true God, and to *wait for His Son from Heaven,* Whom He raised from the dead, even Jesus, Who delivereth us from the wrath to come."

Mr. Moody used to say there were less than twenty passages on baptism, and over three hundred on the second coming, in the New Testament! But, behold, here is a Christendom filled with "Post-millennialists," holders of a heresy invented in the eighteenth century. And here is "A-millennialism," which means *no* Millennium! Which of the two is a greater insult to the Word of God, it would be hard to say. The first would have Christ stay away while one thousand years of "world uplift" go on, which idea of course, is contrary to all the Bible's account of man; and the second would have no Millennium at all, though the Word of God in one chapter alone (Rev. 20), uses the term "thousand years" six times, not to mention many passages, and whole chapters and psalms, describing it.

And then there are the indifferentists, who say, "What does it matter?"

Well, sir, it matters just this: You take away the key of knowledge when you reject prophecy. You enter not in yourself, and those entering, you prevent.

I again press home upon you, Why do you *call yourself* a Christian and reject *Christian revelation?*

APPENDIX G

AUTHORSHIP OF HEBREWS

From Chapter 13.18 to the end of the chapter, Paul, plainly, is speaking, as Peter testifies in II Peter 3.15: "Even as our beloved brother Paul also, according to the wisdom given unto him, wrote unto *you*." Who are the "you" to whom Peter says Paul wrote? I Peter 1.1, Peter's salutation as he begins his epistles, tells us: "To the elect who are sojourners of the Dispersion (Gr., *Diaspora*)"— the dispersed Israelites; and, "This is now, beloved, the *second* epistle that I write unto *you*" (II Pet. 3.1 ff).

This ("Our beloved brother Paul according to the wisdom given unto him wrote unto *you*," "the elect [Israelites] who are sojourners of the Dispersion"—putting the above texts together), this, I say, gives Paul an authority from Peter, the apostle to the circumcision.*

Remember Hebrews 5.11: "Of whom [Melchizedek] we have many things to say and *hard of interpretation*, seeing ye are become dull of hearing," and compare with this, II Peter 3.15-6:

"Even as our beloved brother Paul also, according to the wisdom given to him, wrote unto you; as also in all his epistles, speaking in them of these things; wherein are some things *hard to be understood*, which the ignorant and unstedfast wrest, as they do also the OTHER SCRIPTURES, unto their own destruction."

---

*See Acts 15.25, where "The apostles and [certainly including Peter, who had been speaking at the conference] the elders, with the whole church, chose men" and sent them "to Antioch with Paul and Barnabas . . . and wrote thus by them . . . It seemed good unto us . . . to choose out men and send them unto you *with our beloved* Barnabas *and Paul*" (Acts 15.22-25).

See also Galatians 2.7-9.:

"When they saw that I had been intrusted with the gospel of the uncircumcision, even as Peter with the gospel of the circumcision (for He that wrought for Peter unto the apostleship of the circumcision wrought for me also unto the Gentiles); and when they perceived the grace that was given unto me, James and Cephas and John, they who were reputed to be pillars, *gave to me and Barnabas the* right hands of fellowship, that we should go unto the Gentiles, and they unto the circumcision."

(See Paul's words in I Cor. 3.10, Eph. 3.3: "According to the grace of God which was *given unto me*"; "By revelation was *made known unto me* the mystery.")

We see in this Peter's remarkable testimony to the book of HEBREWS, not only that Paul wrote unto the Hebrews; and that in this writing there were "things hard to be understood"; but also that Peter calls this letter of Paul's to the dispersed among believing Hebrews of Asia Minor, "*Scripture*." Now the only book of Scripture of which the author is not designated directly is the book of **Hebrews,** which, therefore, Paul wrote.*

How beautiful that Peter, whom Paul had "withstood to his face" when Peter "feared them that were of the circumcision" (Gal. 2.12), should so lovingly commend to these Hebrews of Asia Minor Paul's letter to them! The "Dispersion" was in Pontus, Galatia, Cappadocia, Asia, and Bithynia, the very field where most of Paul's labors had been.

---

*"He who wrote the letter desires they should know that Timothy had been set at liberty; he himself was so already; he was in Italy; circumstances which tend to confirm the idea that it was Paul who wrote this letter—a very interesting point, although in nowise affecting its authority." J. N. D., **Synopsis,** p. 349.

APPENDIX H

THE BOOKS WHICH FOLLOW HEBREWS

It is remarkable that the books which follow **Hebrews** are those of "James and Cephas and John," who in Galatians 2.9 are seen *in that order* giving Paul and Barnabas the right hand of fellowship to go to the Gentiles, Peter and others going to the circumcision.

1. James begins his epistle, "To the twelve tribes which are of the Dispersion" (that is, to the dispersed believers coming from the twelve tribes) "greeting" (Gr., wisheth joy—R. V., margin). James was a brother of Jesus (Gal. 1.19), and although we find in Romans that there was "no difference between Jew and Greek," no one having righteousness, yet here we find a brother in the flesh of the Lord having charge of the Jerusalem assembly, and writing to "the twelve tribes" as recognizing that they were remembered by God, though now scattered. (Paul before Agrippa referred to "our twelve tribes earnestly serving God day and night" under Law: Acts 26.7.)

2. Next we have the two epistles of Peter (Cephas), addressed "to the elect who are sojourners of the Dispersion in Pontus, Galatia, Cappadocia, Asia, and Bythinia" (that is, the provinces making up Asia Minor, a relatively small but important province of the Roman Empire, of which Ephesus was the capital, on the western end of Asia Minor).

"He that wrought for Peter unto the apostleship of the circumcision" (Galatians 2.8), shows that Peter was regarded as the chief apostle to the circumcision, although James was set as leader over the assembly at Jerusalem (Acts 21.18).

3. Then we have the epistles of John, the beloved disciple, of whom the Lord Jesus said (Jno. 21.22) "If I will that he tarry till I come, what is that to thee?" Tarry till the Lord comes, John in the Spirit indeed does, speaking first of "fellowship with the Father and with His Son Jesus Christ" (I Jno. 1.3); and a warning of the coming Antichrist—and indeed of many antichrists (2.18, 22); and finally, in the Book of the Revelation, presenting the Lord as Priest-Judge over the seven churches; and seeing the coming believing Remnant of Israel as in Revelation 7.4-8, 11 to 14.

As a FINAL WORD, Remember the last verse of **Hebrews:** "Grace Be With You ALL. Amen."

OTHER RESOURCES
FOR THE STUDY OF THE
BOOK OF HEBREWS

Types in Hebrews   Sir Robert Anderson

An enlightening examination of the Old Testament types found
in Hebrews and their practical relevance for today.

ISBN 0-8254-2129-2   192 pp.   paperback

Great Cloud of Witnesses in
Hebrews Eleven   E. W. Bullinger

A classic exposition including an examination of the great heroes
of the faith. Full of rich, practical applications.

ISBN 0-8254-2247-7   462 pp.   paperback

The Epistle to the Hebrews   Thomas C. Edwards

A complete exposition based upon the English text. Edwards
treats the themes of the Epistle with theological discernment
and spiritual devotion. A clear, convincing presentation of the
all-sufficiency and superiority of Christ.

ISBN 0-8254-5104-3   349 pp.   deluxe hardback

Studies in Hebrews   H. C. G. Moule

This volume, part of the *Popular Commentary Series*, is an
excellent series for personal or group study. Moule was one of
the greatest expositors of all time and one of Keswick's most
valued and admired speakers.

ISBN 0-8254-3223-5   120 pp.   paperback

Hebrews: The Epistle of Warning   John Owen
Preface by Herbert W. Lockyer, Sr.

This one-volume abridgment of Owen's seven-volume *magnum opus* on Hebrews condenses the essential arguments of each chapter.

ISBN 0-8254-3407-6   288 pp.   paperback

Epistle to the Hebrews   Adolph Saphir
Foreword by Herbert W. Lockyer, Sr.

Focusing on the central theme of Hebrews—the new covenant versus the old dispensation—Saphir draws out the practical applications of the Epistle.

ISBN 0-8254-3728-8   924 pp.   hardback

Available from your local Christian bookstore, or

kregel
PUBLICATIONS

P.O. Box 2607, Grand Rapids, MI 49501